W9-BVA-166

When
Perennials
Bloom

When Perennials Bloom

An Almanac for Planning and Planting

Tomasz Aniśko

Timber Press
Portland ▪ London

Published in 2008 by
Timber Press, Inc.

The Haseltine Building
133 S.W. Second Avenue, Suite 450
Portland, Oregon 97204-3527
www.timberpress.com

2 The Quadrant
135 Salusbury Road
London NW6 6RJ
www.timberpress.co.uk

Printed in China
Designed by Christi Payne

Library of Congress Cataloging-in-Publication Data

Aniśko, Tomasz, 1963-
    When perennials bloom : an almanac for planning and planting / Tomasz Aniśko.
        p. cm.
    Includes bibliographical references and index.
    ISBN-13: 978-0-88192-887-7
    1.   Perennials—Flowering.   I. Title.
    SB434.A55 2008
    635.9'32—dc22
                                2008002938

A catalog record for this book is also available from the British Library.

Acknowledgments

I gratefully acknowledge the assistance of many people without whom this book could not have been created. First and foremost, I am especially grateful to Bill Schmitt, a Longwood Gardens' volunteer, who recorded all the bloom data presented here. I also thank Longwood Gardens' volunteers David Child, Diana Cormack, Rita Mulrooney, and Carol Warfel and Longwood Gardens' staff Kristina Aguilar, Venice Bayrd, and David Thompson for their help in preparing and proofreading the manuscript.

Contents

Opposite: *Ophiopogon planiscapus* 'Nigrescens'

What Is a Perennial?

The earliest system for classifying plants, that of Theophrastus (362–287 B.C.), recognized the cardinal categories of plants, such as trees, shrubs, perennials, and annuals. Theophrastus' crude system, grossly inadequate and naïve from the perspective of modern systematists, was founded not so much in morphological similarities within these groups of plants or perceived relationships between them, but in the realization that they represented the principal biological types or life forms of plants. Some 23 centuries after Theophrastus, gardeners continue to rely on his categories to classify cultivated plants and to organize the knowledge about them. The longevity of Theophrastus' categories is even more remarkable when one considers how vaguely they are defined, a rather uncomfortable position for scientifically inclined minds, but of no consequence to the rest of us. With their boundaries blurred and with many plants falling in between the categories, it is not always clear where a tree ends and a shrub begins, what is and what is not a perennial, or when an annual can no longer be called by such a name. Many definitions have been attempted, some more restrictive, others broadly inclusive depending on the needs, reflective of the situation when our language struggles to describe and comprehend the continuum of the natural world.

Perennial or Not

Garden perennials are a very diverse group of plants, which may explain the difficulty of defining their common characteristics with any degree of precision. Instinctually, we position them between annuals and biennials on one side and trees and shrubs on the other. The ability of perennials to live for more than 2 years sets them apart from the earlier group, whereas their herbaceous character distinguishes them from the latter. However, there are many examples of garden perennials that fall somewhat outside this definition. The short-lived perennials may often grow as biennials, whereas those that have woody rootstocks or lower portions of their aerial stems transition to subshrubs or shrublets. Amid the reports of 70-year-old daffodils and fritillaries, we have to recognize that, in some cases, perennials

Helianthus angustifolius

9

persisting in the same location for many years have their parts, such as roots or stems, living for no more than two growing seasons. Aleksander Łukasiewicz (1962) of the Poznań Botanical Garden in Poland, who studied more than 500 perennials representing 70 families, made an important distinction between the longevity of the plants and the longevity of their parts. He defined perennials as plants that are able to repeatedly renew themselves vegetatively, regardless of the longevity of their underground parts.

Perennials, like all plants, are capable of indeterminate growth thanks to the activity of their meristems. The meristems are made up of continually dividing cells, which are located at the tips of the stems and the roots and in a thin layer of cambium around older stems and roots. The indeterminate growth opens a possibility of potential immortality. The shoot system, comprised of stems, leaves, and buds, may grow indefinitely for as long as it remains in the vegetative stage. However, the transition of the stem apical meristem from the vegetative to the

floral state changes the growth from indeterminate to determinate, thus replacing the potential of immortality with the prospect of the end of life for the stem that flowers.

Therefore, the timing and the extent to which apical meristems switch from the vegetative to floral state determine the plant's longevity. In annuals, all active meristems convert to the floral state, leading eventually to the plant's death within a single year, whereas for biennials this event is postponed until the second growing season. Perennials, on the other hand, preserve some of their meristems in the vegetative state each year, while others produce flowers. In some species, such as *Viola odorata*, it is the axillary buds that produce flowers and the terminal bud remains in a vegetative state (monopodial growth). In others, such as *Maianthemum racemosum*, the terminal bud flowers and axillary buds continue to grow (sympodial growth).

Perennials are polycarpic, meaning that they repeatedly flower and fruit, unlike monocarpic plants,

Digitalis purpurea bridges biennials with perennials.

Iris tectorum with stems in various stages of their development.

mostly annuals and biennials, which flower only once in their life and die shortly thereafter. The polycarpic character of perennials results from generations of monocarpic stems flowering successively. These monocarpic stems are formed annually at the base of the stems that already flowered or from the underground parts. The monocarpic stems die back after flowering and fruiting, but perennials have stems that are in various stages of their development, so they do not all flower and die at the same time. In plants that are intermediate between perennials and biennials, such as *Digitalis purpurea*, stems flower and die in their second year, but occasional rosettes of new leaves may form at the base of the flowering stems, extending the plant's life to 3 or 4 years. Thus, the fundamental characteristic of perennials is not the longevity of their underground parts, but the ability to repeatedly regenerate vegetatively.

Morphological Types

Confronted by a much larger diversity of plants than those known in the classical period, botanists of the modern era proposed many systems of classifying biological types of plants that expanded and refined the broad categories recognized by Theophrastus. The early efforts to define the principal morphological types of plants date back to the turn of the 19th century, when Alexander von Humboldt and his followers developed the concept of physiognomic groups based on growth habit. They included such examples as palms, cacti, lilies, or grasses, which were not synonymous with and were understood more broadly than the plant families known by these same names.

The early 20th century saw the emergence of several noteworthy systems, that of Christen Raunkiaer (1934) being perhaps the most influential. Raunkiaer's system of plant life forms was based on the position of dormant buds or shoot apices in relation to the surface of the soil during the unfavorable season, such as cold winter or dry summer. Thus, trees and shrubs, which bear dormant buds on aerial stems, were combined with epiphytes, stem succulents, and large herbaceous plants of the tropics into one group named phanerophytes. Plants that have buds close to the ground, such as shrublets, cushion plants, or many mat-forming perennials, were named chamaephytes. Raunkiaer included in this group suffruticose chamaephytes (or subshrubs),

frequent in warm climates with long dry periods, which die back to near the ground at the beginning of the unfavorable season. Hemicryptophytes are plants that have buds at the soil surface, a condition that applies to the majority of biennial and perennial herbaceous plants living in cold and temperate climates. Raunkiaer further divided hemicryptophytes into those that had no basal rosettes and the largest leaves higher up on the stem, such as *Lysimachia vulgaris*; those with partial rosettes and the largest leaves in the lowest part of the stem, such as *Anthriscus sylvestris*; and those that had all or nearly all of their foliage in basal rosettes and aerial shoots carrying flowers only, such as *Primula veris*. Cryptophytes include plants that have buds concealed below the level of soil or water. Many cryptophytes have storage organs, such as rhizomes, bulbs, corms, or tubers. Within this group, Raunkiaer recognized geophytes, land plants whose buds survive below the ground; helophytes, plants of water edges whose buds survive buried in mud; and hydrophytes, aquatic plants with

In Raunkiaer's system, *Euphorbia cyparissias* could be classified as chamaephyte, hemicryptophyte, or cryptophyte.

submerged or floating leaves, whose buds survive at the bottom of the water. Therophytes, annual plants that survive the unfavorable season as dormant seeds, complete Raunkiaer's classification. Critics pointed out that the main weakness of Raunkiaer's system is the fact that it is founded entirely on one characteristic of only secondary importance, the position of regenerating buds. Especially when it comes to perennials, relatively few species fit well into one of Raunkiaer's life forms, because their regenerating buds are usually located at various levels. Plants such as *Euphorbia cyparissias*, *Rumex acetosella*, or *Saponaria officinalis* each have regenerating buds above, at, and below soil level, which would qualify them as chamaephytes, hemicryptophytes, or cryptophytes.

In a series of publications in the 1950s, Ivan Grigorievich Serebriakov presented a classification based on the longevity of the main and lateral shoots forming a plant's axis. Łukasiewicz (1962) provided a comprehensive review of his works. Serebriakov argued that herbaceous plants evolved from trees by shortening the life cycle of the axis brought about by severity of the climate and soil conditions. Shorter life cycles of the axis accelerated its development and flowering, resulting in various plant life forms. Serebriakov's system has trees, shrubs, shrublets,

perennials, and annuals as the main classes. Within these classes, he recognized variants defined by their growth habit, including prostrate, climbing, succulent, suckering, and arborescent. These special forms, he thought, evolved in response to particular climatic and soil conditions, such as prostrate forms found in severe cold climates with poorly developed soils, or vines and lianas abundant in warm and humid climates. Furthermore, among perennials, Serebriakov distinguished taprooted forms found in dry gravelly soils in deserts, steppe, and arctic tundra; fibrous-rooted forms, which develop adventitious roots from

Paeonia obovata, a rhizocaulophyte, develops both strong primary and adventitious roots.

Eryngium planum, a rhizophyte, has strong primary roots and no adventitious roots.

Regenerating stems of rhizophytes, such as *Papaver orientale*, form on overwintering roots.

Soboliferous rhizocaulophytes, such as *Anemone ×hybrida*, produce adventitious buds on primary and adventitious roots.

the underground or basal portions of erect stems, characteristic of moist sites from arctic tundra south to semi-deserts; loosely clumped forms, also with adventitious roots, but developing many shorter and ascending shoots, frequent on light soils from tundra to southern forests; tightly clumped forms producing even more numerous, shorter, and crowded shoots, typical of plants growing in heavy soils; rhizomatous forms with underground, horizontal rhizomes often found in airy, loose, and moist soils of the forests; and stoloniferous forms, inhabiting forests and wetlands, which have elongated rhizomes, usually ending with storage organs, such as tubers or bulbs. Serebriakov's classification, however, did not take into account the longevity of the underground parts and roots.

The shortcomings of these systems, which for the most part ignored the underground and perennial parts of plants, were addressed by Łukasiewicz (1962), who proposed a classification of perennial plants based on the type of the perennial organ and the morphological and developmental changes during the life of the individual plant; that is, the way in which it regenerates vegetatively and the way in which the perennial organs die off. Łukasiewicz's system recognizes three main types of perennials: rhizophytes, rhizocaulophytes, and caulophytes, which are further divided into 13 groups of lower rank.

Typical rhizophytes, exemplified by *Crambe maritima*, *Eryngium planum*, and *Papaver orientale*, have strong primary taproots and form no adventitious roots. While the oldest central parts of the primary root die off gradually, the peripheral parts increase annually. The aboveground parts of these plants die back completely in the fall, whereas regenerating buds, from which new stems grow in the spring,

Caulophytes, such as *Telekia speciosa*, have a short-lived primary root that is quickly replaced by adventitious roots.

The perennial parts of *Vernonia lettermannii*, a caulophyte, are subterranean stem bases and rhizomes.

In *Penstemon virgatus*, a caulophyte, regenerating stems arise from the youngest parts of the rhizomes, while the oldest parts die off.

Rhizomatous caulophytes, such as *Solidago rugosa* 'Fireworks', develop horizontal subterranean stems.

Aconitum carmichaelii, a typical caulophyte, has regenerating stems formed near the bases of the older stems.

Lilium 'First Lady', a bulbous caulophyte, has subterranean stems modified into bulbs.

form on overwintering roots. As the result of the center of the taproot dying off, in time it splits and several leaf rosettes appear above the ground, leading to a slow spread of these plants. Rhizophytes poorly tolerate transplanting and dividing, which damages their primary roots. In addition to the typical rhizophytes, Łukasiewicz recognized soboliferous rhizophytes, such as *Macleaya cordata*, which can produce adventitious buds on roots; and tuberous rhizophytes, such as *Corydalis cava*, which have tubers developing from the roots or the hypocotyls.

Rhizocaulophytes, such as *Dianthus gratianopolitanus*, *Euphorbia palustris*, or *Paeonia obovata*, initially have strong primary taproots, but later additional adventitious roots develop from the bases of the stems. Gradually the oldest central parts of the primary roots and stems die off, while the peripheral parts increase annually. Rhizocaulophytes are easier to divide than rhizophytes because of their adventitious roots, but dividing requires cutting apart portions of hard taproots. Besides the typical rhizocaulophytes, Łukasiewicz included in this category soboliferous rhizocaulophytes, such as *Anemone* ×*hybrida*, which produce adventitious buds on the roots including adventitious roots; tuberous rhizocaulophytes, such as *Liatris spicata*, which develop long-lived tubers; and rhizomatous rhizocaulophytes, such as *Humulus lupulus*, which have regenerating stems that grow first horizontally underground, then emerge aboveground at some distance from the plant and change orientation to vertical.

Caulophytes, which include *Penstemon virgatus*, *Telekia speciosa*, and *Vernonia lettermannii*, have a weak, short-lived primary root that is quickly replaced by adventitious roots. The most important perennial parts of caulophytes are the subterranean stem bases or storage organs of stem origin, such as rhizomes, tubers, or bulbs. Caulophytes spread fast, form large clumps, and are easy to propagate through division. The regenerating stems arise in the youngest parts of the plants, while the oldest parts progressively die off, leading to the plant's outward expansion. Within this category, Łukasiewicz recognized the typical caulophytes, such as *Aconitum carmichaelii*, which have numerous regenerating stems formed near the bases of the older stems; soboliferous caulophytes, such as *Geranium sanguineum*, which produce adventitious buds on roots; tuberous caulophytes, such as *Helianthus tuberosus*, which have tubers formed from stem bases; rhizomatous caulophytes, such as *Solidago rugosa* 'Fireworks', which develop horizontal subterranean stems; stoloniferous caulophytes, such as *Lysimachia nummularia*, which have stolons creeping along the surface of the soil and taking root; and bulbous caulophytes, such as lilies, which produce bulbs.

Łukasiewicz viewed the change of the perennial organs from the primary root of the rhizophytes to the subterranean stem bases producing adventitious roots in caulophytes as fundamental for the evolution of various types of perennial plants. This process required changing the mode of vegetative regeneration from the concentric growth of layers of the primary taproot outside the senescing central core, characteristic of rhizophytes, to the growth of the youngest parts of the subterranean stems while the oldest parts degenerated at the opposite end, typical of caulophytes. This increased ability to regenerate vegetatively allows caulophytes to better explore and adapt to their environment.

Developmental Types

Aside from classifications based in plant morphology, several systems were proposed to account for the wide variety of developmental types of perennials. Ludwig Diels (1917) classified perennials into three types according to the length and type of their dormancy. Those exhibiting only forced dormancy and having no storage organs were called the Asperula type. Diels thought that they had originated in the tropics and included in this group such examples as *Asperula odorata* (now *Gallium odoratum*) and *Mercurialis perennis*. The Leucojum type, with a short true dormancy followed by forced dormancy and specialized storage organs, was thought to be of Mediterranean origin and was characterized by rapid development in the fall. Diels included here *Leucojum vernum*, *Arum maculatum*, and *Ranunculus ficaria*. Finally, the Polygonatum type, also with specialized storage organs but with longer (up to 8-month-long) true dormancy and rapid development taking place in the spring, included such perennials as *Polygonatum multiflorum*, *Anemone nemorosa*, and *Convallaria majalis*, which were dominant in temperate climate regions.

In 1959 Igor Grigorievich Serebriakov developed an alternative system that classified perennials according to the duration and timing of the development of their stems, from emergence until flowering and fruiting. Thus, monocyclic stems, such as those of *Asarum europaeum*, complete their development during a single growing season. Monocyclic overwintering stems begin their development in late summer or fall, overwinter, and flower the following year, such as those of *Campanula persicifolia*. Bicyclic stems, like those of *Ajuga reptans*, complete their development in two growing seasons: vegetative growth in the first season and flowering in the next. A longer vegetative growth stage of 3 years or more followed by the flowering stage characterizes polycyclic stems, exemplified by *Eriophorum angustifolium*. Serebriakov noted that some species may have stems of more than one type, but even then, one of these types dominates and is characteristic of that species.

Polygonatum odoratum 'Variegatum' produces only a single flush of growth each year.

A few years after publishing his system of morphological types, Aleksander Łukasiewicz (1967) classified perennials according to the characteristics of the phenological development of aerial stems, such as periodicity and timing of stem emergence, number of growth flushes during one growing season, timing of stem senescence, and degree to which the foliage is evergreen.

First, Łukasiewicz distinguished between species that develop aerial stems periodically during a certain time of the year and those that produce aerial stems continually throughout the growing season. He further divided the first group into two categories, those that have only a single flush of growth and those with two (rarely three) flushes of growth in one season. He also recognized evergreen, semi-evergreen, and deciduous types within each of the categories. Łukasiewicz (1967) acknowledged that there are also plants intermediate between these three groups.

The single flush appears only after the old growth dies back and may take place in spring, as in *Polygonatum odoratum*, or fall, as in *Ranunculus ficaria*. This type of development is characteristic of perennials living in habitats where during the summer there is a period unfavorable for growth, brought about by drought in steppes or shading in forests.

With two flushes of growth in a season, the first one begins in the spring and culminates with the flowering in spring or summer, whereas the second flush appears in summer or fall and usually remains vegetative until the end of the season, rarely flowering on the strongest stems. This type of phenology, exemplified by *Pulmonaria*, is typical of plants native to habitats where conditions are favorable for growth during the summer, such as meadows or edges of watercourses. Species capable of producing the second flush of growth take advantage of these conditions, grow faster, and are more tolerant

Pulmonaria 'Blue Ensign' has two flushes of growth, one in spring and the other in late summer or fall.

of damage to the aboveground parts than the species with only a single flush of growth.

Species capable of producing new stems continuously throughout the growing season, such as *Aubrieta deltoidea*, *Carex arenaria*, or *Elymus arenarius*, are characteristic of open plant communities with a sparse plant cover, like sand dunes or stone screes. In such habitats, new growth is not limited by competition, and plants can utilize the entire growing season. Plants exhibiting this phenology are very tolerant of damage to the aboveground parts.

Why Perennials Bloom at Specific Times

Flowering is unquestionably the most anticipated event in any garden. It is the time when our hopes are fulfilled, wishes answered, and hard work rewarded, but it is also the time when occasional disappointments have to be coped with. Each plant opens its flowers at about the same time every year, establishing an annual cycle and succession of bloom that defines the seasons, but it also affects nearly every aspect of our culture, from religious rituals to harvest festivals. Before we had calendars and before we learned to read the stars, flowers were telling us the time of the year. Some languages preserve this ancient connection in their names of months. For instance, the Polish names for July and September are *lipiec*, from *lipa*, linden, and *wrzesień*, from *wrzos*, heather, telling the time when these plants flower.

Agricultural practices from the dawn of civilization were dictated by and timed according to the blooming of cultivated and wild plants. The time of bounty and the time of scarcity, the time of leisure and the time of labor, the time of rejoicing and the time of grieving were all linked to the seasonal phenomenon of flowering. Even our languages reflect this preoccupation with flowering, when we talk about civilizations that flourished or children that blossomed.

This close cultural relationship between us and flowers would probably not have developed if flowers were ubiquitous and plants bloomed continually. It is the awaiting and then the passing of the flowers that makes them so dear to us and creates perhaps a universal metaphor for the fleeting nature of beauty and existence. But why don't plants bloom continually? Why do all flowers on a plant open at about the same time? Why do they mysteriously appear in certain seasons and then vanish?

Clues to the answers become apparent once we realize that the fundamental purpose of having flowers in the first place is plants' sexual reproduction, which provides the tremendous evolutionary advantage of affording a great variety of new gene combinations through which new adaptations can develop. The evolutionary benefits of genetic outcrossing thus justify the Protean diversity and complexity of the developmental processes involved in

The annual cycle and succession of bloom define the seasons.

flowering, followed by formation of fruits and seeds, all aimed at improving the likelihood of successful sexual reproduction.

Maturity

In nearly all plants grown from seed, a certain period elapses before flowers can be initiated, even under conditions that lead mature individuals to bloom. This phase of development that precedes a plant's readiness to flower is known as the juvenile phase. In some plants, the juvenile phase is characterized not only by the plant's inability to flower, but also by growth habit or leaf morphology that is different from that of the mature phase. Although difficult to separate in practical terms, a certain minimum size, rather than age, is thought to be the critical factor for transitioning from the juvenile to the mature phase. To complicate matters, however, in some plants the minimum size required for reproduction may also differ with age. This postponement of flowering until the plant reaches a certain critical size is believed to permit the accumulation of sufficient physiological resources essential for sexual reproduction. Prior to that, during the juvenile phase, directing all of the resources to vegetative growth is advantageous for the plant's ability to compete against other species in its immediate environment.

The juvenile phase may last from a few weeks in some plants to more than a century in others. Environmental conditions affecting growth rate, thus a plant's size, influence the duration of the juvenile phase. Some annual species, such as *Poa annua*, or biennial species, such as *Verbascum thapsus*, may actually flower in the first, second, or third year, depending on the growing conditions. Once the juvenile phase ends, a mature plant is ready to respond to environmental signals, including temperature and light, to initiate flowering. Much variation in plant size at the time of flowering can be explained by varying amount of growth, beyond the critical size, that occurs before flowering is initiated.

Perennial plants usually alternate between vegetative and reproductive phases of development, which permits them to allocate all their resources to vegetative development during those parts of the growing season that are optimal for rapid growth and high productivity, ultimately supporting repro-

ductive development. In many perennials, floral initiation in the meristems occurs only after rapid stem growth has ended. The duration of the vegetative phase may depend on the length of time required to accumulate sufficient reserves needed to flower and then produce fruits and seeds successfully, which in turn is determined by a whole range of environmental factors, including climatic, soil, and biotic.

Mature plants, with age, may also become increasingly responsive to environmental signals to initiate flowering. Young plants of *Anthericum liliago* were observed to flower for the first time in mid-October, whereas older plants of the same species bloomed 4 months earlier (Łukasiewicz 1967). Older plants may even outgrow the need for such signals altogether and flower regardless of the conditions. Such a response is thought to be a fail-safe mechanism, which ultimately permits a plant to succeed in flowering even when the usual environmental triggers fail to occur.

Synchrony and Seasonality

The effective outcrossing among individual plants of the same species in one population requires that they all flower in synchrony. This increases the amount of pollen available, improves chances for cross-pollination, and benefits pollinating insects by reducing the distance they have to fly in search of food. To make synchronous flowering possible, plants combine the internal processes controlling their readiness to flower with an elaborate system for gathering cues from the environment, provided by temperature or day length, to determine the appropriate time to bloom.

For flowering to be successful, it needs not only to be synchronous, it also has to be precisely timed with a particular season. If synchronous flowering were to happen at a different time each year, it could have disastrous consequences for the specialized pollinators unable to find a food source and, therefore, just as catastrophic consequences for a plant species dependent on these pollinators.

Seasonality of bloom thus allows flowering to take place during periods of pollinator availability. When pollinators are active for a brief period, flowering of many species of plants in the same habitat tends to coincide with their presence, but when pol-

Clematis ×jouiniana 'Mrs. Robert Brydon'

Eryngium yuccifolium

Eutrochium fistulosum 'Gateway'

Veronicastrum virginicum

Synchronous and seasonal flowering benefits pollinating insects and improves the chances for cross-pollination.

linators are active over an extended period, various plant species tend to separate their bloom periods to reduce the competition for pollinators. Blooming may also be timed so the flowers are more visible to the pollinators. In forests, such conditions exist when deciduous trees are leafless, causing woodland floras to have numerous species that flower in early spring. In open meadows and prairies, overtopping surrounding vegetation helps to effectively present flowers to the pollinators, resulting in many species blooming late in the season. In other situations, flowering may be timed such that seed production is completed before the onset of winter or drought, so that seed dispersal or germination can take place during the favorable season.

Certain phylogenetic constraints are imposed on flowering time as well. Some plant families, such as Brassicaceae or Ranunculaceae, tend to flower early in the season, whereas others, including Asteraceae or Gentianaceae, tend to flower last, irrespective of the geographic or climatic region. These constraints indicate that modification of flowering time must be an exceedingly slow process and that fine-tuning of flowering times to avoid competition for pollinators is limited by phylogenetically defined boundaries.

Initiation

To fully understand the effect of various environmental factors on the time of flowering, the time when flower buds are first initiated has to be considered, because many plants form their flower buds a long time before flowers emerge. *Convallaria majalis*, for instance, initiates flower buds in June or July that will emerge the following spring. Likewise, most perennials that flower in May, April, or earlier initiate their flower buds in the preceding year and are either evergreen or have reserves stored in rhizomes or taproots. In contrast, most of the species that flower in June or later have limited reserves stored in the underground parts and form their flower buds in the current year.

John Grainger (1939) distinguished three classes of temperate perennials according to the timing of flower initiation, flower bud development, and subsequent flowering. Perennials in which development from floral initiation to flowering proceeds uninterrupted are called direct-flowering plants. Their floral initiation may occur at the time of rapid vegetative growth, as is the case with many summer-flowering species, such as *Epilobium angustifolium*, *Hylotelephium spectabile*, and *Stachys officinalis*. Or, it may occur during the period of minimal vegetative growth, in which case flowers are initiated in late fall or winter and open in the spring, as in *Anthriscus sylvestris*, *Lupinus polyphyllus*, or *Tussilago farfara*.

Another class recognized by Grainger, indirect-flowering plants, include species with a period of rest intervening between floral initiation and flowering. Like the first class, indirect-flowering plants can initiate flower buds during the time of rapid vegetative growth in late summer, but they do not flower until the following spring, as is the case with *Anemone nemorosa*, *Arabis hirsuta*, and *Primula veris*. Or, flower buds can be initiated during a quiescent period in summer and remain dormant until late winter or early spring, when they flower. This pattern is characteristic of many bulbous plants, including tulips and daffodils.

The last class Grainger named cumulative-flowering plants, because they initiate flower buds over a long period, after which they all emerge together and flower over a brief period. This behavior is typical of many weeds, including *Plantago major* and *Taraxacum officinale*.

Flower buds of spring-blooming *Convallaria majalis* 'Aureovariegata' are initiated during the preceding summer.

Floral initiation in *Stachys officinalis* occurs at the time of rapid vegetative growth.

How Perennials Respond to the Environment

In most regions of the world, there is a yearly cycle of changes in temperature, light, and rainfall defining various seasons. These changes can be particularly dramatic at higher latitudes. Perennials living in areas with seasonal climates have evolved many adaptations, which not only allow them to survive periods of severe weather, but also to time their flowering so that it takes place when environmental conditions are favorable for sexual reproduction. Thus, the timing of flowering is determined in response to changes in the environment and through the plant's interactions with its surroundings. But in order for the flowers to open during the optimum period, their initiation needs to commence well in advance of the coming of the conditions favorable for flowering.

Environmental cues can exert control over flower development at various stages. Development begins with termination of the juvenile phase and induction of the reproductive state, through the initiation of floral meristems. Flower buds then develop, with their dormancy regulated by environmental cues, and the process ends with flowering itself. Each of these developmental stages may be triggered by a range of environmental factors that change with the season.

Plant response to an environmental signal can be direct or delayed. If the response is direct, flowers begin to form while the plant is being subjected to particular environmental conditions, but this process stops when these conditions change. In the delayed or inductive response, no changes can be observed in the growth of the plant during the exposure to the conditions necessary for flower development. The flowering occurs after the inducing conditions have been removed. *Xanthium strumarium*, for example, will not flower while it is maintained under long-day conditions. When it is given a single short-day cycle, the processes of flowering are initiated, and several days later, even if the plant has been returned to long days, flowers begin to develop.

The most extensively studied so far have been the effects of temperature and light, but the interactions of plants with their environment appear to be more complex than initially thought. Environmental cues may involve several factors, likely occurring in

Iris pseudacorus

25

a specific sequence, that influences the long chain of physiological events leading to flowering. In addition, there appear to exist alternative physiological pathways permitting the floral development to proceed when one of the stimuli is absent because of extraordinary weather patterns. This indicates that plants have redundant mechanisms to control bloom time, some perhaps inherited when a species migrated out of a climatically different area in recent geological history. In populations inhabiting a climatically stable environment, such redundant mechanisms would be expected to disappear, but when climatic conditions are variable, they offer an adaptive advantage even if used only rarely in extreme situations. With redundant mechanisms existing in the same population, a relatively minor mutation may permit switching from one mechanism to another, which could explain varying flowering times of closely related plants, such as cultivars of one species, which may be triggered by different day lengths.

Temperature

Temperature is among the most important environmental factors controlling flowering in plants growing in temperate and cold climates. Temperature controls flowering by triggering flower induction, as well as through its influence on all other aspects of plant development. Plants usually start growth only when temperature rises above a certain threshold value, higher for plants from warmer climates, lower for those in colder areas. As early as 1735, René de Réaumur, a French naturalist and the inventor of the Réaumur thermometer and temperature scale, introduced the concept of a heat unit to predict plant development. He proposed that the rate of plant development is a function of temperature, such that plants need a certain number of heat units to complete each of the developmental phases. Indeed, high temperature often speeds up the generative development and shortens longevity of certain organs. In hot weather, flowers of *Geranium robertianum*, *Helianthemum chamaecistus*, and *Linum perenne* are usually open for only several hours, whereas during cold weather they may stay open for 3 to 5 days.

It is commonly recognized that each species has a characteristic flowering period, but it is also well known that variation in bloom time occurs

Flowers of *Linum perenne* are open for only several hours in hot weather, but may stay open for several days when temperatures are low.

from year to year, and warm winters and springs are usually credited for bringing forward the date of first flowering. Not all species, however, respond to warm winter and spring weather in the same way. Those that flower early in the season are often influenced most, whereas the later-blooming species tend to be less affected by winter and spring temperatures. Although it is generally accepted that the variation in the bloom start date can be attributed in large extent to the variation in average temperature during the period leading up to flowering, in specific cases, such dependence sometimes cannot be established. For instance, observations of the first flowering date of *Achillea millefolium* in central England over the course of 36 years showed no relationship with average temperature, even though such a relationship was found for 219 of the 243 species (90 percent) of annuals, perennials, shrubs, and trees included in that study (Fitter et al. 1995).

Although nearly all studies of this kind relate time of first flowering to average air temperature, it should be noted that in the case of perennial plants, soil temperature may have a far greater influence on their emergence in the spring and flowering later than the air temperature. Despite the fact that air and soil temperatures are closely related, factors such as type and moisture content of the soil, slope aspect, exposure to sun, or type and thickness of mulch can greatly modify the temperature of the soil. It is especially important in early spring when individual plants of the same species may begin vegetative growth at various times depending on how fast the soil warms up. Observations in Poland showed that mulched plants of *Hemerocallis fulva*, *Pulmonaria obscura*, *Galanthus nivalis*, *Caltha palustris*, and *Pulsatilla vulgaris* emerged in the spring up to 10 days later than those not covered with mulch (Łukasiewicz 1967). In the same study,

various parts of one colony of *Petasites albus* flowered at different times, those with southern exposure blooming 2 weeks earlier than those in a shaded soil depression. A study of *Andropogon gerardii* and *Dactylis glomerata* growing in various locations in Indiana found that appearance of the first leaf was most highly correlated with soil temperature measured at 20 cm below ground level, and the growing season began 6 to 10 days later on heavy moist soil than on dry sandy loam (Benacchio 1970).

Extreme temperatures can be particularly detrimental to plant development. High summer temperatures combined with a drought can lead to wilting, leaf sun scorch, or even desiccation of entire plants. These responses are frequently seen in species that are not adapted to surviving long periods of summer drought. Such conditions can result in the unseasonably early flowering of fall-blooming plants such as *Helianthus* ×*laetiflorus*, *Rudbeckia laciniata*, or *Solidago canadensis*.

Soil temperature has a greater influence on emergence of perennials, such as *Paeonia lactiflora*, in the spring than the air temperature.

Extreme low winter temperatures, especially when combined with the lack of snow cover, can cause injury of the aboveground parts or even the belowground parts of perennials, which in turn can lead to abnormal development during the following growing season. Injured plants may flower weeks or months later than normal, and their bloom can be uneven, sporadic, or extended in time. Severely damaged plants may regenerate their vegetative parts, but may not be able to flower during the season following the injury. Similarly, a damaging late spring frost usually leads to delayed development during the entire growing season. Early fall frost, on the other hand, ends the flowering of late-blooming species and leads to premature deterioration of the aboveground parts of many other perennials.

Flower bud formation and flower emergence can be governed by separate temperature conditions. While most temperature-dependent processes proceed faster at higher temperatures, others are promoted by lower temperatures. In some plants, temperatures prior, during, and shortly after flower bud initiation exert an effect on the time when flowers open. Observations of flowering of *Anemone sylvestris* and *Tussilago farfara*, conducted in England over a 32-year period (Grainger 1939), showed that higher-than-average temperatures between July and October, when flower buds were initiated, delayed flowering, but warmer temperature between January and March, immediately before flowering, accelerated it.

The delay of flowering brought about by high temperatures in the previous fall may also be related to prolonged growth late in the season, which may interfere with the vernalization process. In the early 19th century, the first observations were made that certain plants flowered when planted outdoors in the previous fall, but not when planted in the spring, thus avoiding exposure to winter conditions. A century later, the Ukrainian agronomist Trofim

An early fall frost can lead to premature deterioration of the aboveground parts of *Callirhoe involucrata* and many other perennials that continue growing late in the season.

Denisovich Lysenko demonstrated that this winter effect could be substituted by subjecting the moist seeds to cold, and he proposed the term *jarovization* to describe this treatment. This term was replaced in a German translation of Lysenko's works as *vernalization*, and today it is understood more broadly as the promotion of flowering by exposure to low temperatures.

Temperatures effective in vernalization vary with the species, but generally fall between 0°C (32°F) and 15°C (60°F). The duration of the required exposure varies as well, from a few days to several weeks. High temperatures that follow immediately after vernalization may reverse the effect of low temperature and lead to so-called devernalization.

The response to vernalization can be quantitative or qualitative. Plants that are quantitatively influenced flower under any conditions but are promoted in their flowering by vernalization, whereas plants that respond in a qualitative manner do not flower unless exposed to low temperature. Winter annuals can be vernalized in the seedling or even imbibed seed stage, whereas biennials must grow to a certain size before they are able to respond to low-temperature treatment. Perennial plants, which perhaps are the least studied group in this respect, may show a quantitative or qualitative response to vernalization or none at all.

Light

Plants growing in regions with seasonal climates must modify their activities in advance of the changing weather. Day length provides the most reliable environmental clue forewarning plants of the approaching shift in weather conditions. In the middle latitudes, day length changes between the winter and summer solstices from about 8 to 16 hours of light per day. The amplitude of this oscillation increases at higher latitudes and diminishes toward the equator. For this reason, day length is a more effective environmental signal in temperate and boreal climates than it is in the tropical regions of the world. Therefore, it is in those climates that we find most of the plants whose flowering is controlled by the duration of the light and dark periods in a day.

Day length affects not only flowering time, but also most other aspects of development spanning the entire life cycle of a plant, such as the morphology of its vegetative parts, production of pigments, leaf senescence, cold acclimation, onset of dormancy, and formation of underground storage organs. These responses of plants to the relative length of day and night are referred to as photoperiodism. The length of day precisely times flowering in the most appropriate season and synchronizes the simultaneous flowering of all plants within the same population, facilitating the most effective cross-pollination.

However, when plants bloom upon exposure to long or short days, this does not always mean that the influence is photoperiodic, because in some cases this response can be affected by the amount of light that the plant receives rather than by periodic effects of alternating light and dark conditions. Development of shaded plants often differs from that of plants growing in full sun. *Pulmonaria obscura*, which bloomed in shade on 15 April, flowered 10 days earlier in full sun; and *Rudbeckia nitida*, which began flowering along the south edge of a large clump on 12 July, did not flower on its north side until 20 August (Łukasiewicz 1967).

Like many other biological phenomena, photoperiodism was commonly observed before being scientifically described and quantified. The discovery of photoperiodism was made by Wightman Garner and Harry Allard, who in the 1920s found that certain plants, which they called short-day plants, flowered only when days were sufficiently short. Others, called long-day plants, flowered only when days were long enough, whereas day-neutral plants were not influenced by day length in their flowering. Subsequently, it was shown that plants actually measure the length of the night rather than the length of the day, but the terminology remained unchanged. The difference between short-day and long-day plants is not in the length of the day under which they flower. Instead, the short-day plants flower when the day is shorter than some critical length, whereas the long-day plants flower when the day is longer than the critical value. Both *Xanthium strumarium* and *Hyoscyamus niger* flower when days are 14 hours long, but *Xanthium* is a short-day plant, blooming when days are shorter than about 15 hours, and *Hyoscyamus* is a long-day plant, blooming when days are longer than 11 hours.

Since Garner and Allard made their discovery, research has greatly expanded our understanding and appreciation of the complexity of the photoperiodic control of flowering beyond these basic responses. There is a great degree of plasticity in photoperiodic response. Plants of a long-day species growing in the southern part of the distribution range may have a shorter critical day length than those from the northern part, where summer days are longer. Some species with a very wide north-to-south distribution, such as *Bouteloua curtipendula*, may even have short-day ecotypes at the southern end of their distribution and long-day ecotypes near the northern extreme.

The dependence of flowering on photoperiod can be absolute or qualitative, such that plants will not flower unless their requirement for a particular critical day length is satisfied. In other cases, the response can be relative or quantitative, where flowering can occur regardless of the day length but will be accelerated and more profuse under certain day length. While both *Digitalis purpurea* and *Phlox paniculata* are long-day plants, the response is qualitative in the first species and quantitative in the latter.

Plants can make use of the fact that the day length changes with the seasons, with days becoming longer with the coming of the spring and shorter in the fall. Some plants require exposure to a certain number of short days followed by long days, mimicking the situation encountered in the spring. Others require several long days followed by several short days, as occurs in the fall. Furthermore, some species require intermediate day lengths to flower, whereas exposure to the same intermediate day lengths may inhibit flowering of other plants.

Flowering may be affected simultaneously by photoperiod and temperature. Because the same day length occurs in both spring and fall, plants likely need another environmental signal, such as temperature, to properly time their flowering with the right season. Flower bud formation may be induced by short days in the fall, but their further development is then halted by low temperatures in winter, and resumes only when the temperature increases in the spring.

The photoperiodic monitoring of seasonal changes involves not only the sensing of light and dark conditions, but also requires the referral of these signals to the plant's internal biological clock, whose existence is evidenced by various circadian rhythms, such as changes in enzymatic activity or photosynthetic rates. Although these rhythms are endogenous in nature, they can be reset by appropriate temperature and light signals.

The photoperiod is perceived by leaves and not the apical meristem, where the flowers are formed, indicating that a chemical compound or compounds have to be sent from the leaves to initiate flowering. The existence of such a chemical signal was first postulated in 1882 by the German botanist Julius von Sachs. In 1937 this hypothetical flowering stimulus was christened florigen by the Russian plant physiologist Mikhail Chailakhyan, who demonstrated that the stimulus could be transferred between plants through grafting. The exact nature of such a molecule remained elusive until 2005, when several teams working at the Max Planck Institute in Germany, the Swedish Agricultural University in Umeå, and Kyoto University in Japan announced that they found a molecule, which they called FT protein. The molecule's synthesis was shown to be activated in leaves, which induced flower formation at the growing tip of the plant.

Water

Water availability has a profound effect on the development of perennial plants. It influences the timing of spring growth and duration of subsequent developmental phases, in addition to affecting the size of a plant and its growth habit. In general, high rainfall and high soil moisture content prolong the development and longevity of vegetative organs and delay the onset of flowering and extend its duration. In early spring, soil moisture content appears to have a less significant effect, because it is rarely a limiting factor. Plants are smaller during that time, light intensity and temperatures are lower, and soil moisture content is usually high. During the summer months, however, moist conditions can delay and prolong flowering. Comparing bloom duration of perennials growing in the Poznań Botanical Garden in Poland, Łukasiewicz (1967) found that *Iris sibirica*, *Polygonatum odoratum*, and *Veronica incana* flowered, respectively, for 27, 25, and 32 days in a wet year, but for only 15, 13, and 12 days in a dry year.

In the same study, Łukasiewicz also recorded the effect of soil moisture on the timing of various developmental phases. The vegetative growth of many perennials began earlier on drier sites. For example, the first leaves of *Trollius europaeus* growing in dry soil appeared on 2 April, whereas those of plants growing in wet soil were delayed until 16 April. Similarly, flowering of plants growing in drier conditions was accelerated. *Clematis integrifolia* in dry soil flowered on 14 June, but in moist soil blooming occurred 18 days later, and *Iris pseudacorus* in dry soil flowered from 20 May to 1 June, but in moist soil plants bloomed from 26 May until 16 June.

In contrast, the growth of the replacement leaves in late summer was delayed by dry conditions in Łukasiewicz's study. Those of *Persicaria bistorta*, which appeared on plants growing in a wet situation on 19 August, were halted until 1 September on plants subjected to dry conditions. Drought can also accelerate the process of senescence in the fall. *Helleborus niger*, which in a moist soil retained its foliage until spring, dropped its leaves by early October when grown in a dry soil. Likewise, leaves of *Phalaris arundinacea* growing at the edge of a pond were retained until 3 November, whereas those of plants growing on a drier site deteriorated by 11 September. Łukasiewicz noted that although moist conditions delayed flowering, they also promoted repeat flowering in many species, including *Centaurea jacea*, *Scabiosa lucida*, and *Linum perenne*.

Gardening Practices

Trimming back stems of perennial plants in the early stages of their vegetative growth is often applied by gardeners to encourage additional branching and reduce the ultimate height of a plant, thus making it less prone to flopping in wind or heavy rain later in the season. This practice usually delays flowering and permits gardeners to create new and unexpected plant combinations. Plants that are trimmed back may also flower longer but often not as profusely. The extent of this delay depends on the timing and severity of the trimming. The later the trimming is done and the more severe it is, the greater delay can be expected, and in extreme cases no flowering will occur. An infestation of pests early in the season may have a similar effect on flowering. An aphid infestation delayed flowering of *Aconitum variegatum* by 1 month and that of *Thalictrum lucidum* by 2 weeks (Łukasiewicz 1967).

Cutting back flowering stems when the bloom is nearly complete encourages repeat bloom, although plants whose flowering stems die back naturally, such as *Delphinium grandiflorum* or *Papaver orientale*, are unlikely to flower again. Cutting back prevents fruit and seed development, and instead promotes vegetative growth, rejuvenates plants, and extends the longevity of many short-lived perennials, such as *Centranthus ruber*, *Coreopsis grandiflora*, or *Coreopsis lanceolata*. Removal or deadheading of spent flowers and inflorescences is primarily intended to maintain the neat appearance of those perennials that retain their shriveled flowers or produce unattractive fruits. Removing blooms also prevents the setting copious amounts of seeds that may spread around the garden. Deadheading, however, may also prolong flowering, promote a rebloom, and can extend the longevity of some short-lived perennials.

Injury to the underground parts of a plant may change the rhythm of its development as well. Łukasiewicz (1967) observed that digging around and disturbing roots of several plants, including *Anthericum liliago*, *Solidago canadensis*, *Stachys macrantha*, and *Veronica longifolia*, delayed their growth in the spring by 10 days. Likewise, spring transplanting can delay all developmental phases and prolong growth later into the fall. Established plants of *Clinopodium vulgare*, *Eryngium creticum*, and *Heliopsis helianthoides* flowered in Poznań, respectively, on 4 July, 9 July, and 8 July compared to 12 July, 11 September, and 1 August for those transplanted in the spring. The effect of fall transplanting on flowering was much less pronounced, a 4-day delay of *Linum perenne* and a 5-day delay of *Eryngium planum*.

Perennials and Phenology

Observations of seasonally recurring events, known as phenomena, in the lives of plants and animals were perhaps one of the earliest scientific pursuits of mankind. Since antiquity, farmers have kept such records for the purpose of preparing agricultural calendars. The first botanical records are thought to date back to 1490, when in Kraków, Poland, dates of flowering, fruiting, and other seasonal phenomena of several species growing around that city were inscribed on the pages of *Herbarius*, one of the early herbals published in Mainz, Germany. These notes were made consecutively for the next 37 years. But it was not until the 18th century that such observations were recognized as the scientific discipline of phenology. A branch of ecology, phenology describes the relationship between the timing of periodic biological phenomena and climate and other environmental factors.

The beginning of phenology as a science occurred with the establishment of the first network of observers recording leaf emergence, flowering, fruiting, and leaf fall in Sweden in the 18th century. Subsequently, such networks were organized in other European countries and North America in the 19th and early 20th centuries. The first international conference on phenology was held in 1935 in Gdańsk, Poland, where the ground was laid for adopting a system of standards assuring greater uniformity of phenological observations. Phenological gardens began using vegetatively propagated plants as indicators, providing more precision by eliminating genotypic variation. In the late 20th century, some of these phenological networks and gardens were discontinued because of the perceived low value of their findings for agriculture, but recent years saw a resurgence of interest in phenological records brought about by the growing awareness of global climate change.

The subject of phenology is a wide range of easily observable phenomena, called phenophases, such as bud-break, unfolding of the first leaf, or opening of the first flower. These various stages of plant development are described both quantitatively and qualitatively. In addition, environmental and climatic data are recorded, permitting correlation of the

Rudbeckia laciniata 'Herbstsonne'

variability in phenophase timing with the changes in a plant's habitat. As a result, phenological records offer a useful measure of the conditions in the environment and provide an indication of the impact that climatic changes have on plants.

The dependence of phenophase timing on environmental and climatic conditions explains the variability of bloom start date and bloom duration from one year to another, but also from one region to another. Bloom start date of *Ranunculus ficaria* can vary from March in England to May in Russia. Phenological records of flowering of numerous plants in the United States indicate that the difference between the southernmost and northernmost regions can be more than 10 weeks.

Plants normally spend their entire life in one location; therefore, their development is completely dependent on changes in the local weather and soil conditions. Because of the great number of environmental factors involved and the complex interactions between them, phenological studies are often limited to monitoring only one of these factors, commonly temperature, while trying to keep the other factors constant or ignoring them. In the 18th century, René de Réaumur proposed that every species of plant requires a given quantity of heat units, understood as a sum of temperatures, to reach a certain stage of development and that, with other conditions being equal, this quantity is constant. Later this approach was refined by considering only temperatures above a certain threshold value, which can vary from 0 to 15°C (32 to 60°F), depending on the species. It was also found that the number of heat units required to reach a particular phenophase is not constant, but diminishes with increasing latitude and elevation, and this threshold may be lower in cooler years than in the warmer ones. Northern populations of *Lythrum salicaria* in Sweden, when grown together with the southern populations in a common garden, initiated growth and flowering earlier and bloomed for a shorter period (Olsson and Ågren 2002).

The bloom start date of *Ranunculus ficaria* can vary from March to May across Europe.

Plants can be used as indicators of climatic changes because the timing of their phenophases is influenced by all weather elements. Therefore, bloom start dates collected over extended periods of time can validate meteorological findings regarding changing climate. Analysis of flowering dates of several hundred plants in the United Kingdom recorded between 1954 and 2000 (Sparks et al. 2006) showed that between 1991 and 2000 plants flowered, on average, 4.5 days earlier than during the 1954 to 1990 period. Not all of these plants were equally responsive to the warming weather, but one noteworthy example was *Lamium album*, whose average bloom start date advanced from March 18 to January 23. In addition, the degree to which species advanced their flowering varied: annuals advanced more than perennials, early species advanced more than late ones, and insect-pollinated species advanced more than wind-pollinated ones. Phenological studies indicate that a 1°C (1.8°F) increase of mean temperature in the United Kingdom is expected to advance flowering by 6 to 8 days, on average. Similar studies in the United States recorded bloom dates of designated varieties of *Syringa vulgaris*, *Lonicera tatarica*, and *Lonicera korolkowii* between 1957 and 1994 and concluded that these plants were now flowering about 1 week earlier than in the 1950s. Estimates of temperature increase caused by global warming in the 21st century vary considerably, but all are higher than the 0.7°C (1.3°F) increase recorded during the 20th century, when many regions experienced lengthening of the growing season from 1 to 3 weeks. In light of these predictions, phenologists will continue providing invaluable assessment of the impact that warming of the Earth will have on plant and animal communities.

Encyclopedia of Perennials and Their Bloom Times

The overwhelming majority of phenological studies concentrate on important crop plants, wild flora, or selected indicator plants, usually trees or shrubs. There is a scarcity of phenological observations of perennials, outside those included in the studies of native wild floras. At the same time, many gardening books provide very general information (usually unvalidated) on flowering of perennial plants in cultivation, reflecting an understandable curiosity that gardeners have about this phenomenon, but give only crude guidance as to when flowering can actually occur.

The longest phenological study of perennials in cultivation undertaken thus far appears to be that of Gennadii Nikolaevich Zaitsev (1978), who reported on observations conducted in the Main Botanical Garden in Moscow, Russia, over the course of 21 years, between 1949 and 1970. His study included 1384 taxa, representing 230 genera and 750 species. Moscow is located at about 56°N latitude and 150 m in elevation. The city's annual average temperature is 4.2°C (39.6°F; recorded from 1779 to 1991), and it lies in cold hardiness zone 5, bordering on 4 (this and all subsequent cold hardiness zone information refers to the USDA Plant Hardiness Zone Map, 1990; see the appendix for zone designations according to average annual minimum temperature).

Aleksander Łukasiewicz (1967) presented phenological data for more than 500 species of more than 250 genera of perennials cultivated in the Poznań Botanical Garden in Poland, collected from 1953 to 1956. His study was based on observations of many individual plants of each species growing in various parts of the garden. Poznań is located at about 52°N latitude and 60 m in elevation. Its annual average temperature is 8.1°C (46.6°F; recorded from 1951 to 1990), and it lies in cold hardiness zone 6.

In the United States, the Missouri Botanical Garden (2007) in St. Louis published flowering times of some 1600 perennials, representing about 250 genera, recorded between 2003 and 2006. St. Louis is located at about 39°N latitude and 170 m in elevation. The city's annual average temperature is 12.6°C (54.7°F; recorded from 1961 to 1990), and it lies in cold hardiness zone 6, bordering on zone 5.

Perennial borders at Longwood Gardens in May

June

July

August

September

Longwood Gardens in Kennett Square near Philadelphia, Pennsylvania, began its study in 1993; over the course of the next 14 years, the staff recorded flowering times of some 750 perennials belonging to about 200 genera growing in one location in the gardens. The early results for some 500 taxa were published in 2001 in *Perennials at Longwood Gardens*. The present book discusses in greater detail records for 462 taxa collected during 7 years, from 1999 to 2005. Kennett Square is located at 40°N latitude and about 90 m in elevation. Philadelphia's annual average temperature is 11.6°C (52.9°F; recorded from 1961 to 1990), and it lies in cold hardiness zone 6, bordering on zone 7.

All these locations experience the humid continental climate according to Köppen classification, with Moscow and Poznań having the cool summer subtype of that climate and Longwood and St. Louis having the warm summer subtype bordering on humid subtropical climate.

Observations at Longwood were collected weekly, starting from the first week of April until the first hard frost, usually in November or early December. In a few cases, such as *Helleborus niger*, flowering began before the first week of April; therefore, the true bloom start date was not recorded. Plants grew in a public demonstration garden and were subject to routine maintenance practices, including mulching, weeding, watering, and pruning, that were not always consistent from one year to another, but instead were dictated by esthetic considerations. Although this prevented attempts to formulate a model explaining the dependence of bloom time and duration on temperature and rainfall, it represented a typical garden situation.

With supplemental watering provided on an as-needed basis, the rainfall records had little meaning. The available temperature data were collected at a weather station in Philadelphia about 50 km from Longwood (Franklin Institute 2007); although the

October

data certainly differed from local conditions in the garden, they gave a broad picture of conditions during the period from 1999 to 2005, when bloom dates were recorded. The annual average temperatures ranged from 12.7°C (54.9°F) in 2000 to 15.2°C (59.4°F) in 2002. Another warm year, 2005, had a particularly hot summer with average temperatures staying above 25°C (77°F) from early July to mid-September. In comparison, during the summer of 2000, the coldest during this period, only twice did the weekly average temperature reach 25°C. The year 2004 had an exceptionally warm spring, when the weekly average temperature rose to above 15°C (59°F) at the end of April and reached 25°C (77°F) by the end of May, whereas the more typical change during the same time was from 10 to 20°C (50 to 68°F). During the particularly cold spring of 2003, the average temperature in the last week of May and the first week of June remained around 15°C (59°F). Overall, yearly fluctuations in weekly average temperature for the same week of the year ranged from 5 to 10°C (9 to 18°F).

Not all plants remained in the demonstration garden during the entire period from 1999 to 2005; some were removed before 2005, and others were planted after 1999. Therefore, observations for some plants covered fewer than 7 years. Data from all the years were combined to make charts showing the number of times each plant was in bloom during a given period of the year, with the relative height of each chart corresponding to the number of years the plant remained in the garden. This allows one to assess not only when a particular plant *can* flower, but also the probability that it *will* flower during a certain season. No evaluation of flower quantity was attempted, but one should expect late flowering or rebloom to be less profuse than that in the early part of the bloom period and the bloom peak of most plants to be skewed toward the beginning of the flowering season.

Acanthus

BEAR'S-BREECHES

The name *Acanthus* is derived from *akanthos*, the Greek name of the plant, which in turn has its root in the Greek *akantha*, *akanthes*, meaning a thorn or prickle, in reference to the general spiny character of the plant.

Acanthus balcanicus

BALKAN BEAR'S-BREECHES

This plant is native to the Balkans, from Serbia east to Romania and south to Greece. *Acanthus balcanicus* grows in forests, thickets, and scrubby open places on gravelly or stony hillsides. It has been cultivated since the late 19th century.

Acanthus balcanicus forms dense mounds of arching, bold foliage from which robust, erect, unbranched flowering stems rise to 1.2 m. The dull green, pinnately divided leaves can reach 1 m in length and usually lack spines. The widely spaced

Acanthus balcanicus

leaf lobes are narrowed at the base and have serrated margins. Flowers are 5 cm long and are held in dense, terminal, cylindrical spikes with large, conspicuous, spinose-dentate bracts and entire, lanceolate to linear bracteoles. The single-lipped, three-lobed corolla is white to purplish pink and is surrounded by darker, green or purple calyx lobes. The upper calyx lobe is about equal in size to the corolla and forms a hood over it. Fruits are capsules.

This perennial flowers freely, although after an exceptionally cold winter the leaves may emerge

Acanthus balcanicus

but no flowers will appear. *Acanthus balcanicus* is valued for its strong architectural effect and can be used successfully in both old-fashioned perennial borders and in minimalist contemporary-style gardens. Plant it in full sun, or in partial shade in hotter climates, in average, preferably light and deep, well-drained soil. Avoid sites that stay wet in winter. Control the spread of the plant, as it may encroach on the less vigorous plants around it. Cut back after flowering if the appearance becomes ratty. The plant will respond by sending new attractive leaves, provided the soil is sufficiently moist. *Acanthus balcanicus* is suitable for cutting as fresh flowers or for dry arrangements when in fruit. The plants are hardy to zone 6, but cover them with mulch in colder areas, especially during the first winter after planting.

The natural variability of *Acanthus balcanicus* with regard to its flower color has not been exploited, as no garden selections are available yet, although plants grown from seed collected from plants in cultivation may vary to some degree. Cultivated plants may often be of hybrid origin; see additional comments under *Acanthus spinosus*.

Acanthus balcanicus flowers in Germany and Poland from June to August. In warmer regions further south, it may begin flowering in late spring. At Longwood, it usually began flowering in the second week of June. Only twice in 7 years did it flower earlier, during the first week of June. Rarely, the flowering was delayed until the last week of June. On average it flowered for nearly 13 weeks, sometimes into late September or early October. Cutting back at the end of July or August only once resulted in plants reblooming in November.

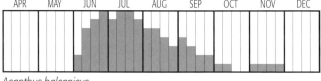

Acanthus balcanicus

Acanthus spinosus

OYSTER-PLANT, SPINY BEAR'S-BREECHES

This perennial is native to southern Europe, from southeastern Italy and the Balkans to the Aegean region and southwestern Turkey, where it is found growing in woodlands and meadows. *Acanthus spi-*

nosus has been cultivated since the early 17th century. It is said that Callimachus, the famous Greek architect, drew the inspiration for the design of the capital of the Corinthian column from the leaves of this plant.

Acanthus spinosus reaches 1.2 m in height when in bloom. Its basal leaves make a dense mound. The leaves are up to 60 cm long, shiny, dark green, deeply and irregularly pinnately dissected. The slim leaf lobes have prominent rigid white veins and jagged teeth tipped with sharp white spines. Flowers, subtended by shiny green, often-fringed bracts tipped with recurved spines, are borne in slender spikes up to 40 cm long. The purple, pink, or sometimes white corolla has an expanded three-lobed lower lip. Calyx lobes are purple tinged, the upper one forming a purplish hood over the corolla.

Acanthus spinosus flowers freely and consistently each year, although extremely cold winters can reduce the number of flowering spikes. Choose a position in the front of the bed to take advantage of the statuesque character of the plant and to show the handsome foliage and the imposing flower spikes. Use *A. spinosus* as a backdrop for lesser plants or display as a specimen in its own right, including planting in large vases or urns, where it performs surprisingly well for such a large plant. Although it will tolerate shady conditions, it flowers best in full sun. In hot climates, partial shade or morning-only sun is preferred. This perennial grows well in any fertile soil as long as it is reasonably well drained, but it performs best in medium, deep soil, in a warm and sheltered position. In cooler climates, the leaves remain fresh all season long. In warmer areas, cut it back in midsummer if the foliage looks ratty. This will soon be replaced by a new flush of growth. In mild winters, this second flush of foliage may last until spring. Be mindful of the stoloniferous nature of this plant, as it can colonize large areas, especially in loose, sandy soils. Dividing every 4 to 5 years helps to control the spread. In contrast, *A. spinosus* is rather slow to establish in clayey and dry soils. The plants are hardy to zone 7, possibly 5. Mulch the plants heavily before winter in colder areas.

Although plants in the wild vary in leaf shape and in the quantity of spines, the true *Acanthus spinosus* always has narrow-lobed and very strongly spiny leaves. Many broader-leaved and less spiny plants cultivated under the name of *A. spinosus* may be of hybrid origin. In fact, it is likely that the majority of bear's-breeches in cultivation are complex hybrids between *A. spinosus*, *A. balcanicus*, and *A. mollis*, the last species being native to southern Europe and northwestern Africa. Garden selections of *A. spinosus* in cultivation offer several choices primarily with regard to the foliage characteristics, including *A. spinosus* 'Lady Moore' with creamy white leaves in the spring, 'Royal Haughty' with leaves strongly

Acanthus spinosus

incised and highly mottled, and 'Spinosissimus' featuring sharply divided leaves, with narrow lobes and white spines.

Acanthus spinosus flowers in Ohio in June and July. In the United Kingdom, the cultivar 'Spinosissimus' flowers a little later, from July to September. At Longwood, the flowering of 'Spinosissimus' began between the first week of June and the first week of July. On average, the plants flowered for nearly 7 weeks, which is 6 weeks less than *A. balcanicus*, and the flowering never extended beyond the last week of July. Cutting back in mid-July did not result in plants reblooming later in the season.

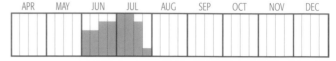

Acanthus spinosus 'Spinosissimus'

Achillea

YARROW

The name *Achillea* is for the mythical Greek hero of the Iliad, Achilles, son of Peleus and Thetis, who learned the healing properties of this plant from Chiron the Centaur.

Achillea clypeolata

YARROW

This plant is native to the Balkans, from the former Yugoslav republics in the north, to Albania in the west, south to Greece, and east to Romania, Bulgaria, and Turkey.

The clump-forming *Achillea clypeolata* grows to 60 cm tall. Its stems are erect, stout, unbranched, and densely felted above. The evergreen, finely and deeply pinnate, long-petiolate basal leaves are silvery gray to gray-green with densely felted hairs and can reach 15 cm in length. Cauline leaves become progressively smaller and less divided up the stem, with the uppermost being only 2 cm long and sessile. The tiny, golden yellow flower heads, comprising three or four ray florets and 10 to 20 disc florets, are borne in compact, flat-topped corymbs to 7 cm wide. Fruits are achenes.

Achillea clypeolata is valued for its exceptionally silvery foliage. It flowers freely, except when injured by extreme cold during the winter. Plant it in a sunny, exposed perennial border, a dry wall, or in a rock garden. Choose a spot in the front of the border where the silvery foliage will be well presented and not hidden by more vigorous plants. It needs excellent drainage year-round, but otherwise it can be grown in average or even dry soils. It tolerates summer heat and drought well. *Achillea clypeolata* is often short-lived unless regularly divided and trans-

Acanthus spinosus 'Spinosissimus'

planted every 4 to 5 years or sooner if flowering weakens. Remove spent flowers to encourage additional bloom from lateral buds. Later cut it back to basal foliage to improve the appearance and for a possible rebloom later in the season. It is excellent for using in dry flower arrangements. The plants are hardy to zone 6, possibly zone 4.

The true *Achillea clypeolata* is rarely cultivated. Plants grown in the gardens under this name are usually of hybrid origin, which are primarily crosses with *A. millefolium*. Some of them are backcrosses with *A. clypeolata*. Cultivars offer limited choices with regard to the intensity of the yellow color of the flowers, such as pale yellow *Achillea* 'Taygetea', sulfur yellow 'Anblo', or lemon yellow 'Moonshine' and 'Schwellenburg'.

Achillea clypeolata starts flowering in Germany and the United Kingdom in June and continues until August, with another possible flush of bloom on deadheaded plants. Younger, vigorous plants usually repeat bloom with deadheading, whereas older ones may not respond to this treatment. Sporadic rebloom may be produced in some years on plants that have been cut back. Flowering continues for a longer time when summers are cooler. At Longwood, the cultivar *Achillea* 'Moonshine' began flowering between the third week of May and the first week of June. It flowered, on average, for 9 weeks, usually into mid to late July, when they were cut back. Rebloom occurred in 3 of 7 years. Plants cut back in the second week of July resumed flowering 2 weeks later and flowered for an additional 5 weeks. Those cut back in the third week of July rebloomed for 2 weeks in late August, whereas those cut back in the end of July rebloomed for only 1 week at the end of October. Therefore, if one is hoping for

Achillea 'Moonshine'

Achillea 'Moonshine'

a meaningful rebloom, 'Moonshine' should be cut back no later than mid-July. The cultivar *Achillea* 'Schwellenburg' flowered on average for 7 weeks, starting at about the same time as 'Moonshine' but continued only until the end of June or, in some years, until the end of July or the first week of August. 'Schwellenburg' did not rebloom in the 6 years of the trials, even when cut back in mid-July.

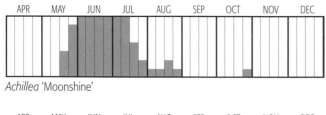

Achillea 'Moonshine'

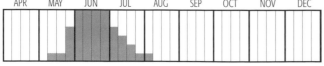

Achillea 'Schwellenburg'

Achillea filipendulina
FERN-LEAF YARROW

This perennial is native to Asia from Armenia and Iran north to the Caucasus and east to central Asia. *Achillea filipendulina* often grows in gravelly or sandy soils in river valleys, along streams, near springs, open dry slopes, forest openings and margins, and in shrubby thickets. It has been cultivated since the early 19th century, when it was introduced from the Caucasus.

Achillea filipendulina grows to 1.5 m tall when in bloom. It forms a clump of feathery, gray-green to green leaves, from which arise erect, stout, leafy stems carrying flower heads in large, dense corymbs. Leaves are alternate, pubescent, and aromatic. Basal leaves are up to 25 cm long, deeply pinnatisect with 10 to 15 linear-lanceolate, toothed segments. Cauline leaves are progressively reduced in size and less divided upward. Flower heads, comprising two to four golden yellow ray florets and 15 to 30 disc florets, are borne in dense compound convex to flat corymbs up to 12 cm wide.

Achillea filipendulina is among the tallest yarrows, with some of the garden selections reaching nearly 2 m in height. Golden yellow flowers with silvery gray foliage provide intense color and contrast when plants are used either as specimens or for massing in the perennial border, wild garden, or meadow. In a perennial border, position them toward the back of the border, as the ferny foliage that appears elegant early in the season may later become untidy. Plant *A. filipendulina* in full sun, in well-drained, rather dry, average soil of moderate fertility. Avoid planting in rich, moist soil or shady locations, where plants may become rank and will require staking. *Achillea filipendulina* tolerates drought but may produce smaller inflorescences under such conditions. This is an excellent cut flower, including dry flower arrangements, as it retains its color for years. For drying, cut stems before flowers begin shedding pollen. Deadhead to prolong the bloom. Cut back after flowering to tidy up the appearance and to encourage a rebloom. Divide every couple of years when clumps become overcrowded. Plants are hardy to zones 3 or 4.

Several botanical varieties of *Achillea filipendulina*, differing in details of the flower heads, have been described, including *leptocline*, *eupatoria*, *filicifolia*, and *szowitziana*, but they are encountered sporadically and

Achillea 'Coronation Gold'

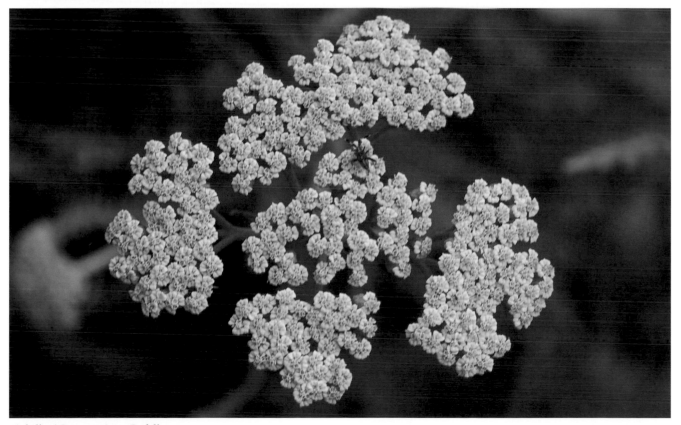

Achillea 'Coronation Gold'

do not have distinct distribution areas. Garden selections of *A. filipendulina* offer a range of colors from sulfur yellow to golden yellow. Many are more vigorous than plants in the wild and produce larger corymbs. Several hybrids have been developed between *A. filipendulina* and other species, such as *A. millefolium*, *A. ptarmica*, or *A. clypeolata*. Hybrid selections tend to be lower growing, about 60 cm in height. Some of the more popular cultivars include *Achillea* 'Altgold', 'Cloth of Gold', 'Coronation Gold', 'Credo', 'Gold Plate', 'Neugold', and 'Schwefelblüte'.

Achillea filipendulina began flowering in Poznań in late June to early July and ended in late August or early September. In Germany, it flowers in June and July, with selections such as 'Altgold' continuing into September. Similarly, it flowers in June and July in Illinois, and reblooms there about 1 month later if cut back. The cultivar *Achillea* 'Coronation Gold' in Ohio flowers from June to August. Removal of spent flowers prolongs the blooming period. Cultivars *Achillea* 'Parker's Variety' and 'Altgold' flower for a long period when regularly deadheaded. At Longwood, the cultivar 'Coronation Gold', which is a hybrid with *A. clypeolata*, began flowering at the end of May and the beginning of June. Rarely, its flowering started as early as the third week of May or as late as the second week of June. On average, it flowered for 8 weeks, usually into mid-July or late July in some years, at which point plants were cut back. No rebloom was observed in this cultivar. The cultivar *Achillea* 'Credo', which is a hybrid with *A. millefolium*, started flowering in early to mid-June and continued into mid-July or mid-August if plants were not cut back. Cutting back in mid-July only rarely resulted in rebloom in September and October. Like 'Coronation Gold', 'Credo' flowered for 8 weeks on average.

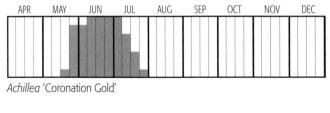

Achillea 'Coronation Gold'

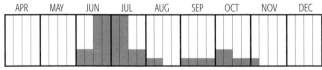

Achillea 'Credo'

Achillea millefolium

CARPENTER'S-WEED, COMMON YARROW, MILFOIL, NOSE-BLEED, SANGUINARY, SOLDIER'S WOUNDWEED, THOUSAND-SEAL

This plant is native to most of Europe and temperate parts of western Asia; it is rare in the Mediterranean region but can be found in the Caucasus and in northern Iran. It grows mostly in grasslands and waste places. *Achillea millefolium* has been cultivated since at least the 15th century, if not earlier. It has spread with European colonists to North America, Australia, and New Zealand, where it is now widely naturalized.

Achillea millefolium grows to 1.2 m tall. Its stems are erect or ascending, usually simple. The leaves are strongly aromatic, more or less pubescent, alternate, simple, finely two- or three-pinnatisect into thread-like segments, and of a soft ferny texture. The basal leaves in rosettes are lanceolate to oblanceolate, to 20 cm long, and have long petioles. The upper cauline leaves are smaller, narrower, and sessile. Flower heads have four to six ray florets and 10 to 20 disc florets and are borne in terminal, flat, dense corymbs to 7 cm wide. Flowers are usually white, rarely pink or red.

The wild types of *Achillea millefolium* are rarely cultivated in the garden due to their ability to spread rapidly, self-seed prolifically, and invade surrounding areas. In contrast, the color selections and hybrids are highly valued and used for massing in perennial borders, in naturalized areas, and for cut flowers. In time it makes large clumps, so avoid planting near slow-growing perennials, but combine this plant with equally vigorous plants. Grow it in full sun to partial shade in any well-drained soil of moderate fertility. *Achillea millefolium* grows successfully in dry soils. In fact, it is better to avoid moist, fertile soils, in which plants will grow too tall and will require staking to prevent flopping. Alternatively, cutting back before flowering will reduce the height and prevent flopping, but flowering will be delayed and corymbs will be smaller. Plant gray-leaved selections, which tend to be short-lived and less hardy, in warmer and drier positions. Deadhead and remove self-sown seedlings to prevent intrusion of plants with inferior colors. Deadheading will also extend the bloom time, whereas cutting back may encourage a rebloom. Divide and discard older parts of the clump every 2 years to keep its spread under control. Plants are hardy to zones 3 or 4.

Achillea millefolium is a polymorphic species, the variability of which is not fully understood. In Europe, two subspecies are recognized: *millefolium* with flowers usually white, found throughout the range; and *sudetica* with flowers usually pink, found in the mountains of central Europe. Garden forms include selections with flowers ranging from white to pink and red, as well as a number of hybrids. Galaxy Hybrids were developed by crossing with *Achillea* 'Taygetea', itself a hybrid between *A. clypeolata* and *A. millefolium*, and include lilac pink 'Apfelblüte', salmon pink 'Lachsschönheit', red 'Fanal', and yellow 'Hoffnung'. Garden selections are less invasive than the wild forms, and they vary in height from 45 cm, such as white 'Snow Sport' or rose 'Fire King', to nearly 1 m, including red 'Feuerland' and yellow 'Martina'.

Achillea 'Fanal'

Achillea 'Fanal'

Achillea 'Lachsschönheit'

Achillea millefolium 'Fire King'

Achillea 'Lachsschönheit'

Achillea millefolium 'Fire King'

Achillea millefolium 'Feuerland'

Achillea millefolium started flowering in Poznań between 13 and 19 June; in Alberta, Canada, on 21 June; and in Moscow around 30 June. It continues flowering in Poznań and Moscow until mid-August. Similarly, in Germany it flowers from June to August, but in the United Kingdom it can continue until November. In Chicago *A. millefolium* flowers in June and July, while in Ohio it can extend its bloom into August or even longer if deadheaded. In Chicago, plants rebloom about a month after being cut back, although flowers are less profuse. At Longwood, the cultivar 'Fire King' began flowering between the second week of May and the second week of June and, when cut back after the first flush of flowers, it continued on average for nearly 24 weeks until late October or the end of November. This cultivar flowers for an exceptionally long time. In Ohio, 'Fire King' flowers for 15 weeks when deadheaded. By comparison, the wild form of *A. millefolium* in Moscow bloomed for 6 or 7 weeks, whereas other selections on trial at Longwood flowered on average for 6 (*Achillea* 'Lachsschönheit') to 10 weeks (*Achillea* 'Fanal'). 'Lachsschönheit' had a relatively short first burst of flowering of 3 to 5 weeks, but after being cut it rebloomed for another 2 to 4 weeks in 3 of 7 years. In contrast, the first bloom of 'Fanal' continued for 5 to 9 weeks and was followed by a rebloom in 4 of 7 years. The cultivar 'Snow Sport', which in St. Louis flowered from late May or early June to mid-July or late August, at Longwood flowered on average for 8 weeks during approximately the same time, except for one year, when it started flowering in the second week of May. Similarly, 'Feuerland' flowered in St. Louis and Longwood from early June to mid or late July, but at Longwood in 3 of 6 years it rebloomed after being cut back in July.

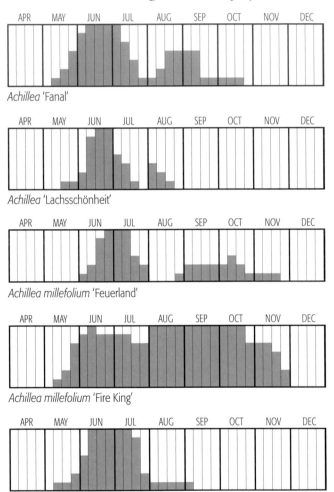

Achillea 'Fanal'

Achillea 'Lachsschönheit'

Achillea millefolium 'Feuerland'

Achillea millefolium 'Fire King'

Achillea millefolium 'Snow Sport'

Aconitum

MONKSHOOD

The name *Aconitum* is derived from *akoniton*, the Greek name used by Theophrastus for this plant. Ancient Greeks believed that the deadly properties of monkshood originated from the saliva of Cerberus (the mythical three-headed dog guarding the entrance to Hades), as it was being strangled by Hercules on the hills of Aconitus.

Aconitum carmichaelii

AUTUMN MONKSHOOD, AZURE MONKSHOOD

This perennial is native to eastern Asia, from northern Vietnam in the south, through most of China, to Kamchatka in the north. *Aconitum carmichaelii* grows in forest margins, scrub, and grassy slopes, up to 2200 m in elevation in the mountains. It has been cultivated since the late 19th century.

Aconitum carmichaelii forms erect, somewhat rigid clumps with tuberous rootstock and stout branched stems to 2 m tall. Its leaves are thinly leathery, deep dark green, glossy, to 15 cm long. They are palmately cleft nearly to the base into three segments, each further lobed and toothed. Panicles terminal, many-flowered, sparsely branched at the base, reach 10 cm (rarely 25 cm) in length. Flowers have large, showy, petal-like sepals, the uppermost forming an erect hood, and rather inconspicuous small petals hidden among the sepals. Flowers are usually light lavender blue. Fruits are follicles to 18 mm long.

Aconitum carmichaelii takes a very prominent position in the garden in the fall, and its rich green foliage is respectable all season long. It combines well with a number of late-blooming perennials. Although its stems are sturdy, staking may be advisable to prevent flopping in high wind at the time of flowering, when the plant becomes top-heavy. Afternoon shade and even moisture are needed for *A. carmichaelii* to show its best. Avoid harsh or dry sites where flowering may be impaired. It is suitable for cut flowers, but caution is warranted, as it is acutely toxic. Deadheading is not required, as it will not result in rebloom. Plants are hardy to zone 3.

Aconitum carmichaelii demonstrates considerable variability in the wild. With regard to height, it can vary from 60 cm to 2 m. In China, several botanical varieties have been recognized within this species, including *hwangshanicum*, *pubescens*, *tripartitum*, and *truppelianum*, but so far they have not been widely cultivated. In gardens, *A. carmichaelii* offers, in addition to the more vigorous and later-flowering Wilsonii Group, several choices with regard to the shade of the blue of the flowers, such as lighter lavender blue 'Spätlese' or deep blue 'Arendsii', as well as the height of the plant, from the 60-cm-tall 'Royal Flush' to the 2-m-tall 'Barker's Variety'.

In its native China, *Aconitum carmichaelii* is reported to flower in September and October. Similar

Aconitum carmichaelii

Aconitum carmichaelii

flowering times were recorded in Germany. In contrast, in Poland it flowered in August and September, and in Moscow even earlier, on average between 11 July and 8 August. At Longwood, the cultivar 'Arendsii' began flowering between the third week of September and the second week of October and continued to bloom for 6 weeks, on average, until the end of October or rarely until the end of November. Flowering of 'Arendsii' in September and October was also reported from Germany. Taller selections, such as those belonging to the Wilsonii Group, flower later (in Poland a month later) than the low-growing types.

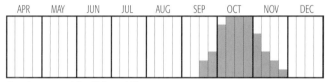

Aconitum carmichaelii 'Arendsii'

Aconogonon

ACONOGONON

The name *Aconogonon* is derived the Greek *acon*, whetstone, and *gone*, seed, in reference to the plant's rough seeds.

Aconogonon weyrichii

WEYRICH'S ACONOGONON

This plant is native to eastern Asia from central Honshu, Japan, north to Sakhalin, Russia. It has also naturalized in parts of Europe. *Aconogonon weyrichii* grows on gravelly slopes, in alpine meadows, margins of marshes, and along roadsides.

Aconogonon weyrichii forms upright clumps of erect, rough, densely pubescent stems to 1.2 m tall, simple or branched above, growing from a stout rhizome. The ovate, short-petiolate leaves, to 27 cm long, are green above and white-tomentose beneath. The dioecious, 2-mm-long, greenish white or white flowers are borne in dense, pyramidal, terminal panicles to 25 cm in length. Fruits are brown, 5- to 8-mm-long achenes.

In the garden, *Aconogonon weyrichii* is valued for its bold, lush foliage and showy flower clusters. Its ability to tolerate a wide range of growing conditions, including the presence of competing roots of nearby trees, makes it a useful companion plant in mixed borders, woodland margins, and similar in-

Aconogonon weyrichii

formal settings. The profuse russet brown seed heads provide a pleasing complement to fall colors of deciduous trees and shrubs. Preferably, plant *A. weyrichii* in light shade, although full sun can be tolerated in moist situations. It thrives in any average garden soil, as long as it is consistently moist. *Aconogonon weyrichii* spreads slowly and rarely needs dividing. Plants are hardy to zone 5.

In the wild in Japan, *Aconogonon weyrichii* flowers from July to September. When cultivated in Moscow it bloomed, on average, from 16 June to 23 September, whereas in Poznań flowering began on 6 June and ended between 19 and 29 August. At Longwood, the bloom start date varied by 6 weeks between the first week of June and the third week of July. Flowering usually continued until the end of July; but when plants that flowered in June were cut back at the end of that month, they rebloomed at the end of July. On average, *A. weyrichii* flowered for a little more than 4 weeks. In comparison, plants in Moscow bloomed for about 15 weeks.

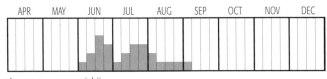

Aconogonon weyrichii

Actaea

BANEBERRY, BUGBANE

The name *Actaea* is derived from the Greek *aktea*, the ancient name for elder (*Sambucus*) because of the similarity of the leaves.

Actaea biternata
JAPANESE BUGBANE

This perennial is native to Japan and South Korea. In Japan *Actaea biternata* grows on the Pacific side of central Honshu in moist deciduous forests from sea level to about 1200 m.

Actaea biternata grows out of a horizontal, cylindrical rhizome and reaches 1 m in height at the time of flowering. Its stems are erect, simple, and glabrous. The basal leaves are dark green above, paler beneath, biternate to ternate, with ovate leaflets to 15 cm long, palmately lobed, and coarsely incised to

Actaea biternata

toothed. Cauline leaves are reduced and scale-like. The inflorescence is a spike to 60 cm long, simple to much branched in the lower part, and densely covered with short yellowish hairs. Flowers are white, appearing sessile. Petal-like sepals are widely elliptic, to 5 mm long, falling early. Petals are entire or emarginated, shortly clawed, to 5 mm long. Numerous showy stamens reach 8 mm in length. Fruits are ellipsoid follicles to 7 mm long.

In the garden, *Actaea biternata* requires some shade. Plant it in a woodland garden, among shrubs, or on the north side of a house. It combines well with other shade-loving plants and ferns. Avoid planting it in full sun, which may lead to leaf scorch, especially when the soil dries out. *Actaea biternata* grows best in soils rich in organic matter that is consistently moist. Apply leaf compost liberally in the spring. This species may be left without dividing for many years. Plants are hardy to zone 5.

Actaea biternata flowers in the wild in Japan from August to October. At Longwood, it began flowering in the first to third week of September and continued, on average, for 4 weeks until late September or early October.

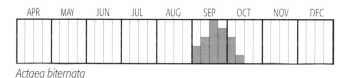

Actaea biternata

Actaea racemosa
BLACK COHOSH, BLACK SNAKEROOT, BUGBANE

This plant is native to the eastern United States and eastern Canada, from Ontario and Massachusetts in the north, to Alabama and Georgia in the south. *Actaea racemosa* grows in moist deciduous forests and along forest margins, on wooded slopes, in ravines, along creeks, in thickets and moist grasslands, from sea level to 1500 m in the mountains. It has been cultivated since the early 18th century.

Actaea racemosa grows to 2.5 m tall. Its erect and glabrous stems bear leaves only in the upper half. The leaves are medium to dark green, glabrous. They are divided, biternate or triternate, often again pinnate, with up to 70 ovate and irregularly serrated leaflets to 12 cm long. The wand-like inflorescences are weakly branched panicles, erect, slightly nodding, to

1 m long, topping wiry stems. The creamy white, unpleasantly scented flowers have four petal-like sepals, up to eight oblong and clawed petals 3 mm long, and up to 110 conspicuous stamens to 10 mm long. Fruits are rather attractive follicles to 10 mm long.

In the garden, *Actaea racemosa* is valued for its summer bloom, as well as for its large, finely divided leaves, which create an attractive clump all season long. Plant in naturalized settings, such as a woodland garden, large informal borders, or along edges of ponds or streams. It is especially effective when used in large masses. Position against a dark background, which helps to show small flowers better, or where they can be backlit by morning or evening sun. This species combines well with many wood-

land perennials. Because of the unpleasant odor of the flowers, choose a location away from paths or windows. *Actaea racemosa* grows best in partial shade but will tolerate deep shade. In cooler climates it can be grown in full sun, provided the soil stays consistently moist. When grown in shade, *A. racemosa* will tolerate drier soil or periodic summer drought. Plant in a woodland-type, rich, slightly acidic soil, high in organic matter that drains freely. After flowering, do not cut back but allow the seed heads to remain for fall and winter interest. *Actaea racemosa* does not require staking, but in windy locations it may be necessary to support individual flowering stems. The plant increases in size slowly, and it rarely needs replanting or dividing. Plants are hardy to zone 3.

Several botanical varieties of *Actaea racemosa* have been named in the past, but currently only the variety *dissecta* is recognized—and even this is of uncertain taxonomic standing. Plants of this variety have extremely dissected leaves and have been found from Connecticut to Delaware and Virginia.

Actaea racemosa flowers earlier than other species in the genus. In the wild, it blooms from June to September. In Germany and Poland, it flowers in July and August. Similarly, in Moscow *A. racemosa* began flowering around 12 July and ended around 17 August. In contrast, in St. Louis it bloomed about a month earlier, from early or late June to mid or late July. At Longwood, flowering began as early as the second week of June in some years, or as late as the second week of July in others. On average, plants were in bloom for almost 5 weeks until late July or early August. The same bloom duration was reported in Moscow.

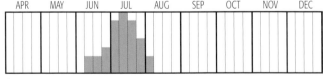

Actaea racemosa

Actaea rubifolia

APPALACHIAN BUGBANE, KEARNEY'S BUGBANE

This perennial is native to the eastern United States, primarily in the central and southern Appalachian Mountains at elevations from 300 to 900 m, but also has disjunct populations from Alabama in the

Actaea racemosa

Actaea rubifolia

south to Illinois in the north. *Actaea rubifolia* is found on wooded, usually north-facing slopes, hilly ridges, river bluffs, ravines, coves, and along rivers and creeks.

Actaea rubifolia grows to 2 m high. Its stems are upright, with several lateral branches, glabrous, usually brown or greenish brown. The leaves are shiny dark green above, paler and somewhat hispid beneath, ternate to biternate. They have three to nine leaflets, rarely more, with the terminal leaflet being much larger than the laterals, to 30 cm long. Leaflets are coarsely and irregularly dentate, two- to three-lobed, with base deeply cordate. The erect inflorescences are panicles of two to six raceme-like branches, to 60 cm long. The pale creamy white flowers are borne on short pedicels. The flowers have five sepals, no petals, and up to 65 stamens, each 6 mm long. Fruits are strongly compressed follicles to 20 mm long.

Actaea rubifolia is one of the easiest bugbanes to grow. Although it grows best under conditions similar to those recommended for *A. racemosa*, this species tolerates more open and drier conditions better than many other bugbanes. Plants are hardy to zone 3.

In the wild, *Actaea rubifolia* flowers from August to October, depending on the region. Similarly, plants in the gardens in Germany bloomed after mid-August. Plants at Longwood began flowering between the last week of July and the second week of August and continued, on average, for a little over 6 weeks, until the first or last week of September.

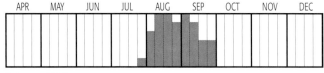

Actaea rubifolia

Actaea simplex

KAMCHATKA BUGBANE, SIMPLE-STEMMED BUGBANE

This plant is a native of western to northeastern China, Japan, Korea, eastern Mongolia, and southeastern Siberia and the Far East of Russia, including Sakhalin, Kamchatka, and the Kuril Islands. *Actaea simplex* grows in woodlands, scrub, along forest margins, on grassy slopes, in damp gulleys, and wet meadows in subalpine zones up to about 3000 m in elevation. This species has been cultivated since the late 19th century.

Actaea simplex grows out of a robust, blackish rhizome. Its erect, arching, usually unbranched, green or purplish stems reach 2.7 m at the time of flowering. The light green or purplish, smooth leaves are biternate or triternate. They consist of up to 80 leaflets, to 7 cm long, oval to ovate, often trilobed, with margins irregularly serrated. Cauline leaves are smaller and only once or twice ternate. The wand-like inflorescences are dense, simple, slightly nodding or arching racemes, rarely sparsely branched, to 30 cm long, with a densely white or gray pubescent rachis and pedicels. The pure white flowers are borne on pedicels to 10 mm long, have five sepals, one to three petals, and up to 42 stamens, each 9 mm in length. Fruits are follicles to 9 mm long.

In the garden, *Actaea simplex* is valued for the late-season bloom. It is most effective when used en masse in a dappled woodland garden or in a partially shaded mixed border, where it can be shown against fall foliage of trees and shrubs. It may be equally attractive when planted in a perennial border situated on the north side of a house. Like other bugbanes, *A. simplex* thrives in partial shade. Direct sunlight, especially in the afternoon, should be avoided, as it may lead to leaf scorch if the soil dries out. Plant *A. simplex* in consistently moist, humus-rich, woodland-type soil. It benefits from a generous addition of leaf compost in the spring. Usually, this plant does not require staking. The clumps increase slowly and do not need to be regularly divided. Plants are hardy to zones 3 or 4.

Actaea simplex is a species with a wide geographic distribution and considerable variability. Low-growing and late-blooming forms from Japan have been recognized as the variety *matsumurae*. But gardeners have capitalized primarily on this species' ability to produce offspring with varying degrees of purplish coloration in the leaves, stems, and flowers. When seed-grown, these plants are referred to as the Atropurpurea Group, but several clonal cultivars have also been introduced over the years, including 'Black Negligee', 'Braunlaub', 'Brunette', 'Elstead', and 'Hillside Black Beauty'.

In the wild, *Actaea simplex* flowers from July to October, depending on the region. Plants in the gardens in Germany bloomed from September to

October, and in the United Kingdom in October and November. But in Moscow they flowered earlier, starting around 17 August and ending around 2 October. *Actaea simplex* flowered in Chicago from late August until October, whereas in St. Louis flowering occurred from early September to mid-October. This species is usually the last bugbane to flower, and in the northern areas flowers may be damaged by early frost. At Longwood, the cultivar 'Brunette' usually bloomed from the first week of September, although in one year its flowering was delayed until the end of September. Flowering continued, on average, for about 4 weeks until the end of September or early October, which is almost 3 weeks less than bloom duration observed in Moscow.

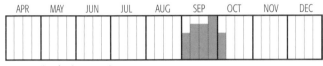

Actaea simplex 'Brunette'

Actaea simplex 'Brunette'

Adenophora

LADYBELL

The name *Adenophora* is derived from the Greek *aden*, a gland, and *phoreo*, to bear, in reference to the sticky nectary in the flower.

Adenophora liliifolia

LILYLEAF LADYBELL

This plant is native from central and eastern Europe east to Siberia, northern Mongolia, and Manchuria, where it grows in forests and moist meadows.

Adenophora liliifolia grows out of deep, fleshy, thick roots. Its leafy, branching stems make an erect clump to 1.2 m tall. The nearly round, long-petiolate, basal leaves senesce before the plant flowers. The medium green, 7-cm-long, cauline leaves are ovate to lanceolate, serrate, with the lowermost short-petiolate, the others sessile. The stems are topped with a terminal, spire-like pyramidal panicle. Fragrant, nodding flowers have a light blue to

Adenophora liliifolia

Adenophora liliifolia

creamy white, broadly campanulate corolla to 2 cm long. Fruits are capsules crowned with a ring of persistent calyx lobes.

In the garden, free-flowering *Adenophora liliifolia* adds blue in midsummer. Because its flowers are rather small and of delicate colors, it is best to use this plant in large groupings and away from brightly colored, large-flowered perennials. Plant it in a border or in a woodland garden, where it can be allowed to naturalize. Because *A. liliifolia* foliage does not appear particularly attractive once the flowering is finished, combine it with plants that can provide foliage interest all season long. It thrives in full sun to partial shade. When given a little shade, at least during the hottest part of the day, *A. liliifolia* will tolerate summer drought. Growing in deep shade may lead to this plant becoming lanky and prone to flopping. In this case, trim the plants in early May, before flowering, to reduce their ultimate height. Choose a site with loose, humus-rich, moderately fertile, moist, well-drained soil. Amend heavier clay soil to improve drainage. Although *A. liliifolia* spreads very slowly, it self-seeds easily. To prevent this and to prolong the bloom, deadhead spent flowers to lateral buds and then cut back when the flowering is over. Avoid disturbing the deep roots, and transplant or divide the plants only when necessary. Plants are hardy to zones 3 or 4.

Adenophora liliifolia blooms in Germany from July to August. In Poznań flowering started between 27 July and 2 August and ended between 26 August and 13 September. It flowered in Chicago in July and August, whereas in St. Louis it flowered from early June to mid-July or mid-August and again from early September to mid or late October. At Longwood, the start of the bloom varied by as much as 5 weeks: in some years was as early as the first week of June, in others as late as the second week of July. On average, the plants flowered for almost 11 weeks, although in most years flowering stopped during the hottest weeks of August, returning with cooler temperatures in September.

APR	MAY	JUN	JUL	AUG	SEP	OCT	NOV	DEC

Adenophora liliifolia

Agastache
GIANT-HYSSOP

The name *Agastache* comes from the Greek words *agan*, much, and *stachys*, ear of grain, in reference to the numerous flower spikes.

Agastache foeniculum
ANISE-HYSSOP, ANISE-MINT, BLUE GIANT-HYSSOP, FRAGRANT GIANT-HYSSOP

This perennial is native to north-central regions of North America, from Manitoba and Wisconsin, south to Kansas, and west to Alberta and Colorado. It grows in dry woodlands and prairies, old fields,

Agastache foeniculum

Agastache 'Blue Fortune'

dry scrub, and hills. *Agastache foeniculum* has become naturalized in parts of eastern North America.

Agastache foeniculum forms clumps of erect, weakly branched stems to 1.5 m tall. Its ovate or lanceolate leaves are strongly aromatic, with licorice or anise aroma when crushed. They have a serrate margin; white, minute, dense hairs beneath; and reach 8 cm in length. The small, 10-mm-long, tubular flowers range in color from lavender blue to bright purple. They are subtended by large violet bracts and tightly arranged in dense terminal, branched spikes to 12 cm long. Fruits are minute yellowish brown nutlets.

In the garden, *Agastache foeniculum* has a bold visual impact in a perennial border, where it provides a strong vertical element. Plant low-growing perennials in front of it to hide its usually bare lower parts of the stems. As an aromatic plant, *A. foeniculum* has its place in an herb garden. Allow it to naturalize in a prairie garden, where it will self-seed and thrive without maintenance. In the spring it develops attractive, purplish new foliage, which later fades to green. Position it in full sun, although it will tolerate partial shade. *Agastache foeniculum* grows well in an average, preferably sandy to loamy, moderately wet, well-drained soil. Avoid clay soil, or at least amend it to improve the drainage. Once established, *A. foeniculum* can tolerate drought and summer heat. Deadhead spent flowers if self-seeding is objectionable. If low-growing and better-branched plants are desired, cut back to about 30 cm in the spring. Its flowers are good not only for cutting but are edible and have sweet licorice taste. Similarly, leaves are used in herbal teas, salads, and drinks. Plants are hardy to zone 6, possibly zone 4.

Agastache foeniculum has been widely used in hybridizing with other species of the genus, including *A. rugosa*, *A. urticifolia*, and *A. cana*. Garden varieties offer a range of flower colors from white, such as 'Honey Bee White' and 'Liquorice White', to various shades of lavender and purple, including 'Blue Fortune' and 'Serpentine', as well as a choice of variegated plants, such as golden-leaved 'Golden Jubilee'. A number of these varieties are seed propagated.

Agastache 'Liquorice White'

Agastache foeniculum blooms for a long time from midsummer into autumn. In Germany, it flowers from June to August. In St. Louis, the cultivar 'Honey Bee Blue' flowered in late August. At Longwood, *A. foeniculum* began to bloom between the first week of July and the third week of August. On average, it continued flowering, without deadheading, for nearly 12 weeks, into late September or early October.

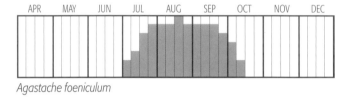

| APR | MAY | JUN | JUL | AUG | SEP | OCT | NOV | DEC |

Agastache foeniculum

Agastache nepetoides

CATNIP GIANT–HYSSOP, YELLOW GIANT–HYSSOP

This perennial is native to southern Canada and the eastern United States, from Vermont to southern Ontario, Wisconsin, and Nebraska, south to Georgia and Arkansas. *Agastache nepetoides* can be found growing in moist, rich, open woodland areas, thickets, scrub, and old fields.

Agastache nepetoides forms clumps of erect, sturdy stems, branched near the top, to 2.5 m tall. Its ovate leaves have coarsely serrate margins and reach 15 cm in length. Small 7-mm-long yellowish green or white flowers are borne in whorls arranged in dense, stiff, cylindrical, spikes, to 20 cm long. Fruits are tiny yellowish nutlets.

Agastache nepetoides

In the garden, *Agastache nepetoides* is valued for its long, late-summer bloom, attracting scores of bees and butterflies. Plant it in large bold groupings in the perennial border or allow it to naturalize in a wildflower or woodland garden. It thrives in any average, moderately wet, well-drained soil in either full sun or partial shade. Once established, *A. nepetoides* tolerates summer heat and humidity. Plants are hardy to zone 5, possibly zone 3.

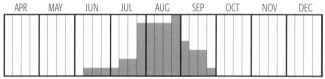

APR	MAY	JUN	JUL	AUG	SEP	OCT	NOV	DEC

Agastache nepetoides

Agastache nepetoides

In the wild, *Agastache nepetoides* blooms typically in August and September, although in St. Louis it may begin flowering in July. At Longwood, it started to flower usually in the last week of July, but in rare instances it bloomed as early as the second week of June. On average, it bloomed for a little over 7 weeks, until early September. Once in 7 years, *A. nepetoides* was still in flower in the last week of September.

Agastache rupestris

ROCK ANISE-HYSSOP, SUNSET-HYSSOP,
THREADLEAF GIANT-HYSSOP

This plant is native to the southwestern United States, from Arizona to New Mexico. *Agastache rupestris* is found growing in open forests, at elevations between 1500 and 2100 m.

Agastache rupestris forms a woody-based clump of slender, branched, and wiry stems to 1 m tall. Its narrow, linear, grayish green, 5-cm-long leaves have a strong mint aroma and are used fresh or dry in herbal teas. Its 2.5-cm-long, tubular, salmon orange flowers with purplish calyxes are sweetly fragrant. The flowers are borne in whorls in erect, terminal spikes. Fruits are tiny nutlets.

Agastache rupestris is grown in perennial borders, herb and rock gardens, and in containers. Its flowers bring bees and butterflies into the garden. Plant it in full sun or partial shade. It thrives in average, moderately moist, or even dry soil, as long as it is well drained. Avoid unamended clay soil that stays wet, especially in winter. Once established, *A. rupestris* can withstand summer heat and drought. Cutting back after flowering may encourage a rebloom in the fall. Plants are hardy to zone 6, possibly zone 4.

Perhaps more commonly cultivated than *Agastache rupestris* are its hybrids with *A. coccinea*, *A. mexicana*, and possibly other species developed as part of the Western Hybrids. They include 'Firebird' with coppery orange-salmon flowers, 'Pink Panther' featuring vivid magenta flowers, and the pink-flowered 'Tutti Frutti'.

Flowers of *Agastache rupestris* appear over a long period from June to September. If cut back in late summer, plants may rebloom in the fall. In St. Louis, 'Firebird', a hybrid of *A. rupestris* and *A. coccinea*, flowered from the first or second week of July until mid-October. At Longwood, 'Firebird' began flowering between mid-June and early July and continued on

Agastache 'Pink Panther'

average for more than 18 weeks, usually until mid-October, rarely mid-November. The cultivar 'Pink Panther' flowered continuously for more than 16 weeks, on average, from late June or mid-July until the end of September or sometimes into mid-November. No deadheading or cutting back was required on these two hybrids to enjoy these extended bloom times.

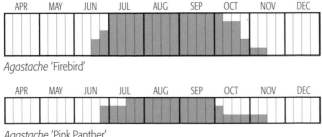

APR	MAY	JUN	JUL	AUG	SEP	OCT	NOV	DEC

Agastache 'Firebird'

APR	MAY	JUN	JUL	AUG	SEP	OCT	NOV	DEC

Agastache 'Pink Panther'

Ageratina

SNAKEROOT

The name *Ageratina* is a diminutive form of a Latin name of another plant, *Ageratum*, which it resembles and was initially classified as such.

Ageratina altissima

RICHWEED, WHITE SANICLE, WHITE SNAKEROOT

This perennial is native to eastern North America, from New Brunswick to Saskatchewan and south to Georgia and Texas. *Ageratina altissima* is found in moist, rich or rocky woods and cove forests, thickets, and woodland margins.

Ageratina altissima grows out of fibrous-rooted, sometimes rhizomatous, crowns to form clumps of erect or ascending, branched above, brown, slender stems to 1.2 m tall. Its deep green, prominently veined, ovate, coarsely and sharply serrate leaves reach 15 cm in length. Brilliant white flowers are arranged in small, 6-mm-wide heads clustered in flat-topped corymbs to 10 cm across, borne at the tips of branches. Fruits are achenes.

In the garden, *Ageratina altissima* provides late-season bloom at a time when choices of white-flowering plants may be limited. Grow it in the informal setting of a cottage garden or allow it to naturalize in a woodland garden, where it can combine with large sweeps of ferns or grasses. Although *A. altissima* is at its best in full sun, it grows successfully in partial shade. Plant it preferably in a rather moist, humus-rich soil that is well drained. However, when grown in a shady corner it will tolerate dry soil conditions. It spreads quickly, thanks to its vigorous rhizomes and prolific seed production. Deadhead or cut back after flowering if self-seeding is not welcomed. Plants are hardy to zones 3 or 4.

Two variants have been described throughout the geographic range of *Ageratina altissima*. Variety *angustata*, distinguished by its narrow leaves, is found at low elevations (up to 800 m) in the southeastern United States, although its taxonomic standing is questioned. The other is variety *roanensis*, with longer and pointier involucral bracts, growing at higher elevations (700–1500 m) in the Appalachian Mountains. Garden varieties include two cultivars with dark purple-brown foliage, 'Braunlaub' and 'Chocolate'.

In the wild, *Ageratina altissima* blooms from late summer until frost. In Germany, it flowers from July to September. In St. Louis, began flowering between the second week of June and the second week of July and to continue until mid-September. At Longwood, the cultivar 'Chocolate' usually started flowering in mid-September. Only once in 7 years, its bloom began a month earlier, in mid-August. On average, 'Chocolate' flowered for 4 weeks into early October, although in some years it was in bloom in the second and third week of October.

Ageratina altissima 'Chocolate'

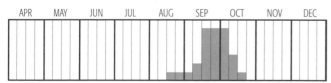

Ageratina altissima 'Chocolate'

Ageratina altissima 'Chocolate'

Ajuga

BUGLEWEED

The name *Ajuga* is derived from the Latin *ajugatus*, not yoked, in reference to the five-toothed, disconnected calyx.

Ajuga reptans

BUGLE, CARPET BUGLEWEED, COMMON BUGLEWEED

This plant is native to most of Europe, northern Africa, Asia Minor, and east to Iran. It grows in meadows and open thickets in deciduous and coniferous woodlands on somewhat moist, fertile soil. *Ajuga reptans* has been cultivated since the early 19th century.

Ajuga reptans forms a prostrate, dense mat of semi-evergreen leafy rosettes, among which appear fast-growing foliate stolons to 40 cm long. The oblong or obovate basal leaves are long-petiolate, nearly entire or slightly crenate, and reach 9 cm in length. The elliptic or ovate upper and floral leaves are sessile and alternate at each node. The large, leaf-like bracts are ovate and often tinged with purple-blue. Flowers, to 17 mm long, are usually violet blue, sometimes purple, pink, or white. The basal flowers are arranged in four- to eight-flowered whorls; the uppermost ones are condensed in a compact, terminal spikes. Fruits are nutlets.

In the garden, *Ajuga reptans* is valued as an excellent ground cover, forming dense mats, vigorous

Ajuga reptans 'Burgundy Glow'

Ajuga reptans 'Burgundy Glow'

and attractive year-round. It is particularly useful in shaded corners of the garden, where it can underplant other vigorous perennials or bulbs. Purple-leaved forms are effective in the company of gray- or golden-foliaged plants. Because of this species' rapid spreading, avoid planting it near the lawn edge. *Ajuga reptans*, especially its color-leaved varieties, performs best in partial shade, but it can be grown in full sun provided the soil is consistently moist. Plant it preferably in a moist to moderately dry humus-rich soil, although *A. reptans* can tolerate poor soils as long as they are well drained. When grown in a shaded position, plants will even tolerate periodic droughts. Control its spread by cutting back spent floral stems and trimming stolons, if necessary. Plants are hardy to zones 3 or 4.

Garden selections, some of which may be hybrids with other species, such as *Ajuga pyramidalis* or *A. genevensis*, offer a wide selection of foliage colors, including dark purple, such as 'Braunherz' and 'Purple Brocade', and variegated, 'Burgundy Glow', 'Multicolor', and 'Variegata' among them. Furthermore, cultivars vary in their flower colors and include white 'Schneekerze', lavender 'Valfredda', blue 'Catlin's Giant', and indigo 'Jungle Beauty'. Many cultivars are also more compact and less invasive than the wild types.

In Germany and Poland, *Ajuga reptans* begins flowering in May or June and may still be in flower from July to September. In Moscow, 'Variegata' flowered from around 13 June to 8 July, whereas 'Multicolor' flowered from around 27 May to 26 June. In the United States, *A. reptans* flowers in Chicago in May and June, but in St. Louis it flowered in the second week of April until the end of that month. At Longwood, 'Catlin's Giant' flowered from the first to the last week of May, for, on average, nearly 4 weeks. In comparison, 'Catlin's Giant' in St. Louis flowered from late March or mid-April until early May and, one year, again from early June until the end of July. No rebloom was observed at Longwood during the 4 years of data collection. The average bloom du-

Ajuga reptans 'Catlin's Giant'

ration of 'Catlin's Giant' at Longwood was similar to that recorded in Moscow for 'Variegata', 25 days, and 'Multicolor', 30 days.

Alchemilla

LADY'S-MANTLE

The name *Alchemilla* is a Latinized form of an Arabic name of the plant, *alkemelych* or *al-kemelih*.

Alchemilla fulgens

PYRENEES LADY'S-MANTLE

This perennial is native to France and Spain, where it grows in the Pyrenees. *Alchemilla fulgens* inhabits montane grasslands and scrub. It has been cultivated since the late 19th century.

Alchemilla fulgens forms a clump of basal leaves and flowering stems up to 30 cm tall, growing out of a woody rhizome. The plants are densely covered with silky hairs, except for nearly glabrous pedicels. The basal, orbicular leaves have nine to 11 lobes and are often silvery beneath and sparsely appressed-hairy above. Stem leaves have fewer lobes. The rounded lobes have short incisions and seven to nine acute teeth. The small green or yellowish flowers are clustered in loose or tight, branched, cymose inflorescences. Perianth consists of four outer epicalyx segments and four sepals, but lack petals. Fruits are achenes.

In the garden, plant *Alchemilla fulgens* in the front of the perennial border or in larger groups as a ground cover, where its silky leaves sparkling with rain or dew droplets can be seen and enjoyed. The attractive foliage of *A. fulgens* is complemented by fine-textured inflorescences, excellent for cutting and drying for winter arrangements. It grows best in areas with cool and moist summers. In hotter climates, provide some shading and moist, fertile soil. In cooler climates, it thrives in full sun or partial shade in any humus-rich, well-drained, evenly moist soil. Under favorable conditions *A. fulgens* may seed itself although not to the point of becoming a problem. Cut back after flowering for a cleaner appearance. Plants are hardy to zone 4.

Alchemilla fulgens flowers in late spring to early summer. The duration of the bloom period is reduced in hot weather. At Longwood, *A. fulgens* began flowering as early as the second week of May or as late as the first week of June. It then flowered, on average, for nearly 5 weeks until early June or late June. In 2 of 7 years, it flowered until the first week of July. Cutting back flowering stems did not lead to a rebloom.

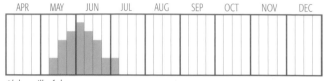

APR	MAY	JUN	JUL	AUG	SEP	OCT	NOV	DEC

Alchemilla fulgens

Alchemilla mollis

Alchemilla mollis
LADY'S-MANTLE

This plant is native to Europe and western Asia, from the Carpathian to the Caucasus Mountains. *Alchemilla mollis* grows in moist meadows and woodland margins. It has been cultivated since the late 19th century.

Alchemilla mollis forms robust, dense, leafy mounds to 80 cm tall when in flower. Its 15-cm-wide leaves are rounded, gray-green, densely felted with soft hairs and have nine to 11 shallow lobes with serrated edges. The greenish yellow, apetalous flowers have epicalyx segments nearly as long as sepals, giving the appearance of tiny stars, to 6 mm wide. The flowers are borne in loose, spreading compound cymes atop stems rising above the foliage.

In the garden, *Alchemilla mollis* makes an excellent ground cover and creates a handsome finish to an edge of the border or path. Its delicate flowers and elegant foliage combine effortlessly with any perennials that thrive under the same conditions. As flowers age, their lime green color changes to a dull brown and, in some situations, may have a desirable, prolonged effect. If not, they can be easily cut back, leaving behind neat, characteristically scalloped leaves. The ability of *A. mollis* (like *A. fulgens*) to cradle dew or rain drops on its leaves only adds to its pleasing appearance. Plant it in partial shade or full sun. In hotter climates avoid sunny, dry sites and provide at least afternoon shade. Otherwise, the leaves may wilt and scorch, and the plants will be short-lived. *Alchemilla mollis* grows well in light shade under a high canopy of trees as long as the soil stays evenly moist. Although it is not demanding with regard to the soil, choose for *A. mollis* a site with preferably moist but well-drained soil. Under optimum growing conditions, it self-seeds freely, but rarely to the point where the seedling could not be enjoyed or easily removed if not needed. Flowering stems can be cut for fresh or dry arrangements. Otherwise, they can be cut back after flowering to better show the neat foliage, prevent self-seeding, and encourage a possibility of a sparse rebloom in late summer. Plants overwinter better when their leaves are not cut back. This plant rarely needs dividing, at most every 6 to 10 years. Plants are hardy to zones 3 or 4.

Alchemilla mollis is the most commonly grown species of *Alchemilla*, although sometimes it is disguised under the name *A. vulgaris*, which belongs to a different plant. Garden selections, such as 'Auslese', 'Robusta', 'Senior', 'Thriller', offer larger, fuller, and more prolific inflorescences, as well as stronger gray-green foliage.

Alchemilla mollis flowers in Poland from June to August. In the United States, it blooms in Chicago and St. Louis from mid-May to late June. When cut back, plants may produce sporadic blooms later in the season. At Longwood, flowering began between the second week of May and the first week of June and continued, on average, for over 6 weeks until late June, rarely the second week of July. Cutting plants back after flowering did not result in repeat bloom later in the season.

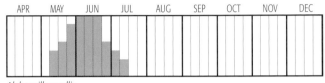

Alchemilla mollis

Alchemilla mollis

Allium

ONION

The name *Allium* is a classical name for garlic, one of the species in this genus.

Allium aflatunense

PERSIAN ONION

This perennial is native to central Asia, in Kazakhstan, Uzbekistan, and Kyrgyzstan. *Allium aflatunense* grows in montane meadows and grasslands. It has been cultivated since the early 20th century, when it was introduced to the trade by Van Tubergen, a Dutch bulb company.

Allium 'Mars'

Allium aflatunense

Allium 'Mount Everest'

Allium aflatunense produces six to eight strap-shaped basal leaves and 1-m-tall erect, flowering scapes growing out of ovoid bulbs covered with a papery tunic. The slightly glaucous leaves, up to 10 cm wide, senesce soon after the flower appears. The star-shaped, lilac and purple-striped flowers are borne in a dense spherical umbel, to 10 cm wide. Fruits are 5-mm-long capsules.

In the garden, plant *Allium aflatunense* in a perennial border among plants that can hide its withering leaves at the time of flowering. Its flowers in shades of lilac blend easily with a variety of color combinations. Choose a sunny spot for it in a well-drained location, preferably with a light, fertile loamy soil. Avoid sites with heavy clay that drain poorly. *Allium aflatunense* is also valued as a long-lasting cut flower, suitable even for dry arrangements. Under optimum growing conditions it often self-seeds. Plants are hardy to zone 4.

Garden varieties are mostly hybrids, some of uncertain parentage, involving such species as *Allium macleanii* and *A. stipitatum*. They offer flower color variants from the white 'Mount Everest' and lilac 'Rien Poortvliet' to the reddish purple 'Mars' and

Allium 'Purple Sensation'

dark violet 'Purple Sensation' and often have large umbels, to 15 cm wide.

Allium aflatunense flowers in late spring. In Germany and the United Kingdom, it blooms in late May. At Longwood, it began flowering between the first and the third week of May and continued, on average, for a little over 3 weeks, into the third or fourth week of May. Only once in 7 years, it flowered until the first week of June. Two hybrid selections, 'Mars' and 'Mount Everest', also flowered for little more than 3 weeks, but about a week later, starting between the second or fourth week of May and ending in early June.

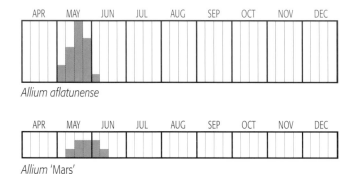

Allium aflatunense

Allium 'Mars'

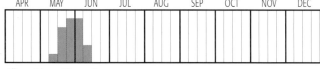

Allium 'Mount Everest'

Allium karataviense

BLUE-TONGUE ALLIUM, TURKISTAN ONION

This plant is native to central Asia in Tajikistan and Kyrgyzstan, where it grows in hot dry steppes, and in western Tien Shan, where it is found on loose limestone screes.

Allium karataviense usually produces two bold basal leaves and an erect flowering stalk to 35 cm long growing out of a rounded bulb covered with a blackish papery tunic. The thick, gray-green, broadly elliptic, up to 15 cm wide, purple-mottled leaves are longer than the stem and rolled outward at tips. The small, stellate, silver-lilac flowers are borne in dense, globose umbels to 15 cm wide. The umbels are subtended by two or three purplish brown bracts. Fruits are reversed heart-shaped capsules.

In the garden, *Allium karataviense* is grown as much for the foliage as for the flowers. Its leaves and

seed capsules persist and remain attractive long after flowering. Plant it in full sun, in any well-drained soil, in a perennial or mixed border, including rock gardens. *Allium karataviense* makes an unusual plant for planting in containers. Flowers can be used in dried arrangements. Once planted, leave it undisturbed for years. Plants are hardy to zone 4.

Allium karataviense flowers in the wild in April and May, becoming dormant by June. In cultivation in Germany it blooms in May and June or earlier if the preceding winter is mild. At Longwood, it began flowering between the second and fourth week of May and continued, on average, for 4 weeks until early June.

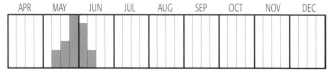

Allium karataviense

Allium senescens

GERMAN GARLIC, MOUNTAIN GARLIC

This perennial is native from central and southern Europe east to Mongolia, northern China, and Korea. *Allium senescens* grows in dry meadows, steppes, forests, on dry rocky, gravelly or sandy soils, up to 800 m in elevation in the mountains.

Allium senescens forms narrow, bottle-shaped bulbs, covered by a blackish gray tunic, that are clustered on rhizomes. Out of the bulbs grow clumps of linear, basal leaves, to 15 cm high, and leafless flowering stems to 45 cm tall. The gray-green leaves are flat, spirally arranged, and slightly twisted, giving the foliage a swirled appearance. When bruised, leaves give off an onion smell. The cup-shaped, lilac or mauve flowers are borne in 5-cm-wide hemispherical umbels subtended by a persistent two- to three-lobed spathe. Fruits are small capsules 4 mm long.

Thanks to its gray-green swirling foliage, *Allium senescens* makes an attractive ground cover or edging plant. Take advantage of the smaller stature of this *Allium* and use it in the intricate knot and herb garden, on top of a stone wall, or in a rock garden. Plant it in full sun, except in areas with hot summers, where some light shade in the afternoon is beneficial. It can tolerate a wide range of soils provided they drain easily. Once established, plants can even withstand summer droughts. Clumps of *A. senescens*

Allium karataviense

Allium senescens ssp. *montanum* var. *glaucum*

Allium senescens 'Summer Beauty'

spread slowly and limited self-seeding may occur. Deadhead flowers before seed sets if self-seeding becomes a nuisance. Plants are hardy to zone 4.

Allium senescens is quite variable in leaves and plant size. The two primary subspecies described in the wild are *senescens* of northern Asia, a taller plant with wider leaves, and *montanum* from Ukraine to northern Portugal, a low-growing plant with narrower leaves. Plants with exceptionally glaucous leaves, frequently in cultivation, are *A. senescens* ssp. *montanum* var. *glaucum*. Plants cultivated under the cultivar name 'Summer Beauty' also represent the same subspecies.

Allium senescens flowers in the wild from July to August. In the United Kingdom, its bloom time may extend to September. In St. Louis, variety *glaucum* flowered from mid-May to early or late September.

At Longwood, the same variety began to bloom between the second week of August and the first week of September. It flowered, on average, for a little over 5 weeks, into mid or late September.

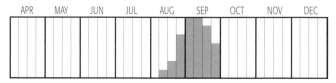

Allium senescens ssp. *montanum* var. *glaucum*

Allium sphaerocephalon

DRUMSTICK CHIVES, ROUND-HEADED GARLIC, ROUND-HEADED LEEK

This perennial is native from central and southern Europe, south to northern Africa, and east to the Caucasus and western Asia. *Allium sphaerocephalon* has been

Allium sphaerocephalon

in cultivation since the late 16th century. It grows in open, dry habitats, including cultivated ground.

Allium sphaerocephalon forms an ovoid bulb, covered by a membranous tunic, and smaller bulblets enclosed in the stem sheath. The bulb produces three to five upright, 5-mm-wide, hollow, semi-cylindrical, broadly grooved leaves, and a flowering stem to 1 m tall. The purple to carmine red, widely campanulate flowers are borne in globose or ovoid, very dense umbels to 6 cm wide, subtended by two persistent spathes. Flowers open from green buds, providing the whole umbel a transient two-color effect. Long stamens give the umbels an airy appearance. Occasionally, the umbels carry small bulbils. Fruits are 4-mm-long capsules.

For a real impact in the garden, plant *Allium sphaerocephalon* in large groupings. Interplant among other perennials with fuller foliage, as the leaves of this *Allium* are rather few and narrow. Plant in full sun, in a warm, protected site, in a well-drained, preferably light, sandy soil. Under favorable conditions, it will increase freely through bulb divisions and aerial bulbils falling on the ground. *Allium sphaerocephalon* is valued as a long-lasting cut flower. Plants are hardy to zones 4 or 5.

In the wild, *Allium sphaerocephalon* is quite a variable species. In Europe, three subspecies have been recognized. Subspecies *sphaerocephalon* has pink or reddish purple flowers and is found throughout the species' range. Subspecies *arvense* has white flowers with a green or yellowish keel on each tepal and is found in the central and eastern Mediterranean region. Subspecies *trachypus* has flowers like those of *arvense* but the pedicels are papillose, rather than smooth, and is found in Greece.

Allium sphaerocephalon flowers in Germany, Poland, and the United Kingdom from July to August for 2 or 3 weeks. At Longwood, plants began flowering usually in the third or fourth week of June. Only once in 7 years, their bloom started as early as the second week of June or was delayed until the first week of July. They flowered, on average, for a little over 4 weeks, into the second or fourth week of July.

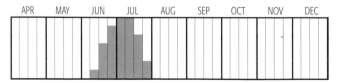

Allium sphaerocephalon

Allium triquetrum

THREE-CORNERED ONION

This plant is native to the western Mediterranean region and naturalized in Great Britain. *Allium triquetrum* grows along streams and in other damp, shady places and woods.

Allium triquetrum forms a spherical or ovate bulb covered with a membranous tunic, out of which grow two to four leaves up to 50 cm long and a distinctly three-sided flowering stem to 45 cm tall. The basal, fleshy, narrow, linear leaves are grooved on the upper side and keeled in the lower. The white, bell-shaped, fragrant, nodding flowers are borne three to 15 in a one-sided, loose umbel up to 6 cm wide and subtended by two spathes. The white tepals of the flowers have distinct green middle stripes. Fruits are 7-mm-long capsules.

In the garden, *Allium triquetrum* is particularly attractive when grown under the canopy of trees and taller shrubs, although it thrives in full sun as well. Under favorable conditions, it will naturalize and spread easily. Plant this species in any well-drained soil. If self-seeding becomes problematic, remove spent flowers before seed set. Plants are hardy to zone 5.

Allium triquetrum flowers in Germany from March to May. At Longwood, flowering began usually in the second week of May, but in 1 of 3 years it was delayed until the last week of May. Plants bloomed, on average, for a little over 4 weeks, into the first or second week of June.

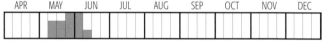

Allium triquetrum

Allium unifolium

ONE-LEAVED ONION

This perennial is native to the United States. *Allium unifolium* grows in the coastal mountain ranges of California and Oregon, in moist, clay soils, including serpentine soils, often along streams, at elevations up to 1700 m.

Despite its name, *Allium unifolium* has two or three leaves growing out of a solitary, ovoid or obliquely ovoid bulb formed annually at the ends of short, thick rhizomes from the outside of the previous year's bulb. The stout, erect, solid flower-

Allium unifolium

Allium unifolium

Amsonia
BLUESTAR
The name *Amsonia* commemorates the 18th-century American physician Charles Amson.

Amsonia ciliata
DOWNY AMSONIA, DOWNY STAR–FLOWER, FRINGED BLUESTAR
This plant is native to the southeastern United States, from North Carolina to Georgia west to Missouri and Texas. *Amsonia ciliata* grows in dry, open woodlands on sandy hills and limestone glades and ledges.

Amsonia ciliata grows from a thickened woody root to form erect clumps of sparsely branched stems to 1.5 m tall. The narrow, linear to linear-lanceolate, dark green leaves are up to 8 cm long and fringed by fine hairs, giving them a silky appearance. The leaves are retained all season and in the fall turn bright yellow. The starry, 1-cm-wide, sky or powder blue flowers are borne in crowded, terminal cymes held above the foliage. Fruits are 10-cm-long, slender follicles.

In the garden, *Amsonia ciliata* is valued for its showy flowers and unique, fine-textured, feathery foliage. Plant large groupings of this *Amsonia* where it can take the center stage in the fall, when its foliage turns brilliant yellow, be it in a perennial border, cottage garden, or an open woodland naturalized area. Choose a spot in full sun or light, dappled shade. In areas with hot summers, flowers will last

ing stems grow to 80 cm tall. The narrow, solid, flattened, sickle-shaped, gray-green leaves reach 50 cm in length and stay green or wither from tip at the time of bloom. Bright pink or rarely white, widely bell-shaped flowers are borne in loose, hemispheric umbels to 5 cm wide, subtended by two spathes.

In the garden, plant large groupings of *Allium unifolium* where its withering foliage will be hidden during the summer months. It thrives in a warm spot in full sun or partial shade, in any average soil that drains easily and stays fairly dry in summer. Plants are hardy to zone 4.

In the wild, *Allium unifolium* flowers from May to July, depending on the region. At Longwood, it started flowering as early as the second week of May or as late as the first week of June. The bloom lasted, on average, for more than 4 weeks and ended between the first and the last week of June.

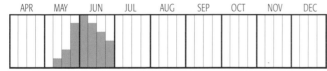

APR	MAY	JUN	JUL	AUG	SEP	OCT	NOV	DEC

Allium unifolium

Amsonia ciliata

longer if shaded in the afternoon, but plants grown in deep shade may tend to flop. It thrives in average, moderately wet, relatively infertile and well-drained soil. Although plants benefit from supplemental watering during dry spells, they are tolerant of heat and drought stress. Cutting back after flowering to about 20 cm will result in new silky growth, creating a bushy mound of foliage. Plants are hardy to zone 7, possibly zone 5.

In the wild, three varieties of *Amsonia ciliata* are recognized. Variety *ciliata* has leaves up to 10 mm wide. Variety *tenuifolia* (also known as *filifolia*) has leaves only 2 mm wide. Both of these varieties are found throughout the range of the species. Variety *texana* grows only to 50 cm tall and has a corolla tube to 12 mm long, as opposed to 6 to 8 mm in the other varieties; its distribution is restricted to Texas and Oklahoma. In addition to the wild types, a couple of garden selections with typical light blue flowers are available, including 'Georgia Pancake' with needle-like leaves, growing to only 12 cm tall, and 'Spring Sky' with larger flowers and strongly ciliate leaves.

Amsonia ciliata var. *tenuifolia*

Amsonia ciliata flowers in Chicago from mid-June to early July, but further south, in St. Louis, it blooms from late April to mid-May. At Longwood, flowering usually began in the second or third week of May. Only once in 7 years, the bloom started in the first week of May. On average, flowering continued for a little over 6 weeks into mid (rarely late) June.

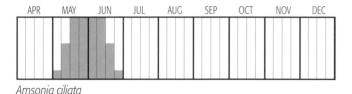

Amsonia ciliata

Amsonia hubrichtii

ARKANSAS AMSONIA, HUBRICHT'S BLUESTAR, NARROW-LEAF BLUESTAR

This perennial is native to the south-central United States, in Arkansas and Oklahoma. *Amsonia hubrichtii* grows in fields, meadows, on dry, rocky outcrops, and in gravely creek bottoms. It has been cultivated since the mid-20th century.

Amsonia hubrichtii forms billowy mounds of erect stems to 1 m tall. The fine-textured, thread-like leaves, less than 2 mm wide but up to 8 cm long, are narrower than those of *A. ciliata* and lack the conspicuous hairs fringing the margins. The leaves, bright green in spring and summer, turn golden yellow in the fall. The stellate, 1-cm-wide, light blue to almost white flowers appear in terminal cymes. Fruits are slender follicles to 15 cm long.

In the garden, *Amsonia hubrichtii* is valued for its starry blue flowers and the feathery foliage, which turns brilliant yellow in the fall. The leaves color up better in cooler climates. Plant it in large groups for striking impact, in either perennial borders or in naturalized woodland areas. Choose a sunny location for better fall color. *Amsonia hubrichtii* grows well in light, partial shade, but avoid deep shade, where plants tend to flop. It is adapted to a wide range of soils provided they drain easily. Once established, this species tolerates periodic drought. If flopping occurs regularly, cut back stems in the spring before flowering. Similarly, cutting back to 20 cm after bloom will stimulate a new regrowth that will form

Amsonia hubrichtii

a neat, dense mound for the rest of the growing season. Plants are hardy to zones 5 or 6.

Amsonia hubrichtii flowers in Chicago from early June to early July, but in St. Louis, it blooms earlier, in mid-May. At Longwood, *A. hubrichtii* began flowering between the second and fourth week of May and continued for nearly 5 weeks, until early June. Only once in 7 years, plants were still in bloom in the third week of June.

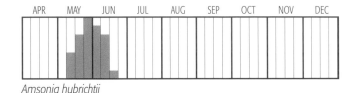

Amsonia hubrichtii

Amsonia tabernaemontana

BLUE DOGBANE, BLUE STAR–FLOWER, BLUE STARS, EASTERN BLUESTAR, WILLOW AMSONIA

This plant is native to the eastern United States, from Pennsylvania to Mississippi and west to Kansas. *Amsonia tabernaemontana* grows in rich open woods and thickets, damp roadside ditches, along streams, and on riverbanks. It has been cultivated since the mid-18th century.

Amsonia tabernaemontana grows out of a short, thick, slightly woody rootstock. It forms erect clumps of stiff, slightly arching stems to 1 m tall. The willow-like, lanceolate to oblong-elliptic, opaquely green leaves reach 15 cm in length and have a conspicuous pale green midvein. In the fall, they turn an attractive yellow color. The star-shaped, 15-mm-wide, pale blue flowers are borne in terminal, pyramidal, slightly drooping cymes to 8 cm long. Fruits are erect, cylindrical, 10-cm-long follicles.

In the garden, *Amsonia tabernaemontana* can be used in a variety of settings, from a low-maintenance open woodland or wildflower garden to a more formal, traditional border and a minimalist contemporary landscape. Plant *A. tabernaemontana* in large groups for stronger impact. Because it requires only minimal care, mass plantings do not add much work to maintain them. Position it so as to take advantage of its attractive fall color, a rare quality among perennials. Plant it preferably in full sun. When grown in shade, especially on moist and fer-

Amsonia tabernaemontana

tile soils, plants will likely require staking or cutting back in the spring to prevent flopping. Choose a site with deep, moderately fertile, moist but well-drained soil. Avoid rich, wet soils in shady spots, where plants will flop and flower sparsely. Once established, *A. tabernaemontana* tolerates periodic drought. Trim the tops of the plant lightly after flowering to encourage a rebloom, or cut back harder to 20 cm to stimulate a flush of new growth to create a neater mound of foliage. This species does not require regular divisions. Plants are hardy to zone 5, possibly zone 3.

In the wild, three varieties of *Amsonia tabernaemontana* are recognized based on leaf shape, size, and hairs. Variety *tabernaemontana* has ovate to oblong-lanceolate leaves, whereas variety *salicifolia* has narrower, lanceolate leaves. Both are found throughout the species' range. Variety *gattingeri*, restricted to Mississippi, Tennessee, and Kentucky, has leaves as narrow as those of variety *salicifolia*, but they are pubescent rather than glabrous like those of *salicifolia*. Garden selections offer several choices of low-growing cultivars, such as 'Blue Ice', 'Montana', and 'Short Stack'.

In the United States, *Amsonia tabernaemontana* flowers from late April to late May in Missouri, in May and June in Ohio, and in early June to early July in Illinois. In Poznań, its bloom began between 25 and 27 May and ended between 14 June and 2 July. Variety *salicifolia* is reported to flower 1 or 2 weeks later than variety *tabernaemontana*. A rebloom later in the summer is seldom observed. At Longwood, flowering of both *tabernaemontana* and *salicifolia* started between the first and the third week of May and continued, on average, for more than 6 weeks, into early, or rarely late, June. This duration is considerably longer than the 2 to 4 weeks reported from St. Louis.

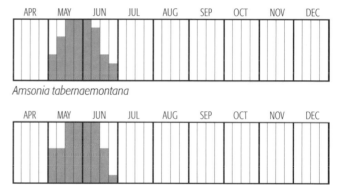

Amsonia tabernaemontana

Amsonia tabernaemontana var. *salicifolia*

Anemone

ANEMONE

The name *Anemone* is an ancient Greek name for this plant.

Anemone ×*hybrida*

HYBRID ANEMONE, JAPANESE ANEMONE

This perennial is a hybrid between *Anemone vitifolia* and *A. hupehensis* var. *japonica*, believed to be raised for the first time in 1848 in Great Britain at the Royal Horticultural Society's garden in Chiswick. Both of the parent species were introduced from Asia, *A. vitifolia* from Nepal in 1829 and *A. hupehensis* var. *japonica* from China in 1844. *Anemone vitifolia* grows at elevations between 1500 and 3000 m in Kashmir east to Yunnan and Sichuan in China. *Anemone hupehensis* var. *japonica* is of garden origin, although it is widely naturalized in the coastal provinces of China and in Japan. The variety differs from *A. hupehensis* in having semi-double flowers.

Amsonia tabernaemontana var. *salicifolia*

Anemone hupehensis

Anemone ×*hybrida* forms large clumps of pubescent leaves and ascending, stiff, flowering stems to 1.5 m tall, growing out of thick, succulent, deep roots. The dark green, long-petiolate, trifoliate leaves have ovate, deeply lobed, and serrate leaflets. The semi-double, flowers to 8 cm wide, have seven to 11 white, pink, or rose tepals with a silky sheen on the backside. A few additional small and distorted tepals may surround the center of the flower, which is filled with prominent golden stamens. Flowers are arranged in large, loose cymes.

In the garden, *Anemone* ×*hybrida* provides a backbone of fall display, together with asters and chrysanthemums. Use it in a perennial border or a woodland garden to create a long-lasting show of flowers. It recovers slowly after transplanting, but once established it spreads from the adventitious buds formed on roots, and flowers freely. Combine it in large groups with other late-season bloomers, or plant it

in front of the shrubs or woodland edge. Choose preferably a site that is partially shaded or at least offers protection from the hot midday sun. Plants growing in full sun may have flowers that become somewhat distorted or faded. *Anemone* ×*hybrida* thrives in deep, fertile, loamy, and well-drained soil with adequate moisture. Avoid dry soils or those that stay excessively wet in winter. Provide supplemental watering during periods of summer drought. The flowers are suitable for cutting. If the plant spreads too aggressively, divide it every few years; otherwise it is better to leave undisturbed. Plants are hardy to zone 6, possibly 4. In colder climates, apply mulch generously, especially to younger plants, to protect the upper portions of the roots from winter injury.

Following the first crossing of *Anemone vitifolia* and *A. hupehensis* var. *japonica* in 1848, a large number of hybrids were introduced by European breeders. Over time, the number of cultivars increased to

Anemone ×*hybrida* 'Königin Charlotte'

about 70, but most of them have probably been lost to cultivation. Still, some of the 19th-century selections, such as white-flowered 'Honorine Jobert' (1858) or pink-purple 'Königin Charlotte' (1898), are popular and widely grown today. Named cultivars offer variously doubled flowers in a range of colors, including white 'Géante des Blanches', creamy white 'Bühler Kind', pink 'Max Vogel', mauve 'Loreley', lilac pink 'Alice', and deep rose 'Stuttgardia'.

In Moscow, one of the parent species, *Anemone vitifolia*, is reported to flower, on average, between 6 September and 9 October, whereas the other parent, *A. hupehensis* var. *japonica*, flowered there a month earlier, between 31 July and 8 September. *Anemone* ×*hybrida* flowers in Poland and the United Kingdom from August until frost in October or November. In the United States, the cultivar 'Königin Charlotte' flowered in St. Louis from mid-July or early September to mid or late October; but in Chicago it bloomed a couple of weeks later, between late September and early November. At Longwood, 'Königin Charlotte' began to flower between the second and the last week of September. It bloomed, on average, for a little over 7 weeks, until the end of October or into early November. In comparison, in Chicago, 'Königin Charlotte' flowered, on average, for 24 days. In Moscow, *A. vitifolia* bloomed for 33

Anemone ×*hybrida* 'Königin Charlotte'

days, whereas *A. hupehensis* var. *japonica* bloomed for 42 days. It appears that the earlier the bloom start date is, the longer bloom duration can be expected.

Anemone tomentosa

HAIRY ANEMONE

This plant is native to China, from eastern Tibet and Sichuan east to Hebei, Henan, and Hubei. It grows on open, grassy slopes in the mountains, at elevations from 700 to 3400 m. *Anemone tomentosa* has been cultivated since the early 20th century.

Anemone tomentosa forms clumps of large basal leaves and erect, flowering stems to 1.5 m tall, growing out of a branched caudex and widely spreading

APR	MAY	JUN	JUL	AUG	SEP	OCT	NOV	DEC

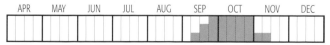

Anemone ×*hybrida* 'Königin Charlotte'

underground stolons. Stems and lower leaf surface have white-tomentose covering when young, becoming less apparent on the mature plant. Long-petiolate, usually trifoliate, basal leaves have deeply lobed leaflets; the middle one may be further subdivided into three leaflets. The whitish to pale pink flowers, up to 8 cm across, have five to six tepals, shaded purple and covered outside with silky hairs, surrounding the central boss of yellow stamens. Flowers are borne on long pedicels in open cymes subtended by an involucre of stalked leaves. Fruits are small, 3-mm-long achenes with tuft of long wooly hairs.

In the garden, *Anemone tomentosa* can be used in similar situations and has similar requirements as *A.* ×*hybrida*. This species grows more vigorously, however, and under favorable conditions can rapidly spread through the stolons, colonizing large areas and becoming invasive in extreme cases. Its fuzzy fruits extend the season of interest. Plants are hardy to zone 5, possibly zone 3.

Anemone tomentosa is quite variable in the wild, but relatively few garden selections have been made so far, and even those have been for the most part overshadowed by the showier cultivars of *A.* ×*hybrida*. Color choices include white 'Albadura', mauve-pink 'Robustissima', and bright pink 'Septemberglanz'.

In the wild in China, *Anemone tomentosa* flowers from July to October, depending on the region. In cultivation, it generally flowers earlier than *Anemone* ×*hybrida*, starting in August in Germany and Poland or in July in the United Kingdom. In the United States, the cultivar 'Robustissima' flowered in Chicago from late August to mid-November, but at Longwood, one year 'Robustissima' flowered a month earlier, from late July to early September. More frequently, its bloom began between the first and the third week of August and continued, on average, for a little over 6 weeks, into September, rarely into the first week of October. The bloom duration at Longwood was thus nearly 3 weeks shorter than the 9 weeks reported for 'Robustissima' from Chicago.

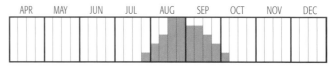

APR	MAY	JUN	JUL	AUG	SEP	OCT	NOV	DEC

Anemone tomentosa 'Robustissima'

Anthriscus

BEAKCHERVIL

The name *Anthriscus* is an ancient Roman name for one of the species.

Anthriscus sylvestris

COW PARSLEY, WILD CHERVIL, WOODLAND BEAKCHERVIL

This perennial is native from Europe east to Pakistan, northern India, Nepal, China, Korea, and Japan. *Anthriscus sylvestris* has been naturalized in parts of North America. It grows in open woodlands, floodplain meadows, ravines, and grassy slopes in the mountains up to 4500 m in elevation.

Anthriscus sylvestris forms robust clumps of erect, slightly furrowed stems to 1.5 m tall. The dull green, long-petiolate, basal leaves are three-pinnate with lobes to 3 cm long and serrate or pinnatifid. The upper cauline leaves are nearly sessile. Tiny white flowers are borne in umbels to 8 cm wide. Fruits are dry, black or dark brown, shiny schizocarps to 1 cm long.

In the garden, *Anthriscus sylvestris* is valued for its airy, ferny foliage and delicate, mist-like flowers. Plant it in average, moisture-retentive soil, in full sun or partial shade. Use it as a foil for larger-flowered or

Anemone tomentosa 'Robustissima'

bolder-leaved perennials. Once established, *A. syl-vestris* can tolerate periodic summer drought when given some shade. It is rather short-lived; in extreme cases it may even be biennial and die after flowering and producing fruits. Deadhead spent umbels to prolong bloom and maintain a neat appearance, unless self-seeding is desired.

There are two subspecies of *Anthriscus sylvestris* recognized among plants in the wild. Subspecies *sylvestris* has glabrous fruits, whereas subspecies *nemorosa* has fruits densely covered with hairs or bristles. Their distribution ranges overlap, although subspecies *nemorosa* tends to be more prevalent in the southern part of the range. The wild forms of *A. sylvestris* are rarely cultivated in the garden. Instead, a few selections offer decorative foliage that is exceptionally dark purple, such as 'Broadleas Blush', 'Moonlit Night', and 'Ravenswing', or yellow-green leaves, including 'Kabir'.

In the wild, *Anthriscus sylvestris* flowers in April and May. In the United States, the earliest flowering date recorded in Cincinnati was 25 April. At Longwood, it began flowering in the first or second week of May, and bloomed, on average, for a little over 5 weeks, until the end of May or into early June.

Anthriscus sylvestris 'Ravenswing'

Anthriscus sylvestris 'Ravenswing'

Anthriscus sylvestris 'Ravenswing'

Aquilegia canadensis

Aquilegia

COLUMBINE

The name *Aquilegia* is derived from Latin *aquila*, eagle, in reference to the spur-like petals resembling an eagle's beak or talons.

Aquilegia canadensis

CANADIAN COLUMBINE, CLUCKIES, ROCK–BELLS, WILD COLUMBINE, WILD–HONEYSUCKLE

This perennial is native to eastern North America, from Quebec, west to Saskatchewan, and south to Georgia and Texas. *Aquilegia canadensis* grows in moist, shaded, or open woods and forest margins, on roadside banks, rock outcrops, and cliffs, at elevations up to 1600 m. *Aquilegia canadensis* has been cultivated since the mid-17th century.

    Aquilegia canadensis forms erect clumps of basal leaves and slender, leafy, branched flowering stems

Aquilegia canadensis

to 1 m tall. Biternately compound, long-petiolate basal leaves have deeply lobed leaflets to 5 cm long, glaucous green undersides. Nodding, 3.5-cm-long flowers have five divergent, petaloid red sepals, and five true petals with yellow limbs and long, backward-projecting red spurs. They are borne several to a stem. Fruits are follicles to 3 cm long.

In the garden, *Aquilegia canadensis* performs best when allowed to naturalize in lightly shaded woodland, but is also well suited for planting as smaller clumps in perennial borders. Its flowers attract hummingbirds, so choose a site where these birds can be easily watched and enjoyed. Plant preferably in a partially shaded area. This species can tolerate full sun when grown in cooler climates in moisture-retentive soil. *Aquilegia canadensis* thrives in a wide range of soils provided they are well drained, but the optimum soil should be fairly rich and moist. Under such conditions, the foliage remains attractive throughout the summer. Otherwise, it may be necessary to cut back the untidy leaves after flowering to stimulate a fresh new growth. *Aquilegia canadensis* self-seeds prolifically and, in time, may form large colonies. Plants are hardy to zones 2 or 3.

As many as five botanical varieties have been proposed in the past for various types differing in the size of plants, sepals, or leaflets. Currently none of them are considered valid, for the reason that these variations are found to be continuous among the wild populations of *Aquilegia canadensis*. Of interest to gardeners are variants with different flower colors, including a white form *albiflora*, an entirely yellow form *flaviflora*, and a salmon-colored form *phippenii*. In addition, a few low-growing cultivars have been selected, including 'Canyon Vista', 'Corbett', 'Little Lanterns', and 'Nana'.

Aquilegia canadensis is one of the earliest columbines to flower. In the wild, it blooms from March to June, depending on the region. In St. Louis, it flowered from late April or early May until the end of May or late June. In contrast, in Moscow, flowering did not start until around 1 June and continued, on average, for 31 days until 2 July. At Longwood, plants

began to bloom usually in the last week of April or the first week of May. Only once in 6 years, they flowered as early as the third week of April. Flowering continued for a little over 5 weeks, into mid or late May. Two years, plants were still in bloom in the first week of June.

Aquilegia chrysantha
GOLDEN COLUMBINE, TEXAS COLUMBINE

This perennial is native to the United States, from Colorado and Utah south to Arizona and Texas, and in northwestern Mexico. *Aquilegia chrysantha* grows in moist, even damp, places in canyons and in coniferous forests and aspen groves, at elevations from 1000 to 3500 m. It has been cultivated since the late 19th century. *Aquilegia chrysantha* is one of the species from which the long-spurred hybrid columbines were developed.

Aquilegia chrysantha forms bushy clumps of basal leaves and freely branched, leafy, silky pubescent stems to 1.2 m tall. The basal leaves are usually triternate, sometimes biternate, with lobed leaflets to 5 cm long and slightly pubescent beneath. The yellow, erect, more or less upward-facing flowers are 7 cm long and wide and have lighter yellow sepals, darker yellow petal blades, and long, slender spurs spreading obliquely outward. Fruits are follicles to 3 cm long.

In the garden, *Aquilegia chrysantha* puts on a spectacular show when in flower. It is at home in traditional borders or cottage-style gardens and in more naturalistic settings, where it can be allowed to self-seed. It is a fairly long-lived and reliable species. Plant it in full sun or partial shade in rich, moisture-retentive and well-drained soil. It tolerates a wide range of soil conditions, but avoid heavy clay. Keep the soil consistently moist to prolong the neat appearance of the foliage through the growing season. Otherwise, if the foliage deteriorates, cut it back to the ground after flowering. Deadhead to encourage additional bloom. Under favorable conditions, *A. chrysantha* may self-seed readily. Be mindful, though, of the possibility of cross-pollination if other columbines grow nearby. Plants are hardy to zone 6, possibly zone 4.

Some of the botanical varieties of *Aquilegia chrysantha* recognized in the past, such as variety *chaplinei* from New Mexico and Texas or variety *hinckleyana*, restricted to Texas, are presently considered to be

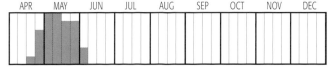

Aquilegia canadensis

Aquilegia chrysantha

Aquilegia chrysantha 'Yellow Queen'

separate species. On the other hand, the variants with shorter spurs, referred to as variety *rydbergii*, found in Colorado, Arizona, and New Mexico, are thought to fall within the range of variation characteristic of the species. Garden selections offer a choice of colors from white 'Alba' and 'Silver Queen' to lemon yellow 'Yellow Queen' and bright yellow 'Denver Gold', including cultivars with double flowers, such as 'Alba Plena' and 'Flore Pleno'.

In the wild, *Aquilegia chrysantha* flowers in spring and summer, from April to September, depending on the region. In cultivation in Germany and Poland, it blooms from May to August. In Moscow, flowering began around 1 June and continued, on average, for nearly 5 weeks, until 4 July. In St. Louis, the cultivar 'Yellow Queen' also bloomed for 5 weeks, but started from early May and continued until early June. Plants of 'Yellow Queen' at Long-

Aquilegia vulgaris

wood bloomed, on average, for more than 7 weeks, starting usually in the third or fourth week of May. Only once in 7 years, flowering began as early as the second week of May. The bloom usually ended in late June or early July. In one year, however, 'Yellow Queen' rebloomed in August.

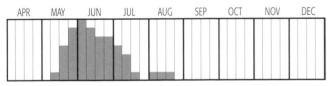

Aquilegia chrysantha 'Yellow Queen'

Aquilegia vulgaris

COMMON COLUMBINE, EUROPEAN CROWFOOT,
GARDEN COLUMBINE, GRANDMOTHER'S-BONNET,
GRANNY'S-BONNET

This plant is native from southern Scandinavia throughout Europe and south to Morocco. *Aquilegia vulgaris* grows in meadows and woodland margins. It has been cultivated since the Middle Ages and has naturalized in North America.

Aquilegia vulgaris forms clumps of basal leaves and flowering stems to 80 cm tall. Stems are usually hairy, especially in the upper part. The basal, biternate leaves have deeply lobed leaflets to 4 cm long, glaucous green on the undersides. The usually blue or violet, nodding, 5-cm-long flowers have spreading sepals and short, strongly hooked spurs ending in small knobs. Fruits are densely hairy follicles to 2.5 cm long.

In the garden, *Aquilegia vulgaris* is a very durable plant that will persist even in less-than-ideal conditions. Because it is able to self-seed freely, use this species in places where it can be allowed to naturalize to form large colonies. When growing it as part of a more formal border, control its spread through

Aquilegia vulgaris

deadheading spent flowers and removing unwanted seedlings. Plant it in full sun or partial shade, where flowers will last longer. *Aquilegia vulgaris* tolerates a wide range of soils provided they drain easily, but it grows best in rich, fertile, and moist soil. Cutting back flowering stems after bloom not only will minimize self-seeding, but may also encourage additional flowering. After flowering, keep the soil consistently moist to keep the foliage looking fresh, or cut it back to the ground to promote a new flush of growth later in the season. Plants are hardy to zones 3 or 4.

Aquilegia vulgaris is extremely variable in its native habitat, which is reflected in the fact that at one time or another, more than 20 botanical varieties were described. Presently, only three subspecies are recognized in addition to the typical subspecies *vulgaris* found throughout the range. Subspecies *dichroa* from western Spain and Portugal differs in having white-tipped sepals and petals. Subspecies *nevadensis* from southern Spain is densely glandular pubescent and has spurs that are not hooked. Finally, subspecies *paui* from northeastern Spain differs in having once-ternate leaves. The natural diversity and long history of cultivation lead to the development of numerous selections of *A. vulgaris* differing in height, foliage color, flower form (including spurless and double) and flower color. In addition, *A. vulgaris* has been involved in development of today's short-spurred hybrid cultivar. Color choices include white 'Nivea', pale yellow 'Sweet Surprise', red 'Raspberry Tart', rose purple 'Woodside', violet 'Plum Pudding', and pale green 'Greenapples'. Several cultivars feature bicolor flowers, such as purple-and-white 'Adelaide Addison', pink-and-white 'Nora Barlow', or rose-and-white 'Trevor Bath'.

Aquilegia vulgaris began its flowering in Moscow around 27 May and ended around 27 June, whereas in Poznań it began between 26 May and 4 June and ended between 20 June and 3 July. In the United States, the cultivar 'Woodside' flowered in St. Louis in mid-May. At Longwood, *A. vulgaris* started bloom usually in the first or second week of May. Only once in 6 years, it flowered in the last week of April. The bloom ended in the first 2 weeks of June or, one year, in the third week of June. In comparison, 'Woodside' began flowering at Longwood about

a week later, and its bloom duration was 1 week shorter than the average 6 weeks for *A. vulgaris*.

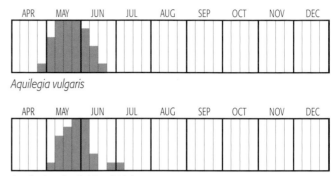

Aquilegia vulgaris

Aquilegia vulgaris 'Woodside'

Aralia

SPIKENARD

The origin of the name *Aralia* is uncertain, although it is thought to be derived from *aralie*, an old French Canadian or American Indian name of one of the species.

Aralia racemosa

AMERICAN SPIKENARD, LIFE-OF-MAN, PETTY-MOREL

This plant is native to North America, from New Brunswick to Manitoba, south to North Carolina, west to Utah, and into northern Mexico. *Aralia racemosa* grows in rich deciduous and coniferous woodlands. It has been cultivated since the mid-17th century.

Aralia racemosa forms widely spreading clumps of branched, brownish stems to 2 m tall, sometimes becoming woody toward the base. The stems grow out of stout rhizomes with thick aromatic roots. The two or three times compound, 1-m-long leaves are layered in overlapping tiers. The ovate leaflets, to 15 cm long, are sharply and often doubly serrate. The greenish white flowers are borne in dense umbels arranged in large panicles to 1 m in length. Fruits are fleshy, deep purple (almost black) berries.

In the garden, *Aralia racemosa* may be mistaken for a shrub because of its impressive stature. Site it to take advantage of its enormous, imposing leaves, lending an almost tropical feel to a garden. Rather modest flowers are followed by showy berries, which are a favorite of many birds. Plant it in light to dense shade, in any humus-rich and moisture-retentive soil. Plants are hardy to zone 5, possibly zone 3.

Aralia racemosa

Aralia racemosa

In the wild, *Aralia racemosa* flowers in July. At Longwood, it flowered, on average, for nearly 5 weeks, starting between the second to the fourth week of July and ending between the early to late August.

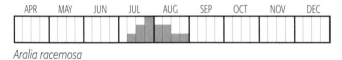

APR	MAY	JUN	JUL	AUG	SEP	OCT	NOV	DEC

Aralia racemosa

Arisaema

JACK-IN-THE-PULPIT

The name *Arisaema* is derived from Greek *aris* or *aron*, arum, and *haima*, blood, in reference to the red blotching present on the spathe or leaves of some species.

Arisaema triphyllum

COMMON-JACK, INDIAN JACK-IN-THE-PULPIT, INDIAN-TURNIP

This perennial is native to eastern North America, from southern Canada south to Florida. *Arisaema*

triphyllum is found at low elevations, growing often in alluvial soils in moist deciduous woodlands, along streams, and in swampy places. This species has been cultivated since the late 17th century.

Arisaema triphyllum forms usually two basal leaves, to 60 cm tall, growing out of a corm. The sheathing leaf bases conceal the lower portion of the inflorescence stalk, thus creating a short pseudostem. The trifoliate leaves have long, often purple-blotched petioles. The sessile, elliptic leaflets reach 20 cm in length. Tiny, unisexual flowers cover the lower portion of an erect, cylindrical to club-shaped spadix subtended by a spathe, which arches over the spadix and varies in color from deep purple to green with a few purple stripes. The whole inflorescence is more or less equal in length or shorter than the leaves. Fruits are orange-red berries about 1 cm in diameter.

In the garden, *Arisaema triphyllum* is valued especially in a moist woodland garden setting. Its large, bold leaves and intriguing inflorescences are especially impressive when they emerge in the spring in large numbers. Because the foliage of *A. triphyllum*

Arisaema triphyllum

dies down in summer, underplant it with shade-loving plants with leaves that will last all season. Its large, showy red berries become visible when the spathe withers, extending the visual interest through the fall. Plant it preferably in partial shade or in places where plants will be shaded during the afternoon hours. It can tolerate even deep shade conditions. Grow it in consistently moist, free-draining, humus-rich, fertile soil. Avoid dry sites or those with heavy clay that are prone to waterlogging. Divide *A. triphyllum* every 3 years if necessary, but it performs best if left undisturbed. Plants are hardy to zone 4.

Arisaema triphyllum is a highly variable species, and a number of subspecies have been described in the past. However, these various morphological types tend to overlap in their characteristics; therefore, they are not presently recognized. Putative hybrid populations between *A. triphyllum* and *A. dracontium*, another species from eastern North America, also occur naturally. These plants do not produce mature fruits but do reproduce vegetatively. Although variations of *A. triphyllum* in color of spathe and spadix are often seen among plants in the wild, this variability has not translated into large numbers of named cultivars. Only a few selections

Arisaema triphyllum

have been made, and even these are only of very limited availability. They include 'Mrs. French' with white veining in the leaflets, 'Zebrinum' featuring well-striped spathe, and the vigorous 'Giant', which grows to 1.2 m tall.

In the wild, *Arisaema triphyllum* flowers in the spring. In St. Louis, it blooms from early April until the end of April for 3 weeks. At Longwood, flowering began usually in the third or fourth week of May. Only once in 7 years, they flowered as early as the second week of May. The bloom continued for nearly 5 weeks, into early or mid-June.

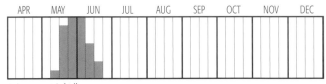

APR	MAY	JUN	JUL	AUG	SEP	OCT	NOV	DEC

Arisaema triphyllum

Arum

ARUM

The name *Arum* is derived from *aron*, the ancient Greek name for this plant.

Arum italicum

ITALIAN ARUM, PAINTED ARUM

This plant is native to southern and western Europe, from the Mediterranean region north to southern England, Belgium, and Sweden. *Arum italicum* grows in woodlands, hedges, and disturbed sites. This species has been cultivated since the late 17th century.

Arum italicum forms clumps of basal leaves to 45 cm tall growing out of horizontal tubers. The simple, hastate to sagittate, long-petiolate leaves are variably marbled with gray and cream or veined with pale green. They emerge in the fall and, in areas with mild climate, remain through the winter. Tiny, unisexual flowers are borne on a yellowish spadix, with male and female flowers in separate zones. The spadix is subtended by a spathe, to 40 cm long, usually greenish white (rarely white) or edged purple. Fruits are bright orange-red berries, to 1 cm long.

Arum italicum makes a valued addition to woodland gardens or perennial borders, especially those that are somewhat shaded. Its bold foliage emerges in the fall, creating a dense ground cover. In colder areas, leaves wither and reappear in the spring to-

Arum italicum

gether with the flowers, only to disappear again as the plants enter summer dormancy. In areas with mild climates, where the leaves remain green until the next season, use *A. italicum* to adorn a winter garden in combination with hellebores, snowdrops, or hardy cyclamen. Plant it in a warm, sheltered site in partial to full shade, where the foliage will stand up to the winter weather better. Give it a light winter cover in colder climates. Plant *A. italicum* in humus-rich soil that stays moist in spring and early summer. It can grow in a variety of soils, even in heavier clay. Clean up the withered leaves in the summer to show better the developing striking fruit clusters. Otherwise, it requires only minimum care. *Arum italicum* spreads gradually through its horizontal tubers and self-seeding, although seedlings may result in inferior plants if one of the improved garden selections is to be maintained. Plants are hardy to zones 5 or 6.

In the wild, *Arum italicum* shows a high degree of variability, and four subspecies have been recognized throughout its range. Subspecies *italicum*, found in much of Europe, northern Africa, and Turkey, has leaves with long and narrow lobes and often prominent pale veining. Subspecies *neglectum*, from western Europe and the western Mediterranean region, has shorter, broader, and partially overlapping lobes. Subspecies *albispathum*, restricted to the Crimea and the Caucasus, has white spathes. Finally, subspecies *byzantinum*, found in the eastern Balkans, has a pale green spathe tinged with purple. In addition, the silver-gray markings on the leaves, so characteristic of subspecies *italicum* in cultivation, vary greatly in wild populations, where forms with unmarked or very weakly marked leaves are common. Most of the garden selections have been derived from the variants of subspecies *italicum* displaying strong leaf markings, including 'Chamaeleon', 'Ghost', 'Marmoratum', 'Sparkler', and 'White Winter'.

Flowers of *Arum italicum* are present for a relatively brief time in late spring. In St. Louis, it flowered in early to late May for 1 to 2 weeks. At Longwood, the cultivar 'Marmoratum' bloomed for 3 to 4 weeks, from mid to late May into early June. The fruit clusters that followed became more conspicuous as their color intensified between early July and mid-September.

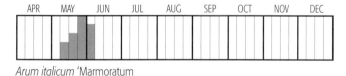

Arum italicum 'Marmoratum

Aruncus

GOAT'S-BEARD

The name *Aruncus* is an ancient Roman name for one of the species.

Aruncus aethusifolius

DWARF GOAT'S-BEARD, KOREAN GOAT'S-BEARD

This perennial is native to Korea, where it is found growing in the alpine zone on Mount Halla on Cheju Island.

Aruncus aethusifolius forms mounded clumps to 30 cm tall when in flower. The finely dissected, three- or four-pinnate leaves are bright green, tinged

bronze when emerging. The tiny, unisexual, creamy white flowers are borne in upright panicles rising above the foliage. Fruits are follicles.

In the garden, *Aruncus aethusifolius* can be used in a variety of situations, in a position in the front of the perennial border, for edging paths, and as a ground cover in a woodland area, or small clumps in a rock garden. In cooler climates, *A. aethusifolius* can be grown in full sun, otherwise partial shade is preferred. Plant it in a consistently moist, fertile, and humus-rich soil. Water during dry spells to prevent the foliage from declining. Although initially *A. aethusifolius* can be slow to establish, in time it will spread slowly to cover larger areas. Cut back the spent flower stalks for a neater appearance of the ferny foliage, or allow them to remain for the extended interest provided by dried follicles. Plants are hardy to zone 5, possibly zone 3.

Several collections have been made on Cheju Island and introduced into cultivation over the years, but only a couple of garden selections have been made so far. Hybrids with *Aruncus dioicus* are also known. Noteworthy are 'Herbstglut' selected for intense yellow to orange fall color, as well as 'Little Gem' and 'Noble Spirit' with deeply cut leaves.

At Longwood, *Aruncus aethusifolius* began flowering between the last week of May and the third week of June. It usually continued to bloom until the end of June or the first week of July. Only once in 7 years, *A. aethusifolius* was still in flower in the second week of July. On average, it bloomed for a little more than 4 weeks.

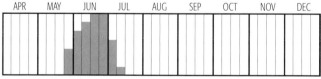

Aruncus aethusifolius

Aruncus dioicus

BRIDE'S-FEATHERS, SYLVAN GOAT'S-BEARD

This perennial is native from Europe east to Korea and Japan, south to Sikkim, Bhutan, and Nepal, and in North America, from Alaska south to California in the west, and in the east from Wisconsin south to Oklahoma, and from Maine south to Georgia. *Aruncus dioicus* grows in shaded, moist places in mixed

Aruncus dioicus

Aruncus dioicus

forests on montane slopes and valleys, at elevations to 3500 m. It has been cultivated since the early 17th century.

Aruncus dioicus grows out of a woody rootstock with a stout much-branched rhizome. It forms a large, shrub-like clump of erect, unbranched stems to 3 m tall. The two- to five-pinnate, glabrous leaves reach 1 m in length. Each ovate to lanceolate leaflet, to 13 cm long, is doubly serrated and prominently veined. The tiny, 3-mm-wide, usually unisexual creamy white flowers are borne in plume-like, pyramidal panicles to 50 cm long. Male and female flowers, with occasional perfect flowers, are on separate plants. Panicles of the male plants are whiter in color, more upright and feathery, and longer lasting; those of the female plants are yellowish white and more drooping. Fruits are pendant follicles.

In the garden, *A. dioicus*—especially the showier male plants—creates a dramatic spectacle when in flower. It is easily grown if provided sufficient moisture, light shade, and plenty of space to spread. Use it as a single specimen or groups of a few plants incorporated into perennial borders, or by themselves in a woodland garden or on the edge of the water. Choose a spot in partial shade or, in cooler climates, in full sun. *Aruncus dioicus* can tolerate deep shade under trees provided the soil is consistently moist. Although it performs best in rich and fertile soil, it can be planted in any soil as long as it is moisture retentive. Under dry and hot conditions, leaves may deteriorate quickly. Spent flowers fade to brown and may be removed to improve the appearance of the plant. *Aruncus dioicus* is slow to establish but long-lived. The plant may decline if transplanted, and it is best to leave it undisturbed indefinitely. Its tough, woody rootstock poses a challenge to anyone attempting to divide it. When female plants are grown, self-seeding may occur freely. Plants are hardy to zone 5, possibly zone 3.

Aruncus dioicus exhibits great variability throughout its distribution range. Many varieties have been described in various parts of that range, including *insularis* with larger flowers, *laciniatus* with leaflets deeply incised, *astilboides* with erect follicles, *subrotundus* with nearly orbicular leaflets, *pubescens* with leaves pubescent beneath, *triternatus* with trifoliate leaves, and a low-growing *kamtschaticus*, among others. A number of these variants have also been con-

sidered to be separate species. In light of this, it is rather surprising that only a few garden selections have been made so far. They include 'Glasnevin' with larger flower panicles, 'Kneiffii' with deeply cut leaves, and 'Zweiweltenkind' with pendulous white flowers and bronzy young foliage.

Aruncus dioicus flowers from late spring through midsummer. In Moscow, its bloom began around 16 July and ended around 7 August, but the cultivar 'Kneiffii' flowered a month earlier, from 19 June to 7 July. Earlier bloom dates were recorded in Poznań, where *A. dioicus* started flowering between 27 May and 17 June and ended between 29 June and 12 July. June and July are given as bloom times in Ohio and Illinois, whereas in St. Louis it flowered from mid or late May until mid or late June. At Longwood, the bloom start date varied by 4 weeks between the second week of May and the first week of June. The flowering continued, on average, for a little over 4 weeks, into early or mid-June. A similar bloom duration was recorded in St. Louis, but in Moscow plants flowered, on average, for only about 3 weeks.

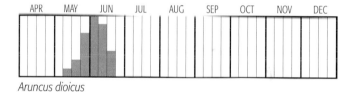

Aruncus dioicus

Asclepias

MILKWEED

The name *Asclepias* is derived from Asklepios, the ancient Greek god of healing.

Asclepias incarnata

SWAMP MILKWEED

This plant is native to North America, from Quebec to Manitoba, south to Georgia, and west to Louisiana, Texas, and New Mexico. *Asclepias incarnata* grows in moist, open areas in wet meadows, river bottomlands, swamps, and roadside ditches.

Asclepias incarnata forms clumps of stout, erect, branched out high or unbranched stems to 1.2 m tall, growing out of deep taproots. Its linear to elliptic leaves reach 15 cm in length and are usually held in whorls of three to six. The rosy pink (rarely white), 6-mm-wide, fragrant flowers are borne in small, tight umbels, mostly paired in the upper leaf axils. Fruits are erect, spindle-shaped, 8-cm-long follicles.

Asclepias incarnata is valued as an addition to sunny naturalistic gardens, especially those low-lying areas that stay moist, where it will attract scores of butterflies. Plant it with other perennials and grasses in a wildflower meadow, on the bank of pond or a stream, or in the back of a perennial border. Choose for it a spot in full sun, although very light shade will also be tolerated. *Asclepias incarnata* thrives in soil that remains consistently moist or even wet, but it will grow successfully in any average garden soil. It requires only minimum maintenance and is best left undisturbed indefinitely. Plants are late to emerge in the spring, so care should be taken when working around it. Staking is not needed except in the most windy locations. Cut back stems in late summer if foliage deteriorates, although no new growth will emerge until the following spring. Flowers are followed by conspicuous, large follicles that split open and release seeds with long, shiny, silky hair. Plants are hardy to zone 3.

Two varieties of *Asclepias incarnata* are recognized in the wild. Variety *incarnata*, found throughout the distribution range, has glabrous stems and leaves,

Asclepias incarnata

Asclepias incarnata 'Ice Ballet'

whereas variety *pulchra*, limited to the eastern part of the range, has pubescent stems and leaves. Several color variants, primarily with white flowers, such as 'Alba', 'Ice Ballet', and 'Milkmaid', have been selected and named.

In the wild, *Asclepias incarnata* flowers between June and August, depending on the region. Similar bloom time is observed in Germany. In Poznań, it started flowering between 21 June and 12 July and ended between 5 and 20 August. In St. Louis, it bloomed from mid-July until late August or mid-September, but the cultivar 'Ice Ballet' flowered in late May. At Longwood, *A. incarnata* began flowering as early as the last week of June or as late as the last week of July. It bloomed, on average, for nearly 8 weeks into late August or early September. By comparison, 'Ice Ballet' flowered earlier, starting between the first week of June and the first week of July and finishing usually before the end of July. 'Ice Ballet' bloom duration was also 2 weeks shorter than that of the typical form.

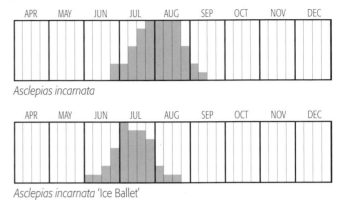

Asclepias incarnata

Asclepias incarnata 'Ice Ballet'

Asclepias tuberosa

BUTTERFLY MILKWEED, BUTTERFLY SILKWEED, CHIGGER–FLOWER, INDIAN PAINTBRUSH, PLEASING ROOT

This perennial is native to North America, from Ontario to New Hampshire and North Dakota, south to Florida, and west to California and northern Mexico. *Asclepias tuberosa* grows in open upland woodlands, in dry fields or prairies, and on rocky

Asclepias tuberosa

slopes or glades. This species has been cultivated since the end of the 17th century.

Asclepias tuberosa forms clumps of villous or hirsute, simple to branched stems to 1 m tall growing out of deep tuberous rootstock. The alternate or opposite, lanceolate or oblong leaves are sessile or short-petiolate, and reach 15 cm in length. Orange, occasionally red or yellow, 6-mm-wide flowers are clustered in terminal umbels or are borne from most of the axils of side branches. Fruits are slender, spindle-shaped follicles, to 15 cm long, held on nodding stalks.

Asclepias tuberosa 'Gay Butterflies'

In the garden, *Asclepias tuberosa* can be used in a variety of situations, from traditional perennial borders in a formal garden to naturalized wildflower areas within rustic settings. Although it cannot compete with the roots of trees, it is adapted to growing among grasses in an open meadow or prairie. Whether used as a single plant or a large drift, it brings scores of butterflies to the garden. Always plant it in full sun. *Asclepias tuberosa* thrives in hot, even dry sites. Plant it in deep, sandy, preferably low-fertility soil that drains easily. Avoid soils that retain excessive amounts of moisture. *Asclepias tuberosa* may decline after injury to its long roots, and it is difficult to transplant and slow to establish. Thus, it is best to leave it undisturbed for years, as transplanting is rarely needed. Plants are late to emerge in the spring, so caution is warranted when working around them. *Asclepias tuberosa* may self-seed under favorable conditions, but never to the point of becoming a nuisance. Both the cut flowers and the dry follicles are valued in arrangements. Plants are hardy to zones 3 or 4.

Asclepias tuberosa is highly variable with respect to its growth habit, leaf characteristics, and flower color. Three subspecies are recognized in the wild. Subspecies *tuberosa*, found in eastern North America, has leaves widest above the middle. Subspecies *interior*, which grows in the western part of the distribution range, has leaves widest below the middle. Subspecies *rolfsii*, restricted to the southeastern part of the United States, has hastate leaves with revolute margins. Garden selections offer choices of flower colors from yellow, such as 'Hello Yellow', to orange or red, including 'Red Wijna' and 'Vermilion'. *Asclepias tuberosa* is often seed grown and colors of certain cultivars may vary, such as 'Gay Butterflies', which offers a mix of yellow-, orange-, and red-flowered plants.

In the wild, *Asclepias tuberosa* flowers over a long period from late spring through the summer. In Chicago, it blooms from June to August for up to 6 weeks. Similar flowering time is given for Germany. In St. Louis, flowering began between late May or early June and continued until late June or early September. Deadheading is reported to result in an additional 4 weeks of flowering later in the season. At Longwood, the cultivar 'Gay Butterflies' varied greatly in its bloom start date from one year to another. The earliest start date was in the last week of May, whereas the latest was in mid-July. Without deadheading, it flowered continuously for 9 weeks, on average, into late August and early September.

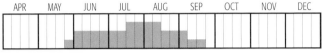

| APR | MAY | JUN | JUL | AUG | SEP | OCT | NOV | DEC |

Asclepias tuberosa 'Gay Butterflies'

Aster

ASTER

The name *Aster* is derived from Latin *aster*, star, alluding to the appearance of the flower heads.

Aster tataricus

TATARIAN ASTER, TATARIAN DAISY

This perennial is native to southern Siberia, northern China, Mongolia, Korea, and Japan, where it inhabits meadows, wetlands, riverbanks, and shrubby thickets. In the United States, *Aster tataricus* has escaped from cultivation in areas from Michigan and Massachusetts in the north to Georgia in the south and Iowa in the west.

Aster tataricus forms dense colonies of erect stems to 2 m (rarely 3 m), tall, growing from short underground fleshy rhizomes, which become woody with age. The basal, spatulate, coarse leaves make up rosettes to 1 m wide, usually withering by the time of flowering. The persistent cauline leaves can be up to 60 cm long and 15 cm wide and taper into long-winged petioles. They have an undulate, few-toothed margin and rugose surface. Leaves gradually diminish in size and become subsessile and entire toward the ends of the stems. Flowering stems branch near the top and bear lax corymbose arrays composed of 3.5-cm-wide flower heads. Flower heads have 14 to 30 bluish purple ray florets and 25 to 30 yellow, turning lavender, disc florets. Fruits are light brown, 2-mm-long achenes topped with a white or cream-colored pappus.

In the garden, the large stature and coarse texture make *Aster tataricus* suitable for planting in the back of the perennial border. Naturalistic meadows offer

Aster tataricus

another situation where one can enjoy the presence of *A. tataricus* without worrying about its vigorous growth. It is valued for exceptional toughness and resistance to pests and pathogens that often plague other asters. Plant it in full sun or partial shade, although shaded plants will grow taller and may require staking. *Aster tataricus* performs well in any garden soil and, although preferring moist sites, it will tolerate periodic drought. Under ideal growing conditions, *A. tataricus* can spread far and smother neighboring plants. Divide it every 3 or 4 years to maintain vigor and to control the spread of rhizomes. If desired, its height can be reduced by cutting stems back in mid-July. This will result in more branched plants and higher bloom count, without much delay in the bloom time. The rigid, sturdy flowering stems hold up well to the vagaries of inclement weather and can be left standing in early winter to provide some interest in the garden. With the first frost threatening,

cut flowers can be brought indoors, where they open easily and last for an exceptionally long time. Plants are hardy to zone 3.

The variability of *Aster tataricus* in the wild has led to several botanical varieties being described, including *minor*, *hortensis*, *vernalis*, *robustus*, *nakaii*, and *fauriei*, but none are currently recognized as valid. Garden selections originating in Japan offer choices of low-growing or even dwarf plants, including 'Jindai', growing to 1.2 m high, 'Blue Lake' reaching 1 m in height, and the shortest of them, 'Violet Lake', only 50 cm tall.

In the wild, *Aster tataricus* flowers between August and October, depending on the area. Cultivated in St. Louis, it bloomed in the first half of October for 2 weeks. At Longwood, *A. tataricus* began flowering as early as the first week of September or as late as the first week of October and continued flowering for more than 7 weeks until the first hard

Aster tataricus 'Jindai'

Aster tataricus

frost in November, unless it was cut back earlier. The floral display peaked in the first 3 weeks of October. In comparison, the cultivar 'Jindai' flowered at Longwood about a week later than the typical form. Although many asters flower until frost, they often look tired and worn out, whereas *A. tataricus* blooms look surprisingly fresh despite the late season.

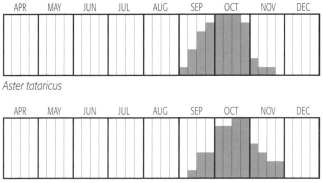

APR	MAY	JUN	JUL	AUG	SEP	OCT	NOV	DEC

Aster tataricus

APR	MAY	JUN	JUL	AUG	SEP	OCT	NOV	DEC

Aster tataricus 'Jindai'

Astilbe

ASTILBE

The name *Astilbe* is derived from Greek *a*, without, and *stilbe*, luster, in reference to the flowers, which are lacking brilliance or, perhaps, to the dull appearance of the leaves of some species.

Astilbe ×arendsii

FALSE SPIREA, HYBRID ASTILBE

This plant is derived from crosses between several eastern Asian species, including *Astilbe chinensis* and *A. chinensis* var. *davidii*, *A. grandis*, *A. japonica*, *A. simplicifolia*, and *A. thunbergii*. The first crosses were performed at the turn of the 20th century in France by Victor Lemoine and in Germany by Georg Arends. In most cases, the male parent was *A. chinensis* var. *davidii* with rose purple flowers, whereas the female parent plants were white-flowered *A. japonica* and *A. thunbergii*.

Astilbe ×arendsii forms clumps of slender stems to 1.5 m tall, growing from stout rhizomes. The two- or three-ternately compound, mostly basal leaves have ovate or oblong, doubly serrate leaflets. Small, slightly fragrant flowers come in white, pink, lavender, or red and are held in spikes arranged in usually erect, dense or open, plumy panicles to 25 cm long. Fruits are 3-mm-long capsules.

In the garden, *Astilbe ×arendsii* makes an impressive show of flowers, whether planted in a woodland, by a stream side, on the edge of a pond, in a perennial border, or in large containers. Its large panicles blooming in a variety of colors have no equal. Furthermore, the graceful, fern-like foliage remains decorative all season long under favorable growing conditions. The red-flowered cultivars have particularly attractive leaves that emerge tinted a rich mahogany in the spring. Combine it with other shade-tolerant and moisture-loving perennials. Plant *A. ×arendsii* in partial shade—or full sun in areas with cooler summers—and consistently moist soil. Where summers are hot, shade is essential, but avoid planting close to trees that might compete for water. Steer clear of dry sites, where plants suffer from chronic stress and respond by shriveling their leaves. Instead choose a location with deep, humus-rich, fertile, moist (but not waterlogged) soil, where foliage will remain attractive throughout the season. To maintain the vigor, topdress the plants annually with compost and divide them every 3 or 4 years. Remove spent flower stalks to enhance the appearance of the foliage, or allow them to develop rusty-brown seed heads that will persist through the winter. Cut flowers do not last long. Plants are hardy to zone 4.

With several species of *Astilbe* involved in hybridization of *A.* ×*arendsii*, its cultivars vary greatly with respect to size of the plants, appearance of the leaves, and habit of the inflorescence, and color of the flowers. While the tall selections can exceed 1.2 m in height, the dwarf ones are less than 40 cm tall. The leaves may be matte or glossy, dark green or suffused with brown or purple. Based on which of the parent species' characteristics are dominant, some of the hybrids have been segregated and classified into

cultivar groups such as Chinensis Hybrids, with stiffly erect and narrow inflorescences flowering in late summer, Japonica Hybrids, with loose inflorescences flowering in early summer, or Simplicifolia Hybrids, which include low-growing, late-flowering plants that have entire rather than serrated leaflets. Color choices include white 'Bergkristall', pale pink 'Peach Blossom', pink 'Europa', rose 'Irrlicht', purple-lilac 'Amethyst', and red 'Fanal'. Plant height ranges from 30-cm-tall 'Dunkellachs', with rich salmon pink flowers, to 1-m-tall coral red 'Feuer', lilac pink 'Hyazinth', and deep salmon red 'Koblenz'.

Cultivars of *Astilbe* ×*arendsii* represent a diverse group of hybrids, some of which flower in late June, whereas others do not begin flowering until early August. 'Amethyst', one of the midseason cultivars, bloomed in Moscow, on average, for nearly 5 weeks between 13 July and 14 August. In comparison, in

Astilbe ×*arendsii* 'Amethyst'

St. Louis, 'Amethyst' bloomed a month and a half earlier, from the end of May and continued for 3 weeks until the middle of June. The bloom duration also varies greatly between cultivars. Of 33 cultivars observed in Moscow, 'Gerbe de Neige' had the shortest average bloom time of a little over 2 weeks, whereas 'Lachskönigin' was the longest flowering, with nearly 7 weeks in bloom. At Longwood, an undetermined white-flowering hybrid bloomed on average for more than 5 weeks, usually between early June and early (rarely late) July. Only once in 7 years, it flowered as early as the end of May.

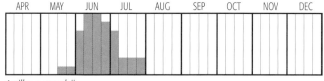

APR	MAY	JUN	JUL	AUG	SEP	OCT	NOV	DEC

Astilbe ×arendsii

Astilbe biternata

AMERICAN ASTILBE, FALSE GOAT'S-BEARD

This perennial is the only North American astilbe and is native to the southeastern United States. *Astilbe biternata* grows in rich, moist woods, and in seepage slopes in the mountains from Virginia to Kentucky and south to Georgia and Tennessee.

Astilbe biternata makes coarse clumps of stems to 2 m tall growing from stout rhizomes. The basal and cauline, petiolate, two- or three-ternate leaves have oblong or ovate, usually three-lobed and sharply serrated leaflets. The small yellowish white flowers are borne in large, elongate, drooping panicles. Fruits are 4-mm-long, erect follicles.

In the garden, *Astilbe biternata* is perhaps more appreciated for its attractive foliage than for its flowers with muted colors. It makes a handsome addition to a shaded perennial border or a woodland garden.

Astilbe ×arendsii 'Peach Blossom'

Astilbe biternata performs best in cooler climates. Plant it in partial shade in humus-rich, fertile soil that is consistently moist. It is relatively slow to establish, so divide it only when necessary. Cut back spent flowering stems to enhance the appearance of the foliage. Plants are hardy to zone 6, possibly zone 4.

In the wild, *Astilbe biternata* flowers from May to July, depending on the region and elevation. At Longwood, its earliest bloom date was recorded in the last week of May, but usually it began flowering around the middle of June. It then flowered, on average, for more than 3 weeks, until the end of June or the first week of July.

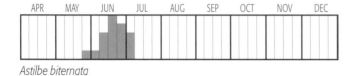

| APR | MAY | JUN | JUL | AUG | SEP | OCT | NOV | DEC |

Astilbe biternata

Astilbe chinensis

CHINESE ASTILBE

This plant is native to eastern Asia, from the Amur River region in Russia, south to Korea, Guangdong and Guangxi in China, and west to Tibet. *Astilbe chinensis* grows in open, moist montane broad-leaved forests, edges of the woods, meadows, and along riversides, at elevations to 3600 m. It has been cultivated since the end of the 19th century.

Astilbe chinensis forms dense clumps of brown-pubescent stems to 1 m tall at the time of flowering, growing from thick, dark brown rhizomes. The two- or three-ternately compound leaves have ovate or oblong, doubly serrate, deep green leaflets covered with reddish pubescence on both sides. The basal and cauline leaves are similar, except for the cauline leaves being smaller. The small, lilac to purple, crowded and almost stalkless flowers are borne in stiff, erect, narrow pyramidal panicles to 35 cm long. Fruits are 3-mm-long capsules.

In the garden, *Astilbe chinensis* makes an imposing plant with its ferny foliage topped by plumy slender panicles. It is at its best either as small groups in a shaded corner of a perennial border or massed in a woodland garden. *Astilbe chinensis* can be grown with good results in wet areas along streams or on pond banks. The lower-growing and faster-spreading cultivar 'Pumila' is also valued as a ground cover

or edging plant for shady areas. Plant it preferably in partial shade, although 'Pumila' can tolerate more sun. *Astilbe chinensis* is more drought tolerant than other astilbes; however, for best performance, choose a cool site with uniformly moist, humus-rich soil. To prevent leaves from declining, water during the periods of drought. To maintain an attractive appearance of the foliage, especially if the plant is used as a ground cover, remove the spent flower stalks. Alternatively, the dried seed heads, if allowed to remain, will provide additional interest later in the season. *Astilbe chinensis* spreads slowly, so divide the clumps only when necessary. Plants are hardy to zones 4 or 5.

Astilbe chinensis is a variable species, as reflected by several botanical varieties described in the past, such as *davidii* or *taquetii*. Although of questionable taxonomic validity, these varieties have been widely

Astilbe chinensis 'Pumila'

cultivated and incorporated through hybridization into many cultivars of *A. ×arendsii*. Those of the hybrids that resemble *A. chinensis* in their erect, stiff, and narrow panicles are often categorized as Chinensis Hybrids, but they can also be listed as selections of that species. Color choices include light pink 'Finale', salmon pink 'Intermezzo', rose 'Spätsommer', lavender 'Pumila', lavender purple 'Superba', and purple-red 'Purpurlanze'.

In the wild, *Astilbe chinensis* flowers between June and September, depending on the region. Cultivated in Germany and the United Kingdom, it blooms from August to September. In Moscow, it began flowering, on average, around 7 July and ended around 7 August. The cultivar 'Pumila' bloomed in Chicago from July through August, but in St. Louis, it started flowering in mid to late June and contin-

ued until the end of July or early August. At Longwood, 'Pumila' flowered, on average, for 7 weeks from early or mid-July until mid to late August. In comparison, the cultivar 'Superba' started flowering at Longwood a little earlier, in late June or the first week of July, but bloomed for only 5 weeks, into late July or the first week of August.

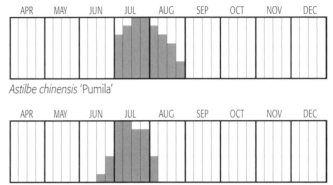

Astilbe chinensis 'Pumila'

Astilbe chinensis 'Superba'

Astilbe thunbergii

THUNBERG'S ASTILBE

This perennial is native to Japan and the Kuril Islands of Russia. *Astilbe thunbergii* grows on sunny, grassy mountain slopes, in open forests and in woodland edges, in moist ravines, and along banks of streams. It has been cultivated since the late 19th century.

Astilbe thunbergii forms clumps of brown-pubescent stems to 1 m tall at the time of flowering, growing from thick, spreading rhizomes. The two- or three-ternately compound leaves have elliptic to ovate, doubly serrate leaflets, to 12 cm long, held on long red petiolules. The white or lilac pink flowers are borne in loose, arching, or nodding panicles to 30 cm long. Fruits are 3-mm-long capsules.

In the garden, *Astilbe thunbergii* is valued for its distinct airy, lax panicles held high above the graceful mounds of fern-like leaves. Once they have gone to seed, the panicles continue to provide interest for an extended period. *Astilbe thunbergii* is at home in any shaded or woodland garden, also at the edge of a pond or stream, where the plants can be used as either small clumps or in large groupings. Grow it in a partially to fully shaded spot. Although it grows easily in any average garden soil that is well drained, it performs best in soils that are moist and rich in humus. Water *A. thunbergii* regularly to avoid leaves declining during summer drought spells. Otherwise, it requires

Astilbe chinensis 'Superba'

Astilbe thunbergii 'Professor van der Wielen'

little care and can be left undisturbed, without dividing for years. Plants are hardy to zone 3.

Astilbe thunbergii is highly variable in its native habitat, and several botanical varieties and forms have been described in Japan. Variety *thunbergii*, with dull green leaves and thick, short rhizomes, grows in central and western Honshu and Shikoku. This variety also has a variant with pinkish flowers, known as form *rosea*. Variety *kiusiana*, distinguished by its lustrous leaves and pinkish flowers, is found on Kyushu. Another variety, *fujisanensis*, with lustrous leaves but white flowers, is known from central Honshu. Variety *shikokiana*, with slender, stoloniferous rhizomes, is found on Shikoku. On Hokkaido and northern Honshu grows variety *congesta*, with broad, dense panicles, a pink variant of which is known as form *roseola*. A dwarf variety called *bandaica* is found in the alpine zones on Hokkaido and northern Honshu. Hybrids developed in cultivation by crossing with *A. thunbergii*, which show strong influence of this species, chiefly in the arching branches of the panicles, are

often classified as Thunbergii Hybrids, but they may also be listed as selections of this species. Noteworthy are white-flowered 'Moerheimii' and 'Professor van der Wielen', 'Betsy Cuperus' with light pink flowers, and 'Straussenfeder' featuring salmon pink flowers.

In the wild, *Astilbe thunbergii* flowers from May to July. Cultivated in Germany and Poland, it blooms from July to August. In Moscow, it began flowering, on average, around 7 July and ended around 3 August. The cultivar 'Professor van der Wielen' bloomed in St. Louis from early June until late June or mid-July. At Longwood, the bloom start date of 'Professor van der Wielen' varied from the first week of June in one year to the first week of July in another. On average, this cultivar flowered for nearly 4 weeks into early or mid-July. A similar bloom duration of 'Professor van der Wielen' was observed in St. Louis.

APR	MAY	JUN	JUL	AUG	SEP	OCT	NOV	DEC

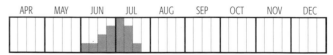

Astilbe thunbergii 'Professor van der Wielen'

Astrantia major 'Margery Fish'

Astrantia

MASTERWORT

The name *Astrantia* is derived from Latin *aster*, star, and *anthos*, flower, because the ring of involucral bracts surrounding the flowers appears to be radiating like a star.

Astrantia major

GREAT MASTERWORT

This plant is native to Europe, from northern Spain east to Russia, and south to Italy and Bulgaria. *Astrantia major* grows in moist, humus-rich soils in open woodlands and mountain meadows. It has been cultivated since the 16th century and has naturalized in parts of Great Britain and Scandinavia.

Astrantia major forms robust clumps of basal leaves overtopped by erect flowering stems to 1 m tall, growing from short rhizomes. The basal, deeply palmately lobed, serrated and long-petiolate leaves reach 15 cm in length and make loose rosettes. The sessile, cauline leaves are smaller and rarely serrated.

The tiny greenish white (rarely pink or rose red) flowers are borne in small, domed umbels to 2 cm wide, subtended by a ruff of 14 to 18 greenish white bracts, sometime tinged purple, equaling or exceeding the umbel, giving a stellate effect. The umbels are held on slender, erect, and branched wiry stems. Fruits are 8-mm-long mericarps.

Astrantia major performs best in relaxed settings of a cottage-style garden, in a shady corner of a perennial border, or naturalized in dappled shade of an open woodland. In time and under favorable conditions, it will spread through the rhizomes and self-seeding to form large colonies. It combines effortlessly with many other perennials, and can weave its wiry stems between them, adding a feel of informality. Showy involucral bracts last long and remain attractive beyond the flowering time. It thrives in climates with cool summers, where it can be grown in full sun, provided soil is consistently moist. Elsewhere, plant it in partial to full shade. Choose a spot with fertile, humus-rich, moisture-retentive soil.

Astrantia major 'Margery Fish'

Avoid light, sandy soils that dry out quickly. Water during dry spells in summer. Deadhead after flowering if self-seeding is not desired. Deadheading may also extend the bloom time. *Astrantia major* is long-lived and does not require to be lifted frequently. If spreading needs to be kept in check, divide and replant every 5 years or so. *Astrantia major* makes an excellent cut flower. Plants are hardy to zone 4.

There are two subspecies of *Astrantia major* currently recognized. Subspecies *major*, distributed throughout the species' range excluding some of the higher mountain areas, has involucral bracts equaling the umbel. Subspecies *carinthiaca*, also known as *involucrata*, which is restricted to higher elevations from the Alps of Carinthia, Austria, to the Cantabrian Mountains of Spain, has bracts twice as long as the umbel and, for this reason, is favored in cultivation. The introduction of selections with larger and

better-colored bracts caused a resurgence of interest in *A. major* as a garden plant. Many of the 50 or so cultivars available are suspected of being hybrids between *A. major* and *A. maxima*, a species from the Caucasus, Turkey, and Iran. Garden selections grow to between 50 cm and 1 m tall, offer showy bracts ranging from white and pink to deep reddish purple, variously combined with green, and similarly colored flowers. Among them are 'Margery Fish' and 'Shaggy', both with white flowers and white green-tipped bracts; 'Rosensinfonie', with rosy pink flowers and silvery white bracts; and 'Hadspen Blood', with reddish purple flowers and bracts. There are also a couple of variegated cultivars, such as 'Sue Barnes', with white-speckled leaves and 'Sunningdale Variegated', featuring leaves with creamy yellow margins.

In the wild, *Astrantia major* flowers from May to July. Cultivated in Poznań, it bloomed starting between 23 and 24 June and ending between 29 and 31 July. In Moscow, flowering began about a week later, on average around 2 July, but continued until 4 September. Similarly, flowering into September was observed in the United Kingdom and in Ohio. At Longwood, bloom time of four cultivars, 'Margery Fish', 'Rosensinfonie', 'Rubra', and 'Shaggy', was recorded. Of these 'Margery Fish' was the earliest flowering, starting between the second week of May

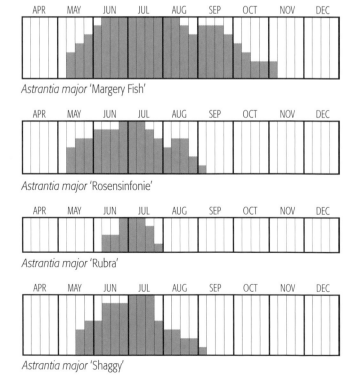

Astrantia major 'Margery Fish'

Astrantia major 'Rosensinfonie'

Astrantia major 'Rubra'

Astrantia major 'Shaggy'

Astrantia major 'Rosensinfonie'

and second week of June, and had the longest bloom period of nearly 20 weeks, which in some years extended into the first week of November. 'Rosensinfonie' and 'Shaggy' had very similar bloom times, starting from the second or third week of May in some years, but being delayed until the last week of June or first week of July in others. They both continued flowering in some years until the end of August or the first week of September, but the average bloom duration of 'Rosensinfonie', close to 12 weeks, was 2 weeks longer than that of 'Shaggy'. In comparison, 'Rubra' was the latest flowering of the four cultivars, starting in mid to late June. Its bloom duration was also the shortest and lasted on average only 5 weeks. Although some claim 'Shaggy' is synonymous with 'Margery Fish', plants sold under these two names showed distinct bloom patterns.

Baptisia
WILD-INDIGO

The name *Baptisia* is derived from the Greek *bapto*, to dye, in reference to the use of certain species as a substitute for indigo.

Baptisia alba
WHITE WILD-INDIGO

This perennial is native to the eastern United States, from New York west to Minnesota and Nebraska, south to Florida and Texas. *Baptisia alba* grows in open lowland forests, along woodland margins, streams and riverbanks, sand ridges, in pastures or open fields, and on roadsides.

Baptisia alba forms robust clumps of erect or divaricate, glabrous or nearly glabrous stems to 2 m tall at the time of flowering, growing from thick rhizomes. The glabrous, often glaucous leaves are divided into three elliptic to obovate leaflets to 6 cm long. The white, sometimes blotched purple, 2.5-cm-long flowers are borne in terminal, elongate racemes to 50 cm long. Fruits are ovoid pods, nearly black at maturity, to 3 cm long, initially held erect, later spreading or pendant.

Baptisia alba can be used as either a single clump or as small groups in traditional perennial borders or in naturalistic prairie- or meadow-style gardens. In the spring, asparagus-like emerging stems, often tinted dark purple, create early interest. These de-

Baptisia alba

velop into attractive mounds of glaucous green foliage topped by large racemes of showy flowers. Flowers are then followed by striking black inflated seed pods, valued in dry flower arrangements. Plant *B. alba* preferably in full sun, although it will tolerate light shade. It thrives in any average garden soil that is well drained. Thanks to its deep and extensive root system, *B. alba* performs well even in dry and poor soils. Plants are long-lived and easy to care for. *Baptisia alba* is rather slow to establish and it is best to leave it undisturbed for years. It seldom requires any staking. Trim after flowering to retain the neat, mounded appearance of the clumps, or allow the flowering stalks to remain and develop the seed pods. Plants are hardy to zone 5, possibly zone 3.

Baptisia alba

Over the large geographic range of *Baptisia alba*, two botanical varieties are recognized. Variety *alba*, found in the southeastern part of the range, from North Carolina to Alabama, has seed pods 15 to 30 mm wide. This variety includes plants previously considered to be a separate species and known as *B. pendula*. In contrast, variety *macrophylla*, native to areas west of Alabama, has narrower seed pods, only 10 to 15 mm wide. This variety, in turn, includes plants referred to as *B. leucantha* in the past. Plants from the southeastern United States, which have erect and cylindrical seed pods, rather than spreading to pendulous and ovoid, were described in older literature as *B. alba* but are now called *B. albescens*.

In the wild, *Baptisia alba* flowers in May and June. In cultivation, similar bloom time was recorded in St. Louis. At Longwood, flowering began in some years as early as the second week of May, but in others it was delayed until the first week of June. Plants flowered for 3 or 4 weeks, with the best show in the second half of May. Rarely, *B. alba* continued flowering until mid-June.

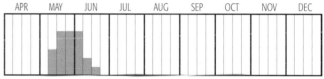

Baptisia alba

Baptisia australis

BLUE FALSE INDIGO, BLUE WILD-INDIGO,
PLAINS FALSE INDIGO

This plant is native to the eastern and southeastern United States, from New Hampshire in the northeast, west to Nebraska and south to Texas and Georgia. *Baptisia australis* grows on moist or dry, often rocky or gravelly soil, in open places, forest glades, rich woods, thickets, prairies, and along streams. *Baptisia australis* has been cultivated since the early 18th century, initially primarily as a substitute for the true indigo.

Baptisia australis forms shrubby mounds of upright or spreading, glabrous and glaucous stems to 1.5 m tall, growing out of thick rhizomes. The glaucous green, trifoliolate leaves have oval leaflets to 8 cm long. The clear blue to purple-blue, 2.5-cm-long flowers are borne in terminal, erect racemes to 40 cm long. Fruits are inflated, ovoid or lanceoloid pods to 7 cm long, turning black at maturity.

Baptisia australis var. *minor*

Baptisia 'Purple Smoke'

In the garden, *Baptisia australis* remains attractive through the whole season from the time its handsome glaucous green leaves emerge in the spring, to be topped later by indigo blue racemes, until the conspicuous seed pods develop and the whole plant turns black after the frost. It is valued both in old-fashioned formal borders or cottage-style gardens, and in naturalistic settings of wildflower gardens. Grow *B. australis* in a sunny location in preferably deep, acidic, well-drained soil, although it can tolerate a wide range of conditions, including poor and dry soils. *Baptisia australis* is slow to establish, but a long-lived and undemanding plant. It is best to leave the plant undisturbed and allow it time to form large groups. When grown in full sun, *B. australis* does not require any support, but shaded plants, especially those grown in fertile soil, may need staking. Removing spent flowers, although laborious, may prolong the bloom period. Trim the plants after bloom if seed pods are unwanted, and to encourage a new flush of growth to maintain the neat appearance of the plant through the rest of the season. Al-

ternatively, allow the seed pods to develop and enjoy them in the garden or in dry flower arrangements. Plants are hardy to zones 3 or 4.

Among the natural populations of *Baptisia australis*, three botanical varieties are recognized. Variety *australis*, found in the eastern part of the range, has nearly symmetric and moderately inflated seed pods. In contrast, variety *minor*, distributed in the western part of the range, grows lower, only to 1 m, and has strongly inflated and asymmetric seed pods. Variety *aberrans*, restricted to the southeastern states of Tennessee, North Carolina, and Georgia, resembles variety *minor*, except for its ascending, rather than spreading or drooping, branches. The diversity found among *B. australis* plants in the wild has yet to result in a wide selection of garden forms. So far, only a few cultivars have been introduced into cultivation, including light blue 'Blue Pearls', dusky purple 'Emma', and deep blue 'Exaltata'. In addition, *B. australis* has been crossed with other wild-indigos, such as *B. albescens* and *B. bracteata*, which led to the developments of hybrid cultivars, including 'Purple

Smoke' with smoky blue flowers, and 'Starlite Prairieblues' featuring bicolor, periwinkle and creamy yellow flowers.

In the wild, *Baptisia australis* flowers in May and June. Cultivated in Poland, it blooms in June. In Moscow, flowering started, on average, around 10 June and continued for nearly 5 weeks, until around 13 July. Cultivated in the United States, *B. australis* bloomed at about the same time, for 2 weeks in Chicago, and for 1 to 4 weeks in St. Louis. At Longwood, flowering began between the second and the fourth week of May and continued, on average, for almost 4 weeks into early or mid-June. In comparison, variety *minor* in some years started to flower 1 or 2 weeks earlier but bloomed for 4 weeks as well. The cultivar 'Purple Smoke' flowered for 4 weeks and during the same period as *B. australis*. While the peak bloom of *B. australis* and 'Purple Smoke' was in late May and early June, in the case of variety *minor* it fell in mid-May.

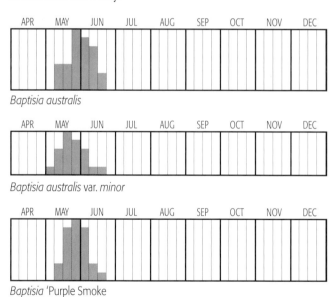

Baptisia australis

Baptisia australis var. *minor*

Baptisia 'Purple Smoke'

Baptisia sphaerocarpa

YELLOW WILD-INDIGO

This perennial is native to southern United States, from Louisiana to Texas north to Missouri and Oklahoma. In Missouri *Baptisia sphaerocarpa* is believed to have been introduced and naturalized. It is found in open places, glades, and prairie remnants in the Ozark and Ouachita Mountains, growing in a variety of poor soils, ranging from sandy and loamy to silty clay.

Baptisia sphaerocarpa forms dense, mounded clumps to 1 m tall, in time often surrounded by a number of vegetatively reproduced offspring. The glabrous stems are erect and branch close to the ground. The rich blue-green trifoliolate leaves have broadly lanceolate to obovate leaflets to 8 cm long. The upper leaves often have only two leaflets or are single. The brilliant yellow, 2-cm-long flowers are borne in erect, terminal or lateral racemes to 35 cm long. Fruits are inflated, spherical, 2-cm-wide pods that turn tan to black-brown when mature.

In the garden, *Baptisia sphaerocarpa* is considered as perhaps the showiest of the yellow-flowered wild-indigos. Outside perennial borders it is suitable for naturalized meadows, including those managed by fire, where a large planting of *B. sphaerocarpa* can be strikingly beautiful. Plant it in any average, well-drained garden soil in full sun, although *B. sphaerocarpa* performs surprisingly well in poor soils. Thanks to its exceptionally extensive and deep root system,

Baptisia sphaerocarpa 'Screamin' Yellow'

Baptisia sphaerocarpa

this species can tolerate summer drought and heat. Avoid overwatering or providing excessive amounts of fertilizer or mulch. Once established, it should not be disturbed by dividing or transplanting. Trimming spent inflorescences helps to maintain the plant's neat appearance, but precludes the spectacle of intriguing seed pods later. Branches with seed pods may be used in dry flower arrangements. Plants are cold hardy to zone 5.

Plants of *Baptisia sphaerocarpa* that have bifoliolate or single upper leaves were described in the past as a distinct species, *B. viridis*, but this designation is no longer considered valid. In cultivation, only a couple of cultivars are available and these resulted from selecting superior forms of the species, such as 'Screamin'

Yellow', or from hybridization with *B. albescens* and *B. australis*, including 'Carolina Moonlight' with light yellow flowers, and 'Twilite Prairieblues' featuring bicolor, chocolate violet and lemon yellow flowers.

In the wild, *Baptisia sphaerocarpa* flowers in May and June. Cultivated in St. Louis, it bloomed for 3 weeks in May. At Longwood, it flowered, on average, for nearly 4 weeks, beginning in the second to the fourth week of May and ending in the second or third week of June. The peak bloom can be expected in the last week of May and the first week of June. In comparison, the cultivar 'Screamin' Yellow' flowered, on average, for 1 week longer. In one year, it flowered until the end of June. The peak bloom of 'Screamin' Yellow' fell in late May.

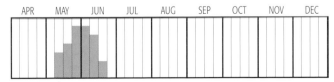

Baptisia sphaerocarpa

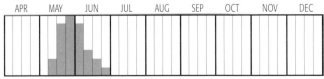

Baptisia sphaerocarpa 'Screamin' Yellow'

Belamcanda

BLACKBERRY–LILY

The name *Belamcanda* is derived from *valamcandam* or *balamtandam*, a Malayalam vernacular name for this plant in Kerala, western India.

Belamcanda chinensis

BLACKBERRY–LILY, LEOPARD–FLOWER

This plant is native to eastern Asia, from the Ussuri region of Russia, Korea, Japan, China, south to the Philippines, Vietnam, Myanmar, and India, although in many areas it is thought to be naturalized. *Belamcanda chinensis* grows in grasslands, pastures, and woodland clearings from near sea level to 2200 m in elevation. It has been cultivated in Asia for centuries as a medicinal plant and elsewhere as an ornamental since the early 19th century. In the United States, *B. chinensis* escaped from cultivation and is found in nearly all states east of the Rocky Mountains.

Belamcanda chinensis forms erect, leafy, branched stems to 1.5 m tall when flowering, growing from fleshy, knobby, usually orange or pale brown rhizomes creeping just below the ground level. The erect, sword-like, glaucous green leaves reach 25 cm in length. They are arranged, up to 14 per stem, in flattened fans. The orange or yellow, red-spotted, 5-cm-wide flowers have six tepals. The flowers are borne in flattened, fan-shaped cymes subtended by green spathes and terminating in forked, wiry stems of a panicle-like inflorescence. Fruits are dry, ovoid, 2.5-cm-long capsules that split to reveal black, shiny, round, fleshy, 5-mm-wide seeds.

In the garden, *Belamcanda chinensis* fits best in a perennial border, grouped for a bold effect. Its rather delicate habit permits it to be used in the front of the border without obscuring lower plants behind. The exotic, leopard-spotted flowers are followed by striking blackberry-like seed clusters that ornament a border for an extended period and provide excellent material for dry flower arrangements. Plant it in a warm, sunny spot, in any average garden soil

Belamcanda chinensis

Belamcanda chinensis

that is well drained, especially during the winter months. In moist and fertile soil, plants will grow taller and may require staking. *Belamcanda chinensis* is short-lived, particularly in areas with cool and damp summers, but it self-seeds readily and small seedlings can be easily transplanted. Its rhizomes spread slowly, and with the short lifespan, plants will usually not grow into large clumps that would require dividing. Mulch before winter in the colder areas. Plants are hardy to zone 5.

No botanical varieties are recognized among the wild populations of *Belamcanda chinensis*, and despite its long history in cultivation, only a handful of garden cultivars are available, including 'Freckle Face' with pale apricot orange flowers spotted red-brown, and 'Hello Yellow' with butter yellow, unspotted flowers.

In its native habitat, *Belamcanda chinensis* flowers from June to August, depending on the region. Individual flowers of *B. chinensis* are short-lived, but they appear over a fairly long period. Cultivated in Moscow, it flowered, on average, for about 7 weeks, between 4 June and 24 July. At Longwood, plants also flowered for nearly 7 weeks, but later than in Moscow, starting usually between the second and the fourth week of July and finishing before the end of August. Only once in 7 years, they flowered as early as the first week of July or as late as the beginning of September.

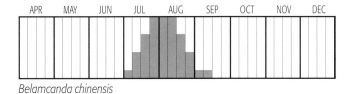

| APR | MAY | JUN | JUL | AUG | SEP | OCT | NOV | DEC |

Belamcanda chinensis

Bergenia

BERGENIA

The name *Bergenia* commemorates Karl August von Bergen (1704–1759), a German physician and botanist.

Bergenia crassifolia

ELEPHANT'S-EARS, HEART-LEAF BERGENIA, LEATHER BERGENIA, MEGASEA, PIGSQUEEK, SIBERIAN-TEA

This perennial is native to central and eastern Asia, from Siberia and the Altay Mountains in Russia south to northern Mongolia and Xinjiang in China.

Bergenia crassifolia grows on rocky cliffs, shaded stony slopes, and in pine forests, at elevations between 1100 and 1800 m. It has been cultivated since the 17th century.

Bergenia crassifolia forms clumps of basal evergreen foliage and branched flowering stems to 50 cm tall, growing from thick, tuberous, scaly rhizomes creeping near the soil surface. The glossy, waxy, leathery, obovate or elliptic leaves, up to 25 cm wide, have wavy or serrate margins and thick, long petioles. The pale rose to dark pink, bell-shaped, 1.5-cm-long flowers are borne in crowded paniculate, corymb-like inflorescences on thick, red-flushed stalks. Fruits are bicornute capsules.

In the garden, *Bergenia crassifolia* is valued for both its early-spring flowers and bold, glossy foliage. Thanks to its adaptability, it has many uses. *Bergenia crassifolia* can serve as a ground cover even in difficult areas, such as those under shallow-rooted trees, or used to soften corners and edges of hard surfaces, such as walls, steps, or walks. Combine it with other foliage plants that offer contrasting textures, including grasses, sedges, or ferns. Plant it in full sun or shade. The evergreen leaves turn attractive hues of red and brown in cold weather, especially when grown in full sun. In colder climates, however, where the leaves may deteriorate during the winter months, they will fare better when grown in shade. *Bergenia crassifolia* tolerates a wide range of soil conditions, but grows best in those that are moist, humus rich, and well drained. In time, the plant spreads by its rhizomes to form extensive clumps, which can be divided every 5 years or so, or more frequently if flowering is reduced. In the spring, trim any damaged leaves that may distract from the emerging flowers. Deadhead after flowering to enhance the appearance of the fresh new foliage. The shiny leaves are valued in cut flower arrangements, as they can last for weeks in water. Plants are hardy to zones 3 or 4.

Some *Bergenia crassifolia* plants in wild populations, particularly those from the Altay Mountains, differ in their leaves having a cordate base. In the past these were described as a distinct species, *B. cordifolia*, but this designation is no longer considered valid. In contrast, narrow-petalled plants, found in Russia's Far East and previously regarded as a variety of *B. crassifolia*, are currently viewed as the species *B. pacifica*. In cultivation, starting from the late 19th century,

Bergenia 'Bressingham White'

Bergenia 'Silberlicht'

Bergenia 'Perfect'

B. crassifolia has been crossed with two Himalayan species, *B. ciliata* to produce *B.* ×*schmidtii* and with *B. purpurascens* to produce *B.* ×*smithii*. These were further hybridized with other species to generate an array of well over 50 cultivars in colors ranging from white 'Bressingham White' and 'Silberlicht', to pink 'Distinction', purple 'Brilliant', rose red 'Perfect', and red 'Morgenröte'. Many of these cultivars develop intense red leaf winter color.

Bergenia crassifolia flowers in early to late spring, from February to March in the United Kingdom but April to May in Germany. In Poznań, it began flowering between 4 and 14 April and ended between 11 and 28 May. In Moscow, it flowered, on average, from 3 to 26 May. Some garden selections, such as 'Morgenröte', are reported to repeat flowering in midsummer if conditions are not too hot. In the United States, *B. crassifolia* flowered in April and May in Chicago, whereas in St. Louis it bloomed from late March until early May. At Longwood, *B. crassifolia* began flowering between the second and fourth week of April and continued, on average, for nearly 5 weeks, into mid (rarely late) May. In comparison, plants in Moscow bloomed for a little over 3 weeks. Of the two hybrid cultivars observed at Longwood, 'Bressingham White' bloomed at about the same time as *B. crassifolia*, whereas 'Silberlicht' flowered somewhat earlier. One year, flowering of 'Bressingham White' was unusually late, in the last week of June and the first week of July, which was likely a response to winter injury.

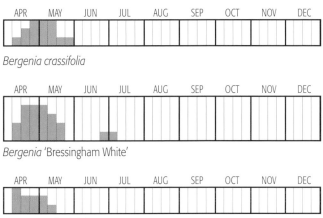

Bergenia crassifolia

Bergenia 'Bressingham White'

Bergenia 'Silberlicht'

Bergenia purpurascens

PURPLE BERGENIA

This perennial is native to the eastern Himalayas, from Sichuan, Xizang, and Yunnan in China, south to northern Myanmar, Bhutan, India, and Nepal. *Bergenia purpurascens* grows in gravelly soils in montane forests, scrub, meadows, and rock crevices, at elevations from 2700 to 4800 m. It has been cultivated since the mid-19th century.

Bergenia purpurascens forms clumps of evergreen, all basal leaves and flowering stalks to 50 cm tall growing from creeping, thick, scaly rhizomes. The dark green, glossy, glabrous (or with only a slightly ciliate margin), leathery leaves are elliptic to ovate and reach 25 cm in length. The leaves are held upright, showing the reddish blushed underside. Deep magenta or bright pink, nodding, 2.5-cm-long flowers are arranged in dense paniculate, corymb-like inflorescences on reddish purple stalks held well above the foliage. Fruits are bicornute capsules.

In the garden, *Bergenia purpurascens* can be used in similar situations as *B. crassifolia*. Its evergreen, shiny leaves turn bright, deep purple in cold weather, providing color during the winter months. Combine it with other perennials of contrasting textures or

Bergenia 'Pugsley's Pink'

colors, and plant under trees, on the bank of a stream or pond, among large rocks, or to soften sharp edges of stone walls or steps. Choose a site in either full sun or shade, but avoid spots that are extremely dark or hot and dry. *Bergenia purpurascens* thrives in any moderately moist and fertile soil. Plants are long-lived and require minimum care, similar to that described for *B. crassifolia* above. Trim old leaves in the spring and deadhead spent flowers after bloom is finished. Plants are hardy to zone 4.

Two botanical varieties of *Bergenia purpurascens* were described in the past, *delavayi* and *macrantha*, but they are no longer recognized. Several hybrids of *B. purpurascens* with other species have been developed in cultivation, including 'Pugsley's Pink' and 'Pugsley's Purple'.

In the wild, *Bergenia purpurascens* flowering varies greatly with elevation and falls between May and October. Cultivated plants are reported to flower in Germany from April to May. At Longwood, its bloom start date varied by a full month. One year plants flowered in the first week of April, while in another their flowering was delayed until the first week of May. On average, they bloomed for close to 5 weeks, into early or late May.

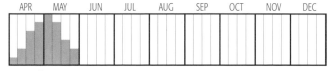

Bergenia purpurascens

Boltonia asteroides

Boltonia

DOLL'S DAISY

The name *Boltonia* commemorates James Bolton (1750–1799), a British naturalist.

Boltonia asteroides

FALSE CHAMOMILE, WHITE BOLTONIA, WHITE DOLL'S DAISY

This plant is native to central and eastern North America, from Manitoba, east to New York, and south to Texas and Florida. *Boltonia asteroides* grows in moist, open sites, in wet pine savannas, on floodplains, along watercourses, in damp meadows, wet prairies, marshes, on roadsides and wet ditches, at elevations from near sea level to 500 m. It has been cultivated since the late 18th century.

Boltonia asteroides forms bold, rounded clumps of much-branched above, erect stems to 2.5 m tall growing from creeping rhizomes. The linear to lanceolate, glabrous, glaucous green leaves reach 15 cm in length but are reduced in size toward the top of the plant. The 2.5-cm-wide flower heads are comprised of up to 60 white to purple ray florets and up to 170 yellow disc florets and are held in terminal, loose corymb-like or panicle-like arrays. Fruits are 3-mm-long, strongly flattened achenes.

In the garden, *Boltonia asteroides* creates impressive displays of delicate flowers among airy, fine-textured foliage. Combine it with other late-summer and fall bloomers in a perennial border or a naturalistic wildflower meadow. Plant it preferably in full sun. It will tolerate partial shade, but plants may grow taller and need support. *Boltonia asteroides* grows best in deep, moist, humus-rich soil. It tolerates drier soils, but plants are less vigorous, grow shorter, and flower less under such conditions. Rich, fertile soil may promote lanky growth that will necessitate staking. As an alternative to staking, plants may be trimmed one-half their height in late spring to prevent flopping. Divide *B. asteroides* every 4 years

Boltonia asteroides

or so, or more often if plants spread rapidly, as may be the case on moist and sandy sites. Flowers are suitable for cutting. Plants are hardy to zone 4.

Boltonia asteroides is a variable species, and three varieties are recognized among wild populations in North America. Variety *asteroides*, found in eastern and southeastern parts of the range, is smaller, less leafy, and produces fewer flower heads than the other two varieties. Varieties *latisquama* and *recognita* occur in western and northern parts of the range. They can be separated by the shape of involucral bracts, which in *latisquama* are spatulate, whereas in *recognita* they are linear. In addition, a few garden selections are available and offer choices with regard to flower color, from white 'Snowbank', to pale pink 'Pink Beauty' and purple or rose-lilac 'Nana'. These cultivars grow lower than the wild forms and, therefore, are not as dependent on staking.

In the wild, *Boltonia asteroides* flowers from July to November, depending on the region. Cultivated in Germany, it blooms from August to September. In Poznań, it began flowering between 23 June and 19 August and ended between 26 August and 19 September. *Boltonia asteroides* bloomed somewhat later in Moscow starting, on average, around 7 August and finishing on 30 September. In St. Louis, flowering occurs from late August until the end of September. Similarly, August and September are reported as flowering times in Chicago. At Longwood, bloom start date of the cultivar 'Snowbank' varied considerably, from the last week of August in some years to the last week of September in others. On average, 'Snowbank' flowered for nearly 6 weeks, into the early part of September. In comparison, *Boltonia asteroides* grown in St. Louis bloomed for 6 weeks, whereas plants in Moscow flowered on average for a little over 7 weeks.

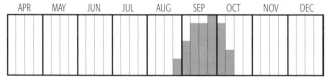

APR	MAY	JUN	JUL	AUG	SEP	OCT	NOV	DEC

Boltonia asteroides 'Snowbank'

Brunnera

BUGLOSS

The name *Brunnera* commemorates Samuel Brunner (1790–1844), a Swiss botanist.

Brunnera macrophylla

FALSE FORGET-ME-NOT, GREAT FORGET-ME-NOT, HEARLEAF BRUNNERA, PERENNIAL FORGET-ME-NOT, SIBERIAN BUGLOSS

This perennial is native to western Asia, in the Caucasus and northeastern Turkey. It grows in oak and spruce forests, on grassy and stony slopes, at elevations from 500 to 2000 m. *Brunnera macrophylla* has been cultivated since the early 19th century and has naturalized in parts of Great Britain.

Brunnera macrophylla grows from a thick, short, black rhizome. It forms spreading, dense clumps of mostly basal leaves and flowering, simple, rather slender and weak stems to 50 cm tall. The basal, long-petiolate leaves are first bright light green but darken later. They are strongly cordate or reniform and reach 15 cm in length and width. The stem leaves are smaller, narrower, and with shorter petioles or nearly sessile. The azure blue, 6-mm-wide, stellate flowers are borne in scorpioid cymes forming a small lax terminal panicles. Fruits are 3-mm-long nutlets.

Brunnera macrophylla

In the garden, *Brunnera macrophylla* is valued as a vigorous deciduous ground cover in shady and moist areas, such as under trees, north sides of buildings, or on banks of streams and ponds. It creates an attractive, lush carpet of soft foliage enhanced in the spring by clear bright blue flowers. Under favorable conditions, it spreads readily through self-seeding. Allow it to naturalize among other shade inhabitants. Although *B. macrophylla* grows best in shade, in cool and moist climates it can be planted in sunny locations. Choose for it preferably a spot with moist, fertile, humus-rich and well-drained soil, but plants can tolerate a wide range of soil conditions. Deadhead after flowering if self-seeding it not desired. Cut back the foliage if it declines as a result of a drought in midsummer. Dividing and transplanting are rarely required unless the spreading needs to be controlled or clumps lose vigor and begin to deteriorate. Plants are hardy to zones 3 or 4.

Although no botanical varieties of *Brunnera macrophylla* are recognized in the wild, gardeners have made a number of selections, most of them with variegated leaves, including 'Gordano Gold' with leaves mottled yellow, 'Hadspen Cream' with light green leaves irregularly bordered creamy white, and 'Variegata' with leaves patterned or edged in cream and white. Several cultivars, such as 'Jack Frost', 'Langtrees', and 'Looking Glass', feature silvery leaves with dark green veining. Others offer a choice of flower colors, white 'Betty Bowring' and 'Marley's White' and pale blue 'Agnes Amez' among them.

In the wild, *Brunnera macrophylla* flowers in March and April. Cultivated in Germany and the United Kingdom, it blooms later, in April and May. Even later flowering was recorded in Moscow, from around 4 May to about 30 May. In the United States, it

Brunnera macrophylla

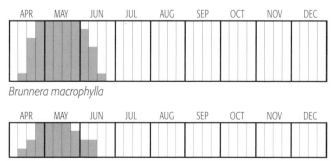

Brunnera macrophylla

Brunnera macrophylla 'Variegata'

Brunnera macrophylla 'Variegata'

bloomed in April and May in Chicago and St. Louis. At Longwood, flowering began usually in the third or fourth week of April. Only once in 7 years, plants bloomed in the second week of April. Flowering at Longwood continued, on average, for over 8 weeks, into late May or early June. In one year, *B. macrophylla* was still in flower during the third week of June. The cultivar 'Variegata' grown at Longwood had the same flowering pattern as the species, but bloomed on average for 7 weeks. In comparison, plants grown in Moscow flowered on average for less than 4 weeks.

Buphthalmum
OXEYE

The name *Buphthalmum* is derived from the Greek *bous*, ox, and *ophthalmos*, eye, in reference to the appearance of the disc of the flower head.

Buphthalmum salicifolium
WILLOWLEAF OXEYE, YELLOW OXEYE

This plant is native to central and southern Europe, from Austria to southeastern France, northern Italy, and Serbia. *Buphthalmum salicifolium* grows primarily in hilly and mountainous regions, often in alpine meadows on alkaline soils. It has been cultivated since the 18th century.

Buphthalmum salicifolium forms a clump of erect, simple or branched stems to 1 m tall, growing from cylindrical, knobby, loosely branched rhizomes. The oblong to lanceolate, entire or sparsely serrate leaves often have white pubescence underneath. The basal petiolate leaves reach 12 cm in length, whereas the cauline leaves become progressively smaller, narrower, and sessile. The 6-cm-wide flower heads are comprised of yellow ray and disc florets and are held

Buphthalmum salicifolium

singly atop thin, leafy stems. Fruits are 4-mm-long achenes topped by a toothed pappus.

In the garden, *Buphthalmum salicifolium* brings brightly colored flowers in midsummer to informal borders, woodland edges, or naturalistic meadows, where it can be permitted to spread widely and lean on neighboring plants. Plant it in full sun. When shaded, *B. salicifolium* will have a stronger tendency to flop. It thrives in moist but well-drained sites. Avoid rich soils and supplemental fertilization, as both will promote lanky growth. Flowers are suitable for cutting. Deadhead to prolong flowering. Dividing and transplanting are rarely needed, except when plants grown in rich soils spread too aggressively. Plants are hardy to zones 4 or 5.

No botanical varieties are recognized among the wild populations of *Buphthalmum salicifolium*. Among plants in cultivation a few low-growing variants have been selected and named, including 'Alpengold' with larger flower heads, 'Dora' with dark purple stems, and 'Sunwheel' featuring golden yellow flowers.

In the wild, *Buphthalmum salicifolium* is a summer bloomer. Cultivated in Germany, it flowers from June to September. In Poznań, flowering began between 13 and 21 June and ended between 1 and 14 August. Similarly, in Chicago, plants flowered in July and August, and when cut back they rebloomed after 3 weeks. At Longwood, flowering started in early June. Only once in 7 years, *B. salicifolium* flowered in the last week of May. The bloom continued, on average, for nearly 11 weeks, usually into early August. In 2 of 7 years, plants rebloomed weakly in late August and early September. Cutting back after the first flush of flowers did not have any effect on their reblooming.

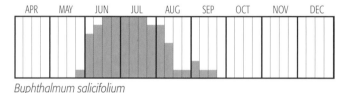

Buphthalmum salicifolium

Calamintha

CALAMINT

The name *Calamintha* is derived from the Greek *kalos*, beautiful, and *mintha*, mint, alluding to the plant's similarity to mint.

Calamintha grandiflora

LARGE-FLOWERED CALAMINT

This plant is native to southern Europe and western Asia, from Spain and France in the west to Turkey, Syria, and Iran in the east. *Calamintha grandiflora* grows in moist and organic soils, often on limestone, in shady montane beech and beech-spruce forests and scrub, at elevations between 300 and 2500 m. It has been cultivated since the 16th century.

Calamintha grandiflora forms dense, bushy clumps of decumbent to erect, usually unbranched stems to 60 cm tall, growing from thin, slowly creeping rhizomes. The soft, aromatic, ovate, coarsely serrate, petiolate leaves reach 8 cm in length. The bright pink, two-lipped, 4-cm-long flowers are borne in small cymes held in the axils of the bracts. Fruits are ovoid nutlets.

In the garden, *Calamintha grandiflora* is at its best in a position in the front of a perennial border and along paths or around patios, where it can spill over, soften the sharp edges of hard surfaces, and allow its aromatic foliage to be fully appreciated. Plant it preferably in a warm, sunny spot, although it will perform well in the filtered light of a woodland. *Calamintha grandiflora* thrives in moist, humus-rich, and well-drained soil.

Buphthalmum salicifolium

Calamintha grandiflora 'Variegata'

It spreads slowly by creeping rhizomes and may occasionally require dividing and replanting to control its growth. Plants are hardy to zone 5.

Despite the large geographic distribution of *Calamintha grandiflora*, accompanied by undoubtedly considerable variability among local populations, hardly any garden selections have been named so far. A couple of examples include 'Elfin Purple' with rose-pink flowers and 'Variegata' featuring foliage with creamy flecks.

In the wild, *Calamintha grandiflora* blooms from early summer to midautumn depending on the region. Cultivated in Germany, it flowers from June to August. At Longwood, cultivar 'Variegata' usually began flowering between the last week of May and the last week of June. On average, it flowered for nearly 17 weeks, typically into September. Only

once in 5 years, plants stopped flowering before the end of August, whereas in one year the bloom continued through October into mid-November.

Calamintha nepeta

LESSER CALAMINT, SAVORY CALAMINT

This perennial is native to southern and central Europe, northern Africa, and western Asia, from Spain in the west to Iran in the east. *Calamintha nepeta* has naturalized in parts of eastern North America. It grows on sandy or rocky limestone slopes, on dry open sites, in beech and chestnut forests, dry riverbanks, grasslands, and on scree, at elevations from 300 to 2100 m.

Calamintha nepeta forms compact, dense, bushy clumps of erect, branching stems to 80 cm tall, growing from short, creeping rhizomes. The pubescent, ovate, shallowly crenate or serrate leaves, to 4 cm in length, release spearmint aroma when crushed. The white to pale lavender, 1.5-cm-long, two-lipped flowers are borne up to 20 in loose, axillary cymes. Fruits are small ovoid nutlets.

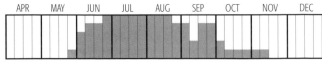

Calamintha grandiflora 'Variegata'

Calamintha nepeta

Calamintha nepeta

Calamintha nepeta 'White Cloud'

In the garden, *Calamintha nepeta* creates a fine foil for larger-flowered perennials and fills spaces in an unobtrusive manner. When thriving, plants can be exceedingly floriferous. The species performs admirably edging walks or patios, spilling over low walls, or sprawling out of containers. Plant *C. nepeta* where its foliage can be brushed against to release the delightful aroma. Position it in a sunny, warm spot, where the flowering will be most profuse. It grows best in well-drained, rather dry soil. Cut it back if the plants stretch too much after bloom and need tidying up, or to prevent unwanted self-seeding. Plants are hardy to zone 4.

Two botanical subspecies of *Calamintha nepeta* are recognized in the wild. Subspecies *nepeta*, from the mountains of southern and south-central Europe, has cymes of up to 20 flowers and peduncles to 22 mm long. In contrast, subspecies *glandulosa*, found in southern and western Europe, has cymes of up to 11 flowers and peduncles only to 10 mm long. In cultivation, only a few color variants have been selected and named so far. Among them are white 'Weisser Riese' and 'White Cloud', blue 'Blauer Riese' and 'Blue Cloud', and mauve-pink 'Gottfried Kühn'.

Calamintha nepeta is a summer bloomer. Cultivated in Germany, it flowers all summer long. In St. Louis, it bloomed from the beginning of July until mid-August. At Longwood, flowering started usually in early or mid-July. Only once in 7 years, it was delayed until the last week of July. Flowering then continued, on average, for 17 weeks. In years when plants were not cut back, flowering continued until the first frost in late November. By comparison, cultivar 'White Cloud' started to flower at Longwood a full month earlier, from early to late June. It bloomed for nearly 18 weeks into late October or, rarely, early November. When plants of 'White Cloud' were cut back in August, they resumed flowering 6 or 7 weeks later.

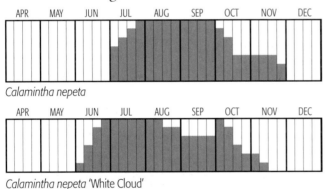

Calamintha nepeta

Calamintha nepeta 'White Cloud'

Calamintha sylvatica
COMMON CALAMINT, WOODLAND CALAMINT

This plant is native to western, southern, and south-central Europe, northern Africa, and western Asia, from northeastern Spain southeast to northern Iran. *Calamintha sylvatica* grows in forests, scrub and coppices, gullies, and along banks of streams and rivers from near sea level to 2000 m in elevation.

Calamintha sylvatica forms bushy clumps of erect or ascendent, pubescent stems to 80 cm tall, growing from branched woody rootstock. The dark green, ovate to orbicular leaves reach 7 cm in length and have coarsely dentate or crenate-serrate margins, with up to 10 teeth on each side. The 2-cm-long, pale pink or lilac and white-spotted flowers are arranged up to nine together in small cymes borne in leaf axils. Fruits are small, ovoid nutlets.

In the garden, *Calamintha sylvatica* can be grown in a variety of situations, from very sunny and open,

to partially shaded. Plant it in the front of a perennial border or kitchen garden, along the edges of patios or walks, where its exceedingly aromatic foliage can be fully enjoyed. *Calamintha sylvatica* thrives in sandy or loamy, well-drained soil. Trim it after the bloom if the appearance needs to be tidied up. Plants are hardy to zone 6.

Two subspecies of *Calamintha sylvatica* are recognized among wild populations throughout its geographic range. Subspecies *sylvatica* has larger flowers with corolla 13 to 20 mm long, whereas subspecies *ascendens* has flowers with corolla less than 15 mm long.

In the wild, *Calamintha sylvatica* blooms from June to September, depending on the region. At Longwood, its flowering began between late July and the first week of August. It continued, on average, for nearly 11 weeks until September or early October, when plants were usually cut back. When plants were left without cutting, they continued to flower weakly until the first frost in late November.

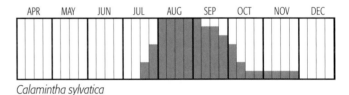

Calamintha sylvatica

Campanula
BELLFLOWER

The name *Campanula* is derived from the Latin diminutive form of *campana*, a bell, in reference to the shape of the flower.

Campanula glomerata
CLUSTERED BELLFLOWER, DANESBLOOD BELLFLOWER

This perennial is native to most of Europe, except the extreme north and south, and across temperate Asia, east to Japan, Korea, Manchuria, and Russia's Far East. It grows on calcareous soils, in forest glades and margins, thickets, scrub, and meadows, reaching the alpine zone in the mountains. *Campanula glomerata* has been cultivated since the 16th century. It has escaped from the gardens in North America and naturalized in the northern United States and southern Canada.

Campanula glomerata forms sturdy clumps of erect, stiff, simple or slightly branched, often reddish stems to 80 cm tall, growing from thick, partly woody, creeping rhizomes. The basal, long-petiolate, oblong or ovate-lanceolate leaves have crenate or dentate margins and reach 13 cm in length. The cauline leaves are narrower, have shorter petioles, and become sessile and clasp the stem upward. The violet blue to white, bell-shaped, upward-facing, 4-cm-long flowers are borne in compact terminal heads. In stronger plants, smaller clusters of flowers are produced in leaf axils, particularly toward the upper part of the stems. Fruits are capsules dehiscing near the base.

In the garden, *Campanula glomerata* is valued as a vigorous and durable summer bloomer. Under optimal growing conditions, it can spread rather rapidly; therefore, in borders combine it with perennials that can match its vigor and spreading tendency and withstand the competition. In less formal settings, allow *C. glomerata* to naturalize, spread widely, and produce more flowers each year. In cooler climates, site it in full sun, but in warmer climates, plants grown in partial shade perform better. *Campanula glomerata* thrives in any average, preferably evenly moist, garden soil. Its growth and spread are especially rapid in rich, fertile soils. Deadhead spent flowers to encourage additional bloom, and cut back to basal foliage when flowering is finished. Divide the plants every 4 to 5 years, or more frequently if they spread too aggressively. *Campanula glomerata* makes an excellent cut flower that lasts up to 2 weeks in water. Plants are hardy to zone 3, possibly zone 2.

With such an extensive geographic range, from Spain to Japan, *Campanula glomerata* is a highly variable species. This is reflected in the large number of variants described among the wild populations. Currently, seven subspecies are recognized, some of which were in the past regarded as distinct species. The typical subspecies *glomerata* is widely distributed in Europe and Siberia. Subspecies *serotina*, growing in the Alps and the Balkans, differs in having very short and decumbent stems. Subspecies *farinosa*, from eastern Europe, is distinct in its grayish tomentose leaves. Two subspecies found in the Carpathians, *elliptica* and *subcapitata*, have flowers arranged mostly in terminal heads, with *elliptica* having more flowers in each inflorescence. Southern European subspecies *cervicarioides* differs in its lanceolate leaves, whereas the Balkan subspecies *hispida* stands out because of its hispid,

Campanula glomerata 'Joan Elliott'

Campanula glomerata 'Joan Elliott'

ovate leaves. In cultivation, numerous variants have been selected primarily for their flower color and more compact growth. Color choices include white 'Schneehäschen' and 'Schneekissen', pink 'Caroline', and purple-violet 'Joan Elliott' and 'Odessa'.

In the wild, *Campanula glomerata* flowers from June to August. Cultivated in Poznań, it began flowering between 23 June and 11 July and ended between 17 July and 4 August. Similarly, in Moscow, flowering started, on average, around 28 June and ended around 26 July. In contrast, at Longwood, cultivar 'Joan Elliott' bloomed nearly 2 months earlier, starting in early May or, in one instance, in the third week of April. Flowering then continued until June, when plants were cut back, which in most years promoted their rebloom in July. On average, 'Joan Elliott' flowered for a little over 8 weeks. In comparison, plants in Moscow bloomed for only 4 weeks.

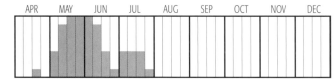

Campanula glomerata 'Joan Elliott'

Caryopteris

BLUEBEARD

The name *Caryopteris* is derived from the Greek *karyon*, nut, and *pteron*, wing, in reference to the winged fruits.

Caryopteris ×*clandonensis*

BLUEBEARD, BLUE-MIST, BLUE-SPIREA

This perennial is a hybrid between *Caryopteris mongholica* and *C. incana*, first raised by Arthur Simmonds in his garden in Clandon, England, in the 1930s. *Caryopteris mongholica*, believed to be the seed parent of this cross, grows in Mongolia and northern China at elevations of 1000 to 1300 m, making it well adapted to water and cold stress. *Caryopteris incana*, growing at elevations below 800 m in southern China, Korea, and Japan, is more tolerant of damp conditions but less cold hardy. The resulting hybrid has shown broader tolerance to climatic conditions than either species.

Caryopteris ×*clandonensis* forms a low-mounded subshrub of soft-wooded stems to 1.5 m tall branched from the woody base. The aromatic, lanceolate, short-petiolate, entire or coarsely serrated leaves are gray-white below and rugose above, and reach 10 cm in length. The bright blue to purplish blue, 1-cm-long flowers are arranged up to 20 in tight cymes, to 5 cm wide, borne in the upper three or four axils. Fruits are small nutlets with winged edges.

In the garden, *Caryopteris* ×*clandonensis* creates misty billows of delicate blue flowers that attract scores of butterflies and bees in late summer and fall. It can be used in either perennial or mixed borders, in small groups, or in large masses. Furthermore, its grayish green, soft-textured, aromatic foliage provides for attractive low hedges. Plant *Caryopteris* ×*clandonensis* in a warm, sunny location. It thrives in any average garden soil as long as it is well drained. In the early spring, prune plants back to the woody framework of branches. In climates colder than zone 7, this pruning will remove soft-wooded stems that died back over the winter, whereas in warmer climates it will promote new, vigorous growth and improve the overall habit. Pruning does not affect

Caryopteris ×*clandonensis* 'Longwood Blue'

Caryopteris ×clandonensis 'Worcester Gold'

Caryopteris ×clandonensis 'Dark Knight'

Caryopteris αclandonensis 'Worcester Gold'

the flowering as the flowers are formed on the new growth. The height at which pruning is done will, however, determine the ultimate size of the plants, which can grow only up to about 80 cm in one season. Plants are root hardy to zone 5.

The hybrid produces seeds freely, and since the 1930s, a whole array of garden selections, often difficult to distinguish, have been introduced into cultivation. These cultivars offer flowers in various shades of blue, from light blue 'Azure' and 'Blue Mist' to dark blue 'Dark Knight' and 'Ferndown'. In addition, some have silvery gray foliage, such as 'Longwood Blue', whereas others feature yellow-variegated leaves, such as 'Worcester Gold'.

In the wild, *Caryopteris mongholica* blooms from August to October, whereas the more southerly *C. incana* flowers from June to October. In St. Louis, cultivar 'Worcester Gold' bloomed for 11 weeks from the end of July until the beginning of October. At Longwood, bloom start date of 'Worcester Gold' varied by 5 weeks, from the second week of July to the third week of August. Irrespective of the start date, flowering then continued until the third week of September, rarely extending into the end of September or the first week of October. The average bloom duration was nearly 8 weeks.

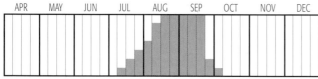

Caryopteris ×clandonensis 'Worcester Gold'

Centaurea

KNAPWEED

The name *Centaurea* commemorates Chiron the Centaur of Greek mythology, who was revered as a great healer.

Centaurea hypoleuca

CORNFLOWER, KNAPWEED

This plant is native to southwestern Asia, from Turkey to northwestern Iran. *Centaurea hypoleuca* grows in oak forests, on screes, and on rocky cliffs, at elevations from 600 to 2600 m. It has been cultivated since the early 20th century.

Centaurea hypoleuca forms vigorous, bushy, mounded clumps of leafy rosettes and flowering

Centaurea hypoleuca 'John Coutts'

stems to 60 cm tall growing from a woody rootstock. The basal leaves, to 45 cm long, are quite variable, but typically deeply lyrate-lobed, dull dark green above and white-tomentose beneath. The cauline leaves are smaller, oblong, and have irregularly and bluntly serrate margins. The 7-cm-wide flower heads are comprised of bright pink outer florets and white central florets and are borne singly on stiff, stout stems. Fruits are 5-mm-long achenes.

In the garden, *Centaurea hypoleuca* is a valued addition to perennial borders because of its ease of cultivation and long summer bloom. Plant it in full sun in any average, preferably moist, garden soil, as long as it is well drained. *Centaurea hypoleuca* performs best in cooler climates. In areas with hot summers, plants may produce weaker stems with a tendency to flop, so some staking may be required. Under optimal growing conditions, it spreads vigorously, and regular transplanting and dividing may be needed to control the spread. Plants are hardy to zone 6, possibly zone 4.

Although *Centaurea hypoleuca* shows great variability of leaf forms among plants in the wild, no varieties have been recognized in the natural populations, and only one color variant, the deep rose-pink 'John Coutts', has been selected in cultivation.

In the wild, *Centaurea hypoleuca* blooms from May to July. In cultivation, it flowers over a long period from late spring to midsummer and sometimes reblooms in the fall. At Longwood, the cultivar 'John Coutts' began flowering usually in the second or third week of May. Only once in 7 years, it flowered in the first week of May. This first flush of bloom ended in early to late June, at which point the spent flowering stalks were cut back. Plants re-

Centaurea hypoleuca 'John Coutts'

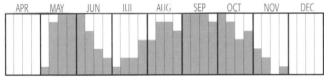

Centaurea hypoleuca 'John Coutts'

sumed flowering 3 to 8 weeks later and continued to bloom, although less profusely, until October or early November, giving, on average, over 20 weeks in bloom in the entire season. One year, plants were still in bloom at the end of November.

Centaurea montana

MOUNTAIN BLUET, MOUNTAIN KNAPWEED, PERENNIAL BACHELOR'S BUTTON, PERENNIAL CORNFLOWER

This plant is native to mountains of Europe, from the Pyrenees east to the Carpathians and south to the Apennines. *Centaurea montana* grows usually on calcareous soils in open woods and meadows. It has been cultivated since the 16th century.

Centaurea montana forms clumps of more or less erect, usually unbranched, broadly winged stems to

Centaurea montana

Centaurea montana

60 cm tall, growing from stoloniferous rhizomes. The simple, oval-lanceolate, entire or serrate leaves reach 18 cm in length. They are covered with silvery gray hairs, which persist on the lower surface of the leaf, whereas the upper surface becomes dark green. The 5-cm-wide flower heads are comprised of rich blue outer florets and reddish violet central florets and have involucral bracts conspicuously fringed in black. The flower heads are borne solitary, terminating upright stems. Fruits are 6-mm-long achenes.

Centaurea montana makes a dense cover of narrow leaves and brings early bloom to the garden. Because only a small number of flowers are open at any time, it has greater impact when planted in large groups or dispersed among other perennials. Under optimal growing conditions *C. montana* can spread aggressively, so it should be planted in company of vigorous plants that will not be choked by it. Grow it in an open and sunny site where flowering will be most profuse. Although it performs best when grown in alkaline soils, *C. montana* thrives in any,

even poor and dry, soil that drains well. Avoid rich, moist, and fertile soils, which promote rapid growth and excessive spreading. *Centaurea montana* is long-lived, but may require rather frequent divisions and replanting to keep its spread in check. Cut the plants back after the first flush of bloom to encourage new growth and flowering. Plants are hardy to zone 3.

The many subspecies ascribed in the past to *Centaurea montana* are presently reclassified as either distinct species or variants of *C. triumfettii*. Cultivated plants, however, proliferated into several selections with flower colors including white 'Alba' and pink 'Carnea', in addition to various shades of blue, such as bright blue 'Coerulea' or amethyst blue 'Violetta'. Furthermore, there are a couple of golden-leaved forms, 'Gold Bullion' and 'Horwood Gold'. These garden selections grow to between 40 and 60 cm tall.

In the wild, *Centaurea montana* flowers for a long time in early to midsummer. Cultivated in Poland and Germany, it blooms in May and June. Similarly, in Moscow, flowering started, on average, around 28 May and ended around 9 July. In Chicago, *C. montana* bloomed from June to July and then sporadically throughout the remainder of the summer, whereas in St. Louis flowering began in mid or late April and continued until mid or late October, with a break in July and August in some years. At Longwood, plants were always in bloom by the first week of May, but in some years they flowered as early as the second or third week of April. Their first flush of bloom was finished in June. At that time, plants were cut back and rebloom was observed 1 to 4 weeks later. The second flowering, less profuse than the first one, continued until September, October, or, in some years, early November, giving, on average, a total of nearly 24 weeks in bloom throughout the season.

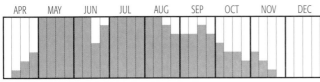

Centaurea montana

Cephalaria

CEPHALARIA

The name *Cephalaria* is derived from the Greek *kephale*, head, in reference to the round inflorescences.

Cephalaria gigantea

GIANT-SCABIES, TATARIAN CEPHALARIA, TREE-SCABIOSA, YELLOW-SCABIOUS

This perennial is native to the Caucasus Mountains. It grows in all regions of both the Greater and Lesser Caucasus, from the grassy areas and forests in the foothills to alpine meadows in high mountains, often in ravines, along stream banks, and on rocky slopes, at elevations up to 2600 m. *Cephalaria gigantea* has been cultivated since the 18th century, also under the names of *C. caucasica* and *C. tatarica*.

Cephalaria gigantea forms coarse, erect, bushy clumps of slender, ribbed, and freely branching stems to 2.5 m tall. The dark green, opposite, serrate leaves reach 40 cm in length. The lower leaves are lyrate to pinnatisect with four to six paired segments, whereas the upper ones are pinnatisect to pinnate. The 6-cm-wide flower heads, comprised of many soft primrose yellow florets, with the marginal flo-

rets enlarged and radiating outward, are held singly at the ends of wiry stems above the foliage. Fruits are ribbed achenes.

In the garden, *Cephalaria gigantea* is grown for its immense size and airy flowers of a rather uncommon soft yellow color, contrasted well by the coarse foliage. Use *C. gigantea* where its vigor and wild appearance will be an asset, in the back of a large perennial border, informal cottage-style garden, or in naturalistic wildflower meadow. Site it so the flowers can be illuminated by low light against a dark background, such as a hedge, shrubbery, or wall. Planting among other tall perennials may alleviate the necessity for staking in certain situations and hide the coarse foliage. Plant *C. gigantea* in full sun in moderately but consistently moist soil. Water during dry periods, because the foliage declines rapidly when plants are subject to drought. If shorter plants are desired, they can be trimmed slightly in the spring. Deadhead to extend bloom period, and cut stems back after flowering, as the plants deteriorates even under optimal conditions. Although *C. gigantea* does not spread particularly fast, it benefits from fairly regular divisions and replanting every 2 or 3 years. Plants are hardy to zone 3.

In the wild, *Cephalaria gigantea* flowers from June to August depending on elevation. Cultivated in Poznań, it began flowering between 27 June and 8 July and ended between 7 and 14 August. Similarly, in Moscow plants bloomed, on average, from about 30 June until 12 August. In the United States, June and July are given as bloom times in St. Louis, whereas July and August are reported for Chicago. At Longwood, bloom start date varied by a whole month, between the first week of June and the first week of July. Plants then flowered, on average, for a little over 5 weeks, into early to late July when they were cut back. Only once in 7 years, plants rebloomed in early October. By comparison, *C. gigantea* grown in Moscow flowered on average for nearly 6 weeks.

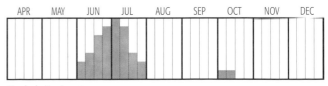

Cephalaria gigantea

Cerastium
MOUSE-EAR CHICKWEED

The name *Cerastium* is derived from the Greek *keras*, horn, in reference to shape of the fruit.

Cerastium biebersteinii
TAURUS CHICKWEED

This plant is endemic to the Crimea. *Cerastium biebersteinii* grows there in dry, open places on stony slopes and rocky cliffs in the mountains. It has been cultivated since the early 19th century.

Cerastium biebersteinii grows from creeping rhizomes, forming compact, dense mats of prostrate, leafy stems, densely covered with white hairs, to 30 cm tall at the time of flowering. The 3-cm-long, silvery tomentose, sessile leaves are linear to lanceolate. The white, 2.5-cm-wide flowers are borne in few-flowered, loose, elongated cymes. Fruits have many-seeded, somewhat curved capsules.

Cerastium biebersteinii

In the garden, *Cerastium biebersteinii* is best suited for exposed borders, among rocks or on dry stone walls, where it can form fast-spreading, profusely flowering, silvery mats. Avoid combining it with slow-growing perennials. Plant it in full sun, preferably in dry, rather poor soil with excellent drainage. Cut back after flowering to prevent excessive spreading and to encourage the regrowth of fresh foliage. Plants are hardy to zones 3 or 4.

In the wild, *Cerastium biebersteinii* flowers from May to June. Cultivated in Poland, plants flower between May and July. In Moscow, flowering began on average around 24 May and ended around 22 June. At Longwood, *C. biebersteinii* started to flower usually in the second or third week of May. Only once in 6 years, plants bloomed as early as the third week of April. Flowering then continued, on average, for 6 weeks into early to late June, although in one year, plants were still in bloom in the second week of July. By comparison, plants in Moscow flowered on average for only 4 weeks.

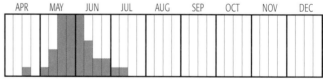

APR	MAY	JUN	JUL	AUG	SEP	OCT	NOV	DEC

Cerastium biebersteinii

Chaerophyllum
CHERVIL

The name *Chaerophyllum* is derived from the Greek *chairo*, to be pleased, and *phyllon*, leaf, in reference to pleasantly scented foliage.

Chaerophyllum hirsutum
HAIRY CHERVIL

This perennial is native to central and southern Europe, east to the Caucasus. *Chaerophyllum hirsutum* grows on moist and shady sites, in boggy meadows and open woodlands, wet ravines, on banks of streams and creeks, from the plains to the higher mountains.

Chaerophyllum hirsutum forms strong clumps of soft ferny, apple-scented foliage and erect or ascending, hairy, hollow, furrowed, branched stems to 1.2 m tall, growing from a deep, branched rootstock. The broadly triangular or pentagonal in outline leaves are two- or three-pinnate, with lobes being broadly

Chaerophyllum hirsutum 'Roseum'

ovate and acute. The tiny, white, sometimes pink flowers are borne in flat umbels. Fruits are narrow, ridged schizocarps, 1 cm long.

In the garden, *Chaerophyllum hirsutum* is valued for its fine-textured and delightfully scented foliage and delicate flowers. It provides an excellent complement to many perennials with its ferny leaves and airy flower stalks weaving in between other plants. It is equally suited to traditional formal borders and naturalized woodlands or meadows. Plant in full sun or partial shade in preferably moist and fertile soil, although *C. hirsutum* can tolerate a wide range of soil conditions. Plants are hardy to zone 6.

Two closely related species *Chaerophyllum elegans* and *C. villarsii*, were in the past treated as subspecies of *C. hirsutum*, but presently no botanical variants are recognized. Among plants in cultivation, only one form has been selected for its pink flowers and named 'Roseum'.

In the wild, *Chaerophyllum hirsutum* blooms in June and July. Cultivated in the United Kingdom, it often produces a second flush of flowers in late summer.

Chaerophyllum hirsutum 'Roseum'

At Longwood, the bloom start date of the cultivar 'Roseum' varied by a month, from the last week of April to the last week of May. Flowering then continued, on average, for nearly 5 weeks, into late May or the first week of June. Only once in 7 years, 'Roseum' bloomed through the first week of July.

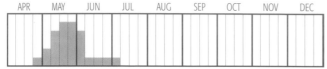

Chaerophyllum hirsutum 'Roseum'

Chelone

TURTLE-HEAD

The name *Chelone* comes from the Greek *chelone*, tortoise, in reference to the flowers resembling a turtle's head.

Chelone lyonii

Chelone lyonii

PINK TURTLE-HEAD, SHELLFLOWER

This plant is native to the eastern United States, where it is found from Maine to Mississippi, although in the northern areas of that range it may be naturalized rather than indigenous. *Chelone lyonii* grows in moist, rich coves, open spruce-fir forests, and on stream banks, primarily in the Appalachian Mountains. It has been cultivated since the early 19th century.

Chelone lyonii forms dense, robust clumps of upright, stiff, sparingly branched stems to 1 m tall, growing from rhizomes. The long-petiolate, ovate to lanceolate, strongly serrated, glabrous and lustrous dark green leaves reach 18 cm in length. The 2.5-cm-long, hooded, purple to rose flowers have curved, tubular, two-lipped, yellow-bearded corollas, subtended by several sepal-like bracts. They are borne in dense, terminal and axillary spike-like racemes. Fruits are 1-cm-long, broadly ovoid capsules.

Chelone lyonii is an ideal candidate for lightly shaded and moist areas, such as near a stream or pond and bog or woodland gardens. It is also very gratifying in a traditional perennial border provided that soil remains consistently moist. Under the right conditions, it is a long-lived plant that requires little maintenance and retains a neat appearance throughout the entire season. Plant *C. lyonii* preferably in partial shade. Avoid planting it in full sun in warmer climates, especially if soil is subject to periodic drought. However, plants in deep shade tend to produce lanky stems that flower poorly and flop easily. Choose a site with moist, rich, preferably organic soil. Usually, *C. lyonii* does not need staking. Low-growing and more-branched plants can be achieved by pinching stems in the spring. Deadheading spent flowers does not lead to rebloom. Rather, allow the seed heads to develop and provide interest through the winter. *Chelone lyonii* spreads slowly by rhizomes and may self-seed under ideal conditions but poses no danger to the neighboring plants. Divide it every 4 or 5 years to maintain the plant vigor. *Chelone lyonii* provides excellent cut flowers. Plants are hardy to zone 3.

No botanical varieties of *Chelone lyonii* are recognized among the natural populations. Among plants in cultivation, only a few selections, such as 'Hot Lips' and 'Pink Temptation', with deeper pink flowers, have been made so far.

In the wild, *Chelone lyonii* flowers from July to September. Cultivated in Germany, it blooms during the same period. August and September are reported as flowering times in Chicago and St. Louis. At Longwood, the bloom start date for the cultivar 'Hot Lips' varied from the third week of August in the second week of September. On average, 'Hot Lips' flowered for over 6 weeks, into late September or early October. Only once in 7 years, plants were still in bloom in the third week of October.

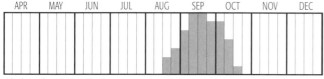

Chelone lyonii 'Hot Lips'

Chelone obliqua

RED TURTLE-HEAD, ROSE TURTLE-HEAD

This plant is native to the eastern United States, from Maryland south to Florida and west to Minnesota and Arkansas. It grows on calcareous, moist, humus-loam soils, along streams, in wetlands, meadows and open woodlands, cypress swamps, and other low-lying areas. *Chelone obliqua* has been cultivated since the middle of the 18th century.

Chelone obliqua forms upright clumps of stiff, sparingly branched, erect or ascending stems to 1 m tall growing from rhizomes. The short-petiolate or sessile, broadly lanceolate, shallowly serrate leaves are dark green, glabrous, distinctly veined, and reach 20 cm in length. The hooded, two-lipped, 3-cm-long, dark pink or purple flowers are borne in tight, terminal, spike-like racemes. The lower lip of the flower has a pale yellow beard. Fruits are ovoid capsules.

In the garden, *Chelone obliqua* is valued for its handsome and long-lasting foliage in all sorts of plant combinations. Like *C. lyonii*, it performs best in moist or even wet situations. *Chelone obliqua* is at home planted in a moist woodland, bog garden, or on the edge of water. It thrives also in any average garden soil as long as it is consistently moist. Plant it in an area that is lightly shaded or receives the afternoon shade. *Chelone obliqua* performs best in moist, fertile, humus-rich soil. Plants do not require staking, except perhaps when grown in deep shade. As an alternative, pinching stems in the spring will result in shorter plants that will be

Chelone obliqua

Chelone obliqua

less prone to flopping. Plants are hardy to zone 6, possibly zone 4.

Three botanical varieties of *Chelone obliqua* are presently recognized. The typical variety *obliqua* grows in the southeastern United States. Variety *speciosa*, found in the western part of the range, has larger flowers, whereas variety *erwiniae*, restricted to North and South Carolina, has duller purple flowers with a nearly white beard. In cultivation, a few color variants and low-growing forms have been selected, including white 'Alba' and pink 'Forncett Poppet' and 'Rosea'.

In the wild, *Chelone obliqua* blooms from August to October. Cultivated in the United Kingdom, it flowers in September and October, whereas in Poland flowering occurs earlier, from June to September. In St. Louis, plants bloom between mid-June and mid-October. At Longwood, *C. obliqua* began flowering usually in mid-August. Only once in 7 years, plants were in bloom in the last week of July. On average, flowering continued for over 9 weeks, into the early part of October. In one year, however, plants were still blooming in the last week of October.

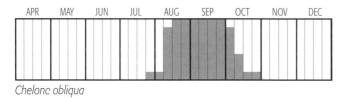

Chelone obliqua

Chrysanthemum

CHRYSANTHEMUM

The name *Chrysanthemum* is derived from the Greek *chrysos*, golden, and *anthos*, flower.

Chrysanthemum ×morifolium

FLORIST CHRYSANTHEMUM, GARDEN CHRYSANTHEMUM

This perennial is a complex hybrid between *Chrysanthemum indicum* and a number of species of the genus from China and Japan, including *C. erubescens*, *C. japonense*, *C. makinoi*, *C. ornatum*, *C. vestitum*, and possibly others. The early hybridization took place in China, perhaps as early as the fifth century B.C. It then continued in Japan starting in the eighth century and in Europe beginning in the 19th century. The first chrysanthemums to reach Europe at the end of the 17th century did not persist in cultivation; and it was not until a century later that several Chinese

varieties were successfully established, first in France. The introduction of the Japanese selections, starting from 1862 in Europe, greatly expanded the variety of flower shapes and colors available, and stimulated the ever-growing interest in chrysanthemums.

Chrysanthemum ×morifolium offers a dazzling variety of plant growth habits and flower forms and colors. It forms mounded clumps to 1 m tall comprised of sturdy, upright or sprawling, branched above, often woody at the base, stems. The petiolate, oval to lanceolate, green above and grayish beneath, strongly aromatic leaves are divided into entire or coarsely serrate lobes, and reach 7 cm in length. The single or variously double flower heads are solitary or held in panicled racemes and come in colors varying from white and lavender to yellow, orange, red, and bronze, whereas their size ranges from 2.5 to 15 cm in diameter. Fruits are achenes, but they seldom develop.

Compared to the vast quantity of *Chrysanthemum ×morifolium* cultivars, only a relatively limited

Chrysanthemum ×morifolium 'Virginia's Sunshine'

number of them are cold hardy enough to be grown outdoors year-round in northern gardens. Choose the early-flowering selections for planting in northern areas with a shorter growing season. They are valued for their wide selection of late-season, prolific flowers that combine with little effort with other fall bloomers and the autumnal leaf colors. Plant *C. ×morifolium* in full sun, in fertile, preferably calcareous and well-drained soil, although it can thrive in any average garden soil. In colder climates, choose a warm, protected site where soil stays rather dry over the winter. With the exception of dwarf varieties, trim the plants back once or more in late spring and early summer to reduce their height and improve branching. To avoid the risk of plants flowering so late that they might be spoiled by early frosts, the last trimming should be done, depending on the length of the growing season, in early to late July. Because *C. ×morifolium* exhausts soil nutrients rapidly, it should be fertilized yearly and transplanted into fertile soil every 2 or 3 years. The hardiest cultivars can overwinter in zones 4 or 5, but results can vary depending on soil conditions and winter protection. Plants grown in a lighter, drier, well-drained soil and given a light mulch cover overwinter better.

Even with the limitations imposed by cold winters and a short growing season, a variety of hardy chrysanthemums available today should satisfy even the most discerning of gardeners. For planting in the garden as hardy perennials, preference is given to early-flowering and low-growing or even dwarf selections that require little or no pinching to encourage branching. *Chrysanthemum ×morifolium* cultivars have been categorized into many classes reflecting the diversity of flower head forms and sizes, as well as the shape, form, and arrangement of individual florets. Color choices include white 'Anneliese Kock' and 'Penelope Pease', pale yellow 'Gethsemane Moonlight' and 'Virginia's Sunshine', soft pink 'Anastasia', lavender pink 'Mei-kyo' and 'Sweet Peg', orange-bronze 'Altgold' and 'Bronze Elegance', and magenta 'J.C. Weigelan'.

Chrysanthemum ×morifolium 'Gethsemane Moonlight'

Chrysanthemum ×*morifolium* 'J.C.Weigelan'

As a group, *Chrysanthemum* ×*morifolium* selections bloom in late summer until frost, but they can be categorized into the early-season varieties, which start flowering before 1 September; mid-season, which starts between 1 and 15 September; and late season, which starts after 15 September. At Longwood, the cultivar 'Virginia's Sunshine' began flowering around mid or late October, although in one year its flowering was delayed until the first week of November. On average, 'Virginia's Sunshine' bloomed for a little over 5 weeks until the first frost in late November or the first week of December.

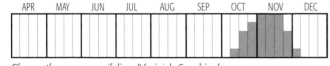

APR	MAY	JUN	JUL	AUG	SEP	OCT	NOV	DEC

Chrysanthemum ×*morifolium* 'Virginia's Sunshine'

Chrysanthemum pacificum

SILVER–AND–GOLD

This plant is native to Japan, where it grows near seashores on the Pacific side of Honshu, from Chiba Prefecture to Shizuoka Prefecture. *Chrysanthemum pacificum* has been cultivated since the latter half of the 20th century.

Chrysanthemum pacificum forms dense, mounded clumps of arcuate, ascending, leafy stems to 40 cm tall, growing from creeping rhizomes. The thick, dark green, oblanceolate to obovate, pinnately lobed leaves are narrowly but sharply white-edged and silvery tomentose underside. They can reach 8 cm in length. The lobes are entire or rarely one- or two-toothed. The lower leaves senesce before flowering. The small, button-like, discoid, 6-mm-wide flower heads, comprised of mostly tubular, rarely ligulate yellow florets, are arranged in corymbs to 10 cm wide. The fruits are achenes 1.5 mm long.

In the garden, *Chrysanthemum pacificum* delights with its uniquely decorative foliage all spring and summer long in borders, containers, or as a low ground cover. It then opens its numerous bright flowers that last well into the fall and can even withstand the early light frost. Plant it in full sun or, in areas with hot summers, partial shade. Choose a site

Chrysanthemum pacificum

Chrysanthemum pacificum

with excellent drainage, as excessive wetness can lead to winter injury. *Chrysanthemum pacificum* thrives in any average garden soil and can tolerate even rather poor soils. It spreads slowly. Divide and replant *C. pacificum* every 3 years or so to maintain the plant's vigor. It is hardy to zone 5.

Among the wild populations of *Chrysanthemum pacificum* occasionally appears a form *radiatum*, which has white ligulate corollas of marginal florets. In cultivation, one selection with light pink ligulate florets surrounding a yellow center has been named 'Pink Ice'.

In its native habitat, *Chrysanthemum pacificum* blooms in October and November. Cultivated in Chicago, it flowers from October until frost, but in St. Louis its bloom starts earlier in mid-September and continues to mid-October. At Longwood, *C. pacificum* began flowering in mid to late October.

Chrysanthemum pacificum

Only once in 5 years, the bloom was delayed until the first week of November. The average bloom duration was a little over 6 weeks, and plants continued to flower until the first hard frost in late November or early December.

Chrysanthemum zawadskii
ZAWADSKI'S CHRYSANTHEMUM

This perennial is native to Europe and Asia, from Poland and Slovakia in the west to Japan in the east. It is found growing in the mountains on stony slopes, often on calcareous soils. *Chrysanthemum zawadskii* has been cultivated since the early 20th century. Its subspecies *coreanum* was introduced in 1917 into the United States, where it was later crossed with *Chrysanthemum* ×*morifolium* to produce the so-called Korean Hybrids. Another subspecies, *latilobum*, was crossed with *C.* ×*morifolium* in 1929 in both Wales and in Germany, and the resulting hybrids are categorized today as Rubellum Hybrids. The distinction between these two hybrid groups, however, is not always clear, and cultivars may often be classified as one or the other.

Chrysanthemum zawadskii forms bushy clumps of simple or branched, somewhat woody at the base, densely leafy stems to 80 cm tall, growing from long, creeping, purplish rhizomes. The basal, two-pinnate, deeply sinuate and toothed, long-petiolate leaves reach 3.5 cm in length. The cauline leaves are gradually smaller and lobed, whereas the uppermost become linear. The 6-cm-wide flower heads, comprised of pink or white ray florets and yellowish disc florets, are held usually singly or in loose corymbs. Fruits are 2-mm-long achenes.

In the garden, the wild type of *Chrysanthemum zawadskii* is rarely cultivated, its place being taken by the Korean and Rubellum Hybrids, often collectively referred to as Korean chrysanthemums. Being exceptionally cold hardy and having simpler flower forms than *C.* ×*morifolium* cultivars, Korean chrysanthemums are well suited for perennial borders. Plant them in a sunny situation, although in warmer climates, plants may benefit from light afternoon shade. Choose a site with fertile, humus-rich, moderately moist, and well-drained soil. If shorter, better-branched plants are desired, stems

Chrysanthemum 'Hillside Sheffield'

can be pinched in late spring and early summer. To maintain good vigor, fertilize the plants regularly and divide every 3 or 4 years. Korean chrysanthemums provide long-lasting cut flowers. Plants are hardy to zone 3.

Chrysanthemum zawadskii is a highly variable species distributed over an immense territory, which is reflected in the large number of subspecies recognized among the natural populations, including *acutilobum, coreanum, latilobum, naktongense, yezoense,* and *zawadskii*. At one point or another, several of these subspecies were considered as separate species. Two of the subspecies, *coreanum,* and *latilobum,* are the most important horticulturally, since they were crossed with *C.* ×*morifolium* to develop a whole range of hardy garden selections classified as Korean and Rubellum Hybrids. Most of these selections have single flowers, although there are some with semi-double or even double flowers. Color choices include white 'Edelweiss', pink 'Pink Procession', apricot-pink 'Hillside Sheffield', yellow 'Citrus', orange-red 'Apollo', carmine 'Duchess of Edinburgh', and wine red 'Fellbacher Wein'.

In the wild, *Chrysanthemum zawadskii* blooms from July to October, depending on the region. Cultivated hybrids may flower even later, into November, but their flowers can tolerate the first light frosts. In St. Louis, the cultivar 'Hillside Sheffield' bloomed from September until the first frost. The same cultivar grown at Longwood began flowering usually in the first week of October. Rarely its bloom was delayed until the second week of October, and only once in 7 years it flowered as early as the last week of September. On average, 'Hillside Sheffield' bloomed for 7 weeks until the time of the first hard frost in November. By comparison, another cultivar grown at Longwood, 'Pink Procession', was far more variable in its bloom start date. In some years, it flowered in the last week of July, whereas in others it was delayed until late August or early September. In years when flowering began early, it diminished or stopped altogether in September, only to resume with greater profusion in October. The first part of October was usually the time when the flowering of 'Pink Procession' peaked, regardless of the bloom start date. On average, 'Pink Procession' flowered for

Chrysanthemum 'Hillside Sheffield'

Chrysanthemum 'Pink Procession'

a little over 9 weeks, into late October. Only in one year, plants were still in bloom in the first week of November.

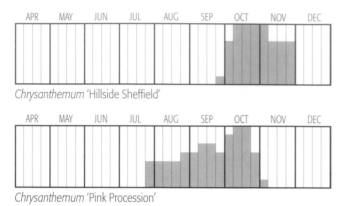

Chrysanthemum 'Hillside Sheffield'

Chrysanthemum 'Pink Procession'

Chrysogonum virginianum

Chrysogonum

GOLDEN STAR

The name of *Chrysogonum* is derived from the Greek *chrysos*, gold, and *gone*, joints, in reference to the flowers being borne in the nodes.

Chrysogonum virginianum

GREEN–AND–GOLD, GOLDEN KNEE, GOLDEN STAR

This plant is native to the eastern United States, from Pennsylvania south to Florida and Louisiana. *Chrysogonum virginianum* grows in moist to dry woodlands, forest clearings and edges, on slopes of ravines, limestone outcrops, and floodplains, at elevations from near sea level to 700 m.

Chrysogonum virginianum forms a dense mat of creeping, branched, leafy stems to 30 cm tall at the time of flowering, growing from stoloniferous rhizomes. The cordate to ovate, 5-cm-long, coarsely serrated, dark green, hairy leaves remain evergreen through the winter months in milder climates. The 3.5-cm-wide, stellate flower heads, comprised of five wide yellow ray florets and a tuft of yellow disc florets, are usually solitary, terminal or axillary. Fruits are 4-mm-long achenes.

In the garden, *Chrysogonum virginianum* is valued as an easy-to-grow ground cover, for edging wood-

Chrysogonum virginianum

land paths, and in a position in the front of shaded borders. In the warmer climates, the usefulness of *C. virginianum* extends through the winter months, as its foliage is semi-evergreen. Plant it preferably in partial shade. Sunny sites are suitable only when the soil is consistently moist, whereas deep shade may diminish flowering. *Chrysogonum virginianum* grows best in moist, porous, humus-rich, well-drained soil. It tolerates periodic drought as long as the plants are shaded. Trim the spent flowers to maintain the plant's neat appearance. *Chrysogonum virginianum* spreads gradually by rhizomes and self-seeding, but it can be easily controlled and does not become invasive. Plants are hardy to zone 5.

Three botanical varieties of *Chrysogonum virginianum* are recognized among the natural populations. Variety *virginianum*, which grows in the northern part of the geographic range, is not stoloniferous. Variety *brevistolon*, found in the middle part of the range, produces stolons with internodes less than 6 cm long, whereas the most southerly, variety *australe*, has stolons with internodes longer than 12 cm. The latter two stoloniferous varieties produce more prostrate, lower-growing, and faster-spreading plants than the northerly variety *virginianum*. In cultivation, several lower-growing selections differing primarily in leaf characteristics have been named, including 'Allen Bush', 'Pierre', and 'Springbrook', with light green leaves, and 'Eco Lacquered Spider', with shiny gray-green foliage.

In the wild, *Chrysogonum virginianum* flowers from late March until June or, in a moist site, until July. Cultivated in the United States, it flowers in the southern states primarily in March but stops in the heat of summer, although it may rebloom when cooler weather returns. In northern states it blooms later, starting in June, and then continues sporadically until September. At Longwood, the bloom start date varied by a month between the third week of April and the third week of May. On average, *C. virginianum* flowered for nearly 8 weeks, into mid or late June. No rebloom was recorded later in the summer or fall.

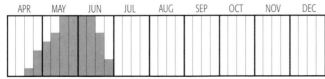
Chrysogonum virginianum

Clematis
CLEMATIS
The name *Clematis* is derived from the Greek *klema*, a vine branch, referring to the vine-like growth habit.

Clematis heracleifolia
HYACINTH–FLOWER CLEMATIS, TUBE CLEMATIS
This plant is native to eastern Asia, in eastern China, Korea, and Japan. It grows in forest edges and scrub, from 300 to 2000 m in elevation. *Clematis heracleifolia* has been cultivated since the early 19th century.

Clematis heracleifolia forms a sprawling, mounded subshrub of stiff, leafy stems, persistent and woody at the base, falling outward from the middle, to 1 m tall. The ternately compound leaves have broadly ovate, somewhat tomentose and prominently veined beneath, coarsely serrated leaflets to 15 cm long. The fragrant, 2.5-cm-long, tubular, nodding, hyacinth-like, blue to pink flowers have four reflexed, oblong sepals. They are borne in six- to 12-flowered terminal or axillary compound cymes. Fruits are elliptic,

Clematis ×jouiniana 'Mrs. Robert Brydon'

Clematis ×jouiniana 'Mrs. Robert Brydon'

Clematis ×jouiniana 'Praecox'

4-mm-long achenes with persistent, plumose styles 2.5 cm in length.

In the garden, sweetly scented *Clematis heracleifolia* attracts scores of bees, butterflies, and other insects. It is a vigorous grower that makes coarse and bushy mounds of foliage. Train it onto a support or plant it among other strong growing perennials or shrubs and allow the stems to sprawl between them. *Clematis heracleifolia* is valued in borders for its hardiness, reliability, and profuse late-summer flowering. Plant it in full sun, in consistently moist, cool, humus-rich soil. It may be slow to establish initially, but in time forms a substantial clump. Pinch in spring when stems reach 30 cm, to encourage better-branched and denser growth that will be less inclined to ramble. After flowering, allow the silvery, fluffy fruits to develop to extend the season of interest. Cut back in late winter, leaving the woody bases of the stems. Plants are hardy to zone 5, possibly zone 3.

Clematis heracleifolia is a highly variable species. Its many variants are by some botanists given varietal designations or even a status of distinct species. Horticulturally, the most significant of those is variety *davidiana*, also known as *C. tubulosa*, which has larger, widely flared, more tightly clustered and strongly scented flowers. This variety, crossed with *C. vitalba* from Europe and western Asia, produced a hybrid *C. ×jouiniana*, from which many popular garden selections originated. Color choices include pale blue 'Mrs. Robert Brydon' and 'Praecox', purplish blue 'China Purple' and 'Cassandra', and dark blue 'Roundway Blue Bird' and 'Wyevale'.

In its native habitat, *Clematis heracleifolia* blooms in August and September. Cultivated in Poznań, it started flowering between 13 and 19 July and ended between 16 and 22 September. In St. Louis, *C. heracleifolia* bloomed from late May or late August until early July or late September. At Longwood, the cultivar 'Mrs. Robert Brydon' began flowering in early to mid-July. Only once in 7 years, it bloomed as early as the last week of June. Its flowering then continued, on average, for a little more than 9 weeks, into late August or early September. The latest that the flowers were observed was in the third week of September. In comparison, the hybrid selection 'Praecox' flowered at Longwood about 2 weeks later, starting in mid to late July and ending, on average, 8 weeks later, in mid to late September.

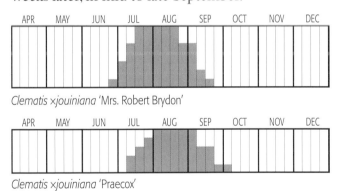

APR	MAY	JUN	JUL	AUG	SEP	OCT	NOV	DEC

Clematis ×jouiniana 'Mrs. Robert Brydon'

APR	MAY	JUN	JUL	AUG	SEP	OCT	NOV	DEC

Clematis ×jouiniana 'Praecox'

Clematis integrifolia

SOLITARY CLEMATIS

This perennial is native to Europe and Asia, from Austria and Italy in the west to Kazakhstan, Russia, and the Chinese province of Xinjiang in the east. *Clematis integrifolia* grows on grassy slopes, meadows, forest openings, scrub, and along rivers and streams in the mountains, at elevations from 1200 to 2000 m. It has been cultivated since the 16th century.

Clematis integrifolia initially forms an upright, then sprawling mound of wiry, slender, often unbranched, woody at the base or entirely herbaceous stems to 60 cm, rarely to 1.5 m tall. The simple,

Clematis integrifolia

Clematis integrifolia

Clematis integrifolia 'Alba'

ovate to oblong, conspicuously veined sessile, widely spaced leaves have entire margin and reach 10 cm in length. The blue-to-purple, nodding, 4-cm-long, urn-shaped, solitary or occasionally two or three together, terminal flowers have four flaring, slightly twisted sepals and a prominent tuft of stamens. Fruits are narrowly obovate achenes to 1 cm long, tipped with plumose, 5-cm-long, persistent styles.

Clematis integrifolia is at home in either a position in the front of traditional perennial borders or in more informal cottage-style gardens and naturalistic wildflower meadows. It puts on a better show when it is grouped in larger clumps. It starts with attractive, dense leafy mounds in the spring, which are later topped by fairly large and strongly colored flowers, followed by showy silvery green fruits. Plant *C. integrifolia* in full sun or partial shade in uniformly moist, cool, fertile, well-drained soil. When grown in full sun, cover soil with mulch to keep its temperature lower. Shaded plants tend to send weaker stems that are more prone to sprawling. Allow the stems to drape over other surrounding plants or support them by staking. Plants are hardy to zones 3 or 4.

There are no botanical varieties of *Clematis integrifolia* recognized in the wild. Occasional color variants with white, blue, or pink flowers have been given varietal status as, respectively, *alba*, *caerulea*, or *rosea* in the past but are usually treated as cultivars. In cultivation, a number of more refined clonal selections with varying flower colors have been introduced. Furthermore, *C. integrifolia* has been extensively hybridized with other species, including *C. lanuginosa*, *C. flammula*, and *C. viticella*, to produce an even larger range of cultivars, many of which may be offered under its name. Color choices include light blue 'Olgae', bright pink 'Pangbourne Pink', rose-pink 'Rose Colored Glasses', purple-red 'Tapestry', and dark blue 'Hendersonii'.

In the wild, *Clematis integrifolia* flowers in June and July. Cultivated in Moscow, it bloomed, on average, from around 22 June until 14 August. In Poznań, flowering began a little later, between 24 June and 6 July and ended between 28 July and 20 August. In St. Louis, *C. integrifolia* bloomed from early May until the end of August or early September. At Longwood, bloom start dates varied a month, from the second week of May to the second week of June. Plants flowered, on average, for more than 15 weeks into mid-August or mid-September, although flowering was often weak after June. In comparison, plants in Moscow bloomed for less than 8 weeks.

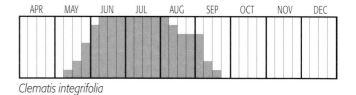

Clematis integrifolia

Clematis recta

GROUND CLEMATIS

This plant is native to Europe, from northern Spain in the west to the Caucasus in the east. *Clematis recta* has been naturalized in parts of northeastern North America. This species grows in forests, scrub, thickets, old fields, and in river valleys. It has been cultivated since the 16th century.

Clematis recta forms bold clumps of thin, sturdy, erect or rambling, leafy stems to 1.5 m (rarely 2 m) tall. The odd-pinnately compound leaves are divided into five to nine deep green, lanceolate to ovate, glabrous leaflets, each to 9 cm long. The

Clematis recta 'Lime Close'

Clematis recta 'Purpurea'

stellate, 2.5-cm-wide, fragrant, white flowers are borne in large, terminal and axillary corymbiform inflorescences. They have four narrow, wide-spreading, not recurved sepals. Fruits are broad, flat achenes with plumose-pubescent, persistent styles to 2 cm long.

In the garden, *Clematis recta* looks best if it is provided with some sort of support for its rambling stems. It envelops itself in a cloud of airy, white, scented flowers in summer, later followed by the silvery, fluffy fruits. Delicate flowers and neat foliage provide attractive foil for other, more brightly colored perennials. In less formal settings, allow it to scramble over low shrubs or sprawl over the ground. Plant it in full sun, in preferably fertile, humus-rich, well-drained soil that stays cool and uniformly moist. After bloom, allow the attractive seed heads to develop and extend the season of interest, or cut the stems back to encourage another flush of growth and possibly a second bloom. Plants are hardy to zone 5, possibly zone 3.

Although *Clematis recta* is a variable species, no botanical varieties are presently recognized among the natural populations. In cultivation, however, plants grown from seed vary considerably with respect to the quantity and fragrance of the flowers. Named garden selections offer choices of plants with larger, longer lasting flowers, such as 'Grandiflora' and 'Peveril', or even double flowers, including 'Plena'. In addition, several cultivars, including 'Lime Close', 'Purpurea', and 'Velvet Night', feature purple-tinted foliage.

In the wild, *Clematis recta* flowers in June and July. Plants cultivated in Germany sometimes bloom into August. In Poznań, flowering started between 29 May and 11 June and ended between 15 and 31 July. In contrast, the cultivar 'Purpurea' bloomed in St. Louis until mid-September or even mid-October. At Longwood, 'Purpurea' began flowering in mid or late May and continued, on average for nearly 12 weeks, usually into the end of July, but sometimes through the middle of September. Regardless of the bloom duration, the peak of flowering was observed in late May and early June.

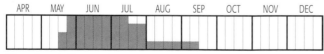

Clematis recta 'Purpurea'

Conoclinium

THOROUGHWORT

The name *Conoclinium* is derived from the Greek *konos*, cone, and *klinion*, a little bed, alluding to conical receptacle of the flower head.

Conoclinium coelestinum

BLUE BONESET, HARDY-AGERATUM, MIST-FLOWER

This perennial is native to eastern North America, from New York and Michigan in the north, to Nebraska and Texas in the west, and south to Cuba. *Conoclinium coelestinum* grows at elevations up to 400 m in moist soils in bogs, ravines, on wet slopes, banks of streams and lakes, in low woods, floodplains, along roads, and in ditches. It was formerly cultivated under the name *Eupatorium coelestinum*.

Conoclinium coelestinum forms vigorous clumps of red-brown, erect or decumbent, branching stems to 1 m tall, growing from slender, spreading rhizomes. The light green, triangular-ovate, petiolate, coarse-

Conoclinium coelestinum

ly serrate leaves reach 10 cm in length. The bright violet blue (rarely white), 1-cm-wide flower heads, comprised of 35 to 70 disc florets, are arranged in dense racemes and corymbs. Fruits are 1-mm-long black achenes tipped with a pappus of bristles.

Conoclinium coelestinum is valued for its late-season prolific bloom, which attracts butterflies into the garden and provides long-lasting cut flowers. It combines easily with other late-flowering perennials in a border, but its rapid spreading warrants some consideration to prevent it from smothering less vigorous plants. The colonizing character of *C. coelestinum* becomes a virtue, however, in wildflower gardens, meadows, and other similar naturalistic settings. Plant it in full sun or in very light shade. Although *C. coelestinum* performs best in moist to wet soils, it can tolerate periodic drought. If the procumbent growth habit is viewed as too rangy, stake the plants, position them among other sturdier perennials, or trim a couple of times in spring and early summer

to encourage lower and more branched growth. To control the spreading, divide the plants every 2 to 4 years, more often in fertile soils. Plants are hardy to zones 5 or 6.

Although *Conoclinium coelestinum* has a large distribution range covering nearly half of the North American continent, there are no botanical varieties presently recognized among the natural populations. Similarly, in cultivation only a couple of improved selections have been made so far, including 'Corey' with lighter blue flowers and the lower-growing 'Wayside Variety'.

In the wild, *Conoclinium coelestinum* flowers between June and November, depending on the region. Cultivated in Germany, it blooms from July to October. Planted in St. Louis, *C. coelestinum* flowered from late September until mid or late October. At Longwood, the bloom start date varied greatly between years, ranging from the last week of June to the third week of August. On average, plants flowered for 12 weeks into early to late October.

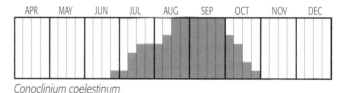

APR	MAY	JUN	JUL	AUG	SEP	OCT	NOV	DEC

Conoclinium coelestinum

Coreopsis

TICKSEED

The name *Coreopsis* is derived from the Greek *korios*, bedbug, and *opsis*, resemblance, in reference to the appearance of the achenes.

Coreopsis rosea

PINK COREOPSIS, PINK THREADLEAF COREOPSIS, PINK TICKSEED, ROSE TICKSEED

This perennial is native to coastal areas of eastern North America, from Nova Scotia south to Georgia. *Coreopsis rosea* grows in damp, often acidic soil, on sandy shores, marsh edges, along water margins, in shallow waters, at elevations of up to 50 m.

Coreopsis rosea forms dense, bushy clumps of erect, delicate, finely branched stems to 60 cm tall, growing from creeping rhizomes. The bright green, 5-cm-long leaves are mostly cauline. The upper leaves are linear, whereas the lower ones are two- or three-pinnate with linear segments. The 2.5-cm-

Conoclinium coelestinum

Coreopsis rosea 'Sweet Dreams'

wide flower heads, comprised of rose-pink (rarely white) ray florets and yellow disc florets, are held singly on short stalks. Fruits are 1.5-mm-long, narrow achenes with a minute or obsolete pappus.

In the garden, *Coreopsis rosea* creates fine-textured and airy mounds of light green foliage cover over a long period with pink flowers, a color unseen in other *Coreopsis*. It performs well in the front of a perennial border, edging paths or patios, in containers, or as a ground cover for a smaller area. It can also be allowed to naturalize in a wildflower garden. Plant it in full sun, in moderately fertile but consistently moist soil. Avoid sites where plants will be exposed to intense heat and drought. Deadheading encourages prolonged flowering but is tedious. Instead, trim the plants after the first bloom flush to encourage additional flowering. *Coreopsis rosea* can spread quickly under optimum conditions through the rhizomes and self-seeding. Divide and replant regularly if this spreading becomes excessive. Plants are hardy to zone 5, possibly zone 3.

There are no botanical varieties of *Coreopsis rosea* presently recognized in the wild populations, although the occasional white-flowered variants are described as form *leucantha*. Among cultivated plants, several improved selections have been made, some with flower heads 4 cm wide, offering a choice of colors of ray florets, including white 'Alba', pink 'Nana', and rose-pink 'American Dream'. In addition, a couple of cultivars feature bicolor flowers, 'Heaven's Gate', with pink and rose red florets, and 'Sweet Dreams', with white and raspberry red florets, among them.

In the wild, *Coreopsis rosea* blooms in August and September. Cultivated in Germany, it flowers earlier, from June to July. Plants grown in St. Louis bloomed from mid or late June until late August or early September. At Longwood, the white-flowered form *leucantha* began flowering in mid-July, except one year when it did not flower until the second week of August. On average, it bloomed for 12 weeks into early October.

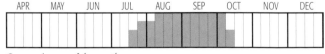

Coreopsis rosea f. *leucantha*

Coreopsis tripteris

Coreopsis tripteris

TALL COREOPSIS, TALL TICKSEED

This plant is native to eastern North America, from Ontario and Quebec south to Florida and west to Kansas. *Coreopsis tripteris* grows in moist sandy and loamy soils, boggy meadows, woodland edges, fields, and along streams, at elevations of up to 500 m.

　　Coreopsis tripteris forms upright clumps of strong stems branched in upper parts, to 2 m (rarely 3 m) tall, growing from a stout rhizome. The mostly three-foliate leaves have narrow, simple, or sometimes pinnately lobed segments to 10 cm long. The anise-scented, 5-cm-wide flower heads are comprised of lemon yellow ray florets and yellow, turning purple, disc florets. They are arranged in open, terminal, corymb-like inflorescences. Fruits are 5-mm-long achenes tipped with a pappus of a few minute bristles.

　　In the garden, *Coreopsis tripteris* is valued as an easily grown, long-lived, imposing perennial that fits well in the back of a perennial border, along the edge of a woodland, or in a tall meadow. If space permits, allow it to self-seed and naturalize. Plant it in full sun

Coreopsis tripteris

Coreopsis verticillata 'Crème Brûlée'

or partial shade. *Coreopsis tripteris* adapts to a wide range of soils, dry or wet, even poor. Plants grow taller in moist environments and may need staking there, especially in open situations where they will be exposed to wind. If self-seeding is not desired, deadhead spent flowers to prevent seed set. Divide *C. tripteris* every 2 or 3 years to maintain vigor. Plants are hardy to zone 4.

Several botanical varieties of *Coreopsis tripteris* described in the past, such as variety *deamii* with densely pubescent leaves, or variety *smithii* with simple leaves, are no longer recognized. Available garden selections are limited to a couple of cultivars, among them 'Pierre Bennerup' with broader ray florets and the lower-growing 'Mostenveld'.

In the wild, *Coreopsis tripteris* blooms from July to September. The same period is given for plants cultivated in Germany. At Longwood, flowering began in the second half of July. Only once in 7 years, it was delayed until the first week of August. On av-

erage, plants bloomed for 8 weeks, until, in some years, late September or the first week of October. In other instances, however, they had to be cut back at the end of August or in early September because of excessive flopping.

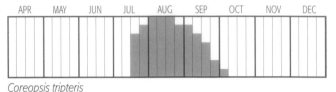

Coreopsis tripteris

Coreopsis verticillata

POT–OF–GOLD, THREAD–LEAF COREOPSIS, WHORLED TICKSEED

This perennial is native to the eastern United States, from Massachusetts and New York south to Florida, Alabama, and Arkansas, although populations north of Maryland are said to be the result of introduction. *Coreopsis verticillata* grows in sandy soils, in dry and open oak forests, at elevations up to 500 m. It has been cultivated since the late 18th century.

Coreopsis verticillata forms bushy, upright clumps of sparsely branched or unbranched stems to 80 cm tall, growing from thin, yellow, dense and tangled rhizomes. The sessile leaves, to 7 cm long, are palmately three-parted, with divisions dissected into nearly filamentous segments. The 5-cm-wide yellow flower heads, comprised of about eight disc and 30 to 40 ray florets, are arranged in loose corymbs on slender stalks. Fruits are oblong, 4-mm-long, blackish achenes.

In the garden, *Coreopsis verticillata* creates fine-textured mounds of delicate, thread-like foliage, covered throughout the summer with profuse small bright yellow flowers. Thanks to the overall airy appearance, *C. verticillata* fits agreeably in the front of a perennial border or at the edge of a planter, but also fills gaps left by the early-spring perennials that die off by summer. Plant it in full sun in any light, well-drained soil. *Coreopsis verticillata* thrives even in poor, sandy, or rocky soils. It tolerates drought and summer heat. Except when grown in moist and rich soils, *C. verticillata* is slow to increase and rarely needs dividing to control spreading. Deadheading spent flowers prolongs bloom period, but is rather laborious. Instead, cut the plants back after the first flush of flowers in midsummer to encourage a rebloom

Coreopsis verticillata 'Golden Showers'

Coreopsis verticillata 'Moonbeam'

Coreopsis verticillata 'Zagreb'

Coreopsis verticillata 'Zagreb'

in the fall, and to remove the foliage that may look tired and untidy by then. Plants are hardy to zone 5, possibly zone 3.

There are no botanical varieties of *Coreopsis verticillata* recognized among the natural populations. In cultivation, however, several color variants, ranging from pale to deep yellow, and lower-growing forms have been selected, including 'Crème Brûlée', 'Golden Gain', 'Golden Showers', 'Moonbeam', and 'Zagreb'.

In the wild, *Coreopsis verticillata* blooms from June to August. Cultivated in Germany, it flowers from June to September. Plants grown in Poznań began blooming on 9 or 10 July and finished between 6 September and 14 October. In Moscow, flowering started, on average, around 5 July and ended around 3 September. In the United States, June to August, with possible rebloom in September and October, are given as flowering times for plants in cultivation. Some cultivars such as 'Moonbeam' rebloom even without being cut back. In St. Louis, 'Moonbeam' flowered from mid-May or late June until early September or mid-October. At Longwood, 'Moonbeam' began flowering in mid to late June. Only once in 7 years, its flowering was delayed until the first week of July. It then continued, on average, without plants being cut back, for more than 15 weeks, into late September or the first week of October. Two other cultivars observed at Longwood, 'Zagreb' and 'Golden Showers', began flowering at about the same time in June, but had shorter bloom

period, 14 and 11 weeks, respectively. In comparison, *C. verticillata* grown in Moscow flowered, on average, for nearly 9 weeks.

Crocosmia
CROCOSMIA

The name *Crocosmia* is derived from the Greek *krokos*, saffron, and *osmea*, smell, alluding to the fact that dried flowers smell of saffron when soaked in warm water.

Crocosmia ×crocosmiiflora
CROCOSMIA, MONTBRETIA

This plant is a cross between *Crocosmia aurea*, a yellow-flowered, tender species, and *C. pottsii*, a vivid red, hardy species, made first in 1879 by Victor Lemoine in France. The parent species are native to South Africa, where they grow along riverbanks and other moist situations. *Crocosmia aurea* was the first of the two to be introduced in Europe, around 1847. It quickly gained popularity, but its use was limited by this species' lack of hardiness. In 1877

Crocosmia 'Lucifer'

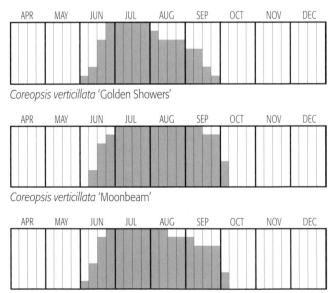

Coreopsis verticillata 'Golden Showers'

Coreopsis verticillata 'Moonbeam'

Coreopsis verticillata 'Zagreb'

the hardier *C. pottsii* was introduced in Europe, and hybrids between the two parents began to appear, starting with those developed by Lemoine. Since then, *C. ×crocosmiiflora* has naturalized in western Europe, parts of North and Central America, Hawaii, Australia, New Zealand, the Philippines, and parts of tropical Asia.

Crocosmia ×crocosmiiflora forms erect clumps of stiffly ascending and arching, sometimes laxly branched stems to 1 m tall at the time of flowering; the stems rise above the basal leaves, growing from corms and rhizomes. The narrow, sword-shaped, 1.5-cm-wide leaves reach 1 m in length. The orange to orange-red, tubular, 3.5-cm-wide, nodding to erect flowers are held in dense spikes along the upper portion of arching stems. Fruits are globose capsules splitting lengthwise.

In the garden, *Crocosmia ×crocosmiiflora* provides some of the most fiery flowers in midsummer. Lush clumps of grassy foliage and graceful, brightly colored flowers can cheer up any plant composition, be it in a perennial border or in containers. For the best effect, plant good-sized groups. Grow it preferably in full sun, although partial shade is acceptable. *Crocosmia ×crocosmiiflora* tolerates summer heat and high humidity well. It can thrive in any average garden soil that is well drained, but performs best in moist and humus-rich soils. Under favorable conditions, plants spread through the rhizomes and can colonize large areas rapidly, which leads to its becoming invasive in warmer climates. To control the spread, divide every 2 or 3 years, and weed out the inferior plants that may have self-seeded. No deadheading is required, as the spent flowers drop cleanly. Cut flowers are valued in floral arrangements. Plants are hardy to zones 5 or 6, but in colder areas they should be well mulched before winter, or corms should be dug out and stored indoors.

Since Lemoine made his first cross, some 400 crocosmia hybrids have been introduced, about half of which are still cultivated. Many cultivars were developed by crossing *Crocosmia ×crocosmiiflora* with it-

Crocosmia 'Lucifer'

self or by backcrossing to one the parents, and more recently by crossing with other wild species, such as *C. masoniorum* or *C. paniculata*. The profusion of named selections may be explained by the fact that crocosmia are relatively easy to cross. Cultivars offer many flower color choices, including pale yellow 'Canary Bird', rich yellow 'Voyager', apricot yellow 'Solfatare', soft orange 'Coleton Fishacre', rusty orange 'Dusky Maiden', and scarlet red 'Lucifer'.

Crocosmia ×crocosmiiflora blooms from June to August in St. Louis and from July to August in Chicago. In the United Kingdom, the cultivar 'Lucifer' starts bloom in the first half of July. At Longwood, 'Lucifer' began flowering in the last week of June or the first week of July. Only once in 7 years, its bloom was delayed until the second week of July. On average, 'Lucifer' flowered a little more than 5 weeks, into the last week of July or the first week of August. In comparison, 'Coleton Fishacre', another cultivar observed at Longwood, came into bloom in the latter half of July or in early August and continued for more than 7 weeks into late August or September.

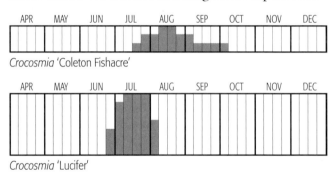

APR	MAY	JUN	JUL	AUG	SEP	OCT	NOV	DEC

Crocosmia 'Coleton Fishacre'

APR	MAY	JUN	JUL	AUG	SEP	OCT	NOV	DEC

Crocosmia 'Lucifer'

Delphinium

LARKSPUR

The name *Delphinium* is derived from the Greek *delphin*, dolphin, for the resemblance of flowers of some species to classical sculptures of these mammals.

Delphinium exaltatum

TALL LARKSPUR

This perennial is native to the eastern United States, where it is found primarily in the Appalachian Mountains, from Pennsylvania south to Alabama. Isolated populations also exist in the Ozark Mountains in Missouri. *Delphinium exaltatum* grows mainly in calcareous soils, on rocky slopes, in woodland margins, and in open deciduous forests and fields, at elevations between 150 and 2000 m.

Delphinium exaltatum forms clumps of unbranched, glabrous, leafy stems to 2 m tall, growing from a small crown of slender, fibrous roots. The deep green, palmately divided, three- to seven-lobed leaves have narrow, lanceolate segments, and reach 7 cm in length. The lower cauline leaves wither by the time of flowering. The whitish to pale lavender or purple, 2.5-cm-long, spurred flowers are held in loose, elongate, often branched, terminal racemes to 30 cm long. Fruits are 1-cm-long pubescent follicles.

In the garden, *Delphinium exaltatum* is valued for its lush, deep green foliage that remains attractive throughout most of the season and its late flowers in delicate shades of blues and purples. Plant groups of at least several together in perennial borders, cottage-style gardens, or in wildflower areas. In cooler climates, *D. exaltatum* performs best in full sun. Further south, however, it benefits from afternoon shade. Preferably, grow it in calcareous, fertile, mod-

Delphinium exaltatum

erately wet, and well-drained soil. Choose a spot that is protected from strong winds to avoid the need to stake the plants. Prompt deadheading of spent flowers helps the foliage to retain its lush appearance and encourages possible sporadic rebloom. Allow the fruits to develop, however, if self-seeding and naturalizing is desired. Plants are hardy to zone 5.

In the wild, *Delphinium exaltatum* blooms in July and August. Cultivated in Germany, however, it begins to flower in late spring. Similarly, plants grown in St. Louis began bloom in mid-April. At Longwood, *D. exaltatum* started to flower between mid-July and the first week of August. On average, the bloom continued for over 5 weeks, into mid or late August, and in one instance even into early September.

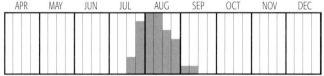

Delphinium exaltatum

Delphinium exaltatum

Dianthus

PINK

The name *Dianthus* was used by ancient Greeks to denote a flower of the gods, from the Greek *dios*, genitive of Zeus, and *anthos*, flower.

Dianthus gratianopolitanus

CHEDDAR PINK

This plant is native to western and central Europe, from France and the United Kingdom in the west to Ukraine in the east. *Dianthus gratianopolitanus* grows on sunny, well-drained sites, on rocks, and in open thickets.

Dianthus gratianopolitanus forms compact, dense tussocks of gray-green, lax, usually unbranched, leafy stems to 25 cm tall, growing from a woody stock. The entire, linear, glaucous gray-green leaves reach 5 cm in length. The fragrant, 2.5-cm-wide, rose to pink flowers are usually held singly on erect, wiry stems. The petals are mostly toothed and sometimes slightly bearded. Fruits are dehiscent capsules.

Dianthus gratianopolitanus finds a variety of uses, from filling little nooks in rock gardens and dry stone walls, edging perennial borders, paths, or patios to covering ground in smaller, especially sloped, areas. It is grown as much for the masses of elegant, fragrant flowers, as it is for its neat, dense, bluish foliage. Plant it in full sun. *Dianthus gratianopolitanus* tolerates summer heat and drought better than many other pinks. It can be easily satisfied with any average soil as long as it is well drained. Avoid sites that stay damp during the winter months. Improve heavier soils with amendment of crushed limestone. Deadheading prolongs flowering but is too laborious to be practical. Instead, trim the entire plants after flowering to remove spent flowers and untidy foliage. This will encourage a new flush of growth and another bloom. Under favorable conditions, *D. gratianopolitanus* is long-lived and rarely requires dividing to maintain vigor. Plants are hardy to zone 5, possibly zone 3.

There are no botanical varieties of *Dianthus gratianopolitanus* recognized among the natural populations. Nevertheless, among the plants in cultivation, a number of color variants and double-flowered forms have been selected. In addition, *D. gratianopolitanus* has been used in breeding hybrid cultivars. Color choices include white 'Dottie', soft pink 'Bath's Pink', medium pink 'Blue Hills', carmine-

Dianthus gratianopolitanus

Dianthus gratianopolitanus 'Bath's Pink'

Dianthus gratianopolitanus 'Grandiflorus'

pink 'Blauigel', rose-pink 'Grandiflorus', and magenta 'Feuerhexe'.

In the wild, *Dianthus gratianopolitanus* blooms in the summer. Plants cultivated in Germany and Poland flower from May to June. In the United States, it blooms from late spring into early summer, then repeats intermittently through the summer, sometimes until frost. In St. Louis, the cultivar 'Grandiflorus' flowered from mid to late May until late July and August, whereas the cultivar 'Bath's Pink' was in flower in May and again, in some years, from mid-June until early July. At Longwood, 'Grandiflorus' had the first flush of bloom in the latter half of May and in early June. After being cut back, it rebloomed in July. Rarely, sporadic flowers continued to appear through August until September. Cutting plants back after the second flush of flowers did not result in additional rebloom in the fall. On average, throughout the season, 'Grandiflorus' was in flower for a little more than 9 weeks. In contrast, 'Bath's Pink' grown at Longwood flowered only in the spring, for less than 5 weeks, between mid-May and mid-June. It did not rebloom later in the summer. 'Blue Hills', another cultivar observed at Longwood, flowered in the spring at about the same time as 'Grandiflorus' and 'Bath's Pink'. In some years it rebloomed in the summer, although less reliably than 'Grandiflorus', giving, on average, a little more than 7 weeks in bloom.

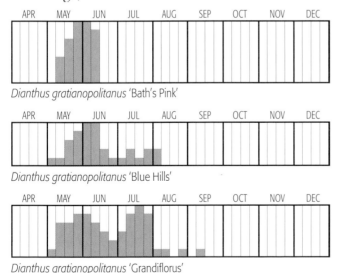

Dianthus gratianopolitanus 'Bath's Pink'

Dianthus gratianopolitanus 'Blue Hills'

Dianthus gratianopolitanus 'Grandiflorus'

Dianthus plumarius

BORDER PINK, COTTAGE PINK, GARDEN PINK, GRASS PINK, PHEASANT'S-EYE PINK, SCOTCH PINK

This perennial is native to central and southern Europe, from Poland in the north to Serbia in the south. It has naturalized in other parts of Europe, including Germany and the United Kingdom. It grows primarily in the mountains in calcareous soils. *Dianthus plumarius* has been cultivated since before the 16th century. Initially it was grown as a substitute for imported cloves for flavoring wines.

Dianthus plumarius forms dense, rounded, cushion-like clumps of procumbent, branched, glabrous and glaucous, wiry stems to 40 cm tall, growing from a woody base. The evergreen, gray-green, linear or narrowly lanceolate leaves reach 10 cm in length. The 3.5-cm-wide, very fragrant, rose to white flowers are borne solitary or two to five together in terminal clusters. Petals are usually deeply fringed and are usually bearded with long hairs. Fruits are dehiscent capsules.

In the garden, *Dianthus plumarius* brings a delightful spicy fragrance, a profusion of flowers, and neat, low mounds of bluish evergreen foliage. It fits agreeably planted among rocks, on top of a low stone wall, at the edge of paths or steps, or in a position in the front in a perennial border. Choose for *D. plumarius* a sunny spot, although in southern climates light afternoon shade may help it to cope with the effects of the summer heat and humidity. Plant it in preferably humus-rich, calcareous, moderately moist and well-drained soil. Avoid sites that remain damp during the winter months. Regular deadheading prolongs flowering, especially in cooler climates. Trim plants back after flowering to tidy up the appearance and to encourage a new flush of growth. Divide the plants every 2 or 3 years to maintain their vigor. Plants are hardy to zones 3 or 4, but they benefit in colder climates from a light cover of evergreen boughs.

Although a few botanical varieties of *Dianthus plumarius*, such as *blandus* or *semperflorens*, have been described in the past, they are no longer considered valid. One variant still recognized is designated as subspecies *praecox*. It differs in its early white flowers, and it is found in the mountains of Poland, the Czech Republic, and Slovakia. The species *D. plumarius* is rarely cultivated today and has been mostly replaced by its cultivars. It has also been extensively hybridized with other species, including *Dianthus caryophyllus*, *D. gratianopolitanus*, and *D. barbatus*, resulting in a wide array of cultivars with colors ranging from carmine 'Casser's Pink' and pink 'Altrosa'

Dianthus 'Itsaul White'

to white 'Itsaul White' or bicolored with a darker center, 'Excelsior' and 'Maggie', among them. Flowers come also in various forms including single, such as 'Duchess of Fife', semi-double, like 'Agatha', and double, including 'Inchmery', 'Mrs. Sinkins', and 'White Ladies', many with fringed petals.

In the wild, *Dianthus plumarius* blooms in late spring and early summer. Cultivated in Germany, it flowers from May to July, whereas in Poland from June to August. Plants grown in Moscow began flowering on average around 9 June and ended around 8 July. In the United States, the cultivar 'Itsaul

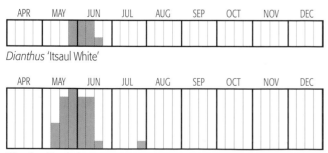

White' cultivated in St. Louis bloomed from mid-May until the end of May or into the latter half of June. At Longwood, 'Itsaul White' flowered at about the same time, from late May until mid-June, on average, for a little more than 3 weeks. In comparison, another cultivar observed at Longwood, 'Agatha', which is a hybrid between *D. plumarius* and *D. caryophyllus*, bloomed about 1 or 2 weeks earlier than 'Itsaul White', starting in the second or third week of May. Only once in 7 years, flowering of 'Agatha' was delayed until the last week of May. On average, 'Agatha' flowered for a little over 4 weeks, until mid-June, but in one year, it also sent sporadic flowers in the last week of July. Similar 4-week bloom duration was reported for *D. plumarius* from Moscow.

Dicentra

BLEEDING–HEART

The name *Dicentra* is derived from the Greek *dis*, twice, and *kentron*, spur, in reference to the shape of the corolla.

Dicentra eximia

FRINGED BLEEDING–HEART, PLUME BLEEDING–HEART,
STAGGERWEED, TURKEY–CORN, WILD BLEEDING–HEART

This perennial is native to the Appalachian Mountains in the eastern United States, from Pennsylvania south to Georgia. Populations established further north and west are said to be the result of introduction. *Dicentra eximia* grows in dry to moist, montane forests, often on rocks, ledges or cliffs, at elevations of up to 1700 m. It has been cultivated since the early 19th century.

Dicentra eximia forms clumps of ferny basal foliage and lax flowering stems to 30 cm tall, growing from stout, fleshy, creeping, scaly rhizomes. The gray-green, 30-cm-long leaves are broadly ovate in outline. The basal leaves are ternately compound with lanceolate or oblong leaflets, whereas the cauline leaves are finely dissected into narrow segments. The heart-shaped, nodding, 2.5-cm-long, rosy pink flowers are held in pendant, loose panicles terminating slender scapes to 50 cm long. Fruits are oblong or ovoid, 2-cm-long capsules.

In the garden, thanks to its delicate but persistent foliage and softly colored flowers, *Dicentra eximia* elegantly fills spaces between other perennials thriving in shady situations. Preferably, choose a spot that is at least partially shaded, although in cooler climates plants succeed in full sun if soil is consistently moist. Plant *D. eximia* in humus-rich, moderately moist, and well-drained soil. Avoid sites that stay damp during the winter. Under favorable conditions, *D. eximia* increases gradually primarily through self-seeding. Plants are hardy to zones 3 or 4.

There are no botanical varieties of *Dicentra eximia* recognized among the natural population. In cultivation several selections have been introduced over the years, many of which are the result of hybridization with *D. formosa*, which is native to the west coast of North America. Some of the cultivars are difficult to assign to one of the species or their hybrids. Garden selections offer larger, more prolific flowers, ranging from white 'Aurora', 'Angel Heart', and 'Langtrees' to carmine red 'Luxuriant', cherry red 'Adrian Bloom', and 'Bacchanal'. Some cultivars can also tolerate summer heat and drought better than *D. eximia*.

In the wild, *Dicentra eximia* has a long bloom season, especially in cooler climates, from the middle of spring to early fall. Cultivated in Germany, it flowers from May to September. Plants grown in Moscow flowered, on average, for 12 weeks, starting around 16 May and finishing around 19 August. In hotter

Dicentra eximia

Dicentra eximia

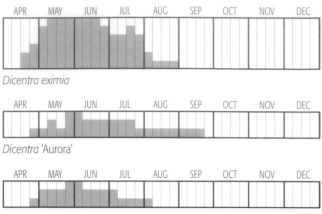

APR	MAY	JUN	JUL	AUG	SEP	OCT	NOV	DEC

Dicentra eximia

APR	MAY	JUN	JUL	AUG	SEP	OCT	NOV	DEC

Dicentra 'Aurora'

APR	MAY	JUN	JUL	AUG	SEP	OCT	NOV	DEC

Dicentra 'Luxuriant'

Dicentra spectabilis

climates, bloom may stop in the heat of the summer and possibly resume later in the season with the return of cooler temperatures. At Longwood, *D. eximia* began flowering between the third week of April and the second week of May. It then continued, on average, for 13 weeks, into late June or July. Only once in 6 years, plants flowered through August. In one year, flowering stopped for 2 weeks in the heat of July. The cultivar 'Aurora' had a comparable bloom duration of 11 weeks, but sometimes its flowering was delayed until the last week of May and then continued through September. Another cultivar observed at Longwood, 'Luxuriant', had a similar bloom season but the shortest bloom duration of the three taxa, only 9 weeks, on average.

Dicentra spectabilis

COMMON BLEEDING-HEART, DUTCHMAN'S-BREECHES, DUTCHMAN'S-TROUSERS, JAPANESE BLEEDING-HEART, LADY-IN-THE-BATH, LADY'S-LOCKET, LYRE FLOWER, OUR-LADY-IN-A-BOAT

This plant is native to eastern Asia, from China to Korea and Japan, although populations in Japan are said to be the result of introduction. *Dicentra spectabilis* grows in shady, moist forests. It has been cultivated outside Asia since around the mid-19th century.

Dicentra spectabilis forms round, loose clumps of arching, leafy, reddish stems to 1 m tall, growing from a stout, elongated rhizome. The gray-green, long-petiolate leaves are two-ternately compound with leaflets dissected into three or five obovate segments. The heart-shaped, pendant, 3-cm-long flowers are held in one-sided racemes to 25 cm long on arching stems. The white inner petals protrude from rosy pink outer petals. Fruits are oblong capsules.

In the garden, *Dicentra spectabilis* is among the most-loved spring flowering perennials. Its soft, ferny foliage delights from the time when it is barely out of the ground until it dies back by summer. In cooler climates, plants grown in moist soil may retain the leaves longer through the summer months. *Dicentra spectabilis* performs best planted in larger groups in a shaded part of a perennial border or in a woodland garden. Site it among later-developing perennials, which can cover the bare spots left after the foliage dies down. Plant it in partial to full shade, although in mild climates with cooler and cloudy springs, it can be grown in open situations. It thrives in humus-rich, loose, moist but well-drained soils. Avoid sites where soil stays damp during the winter. *Dicentra spectabilis* is very long-lived and requires no regular transplanting or dividing. Plants are hardy to zone 3, possibly zone 2.

There are no botanical varieties of *Dicentra spectabilis* described in the wild. Also, despite being cultivated for a long time, this species did not sport many variants. Only a couple of white-flowered selections, 'Alba' and 'Pantaloons', and one yellow-leaved cultivar, 'Gold Heart', have been selected so far. No hybrids with other species have been developed yet.

In the wild, *Dicentra spectabilis* flowers from April to June. Cultivated in Poznań, it bloomed starting between 11 and 22 May and ending between 22 and 25 June. Plants grown in Moscow flowered, on average, between 19 May and 4 July. *Dicentra spectabilis* bloomed in St. Louis from late March or mid-April until late April or May. At Longwood, flowering began in mid

Dicentra spectabilis

Dicentra spectabilis 'Gold Heart'

Dicentra spectabilis 'Pantaloons'

Dicentra spectabilis 'Gold Heart'

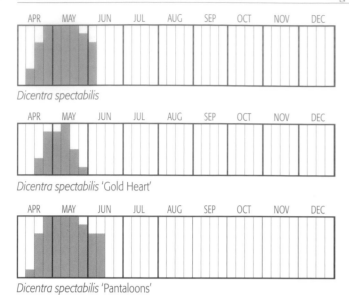

APR MAY JUN JUL AUG SEP OCT NOV DEC

Dicentra spectabilis

APR MAY JUN JUL AUG SEP OCT NOV DEC

Dicentra spectabilis 'Gold Heart'

APR MAY JUN JUL AUG SEP OCT NOV DEC

Dicentra spectabilis 'Pantaloons'

to late April and continued, on average, for 7 weeks into late May or early June. Two cultivars observed at Longwood, the white-flowered 'Pantaloons' and yellow-leaved 'Gold Heart', started to bloom at about the same time as the straight species. 'Pantaloons' continued to flower for 8 weeks, but 'Gold Heart' bloomed, on average, for only 4 weeks. In comparison, plants in Moscow were in flower for nearly 7 weeks.

Digitalis

FOXGLOVE

The name *Digitalis* is derived from the Latin *digitus*, finger, in reference to the form of the flower.

Digitalis grandiflora

YELLOW FOXGLOVE

This plant is native to Europe and Asia, from Belgium and France in the west to Russia's Altai Mountains in the east. It has naturalized in parts of the northeastern United States. *Digitalis grandiflora* grows in deciduous and mixed forests, woodland edges and glades, in meadows, on open stony slopes and stream banks, at elevations to 500 m. It has been cultivated since the 16th century.

Digitalis grandiflora forms clumps of erect, simple or rarely branched stems to 1.2 m tall, growing from short, much-branched rhizomes. The shiny, ovate-lanceolate, finely serrate or entire leaves are arranged in basal rosettes and alternately higher on the stem. The lowermost leaves have short, broad petioles and reach 25 cm in length, but the cauline leaves become sessile and smaller as they ascend the stem. The flowers are widely campanulate, pendant, pale yellow, and sometimes brown-netted inside. The 5-cm-long flowers are borne in loose, one-sided terminal racemes to 30 cm long. Fruits are ovoid, 1-cm-long, densely hairy capsules.

In the garden, *Digitalis grandiflora* fits admirably in a wide variety of settings. Its vertical spires of lightly colored flowers combine effortlessly with other perennials in both a formal border and in a naturalistic-style woodland garden. To show the flowers best, position it in front of a darker background of taller plants or in shade cast by the trees. The overall adaptability and the ease of growing *D. grandiflora* only add to its value, as does the evergreen basal rosettes of foliage, which remain attractive through the winter. Plant it in full sun or partial shade, preferably in calcareous, fertile, humus-rich, moist, and well-drained soil. Deadhead spent flowers to pro-

Digitalis grandiflora

long flowering. Cut back later to basal rosettes to encourage possible rebloom, or allow at least some fruits to develop if self-seeding is desired. *Digitalis grandiflora* persists long in the garden and does not require frequent transplanting and dividing. Plants are hardy to zone 3.

Despite the wide geographic distribution of *Digitalis grandiflora*, there are no botanical varieties described in natural populations. Similarly, in cultivation only a handful of improved selections, such as 'Carillon' and 'Temple Bells', have been introduced, and even these are not very distinct from the wild form. In addition, a hybrid between *D. grandiflora* and *D. purpurea* (another European species) named *D. ×mertonensis* is cultivated.

In the wild, *Digitalis grandiflora* blooms in June and July. Cultivated in Germany, it flowers from June to August. Plants grown in Poznań began flowering between 31 May and 22 June and ended between 29 June and 29 July. *Digitalis grandiflora* flowers in Missouri from May to June and in Ohio from June to July. At Longwood, flowering started in the end of May or in early June. Only once in 7 years, plants bloomed as early as the second week of May. They continued to flower until late June or early July, when they were cut back. In 3 of 7 years, a second bloom was observed beginning in August or September, 7 to 11 weeks after cutting plants back. As a result, *D. grandiflora* was in flower, on average, for nearly 8 weeks. In one year, the second bloom continued until the first frost in November.

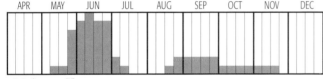

APR	MAY	JUN	JUL	AUG	SEP	OCT	NOV	DEC

Digitalis grandiflora

Digitalis lutea

SMALL YELLOW FOXGLOVE, STRAW FOXGLOVE

This perennial is native to Europe, from Germany west to Spain and south to Italy, and in northwestern Africa. It has also naturalized in parts of eastern North America. *Digitalis lutea* grows on sandy soils in open forests, woodland edges, hedgerows, and old fields.

Digitalis lutea forms clumps of slender, glabrous or slightly pubescent, leafy stems to 1 m tall, growing from much-branched rhizomes. The dark green, glossy, glabrous, oblong-lanceolate, acutely serrate or nearly entire leaves reach 15 cm in length. The pale yellow, sometimes almost white, 2.5-cm-long, tubular to campanulate, pendant flowers are borne in one-sided, slender, dense, branched racemes. Fruits are ovoid capsules.

In the garden, *Digitalis lutea* appears as a lesser, yet perhaps more graceful, version of *D. grandiflora* and can be used in a similar situations, while taking its smaller stature into consideration. Plants are very adaptable and persist in a garden for years without particular care. Plant *D. lutea* in full sun or light shade. It thrives in any average garden soil, although its performance is best in those that are moist and rich in humus. Once established, plants are quite drought-tolerant. Cut back after flowering, or allow fruits to develop if self-seeding is desired. Plants are hardy in zones 3 or 4.

Digitalis lutea

Digitalis lutea

There are two subspecies of *Digitalis lutea* recognized in the wild. Subspecies *lutea*, found throughout most of the distribution range except the southernmost part, has recurved lateral corolla lobes and one-sided racemes. In contrast, subspecies *australis*, found in Italy and Corsica, has straight lobes and racemes with flowers on all sides. In gardens, besides the straight species, only a couple of variegated selections, such as 'Flashing Spires' and 'Yellow Medley', are cultivated. Hybrids between *D. lutea* and *D. purpurea*, called *D.* ×*purpurascens*, are also known.

Digitalis lutea is a summer bloomer. Cultivated in Poznań, it began flowering between 14 and 20 June and ended between 23 and 29 July. Plants grown in Germany may continue blooming intermittently into September. At Longwood, *D. lutea* started to flower in late May or early June. Only once in 7 years, it began to flower earlier, in the second week of May. Bloom period, on average, continued for 4 weeks into late June or, rarely, to the first week of July. No rebloom was observed despite cutting plants back.

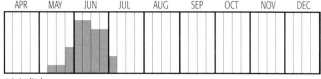

Digitalis lutea

Disporum

FAIRY-BELLS

The name *Disporum* is derived from the Greek *di*, two, and *spora*, seeds, in reference to the two-seeded fruits.

Disporum sessile

JAPANESE FAIRY-BELLS

This plant is native to eastern Asia, from Japan north to Sakhalin. *Disporum sessile* grows in the foothills, in shaded low-elevation woodlands, and on stream banks.

Disporum sessile forms erect or mounded clumps of arching, branched stems to 75 cm tall, growing from relatively short rhizomes. The sessile, clasping, ovate to lanceolate leaves reach 15 cm in length. The

Disporum sessile

Disporum sessile 'Variegatum'

creamy white, green-tipped, 3-cm-long, tubular, pendant flowers are borne singly or up to three in small terminal clusters. Fruits are 1-cm-wide blue-black berries.

In the garden, *Disporum sessile* finds its place as a vigorously spreading ground cover for any woodland or other lightly shaded situation. Although plants prefer partial to full shade, they can tolerate sun during the morning hours. Plant it in any average garden soil that is moist, rich in humus, and well drained. *Disporum sessile* may spread rapidly under favorable conditions, so regular dividing may be advisable if space is limited. Otherwise, it can be left undisturbed to increase freely through rhizomes. Plants are hardy to zone 4.

There are no botanical varieties of *Disporum sessile* described in the natural populations. In cultivation, there is a wealth of selections, all with variously variegated leaves. In addition to the most commonly grown 'Variegatum', newer cultivars include 'Awa-no-tsuki', 'Chigger', 'Kinga', 'Sunray', 'Tightwad', 'Tweetie', and 'White Lightning', to name just a few.

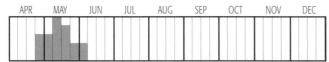

APR	MAY	JUN	JUL	AUG	SEP	OCT	NOV	DEC

Disporum sessile 'Variegatum'

In the wild, *Disporum sessile* blooms in April and May. In cultivation, its flowering may extend to early summer in some areas. At Longwood, cultivar 'Variegatum' began to flower in the end of April or in early May. On average, it bloomed for 4 weeks, into the latter half of May or, rarely, the first week of June.

Doellingeria

WHITETOP

The name *Doellingeria* commemorates a German botanist, Ignatz Doellinger (1770–1841).

Doellingeria umbellata

FLAT–TOPPED ASTER, PARASOL WHITETOP

This plant is native to North America, from Newfoundland west to Alberta and south to Georgia and Alabama. *Doellingeria umbellata* is found in moist woods, thickets, clearings, floodplains, wet fields, and along streams, at elevations to 1800 m. It has been cultivated since the middle of the 18th century.

Doellingeria umbellata forms colonies or spreading clumps of ascending to erect, dense, bushy, wiry, glabrous stems to 2 m tall, growing from a creeping rootstock of short to long rhizomes. The broadly lanceolate, short petiolate, entire leaves can be to 11 cm long, but become gradually reduced in size toward the ends of the stems. The basal leaves are smaller and usually wither early. The 2-cm-wide

Disporum sessile 'Variegatum'

Doellingeria umbellata

flower heads are comprised of five to 10 white ray florets and 11 to 26 yellow disc florets. They are borne in loose or dense, flat-topped corymb-like arrays. Fruits are 3-mm-long achenes topped by a silvery white pappus.

In the garden, *Doellingeria umbellata* is valued for its clean, attractive foliage and creamy yellow flowers followed by silvery white, fluffy fruits. It is best used in informal gardens, along woodland edges, wildflower meadows, and other naturalized settings. Plant it in full sun or partial shade, preferably in consistently moist or evenly damp soil. Plants are hardy to zones 3 or 4.

Currently, two botanical varieties of *Doellingeria umbellata* are recognized within natural populations. Variety *umbellata*, common in the eastern part of the distribution range, has glabrous or sparsely hairy leaves, whereas variety *pubens*, found in the western part of the range, has densely hairy leaves. In addition, a number of minor variants or forms have been described in the past, including *convexa*, *discoidea*, *flexicaulis*, and *intercedens*; these may be of questionable botanical validity but nevertheless suggest some potential for making garden selections in the future.

In the wild, *Doellingeria umbellata* flowers in late summer and fall. Cultivated in Germany, it blooms from August to September. It is noted for its long flowering period. In the United States, it is reported to flower for more than 8 weeks in Georgia. At Longwood, *D. umbellata* bloomed, on average, for more than 9 weeks, starting in mid to late July and finishing in early to late September. Only once in 7 years, plants were in flower during the first 2 weeks of July.

Echinacea

PURPLE CONEFLOWER

The name *Echinacea* is derived from the Greek *echinos*, hedgehog or sea-urchin, in reference to prickly receptacular bracts.

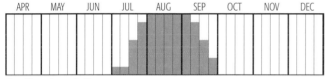

Doellingeria umbellata

Doellingeria umbellata

Echinacea paradoxa

BUSH'S CONEFLOWER, YELLOW CONEFLOWER

This perennial is native to the south-central United States, in Arkansas, Kansas, Missouri, and Texas. *Echinacea paradoxa* grows in open sites in the Ozark Mountains, wooded hillsides, glades, bald knobs, and rocky prairies, at elevations to 400 m.

   Echinacea paradoxa forms strongly upright clumps of unbranched or sparsely branched, nearly glabrous, yellowish green stems to 1 m tall, growing from thick, branched, spindle-shaped rootstock. The smooth, dark green, lanceolate to linear, strongly three- to five-nerved leaves reach 35 cm in length. Flower heads, held on rigid, glabrous stalks, are comprised of yellow or pinkish to white, strongly reflexed ray florets to 7 cm long, surrounding the high-domed chocolate brown disc. Fruits are tan or brown, 5-mm-long achenes tipped with a short pappus.

   In the garden, the yellow-flowering *Echinacea paradoxa* brings a color that is unusual among *Echinacea* species, which are commonly called purple coneflowers. It is an ideal candidate for prairie- and

Echinacea 'CBG Cone 3'

Echinacea 'Sunrise'

steppe-style informal gardens but fits equally well in traditional perennial borders or cottage-style gardens. Plant it in full sun, in any average, rather dry to moderately moist, well-drained soil. *Echinacea paradoxa* tolerates summer drought and heat well. Deadhead to prolong flowering and improve the overall appearance. Alternatively, allow the seed heads to develop to attract birds into the gardens and to permit self-seeding to take place. *Echinacea paradoxa* spreads gradually, and dividing is needed only if clumps become too crowded. Plants are hardy to zones 4 or 5.

There are two botanical varieties of *Echinacea paradoxa* described in the natural populations. The yellow-flowered variety *paradoxa* is found in Arkansas and Missouri, whereas variety *neglecta* with pink or white flowers grows in Oklahoma and Texas. In cultivation, although no superior selections have been made, several hybrids between *E. paradoxa* and *E. purpurea*, as well as other species, have been developed, including pale yellow 'Sunrise', mango yellow 'CBG Cone 3', salmon orange 'Sunset', deep orange 'Art's Pride', orange-red 'Evan Saul', pink 'CBG Cone 2', and rose 'Twilight'.

In the wild, *Echinacea paradoxa* blooms in late spring to early summer. The same season is given as bloom time for plants cultivated in Germany. In the United States, *E. paradoxa* grown in St. Louis flowered from late May until early July. It has been said that plants may sporadically rebloom throughout the summer. At Longwood, however, this was not observed. The bloom start date varied at Longwood by 3 weeks, between the last week of May and the third week of June. On average, *E. paradoxa* bloomed for 8 weeks, into late July and, on one occasion, into the first week of August.

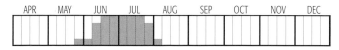

Echinacea paradoxa

Echinacea purpurea

BLACK SAMPSON, EASTERN PURPLE CONEFLOWER, HEDGE CONEFLOWER

This plant is native to the central United States, from Louisiana, the northwestern tip of Texas, and eastern Oklahoma, north through Ohio and Michigan, and east to Virginia. Populations established elsewhere in North America are believed to be a result of introduction. *Echinacea purpurea* grows in moderately rich, calcareous soils along creek beds, often under dappled shade, in rocky open woodlands, prairies, and thickets, at elevations of up to 400 m. It has been cultivated since the early 18th century.

Echinacea purpurea forms clumps of stiff, erect, brownish green, sparsely branched stems to 1.2 m tall, growing from numerous short, creeping rhizomes. Stems and leaves are covered with short rough hairs. The ovate to broadly lanceolate lower leaves are coarsely toothed, have long petioles, and reach up to 30 cm in length. The upper leaves are narrower, nearly entire, and sessile. Slightly fragrant flower heads, to 15 cm wide, appear singly at the end of a rigid stem. Drooping, reflexed ray florets are rose to deep purple (rarely white). The orange-brown disc florets are borne on a prominent conical receptacle. Fruits are off-white, 4-mm-long achenes tipped with a short pappus.

In the garden, *Echinacea purpurea* is usually planted in perennial borders where its rigid, strong stems and large flower heads contrast well with softer-textured plants. Similarly, it fits splendidly in naturalized meadow-like plantings. Although it performs well in full sun, partial shade will prevent richer flower colors from fading in hot weather. *Echinacea purpurea* grows best in moderately fertile, free-draining soil. Even though it is a lime-loving plant, it tolerates slightly acidic soils. Avoid planting in very fertile soils, which may result in leggy plants subject to flopping. This species is exceptionally drought and heat tolerant. Deadhead spent flowers to maintain a neat appearance. Otherwise, allow the seed heads to mature and provide food for birds. Plants spread gradually and require dividing only when clumps become too crowded. Plants are cold hardy to zones 3 or 4.

There are no botanical varieties of *Echinacea purpurea* recognized among plants in natural populations. Nevertheless, cultivated plants show remarkable diversity, which has led to the selection of numerous cultivars. Perhaps as many as 50 variants have been introduced over the years. Their colors range from white 'White Swan' to rose-pink 'Leuchtstern', purple-pink 'Magnus', and deep crimson red 'Crimson Star'; many have ray florets held in horizontal position rather than pendant. Cultivars such as 'Doppelganger' and 'Razzmatazz' have enlarged and showy

Echinacea purpurea 'Leuchtstern'

Echinacea purpurea 'Magnus'

Echinacea purpurea 'White Swan'

disc florets. The color of the conical receptacles varies from the greenish yellow 'Fragrant Angel' to the orange 'Little Giant' to the brown 'Hope' or nearly black 'Taplow Crimson'. There are a few variegated selections as well, such as 'Sparkler'.

In the wild, *Echinacea purpurea* blooms in late spring and summer. Cultivated in Poznań, it began flowering between 6 and 24 July and ended on 20 September. Similarly, plants grown in Moscow started to flower, on average, about 28 July and continued until about 19 September; a July-to-September bloom period is reported for Illinois, Missouri, and Ohio as well. At Longwood, three cultivars of *E. purpurea*, 'Leuchtstern', 'Magnus', and 'White Swan', started to flower between the last week of May and the last week of June. Their flowering continued until September or October, depending on the cultivar. 'Leuchtstern' flowered in the last week of May in 3 of 7 years, often 3 weeks ahead of 'Magnus', but also finished flowering earlier than the latter cultivar. 'White Swan' began flowering with 'Leuchtstern' but it continued to flower in some years through the end of October. On average, 'Leuchtstern' and 'Magnus' flowered for about 13 to 14 weeks, but 'White Swan' was in flower for nearly 17 weeks. In comparison, plants in Moscow bloomed for about 8 weeks.

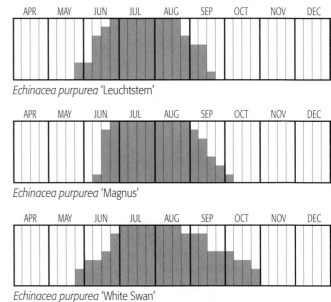

Echinacea purpurea 'Leuchtstern'

Echinacea purpurea 'Magnus'

Echinacea purpurea 'White Swan'

Echinacea tennesseensis

TENNESSEE PURPLE CONEFLOWER

This plant is found only in a very restricted area of Tennessee. *Echinacea tennesseensis* grows on limestone soil, in open clearings, glades in coniferous forests, and on dry rocky hills and barrens, at elevations between 100 and 200 m.

Echinacea tennesseensis forms clumps of yellowish green to tan, hairy stems to 60 cm tall, growing from short rhizomes. The dark green, linear to lanceolate leaves have entire, usually ciliate, margins and reach 18 cm in length. The flower heads are comprised of narrow, horizontal or slightly upturned, 3-cm-long, pinkish to purple ray florets and usually purple disc florets. They appear solitary at the end of rigid stems. Fruits are tan-colored, 5-mm-long achenes, tipped with a short pappus.

In the garden, *Echinacea tennesseensis* may be used in a fashion similar to other *Echinacea* species in borders, wildflower meadows, and lightly shaded woodland edges. It lacks, however, the vigor of many other members of the genus. Because it neither forms very large clumps nor spreads rapidly, start with a good size grouping for maximum effect. Avoid planting

E. tennesseensis mixed among other *Echinacea*, to prevent the faster-growing species from crowding it out. Plant it in full sun or partial shade, in any average, moderately moist garden soil that is well drained. Plants are hardy to zone 5, possibly zone 3.

There are no botanical varieties of *Echinacea tennesseensis* recognized among the natural populations. In cultivation this species easily crosses with *E. purpurea*, so true-to-type plants may be grown rarely. Only one seed strain has been introduced into the garden so far, 'Rocky Top', with dark red, curved upward ray florets.

In the wild, *Echinacea tennesseensis* blooms for a long time during the summer months. Cultivated in St. Louis, it flowered from late May until mid-October. At Longwood *E. tennesseensis* began flowering in the latter half of June. Only once in 6 years, plants bloomed in the second week of June. On average, they flowered for 11 weeks, usually until the middle of August, rarely through the end of September.

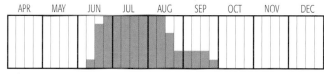

Echinacea tennesseensis

Echinacea tennesseensis

Epimedium

BISHOP'S-HAT

The name *Epimedium* was taken from Dioscorides, an ancient Greek author, but its meaning is obscure.

Epimedium Hybrids

BARRENWORT, BISHOP'S-HAT, BISHOP'S-MITRE, FAIRY-WINGS

There are about 50 species of *Epimedium* found in Asia, Europe, and northern Africa. A number of hybrids have been raised since the middle of the 19th century by crossing several of those species, including *E. alpinum* from Europe, *E. diphyllum* and *E. grandiflorum* from Japan, *E. perralderianum* from Algeria, and *E. pinnatum* from Iran and the Caucasus. The hybrid *E. ×perralchicum* is a cross between *E. perralderianum* and *E. pinnatum* ssp. *colchicum*. The latter species crossed with *E. grandiflorum* resulted in a hybrid *E. ×versicolor*, whereas crossing it with *E. alpinum* led to the development of *E. ×warleyense*. Furthermore, *E. alpinum* and *E. grandiflorum*, crossed with each other, produced *E. ×rubrum*. The hybrid

E. ×*youngianum* was raised by crossing *E. diphyllum* and *E. grandiflorum*.

With such a mixed background, hybrid *Epimedium* plants vary greatly with regard to their appearance. They form dense, mounded clumps of basal leaves and flowering stems to 50 cm tall growing from tough, creeping, branched rhizomes. The leaves are usually bi- or triternate, often tinged red in spring and, in the evergreen types, changing to yellow, reddish, or bronze during the winter months. The leaflets are typically ovate or acuminate with cordate base and have serrate margins. The delicate flowers have four petals and eight sepals. The four outer sepals are small and soon fall, whereas the four inner are colored, long lasting, and petal-like. The petals may be extended to form nectar-producing pouches or spurs. The flowers are borne in loose panicles on wiry stems and appear just before or during the leaf emergence. Fruits are slender dehiscent capsules.

In the garden, *Epimedium* hybrids are valued primarily as ground covering plants that provide year-round interest and can persist even in difficult sites, such as those existing under shallow-rooted trees. Their distinct spidery flowers appear in the spring in large numbers to complement the newly emerging, often attractively tinted or veined foliage. The leaves turn dark green in summer, and later, in evergreen forms, acquire a bronze blush during the cold season. Those that spread quickly, such as *E.* ×*versicolor*, can be used to fill larger areas, whereas the slower-growing *E.* ×*youngianum* will form compact clumps useful in smaller spaces. Use *Epimedium* hybrids in any lightly shaded situation. Although these plants tolerate deep shade, they will increase very slowly under such conditions. To create a dense ground cover in deep shade, start with an adequate number of plants, as they will be unlikely to spread rapidly. Plant them preferably in moist, humus-rich soil that is well drained. *Epimedium* species that are native to

Epimedium ×*rubrum*

Epimedium ×perralchicum 'Frohnleiten'

Epimedium ×versicolor 'Sulphureum'

Epimedium ×youngianum 'Niveum'

Epimedium ×youngianum 'Roseum'

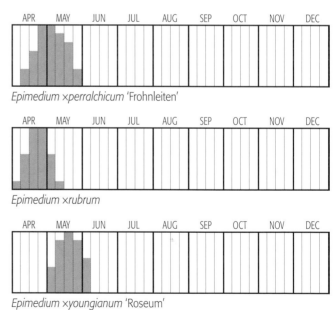

APR	MAY	JUN	JUL	AUG	SEP	OCT	NOV	DEC

Epimedium ×perralchicum 'Frohnleiten'

APR	MAY	JUN	JUL	AUG	SEP	OCT	NOV	DEC

Epimedium ×rubrum

APR	MAY	JUN	JUL	AUG	SEP	OCT	NOV	DEC

Epimedium ×youngianum 'Roseum'

the Mediterranean region and the Caucasus, such as *E. alpinum*, *E. perralderianum*, and *E. pinnatum*, tolerate summer heat and drought, and some of this ability is transferred to their offspring. Most of the hybrids, once established, are resilient, long-lived, and seldom require dividing. In colder climates, the evergreen foliage of some *Epimedium* may have a

Eremurus ×*isabellinus* Spring Valley Hybrids

somewhat worn-out appearance by spring. Trim off the old leaves to show the new emerging foliage and flowers better. No deadheading is needed as the expanding leaves hide the spent flowers. Plants are hardy to zone 5.

In cultivation, *Epimedium* plants hybridize easily. In addition to unspecified often seed-grown hybrid stock, several clonal selections have been introduced. These usually offer variations in color of the flowers and of the young, emerging foliage. Noteworthy examples include *E.* ×*perralchicum* 'Frohnleiten' with yellow flowers and red-tinted leaves, *E.* ×*versicolor* 'Sulphureum' with yellow flowers and red-mottled leaves, *E.* ×*warleyense* 'Orangekönigin' with pale orange flowers, *E.* ×*youngianum* 'Niveum' with white flowers and red-tinged leaves, and *E.* ×*youngianum* 'Roseum' with pinkish lilac flowers.

Epimedium ×*rubrum* blooms in Germany and Poland from April to May. In the United States, it flowers in St. Louis in April, but in Chicago in May and June. At Longwood, *E.* ×*rubrum* started flowering usually in the second or third week of April. Only once in 7 years, it bloomed in the first week of April. Flowering continued, on average, for a little more

than 3 weeks into the last week of April or the first week of May. In one year, plants were still in bloom in the second week of May. In contrast, another hybrid observed at Longwood, *E.* ×*youngianum* 'Roseum', flowered almost a month later, starting in early May and finishing nearly 4 weeks later. In St. Louis, flowering of *E.* ×*youngianum* coincided with that of *E.* ×*rubrum*. A third hybrid observed at Longwood, *E.* ×*perralchicum* 'Frohnleiten', was intermediate between the first two, beginning usually in the latter half of May and continuing into mid or late May. It was the longest blooming of the three, with an average of nearly 5 weeks of flowering time.

Eremurus
DESERT-CANDLE

The name *Eremurus* is derived from the Greek *eremos*, solitary, and *oura*, tail, in reference to the inflorescence.

Eremurus ×*isabellinus*
FOXTAIL-LILY, GIANT-ASPHODEL

Eremurus is a genus of about 50 species native to the drier regions of western and central Asia. Many

Eremurus ×isabellinus Shelford Hybrids

cm-wide flowers come in yellow, orange, pink, or white. They are borne in slender, dense, unbranched racemes. Fruits are spherical capsules.

In the garden, *Eremurus ×isabellinus*, when well grown, can create a breathtaking sight. Its pastel flowers rising high on imposing stalks cannot be rivaled. Because the plants become dormant in summer, position them among perennials that flower later and remain attractive through the rest of the season, yet thrive under the same growing conditions. Plant *E. ×isabellinus* in full sun in light but fertile soil that drains well. Avoid planting in heavy soils where, even under the best of care, plants tend to be short-lived. When drainage is in question, plant the rhizomes over a thick layer of gravel and cover with sand. Special attention needs to be given during planting in order not to damage the brittle roots, which can rot easily. Protect the dormant plants from excessive moisture during the periods of extended summer or winter rains by covering the ground with plastic sheeting. In colder climates, young emerging leaves may be subject to late frost injury. Plants are hardy to zone 5.

Most commonly seen in the gardens are seed-grown strains, such as Shelford Hybrids, Ruiter Hybrids, or Spring Valley Hybrids. They all offer a mix of flowers in shades of pink, yellow, orange, and white. In addition, a number of clonal cultivars with unique flower colors have been selected. Color choices include orange-red 'Feuerfackel', orange 'Cleopatra', pink-orange 'Isobel', pink 'Rosalind', yellow 'Image', pale yellow 'Moonlight', and several whites, 'Obelisk', 'Schneelanze', and 'White Beauty', among them. These cultivars are sometimes grown from seeds, however, so their flower color may vary somewhat.

Flowers of *Eremurus ×isabellinus* open from the bottom to top of the racemes and remain in flower for 2 or 3 weeks. In St. Louis, flowering takes place in May and June. When cultivated in Moscow, *E. olgae* (one of the parent species of the hybrid) began to bloom on 11 June, on average, and ended around 14 July. At Longwood, bloom start date of Shelford

species grow in steppes or rocky semi-deserts, often on mountain slopes, in areas with long, hot summers. *Eremurus ×isabellinus* is a hybrid between the pink-flowered *E. olgae* from Iran, Tadzhikistan, and Kyrgyzstan and the yellow-flowered *E. stenophyllus* native to Afghanistan, Iran, and Turkmenistan. The early crosses were made in 1902 by Michael Foster of Great Shelford, England, and were previously known as *E. ×shelfordii*.

Eremurus ×isabellinus forms tufts of bold, basal leaves and robust unbranched, leafless flowering stems to 1.8 m tall, growing from a short rhizome with fleshy, brittle roots radiating from all sides. The narrow, lanceolate, keeled, 30-cm-long leaves die back in early summer. The stellate, short-stalked, 1-

APR	MAY	JUN	JUL	AUG	SEP	OCT	NOV	DEC

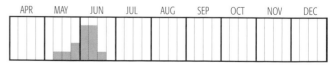

Eremurus ×isabellinus Shelford Hybrids

Hybrids varied by 3 weeks, between the second week of May and the first week of June. On average, plants flowered a little more than 2 weeks, usually into mid-June. By comparison, *E. olgae* in Moscow bloomed for nearly 5 weeks.

Eryngium

ERYNGO

The name *Eryngium* is derived from the Greek *eyringion*, a name used by Theophrastus for an undetermined species of thistle.

Eryngium agavifolium

SEA-HOLLY

This perennial is native to Argentina, from San Luis in the south to Santiago del Estero in the north. *Eryngium agavifolium* grows in wet, often gravelly, soils along rivers and on stream banks.

Eryngium agavifolium forms clumps of sturdy, stout, ascending stems to 1.5 m tall, branched toward the tip and growing from a thick, fleshy rootstock. The evergreen, oblong to linear, sharply and spiny serrated, 0.5-m-long leaves are mostly in basal rosettes. The small flowers are arranged in cylindrical, greenish blue, terminal flower heads to 5 cm long, subtended by an involucre of somewhat spiny bracts. Fruits are mericarps.

In the garden, thanks to its bold, sword-like foliage and coarse habit, *Eryngium agavifolium* is used as a statuesque accent to create contrast to softer-textured plants. It also provides cut stems for either fresh or dry flower arrangements. Plant it in full sun in any average, well-drained soil. *Eryngium agavifolium* thrives in poor and dry sites. It tolerates even saline soils. It grows poorly, however, in rich and excessively wet soil, especially if it remains damp over the winter. Under such conditions, plants tend to be poorly colored and have weak stems subject to flopping. It is a long-lived species and, as it resents root disturbance, transplanting should be done only when necessary. Plants are hardy to zones 6 or 7.

In its native habitat in Argentina, *Eryngium agavifolium* blooms for a long time from mid-December until March, which in the Northern Hemisphere corresponds with mid-June until September. Cultivated in Poznań, it started flowering on 24 June and ended on 7 August. At Longwood, plants had two flushes of bloom. They began to flower usually

Eryngium agavifolium

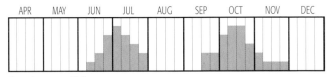

Eryngium agavifolium

in the latter half of June. Rarely the bloom start date was as early as the second week of June or as late as the first week of July. This first flush of flowers lasted through mid or late July. The second bloom began in late September or early October and lasted through the end of October or, on one occasion, through the end of November. On average, *E. agavifolium* was in flower for 8 weeks. In comparison, plants in Poznań bloomed for a little more than 6 weeks.

Eryngium planum

BLUE ERYNGO, FLAT SEA–HOLLY

This plant is native to Europe and western and central Asia, from Germany and Austria in the west to the Altai Mountains in Russia in the east, south to the Caucasus and Kashmir. It grows in poor soils on dry hills, at elevations from 500 to 1500 m. *Eryngium planum* has been cultivated since the 16th century.

Eryngium planum forms clumps of stiffly erect, branched stems to 1 m tall, growing from stout, fleshy taproots. The leathery, dark green leaves reach 10 cm in length. The basal leaves are petiolate, entire, oblong to ovate, and have serrated but not spiny margins. The cauline leaves are sessile, palmately parted, and have three to five spiny lobes. The small, pale blue flowers are arranged in silver-blue, ovate, terminal, 1.5-cm-long flower heads subtended by six to eight involucral, narrowly lanceolate, spiky bracts to 2.5 cm in length. Fruits are 3-mm-long mericarps.

In the garden, *Eryngium planum* excels in informal borders or naturalistic-style plantings, where its coarse, steel blue foliage and flowers complement the extravaganza of brightly colored summer flowers. The plant's longevity, ease of cultivation, and suitability for dry flower arrangements contribute to its popularity with gardeners. Plant *E. planum* in a warm, sunny spot in any average, deep, and well-drained soil. It tolerates even dry, poor, sandy or gravelly soils. Avoid planting in moist and fertile soil, where plants tend to stretch, flop and sprawl, and may require support. If desired, deadhead to maintain the neat appearance. Cut back in late summer, when all flowering is finished. New basal leaves resprout and remain evergreen during the winter. *Eryngium planum* recovers slowly after transplanting, so leave it undisturbed for years. Dividing is seldom

Eryngium planum

Eryngium planum 'Blaukappe'

required. Self-seeding may happen under optimum growing conditions, but it rarely becomes a nuisance. Plants are hardy to zones 4 or 5.

There are no botanical varieties of *Eryngium planum* recognized in the natural populations. In cultivation, a number of selections have been made, most of them having stronger blue color in the flowers and intensely glaucous leaves. Noteworthy examples include 'Blaukappe', 'Flüela', and 'Seven Seas'. Others exhibit variegated foliage, such as 'Calypso' and 'Jade Frost', or unusually compact growth habit, including the 45-cm-tall 'Blauer Zwerg' and 'Blue Diamond'.

In the wild, *Eryngium planum* is a summer bloomer. Cultivated in Poznań, it began flowering between 22 June and 3 July and ended between 7 and 29 August. Plants grown in St. Louis bloomed from the first week of June until early August, occasionally again in early October. At Longwood, both the species

and the cultivar 'Blaukappe' started to flower usually in the latter half of June or the first week of July. Only once in 7 years, either one of these bloomed in the second week of June. 'Blaukappe' bloomed, on average, for 7 weeks, nearly a week longer than the species, finishing in late July or early August, and only rarely flowering through the end of August.

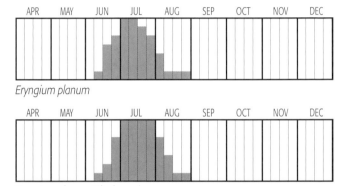

Eryngium planum

Eryngium planum 'Blaukappe'

Eryngium planum 'Blaukappe'

Eryngium planum 'Flüela'

Eryngium yuccifolium

BUTTON ERYNGO, BUTTON SNAKE-ROOT,
RATTLESNAKE MASTER

This plant is native to the United States, from New Jersey and Connecticut west to Minnesota, and south to Texas and Florida. *Eryngium yuccifolium* grows in dry, rocky soils in open woodlands, thickets, forest edges, prairies, and glades. It has been cultivated since the end of the 17th century.

Eryngium yuccifolium forms clumps of basal foliage and sparingly branched, erect, mostly leafless stems to 1.8 m tall, growing from a deep taproot. The blue-gray, stiff, narrow leaves have widely spaced bristles along the margins. The basal leaves reach 1 m in length, whereas the cauline leaves become progressively smaller up the stems. The small, creamy white flowers are arranged in globose, whitish or green flower heads to 2.5 cm long, subtended by five to 10 short, serrated bracts, and held in terminal, branched inflorescences. Fruits are mericarps to 8 mm long.

In the garden, *Eryngium yuccifolium* is grown for bold stature and yucca-like foliage rather than for the flowers. Although it can be effective even in small numbers, it creates the most dramatic display when used in large groupings in naturalistic gardens and meadows. Plant it preferably in full sun, but light afternoon shade is tolerated. Choose a warm site, with moderately fertile, light, rather dry, and well-drained soil. Avoid situations with heavy, overly fertile, and moist soil, which will promote lanky growth with a tendency to flop. It does not require transplanting and is best left undisturbed for years. Plants may self-seed under favorable conditions. *Eryngium yuccifolium* is hardy to zone 5, possibly zone 3.

Eryngium yuccifolium

Eryngium yuccifolium

There are two varieties of *Eryngium yuccifolium* described among the natural populations. Variety *yuccifolium*, which has leaves wider than 1.5 cm and margined with solitary bristles, is found throughout the species' range, whereas variety *synchaetum*, with narrower leaves margined with clustered bristles, has distribution limited to the southern part of the range. No garden selections have been introduced into cultivation.

In the wild, *Eryngium yuccifolium* blooms from June to August. Cultivated in St. Louis, plants flowered from June until the end of August or mid-September. At Longwood, the bloom start date varied by a month, between the second week of June and the second week of July. On average, flowering continued for 8 weeks through the end of July or the end of August. One year, when plants were cut back at the end of July, they rebloomed, though less profusely, in October.

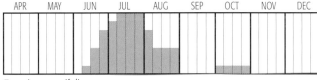

Eryngium yuccifolium

Eupatorium

THOROUGHWORT

The name *Eupatorium* commemorates Mithridates Eupator (132–63 B.C.), king of Pontus.

Eupatorium hyssopifolium

HYSSOPLEAF THOROUGHWORT

This perennial is native to the United States, from Massachusetts and New York south to Florida and west to Illinois and Texas. *Eupatorium hyssopifolium* often grows in dry, sandy soils, in old fields, open disturbed sites, and along roadsides, at elevations of up to 200 m.

Eupatorium hyssopifolium forms clumps of single or sparsely branched, pubescent stems to 1 m tall, growing from short caudices or rhizomes. The simple, sessile, lanceolate or linear leaves have entire or serrate margins and reach 10 cm in length. They are usually arranged in whorls of four, but are sometimes opposite or even alternate. Flower heads, comprised of five white disc florets, are held in corymbiform arrays. Fruits are 3-mm-long achenes tipped with a pappus of short bristles.

In the garden, *Eupatorium hyssopifolium* performs best when used in large groupings in informal settings, where its narrow, fine-textured foliage and masses of tiny flowers can truly shine. Plant it in full sun in any average, moderately moist soil. *Eupatorium hyssopifolium* tolerates poor, infertile soils and periodic drought. Cut back after flowering if self-seeding becomes a nuisance. Plants are hardy to zone 5.

There are two botanical varieties of *Eupatorium hyssopifolium* currently recognized among natural populations. Variety *hyssopifolium*, found throughout the species' range, is distinguished by its very narrow, linear leaves, which are less than 5 mm wide. In contrast, variety *laciniatum*, which is absent in Texas, Missouri, and Illinois, has broader, lanceolate leaves,

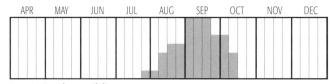

Eupatorium hyssopifolium

Eupatorium hyssopifolium

Eupatorium hyssopifolium

which measure 5 to 15 mm wide. In cultivation, no improved selections have yet been introduced.

In the wild, *Eupatorium hyssopifolium* flowers from August to October. At Longwood, the bloom start date varied by more than a month, between the last week of July and latest in the first week of September. On average, plants flowered for 7 weeks, into late September or early October.

Euphorbia
SPURGE

The name *Euphorbia*, used for these plants by ancient Romans, was derived from Euphorbus, a Greek physician to Iuba II, king of Mauritania in the first century A.D.

Euphorbia dulcis
SWEET SPURGE

This plant is native to Europe, from Portugal in the west, east to Russia, and north to Germany and Poland. *Euphorbia dulcis* grows in damp and shady places.

Euphorbia dulcis forms tight, mounded clumps of erect, often purple, pubescent, slender stems to 70 cm tall, growing from long, thick, fleshy rhizomes. The oblong, matte green, sometimes purple-tinged cauline leaves reach 7 cm in length. The inconspicuous female and male florets are fused to form flower-like cyathia subtended by yellowish triangular bracts and arranged in false, much-branched but compact umbels. Fruits are warty capsules to 4 mm long.

In the garden, *Euphorbia dulcis* is valued as an easily grown, reliable perennial that provides attractive, long-lasting chartreuse flowers backed by neat, often purplish, foliage. It fits splendidly in the front of perennial borders and can even be used as a ground cover in smaller areas. Plant *E. dulcis* in full sun, where the purple-leaved forms color better, or partial shade. In warmer climates, a somewhat

Euphorbia dulcis 'Chameleon'

Euphorbia dulcis 'Chameleon'

APR	MAY	JUN	JUL	AUG	SEP	OCT	NOV	DEC

Euphorbia dulcis 'Chameleon'

shaded situation may help the plants to cope with hot and humid summers. *Euphorbia dulcis* thrives in any average garden soil, preferably fertile and well drained. Under favorable conditions it may self-seed. Cut the plants back after flowering to promote a second flush of new leaves and to eliminate the possibility of seeds forming. Plants are hardy to zones 4 or 5.

There are no botanical varieties of *Euphorbia dulcis* recognized in the wild. In cultivation, a purple-leaved form found in France and named 'Chameleon' is grown most often.

Euphorbia dulcis is a spring bloomer. In St. Louis, it flowers from the second week of April until the end of May. At Longwood, the cultivar 'Chameleon' bloomed from the last week of April or the first week of May until the end of that month, but in one year, flowering was delayed until early June. The average bloom duration was a little more than 4 weeks.

Euphorbia palustris

SWAMP SPURGE

This perennial is native to Europe and western Asia, from Spain north to Finland and Norway and east to Russia and the Caucasus region. It grows in moist and wet soils, in swampy woodlands, along rivers and streams, even in shallow water. *Euphorbia palustris* has been cultivated since the 16th century.

Euphorbia palustris forms large, robust clumps of erect, thick, pale green and glaucous, well-branched stems to 1.5 m tall, growing from creeping rhizome. The bright green, glabrous, lanceolate or elliptic leaves have minutely serrate margins and reach 8 cm in length. The male and female flowers fuse to form dark yellow cyathia subtended by bright yellow-green, rounded bracts. The cyathia are arranged

Euphorbia palustris

Euphorbia palustris

in terminal, umbellate, rounded inflorescences to 30 cm wide. Occasionally, axillary flowering branches develop below the terminal inflorescence. Fruits are warty capsules to 6 mm long.

In the garden, *Euphorbia palustris* is admired for its lush, airy, willow-like foliage held on tall, strong stems that wave gracefully and are complemented by large yellowish flower heads in spring. The leaves may turn showy yellow-orange or purplish red color in the fall. Plant preferably in full sun, where the fall color will be the most vivid, although this species can tolerate partial shade. *Euphorbia palustris* performs best in moist places, such as bog gardens and edges of ponds or streams, but it can thrive in average, moderately moist soils as well. Plants are hardy to zone 7, possibly zone 5.

Although *Euphorbia palustris* shows a considerable variability in the natural populations, no botanical varieties are recognized. In cultivation, a couple of improved selections are available, including 'Walenburg's Glorie', with brighter yellow flower heads and growing to 1 m tall, and 'Zauberflöte', with lime yellow flower heads, reaching 1.2 m in height.

In the wild, *Euphorbia palustris* blooms in May and June. Cultivated in Poznań, it started to flower between 25 May and 6 June and finished between 1 and 6 July. Occasionally, a second flush of flowers may appear in late summer. Plants grown at Longwood began flowering in the last week of April or the first week of May. On average, they bloomed for 5 weeks, into late May or the first week of June, but no rebloom was observed.

APR	MAY	JUN	JUL	AUG	SEP	OCT	NOV	DEC

Euphorbia palustris

Eurybia

ASTER

The name *Eurybia* is derived from the Greek *eurys*, wide, and *baios*, few, in reference to the few, widespreading ray florets.

Eurybia divaricata

WHITE WOOD ASTER

This perennial is native to eastern North America, from Quebec and Ontario, south to Georgia and Alabama. *Eurybia divaricata* grows in open, dry

Eurybia divaricata

to mesic woodlands, forest edges, thickets, clearings, and shady roadsides up to 1700 m in elevation.

Eurybia divaricata forms loose clumps of sprawling, simple, thin, nearly black stems to 1 m tall, growing out of branched, elongated rhizomes. The long-petiolate, heart-shaped, to 13-cm-long leaves are coarsely toothed. The lower leaves wither by the time of flowering. The 2-cm-wide flower heads, comprised of five to 10 white ray florets and up to 25 yellow to red disc florets, are arranged in mostly terminal, flat-topped, loose corymbs. Fruits are brown achenes, to 4 mm long, topped with a pappus of reddish to cream bristles.

In the garden, *Eurybia divaricata* is valued primarily for underplanting in wooded areas or in shaded borders. Its profuse starry flowers showing in between other plants can not only brighten darker corners but also attract butterflies. Plant it, preferably in large groupings, in partial shade. *Eurybia divaricata* has a rare quality of being able to tolerate drier shade conditions caused by the competing roots of trees and shrubs. This species thrives in any average, moderately moist, and well-drained soil. Stems arch

Eurybia divaricata

under the weight of the flowers, but staking is futile, and it is best to allow it to cascade over sturdier plants. If this is not desired, cut stems back in late spring to 20 cm in order to improve branching and reduce the height, although this will delay flowering. Plants are hardy to zones 3 or 4.

Eurybia divaricata is a highly variable species from which numerous variants have been proposed in the past, but because they were weakly defined, they are no longer recognized. The natural variability of this species has not yet been exploited by gardeners. Only a few selections have been made, some with showier flowers, such as 'Eastern Star', others with variegated foliage, including 'Fiesta' and 'Snow Heron'.

In the wild, *Eurybia divaricata* flowers for several weeks in late summer to early fall. In cultivation in St. Louis, it blooms from the beginning of September until the end of October. At Longwood, the flowering began usually in mid to late August. Only once in 7 years, plants flowered in the last week of July. Their bloom continued, on average, for a little over 7 weeks, into mid to late September or rarely into mid-October.

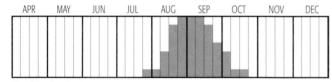

Eurybia divaricata

Eutrochium

JOE PYE WEED

The name *Eutrochium* is derived from the Greek *eu*, well, truly, and *trocho*, wheel-like, in reference to whorled leaves.

Eutrochium fistulosum

HOLLOW-STEMMED JOE PYE WEED, TRUMPETWEED

This plant is native to the eastern United States, from Maine south to Florida and west to Michigan and Texas. *Eutrochium fistulosum* grows usually in moist organic soils, in floodplains, meadows, bogs, marshes, wet thickets, woodlands, and along streams, at elevations of up to 1400 m. This and other *Eutrochium* species were previously classified as belonging to the genus *Eupatorium*.

Eutrochium fistulosum forms clumps of erect, hollow, purple, greenish or purple-spotted, strongly glaucous stems to 3.5 m tall. The lanceolate, finely serrate, leaves have four to seven whorls and reach 25 cm in length. The bright or dull pinkish purple flower heads, comprised of five to seven disc florets, are borne in dome-shaped, corymb-like compound arrays to 40 cm wide. Fruits are 4-mm-long achenes.

In the garden, thanks to its imposing height and stature, *Eutrochium fistulosum* commands attention but requires plenty of room to form substantial clumps. It fits splendidly in larger perennial borders, informal cottage-style gardens, and wildflower meadows. It rewards a gardener not only with the immense inflorescences, but also with a kaleidoscope of butterflies it attracts. Plant *E. fistulosum* in full sun to partial shade, preferably in moist, fertile, and humus-rich soil. It requires little care during the growing season. Allow it to form seed heads that will persist and provide interest well into winter. Plants are hardy to zone 3.

Eutrochium fistulosum 'Gateway'

Eutrochium fistulosum 'Big Umbrella'

Eutrochium fistulosum 'Gateway'

Eutrochium maculatum 'Purple Bush'

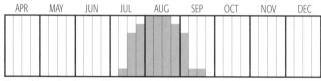

Eutrochium fistulosum 'Gateway'

Eutrochium maculatum 'Purple Bush'

There are no botanical varieties of *Eutrochium fistulosum* recognized among the natural populations. In cultivation, only a few garden selections have been introduced, although their affiliation with *E. fistulosum* is not always clear, and they often may be ascribed to related species *E. maculatum* or *E. purpureum*. These cultivars offer some choices with regard to flower color, from the white-flowered 'Album', to the lighter lavender purple 'Gateway', the rich lavender-pink 'Big Umbrella', and the darker purple 'Atropurpureum'.

In the wild, *Eutrochium fistulosum* blooms from July to October, depending on the region. Cultivated in St. Louis, it flowered from July to September. At Longwood, the cultivar 'Gateway' usually began flowering in late July. Only once in 7 years, it bloomed in the second week of July. On average, plants flowered for nearly 7 weeks to late August or early September. One year, they even continued blooming through the third week of September.

Eutrochium maculatum

SMOKEWEED, SPOTTED JOE PYE WEED

This perennial is native to North America, from Newfoundland west to British Columbia and south to North Carolina and New Mexico. *Eutrochium maculatum* grows in moist and often calcareous soils, in thickets, bogs, swamps, wet meadows, and banks of ponds and streams, at elevations of up to 2500 m.

Eutrochium maculatum forms clumps of usually erect, solid, purple-spotted or mottled, rarely uniformly purple stems to 2 m tall. The lanceolate or oval, unevenly and sharply serrate leaves are held in whorls of four or five and reach 25 cm in length. Flower heads are comprised of nine to 30 red-purple disk florets and are borne in flat-topped corymbiform arrays. Fruits are 4-mm-long achenes.

In the garden, *Eutrochium maculatum* is valued for its tall and bold stature, making a strong statement in a variety of settings from borders, wildflower meadows, woodland edges, to the margins of ponds and streams. The constant presence of butterflies flurrying around the flower heads animates what otherwise could appear as a rather somber-looking plant. Site *E. maculatum* in full sun, in moisture-retentive, fertile, humus-rich soil. Established plants can tolerate brief periods of drought and do not require special care. Trimming back or pinching in late spring will result in shorter and more branched plants, if such are desired, without delaying flowering. Allow spent flowers to remain on the plant and develop into conspicuous seed heads, which can persist through most of the winter. Regular dividing is not required, except when plants outgrow the space allocated for them. *Eutrochium maculatum* is hardy to zone 5, possibly zone 3.

Eutrochium maculatum has a wide geographic distribution and corresponding morphological variability. Three botanical varieties are described among the natural populations. The typical variety *maculatum* is native to the eastern part of the range, primarily east of the Mississippi River. Variety *bruneri*, found mostly in areas west of the Mississippi, differs in pubescent stems and leaves. Variety *foliosum*, restricted to the northeastern part of the range, east and north of Wisconsin, is distinct in its long leaves subtending the inflorescences. A handful of color variants have been selected for cultivation, including 'Glutball', with mauve-pink flowers, and the wine red 'Riesenschirm'. Furthermore, lower-growing forms such as 'Purple Bush' are available.

In the wild, *Eutrochium maculatum* blooms from July to September. Cultivated in Germany, it flowers during the same period. In Poznań, *E. maculatum* bloomed between 17 August and 25 September. In comparison, plants grown in St. Louis flowered from the last week of June until late August. At Longwood, the cultivar 'Purple Bush' usually began flowering in late July. Only twice in 7 years, it bloomed in the second week of July. It continued to flower until late August or, rarely, early September. Plants that were cut back in the third week of August rebloomed 6 weeks later, in the last week of September and, in one year, flowered until the end of October. On average, 'Purple Bush' was in flower for 7 weeks.

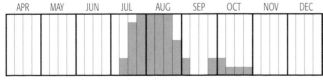

Eutrochium maculatum 'Purple Bush'

Eutrochium purpureum

HEMP-AGRIMONY, SWEET JOE PYE WEED

This plant is native to eastern North America, from Quebec and southern Maine, south to the mountains of northern Georgia, and west to Texas. *Eutrochium purpureum* grows in rich open deciduous woods, thickets and brushy clearings, meadows, and along streams, at elevations to 1200 m. It has been cultivated since the 17th century.

Eutrochium purpureum forms clumps of robust stems, which are greenish and dark purple at nodes or, rarely, entirely purplish. The stems, reaching 2 m in height, are usually solid, rarely hollow near bases. The coarsely serrated, lanceolate or elliptic, to 30 cm long leaves are held in whorls of three to five. The leaves emit a vanilla-like scent when crushed. Flower heads, comprised of five to nine pink to purple florets, are arranged in slightly domed loose, terminal, corymbose arrays to 45 cm wide. Fruits are 4-mm-long achenes.

In the garden, *Eutrochium purpureum* makes a striking display when properly sited with other taller perennials in a large, informal border or allowed to naturalize in a meadow, along a woodland edge, or near water. Its flowers, like those of other *Eutrochium*, attract scores of butterflies. Plant it in full sun or very light afternoon shade. Choose a spot with moist, fertile, and humus-rich soil. If lower plants are desired, trim or pinch them in late spring. Allow the spent flowers to mature into attractive seed heads, which can extend the season of interest through the winter. Plants are hardy to zones 3 or 4.

The natural populations of *Eutrochium purpureum* are morphologically variable. Several infraspecific taxa have been described, but currently only two botanical varieties are recognized. The typical variety *purpureum*, which has leaves usually glabrous beneath, is found throughout the geographic range of the species, whereas variety *holzingeri*, with densely hairy leaves, is found primarily west of the Mississippi River. Furthermore, *E. purpureum* is known to produce hybrids with other species, which may explain to some degree the confusion that exists with regard to the affiliation of many of the cultivated varieties. One should be prepared to find any of the cultivars mentioned under *E. fistulosum* and *E. maculatum* listed also as a selection of *E. purpureum*. In addition, the white-flowered 'Bartered Bride' and

Eutrochium purpureum 'Bartered Bride'

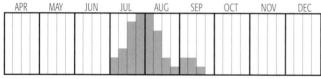

Eutrochium purpureum 'Bartered Bride'

'Joe White' and the lower-growing 'Little Red', are attributed to *E. purpureum*.

In the wild, *Eutrochium purpureum* blooms from July to September. Plants cultivated in Germany and Poland flower during the same period, but those grown in the United Kingdom bloom later, in September and October. In Moscow, *E. purpureum* started flowering, on average, around 8 August and finished around 16 September. A similar August-to-September bloom season was reported from Chicago. At Longwood, the cultivar 'Bartered Bride' began flowering between the first and last week of July. It continued blooming into early August or September. In one instance, plants that were cut back in early August rebloomed 3 weeks later. On average, 'Bartered Bride' was in flower for 6 weeks. Similarly, occasional rebloom of *E. purpureum* in September was observed in St. Louis.

Filipendula

MEADOWSWEET

The name *Filipendula* is derived from the Latin *filum*, thread, and *pendulus*, hanging, in reference to the plant's many small tubers fastened together by long threads.

Filipendula rubra

QUEEN–OF–THE–PRAIRIE

This plant is native to the central and eastern United States, from Maine west to Minnesota and south to North Carolina and Missouri. *Filipendula rubra* grows in lowland woods, thickets, moist meadows, and prairies. It has been cultivated since the 18th century.

Filipendula rubra forms massive clumps of upright stems to 2.5 m tall. The pinnately compound leaves have large stipules fused to the petiole, pairs of tiny leaflets interspersed with the larger ones, and a terminal leaflet, to 20 cm wide, deeply cleft into five to nine serrate lobes. The fragrant, pink to peach, 8-mm-wide flowers are arranged in broad paniculate, terminal cymes to 30 cm wide. Fruits are achenes to 8 mm long.

Filipendula rubra 'Venusta'

Filipendula rubra 'Venusta'

Filipendula rubra can create an impressive spectacle, especially when used in large groupings in bog or woodland gardens, wildflower meadows, along streams and ponds, or as a tall accent in the rear of traditional perennial borders. It is valued for the bold, jagged foliage and large plumes of pink flowers. Plant in full sun or, especially in warmer climates, partial shade. *Filipendula rubra* thrives in any fertile garden soil that is consistently moist or even wet. In dry situations, foliage may scorch and decline in the heat of the summer. Despite its height, *F. rubra* rarely needs staking. If the moisture supply is inadequate and foliage deteriorates after flowering, cut it back to encourage a new flush of growth later in the summer. Otherwise, allow the spent flowers to develop into attractive seed heads showing a pinkish cast. Under favorable conditions, *F. rubra* may self-seed freely. If this becomes a nuisance, deadhead spent flowers. Plants increase

over time to form large colonies, which are best left undisturbed for years. Plants are hardy to zone 3, possibly zone 2.

There are no botanical varieties of *Filipendula rubra* recognized among natural populations. In cultivation, a few color variants have been selected, offering choices of flowers from white 'Albicans' to dark pink 'Venusta' to dark carmine 'Magnifica', although the last one is often considered synonymous with 'Venusta'.

In the wild, *Filipendula rubra* flowers in June and July. Cultivated in Germany and Poland, it blooms during the same period, whereas plants in the United Kingdom may flower through August. Similarly, plants grown in Chicago bloomed in June and July, whereas those in St. Louis continued until August. At Longwood, the cultivar 'Venusta' usually began flowering in late June. It seldom started to flower as early as the second week of June or as late as the first week of July. On average, the bloom continued for 5 weeks into mid-July or, rarely, into the first week of August. On one occasion, plants that were cut back in mid-July rebloomed in mid-October.

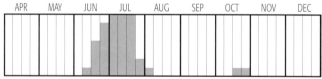

APR	MAY	JUN	JUL	AUG	SEP	OCT	NOV	DEC

Filipendula rubra 'Venusta'

Filipendula ulmaria

EUROPEAN MEADOWSWEET, QUEEN-OF-THE-MEADOW

This perennial is native to Europe and western and northern Asia, from Portugal in the west, north to Norway, south to Greece, and east to Siberia. *Filipendula ulmaria* has also naturalized in parts of northeastern North America. It grows in moist meadows or dry grasslands, steppes, and scrub.

Filipendula ulmaria forms upright clumps of erect, simple or branched, leafy stems to 1.8 m tall. The irregularly pinnate leaves have seven to 11 serrated leaflets, with the terminal leaflet larger than the lateral ones and palmately divided into three or five lobes. The leaflets are white-tomentose beneath and have strongly impressed venation. The basal leaves reach 60 cm in length, whereas the cauline ones become gradually reduced, with the uppermost being simple. The fragrant, 6-mm-wide, white or yellow-

Filipendula ulmaria

Filipendula ulmaria

ish white flowers are borne in dense, branched, terminal paniculate cymes to 25 cm long. Fruits are 3-mm-long twisted achenes.

In the garden, *Filipendula ulmaria* is highly desirable for naturalizing in wet meadows and along water edges, or as a taller accent in the back of more formal perennial borders. In cooler climates or in moist sites, plant *F. ulmaria* in full sun; otherwise, partial shade will be more beneficial, especially for selections with variegated foliage. It performs best in deep, moist, humus-rich soils. It thrives even in boggy sites but is intolerant of drought. Its tall stems do not require staking. In case of variegated selections, stems may be removed before flowering to enhance the appearance of the basal foliage. If the foliage declines by midsummer, cut it back to encourage a new flush of fresh growth. Deadheading may promote sporadic rebloom and prevent self-seeding. *Filipendula ulmaria* increases gradually and

does not need regular dividing. Plants are hardy to zone 3.

Three subspecies of *Filipendula ulmaria* are described throughout its range, reflecting the variability of the indumentum and serration of the leaves. Subspecies *ulmaria* has leaflets white-tomentose beneath with crenate-serrulate to shallowly biserrate margins. Subspecies *denudata* has green leaflets with sparse hairs. Both of these variants grow primarily in wet places. In contrast, subspecies *picbaueri*, which has white-tomentose leaflets that are deeply serrate or even lobed, is found growing in dry grasslands and scrub. In cultivation, a double-flowered selection known as 'Flore Pleno' is popular. In addition, 'Aurea', with golden yellow leaves, and 'Variegata', which has leaves marked with a yellow stripe in the middle, are frequently grown.

In the wild, *Filipendula ulmaria* blooms in late spring or summer, depending on the region.

Filipendula ulmaria 'Variegata'

Filipendula vulgaris 'Multiplex'

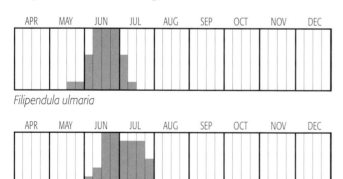

Filipendula ulmaria

Filipendula ulmaria 'Variegata'

Cultivated in Poznań, it started to flower between 21 June and 4 July and ended between 17 July and 1 August. Similarly, in Moscow, flowering began, on average, around 21 June and continued until 17 July. The cultivar 'Plena', however, bloomed in Moscow some 2 weeks later, starting around 5 July and ending around 1 August. Plants flowered in June in Chicago and St. Louis. At Longwood, flowering began usually in the first 2 weeks of June. Only once in 7 years, plants were in flower in the third week of May.

On average, flowering continued for a little more than 4 weeks into the last week of June or the first week of July. Similar bloom duration was reported from Moscow. In comparison, the cultivar 'Variegata' flowered at Longwood nearly 2 weeks later and often continued into the end of July, giving almost 6 weeks in bloom.

Filipendula vulgaris

DROPWORT

This perennial is native to Europe, northern Africa, and western and northern Asia, from Portugal in the west to western Siberia in the east. *Filipendula vulgaris* grows in dry grasslands. It has been cultivated since the 16th century.

Filipendula vulgaris forms a low mound of basal foliage topped by slender, unbranched, sparsely leafed flowering stems to 1 m tall, growing from a tuberous rootstock. The pinnately divided, shiny leaves are comprised of as many as 25 pairs of 2-cm-long, sessile, deeply serrate or incised lateral leaflets

Filipendula vulgaris 'Multiplex'

and a somewhat larger terminal one. The numerous basal leaves reach 45 cm in length, whereas the cauline leaves are few and smaller. The 15-mm-wide, creamy white, often tinged pink, flowers are held in loose, terminal umbellate panicles 15 cm wide. Fruits are 4-mm-long, straight erect achenes.

In the garden, *Filipendula vulgaris* can be used in locations that are too dry for other meadowsweets. It is valued for its rich green, soft, ferny foliage and delicate white flowers. Use it in large groups in the front in a perennial border, as an edging plant, or as a ground cover in more naturalistic settings, where it can be allowed to self-seed and spread freely. Plant it in full sun or partial shade, in any average garden soil that is well drained. Although *F. vulgaris* performs best under uniformly moist conditions, it can tolerate drier sites with infertile soils. It self-seeds freely, but rarely to the degree of becoming a problem. Plants are hardy to zones 3 or 4.

Despite the very large geographic distribution, no botanical varieties of *Filipendula vulgaris* are rec-

ognized among natural populations. In cultivation, the most commonly grown is the double-flowered 'Multiplex'. Less popular are 'Grandiflora' with larger flowers and 'Rosea' with light pink flowers.

In the wild, *Filipendula vulgaris* blooms in late spring to early summer. Cultivated in Poznań, it began flowering between 27 May and 15 June and finished between 26 June and 10 July. In Moscow, the bloom started somewhat later, around 19 June and continued until around 11 July. At Longwood, the double-flowered cultivar 'Multiplex' began flowering as early as the second week of May or as late as the first week of June. On average, plants bloomed for nearly 4 weeks, into mid or late June. In one year, plants that were cut back in the second week of June rebloomed in late July. A similar bloom duration was reported in Poznań and Moscow, but in Chicago, *F. vulgaris* flowered for only 2 or 3 weeks.

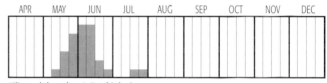

APR	MAY	JUN	JUL	AUG	SEP	OCT	NOV	DEC

Filipendula vulgaris 'Multiplex'

Gaillardia

BLANKET-FLOWER

The name *Gaillardia* commemorates Gaillard de Charentonneau, an 18th-century French magistrate, naturalist, and patron of botany.

Gaillardia ×grandiflora

FIRE-WHEELS, HYBRID BLANKET-FLOWER, INDIAN-BLANKET

This perennial is a hybrid between *Gaillardia pulchella*, an annual species from the southwestern United States, and *G. aristata*, a perennial species from the northwestern United States. *Gaillardia pulchella* was introduced in Europe in the late 18th century by M. le Comte d'Essales, chevalier de Saint-Louis, from what was then French Louisiana. *Gaillardia aristata* was introduced in the early 19th century by David Douglas, who collected it along the Columbia River. Both species grew in European gardens for years until they spontaneously hybridized in a garden near Liège, Belgium, around the middle of the 19th century.

Gaillardia ×*grandiflora* combines the richly colored flowers of *G. pulchella* with the perennial nature of *G. aristata*. It forms bushy clumps of erect or sprawling stems to 1 m tall. The gray-green and soft-textured leaves are oblong to pinnately cleft or deeply partite, coarsely serrated, and reach 25 cm in length. The solitary, 10-cm-wide flower heads are comprised of yellow to brown-red ray and disc florets, often bicolored with a darker center. The ray florets are three- to five-toothed, giving a fringed appearance to the flower head. Fruits are densely hairy achenes.

In the garden, *Gaillardia* ×*grandiflora* produces some of the most brightly colored and longest blooming flowers. Especially the bicolored forms may dominate visually over other more pastel-colored perennials. Therefore, combine it with plants that have equally strongly colored flowers, or give preference to single-color cultivars, which are easier to blend in borders. Be prepared to replant or reseed *G.* ×*grandiflora*, as it rarely lives more than 3 or 4 years, particularly when subject to wet winter conditions. Flowers bring butterflies into a garden and last long after cutting. Plant it in full sun, in moderately fertile, light, warm, and well-drained soil. Avoid sites with heavy, rich, and damp soils, where *G.* ×*grandiflora* tends to be short-lived. Deadheading is not necessary, although it improves the plant's overall appearance. Cut back untidy flowering stems just above the basal leaves in late summer. This encourages a flush of new growth, which improves plant's overwintering, as well as stimulates reblooming in the fall. Divide every 2 or 3 years, or allow plants to regenerate through self-seeding. *Gaillardia* ×*grandiflora* is hardy to zone 3, but in colder areas it benefits from a light cover during the winter.

Numerous cultivars of *Gaillardia* ×*grandiflora* offer a wide variety of color combinations: ray florets range from yellow of 'Chloe' to orange of 'Tokajer' and wine red of 'Burgunder', often with maroon to orange bases and yellow to dark burgundy disc florets. In addition, a number of double-flowered forms, such as 'Lollipop', and low-growing cultivars, including 20-cm-tall 'Baby Cole' and 'Büble', have been developed. Because many selections are seed grown, a certain variability among them is to be expected.

Gaillardia ×*grandiflora* inherited from *G. pulchella*, its annual parent, the ability to flower continuously over several months from late spring to fall, even without deadheading. *Gaillardia aristata*, the other parent species, also has a fairly long bloom season. In Poznań, it was in bloom for almost 8 weeks, whereas in Moscow it flowered for nearly 11 weeks. This species started flowering in Poznań between 12 and 26 June, whereas in Moscow it began around 20 June. A similar average bloom start date, 21 June, was reported in Alberta, Canada. June was also the month when the hybrid *G.* ×*grandiflora* began flowering in St. Louis and Chicago. At Longwood, *G.* ×*grandiflora* started to flower around mid or late May. Only once in 6 years, its flowering was delayed until the first week of June. It continued to flower throughout the remainder of the growing season until the first hard frost, sometimes into early December, giving, on average, more than 21 weeks in bloom. When cut back during the summer, it resumed flowering 1 to 5 weeks later.

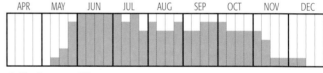

Gaillardia ×*grandiflora*

Galium
BEDSTRAW

The name *Galium* is derived from the Greek *galion*, which was the name used for a plant used to curdle milk in cheese making.

Galium odoratum
LADIES' BEDSTRAW, SWEET WOODRUFF

This plant is native to most of Europe, south to northern Africa, and east to Siberia. *Galium odoratum* grows in deciduous forests, usually in moist, fertile, and humus-rich soils. It was known previously as *Asperula odorata*.

Galium odoratum forms sprawling clumps of many weak, erect, square stems to 25 cm tall, growing from slender, creeping rhizomes. The entire plant is pleasantly aromatic. The 3-cm-long leaves are sessile, lanceolate, entire or finely serrate, and are held in whorls of six to nine. The 6-mm-wide white flowers are borne in loosely branched terminal cymes. Fruits are hairy schizocarps.

Galium odoratum

Galium odoratum

In the garden, *Galium odoratum* is valued primarily as an attractive ground cover for shady areas. Under optimal growing conditions, it spreads rapidly through both its rhizomes and self-seeding, so in more confined spaces it may need to be restrained. Use it to underplant trees or shrubs, edge a shaded border, fill crevices among rocks or in a dry stone wall, or allow it to roam freely through a woodland garden. Strongly aromatic dry leaves have found applications in fragrant sachets, potpourris, and moth deterrents, whereas fresh leaves are used to flavor drinks and desserts. Plant *G. odoratum* in partial to full shade. Avoid sunny locations, where plants tend to die down and become dormant by midsummer. Grow it where soil is rich in humus, preferably slightly acidic, and consistently moist. Plants are hardy to zones 4 or 5.

In the wild, *Galium odoratum* blooms from April to June. Cultivated in St. Louis, it flowered from late April or early May until the second or third week of May, and occasionally again in the second week

of June. In comparison, plants grown in Chicago bloomed during June and July. At Longwood, *G. odoratum* began flowering in late April or the first week of May. It continued blooming, on average, for a little more than 5 weeks (about 2 weeks longer than plants in St. Louis), until late May or, rarely, the first week of June.

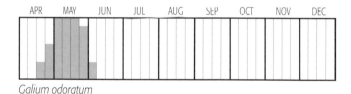

Galium odoratum

Gaura

BEEBLOSSOM

The name *Gaura* is derived from the Greek *gauros*, superb, in reference to the flowers.

Gaura lindheimeri

LINDHEIMER'S BEEBLOSSOM, WHIRLING BUTTERFLIES, WHITE GAURA

This perennial is native to North America, from Louisiana and Texas south to Mexico. It has become naturalized in parts of Australia. *Gaura lindheimeri* grows in open areas and black-soil prairies. This species has been cultivated since the middle of the 19th century.

Gaura lindheimeri forms open, bushy, vase-shaped clumps of erect or arching, slender stems to 1.5 m tall, growing from a deep taproot. The 7-cm-long,

Gaura lindheimeri

Gaura lindheimeri 'Dauphin'

Gaura lindheimeri 'Whirling Butterflies'

gray-green leaves are lanceolate to spathulate, sessile, and have somewhat wavy and serrate margins. The 2.5-cm-long flowers have four white, aging to pink, petals and are borne in open, loose panicles. The petals are held upward, giving the flowers the appearance of tiny butterflies. Although only a few, short-lived flowers are open at any one time, the panicles continue to produce new flowers over a long period. Fruits are four-angled capsules to 9 mm long.

Gaura lindheimeri finds a variety of uses, including formal borders, rock gardens, naturalistic meadows, or containers. It can be grown in small groups, or where space permits, in large bold drifts. It is valued for its distinct, willowy, graceful habit and long flowering period. Because *G. lindheimeri* might not have a great many flowers open at the same time, it benefits from being planted among other perennials that will enhance its unique qualities. Plant it in full sun to partial shade. *Gaura lindheimeri* is very durable and continues to flower despite the summer heat and humidity. Grow it in moderately fertile and moist soil that drains well. Supplemental watering is needed only during extended drought periods. *Gaura lindheimeri* does not require staking; rather, use the neighboring plants for support and allow the long stems to arch over or through them. Deadheading prolongs flowering, but is too tedious to be practical. Besides, spent flowers drop off neatly, leaving pink-tinted capsules behind. Plants seldom need division. *Gaura lindheimeri* produces

a long taproot, so it is best to leave it undisturbed for years after planting. This species may self-seed under favorable conditions, and young seedlings can be transplanted easily. Plants are hardy to zone 7, possibly zone 5.

There are no botanical varieties of *Gaura lindheimeri* recognized in the wild. Nevertheless, in cultivation, a wide array of selections is available. Hybrids between *G. lindheimeri* and *G. coccinea*, another North American species, are also being introduced. Some of them are low-growing plants, including 40-cm-tall 'Blaze', 'Crimson Butterflies', and 'Nugauwhite'. Others are variegated, like 'Corrie's Gold' and 'Passionate Rainbow', or with foliage tinged pink to burgundy, such as 'Bijou Butterflies' and 'Passionate Blush', whereas still others offer a choice of flower colors from white 'Dauphin' and 'Whirling Butterflies' to various shades of pink, like 'Siskiyou Pink' and 'Val's Pink'.

Although most *Gaura* species are night blooming, *G. lindheimeri* opens its flowers in the morning. Only a few flowers are open in each panicle at any given time, but new flowers are produced over a long period. In cooler climates, *G. lindheimeri* may bloom continuously through the summer, especially if plants are deadheaded. If flowering ceases in mid-summer, cut plants back to encourage a rebloom a few weeks later. Cultivated in St. Louis, the cultivar

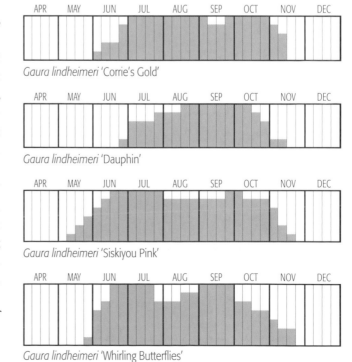

Gaura lindheimeri 'Corrie's Gold'

Gaura lindheimeri 'Dauphin'

Gaura lindheimeri 'Siskiyou Pink'

Gaura lindheimeri 'Whirling Butterflies'

'Siskiyou Pink' flowered from late May until October, whereas 'Whirling Butterflies' bloomed from May to September. At Longwood, four cultivars were grown, 'Corrie's Gold', 'Dauphin', 'Siskiyou Pink', and 'Whirling Butterflies'. Of those, 'Dauphin' was the latest to flower, beginning to bloom between the last week of June and mid-August. This cultivar also had the shortest flowering season of 16 weeks, on average. In contrast, the earliest to flower, 'Siskiyou Pink', had the longest flowering season. It bloomed on average for 22 weeks. 'Corrie's Gold' and 'Whirling Butterflies' were intermediate with regard to the bloom start date and bloom duration. With the exception of 'Corrie's Gold', the remaining three cultivars, in some years, halted their flowering in summer, but after being trimmed back rebloomed within 3 to 8 weeks. All cultivars usually flowered through October, sometimes into early November.

Geranium

CRANESBILL

The name *Geranium* is derived from the Greek *geranos*, crane, in reference to the long beak-like tips of the fruits.

Geranium asphodeloides

CRANESBILL

This perennial is native to southern Europe and southwestern Asia, from Italy east to the Caucasus and Iran. It grows in open woods, thickets, scrub, meadows, on stream banks, and on rocky slopes, at elevations up to 1800 m.

Geranium asphodeloides forms mounded clumps of basal foliage and erect stems to 75 cm tall, growing from short, stout rhizomes with fleshy, thick roots. The rounded, 4- to 12-cm-wide leaves are deeply divided into five or seven segments, these being further lobed and serrate. The 3-cm-wide flowers have entire or slightly emarginated narrow petals that are purple to white, often darker veined. The flowers are borne in diffuse inflorescences. Fruits are 2-cm-long mericarps with slender tips.

In the garden, *Geranium asphodeloides* makes an attractive ground cover that spreads and self-seeds easily, weaving through and around other plants. Use it in a position in the front of a perennial border, on top of a stone wall, or on low banks. Plant it preferably in full sun or partial shade. *Geranium asphodeloides*

thrives in any average garden soil that is well drained, and it can tolerate periodic drought without adverse effects. Cut it back after the first flush of flowers to tidy up the plants and to encourage new growth and possible rebloom. Plants are hardy to zone 6.

Geranium asphodeloides is a variable species. There are three subspecies recognized among natural populations. Subspecies *asphodeloides*, widespread in southern Europe, has narrow petals of white, pale pink, or deep pink. Subspecies *crenophilum*, found in Lebanon and Syria, has broader overlapping deep rosy pink petals with darker veins. Restricted to northern Turkey, subspecies *sintenisii*, has pale pink or deep purple flowers with wavy petals. Considering the diversity of *G. asphodeloides* in the wild, surprisingly few garden selections have been introduced so far, among them 'Prince Regent' with pale lilac flowers and 'Starlight' with pure white flowers.

In the wild, *Geranium asphodeloides* flowers in late spring and early summer. In cultivation, occasionally a late-summer rebloom is observed. At Longwood, the cultivar 'Starlight' began to flower between the second and fourth week of May and continued, on average, for nearly 3 weeks into early June. No rebloom, however, was noted during the 4 years in the garden.

Geranium asphodeloides 'Starlight'

Geranium endressii

ENDRESS' GERANIUM, PYRENEAN CRANESBILL

This plant is native to western Europe, mainly in southwestern France but also extending into Spain. It grows in wet places in the Pyrenees, but has naturalized elsewhere in Europe. *Geranium endressii* has been cultivated since the early 19th century.

Geranium endressii forms leafy mounds to 50 cm tall with mostly procumbent stems to 80 cm long, growing from elongated, creeping rhizomes. The somewhat glossy and wrinkled leaves are deeply cut into five segments, which are further lobed and serrate, and reach 12 cm in width. In milder climates, the leaves are evergreen. The 3-cm-wide, funnel-shaped flowers have light to deep pink, notched or entire petals. They are held in two-flowered cymules above the foliage. Fruits are 2-cm long mericarps.

In the garden, *Geranium endressii* is used as a ground cover or as large groupings in the front of a perennial border. It is valued for its neat, partially evergreen foliage, long flowering season, and the ability to spread vigorously. Plant it in either full sun or partial shade, but in warmer climates some shade is required. Choose a site with moist, humus-rich, and well-drained soil, although *G. endressii* can tolerate periods of drought given some shading, especially in colder climates. Avoid heavy clay and poorly drained soils, in which plants tend to be short-lived. If plants look unkempt after the first flush of bloom, cut them back and new foliage will return within 2 weeks, provided the soil is consistently moist. This may also encourage sporadic rebloom. *Geranium endressii* seldom needs dividing, except to control its spread. Plants are hardy to zone 4.

The are no botanical varieties of *Geranium endressii* recognized in the wild, and only one garden selection, 'Wargrave Pink' with deeper pink flowers, is widely cultivated. *Geranium endressii* has been hybridized, however, with *G. psilostemon*, *G. sessiliflorum*, *G. traversii*, and *G. versicolor*. The fertile hybrids with the last species, known as *G. ×oxonianum* (see that section), are commonly cultivated and have naturalized in parts of southwestern England and northwestern France.

In cooler climates, *Geranium endressii* blooms through most of the summer, but in warmer areas flowering may end by mid-June. Cultivated in Poland and the United Kingdom, it blooms from May or June until September. In contrast, the cultivar 'Wargrave Pink' grown in the warmer climate of St. Louis flowered only until June. At Longwood, 'Wargrave Pink' began bloom in mid or late May. In some years, it continued flowering through the summer

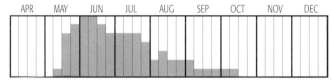

Geranium endressii 'Wargrave Pink'

Geranium endressii 'Wargrave Pink'

until September or October. In others, it ceased to flower in June or July and was cut back at that time. Only one year, a sporadic rebloom was observed 8 weeks after cutting plants back. On average, 'Wargrave Pink' was in flower for nearly 12 weeks.

Geranium macrorrhizum

BIGROOT GERANIUM

This perennial is native to the mountains of southern Europe, from the Apennines in the west, north to the south side of the Alps, through the Balkans, and east to the southeastern Carpathians. It has also naturalized in other parts of Europe. *Geranium mac-*

rorrhizum grows usually on calcareous soils, in shaded montane woodlands and scrub. It has been cultivated since the 16th century.

Geranium macrorrhizum forms dense, bushy, widespreading mounds of thick, erect or ascending stems to 45 cm tall, growing from fleshy, creeping rhizomes. The long-petiolate and rounded leaves are cut deeply into five or seven segments, each further irregularly lobed and incised, and reach 20 cm in width. They are covered with sticky, glandular hairs, responsible for the leaves being strongly aromatic. The older leaves turn red or yellow in the fall, whereas the youngest overwinter as evergreen

Geranium ×cantabrigiense 'Biokovo'

Geranium macrorrhizum 'Album'

Geranium ×cantabrigiense 'Karmina'

rosettes. The 2.5-cm-wide purple-pink to white flowers have dark red inflated calyces and are held in dense terminal inflorescences. Fruits are 3.5-cm-long, ribbed mericarps with slender tips.

In the garden, *Geranium macrorrhizum* is considered to be one of the easiest cranesbills to grow. It performs admirably as a ground cover. The plant spreads vigorously, and its dense scented foliage remains attractive during the summer and, in milder climates, even through the winter, when it colors with tints of yellows and reds. It tolerates competition from the roots of trees and shrubs. Slower-spreading varieties can also be used in perennial borders or on dry stone walls. In cooler climates, plant *G. macrorrhizum* in full sun or light shade. In areas with hot summers, partial shade is preferred. Grow it in any average garden soil that is well drained. *Geranium macrorrhizum* can thrive even in low-fertility soils that are subject to occasional drought. Although this species does not require cutting back after flowering, like many other cranesbills, deadheading spent flowers improves the plant's appearance. *Geranium macrorrhizum* rarely needs dividing. Plants may self-seed, but never to the point of becoming a nuisance. They are hardy to zones 3 or 4.

Within the wide distribution range, many geographic forms of *Geranium macrorrhizum* have been described, but none are recognized as taxonomically valid today. Plants in the wild show considerable variation in their height, evergreen character, pubescence, and petal color. A hybrid of *G. macrorrhizum* with *G. dalmaticum*, a closely related species from Montenegro and Albania, named *G.* ×*cantabrigiense*, has been found in Biokovo Mountains in Croatia and has also arisen in cultivation. Color variants of this hybrid include several cultivars, such as 'Biokovo' with white flowers tinged pink, 'Karmina' with deep carmine red flowers, and pure white 'St. Ola'. A number of selections of *G. macrorrhizum* have been introduced as well. They vary with respect to the color of the petals from white 'Album' and 'Spessart' to magenta-red 'Czakor' and 'Bevan's Variety'; the colors of the inflated calyx range from green to deep red. Their heights vary little, from 30 to 45 cm.

Geranium macrorrhizum flowers in late spring to early summer and occasionally reblooms later.

Geranium macrorrhizum 'Spessart'

Cultivated in Moscow, it started to flower, on average, around 9 June and ended around 3 July; but in Poland and the United Kingdom, it blooms earlier, in May and June. Similarly, in St. Louis the hybrid cultivars 'Biokovo' and 'Karmina' flowered in May and June. At Longwood, in addition to *G. macrorrhizum*, two of its selections, 'Album' and 'Spessart', as well as two hybrids, 'Biokovo' and 'Karmina', were observed. All of these plants began flowering between the first and last week of May. While the typical *G. macrorrhizum* bloomed on average for only 4 weeks, the hybrid 'Biokovo' and 'Karmina' flowered for 8 and 9 weeks, respectively. Whereas *G. macrorrhizum* finished flowering in early June and never rebloomed, its two selections 'Album' and 'Spessart' occasionally flowered again in July, August, or September. In comparison, 'Biokovo' and 'Karmina', which ended their first flush of bloom in late June, in most years rebloomed within 2 to 7 weeks.

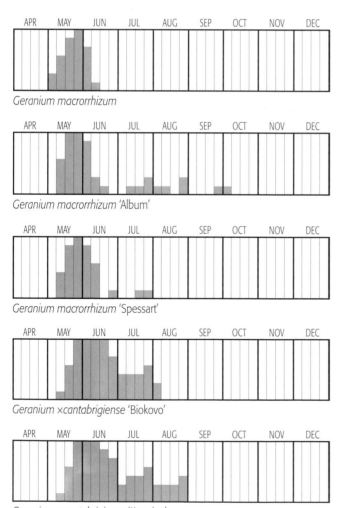

Geranium macrorrhizum

Geranium macrorrhizum 'Album'

Geranium macrorrhizum 'Spessart'

Geranium ×*cantabrigiense* 'Biokovo'

Geranium ×*cantabrigiense* 'Karmina'

Geranium maculatum

SPOTTED CRANESBILL, WILD CRANESBILL, WILD GERANIUM

This plant is native to eastern North America, from Quebec, west to Manitoba, and south to Georgia and Louisiana. *Geranium maculatum* grows in rich, moist soils, in old fields, meadows, thickets, open woods, and along forest edges. It has been cultivated since the 18th century.

Geranium maculatum forms loose mounds of foliage and slender erect stems to 60 cm tall, growing from a compact, stout, sometimes-woody rootstock. Leaves are deeply cut into five or seven widely spaced segments, each segment acutely lobed and serrated, and reach 20 cm in width. The 3-cm-wide, purple-pink to white, upward-facing flowers are held in erect, branched, terminal umbel-like inflorescences. Fruits are 3-cm-long mericarps with slender beaks.

Geranium maculatum

Geranium maculatum

Geranium maculatum 'Espresso'

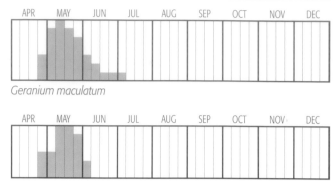

Geranium maculatum

Geranium maculatum 'Espresso'

Geranium maculatum 'Espresso'

Geranium maculatum is well suited for naturalizing in a woodland, wild garden, or along a stream, especially combined with spring bulbs and other perennials. It can also be included in more formal borders and planted as a ground cover. Grow it preferably in lightly shaded areas. In cooler climates, plants can also thrive in full sun, provided adequate moisture is available. Plant *G. maculatum* in moist, humus-rich, and well-drained soil. Deadheading is not necessary, as it will not stimulate a second bloom. If foliage declines as a result of summer drought, cut it back to encourage a new flush of growth. Under favorable conditions, *G. maculatum* self-seeds and spreads easily. Plants are hardy to zone 5, possibly zone 3.

There are no botanical varieties of *Geranium maculatum* recognized among the natural populations. In cultivation, a handful of cultivars have been selected, including the white-flowered 'Album', 'Beth Chatto' with pale lilac flowers, bronze- to purple-leaved 'Elizabeth Ann' and 'Espresso', as well as golden-leaved 'Heronswood Gold'.

In the wild, *Geranium maculatum* blooms from April to June, depending on the region. Cultivated in the United Kingdom, it flowers from May to July, whereas plants grown in St. Louis bloomed from late April until the end of May, rarely until mid-June or even July. Similarly, at Longwood *G. maculatum* began flowering in late April or early May and continued usually until late May and early June. Only once in 7 years, it rebloomed in late June and early July. On average, *G. maculatum* flowered at Longwood for close to 6 weeks. The cultivar 'Espresso' bloomed at Longwood at about the same time as the species, but its flowering time was 1 week shorter.

Geranium ×*magnificum*

SHOWY CRANESBILL, SHOWY GERANIUM

This plant is a hybrid between two species from southwestern Asia, *Geranium ibericum* and *G. platypetalum*. The exact time and place of its origin are not known, but the earliest records date back to 1871 and come from the Botanic Garden in Geneva, Switzerland.

Geranium ×*magnificum* forms vigorous, bushy mounds of soft foliage and upright stems to 70 cm tall, growing from a compact rootstock. The softly hairy leaves reach 20 cm in width and are cut into seven to 11 broad overlapping, lobed, and serrated divisions. The leaves turn yellow and red in the fall. The 4-cm-wide, saucer-shaped flowers have intensely blue-violet, dark-veined, often notched petals. The flowers are held mostly in umbels. Fruits do not fully develop.

In the garden, *Geranium* ×*magnificum* is admired for a splendid display of brilliantly colored and profuse flowers. Thanks to its hardy and vigorous nature, it performs reliably in a variety of situations, including formal borders, cottage-style, or even

Geranium ×magnificum

naturalistic gardens. Where space permits, it forms a dense ground cover that can be combined with a wide range of other perennials or shrubs. Plant *G. ×magnificum* in full sun or, in warmer areas, in partial shade. It grows best in moist, humus–rich, and well-drained soils, but can thrive in any average garden soil. If plants become too leggy or floppy after flowering, cut them back to encourage a new flush of foliage and possible rebloom. *Geranium ×magnificum* spreads gradually, making larger clumps, and can be left without dividing for years. Plants are hardy to zone 5, possibly zone 3.

Geranium ×magnificum is a sterile hybrid; nevertheless several clones are cultivated, some of which have been named. These include 'Hylander' with purple-violet flowers, 'Peter Yeo' with bluer tones, and 'Rosemoor' with lavender blue flowers.

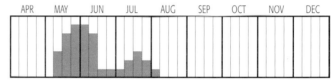

Geranium ×magnificum

Geranium ×magnificum

Geranium ×*magnificum* flowers profusely over a relatively short period in early summer. In the United Kingdom, it blooms in June and does not repeat flowering later in the season. At Longwood, its bloom start date varied by 3 weeks, from the second week of May to the first week of June. The first flush of bloom ended usually in early June, but in some years a rebloom was observed in July. On average, G. ×*magnificum* was in flower for 5 weeks.

Geranium ×*oxonianum*

DRUCE'S CRANESBILL, OXFORD GERANIUM

This perennial is a hybrid between *Geranium endressii* and *G. versicolor*, which arises spontaneously where the parent species grow together. It was not formally named until 1985, but has been cultivated long enough to escape from the gardens and naturalize in parts of France and the United Kingdom.

Geranium ×*oxonianum* forms vigorous, broad mounds of gray-green foliage and stems to 60 cm tall. The wrinkled, downy or hairy leaves are cut into five coarsely lobed segments and reach 20 cm

Geranium ×*oxonianum* 'Pearl Boland'

Geranium ×*oxonianum* 'Pearl Boland'

in width. The notches between segments are sometimes tinged reddish or brown. The funnel-shaped, 3.5-cm-wide flowers have slightly notched pink petals with darker veins. Fruits are mericarps.

Geranium ×*oxonianum* is valued as a dense, easy-to-grow ground cover. It performs admirably when allowed to spread freely in naturalistic, wild gardens. Plant it preferably in dappled, light shade. *Geranium* ×*oxonianum* tolerates full sun exposure, but colors of the flowers of some cultivars may fade under such conditions. Grow it in any well-drained garden soil with adequate moisture. Cut the plants back after the first flush of flowers to encourage new growth. *Geranium* ×*oxonianum* may self-seed under favorable conditions. Plants are hardy to zone 4.

Geranium ×*oxonianum* is a fertile hybrid, which has led to numerous selections. Named cultivars offer larger flowers with longer blooming; these vary in color from white 'Ankum's White' and pink 'A. T. Johnson' to purple 'Lady Moore', often with prominent darker veining, like 'Hollywood' and 'Pearl Boland'. Some, such as 'Walter's Gift', stand out because of the distinct foliage showing bronze blotching or undertones. In addition, *G.* ×*oxonianum* has been further crossed with other species, including *G. psilostemon*.

Geranium ×*oxonianum* blooms heavily in early summer and then reblooms sporadically later. Flowering begins in June in Cambridge, the United Kingdom. At Longwood, the cultivar 'Pearl Boland' started to bloom usually in mid or late May. Flowering then continued, with short breaks, through the end of July, rarely into early August. The May and June bloom was heavy, whereas in July and August flowers were produced sparingly. On average, plants were in bloom for 10 weeks.

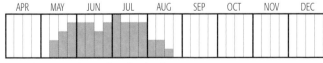

APR	MAY	JUN	JUL	AUG	SEP	OCT	NOV	DEC

Geranium ×*oxonianum* 'Pearl Boland'

Geranium phaeum
DUSKY CRANESBILL, MOURNING WIDOW

This perennial is native to the mountains of Europe, from the Pyrenees in the west, through the Alps, to the Balkans and the Carpathians in the east. *Geranium phaeum* grows in damp meadows, woodland margins, and on shady roadsides. It has also naturalized further north in Europe.

Geranium phaeum forms clumps of erect, branched stems to 60 cm tall, growing from thick, stout rhizomes. The soft, bright green leaves are deeply cut into seven or nine shallowly lobed and serrate segments and reach 20 cm in width. They are often blotched purple or brown in the notches between the segments. The nodding, 2.5-cm-wide flowers have dark purple, almost black, reflexed petals with pale or white bases. The flowers are held in terminal and lateral one-sided racemes. Fruits are mericarps.

In the garden, *Geranium phaeum* is valued primarily for its unusually dark, nearly black flowers. It is best positioned to contrast against a lighter colored background. It is a reliable easy-to-grow ground cover, which retains its basal foliage throughout most of the year. It fits best in informal cottage-style

Geranium phaeum 'Lily Lovell'

Geranium phaeum 'Lily Lovell'

or woodland gardens. Plant it in full or partial shade, in moist, humus-rich, reasonably fertile, and well-drained soil. In cooler climates, given some shade, *G. phaeum* can tolerate periodic drought. If foliage declines in hot summers following flowering, cut it back to encourage a new flush of growth. When fruits are permitted to develop, moderate self-seeding may take place. Plants are hardy to zones 4 or 5.

Geranium phaeum is a variable species, and numerous regional variants have been described in the past. None of them, however, are recognized currently as valid botanical varieties. Nevertheless, this considerable variability has permitted the selection of a large number of cultivars. Their flower color varies from the typical dark purple of 'Chocolate Chip' and deep mauve of 'Lily Lovell' to pale lilac of 'Joan Baker', dusky pink of 'Rose Madder', and white of 'Album'. The white center is sometimes surrounded by a purplish ring or zone, as in 'Blauw-voet'. Several cultivars, including 'Calligrapher' and 'Samobor', have leaves blotched bronze or purple,

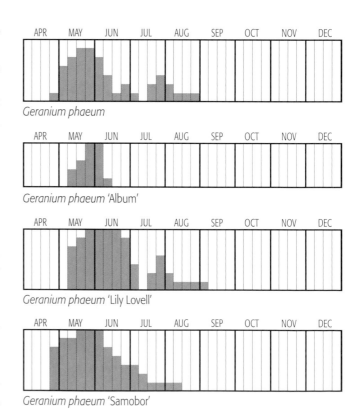

Geranium phaeum

Geranium phaeum 'Album'

Geranium phaeum 'Lily Lovell'

Geranium phaeum 'Samobor'

Geranium phaeum 'Samobor'

whereas others, such as 'Golden Spring' and 'Mrs. Withey Price', have leaves that emerge yellow-green in spring and later fade to green.

Geranium phaeum blooms from late spring to early summer, with possible sporadic rebloom later. When cultivated in the United Kingdom, its main flowering period occurs in May and June. Similarly, plants grown in Poznań bloomed between 18 May and 10 June. In St. Louis, *G. phaeum* flowered from mid or late May until mid or late July. At Longwood, in addition to *G. phaeum*, three of its cultivars were observed: 'Album', 'Lily Lovell', and 'Samobor'. Of these, 'Samobor' bloomed the earliest, beginning in most years in the last week of April. In contrast, 'Album' and 'Lily Lovell' were never in flower before the second week of May. 'Samobor' was also the longest flowering, with nearly 10 weeks in bloom, compared to only 4 weeks of 'Album'. The latter cultivar never rebloomed, whereas the typical *G. phaeum* and 'Lily Lovell' often flowered again in July and August. Although 'Samobor' rebloomed

only once during 7 years, its early bloom start and continuous flowering through June resulted in its long bloom duration.

Geranium pratense
MEADOW CRANESBILL

This plant is native to Europe and western and central Asia, from Spain in the west, east to the Altai Mountains in Russia, and south into the Himalayas. *Geranium pratense* often grows on calcareous soils, in meadows, and along roadsides. It has naturalized in parts of northeastern North America.

Geranium pratense forms dense upright clumps of erect branched stems to 1 m tall, growing from a compact rootstock made up of the permanent stem and attached fleshy roots. Leaves are deeply cut into seven or nine lobed and serrated segments and reach 20 cm in width. The 4-cm-wide, saucer-shaped flowers have violet blue (rarely white or pink) flowers with paler reddish veins and are borne in crowded terminal inflorescences. Fruits are 3-cm-long mericarps with slender beak-like tips.

In the garden, *Geranium pratense* stands out as one of the tallest and most vigorous cranesbills. It is well suited for informal gardens and for naturalizing in meadows or open woodlands. Plant it preferably in full sun, although it will tolerate light partial shade. *Geranium pratense* thrives in any average garden soil that is consistently moist. In hotter climates, foliage tends to decline after flowering. If this happens, cut the foliage back to encourage a new flush of growth and possible rebloom. The tall flowering stems may need staking, especially on richer soils and in partially shaded areas. Single-flowered varieties may self-seed prolifically. If this is objectionable, deadhead spent flowers or choose double-flowered cultivars instead. Plants are hardy to zones 4 or 5.

Geranium pratense shows considerable variability over its expansive geographic range. One variety found in the Himalayas and differing in purple-pink flowers has been named *stewartianum*. White-flowered variants are known as form *album*. In cultivation, many additional color variants have been selected. Their flower colors range from white 'Galactic' and mauve-pink 'Bittersweet' to deep purple-blue 'Plenum Violaceum'. Several selections, such as 'Nodbeauty', feature purple-tinted foliage. Furthermore, *G. pratense* has been hybridized with other species to

Geranium pratense

Geranium 'Johnson's Blue'

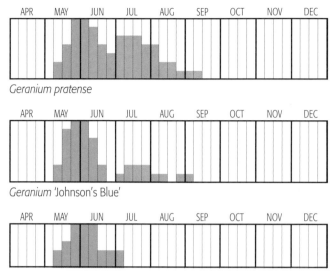

Geranium pratense

Geranium 'Johnson's Blue'

Geranium 'Spinners'

Geranium 'Spinners'

produce such cultivars as lavender 'Johnson's Blue', a cross with *G. himalayense*, or purplish blue 'Spinners', a cross with *G. clarkei*.

In the wild, *Geranium pratense* blooms in late spring or early summer. Cultivated in the United Kingdom, it flowers in July and sometimes again in August. In contrast, plants grown in Poznań bloomed earlier, between 9 and 28 June, and did not rebloom. At Longwood, *G. pratense* started to flower between the second and the last week of May. It bloomed usually until mid-June, and then, after a short break, rebloomed from early July until early August, or rarely in early September. Cutting plants back after the first flush of flowers did not have an effect on the later rebloom. Only once in 7 years, *G. pratense* bloomed continuously between late May and early August. On average, it was in flower for nearly 10 weeks. In comparison, two hybrids of *G. pratense* observed at Longwood, 'Johnson's Blue' and 'Spinners', bloomed for 7 and 5 weeks, respectively.

This shortened bloom season reflected the fact that 'Johnson's Blue' rarely rebloomed, and 'Spinners' did not rebloom at all.

Geranium psilostemon

ARMENIAN CRANESBILL, ARMENIAN GERANIUM

This perennial is native to southwestern Asia, from northeastern Turkey east to Armenia and Azerbaijan, and north to Dagestan in Russia. *Geranium psilostemon* grows in spruce forests, woodland margins, scrub, and meadows, at elevations between 1400 and 2400 m. It has been cultivated since the late 19th century.

Geranium psilostemon forms broad, upright clumps of erect stems to 1.2 m tall, growing from a compact rootstock. Leaves are deeply cut into five or seven lobed and serrate segments and reach 20 cm in width. The 4-cm-wide bright magenta-crimson flowers have conspicuous black centers and black venation. They are borne in erect, diffuse inflorescences. Fruits are 3–cm-long mericarps.

In the garden, *Geranium psilostemon* performs admirably in both formal perennial borders or when allowed to spread through a woodland or in other naturalistic settings. It is valued for its striking, brightly colored, black-eyed flowers and elegant, lush foliage that acquires attractive red and yellow tints in the fall. Although individual flowers are short-lived, they are produced in great abundance over a long period. Their bright colors offer many opportunities when it comes to creating plant combinations. Position *G. psilostemon* in full sun or dappled partial shade. It grows best in deep, nutrient-rich soil, yet

Geranium psilostemon

Geranium 'Anne Thomson'

Geranium 'Anne Thomson'

any average garden soil will suffice. Being one of the tallest cranesbills, *G. psilostemon* may require support for its flowering stems, but if it is grown among other sturdier plants, it may lean on them instead. Plants are hardy to zone 5.

There are no botanical varieties of *Geranium psilostemon* recognized in the wild. In cultivation, only a handful of selections of *G. psilostemon* are known.

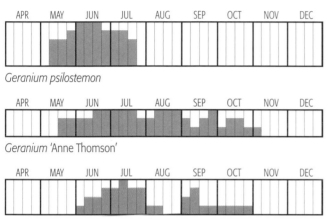

APR	MAY	JUN	JUL	AUG	SEP	OCT	NOV	DEC

Geranium psilostemon

APR	MAY	JUN	JUL	AUG	SEP	OCT	NOV	DEC

Geranium 'Anne Thomson'

APR	MAY	JUN	JUL	AUG	SEP	OCT	NOV	DEC

Geranium 'Ann Folkard'

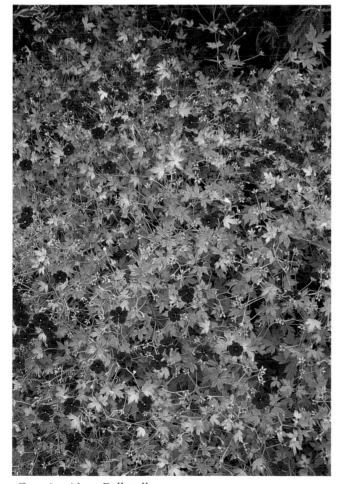

Geranium 'Ann Folkard'

Its hybridization with other species, however, has led to the development of some of the more popular cultivars, including magenta-flowered 'Ann Folkard' and 'Anne Thomson', both crosses with *G. procurrens*, as well as soft purple-magenta 'Eva', a cross with *G. pratense*, and bright magenta 'Brempat', a cross with *G. endressii*.

Geranium psilostemon blooms from late spring to early summer. Cultivated in the United Kingdom, it flowers in June until August. In St. Louis, it bloomed earlier, from mid-May until the end of July. At Longwood, flowering also began in mid to late May. It then continued on average for 8 weeks into mid-July. Cutting plants back after flowering was finished did not result in a rebloom later in the season. In contrast, two hybrids of *G. psilostemon* observed at Longwood, 'Ann Folkard' and 'Anne Thomson', repeated bloom regularly even without being cut back. 'Anne Thomson' began flowering usually in mid-May and continued until late July or August. After a break of 2 to 4 weeks, it then resumed blooming until late October or even early November, giving it on average a very impressive 19 weeks in bloom. In comparison, 'Ann Folkard' did not fare as well. It started to flower later and its rebloom was not as long, which resulted in the average bloom duration of only 9 weeks.

Geranium renardii

RENARD'S GERANIUM

This plant is native to the Caucasus Mountains, where it grows often on rock cliffs. *Geranium renardii* has been cultivated since the early 20th century.

Geranium renardii forms dense clumps of slender, branched stems to 30 cm, growing from a thick woody rootstock trailing along the ground. The long-petiolate, reniform leaves are shallowly cut into five or seven barely lobed segments, deeply veined, wrinkled, and velvety gray-green. They reach 12 cm in width. The 3- to 4-cm-wide, starry flowers have white, purple-veined petals. They are borne in dense, erect, terminal, umbel-like clusters. Fruits are 3-cm-long mericarps with slender beak-like tips.

In the garden, *Geranium renardii* is valued primarily for its unique sage green, soft foliage, creating low-growing mounds that remain attractive throughout the entire season. It is used in the front of perennial borders, for softening hard corners or edges of patios

Geranium renardii

or stone walls, or for naturalizing along woodland edges. Plant it preferably in full sun, although some shade is tolerated. *Geranium renardii* grows best in rather dry, low-fertility, and well-drained soil, which enhances foliage qualities, improves flowering, and keeps the plant's habit compact. It increases slowly and rarely requires dividing. Under favorable conditions, self-seeding may occur. Plants are hardy to zones 5 or 6.

A number of color variants of *Geranium renardii* have been selected in cultivation. They feature flowers that, in addition to the typical white, have pale lilac or lavender petals, usually with heavier purple venation. Examples include the light violet 'Tcschelda', opal white 'Walter Ingwersen', bluish purple 'Whiteknights', and pale lilac 'Zetterlund'. *Geranium renardii* has also been crossed with other species, such as *G. platypetalum*, which led to the development of additional cultivars.

Geranium renardii blooms in late spring. Cultivated in Poland and the United Kingdom, it flowers in June. Plants grown at Longwood began flowering in the second or third week of May and continued, on average, for 7 weeks into the end of June. Cutting plants back at that time did not result in additional bloom later in the season.

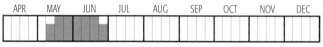

APR	MAY	JUN	JUL	AUG	SEP	OCT	NOV	DEC

Geranium renardii

Geranium sanguineum

BLOODRED GERANIUM, BLOODY CRANESBILL

This plant is native to Europe and western Asia, from Portugal east to northern Turkey and the Caucasus Mountains. *Geranium sanguineum* grows often in calcareous soils, in dry woodlands, scrub, and on open, rocky slopes.

Geranium sanguineum forms mounded bushy clumps of slender, stiff, procumbent to erect, branched stems to 30 cm tall, growing from thick fleshy rhizomes. Leaves are deeply cut into five or seven narrow, lobed, and serrate segments and reach 10 cm in width. The 3.5-cm-wide, saucer-shaped flowers have rich magenta (rarely pink or white) petals, mostly with darker veins. They are held in leafy, diffuse inflorescences of single-flowered cymules. Fruits are 3-cm-long mericarps.

In the garden, *Geranium sanguineum* is valued for its handsome, deep green, deeply divided foliage that turns crimson red in the fall, as well as for its prolific brightly colored flowers. It is well suited for the

Geranium sanguineum 'John Elsley'

front of the perennial border or along the margins of shrubbery or woodland. *Geranium sanguineum* makes a tough, adaptable, and long-lived ground cover. Plant it in full sun or light partial shade. Avoid shaded areas, where plants are less compact and not as floriferous. This species thrives in any well-drained soil, even the drier ones. Cut it back after flowering to encourage a flush of fresh foliage and a possible rebloom. Otherwise, allow plants to develop mature seeds if self-seeding is desired. *Geranium sanguineum* increases gradually and does not require regular dividing. Plants are hardy to zones 3 or 4.

Geranium sanguineum is a diverse species showing variation with respect to the flower size and color, leaf forms and pubescence, and growth habit. One variety, *striatum*, found along the northwestern coast of England, differs in light pink flowers and very compact growth habit. Many garden selections offer choices of colors ranging from white 'Album', pink 'Aviemore', and rose red 'Alpenglow' to magenta

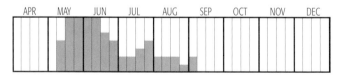

Geranium sanguineum 'Album'

'John Elsley' and 'New Hampshire Purple', some featuring larger flowers as well.

In the wild, *Geranium sanguineum* blooms from May to September, depending on the region. Cultivated in Moscow, it started to flower on average around 13 June and ended around 16 July. In comparison, plants grown in Poznań began blooming between 23 May and 2 June and finished between 30 June and 14 July. An even earlier bloom start date is reported in St. Louis, where flowering began between the end of April and mid-May. At Longwood, the cultivar 'Album' started to flower in the second or third week of May and continued usually through late June or early July. In 3 of 7 years, 'Album' rebloomed, without being cut back, from late July, sometimes into the first week of September. On average, it was in flower for nearly 9 weeks. In comparison, *G. sanguineum* in Moscow bloomed for 5 weeks.

Geranium sylvaticum
WOOD CRANESBILL

This perennial is native to Europe and northern Asia, from Portugal in the west to Siberia in the east. *Geranium sylvaticum* grows in meadows, open woodlands, forest edges, thickets, on stream banks, and along roadsides.

Geranium sylvaticum forms upright clumps of basal foliage and erect, somewhat angular stems to 80 cm tall, growing from short rootstock made up of permanent stems and fleshy roots. The round leaves are deeply cut into seven or nine lobed and serrate segments and reach 20 cm in width. The 3-cm-wide, saucer-shaped flowers are purplish violet with white centers, rarely pink or entirely white. They are borne in dense, cyme-like inflorescences. Fruits are 2-cm-long mericarps.

In the garden, *Geranium sylvaticum* is well suited for planting in the perennial borders, where it is valued for its early flowering, which fills the gap between the display of the early-spring bulbs and the riot of perennial flowers in late spring. It performs admirably also when allowed to naturalize in open woodlands. *Geranium sylvaticum* can tolerate some competition from tree roots as long as the site is not too dry. Preferably, plant it in partial shade, although full shade is acceptable. This species thrives in any average garden soil, provided it is consistently moist. Plants are hardy to zones 4 or 5.

Geranium sylvaticum is a variable species with several subspecies recognized in different parts of its geographic range. The typical subspecies *sylvaticum*, found throughout the distribution range, usually has reddish purple flowers. Subspecies *rivulare*, from the Alps, has white flowers with red veins. Subspecies *caeruleatum*, with violet blue flowers, grows in the Carpathians and the Balkans. Subspecies *pseudosibiricum*, native to the Ural Mountains in Russia, has pale blue flowers. The naturally occurring white-flowered forms are referred to by the name *albiflorum*. In cultivation, the considerable color variation of *G. sylvaticum* has led to the selection of several cultivars ranging from white 'Album' to pink 'Angulatum' and 'Baker's Pink', lavender 'Birch Lilac', blue 'Amy Doncaster', and violet blue 'Mayflower'.

Geranium sylvaticum is among the earliest flowering cranesbills. In the wild, it blooms for several weeks from April to June, depending on the region. At Longwood, the cultivar 'Album' began flowering usually in the second week of May, although one year it was in flower in the first week of May. The first flush of bloom lasted until late May or early June. It then resumed flowering intermittently between mid-July and the end of November. Throughout the season, the cultivar 'Album' was in flower for a little over 8 weeks, on average.

Geranium wlassovianum
WLASSOV'S CRANESBILL

This plant is native to central and eastern Asia, from Siberia east to Russia's Far East and south to Mongolia and northern China. *Geranium wlassovianum* grows often in wet meadows, marshes, scrub, and on banks of rivers and streams.

Geranium wlassovianum forms dense, bushy clumps of procumbent, velvety stems to 40 cm long, growing from a stout, compact rootstock. The soft, velvety leaves are shallowly cut into five- or seven-lobed and serrate segments and reach 15 cm in width. They emerge tinted or blotched reddish in spring, later fade to dark green, but change color again to yellow and red in the fall. The 4-cm-wide flowers have pale pink to dark violet, heavily veined petals with white bases. They are held in diffuse inflorescences. Fruits are 2.5-cm-long mericarps.

In the garden, *Geranium wlassovianum* performs admirably in both traditional perennial borders and when allowed to spread among other plants in an open woodland or similar naturalistic settings. In either situation, it is valued for prolonged flowering and bright fall colors. Plant it in partial shade or, in cooler climates, in full sun. *Geranium wlassovianum* thrives in any average garden soil that stays moist, although it can tolerate periodic drought. Cut it

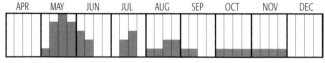

Geranium sylvaticum 'Album'

Geranium wlassovianum

Geranium wlassovianum

back after the first flush of flowers to encourage additional bloom later. It can self-seed under favorable conditions. Plants are hardy to zones 3 or 4.

There are no botanical varieties of *Geranium wlassovianum* recognized among wild populations. In cultivation, it shows variability with respect to the flower color, which can range from pale pink to purple. One lavender blue variant has been selected and named 'Blue Star'.

Geranium wlassovianum flowers for months starting in late spring. In the United Kingdom, peak bloom occurs in July and August. In St. Louis, flowering began between the last week of May or the first week of June and ended between late August and mid-October. Plants grown at Longwood started to bloom usually in late June. The earliest flowering was recorded in the second week of June. They continued to bloom through September, sometimes even into the first week of October. In some years, plants briefly ceased to flower during July or August for a period of 1 to 2 weeks. On average, *G. wlassovianum* was in bloom for 14 weeks.

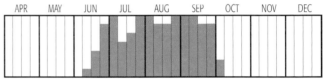

Geranium wlassovianum

Geum

AVENS

The name *Geum* was used by ancient Romans for one of the species of avens.

Geum Hybrids

HYBRID AVENS

Geum species in cultivation intercross easily. This has given rise to a number of interspecific hybrids. *Geum* ×*heldreichii* is a cross between two European species, *G. montanum* and *G. coccineum*. Crossing of the latter species with the Chilean *G. chiloense* resulted in a large number of popular cultivars grouped under the name *G.* ×*hybridum*. *Geum montanum*, in turn, hybridized with *G. reptans* from the Alps produced *G.* ×*rhaeticum*, whereas crosses of *G. montanum* with *G. rivale* from Europe, Asia, and North America have been named *G.* ×*tirolense*. Additional crosses are

Geum coccineum

Geum 'Georgenberg'

Geum coccineum

Geum 'Mrs. Bradshaw'

known involving European species *G. bulgaricum*, *G. coccineum*, *G. reptans*, and *G. urbanum*.

Geum hybrids form clumps of basal foliage held in rosettes and leafy stems to 60 cm tall, growing from a thick rootstock. The basal leaves are usually unequally pinnately divided, with the terminal leaflet much larger than the lateral ones, and reach 30 cm in length. The cauline leaves are reduced in size, unevenly lobed, sometimes bract-like. The 3.5-cm-wide, scarlet red, orange, or yellow flowers may be single or variously double. They are either held singly or in few-flowered racemes. Fruits are clusters of achenes with long persistent styles.

In the garden, *Geum* hybrids create some of the most brightly colored displays. Large groupings incorporated into perennial borders or in the foreground of shrubbery are especially effective. Avoid planting them among vigorous neighbors, as *Geum* does poorly under competitive and crowded conditions. Site *Geum* in full sun or, in warmer climates, in partial shade. Plants thrive in average garden soils that drain well but remain consistently moist. Stay away from locations that remain damp during the fall and winter months. *Geum* hybrids are usually short-lived and require frequent replanting, every 3 years or so, to prolong longevity. Plants are hardy to zones 4 or 5.

Many hybrid cultivars have been selected and introduced into cultivation. Because plants are often produced from seed, a certain degree of variability among plants grown under the same name is to be expected. Unfortunately, the ease of intercrossing among various *Geum*, which led to the development of so many cultivars, is also the cause of considerable mix-up of plants in the trade. Cultivated selections feature single or variously double flowers in colors ranging from the yellow 'Lady Stratheden' to the orange 'Georgenberg' and 'Starker's Magnificum' and the red 'Blazing Sunset', 'Mrs. Bradshaw', and 'Rubin'.

Because *Geum* hybrids and their parent species are a diverse group, they vary with regard to their flowering season. *Geum coccineum* cultivated in Poznań began flowering between 20 April and 18 May. *Geum chiloense* grown in Moscow bloomed starting around 30 May; but its two hybrids 'Mrs.

Geum 'Georgenberg'

Geum 'Starker's Magnificum'

APR	MAY	JUN	JUL	AUG	SEP	OCT	NOV	DEC

Geum 'Georgenberg'

APR	MAY	JUN	JUL	AUG	SEP	OCT	NOV	DEC

Geum 'Lady Stratheden'

APR	MAY	JUN	JUL	AUG	SEP	OCT	NOV	DEC

Geum 'Mrs. Bradshaw'

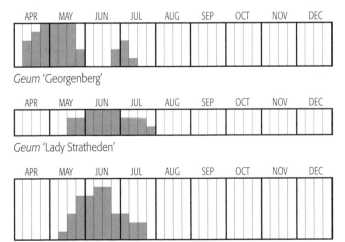

Bradshaw' and 'Lady Stratheden' began later, around 14 June and 18 June, respectively. At Longwood, these two cultivars started flowering usually in mid or late May. As in Moscow, 'Mrs. Bradshaw' flowered at Longwood a little earlier than 'Lady Stratheden', but its average bloom season of 6 weeks was more than 1 week shorter than that of 'Lady Stratheden'. In comparison, 'Mrs. Bradshaw' in Moscow flowered for about 4 weeks. Cutting plants back after flowering did not result in additional rebloom. Another *Geum* hybrid observed at Longwood was 'Georgenberg'. Its bloom start date was more than a month earlier than 'Mrs. Bradshaw' and 'Lady Stratheden'. Unlike these two cultivars, 'Georgenberg' rebloomed at the end of June in some years. On average, 'Georgenberg' was in flower for 7 weeks.

Gillenia

INDIAN–PHYSIC

The name *Gillenia* commemorates Arnold Gillen (or Gille), a 17th-century German physician and botanist.

Gillenia trifoliata

BOWMAN'S ROOT, INDIAN–HIPPO, INDIAN–PHYSIC, THREE–LEAVED GILLENIA, WESTERN DROPWORT

This perennial is native to eastern North America, from Ontario, east to New York, and south to Georgia and Alabama. *Gillenia trifoliata* grows in open woodlands, clearings, thickets, on rocky slopes, and along roadsides, at elevations to 1500 m. It has been cultivated since the early 18th century.

Gillenia trifoliata forms upright, bushy clumps of erect, slender, branched, glabrous or somewhat pubescent stems to 1.2 m tall, growing from a thick and deep rootstock. The sessile, trifoliate to three-parted leaves have lanceolate to ovate, sharply and irregularly serrate leaflets to 10 cm long. The starry, white or pink-blushed, 2.5-cm-wide flowers have five very narrow, slightly contorted petals, surrounded by a persistent reddish calyx. They are held on long pedicels in loose panicles. Fruits are subulate-tipped follicles.

In the garden, *Gillenia trifoliata* gives an airy texture to a border and makes a charming companion

Gillenia trifoliata

in mixed planting with shrubs or along the edge of the woodland. Its rather small and delicate flowers are contrasted by reddish calyces and stems. The handsome foliage often acquires bronzy or reddish tints in the fall. *Gillenia trifoliata* performs best in partial shade but can tolerate both fully shaded and sunny conditions. Preferably, plant it in deep, moist, humus-rich, and well-drained soil, although it can adapt to a wide range of situations. *Gillenia trifoliata* is slow to establish but long-lived; it does not need to be transplanted regularly and is best left undisturbed for years. Plants are hardy to zones 4 or 5.

There are no botanical varieties of *Gillenia trifoliata* recognized among natural populations. In cultivation, the only variant selected so far is the dwarf 'Pixie', which produces normal size flowers on 15-cm-tall plants.

In the wild, *Gillenia trifoliata* blooms from May to July. Cultivated in Poland, it flowers during June and July, whereas in the United Kingdom somewhat later, between June or July and August. Plants grown in St. Louis bloomed in June. At Longwood, flowering began between the third week of May and the first week of June. It continued, on average, for a little more than 3 weeks, usually into the third week of June, rarely until the last week of that month.

Gillenia trifoliata

Helenium

SNEEZEWEED

The name *Helenium* is derived from *helenion*, an ancient Greek name for a plant that sprang from the ground, watered by the tears of Helen of Troy.

Helenium autumnale

COMMON SNEEZEWEED, FALSE SUNFLOWER,

HELEN'S-FLOWER, SWAMP SUNFLOWER, YELLOW STAR

This plant is native to eastern North America, from Quebec, west to British Columbia, and south to Florida and California. It grows in old fields, moist prairies, forest edges, on the banks of lakes and streams, and along roadsides, at elevations up to 2600

Helenium 'Moerheim Beauty'

m. *Helenium autumnale* has been cultivated since the early 18th century.

Helenium autumnale forms upright clumps of stout, erect, branched, and winged stems to 1.5 m tall. The sessile, decurrent, lanceolate leaves have sparsely serrate margins and reach 15 cm in length. The 7-cm-wide flower heads, comprised of up to 20 yellow ray florets and several hundred yellow-brown disc florets, are borne on a globoid receptacle. The flower heads are held in open, branched corymbs. Fruits are 2-mm-long achenes tipped by a pappus of short bristles.

Helenium autumnale is well suited for more formal perennial borders, as well as cottage gardens or naturalistic prairie-style plantings. Although it provides little interest in early summer, once in bloom *H. autumnale* becomes one of the showiest plants in any

Helenium 'Helbro'

plant composition. It can be easily combined with a wide variety of mid- to late-summer perennials, but it benefits from the company of those plants that disguise its bare lower stems. Plant *H. autumnale* in full sun, in any average, preferably consistently moist, and moderately fertile soil. Avoid dry sites, where plants will be subject to excessive lower leaf senescence. Lower-growing cultivars usually do not require staking, but the taller ones, especially in warmer climates and on richer soils, may easily topple over without support. Alternatively, plants can be cut back in early summer to encourage lower and fuller growth. Deadhead spent flowers to extend bloom time. Because *H. autumnale* has little to offer after flowering, cut it back to tidy up the appearance. Divide the plants every 3 years or so to prevent overcrowding and to maintain vigor. Plants are hardy to zone 3.

In the past, several botanical varieties of *Helenium autumnale* were described, among them variety *autumnale*, found in the eastern half of the distribution range; variety *montanum*, growing in the western part of the range; and variety *grandiflorum*, restricted to the west coast of North America. Presently, none of these varieties are recognized as valid. In cultivation, many cultivars are putative hybrids between *H. autumnale* and two other North American species, *H. bigelovii*, with dark yellow flowers, and *H. hoopesii*, with dark orange flowers. Over the years, more than a hundred cultivars have been introduced into gardens. They vary in height from 80-cm-tall 'Blütentisch' to 1.7-m-tall 'Kugelsonne'. The shorter cultivars tend to flower earlier than the tall ones. Their flower colors range from yellow 'Kanaria' to red 'Moerheim Beauty' and include bicolored variants, such as yellow-and-red 'Helbro' and 'Waltraut'.

In the wild, *Helenium autumnale* blooms from July to November, depending on the region. Cultivated in Germany, most cultivars flower from August to October, but the early types, such as 'Waltraut', start blooming in late June. The midseason variety 'Kanaria' flowers in Germany from mid-July to late August. *Helenium autumnale* grown in Poznań began flowering between 18 and 27 July, but flowering began in Moscow around 3 August. Plants in Poznań continued their bloom until 7 to 14 October, whereas those in Moscow finished flowering around 20 September. At Longwood, the cultivar 'Kanaria' started flowering between the first week of August and the first week of September. On average, it bloomed for 6 weeks, into mid or late September. In comparison, plants in Moscow flowered for more than 7 weeks.

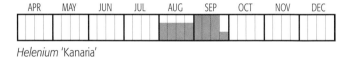

Helenium 'Kanaria'

Helianthemum
SUN–ROSE

The name *Helianthemum* is derived from the Greek, *helios*, sun, and *anthemon*, flower, referring to the flowers opening for a brief time in the sun.

Helianthemum Hybrids
HYBRID SUN–ROSE, ROCK–ROSE

Helianthemum hybrids have been developed by crossing a number of European species, including *H. apenninum, H. croceum, H. nummularium, H. oelandicum,*

Helianthemum 'Golden Queen'

Helianthemum 'Rushfield's White'

and others. In the wild, these species grow in rocky soils, in meadows and scrub, in the mountains of southern Europe and the Mediterranean region.

Helianthemum hybrids form mounded, spreading shrublets with procumbent, ascending or erect stems to 60 cm tall. The semi-evergreen, 5-cm-long leaves are mostly narrow oval and entire. They are often gray-tomentose and may have revolute margins. The flowers vary from 2 to 5 cm wide and have five silky petals that range from white and yellow to pink and red. The petals surround a conspicuous tuft of yellow stamens. The flowers are borne in loose, often one-sided, racemose cymes. Fruits are ovoid capsules.

In the garden, *Helianthemum* hybrids are well suited for planting in perennial borders, for softening hard edges of stone walls, paths, steps or patios, and for covering ground, especially on open slopes. They are valued for the profuse, brightly colored flowers, as well as the pleasing grayish green foliage. Plant *Helianthemum* in warm, sunny locations in any well-drained and calcium-rich soil. Avoid sites with damp, nutrient-rich, or acidic soils. Excellent drainage is essential, especially in areas where *Helianthemum* is only marginally hardy. Trim the plants in early spring to encourage a denser habit and to remove stems that may have been damaged during winter. Cut back again after flowering to promote a new flush of growth and occasional reblooming. Plants are hardy to zone 5, but in colder areas benefit from a light covering with evergreen boughs.

More than 200 cultivars of *Helianthemum* have been selected over the years. With that many named hybrids, they are often quite similar to each other and not easy to tell apart. The selections offer a wide range of flower colors that include white 'Rushfield's White', yellow 'Golden Queen', orange 'Ben Nevis', pink 'Wisley Pink', red 'Red Orient', as well as various bicolor combinations, such as red-and-yellow 'Blutströpfchen' or red-and-white 'Raspberry Ripple'. Flowers can be either single or variously double. The double-flowered varieties hold their flowers longer, but are thought to be less graceful by some.

Helianthemum hybrids flower during late spring and early summer, sometimes into the fall. Although individual flowers are open for only one day, they continue to appear for weeks. Initially, flowers are very prolific, but their numbers decline later in the season. Cultivated in Germany and Poland, *Heli-*

anthemum hybrids bloom between June and September, with single-flowered cultivars finishing sooner than the double-flowered ones. In Moscow *H. nummularium*, one of the hybrids' parent species, bloomed between 11 June and 3 August, on average. At Longwood, the cultivar 'Ben Nevis' began flowering between the second week of May and the first week of June. It usually finished blooming by mid-June or mid-July, but one year it continued to produce flowers into mid-October. The average bloom duration of 'Ben Nevis' was close to 10 weeks. In comparison, *H. nummularium* in Moscow flowered for almost 8 weeks.

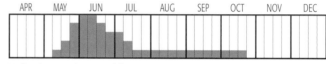

APR	MAY	JUN	JUL	AUG	SEP	OCT	NOV	DEC

Helianthemum 'Ben Nevis'

Helianthus
SUNFLOWER

The name *Helianthus* is derived from the Greek *helios*, sun, and *anthos*, flower, referring to the appearance of the flower heads.

Helianthus angustifolius
SWAMP SUNFLOWER

This perennial is native to the eastern United States, from New York, south to Florida, and west to Texas. *Helianthus angustifolius* grows in wet areas, damp meadows, low wetlands, thickets, and pinelands, at elevations of up to 700 m.

Helianthus angustifolius forms clumps of erect, branched above, hairy stems to 2 m tall, growing from a crown with fibrous roots and sometimes slender rhizomes. The narrowly lanceolate to linear leaves have entire margins and grow to 20 cm long. They are dark green and usually covered with stiff hairs. The 6-cm-wide flower heads are comprised of 10 to 20 yellow ray florets and many purple-red or yellow disc florets. They are held singly or in few-flowered arrays. Fruits are 3-mm-long achenes tipped by two bristly scales.

In the garden, *Helianthus angustifolius* displays a great profusion of flowers in late season. Its imposing height requires careful consideration when selecting a site. It is well suited for the back of a larger perennial border, or for planting in wet areas in meadows

Helianthus angustifolius

Helianthus angustifolius 'Mellow Yellow'

Helianthus ×*laetiflorus* 'Lemon Queen'

or along streams and ponds. Choose a location in full sun. Shaded plants tends to be less floriferous, taller, more open, and subject to flopping. Plant *H. angustifolius* in fertile soil that stays consistently moist. If lower, fuller plants are desired, pinch or trim stems in early summer to encourage branching. *Helianthus angustifolius* spreads rapidly but is short-lived and can be removed easily. In some cases, it may behave as a biennial. Plants are hardy to zones 5 or 6.

There are no botanical varieties of *Helianthus angustifolius* recognized among plants in the natural populations. A lower-growing variety *planifolius*, found from Virginia to New Jersey, is no longer considered valid. In cultivation, several improved selections are known, including 'Mellow Yellow', with pale yellow flowers, and a lower-growing 'Gold Lace'.

In the wild, *Helianthus angustifolius* blooms from August to October, depending on the region. In cultivation, it is among the last perennials to flower. At Longwood, it began to bloom between the last week of September and mid–October and continued, on average, for 4 weeks, into late October or early November. The bloom season for the cultivar 'Mellow Yellow' was nearly identical.

Helianthus ×laetiflorus

CHEERFUL SUNFLOWER, SHOWY SUNFLOWER

This plant is a natural hybrid between *Helianthus pauciflorus* and *H. tuberosus*. It is found in eastern North America, from Newfoundland, west to Ontario, and south to Georgia and New Mexico, although in some parts of this range it is thought to be a result of introduction. It grows on dry prairies, in old fields, and along roadsides, at elevations of up to 300 m.

Helianthus ×laetiflorus forms upright, bushy clumps of erect, stiff, hairy stems to 2 m tall, growing from creeping rhizomes. The broadly oval to lanceolate, coarsely serrate leaves reach 25 cm in length. The 8- to 12-cm-wide flower heads are comprised of 15 to 20 pale yellow ray florets and numerous darker yellow or reddish disc florets. They are held on short peduncles, three to six together in open clusters. Fruits are 4-mm-long achenes tipped with two bristly scales.

In the garden, *Helianthus ×laetiflorus* is best planted in larger perennial borders or allowed to naturalize in open and dry sites, meadows, woodland edges, or similar informal settings. Plant it in full sun, preferably in moderately moist soil. This hybrid grows vigorously and can spread rapidly both through its rhizomes and by self-seeding. Despite its vigor, *H. ×laetiflorus* rarely becomes invasive. It usually can be grown without staking. Plants are hardy to zone 4.

A couple of garden selections are attributed to *Helianthus ×laetiflorus*. The best-known cultivars are 'Lemon Queen', with lighter yellow flowers, and the semi-double 'Miss Mellish'.

In the wild, *Helianthus ×laetiflorus* blooms in late summer and fall. At Longwood, the cultivar 'Lemon Queen' usually began flowering between the first and

Helianthus angustifolius

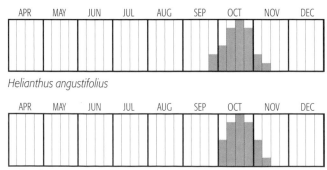

Helianthus angustifolius

Helianthus angustifolius 'Mellow Yellow'

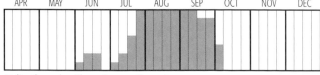

Helianthus ×laetiflorus 'Lemon Queen'

Helianthus ×*laetiflorus* 'Lemon Queen'

the last week of July. In 2 of 7 years, however, sporadic flowers were recorded in early June. Flowering continued, on average, for 11 weeks, through the end of September or even the first week of October.

Helianthus salicifolius

GRACEFUL SUNFLOWER, WILLOWLEAF SUNFLOWER

This perennial is native to the central United States, from Texas north to Nebraska and Missouri. It has also naturalized in areas to the north of this range. *Helianthus salicifolius* grows usually in dry, calcareous soils, on prairies, in glades and plains, at elevations of 100 to 300 m. It has been cultivated since the early 19th century.

Helianthus salicifolius forms erect clumps of stout, smooth, green or glaucous, leafy stems to 2.5 m tall, growing from creeping, thick rhizomes. The linear to lanceolate leaves grow to 20 cm long and are distinctly crowded and drooping. The 6-cm-wide flower heads are comprised of 10 to 20 yellow ray florets and many yellow or brown disc florets. They are held in loosely branched racemes. Fruits are 5-mm-long achenes tipped with a pappus of a few scales.

In the garden, *Helianthus salicifolius* is perhaps valued more for its unusual, willow-like foliage and stems growing to impressive heights. Late-season flowering adds to the picturesque character of the plant. Because of its willowy appearance, it is often grown near water, but it grows better on higher and drier ground. *Helianthus salicifolius* creates an effective backdrop for shorter plants in either formal borders or as part of naturalistic plantings. Thanks to its distinct habit, *H. salicifolius* lends itself to being given a prominent position as a specimen, or it can be grown in a large grouping in contemporary, minimalist-style gardens. Plant it in full sun. Shaded conditions promote lanky, open growth and lead to fewer flowers. *Helianthus salicifolius* tolerates a wide range of soil conditions, including dry soils. It does not require staking when grown in a dry and sunny location. Otherwise, support should be provided, or plants can be pinched or trimmed in late spring to

Helianthus salicifolius

Helianthus salicifolius

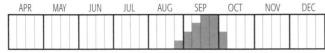

APR	MAY	JUN	JUL	AUG	SEP	OCT	NOV	DEC

Helianthus salicifolius

encourage lower and more branched growth. *Helianthus salicifolius* spreads over time to create dense colonies. Divide it every 4 years or so to control the spread and to maintain the plant's vigor. *Helianthus salicifolius* is hardy to zone 6, possibly zone 4.

There are no botanical varieties of *Helianthus salicifolius* recognized among the wild populations. In cultivation, however, several dwarf cultivars have been named and introduced, among them 'First Light', 'Golden Pyramid', 'Low Down', and 'Table Mountain'.

Helianthus salicifolius is one of the latest sunflowers to bloom. In the wild, it blooms from August to October. In cultivation, September to October flowering season has been recorded in Poland, the United Kingdom, and in Missouri and Ohio. At Longwood, *H. salicifolius* began to bloom as early as the last week of August or as late as the third week of September. On average, it flowered for a little more than 4 weeks, into late September or the first week of October.

Heliopsis

OXEYE

The name *Heliopsis* is derived from the Greek *helios*, sun, and *opsis*, like, in reference to the flowers resembling sunflowers.

Heliopsis helianthoides

FALSE SUNFLOWER, HARDY ZINNIA, ORANGE
SUNFLOWER, SMOOTH OXEYE, SUNFLOWER HELIOPSIS

This plant is native to eastern North America, from New Brunswick, west to Manitoba, south to Florida and New Mexico. *Heliopsis helianthoides* grows in dry open woodlands, thickets, prairies, marshes, meadows, along roadsides and railroads, at elevations of up to 2300 m. It has been cultivated since the early 19th century.

Heliopsis helianthoides forms upright clumps of stiff, erect, loosely branched stems to 1.8 m tall, growing from thick, creeping rhizomes. The ovate to oval lanceolate leaves are sharply and coarsely serrate and reach 12 cm in length. The 7-cm-wide flower heads are comprised of 10 to 18 golden yellow ray florets and numerous brownish yellow disc florets. They are held singly or a few together on long peduncles. Fruits are 4-mm-long achenes.

In the garden, *Heliopsis helianthoides* offers a wide range of possibilities, from traditional perennial borders to prairie-style or container plantings, as well as cut flowers. Plant it in full sun. Although *H. helianthoides* can tolerate light shade, it tends to grow taller and flop easily under such conditions. It tolerates a wide range of soils, but performs best in those that are reasonably fertile, consistently moist, rich in humus, and well drained. Avoid sites where plants will be exposed to a prolonged drought in summer or excessive dampness in winter. If staking is objectionable, stay away from shady and windy locations, where plants are more likely to fall over, or trim them back in late spring to encourage a sturdier and shorter habit. This approach, however, may delay the flowering somewhat. Deadheading prolongs the bloom season, although younger plants can bloom all summer even without it. Cut plants back after flowering to tidy up the appearance. Otherwise, allow the seeds to mature and be picked up by the birds. *Heliopsis helianthoides* can be short-lived. Divide it about every 4 years, more frequently when

Heliopsis helianthoides 'Ballerina'

it is grown in richer soils. Plants are hardy to zones 3 or 4.

There are two subspecies of *Heliopsis helianthoides* currently recognized among the natural populations. The subspecies *helianthoides*, found mostly in the eastern part of the range, has glabrous leaves, whereas the leaves of subspecies *scabra*, with a more western distribution, are scabrous. In addition, forms intermediate between these subspecies also occur. In cultivation, the wild type of *H. helianthoides* has been largely replaced by its cultivars. They feature larger flower heads that are single, as in 'Jupiter' and 'Karat', semi-double, as in 'Lohfelden' and 'Spitzentänzerin', or double, as in 'Goldgefieder' and 'Goldgrünherz'. Their flower colors range from yellow 'Sommersonne' to orange 'Hohlspiegel'. Many grow shorter, such as the 60-cm-tall 'Ballerina' and 'Tuscan Sun',

Heliopsis helianthoides 'Sommersonne'

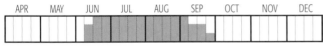

APR	MAY	JUN	JUL	AUG	SEP	OCT	NOV	DEC

Heliopsis helianthoides 'Ballerina'

and have stronger stems less prone to flopping. A few, such as 'Prairie Sunset' and 'Summer Nights', develop purple- or bronze-tinted foliage.

In the wild, *Heliopsis helianthoides* blooms over a long period from late spring to early fall, depending on the region. Cultivated in Poznań, it began flowering between 19 June and 13 July and finished between 3 and 18 September. In Moscow, bloom season started around 7 July and ended around 19 September. At Longwood, the cultivar 'Ballerina' began to flower in the second or third week of June and continued on average for 14 weeks, into September. In comparison, *H. helianthoides* grown in Moscow was in bloom for close to 11 weeks, on average. In Illinois and Ohio, it also flowers from June to September.

Helleborus niger

Helleborus

HELLEBORE

The name *Helleborus* is derived from the Greek *hellein*, to kill, and *bora*, food, in reference to the plant's poisonous properties.

Helleborus niger

BLACK HELLEBORE, CHRISTMAS-ROSE

This plant is native to the mountains of southern Europe and western Asia, from the Apennines, Dolomites, and Alps in the west to the Carpathians in the east. *Helleborus niger* grows often in calcareous soils, in montane woods, thickets, and meadows. It has been cultivated since antiquity.

Helleborus niger forms rounded tufts of evergreen leaves and fleshy, red-spotted flowering stems to 45 cm tall, growing from a short, branched rhizome. The dark, dull green, thick, and leathery leaves are deeply cut into seven or nine irregularly serrate segments and reach 20 cm in length. The 6-cm-wide, saucer-shaped flowers have white or tinted pink petal-like sepals surrounding a ring of true petals modified into nectaries and a tuft of conspicuous stamens. The flowers are held singly or two or three together on a stem. Fruits are clusters of follicles.

In the garden, *Helleborus niger* develops into large and floriferous clumps when grown under proper conditions. It is usually combined with other shade-tolerant, smaller perennials and spring bulbs. Plant in light shade in a warm location sheltered from winter winds, which can ravage the evergreen foliage and early-season flowers. Avoid planting close to shallow-rooted trees casting dense shade. Choose a site with consistently moist, humus-rich, and preferably calcareous soil. Where flowers get spoiled in the rain by splashing mud, spread a layer of coarse sand around the plants. After flowering, apply a generous dressing of compost. *Helleborus niger* is very long-lived but sometimes difficult to establish. This species responds poorly to disturbance and recovers slowly from root damage during transplanting, so it is best to leave plants without dividing for years. *Helleborus niger* may occasionally self-seed under favorable conditions. Plants are hardy to zones 3 or 4.

Helleborus niger exhibits great variation in flower size and color, as well as time of flowering. Several variants from the wild populations were described, but presently only two subspecies are recognized. The typical subspecies *niger*, is found throughout the distribution range of the species, whereas subspecies *macranthus*, distinguished by its larger flowers and bluish tinted, spiny leaves, is restricted to parts of Italy and Slovenia. In cultivation, several variants of *H. niger* have been named. Those selected for larger flowers include 'Allerseelen', 'Saint Bridgid', and 'Potter's Wheel'. Some cultivars, such as 'Louis Cobbett', have flowers more strongly suffused with pink. Most are seed-propagated strains, so a certain amount of variability among them is to be expected. In addition, *H. niger* has been crossed with several other hellebores, including *H. argutifolius*, *H. lividus*, and their hybrid, *H.* ×*sternii*.

Helleborus niger may flower any time between November and April, depending on the weather conditions. The autumn flowering occurs typically in sheltered locations in areas with milder climates. In colder regions, *H. niger* flowers usually in early

Helleborus niger

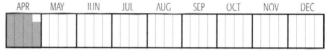

Helleborus niger

spring as soon as snow recedes. Cultivated in Poznań, it bloomed starting between 17 February and 24 March and ending between 1 April and 3 May. A similar February-to-April bloom time was reported from St. Louis. In contrast, in Moscow flowering began several weeks later, around 15 April on average, and continued until 6 May. At Longwood, *H. niger* was always already in flower the first week of April, when data collection began, so the bloom start date was not recorded. Plants then continued to flower through the end of April.

Helleborus orientalis

EASTERN HELLEBORE, LENTEN-ROSE

This perennial is native to southern Europe and western Asia, from Greece and Bulgaria east to northern Turkey and the Caucasus. *Helleborus orientalis* has been cultivated as an ornamental since the early 19th century, but the plant has been known for its medicinal and poisonous qualities since antiquity.

Helleborus orientalis forms dense, bold clumps of evergreen or semi-evergreen foliage and upright flowering stems to 45 cm tall growing from a woody crown. The dark green, leathery leaves are deeply cut into seven to 11 coarsely serrate segments and reach 40 cm in length. The nodding flowers are 7 to 10 cm wide and have showy, petal-

Helleborus orientalis

like sepals that vary from white to purple-tinted, often with darker spots inside. The flowers are held a few together on branched stems. Fruits are clusters of follicles.

In the garden, *Helleborus orientalis* is valued for its early flowering and handsome foliage. The leaves form an effective ground cover that remains attractive throughout the growing season and, in mild climates, even during the winter months. It is very adaptable and can thrive under a wide range of conditions. Use *H. orientalis* in perennial borders, for underplanting deciduous shrubs and trees, edging paths or patios, and in combinations with bulbs that flower in early spring. Plant it in partial to full shade, or in northern climates site in full sun. It performs best in moist, fertile, humus-rich, preferably calcareous soil, but it tolerates less-than-ideal situations. Although *H. orientalis* is very resilient, its leaves can easily be scorched during winter in colder climates unless protected by snow. Cut them off in spring to tidy up the appearance and to show the flowers better. Deadheading will not prolong the bloom.

Rather, allow the persistent sepals to fade to green and provide extended interest. *Helleborus orientalis* is long-lived and does not require regular division or transplanting. Under favorable conditions, it can self-seed. Plants are hardy to zones 4 or 5.

Helleborus orientalis is a variable species with many regional variants described in the past, some of which were even considered to be separate species. Among them are subspecies *abchasicus* in the western Caucasus, with flowers suffused purple-red, and subspecies *guttatus* from the eastern Caucasus, with white flowers spotted purple-red. In cultivation, *H. orientalis* has been hybridized with other hellebores, chiefly *H. multifidus* and *H. odorus*, to produce a plethora of cultivars known as *H.* ×*hybridus* or Orientalis Hybrids. These selections, which are mostly seed-raised strains, offer a range of colors from white and nearly yellow to deep purple and nearly red, as well as various patterns, speckled, blotched, pecotee, and dark-centered. Furthermore, double-flowered and anemone-centered forms, in which the nectaries become enlarged, are available.

Helleborus orientalis

Helleborus orientalis may flower any time between December and May, depending on the region. In mild climates, such as that of the United Kingdom, flowering may begin in December, but in colder areas, such as Poland or the central United States, bloom usually starts in March or April. At Longwood, *H. orientalis* began flowering before the first week of April, the start point for collecting observations. It then bloomed through the end of April or, on rare occasions, into early May.

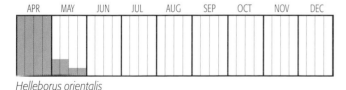

Helleborus orientalis

Hemerocallis

DAYLILY

The name *Hemerocallis* is derived from the Greek *hemeros*, day, and *kallos*, beauty, referring to short-lived flowers, which are open for only one day.

Hemerocallis citrina

Hemerocallis citrina

CITRON DAYLILY, LONG YELLOW DAYLILY

This plant is native to eastern Asia, from Sichuan in China east to Korea and Japan. *Hemerocallis citrina* is found on grassy slopes and along woodland edges, at elevations up to 2000 m. It has been cultivated as an ornamental plant in the West since the early 20th century, but in Asia it has been grown for culinary purposes for many centuries.

Hemerocallis citrina forms stout, fountain-like clumps of coarse leaves and stiff, erect, and branched flowering scapes to 1.2 m tall, growing from a root crown with club-shaped tubers. The narrow, grass-like leaves have a glaucous green sheen, purple-flushed bases, and grow to 1.3 m in length. The night-blooming fragrant flowers, to 12 cm wide, have pale lemon yellow, flaring, stiff tepals. They open in late afternoon and close the next morning. The flowers are held in few-flowered cymes, which terminate scapes slightly longer than the leaves. Fruits are 2-cm-long ellipsoid capsules.

In the garden, *Hemerocallis citrina* has many virtues, including elegant fountain-like foliage, fragrance, and soft coloring of the nocturnal flowers. Single plants can be effectively combined with many perennials in borders, whereas massed groupings can provide a handsome ground cover for larger areas. Plant it in full sun or partial shade. *Hemerocallis citrina* thrives in any average garden soil that is moderately moist and well drained. Established plants are quite drought tolerant. Deadhead spent flowers and cut back entire scapes when flowering is finished. If foliage deteriorates in late summer, cut it back to the ground. *Hemerocallis citrina* grows rapidly and in time clumps may become overcrowded. Divide them every few years to maintain vigor. Plants are hardy to zone 5.

Hemerocallis citrina

Hemerocallis fulva

Two botanical varieties are distinguished among natural populations of *Hemerocallis citrina*. In addition to the typical variety *citrina* from China, the taller variety *vespertina* is found in Japan. Furthermore, exceptionally tall plants introduced from Nanjing, China, known as *H. altissima*, are now considered to belong to *H. citrina*. Although the wild type is rarely cultivated, *H. citrina* has been used often in hybridizing because of its fragrance. Crosses with *H. thunbergii*, include such cultivars as 'Baroni' and 'Autumn Minaret'.

In the wild, *Hemerocallis citrina* blooms from May to August, depending on the region. Cultivated in Germany and Poland, it flowers in July and August. Plants grown in Moscow bloomed, on average, from 13 July until 22 August. At Longwood, *H. citrina* began flowering usually in early to mid-July, although in one year it was in bloom in the last week of June. Flowering continued, on average, for nearly 6 weeks through the end of July or into early (rarely late) August.

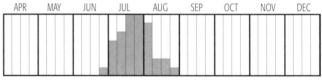

APR	MAY	JUN	JUL	AUG	SEP	OCT	NOV	DEC

Hemerocallis citrina

Hemerocallis fulva

ORANGE DAYLILY, TAWNY DAYLILY

This perennial is native to eastern Asia, from Xizang in China, south to India, north to Russia, and east to Korea and Japan. It grows in open forests, thickets, meadows, and along streams and roadsides, at elevations from 300 to 2500 m. *Hemerocallis fulva* was introduced in the West during the Middle Ages, but has been cultivated in Asia for medicinal and culinary purposes since antiquity. It has since naturalized in parts of Europe and North America.

Hemerocallis fulva forms clumps of bold foliage and strong, erect flowering scapes to 1.5 m tall, growing from creeping, fleshy rhizomes with spindle-shaped, tuberous roots. The arching and strongly keeled, linear leaves grow to 1 m long. The diurnal, unscented flowers, to 12 cm wide, have flaring and wavy, orange-red to purplish tepals, often with a darker zone in the throat and a stripe along the midrib. They are held six to 12 together in helicoidal cymes, which terminate branched scapes. Fruits are 2-cm-long capsules but rarely develop.

In the garden, *Hemerocallis fulva* is valued primarily for its exceptional adaptability and vigor. It can be grown even where many other perennials fail. It spreads rapidly, colonizing even difficult sites. Plant it in full sun or partial shade. It tolerates shady conditions better than other daylilies. *Hemerocallis fulva* thrives in any average soil and can grow well even in poor soils and dry situations. Deadhead spent flowers to maintain a tidy appearance. Cut the scapes after flowering is finished. *Hemerocallis fulva* is long-lived and increases rapidly. Divide it every few years to control the spread and to maintain the plant's vigor. Plants are hardy to zone 4.

Hemerocallis fulva shows significant variability throughout its geographic range. In China, four botanical varieties are recognized. The typical variety *fulva* has rather stout flowers with broad tepals. Variety *angustifolia* has slender flowers with narrower petals. Variety *kwanso* differs in having double flowers, whereas variety *aurantiaca* is distinguished by its evergreen foliage. In cultivation, *H. fulva* has been mostly replaced by hybrid daylilies, many of which derive from this species. Several variants of *H. fulva* exist, some with double flowers, others with darker-colored midribs on petals. The most commonly grown cultivar is 'Europa', a sterile clone with yellow-orange flowers.

In the wild, *Hemerocallis fulva* blooms from June to November, depending on the region. Cultivated in Poznań, it started to flower between 24 July and 1 August and ended between 31 August and 11 September. Plants grown in Moscow bloomed earlier, starting, on average, around 14 July and finishing by 23 August. An even earlier bloom time was recorded in St. Louis, where plants were in flower from mid-June to mid-July. At Longwood, flowering began in the last week of June or in early July. On average, plants were in bloom for a little more than 5 weeks, through the end of July or into early August. Similar bloom duration was recorded in Moscow.

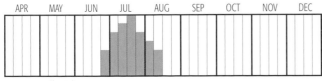

APR	MAY	JUN	JUL	AUG	SEP	OCT	NOV	DEC

Hemerocallis fulva

Hemerocallis hakuunensis

HAKUUN DAYLILY

This perennial is native to the Korean Peninsula. *Hemerocallis hakuunensis* grows on the hillsides, in deciduous and mixed forest, and in grasslands, at elevations from 500 to 800 m. It has been cultivated since the late 20th century.

Hemerocallis hakuunensis forms short, compact clumps of leaves and upright, branched flowering scapes to 1 m. The narrow-keeled, glossy green leaves reach 75 cm in length. The diurnal flowers have 7-cm-long orange-yellow tepals and are borne up to 16 in terminal cymes. Fruits are capsules.

In the garden, *Hemerocallis hakuunensis* can be used like other daylilies described earlier. It flowers in early summer. In St. Louis, it began to bloom

Hemerocallis hakuunensis

Hemerocallis hakuunensis

in the third week of June. At Longwood, flowering began in either the third week of June or in the first 2 weeks of July. On average, it bloomed for 4 weeks into mid or late July. Only once in 5 years, it continued to flower through the second week of August.

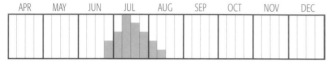

APR	MAY	JUN	JUL	AUG	SEP	OCT	NOV	DEC

Hemerocallis hakuunensis

Hemerocallis Hybrids

HYBRID DAYLILY

Daylilies have been cultivated in eastern Asia as vegetables and medicinal plants for thousands of years. *Hemerocallis fulva* and *H. lilioasphodelus* were the first daylilies to be introduced in Europe during the Middle Ages. They spread and naturalized there quickly. Additional species arrived from Asia during the 19th century, and the first hybrids were developed around 1890. The next century witnessed daylily hybridizing being taken to new heights and the creation of some 50,000 named cultivars.

Being such an immense group of plants with a complex parentage, *Hemerocallis* hybrids are diverse in their appearance. They usually form dense, tight clumps of lush foliage and stiff, upright stems, growing from short rhizomes with fleshy, often tuberous roots. The linear, arching leaves can be deciduous or evergreen. Flowers vary from campanulate to funnel-shaped and from nodding to upward facing. Typically they are held in cymes terminating leafless scapes. Flowers of *Hemerocallis* hybrids come in almost every color, except blue. Many combine two or three colors. Furthermore, flower size and form vary greatly.

Hemerocallis hybrids enjoy well-deserved popularity because of their versatility and adaptability. They perform admirably in almost every situation, mixed in borders with other perennials, as companions for shrubs, planted near water, in rock gardens, for edging paths and patios, naturalized in meadows, and even as ground covers for larger areas. With so many choices of flower sizes, forms, and color, choosing a favorite variety is not an easy task. When in doubt, start with flowers of simpler forms with lighter and clear colors, which are less challenging to blend in with the surrounding plants than the darker, multi-colored, and unusually shaped ones. Preferably, plant

Hemerocallis hybrids in full sun, although they can tolerate partial shade. They thrive in any average garden soil, especially if fertilized regularly. Deadhead spent flowers and cut back scapes when flowering is finished. Plants are cold hardy to zones 3 or 4.

In cultivation, *Hemerocallis* has undergone a complete transformation. Since the 1890s, a staggering number of *Hemerocallis* hybrids have been developed. Many of the more than 50,000 named selections never became widely used; others, although met with acceptance, were later replaced by better varieties. This process continues until this day and results in hundreds of new cultivars named and introduced each year. In addition to single flowers, resembling the wild form, breeders developed spider types, with exceptional long and narrow tepals; double types, with additional inner tepals formed from stamens; polypetal types, with four or more inner and outer tepals, rather than the normal three; and so-called unusual types, with tepals variously twisted or pleated. Besides the nearly complete rainbow of single colors, such as pale yellow 'Happy Returns' or persimmon orange 'Bertie Ferris', flowers may feature

Hemerocallis 'Bertie Ferris'

Hemerocallis 'Krakatoa Lava'

Hemerocallis 'Happy Returns'

Hemerocallis 'Spindazzle'

Hemerocallis 'Russian Rhapsody'

combinations of two or three colors and patterns of contrasting stripes, edges, or throats, such as 'Russian Rhapsody', which has violet purple flowers with a dark eye and a yellow throat, 'Krakatoa Lava', featuring orange flowers with a yellow throat and a darker halo, and 'Spindazzle' with copper yellow flowers veined red.

The overall flowering season for *Hemerocallis* hybrids is May to September, but cultivars differ considerably with regard to their bloom start dates. In Moscow, in a group of 33 cultivars, the earliest, 'Dr. Regel', began flowering on 7 June, whereas the latest, 'Hellbraun mit Gelb', began on 30 July. Some may be in bloom for less than 3 weeks; others may flower continuously from June until frost. Cultivars vary also in their ability to rebloom. While some never rebloom, others are dependable rebloomers, provided the growing season is long enough. Diurnal flowers open in the morning and close in the evening, whereas the nocturnal ones open in the afternoon or early evening and remain open until the following morning. At Longwood, 'Bertie Ferris', 'Russian Rhapsody', and 'Spindazzle' began blooming in late June or the first week of July. In comparison, 'Happy Returns' started to flower about 2 weeks earlier, in early to mid-June; and 'Krakatoa Lava' bloomed about 2 weeks later, beginning in early to mid-July. With exception of 'Happy Returns', these cultivars were in flower for 4 or 5 weeks and never rebloomed. In contrast, 'Happy Returns', after the first flush of flowers in June and July, rebloomed within 1 to 3 weeks and continued until September or October, giving, on average, more than 15 weeks in bloom.

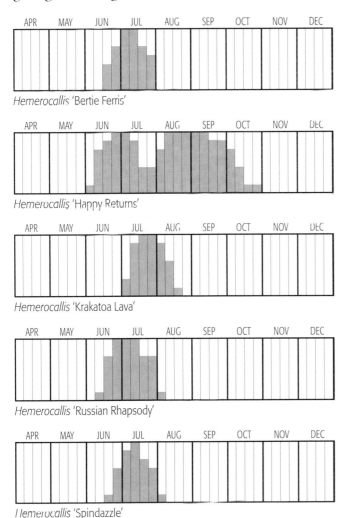

Hemerocallis 'Bertie Ferris'

Hemerocallis 'Happy Returns'

Hemerocallis 'Krakatoa Lava'

Hemerocallis 'Russian Rhapsody'

Hemerocallis 'Spindazzle'

Hemerocallis lilioasphodelus

CUSTARD-LILY, LEMON DAYLILY, LEMON-LILY

This plant is native to central and eastern Asia, from Siberia, south to China, and east to Korea and Japan. *Hemerocallis lilioasphodelus* grows in moist meadows, open woods, woodland clearings, thickets, and along roadsides, at elevations up to 2000 m. It was introduced to Europe during the Middle Ages but had been used in China as food and medicine for centuries before that. It has been naturalized in parts of Europe and North America.

Hemerocallis lilioasphodelus forms loose, fountain-like clumps of arching leaves and rather weak, slender, and leaning stems to 1 m tall, growing from a rhizome with occasional tuberous or spindle-like roots. The deciduous, linear, and dark green leaves reach 70 cm in length. The fragrant, campanulate or funnel-like flowers, to 10 cm long, have uniformly light or bright yellow, recurving tepals. They are held five to 12 in branched terminal cymes. Flowers open in the afternoon and may last up to 3 days. Fruits are 3-cm-long ellipsoid capsules.

In the garden, *Hemerocallis lilioasphodelus* is valued primarily for its early and delightfully fragrant flowers, which come in clear colors and last longer than daylily flowers usually do. It grows vigorously and spreads rapidly, making it a good ground cover, even in rather difficult sites, such as steep slopes. This species is well suited for planting individually or in smaller groups in spring borders or for massing and naturalizing in larger areas. Plant it in full sun or partial shade. *Hemerocallis lilioasphodelus* can tolerate summer heat and humidity. It thrives in any average garden soil and can adapt even to somewhat damp or dry situations. Deadhead spent flowers and cut back flower scapes after the bloom is completed. Divide it regularly where space is limited and the plant's spread needs to be controlled. Plants are hardy to zones 3 or 4.

There are no botanical varieties of *Hemerocallis lilioasphodelus* recognized in the wild. In cultivation, one selection with darker leaves and larger, deeper yellow flowers has been named 'Major'. Furthermore, *H. lilioasphodelus* has been used in hybridizing with other daylilies to develop early-blooming cultivars with fragrant and long-lasting flowers.

In the wild, *Hemerocallis lilioasphodelus* blooms from June to August, depending on the region. In cultivation, it is among the earliest flowering daylilies. Plants grown in Moscow bloomed starting, on average, around 12 June and ending around 6 July. In St. Louis, *H. lilioasphodelus* flowered from late June until mid-July. At Longwood, plants began to bloom in the last week of May or the first week of June. On average, they were in flower for only a little over 2 weeks, and their bloom never extended beyond the second week of June. Similar bloom duration was observed in St. Louis, but in Moscow *H. lilioasphodelus* flowered for about 4 weeks.

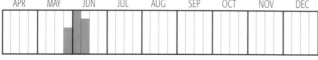
Hemerocallis lilioasphodelus

Hemerocallis thunbergii

LATE YELLOW DAYLILY, THUNBERG'S DAYLILY

This perennial is native to the Korean Peninsula, and plants reported in China and Japan probably have been introduced. *Hemerocallis thunbergii* has been cultivated in the West since the late 19th century.

Hemerocallis thunbergii forms robust but compact clumps of mounded foliage and slender, stiff, erect, and branched scapes to 1.2 m tall, growing from short rhizomes with slender, seldom swollen roots. The dark green, ascending or arching, semi-evergreen leaves reach 60 cm in length. The fragrant, nocturnal, funnel-like flowers have lemon yellow tepals, darker yellow or greenish in the throat. Flowers are held eight to 10 together in terminal cymes.

In the garden, *Hemerocallis thunbergii* can be used the same way as most other daylilies. It is equally versatile and adaptable. It is valued for its simple, fragrant flowers that stay open for a relatively long time. *Hemerocallis thunbergii* does not spread rapidly and clumps improve gradually with age; therefore it is better to leave them undisturbed for a good number of years. Preferably, plant it in full sun, as shaded conditions tend to diminish the number of flowers. Plants are hardy to zone 4.

No botanical varieties of *Hemerocallis thunbergii* are known in the wild. Likewise, no superior selections are cultivated, but this species has been used extensively in breeding with other daylilies because of its desirable traits, such as the fragrance and longevity of its flowers.

Cultivated in Germany and Poland, *Hemerocallis thunbergii* blooms in July and August. Plants grown in Moscow flowered starting, on average, around 28 June and finishing around 31 July. At Longwood, the bloom start date of *H. thunbergii* varied by 4 weeks,

between the third week of June and the third week of July. Flowering then continued into late July or early August. In 1 of 5 years, a rebloom was observed in the last week of August and the first week of September. On average, *H. thunbergii* was in flower for a little more than 4 weeks. In comparison, plants in Moscow averaged over 5 weeks in bloom.

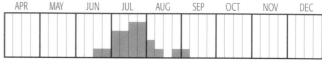
Hemerocallis thunbergii

Heuchera

ALUMROOT

The name *Heuchera* commemorates Johann Heinrich von Heucher (1677–1747), a German professor of medicine at the University of Wittenberg.

Heuchera americana

AMERICAN ALUMROOT, ROCK-GERANIUM

This plant is native to eastern North America, from Ontario, south to Georgia, Louisiana, and Missouri. *Heuchera americana* grows often in calcareous soils, in dry upland woods, shaded slopes, ledges, and bluffs. It has been cultivated since the late 17th century.

Heuchera americana forms mounded clumps of basal foliage and thin, erect flowering scapes to 1 m tall, growing from a stout caudex. The rounded, cordate, long-petiolate leaves have five to nine lobes and reach 15 cm in width. The young leaves are often flushed, mottled or veined reddish brown, later maturing to deep green with a glistening sheen. The 6-mm-long, urn-shaped, greenish white or red-tinged flowers are held in airy panicles to 60 cm long. Fruits are 6-mm-long ovoid capsules.

In the garden, *Heuchera americana* is grown primarily for its attractive foliage, although the tiny flowers are produced in such quantities that they create a welcome change in what otherwise could be a rather static display. Being an adaptable and reliable performer, *H. americana* finds a variety of uses, from perennial borders and containers to underplanting shrubs, edging paths, and ground covering. In warmer areas, the foliage remains attractive through January, making this plant a valuable element in winter gardens or planters. Preferably grow it in partial shade, although full sun is acceptable in northern climates provided soil moisture level is adequate. Deep shade tends to weaken the coloration of the leaves. *Heuchera americana* thrives in a wide range of soils as long as they are well drained, but it performs best in fertile, humus-rich, and consistently moist soil. Cutting back scapes that finished flowering encourages production of additional scapes and extends bloom season, especially in cooler climates. Replant every 3 years or so, and in the process discard the oldest parts of the caudex. Replanting can be somewhat delayed if a fresh layer of organic soil or compost is added around the plants to cover the exposed part of the caudex. *Heuchera americana* is

hardy to zone 4, although in colder areas it is advisable to cover plants lightly with mulch.

Heuchera americana is a highly variable species, and many botanical varieties have been described in the natural populations in the past. Some of these were at times classified as separate species. Currently, only three botanical varieties are recognized. The typical variety *americana*, found throughout the species' range, has glabrous or minutely pubescent petioles. Native to the central United States, variety *hirsuticaulis* has petioles that are densely hirsute. Variety *hispida*, distributed from North Carolina north to Ohio, is distinguished by its oblique flowers. In cultivation,

Heuchera americana 'Dale's Strain'

Heuchera 'Pewter Veil'

Heuchera americana 'Dale's Strain'

the wild types of *H. americana* have been mostly replaced by numerous cultivars, which have leaves entirely suffused purple, such as 'Molly Bush' and 'Montrose Ruby', or showing various purple and silver patterns, including 'Dale's Strain', 'Pewter Veil', and 'Plum Pudding'. In addition, some cultivars, such as 'Can Can' and 'Chocolate Ruffles', have variously ruffled or cut leaves. Many of these selections resulted from hybridization with other species.

In the wild, *Heuchera americana* blooms from late April to June, depending on the region. Cultivated in the United Kingdom, it flowers in May and June and often continues sporadically until fall. Plants grown in Moscow began flowering, on average, around 14 June and ended around 8 August. In St. Louis, cultivars 'Dale's Strain' and 'Pewter Veil' bloomed in mid to late May. At Longwood, 'Dale's Strain' flowered for a little over 2 weeks, starting in the second or third week of May. In comparison, 'Pewter Veil' was somewhat later, rarely flowering before the first week of June. It also bloomed for about a week longer, usually through late June, and in some years rebloomed sporadically in July and August. In addition, three other cultivars were observed at Longwood, 'Molly Bush', 'Montrose Ruby', and 'Plum Pudding'. While both 'Montrose Ruby' and 'Plum Pudding' began flowering at about the same time, in late May or early June, the first cultivar bloomed for 8 weeks, on average, compared to 5 weeks for the latter one. In comparison, *H. americana* in Moscow flowered for 8 weeks. 'Molly Bush' stood out from this group as the last to flower. It began in early to mid-July and continued, on average, for 5 weeks, through the end of July, rarely through the end of August. In one year, 'Molly Bush' rebloomed in September.

Heuchera 'Plum Pudding'

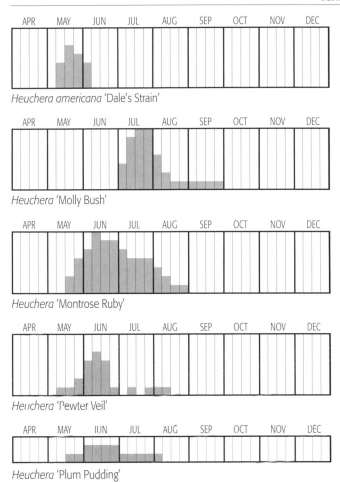

APR	MAY	JUN	JUL	AUG	SEP	OCT	NOV	DEC

Heuchera americana 'Dale's Strain'

Heuchera 'Molly Bush'

Heuchera 'Montrose Ruby'

Heuchera 'Pewter Veil'

Heuchera 'Plum Pudding'

Heuchera cylindrica

POKER ALUMROOT, ROUNDLEAF ALUMROOT

This perennial is native to western North America, from California, north to British Columbia and east to Alberta, Montana, and Wyoming. *Heuchera cylindrica* grows usually in rocky soils, on cliffs and talus slopes in the mountains. It has been cultivated since the mid-19th century.

Heuchera cylindrica forms dense mounds of tufted, basal foliage and stiff, erect flowering stems to 80 cm tall, growing from branched caudex and short rhizomes. The 6-cm-wide, ovate to rounded, cordate leaves have five to seven blunt, serrate lobes. The 6-mm-wide, creamy yellow to brownish flowers are held in spike-like, slender panicles to 15 cm long. Fruits are capsules to 1 cm long.

In the garden, *Heuchera cylindrica* is grown primarily for its attractive tufted foliage. It spreads faster than other alumroots, and it is often used to make an effective ground cover or for edging of paths and beds. Plant it in partial shade in any average garden soil that is well drained but provides consistent moisture. Cut the stems back after flowering to maintain a tidy appearance. Plants are hardy to zone 5, possibly zone 3.

Heuchera cylindrica 'Greenfinch'

In the wild, five botanical varieties of *Heuchera cylindrica* are recognized. Of those, a small-leaved variety *alpina* grows in the southern part of the species' distribution range; the varieties with larger leaves, including *cylindrica* and *orbicularis*, with petioles stiffly hairy, as well as *glabella* and *septentrionalis*, with glabrous petioles, are found in the northern part of the range. In cultivation, a few color variants have been selected, among them cream-colored 'Alba', 'Greenfinch', and 'Green Ivory', as well as 'Hyperion' with soft rosy red flowers.

In the wild, *Heuchera cylindrica* blooms from April to August, depending on the region. Cultivated in Poznań, it began to flower between 8 and 12 June and finished between 29 June and 4 July. At Longwood, the bloom start date of the cultivar 'Greenfinch' varied by 3 weeks between the last week of May and the third week of June. It bloomed, on average, for 3 weeks, sometimes through the end of June.

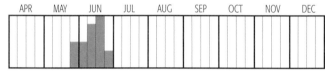

Heuchera cylindrica 'Greenfinch'

Heuchera sanguinea

CORALBELLS, CRIMSONBELLS

This perennial is native to southwestern North America, from New Mexico and Arizona south to Chihuahua in Mexico. *Heuchera sanguinea* grows often on rocky outcrops in the mountains. It has been cultivated since the late 19th century.

Heuchera sanguinea forms mounded clumps of tufted basal foliage and upright flowering stems to 50 cm tall, growing from a stout caudex. The 5-cm-wide, ovate to rounded and cordate leaves have five to nine shallow, serrate, blunt lobes. The 1-cm-long, campanulate flowers have showy red or pink sepals and short, inconspicuous petals. Flowers are borne in loose panicles to 15 cm long. Fruits are capsules.

In the garden, *Heuchera sanguinea* is valued for its decorative, often marbled, foliage and airy, bright red or pink, midsummer flowers. In warmer areas, the leaves are retained through the winter. *Heuchera sanguinea* is often used in a position in the front of perennial borders, for edging paths and other hard surfaces, in rock gardens, and for naturalizing among other lower-growing plants. Plant it in full sun, or in warmer climates in partial shade. Choose a site with excellent drainage, preferably with moist, humus-rich soil. Avoid drought-prone locations with heavy or acidic soil. Deadhead spent flowers to prolong bloom. Cut back flowering stems when the bloom is finished to tidy up the appearance. Add organic soil or compost to keep the caudex covered. Replant about every 3 years, discarding the oldest parts of the caudex. Plants are hardy to zones 3 or 4, but in colder climates a light cover during the winter is advisable.

A few color variants of *Heuchera sanguinea* have been selected and introduced into gardens, but they have been surpassed by hybrids. These hybrid plants are usually classified as *H.* ×*brizoides*, developed by crossing *H. sanguinea* with *H. micrantha*, from western North America, and possibly with other species.

Heuchera ×*brizoides* 'Northern Fire'

These hybrids combine the bright colors of *H. sanguinea* with larger panicles of other alumroots. They offer choices of flowers colors ranging from white 'June Bride', pink 'Chatterbox' and 'Raspberry Regal', to red 'Northern Fire'.

Heuchera sanguinea blooms for 4 to 8 weeks during late spring to early summer, longer on moist

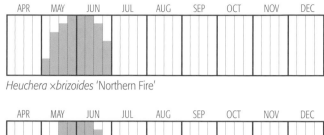

Heuchera ×brizoides 'Northern Fire'

Heuchera ×brizoides 'Raspberry Regal'

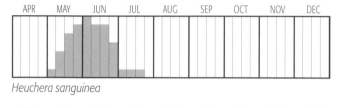

Heuchera sanguinea

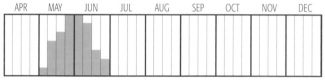

Heuchera ×brizoides 'June Bride'

Heuchera ×brizoides 'Raspberry Regal'

Heuchera ×brizoides 'June Bride'

sites. Cultivated in Moscow, it bloomed from around 15 June until around 12 August. Plants grown in Poznań flowered about 2 weeks earlier, starting between 28 and 30 May and finishing between 15 and 26 July. An even earlier bloom time was observed in St. Louis, where flowering started in late April or early May and continued through the end of May or early June. At Longwood, *H. sanguinea* began to flower between the first and the last week of May. On average, they were in bloom for almost 7 weeks, often through the end of June, or in one year until the third week of July. In comparison, plants in Moscow flowered for about a week longer. The three hybrid cultivars observed at Longwood, including 'June Bride', 'Northern Fire', and 'Raspberry Regal', started to flower at about the same time as the species *H. sanguinea*. Their average bloom duration varied somewhat, from 6 weeks of 'June Bride' to 8 weeks of 'Raspberry Regal'.

Heuchera villosa

HAIRY ALUMROOT

This plant is native to the eastern United States, from New York, south to Georgia, and west to Missouri. *Heuchera villosa* grows in moist, shaded sites on wooded slopes, rock ledges, and cliffs. It has been cultivated since the early 19th century.

Heuchera villosa forms clumps of mounded foliage and slender, wiry flowering stems to 1 m tall, growing from a strong rhizome. The ovate to rounded, cordate leaves are deeply or shallowly cut into five or seven sharply serrate lobes. The 3-mm-long flowers have white to pinkish petals and are borne in large, open panicles. Fruits are 5-mm-long, ovoid capsules.

In the garden, *Heuchera villosa* stands out among other alumroots for its larger stature, bold and velvety foliage, and exceptionally late and profuse flowering. It is well suited for planting as small groups in perennial borders and cottage-style gardens or as a ground cover in larger areas such as open woodlands or rocky slopes. In warmer areas foliage remains evergreen through the winter. Preferably, plant *H. villosa* in partial shade, but in northern climates, plants will thrive in full sun, provided conditions are adequately moist. Choose a site with moist, humusrich, well-drained soil. Leaves will become scorched

Heuchera villosa

if the soil is allowed to dry out for extended period. Deadheading may prolong the flowering season. Divide and replant *H. villosa* every 3 years or so. Plants are hardy to zone 6, but in colder areas apply a light cover after the ground freezes.

There are two botanical varieties of *Heuchera villosa* currently recognized. The typical variety *villosa*, which includes the larger-leaved plants described in the past as variety *macrorhiza*, is found throughout the species' range. The other is a more pubescent variety *arkansana*, previously regarded as a separate species, which has distribution restricted to the Ozark Mountains in Arkansas. In cultivation, several variants have been selected for their leaf color, including pale green 'Autumn Bride' and 'Chantilly'; purple-suffused 'Brownies', 'Bronze Wave' and 'Purpurea'; and the amber-colored 'Caramel'.

Heuchera villosa is the last alumroot to bloom. Cultivated in the United Kingdom, it flowers from

Heuchera villosa

August onward. Plants grown in St. Louis bloomed from the last week of June until mid-October. At Longwood, *H. villosa* began flowering between the first and the third week of August and continued for more than 10 weeks, through the end of September or, rarely, through the end of October. Only once in 7 years, plants were still in flower in early November.

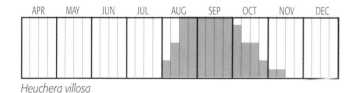

Heuchera villosa

×*Heucherella*

FOAMYBELLS

The name ×*Heucherella* is derived from the names of the two parent genera, *Heuchera* and *Tiarella*.

×*Heucherella tiarelloides*

FOAMYBELLS

The intergeneric hybrid, ×*Heucherella*, was developed in 1912 in Nancy, France, by crossing *Heuchera* ×*brizoides*, itself a hybrid between two North American species of *Heuchera*, and a related plant, *Tiarella cordifolia*, also from eastern North America. In the 1950s additional hybrids were obtained when *H.* ×*brizoides* was crossed with *T. cordifolia* var. *collina*, also know as *T. wherryi*.

×*Heucherella tiarelloides* forms dense clumps of mounded, basal foliage and upright, wiry flowering stems to 60 cm tall. The clumps can be either compact or spreading by stolons. The rounded, cordate leaves have seven or nine shallow or deeply serrated lobes and grow to about 9 cm wide. The 6-mm-long, white or pink flowers are held in slender, open panicles. Fruits are not produced, as this hybrid is sterile.

×*Heucherella tiarelloides* makes an attractive ground cover, but also fits well in perennial borders, along paths, on stone walls, and in naturalistic settings of a woodland garden. It is valued for its prolonged bloom and handsome foliage, which in warmer areas is retained through the winter months. Preferably, plant this hybrid in partial shade, although it will flower satisfactorily even in full shade. In cooler climates, sunny situations are appropriate as long as they are adequately moist. ×*Heucherella tiarelloides* thrives in deep, moist, humus-rich and fertile soils. Avoid overly wet or drought-prone, heavy soils that drain poorly. ×*Heucherella tiarelloides* spreads gradually and may initially be slow to establish. In areas with hot summers, it tends to be short-lived. Plants are hardy to zone 5, possibly zone 3.

×*Heucherella* hybrids combine the features of the parent species in a variety of ways. Those obtained from crosses with a stoloniferous *Tiarella cordifolia* var. *cordifolia* have a tendency to spread, whereas those developed from the nonstoloniferous *T. cordifolia* var. *collina* form compact clumps. Their leaves often display silvery, purple, and green color patterns, whereas the flowers vary from white in 'Heart of Darkness' and 'Quicksilver' to shades of pink in 'Bridget Bloom' and 'Rosalie'.

×*Heucherella tiarelloides* blooms for several weeks in early to late spring, and occasionally repeats flowering in the fall. In Germany and the United Kingdom, it blooms in May and June and sometimes again in September. Plants grown in Moscow began flowering, on average, around 19 June and finished around 7 August. In St. Louis, the cultivar 'Bridget Bloom' bloomed from the last week of April until mid or late May and occasionally again in mid-June. At Longwood, 'Bridget Bloom' began flowering in the last week of April or in early May and continued, on average, for 7 weeks, through the end of May or June. ×*Heucherella tiarelloides* in Moscow also had a 7-week-long bloom season.

×*Heucherella tiarelloides* 'Bridget Bloom'

Hibiscus

ROSE-MALLOW

The name *Hibiscus* is derived from the Greek *hibiskos*, an ancient name for related plants.

Hibiscus coccineus

SCARLET ROSE-MALLOW, SWAMP HIBISCUS

This perennial is native to the southeastern United States, from Virginia, south to Florida, and west to Louisiana. *Hibiscus coccineus* grows in wet areas, coastal swamps, and tidal marshes.

Hibiscus coccineus forms narrow, upright, open clumps of glabrous, sturdy, and glaucous stems to 2.5 m tall, growing from a woody base. The 15-cm-wide leaves are palmately cut into three to seven slender, remotely serrate lobes or sometimes are palmately compound. The funnel-shaped, five-petalled, bright

×*Heucherella tiarelloides* 'Bridget Bloom'

Hibiscus coccineus

Hibiscus coccineus 'Davis Creek'

Hibiscus coccineus
'Davis Creek'

red flowers reach 20 cm in width and are borne singly on long peduncles in the upper leaf axils. Fruits are capsules subtended by a persistent calyx.

In the garden, *Hibiscus coccineus* is valued for its striking, brightly colored, and large flowers. It is best suited for wet areas near ponds or streams, but it is also good for larger perennial borders or planted singly, framing patios or inside courtyards. Despite its imposing height, *H. coccineus* is open enough not to shade out neighboring plants. Preferably, plant it in full sun, as in shade stems become leggy and flowering is reduced. *Hibiscus coccineus* thrives in wet situations, although average garden soil is also acceptable provided it is kept consistently moist. After flowering, allow the conspicuous capsules to develop and remain on the rigid stems through the winter to provide additional interest. Cut the stems back in the spring. Plants are hardy to zone 7, possibly 5, but in colder areas choose a sheltered site and cover lightly with mulch.

No botanical varieties of *Hibiscus coccineus* are recognized among the natural populations. In cultivation, a pink-flowered variant (or possibly a hybrid) has been named 'Davis Creek'.

In the wild, *Hibiscus coccineus* blooms over a long period in mid to late summer. Cultivated in St. Louis, it flowered from the last week of July until mid-October. At Longwood, *H. coccineus* began flowering usually in the last week of July or early August. Only once in 7 years, bloom began as early as the third week of July or the third week of August. On average, plants flowered for 10 weeks, through the end of September or into early October. One year, they were still in bloom in the third week of October. The cultivar 'Davis Creek' flowered during the same season as the species.

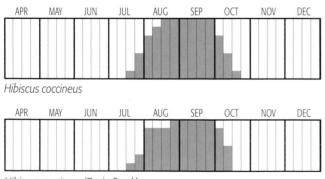

Hibiscus coccineus

Hibiscus coccineus 'Davis Creek'

Hibiscus moscheutos

COMMON MALLOW, MALLOW-ROSE, MARSH-MALLOW, ROSE-MALLOW, SWAMP ROSE-MALLOW

This plant is native to eastern and southeastern North America, from Massachusetts in the United States, west to Ontario in Canada, and south to Florida and Texas. *Hibiscus moscheutos* grows in saline, brackish, or freshwater marshes, sloughs, and wet ditches along the coast and inland. It has been cultivated since the 16th century.

Hibiscus moscheutos forms vigorous, robust clumps of erect, softly pubescent stems to 2 m tall, growing from a woody base. The ovate to lanceolate, serrated leaves are unlobed or cut into three or five lobes and reach 25 cm in length. Flowers are usually creamy to pink and have a darker red or purple center. They are up to 20 cm wide and are borne singly in the axils of the upper leaves. Fruits are conical capsules tapering to a narrow beak.

In the garden, *Hibiscus moscheutos* is grown for its immense flowers backed by bold foliage. Individual flowers last only one day, but they are produced continuously over a long period. Plants are slow to emerge in the spring but then increase rapidly. Naturalize *H. moscheutos* in wet areas, on banks of ponds and streams, or combine with other perennials in borders. Site it in a warm spot in full sun. Shaded plants develop lanky stems and flower less. Plant it in any fertile soil, provided it is consistently moist. *Hibiscus moscheutos* produces strong stems that require no staking. If lower-growing plants are desired, trim stems in late spring to encourage more branched and shorter growth. Deadhead spent flowers to keep the appearance neat and prevent self-seeding. Otherwise, allow the capsules to develop and extend the interest through the winter months. Cut stems back in the spring. *Hibiscus moscheutos* does not require regular dividing and is best left undisturbed for years. Plants are hardy to zone 5.

Although *Hibiscus moscheutos* is a variable species, there are no botanical varieties recognized among the natural populations. Previously described subspecies *palustris*, with broader and more lobed leaves and pink flowers, is currently considered synonymous with the species. In cultivation, the wild types of *H. moscheutos* have been largely replaced by cultivars, many of which are the result of hybridization with other species, including *H. coccineus*, *H. laevis*, and others, that began in the early 20th century. The cultivars offer flowers up to 30 cm wide, in colors ranging from white 'Blue River II' and pink 'Lady Baltimore' to rose-purple 'Plum Crazy' and red 'Lord Baltimore', often with a dark purple center. Plants of the seed-propagated strains, such as 'Dixie Belle', 'Disco Belle', and 'Southern Belle', have assorted colors.

In the wild, *Hibiscus moscheutos* blooms from June to September, with the bloom start date varying by region. In the southern United States, flowering begins in June, but in Illinois, Ohio, and Missouri, it begins in July. Even later bloom, starting around 11 September, was recorded for plants cultivated in Poznań. At Longwood, four cultivars were observed, 'Blue River II', 'Lady Baltimore', 'Lord Baltimore', and 'Plum Crazy'. They all began flowering between mid-July and the first week of August. Of this group, 'Plum Crazy' had the shortest bloom season of 8 weeks. It usually ended flowering in mid

Hibiscus moscheutos 'Blue River II'

Hibiscus 'Lady Baltimore'

Hibiscus 'Lord Baltimore'

Hibiscus 'Plum Crazy'

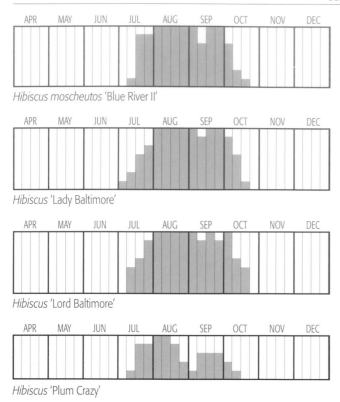

APR | MAY | JUN | JUL | AUG | SEP | OCT | NOV | DEC

Hibiscus moscheutos 'Blue River II'

APR | MAY | JUN | JUL | AUG | SEP | OCT | NOV | DEC

Hibiscus 'Lady Baltimore'

APR | MAY | JUN | JUL | AUG | SEP | OCT | NOV | DEC

Hibiscus 'Lord Baltimore'

APR | MAY | JUN | JUL | AUG | SEP | OCT | NOV | DEC

Hibiscus 'Plum Crazy'

Hosta lancifolia

or late August, but in some years plants rebloomed in September. In contrast, the other three cultivars bloomed, on average, for 12 or 13 weeks, through the end of September or into early October. Only sporadically, they were without flowers for 1 week in September. In comparison, 'Lord Baltimore' bloomed in St. Louis for 10 weeks.

Hosta

PLANTAIN-LILY

The name *Hosta* commemorates Nikolaus Thomas Host (1761–1834), an Austrian botanist and physician to Emperor Francis I.

Hosta lancifolia

LANCE-LEAF HOSTA, NARROW-LEAF PLANTAIN-LILY

This plant is believed to have originated in Japan, but today all its populations are near places of human habitation, which probably resulted from plants that escaped from the garden. It has been cultivated in Japan for centuries and in the West since the early 19th century. *Hosta lancifolia* has naturalized in parts of the northeastern United States. Because no unquestionably natural populations are known, this plant is sometimes classified as *Hosta* 'Lancifolia'.

Hosta lancifolia forms open clumps of mounded, glossy foliage and erect wiry flowering scapes to 60 cm tall, growing from short, sometimes stoloniferous rhizomes. The long-petiolate, wavy-margined, lanceolate leaves have distinct, often curving venation and reach 25 cm in length. The deep lilac blue, trumpet-shaped, 4-cm-long flowers are held nearly horizontally in open, one-sided, slender racemes to 20 cm long. Fruits are capsules, but they are sterile and seldom develop.

Thanks to its handsome deep green, glossy leaves, and dense vigorous growth, *Hosta lancifolia* creates an excellent ground cover. The leaves of *H. lancifolia* develop late in spring, permitting interplanting with spring bulbs and other early-flowering and summer-dormant perennials. Its late and profuse flowers are a valued addition to a perennial border or a woodland garden. Use *H. lancifolia* for edging paths, or allow it to mingle with other low perennials under trees or near water. Preferably, plant it in partial shade, although full sun is tolerated on sites that remain consistently moist. *Hosta lancifolia* thrives in moist, humus-rich, slightly acidic soil, but can adapt to drier conditions better than most plantain-lilies. It increases gradually, but not to the point of being invasive. Divide it only when plants outgrow their space. Plants are hardy to zones 3 or 4.

A few variegated forms of *Hosta lancifolia*, such as 'Viridis Marginata' and 'Aurea', are known. This species has been used extensively in breeding of many modern hybrids.

Hosta lancifolia blooms in late summer and sometimes into early fall. In Moscow, it started flowering,

Hosta lancifolia

on average, around 12 July and ended around 13 August. Plants grown in St. Louis bloomed later, beginning between the last week of August and early September and finishing between late September and mid-October. At Longwood, the bloom start date varied by 3 weeks, between the second week of August and the first week of September. Flowering continued, on average, for nearly 7 weeks, through the end of September or the first week of October. A hybrid cultivar, 'So Sweet', derived from crosses involving *H. lancifolia*, also averaged 7 weeks in bloom, but it began flowering about 2 weeks earlier than this species. In comparison, *H. lancifolia* bloomed in Moscow for 5 weeks, whereas in St. Louis bloom time varied from 2 to 8 weeks.

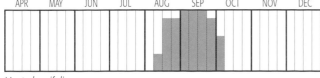

Hosta lancifolia

Hosta plantaginea

AUGUST–LILY, FRAGRANT HOSTA, FRAGRANT PLANTAIN–LILY, FUNKIA, WHITE PLANTAIN–LILY

This perennial is native to southeastern China, from Guangdong north to Hebei and west to Yunnan and Sichuan. It grows in forests and on grassy or rocky slopes, at elevations of up to 2200 m. *Hosta plantaginea* has been cultivated in China and Japan for centuries, and it was introduced in the West at the end of the 18th century. It was so widely planted in Paris that it became known as "Parisian funkia."

Hosta plantaginea forms large clumps of mounded, lustrous green foliage and erect stout flowering scapes to 80 cm tall, growing from thick, stout rhizomes. The long-petiolate, ovate to broadly cordate leaves have six to 10 pairs of prominent veins and reach 25 cm in length. The fragrant, white, funnel-shaped, 12-cm-long flowers are the largest of any *Hosta*. They are held horizontally, up to 50, in dense racemes to 25 cm long. Fruits are 6-cm-long, cylindrical capsules.

Hosta 'Guacamole'

Hosta 'Guacamole'

In the garden, *Hosta plantaginea* is valued for both its elegant shiny foliage and large flowers, unique among plantain-lilies in that they are sweetly scented and open in the evening. Site it near patios or paths, where the fragrance of the flowers can be easily enjoyed. It is well suited for planting as a specimen or small groups in perennial borders, as well as for larger groupings in woodland gardens or as ground cover. Plant it in partial shade or, in cooler climates and in moist situations, in full sun. *Hosta plantaginea* thrives in moist, humus-rich, and well-drained soils. Plants increase gradually but require no regular dividing. This species may self-seed under favorable conditions. Plants are hardy to zone 3.

A few variants of *Hosta plantaginea* are know in cultivation, including 'Grandiflora' with larger flowers, double-flowered 'Aphrodite', narrow-leaved 'Japonica', 'Stenantha' with shorter and narrow flowers, and variegated 'Chelsea Ore'. In addition, numerous hybrids with fragrant flowers, such as 'Guacamole', 'Honeybells', and 'Royal Standard' were developed from *H. plantaginea*.

In the wild, *Hosta plantaginea* blooms from August to October. Plants cultivated in Germany and Poland flower during a similar season, starting in August; but in Moscow, they bloomed later, beginning on average around 8 September. In St. Louis, *H. plantaginea* flowered from late August until mid or late September. At Longwood, the cultivar 'Aphrodite' began flowering in late August or early September. On average, it bloomed for nearly 4 weeks, into mid or late September. One year, it was still in flower in the first week of October. In comparison, 'Guacamole', a hybrid cultivar derived from *H. plantaginea*, bloomed at Longwood for more than 6 weeks, starting usually in late July or early August.

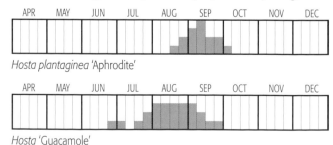

Hosta plantaginea 'Aphrodite'

Hosta 'Guacamole'

Hosta ventricosa

Hosta ventricosa

BLUE HOSTA, BLUE PLANTAIN-LILY

This perennial is native to southeastern China, from Guangdong, north to Jiangsu, and west to Sichuan. It grows on the hillsides, in open forests, and on grassy slopes, at elevations between 500 and 2400 m. *Hosta ventricosa* has been cultivated in the West since the end of the 18th century. It has naturalized in parts of northeastern North America.

Hosta ventricosa forms lush broad clumps of mounded foliage and stiffly erect flowering scapes to 1 m tall, growing from thick, stout rhizomes. The broadly ovate to cordate, shiny green leaves have slightly wavy margins, seven to 11 pairs of veins, and reach 25 cm in length. The 5-cm-long campanulate flowers are dark purple with even darker stripes within. They are held horizontally or nodding, up to 30 in loose racemes. Fruits are 4-cm-long cylindrical capsules.

In the garden, *Hosta ventricosa* can be used in similar situations as the plantain-lilies described earlier. This species is very adaptable to various soils as long as they are adequately moist. Its thin leaves are easily scorched along the edges in hot weather; therefore, shady conditions are preferred. *Hosta ventricosa* is long-lived, requires little care, and is best left undisturbed for years. It freely produces apomictic seeds, without fertilization. Plants are hardy to zones 3 or 4.

There are no botanical varieties of *Hosta ventricosa* recognized among natural populations. In cultivation, a number of variegated forms, such as 'Aureomaculata' and 'Aureomarginata', were selected. *Hosta ventricosa* cannot be used as a seed parent in hybridizing, because it produces apomictic seeds without fertilization, but it has been used extensively as a pollen parent.

In the wild, *Hosta ventricosa* blooms from June to September, depending on the region. Cultivated in Poznań, it flowered between 5 July and 17 August. Plants grown in Moscow started to bloom, on average, 1 week later, around 12 July, and finished 1 week earlier, around 10 August. At Longwood, flowering usually began at about the same time as in Poznań and Moscow, in early to mid-July, although in one year plants were already in bloom in the last week of June. The bloom continued through the end of July, sometime into the first week of August. The average bloom season at Longwood was about 1 week shorter than in Moscow and 3 weeks shorter than in Poznań.

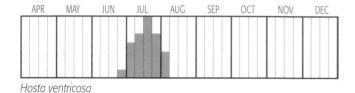

Hosta ventricosa

Hylotelephium

STONECROP

The name *Hylotelephium* is derived from the Greek *hyle*, forest, and *telepheion*, health, in reference to the medicinal use of some of the species.

Hylotelephium spectabile

BUTTERFLY STONECROP, ICE PLANT, LIVE-FOREVER, SHOWY STONECROP

This plant is native to eastern Asia, from Shanxi in China east to Korea. It grows in woodland margins and rocky slopes at low elevations. *Hylotelephium spectabile* has been cultivated in Asia for centuries, and in the West since the late 19th century. This and other *Hylotelephium* were previously classified as species of *Sedum*.

Hylotelephium spectabile forms upright rounded clumps of erect, smooth, glaucous, light green stems to 60 cm tall, growing from thick fleshy rhizomes. The broadly obovate, sessile leaves, to 13 cm long, are glaucous, fleshy, and weakly serrate. They are opposite or whorled in threes and fours. The starry, 1.2-cm-wide, pink flowers are held in dense, flat or convex, corymbose cymes to 15 cm wide. Fruits are follicles.

In the garden, *Hylotelephium spectabile* is valued as a versatile and adaptable perennial that remains attractive throughout the growing season and even into the winter months. It can be used in the front of a perennial border, in tight corners near paved areas or stone walls, and in various containers. Plant it in full sun. Light shade is tolerated but may lead to stem flopping at the time of flowering. *Hylotelephium spectabile* thrives in any average garden soil that

is well drained, and once established it can tolerate drought. It is long-lived and spreads slowly. Regular dividing is not needed, unless intended for propagation purposes. Plants are hardy to zones 3 or 4.

In the wild, plants of *Hylotelephium spectabile* with narrow and serrate leaves, found in northeastern China, have been designated as the variety *angustifolium*. In cultivation, numerous superior selections have been named. Their flower colors range from white 'Iceberg'; various shade of pink, including pale pink 'Stardust', magenta-pink 'Neon', deep carmine-pink 'Brilliant', and rose-pink 'Autumn Fire'; to dark red 'Septemberglut'.

In its native habitat in Japan and China, *Hylotelephium spectabile* blooms from August to September. When cultivated in Germany and the United Kingdom, it flowers at about the same time. Plants grown in Poznań began flowering around 27 August and ended between 7 and 14 October, whereas those in Moscow bloomed a couple of weeks later, on average, from 11 September to 12 October. At Longwood, three cultivars of *H. spectabile* were observed, 'Autumn Fire', 'Brilliant', and 'Neon'. All three started to bloom between late August and early September, but they differed in bloom duration. While 'Neon' averaged nearly 6 weeks in bloom, 'Brilliant' flowered for 1 week longer, and 'Autumn Fire' for 2 weeks longer. They all usually continued blooming into early October, but 'Autumn Fire' was still in flower in the first week of November in 3 of 6 years.

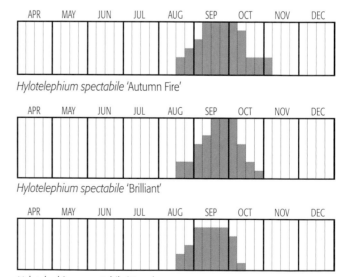

Hylotelephium spectabile 'Autumn Fire'

Hylotelephium spectabile 'Brilliant'

Hylotelephium spectabile 'Neon'

Hylotelephium spectabile 'Brilliant'

Hylotelephium spectabile 'Autumn Fire'

Hylotelephium spectabile 'Brilliant'

Hylotelephium spectabile 'Neon'

Hylotelephium telephium

LIVE–FOREVER, LIVE–LONG, MIDSUMMER–MEN, ORPINE, STONECROP, WITCH'S MONEYBAGS

This perennial is native to temperate regions of Europe and Asia, from Portugal east to Japan. *Hylotelephium telephium* grows in woods and forest glades, hedgerows, meadow margins, rocky slopes, and stream banks.

Hylotelephium telephium forms upright clumps of erect, stiff, leafy, usually simple stems to 80 cm tall, growing from rhizomes with tuberous thickened roots. The glaucous green, fleshy leaves, to 10 cm long, are alternate, oblong to ovate, sessile and irregularly serrate. The 1-cm-wide, pink to purple-

Hylotelephium 'Herbstfreude'

Hylotelephium 'Matrona'

Hylotelephium 'Vera Jameson'

red flowers are held in crowded, axillary and terminal broadly conical cymes to 12 cm wide. Fruits are erect follicles.

Like *Hylotelephium spectabile*, in the garden *H. telephium* provides nearly year-round interest, thanks to its succulent, often purple-tinged foliage and richly colored sumptuous flower clusters, followed by conspicuous seed heads standing up to the brutal forces of winter weather. Use it in traditional perennial borders, dry gravel gardens, near patios and other hard surfaces, and in containers. Plant it in full sun, although in hot southern climates, partial shade may be preferred. Excessive shading will lead to lanky growth subject to flopping. *Hylotelephium telephium* grows best in loose, light, moderately fertile and moist soil, but it can adapt to almost any soil provided it drains well. Established plants are drought tolerant. Allow seed heads to mature and stand through the winter months or until they give in under the weight of snow. This species is long-lived and rarely

Hylotelephium 'Vera Jameson'

needs dividing. It may self-seed but not to the point of becoming a nuisance. Plants are hardy to zones 3 or 4.

Hylotelephium telephium is a variable species and numerous variants have been described throughout its huge distribution range. In Europe, four subspecies are recognized. The typical subspecies *telephium* has erect stems, sessile leaves, and purplish flowers. Yellowish white flowers distinguish subspecies *maximum*, and procumbent stems are characteristic of subspecies *ruprechtii*. Subspecies *fabaria* stands out because of its lower leaves being petiolate. Intermediate forms, some developed in cultivation, are also known. Numerous garden selections have been developed, many through hybridization with other stonecrops. Their flowers come in various shades of pink, such as 'Herbstfreude' and 'Matrona', or reddish purple, including 'Lynda Windsor' and 'Mohrchen'. Some cultivars feature leaves with varying degrees of purple coloration, from slightly red-flushed 'Gooseberry Fool' to black-purple 'Black Jack'. Hybrids between *H. telephium* and *H. cauticola*, such as 'Purple Emperor', 'Ruby Glow', and 'Vera Jameson', have procumbent stems.

In the wild, *Hylotelephium telephium* blooms from August to October. Cultivated in Germany and Poland, it flowers at about the same time. At Longwood, three cultivars were observed, 'Herbstfreude', 'Matrona', and 'Vera Jameson'. All three began flowering between mid-August and the first week of

September. They usually continued to bloom until the end of September or the first week of October. 'Matrona' and 'Vera Jameson' averaged around 6 weeks in bloom, whereas 'Herbstfreude' flowered for about 1 week longer. In comparison, 'Herbstfreude' in St. Louis was in bloom for 5 weeks.

Iberis

CANDYTUFT

The name *Iberis* is derived from Iberia, the ancient name of Spain, where many species are found.

Iberis sempervirens

EDGING CANDYTUFT, EVERGREEN CANDYTUFT, PERENNIAL CANDYTUFT

This plant is native to the Mediterranean regions of northern Africa, Asia Minor, and southern Europe, from Algeria, Morocco, and Spain in the west to Syria and Turkey in the east. *Iberis sempervirens* grows among rocks in high mountains. It has been cultivated since the early 18th century.

Iberis sempervirens forms a dense, bushy, sometimes mat-forming subshrub of procumbent, spreading, branched, semi-woody stems to 30 cm tall, growing from a woody base. The semi-evergreen, entire, lanceolate leaves reach 5 cm in length. The small, four-petalled flowers are white, sometimes aging to pink, and are borne in dense corymbs to 5 cm wide. Fruits are flat, round silicles to 7 mm long.

In the garden, *Iberis sempervirens* has traditionally been used for edging beds and paths, but can perform equally well planted in a position in the front of a perennial border, on a stone wall, among rocks, or as a ground cover in a smaller area. In milder climates, its foliage remains evergreen, but in colder areas plants partially defoliate during the winter. Choose a spot in full sun. Plants grown in shade flower less and are more prone to winter injury. *Iberis sempervirens* can thrive in any average soil, provided it is well drained, especially in winter. Trim plants back after flowering to encourage dense habit. Being a subshrub, *I. sempervirens* requires no dividing. Procumbent stems, which root after touching soil, can be separated and transplanted if desired. Plants are hardy to zones 3 or 4, but in colder climates they benefit from a light cover of evergreen boughs to minimize desiccation over the winter months.

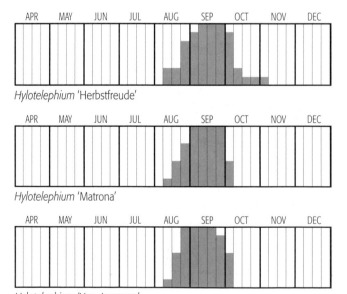

Hylotelephium 'Herbstfreude'

Hylotelephium 'Matrona'

Hylotelephium 'Vera Jameson'

There are no botanical varieties of *Iberis semper-virens* recognized among the natural populations. In cultivation, numerous selections with improved flowering and often more compact growth habit have been introduced. The differences between them are small, however. Many, including 'Alexander's White' and 'Purity', were selected for their exceptionally pure, sparkling white flowers. 'Winterzauber' was named for its very early (March) bloom, whereas other cultivars, such as 'Autumn Beauty' and 'October Glory', show a tendency to rebloom in the fall. The height of the cultivars varies from 10 cm in 'Pygmea' and 'Zwergschneeflocke' to 30 cm in 'Snowflake' and 'Climax'.

In the wild, *Iberis sempervirens* flowers in March or April, depending on the region. Cultivated in Moscow, it bloomed, on average, between 9 May and 6 June, whereas the cultivar 'Snowflake' flowered a few days later, between 14 May and 8 June. In Poznań, *I. sempervirens* bloomed at about the same time, starting between 6 and 9 May and ending between 4 and 15 June. In St. Louis, flowering began a couple of weeks earlier, in mid to late April. At Longwood, the bloom start date of 'Snowflake' varied by 4 weeks, between the third week of April and the third week of May. On average, plants were in flower for 6 weeks, through the end of May or until the second week of June, about 2 weeks longer than in Moscow.

Iberis sempervirens 'Snowflake'

Iberis sempervirens 'Purity'

Inula

INULA

The name *Inula* was used by ancient Romans for one of the species.

Inula ensifolia

SWORDLEAF INULA

This perennial is native to southern and central Europe and western Asia, from Italy, north to Sweden, and east to Turkey and the Caucasus. *Inula ensifolia* grows on dry, grassy slopes. It has been cultivated since the late 18th century.

Inula ensifolia forms compact, dense, bushy, round clumps of erect, slender, leafy stems to 60 cm tall, growing from a rootstock of short rhizomes. The lanceolate, entire or serrulate, sessile leaves grow to 10 cm long. The 5-cm-wide, golden yellow to orange flower heads, comprised of numerous ray and disc florets, are borne singly or in small clusters at the end of the stems. Fruits are 3-mm-long achenes.

In the garden, *Inula ensifolia* is valued for its prolific floral display and the ability to succeed even under the most Spartan conditions. Use in a posi-

Inula ensifolia

Inula ensifolia

tion in the front of a traditional perennial border or in more informal settings of a wildflower meadow or forest edge. Plant it in full sun, in any well-drained garden soil. *Inula ensifolia* is noted for its drought tolerance. It is rather short-lived, especially in warmer climates, and requires frequent divisions and replanting to maintain vigor. Plants are hardy to zone 5, possibly zone 3.

There are no botanical varieties of *Inula ensifolia* recognized among the wild populations. In cultivation, several lower-growing forms have selected, among them 'Compacta', 'Goldammer', and 'Gold Star'.

Inula ensifolia blooms in early to midsummer, depending on the region. Cultivated in Poznań, it flowered starting between 2 and 4 July and ending between 4 and 14 August. Similarly, plants grown in Moscow bloomed, on average, from 6 July until 8 August. At Longwood, *I. ensifolia* usually began flowering in mid to late June, although in one year plants were in bloom as early as the first week of June. In most years, they stopped flowering in early August but rebloomed within 2 to 6 weeks. This second flush of flowers lasted until mid or late September, rarely into the first week of October. In 2 of 7 years, *I. ensifolia* bloomed continuously from June through September. It averaged nearly 13 weeks in bloom. In comparison, *I. ensifolia* in Moscow, where it did not rebloom, flowered for less than 6 weeks on average.

bluffs and outcrops, in ravines and floodplains. It has been cultivated since the 18th century.

Iris cristata forms dense, broad clumps of clustered leaves and simple stems to 20 cm tall, growing from shallow, slender, creeping rhizomes. The sword-shaped, slightly falcate, pale green leaves elongate after flowering to 40 cm. The fragrant, 5-cm-wide flowers have three sepals, three petals, and three petaloid styles. The blue to violet, spreading sepals (known as falls) are marked with a white or yellow band and crested ridges. The slightly shorter and more upright, unmarked petals (known as standards) are the same color as the falls. The petaloid styles lie over the falls. The flowers are held singly or in pairs, surrounded by a spathe of three somewhat inflated, modified leaves, and terminating the stems. Fruits are oval, ridged capsules to 1.5 cm long, enclosed in spathes.

In the garden, *Iris cristata*, when properly sited, creates attractive ground cover. It can withstand drier situations and competition from tree roots, but grows poorly when crowded out by other plants or smothered by a thick layer of leaf litter. Allow it to spread and naturalize on slopes, in woodland or rock gardens, and on banks of streams or to form smaller groups in traditional perennial borders. *Iris cristata* grows best in partial shade. Full shade is also tolerated, but flowering will be diminished there. It can be grown in sunny situations provided plants are

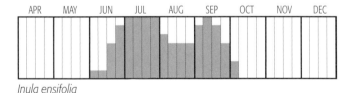

APR	MAY	JUN	JUL	AUG	SEP	OCT	NOV	DEC

Inula ensifolia

Iris

FLAG, IRIS, SWORD–LILY

The genus *Iris* is named for the Greek mythological messenger, Iris, who came to earth over a rainbow and from whose footsteps sprang flowers.

Iris cristata

DWARF CRESTED IRIS

This plant is native to eastern North America, from Pennsylvania, south to Georgia and Mississippi, and west to Missouri and Oklahoma. *Iris cristata* grows in rich open woodlands, on rocky or gravelly slopes,

Iris cristata

Iris cristata

Iris cristata 'Alba'

well watered. Plant it in moist, humus-rich, moderately fertile, and well-drained soil. *Iris cristata* spreads slowly through the rhizomes and rarely requires dividing. Plants are hardy to zones 3 or 4.

Iris cristata is a highly variable species, but there are no botanical varieties recognized among the native populations. However, several cultivars varying in color and size of flowers have been selected. Most feature flowers in shades of blue, among them 'Caerulea', 'Eco Bluebird', 'Edgar Anderson', 'Little Jay', and 'Powder Blue Giant'. Less common are variants with violet flowers, such as 'Abbey's Violet' and 'Dick Redfield', or white flowers, such as 'Alba'.

In the wild, *Iris cristata* blooms from April to July, depending on the region. Cultivated in Germany, it flowers in April and May. A similar bloom season was observed in St. Louis. At Longwood, *I. cristata* began to flower in the first or second week of May and continued for nearly 3 weeks, on average, through the end of May. Its cultivar, 'Eco Bluebird', had simi-

lar bloom time and duration, although its flowering continued into the first week of June one year. Another cultivar, 'Alba', was a little earlier, sometimes starting flowering in the last week of April. Its bloom duration, however, averaged only 2 weeks.

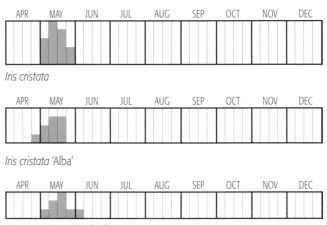

Iris cristata

Iris cristata 'Alba'

Iris cristata 'Eco Bluebird'

Iris fulva

COPPER IRIS

This perennial is native to the central United States, from Ohio, south to Florida, and west to Texas. It grows in shallow water, bottomlands, cypress swamps, sloughs, ditches, and other low wet areas. *Iris fulva* is often found in soils that are inundated with water in the spring but become completely dry by summer.

Iris fulva forms clumps of mostly basal, arching foliage and simple (rarely branched) flowering stems to 1.2 m tall, growing from compact, branched, creeping rhizomes. The linear, sword-shaped, lightly ribbed leaves grow to 1 m long and 2.5 cm wide. The coppery orange flowers have all perianth segments held horizontally or pendulous. The flowers are held usually in pairs and subtended by two spathes. Fruits are green, oblong, ribbed capsules to 8 cm long.

In the garden, *Iris fulva* offers flowers in rarely seen coppery colors. It is well suited to any wet or moist situation, including shallow standing water. Use it in water or bog gardens and containers, along edges of ponds and streams, as well as in perennial borders. Plant *I. fulva* in full sun, although in warmer climates partial shade may be beneficial. Choose a site with fertile, humus-rich, rather heavy, moist or even boggy soil. An ample supply of water is especially critical during the early part of the growing

Iris cristata 'Alba'

season. *Iris fulva* exhausts the soil rather fast. Fertilize it regularly and replant every 3 years or so. Plants are hardy to zone 5, but in colder areas may overwinter better when lightly covered.

There are no botanical varieties of *Iris fulva* recognized among natural populations, although a yellow-flowered variant has been described as form *fulvaurea*. *Iris fulva* hybridizes spontaneously in the wild with a number of species, including *I. brevicaulis*, *I. giganticaerulea*, and *I. savannarum*. In gardens, these species were further intercrossed to produce a range of cultivars known as Louisiana Hybrids, such as 'Black Gamecock', with inky purple flowers, and 'Dorothea K. Williamson', featuring very large plum purple flowers.

In the wild, *Iris fulva* blooms from April to June, depending on the region. Cultivated in Germany, it flowers in June. Plants grown in St. Louis bloomed somewhat earlier, starting in May. At Longwood, two hybrid cultivars were observed, 'Black Gamecock' and 'Dorothea K. Williamson'. The bloom start date of 'Black Gamecock' was highly variable, from the last week of May to the last week of June. In contrast, 'Dorothea K. Williamson' began flowering between the third week of May and the first week of June. The average bloom duration of both cultivars slightly exceeded 2 weeks, but 'Black Gamecock' often flowered through the end of June, whereas 'Dorothea K. Williamson' never bloomed past the second week of June.

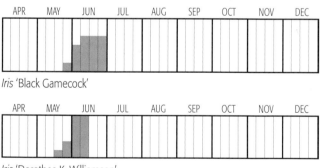

Iris 'Black Gamecock'

Iris 'Dorothea K. Williamson'

Iris pallida

DALMATIAN IRIS, ORRIS ROOT, SWEET IRIS

This perennial is native to southern Europe, in Italy, Slovenia, Croatia, and Bosnia, but it is also commonly naturalized elsewhere in the Mediterranean region. *Iris pallida* has been cultivated as a source of orris root, which has been used in perfumery since antiquity.

Iris pallida forms erect clumps of mostly basal foliage and stiff, stout, and sparsely branched stems to 1 m tall, growing from thick rhizomes. The sword-shaped, gray-green leaves grow to 60 cm long and 3.5 cm wide. The fragrant lavender blue flowers have contrasting yellow beards on the falls, are up to 10 cm wide, and are held two or three together, subtended by a papery spathe.

In the garden, *Iris pallida* is valued for its graceful, sweetly scented flowers. Their delicate colors make it easy to combine this species with other plants. The gray-green foliage remains attractive throughout the growing season, and in warm climates even through the winter. The durable and undemanding *I. pallida* is well suited not only for perennial borders and woodland gardens, but also for difficult sites such as open, dry, steep slopes. Preferably, plant it in full sun, although partial shade is also tolerated. It thrives in any average garden soil that is well drained. Established plants can withstand periodic droughts. *Iris pallida* increases slowly and division is

Iris pallida 'Variegata'

rarely required. Plants are hardy to zone 6, possibly zone 4.

Iris pallida is extremely variable in the wild, with flower colors sometimes ranging from violet to pink and white within the same population. Two subspecies are recognized. The typical subspecies *pallida*, which has pale flowers and whitish bracts, is found throughout the species' range, whereas the distribution of subspecies *cengialti*, distinguished by its more deeply colored flowers and brownish bracts, is limited to northeastern Italy and neighboring Slovenia. In cultivation, two variegated forms have been selected, a white-striped 'Argentea Variegata' and yellow-striped 'Variegata'. Most importantly, *I. pallida* was one of the species used in developing the tall bearded hybrids, the Barbata Elatior Group, the most commonly grown group of *Iris* cultivars.

Iris pallida blooms in late spring or early summer. Cultivated in Poznań, it flowered between 2 and 14 June, but in Germany it bloomed in the end of May. The cultivar 'Variegata', grown in St. Louis, was in bloom for 1 week in the second week of May. At Longwood, 'Variegata' began to flower in mid to late May, but in 1 of 5 years it was in flower as early as the second week of May. It flowered for 3 to 4 weeks, into early June.

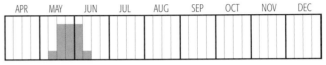

APR	MAY	JUN	JUL	AUG	SEP	OCT	NOV	DEC

Iris pallida 'Variegata'

Iris sanguinea

ORIENTAL IRIS

This plant is native to Asia, from Siberia, south to northeastern China, and east to Japan. *Iris sanguinea* grows in wet meadows, on banks of streams and ponds, at elevations of up to 500 m. It has been cultivated since the late 18th century.

Iris sanguinea forms clumps of erect, reed-like foliage and stiff, short-branched flowering stems to 60 cm tall, growing from thick, creeping rhizomes. The linear, 1-cm-wide leaves equal the length of the

Iris pallida 'Variegata'

flowering stems. The 7-cm-wide, intensely violet blue, sometimes white flowers have erect standards and rounded, beardless falls. They are held in pairs, subtended by spathes that are often suffused pink or red. Fruits are ellipsoid or cylindrical capsules to 5 cm long.

In the garden, *Iris sanguinea* is valued as an adaptable, easy-to-grow prolific bloomer. Use it in a traditional perennial border or in naturalistic settings of a seasonally wet meadow, forest edge, or near a pond or lake. Plant it in full sun or, in warmer areas, partial shade. *Iris sanguinea* thrives in moist situations but is also tolerant of poor, dry soils. Deadheading is not necessary unless self-seeding becomes a nuisance. *Iris sanguinea* spreads slowly and can be left without dividing or transplanting for years. Plants are hardy to zone 4.

Iris sanguinea is closely related to *I. sibirica*, and in the past was considered to be a variety of the latter. A white-flowered form found occasionally among the wild populations of *I. sanguinea* has been described as form *albiflora*, and those with deep violet

Iris sanguinea

Iris sanguinea

flowers are known as form *violacea*. In cultivation, *I. sanguinea* has been extensively hybridized with *I. sibirica* and other species.

In the wild, *Iris sanguinea* blooms during May and June. Cultivated in Germany, it flowers during a similar season. *Iris sanguinea* usually flowers for about 3 weeks, although forms with unbranched stems— and therefore fewer flowers on each stem—may have a shorter bloom period. At Longwood, flowering began as early as the second week of May or as late as the first week of June. It continued, on average, for a little more than 3 weeks, through the end of May or into early June, rarely until the third week of June.

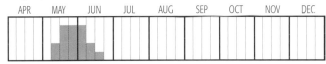

APR	MAY	JUN	JUL	AUG	SEP	OCT	NOV	DEC.

Iris sanguinea

Iris sibirica

SIBERIAN IRIS

This perennial is native to Europe and Asia, from France, south to northern Turkey and the Caucasus, and east to Lake Baikal in Russia. *Iris sibirica* grows in moist meadows, forest clearings and margins, at elevations to 2300 m. It has been cultivated since the 16th century, and this species has been naturalized in parts of North America.

Iris sibirica forms upright clumps of grassy, slightly arching foliage and strong, erect, usually branched, flowering stems to 1.2 m tall, growing from compact, branched rhizomes. The linear, 80-cm-long, slightly glaucous leaves are ribbed and thickened along the midrib and are often tinged pink at the base. The purple-blue (rarely white), 5-cm-wide flowers have erect, elliptic standards and dark-veined, reflexed, oblong and beardless falls. They are held two to three together, subtended by brown, papery spathes. Fruits are dark brown elliptical capsules to 5 cm long.

In the garden, *Iris sibirica* is well suited to a wide variety of situations, but perhaps the most spectacular is large groupings placed near water. Whether grown in shallow water, a bog garden, moist meadow, or perennial border, *I. sibirica* develops into handsome clumps that remain attractive all season. Plant it in sunny locations or, in warmer climates, partial shade. Avoid deep shade, as plants flower less and tend to flop under such conditions. Preferably, choose a cool,

Iris sibirica 'Reprise'

moist site, although *I. sibirica* can thrive in any average garden soil as long as it is well watered. Deadheading is not necessary, and it is best to allow the capsules to develop in order to provide some interest through the winter months. *Iris sibirica* is long-lived and can be left without dividing or transplanting for years, unless flowering decreases. Plants are hardy to zones 3 or 4.

There are no botanical varieties of *Iris sibirica* recognized among the natural populations. In cultivation, however, numerous variants have been selected. Furthermore, hundreds of hybrids between *Iris sibirica*, *I. sanguinea*, and related species have been developed over the years, and these are conventionally often listed under the name of *I. sibirica*. The color choices include violet 'Caesar's Brother' and 'Reprise', rich blue 'Ego', pale blue 'Soft Blue', purple 'Lady Vanessa', rose-pink 'Helen Astor', and white with a touch of yellow in 'White Swirl'. Older cultivars have narrow and drooping falls, whereas the newer ones have broader falls held horizontally.

Iris sibirica 'Caesar's Brother'

Iris sibirica 'Lady Vanessa'

In the wild, *Iris sibirica* blooms in May or June, depending on the region. Cultivated in Poznań, it began flowering between 22 May and 5 June and ended between 9 and 24 June. Bloom duration varied there from 2 weeks in a dry year to 4 weeks in a wet one. At Longwood, four cultivars of *I. sibirica* were observed: 'Caesar's Brother', 'Lady Vanessa', 'Reprise', and 'White Swirl'. They all averaged between 3 and 4 weeks in bloom. Their flowering began in mid to late May, and only rarely was it delayed until the first week of June. It continued usually through early June. Flowers were seldom observed in the third or fourth week of June.

Iris ×*germanica*

BEARDED IRIS, FLAG IRIS, GERMAN IRIS

This plant is thought to be a hybrid that originated in antiquity from crossing *Iris pallida*, from southern Europe, with *I. variegata*, from central and eastern Europe. Where these two species grow together, they hybridize spontaneously. Once moved into gardens, the hybrids further intercrossed and segregated into color variants. By the end of the 16th century, 28 varieties were described. Beginning in the early 19th century, hybridizing of *I.* ×*germanica* with several Near Eastern species, such as *I. cypriana*, *I. trojana*, and *I. mesopotamica*, gave impetus to the breeding of new cultivars, which by the 1830s amounted to hundreds. Crosses with a Balkan *I. pumila* and other lower-growing species resulted in the development of an even wider range of cultivars, with their numbers swelling to tens of thousands and still growing.

Iris ×*germanica* forms upright clumps of sword-shaped, two-ranked foliage and usually well-branched flowering stems to 1.2 m tall, growing from thick, fleshy rhizomes. The glaucous green leaves reach 60 cm in length and 4 cm in width. Flowers are up to 10 cm wide and usually in shades of violet blue, with the erect and arching standards often paler than the yellow-bearded, drooping falls. Flowers are held two or three together subtended by green or purplish, papery spathes. Fruits are capsules.

In the garden, *Iris* ×*germanica* cultivars are regarded as some of the showiest perennials. Few plants offer a spectrum of colors and color combinations that equals that of bearded iris. Furthermore, the adaptability and the ease of growth make *I.* ×*germanica*, whether used as a single plant or massed in bold groupings, suitable

Iris sibirica 'Soft Blue'

| APR | MAY | JUN | JUL | AUG | SEP | OCT | NOV | DEC |

Iris sibirica 'Caesar's Brother'

| APR | MAY | JUN | JUL | AUG | SEP | OCT | NOV | DEC |

Iris sibirica 'Lady Vanessa'

| APR | MAY | JUN | JUL | AUG | SEP | OCT | NOV | DEC |

Iris sibirica 'Reprise'

| APR | MAY | JUN | JUL | AUG | SEP | OCT | NOV | DEC |

Iris sibirica 'White Swirl'

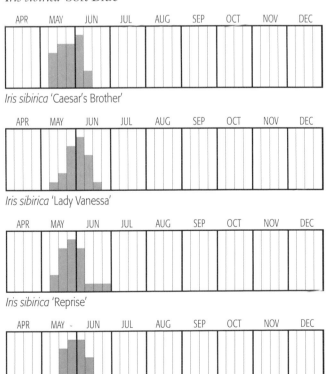

Iris ×germanica 'Immortality'

for a wide range of situations. Plant it in a warm, sunny location, in well-drained, fairly fertile, and moderately moist soil. Avoid sites with heavy, acidic, or waterlogged soil. Deadhead individual flowers to keep the plant's neat appearance. Cut back stems to the ground after flowering is completed. Divide and transplant clumps every 3 years or so, while discarding the oldest parts of the rhizomes. Plants are hardy to zone 5, possibly zone 3.

In less than 200 years of breeding, tens of thousands of cultivars of *Iris ×germanica* have been selected. Although only a fraction of this number is still cultivated today, this leaves a gardener with at least a couple thousand forms to choose from. One can find a bearded iris in nearly every color, some single-colored, others with multicolored flowers in every imaginable color combination. Based on their height, *I. ×germanica* cultivars are divided into tall (Barbata Elatior Group), including those exceeding 70 cm; intermediate (Barbata Media Group), between 40 and 70 cm; and dwarf (Barbata Nana Group), comprised of varieties shorter than 40

Iris ×germanica 'Harvest of Memories'

cm. These main classes are further subdivided into smaller categories. Remontant cultivars, such as yellow 'Harvest of Memories', white 'Immortality', and creamy yellow 'La Perle', can be found in each of these height categories.

Iris ×*germanica* blooms in late spring to early summer. Generally, the lower-growing cultivars flower earlier than the taller ones. In Poland, the dwarf selections bloom in early May, the intermediate ones in late May, and the tall forms are in flower at the end of May and in early June. Cultivars known as remontant tend to repeat bloom, provided the conditions are conducive to vigorous growth later in the season. At Longwood, three cultivars were observed: 'Harvest of Memories', 'Immortality', and 'La Perle'. The dwarf 'La Perle' began flowering in mid to late April, whereas the taller 'Harvest of Memories' and 'Immortality' started about a month later. The spring bloom of all three selections averaged a little more than 3 weeks, but they showed noteworthy differences in their ability to rebloom. 'Immortality' never repeated flowering. 'La Perle' rebloomed

briefly twice in 7 years, one time in late May for a period of 2 weeks and another in late October for 1 week. In contrast, 'Harvest of Memories' rebloomed in 3 of 7 years, for a period of 2 to 9 weeks, between late September and late November.

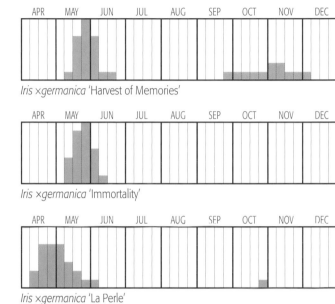

Iris ×*germanica* 'Harvest of Memories'

Iris ×*germanica* 'Immortality'

Iris ×*germanica* 'La Perle'

Iris ×*germanica* 'La Perle'

Kalimeris

KALIMERIS

The name *Kalimeris* is derived from the Greek *kalos*, beautiful, and *meris*, a portion or part, in reference to the attractive flowers.

Kalimeris pinnatifida

JAPANESE-ASTER, ORPHANAGE PLANT

This plant is native to Japan's Honshu Island, where it grows in the hills and low mountains.

Kalimeris pinnatifida forms upright, bushy, oval clumps of strongly erect, openly branched stems to 1 m (rarely 1.5 m) tall, growing from creeping rhizomes. The leaves on the main stems are ovate, deeply pinnately lobed, and reach 8 cm in length, whereas those on side branches are linear, entire, and shorter. The 3-cm-wide flower heads have pale pink or bluish ray florets and yellow disc florets. They are held in loose corymbs. Fruits are 2.5-cm-long achenes tipped with short bristles.

In the garden, *Kalimeris pinnatifida* is well suited for planting in a perennial border, meadow, or an open woodland. Although only modestly colored itself, thanks to the airy fine texture, *K. pinnatifida* provides an excellent foil for other perennials. It is very adaptable and can be grown in a wide range of conditions. It thrives in full sun, but some afternoon shade may be beneficial in warmer climates. Plant it in any average garden soil that is well drained, although it can tolerate damp situations. Plants are hardy to zones 4 or 5.

There are no botanical varieties of *Kalimeris pinnatifida* recognized among the natural populations. In cultivation, the typical form of the species is largely replaced by the cultivar 'Hortensis', which has white, semi-double flowers with pale yellow centers.

In the wild, *Kalimeris pinnatifida* blooms from July to October. Cultivated in St. Louis, the cultivar 'Hortensis' flowered beginning in late May, fin-

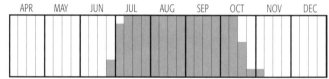

Kalimeris pinnatifida 'Hortensis'

Kalimeris pinnatifida 'Hortensis'

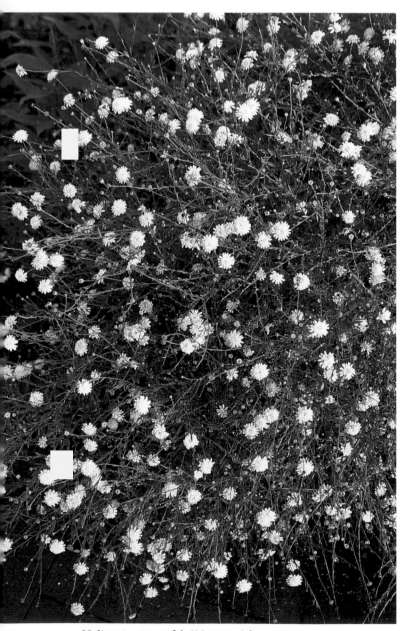

Kalimeris pinnatifida 'Hortensis'

ishing between late August and mid-October. At Longwood, 'Hortensis' started blooming in the first week of July, rarely a week earlier or later. Flowering continued, on average, for 17 weeks, usually into mid-October. Once in 7 years, plants were still in bloom in the first week of November.

Kalimeris yomena
KALIMERIS

This perennial is native to Japan and South Korea, where it grows in lowland areas and open fields.

Kalimeris yomena forms clumps of erect stems to 1 m tall, growing from creeping rhizomes. The ovate to oblong, serrate leaves grow to 7 cm long. The lowermost leaves wither at the time of flowering. The 4-cm-wide flower heads have 10 to 20 lavender blue ray florets and yellow disc florets. They are borne in loose, few-flowered corymbs. Fruits are 3-mm-long, bristly achenes.

In the garden, *Kalimeris yomena* is used primarily in perennial borders, either as individual plants or in large groups. It is valued for its handsome, glossy, fine-textured foliage and delicate, late-blooming flowers. It can be easily grown in a variety of conditions, from full sun to partial shade. Plant it in any average garden soil that drains well. Plants are hardy to zones 5 or 6.

There are no botanical varieties of *Kalimeris yomena* recognized currently, but plants with deeply incised leaves, found on Honshu, were known in the past as variety *dentata*. In cultivation, several variegated forms have been selected and named, among them 'Aurea', 'Fuji Snow', 'Geisha', and 'Shogun'.

In the wild, *Kalimeris yomena* blooms from July to October. Cultivated in the United Kingdom, it flowers during a similar season. The cultivar 'Aurea', grown in St. Louis, began blooming between late July and the second week of September and continued until mid-October. At Longwood, 'Aurea' flowered a couple of weeks later, starting in mid to late September and finishing in mid-October. Occasionally, it bloomed through the first week of November. *Kalimeris yomena* 'Aurea' averaged 5 weeks in bloom.

APR	MAY	JUN	JUL	AUG	SEP	OCT	NOV	DEC

Kalimeris yomena 'Aurea'

Knautia
KNAUTIA

The name *Knautia* commemorates Christian Knaut (1654–1716), a German botanist.

Knautia arvensis
BLUE BUTTONS, FIELD-SCABIOUS

This perennial is native to Europe and southwestern Asia, from Portugal, north to Norway, and east to the Caucasus, Iran, and Pakistan. *Knautia arvensis* has also naturalized in parts of North America. It grows commonly in calcareous soils, in open woods, meadows, pastures, old fields, and waste ground.

Knautia arvensis

Knautia arvensis

eastern and central Europe. In addition, *K. arvensis* easily hybridizes with other species, such as *K. arvernensis* and *K. basaltica*. In cultivation, plants can vary in their flower color from bluish violet and lilac, to pink, or rarely white, but only a handful of selections have been named, including 'Lawley's White' and 'Rachael'.

Knautia arvensis blooms for a long time from early summer onward. Plants grown at Longwood usually began to flower in late May or early June, rarely as early as in the third week of May or as late as in the third week of June. When flowering declined in July, plants were often cut back. They typically rebloomed within 2 to 8 weeks and continued flowering through the end of October. Plants that rebloomed later, in the end of September, kept flowering until the hard frost, sometime into the first week of December. Plants that were cut back in August or later did not flower again. On average, *Knautia arvensis* was in bloom for 19 weeks.

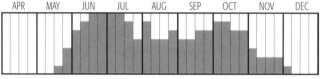

Knautia arvensis

Knautia arvensis forms clumps of basal foliage and lax, hirsute stems to 1 m (rarely 1.5 m) tall, growing from a deep, woody rootstock. The dull green, hispid leaves are entire or pinnately cut into 12 to 16 lobes. The pale purple flowers are borne in 4-cm-wide, globose heads, subtended by leafy, involucral bracts. Fruits are achenes.

Knautia arvensis is best suited for informal areas, such as a meadow or a wildflower or cottage-style garden. It is valued for its soft-textured foliage and exceptionally long bloom season. Plant it in full sun, preferably in sandy soil that is well drained. It tends to be short-lived or, in colder climates, biennial. Plants are hardy to zones 4 or 5.

Knautia arvensis is a highly variable species. A number of its formerly recognized subspecies are currently classified as separate species, but two are still considered to belong to *K. arvensis*. Subspecies *pannonica* has bluish lilac flowers and grayish subtomentose, deeply multipinnate leaves, whereas subspecies *rosea* has lilac-pink flowers and wide, undivided greenish leaves. They are both found in

Knautia macedonica

MACEDONIAN-SCABIOUS

This plant is native to the Balkans in southern Europe, from Albania, south to Greece, and east to Romania. *Knautia macedonica* grows in open woods and scrub.

Knautia macedonica forms loose, erect clumps of basal foliage and slender, curving, branched stems to 80 cm tall, growing from a tough, deep rootstock. The basal leaves are lyrate, whereas the cauline leaves are entire to pinnately lobed. The deep purple or crimson flowers are borne in dense, domed, 5-cm-wide heads. Fruits are achenes.

In the garden, *Knautia macedonica* is valued for abundant and long-lasting flowers of a rather uncommon intense purple or crimson color. It is best suited for informal grouping in perennial borders, cottage-style gardens, or meadows. Thanks to its fine texture and delicate flowers, *K. macedonica* combines well with bold perennials, roses, or other shrubs that have a framework of strong stems. Plant it in a warm and sunny spot, in any well-drained, or even dry

Knautia macedonica

soil. In warmer climates, where *K. macedonica* tends to grow taller, trim plants in spring to prevent flopping later. Deadhead or cut back after the first flush of flowers to encourage a rebloom. *Knautia macedonica* is rather short-lived, sometimes biennial, but it self-seeds easily and young seedlings can be saved as replacements. Plants are hardy to zone 6, possibly zone 4.

There are no botanical varieties of *Knautia macedonica* recognized among natural populations. In cultivation, plants vary in their flower color from the typical dark purple or crimson to lilac and pink. Named seed-propagated cultivars include 'Melton Pastels', which offers a range of colors from pink to crimson red, and 'Mars Midget', a dwarf with ruby red flowers.

Knautia macedonica flowers for a long time, from early summer to fall. Cultivated in Germany, it blooms from July until September. Plants grown in St. Louis began flowering between late May and the first week of June and bloomed through the end of September or October. At Longwood, flowering usually started in early June. Only once in 7 years, plants were in flower in late May. The first burst of

Knautia macedonica

flowers subsided by mid to late July, at which point plants were often cut back. Rebloom occurred within 2 to 7 weeks and continued through the end of October or into November. One year, *K. macedonica* was still in bloom in early December. On average, it flowered for 22 weeks.

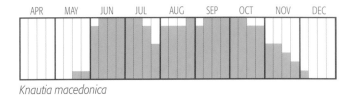

Knautia macedonica

Kniphofia

TORCHLILY

The name *Kniphofia* commemorates Johann Hieronymus Kniphof (1704–1763), a German botanist.

Kniphofia Hybrids

POKER PLANT, RED-HOT-POKER, TORCHLILY, TRITOMA

Kniphofia hybrids were developed, beginning in the mid-19th century, by crossing *K. uvaria* with several other African species, including *K. bruceae*, *K. galpinii*, *K. macowanii*, *K. nelsonii*, and *K. pauciflora*. In their native habitat, torchlilies are often found growing in moist or marshy ground, along streams, and in higher elevation grasslands. The hybrids first gained wide recognition when Max Leichtlin, a German nurseryman at Baden Baden, introduced several bold and brightly colored hybrids in the late 19th century.

Kniphofia hybrids form typically erect, tight, tufted clumps of arching, grassy leaves and stout flowering scapes to 1.2 m tall, growing from short rhizomes with thick, fleshy roots. The gray-green,

Kniphofia 'Border Ballet'

Kniphofia 'Alcazar'

linear, strongly keeled leaves reach 1 m in length. The drooping, tubular flowers range in color from pale creamy yellow to dark scarlet red. They are borne in dense, tapering, terminal racemes to 30 cm long. Fruits are spherical capsules.

Kniphofia hybrids are used primarily in traditional perennial borders, but they are well suited to a variety of settings from naturalistic, woodland or water edges to brightly colored, exotic, tropical-style combinations to minimalist, contemporary gardens. Their flowers are very decorative and usually two-toned, with unopened flowers being darker than the fully open ones. Plant *Kniphofia* hybrids in warm, sunny locations. Choose a spot with preferably humus-rich, moist, fertile, and well-drained soil. Avoid sites where soil is excessively dry in summer, or becomes waterlogged in winter. To maintain the neat appearance and to extend bloom season, cut back individual scapes when they finish flowering. Clean up and trim any damaged old leaves in the spring. *Kniphofia* hybrids are long-lived, unless subject to winter injury. They are best left undisturbed, without dividing or transplanting, for years. Some cultivars may self-seed under favorable conditions.

Plants are hardy to zone 5; in colder climates, protect roots with a thick layer of mulch, while leaving the tips of leaves uncovered.

Since the first *Kniphofia* hybrids were introduced in the 19th century, hundreds of selections have been named. Their heights vary from 60 cm to 1.5 m. Most feature bright colors, such as yellow 'Star of Baden Baden' and 'Yellow Hammer', orange-red 'Alcazar' and 'Fyrverkeri', and scarlet-red 'Lord Roberts' and 'Prince Igor'. However, other cultivars have softer, pastel-colored flowers, including greenish ivory 'Green Jade' and 'Ice Queen', creamy 'Jenny Bloom' and 'Little Maid', pale lemon 'Candlelight', and primrose yellow 'Primrose Beauty'. The cultivar 'Innocence' changes from coppery orange to pale yellow and cream. Furthermore, seed-propagated cultivars, such as 'Border Ballet', offer a mix of colors from red and pink to yellow and cream.

Kniphofia hybrids have a wide range of flowering times. In Poland, bloom season varies from June to October, depending on the cultivar. In the United Kingdom, some of the cultivars start flowering in April, whereas others may not bloom before July.

Kniphofia 'Primrose Beauty'

Younger plants tend to bloom later than older ones. Some cultivars may also rebloom sporadically later in the season. Individual flowers of *Kniphofia* open in succession, over a fairly long time, from the bottom of the racemes to the top. The cultivar 'Alcazar' began flowering in Moscow around 15 July and ended around 7 September. 'Alcazar' grown at Longwood started to bloom several weeks earlier, between the first week of June and the first week of July and continued through mid-August, rarely mid-September. Twice in 7 years, it rebloomed between late August and early October. 'Alcazar' at Longwood averaged a little more than 11 weeks in bloom. In comparison, 'Alcazar' in Moscow flowered for 8 weeks, on average. Two other cultivars observed at Longwood were 'Border Ballet' and 'Primrose Beauty'. They showed very distinct flowering patterns. While 'Border Ballet' began flowering in mid to late May, 'Primrose Beauty' did not come into bloom before late June or early July, by which time flowering of the first cultivar was already finished. 'Border Ballet' never rebloomed, whereas 'Primrose Beauty' repeated flowering in 3 of 4 years. On average, 'Border Ballet' was in bloom for 5 weeks, and 'Primrose Beauty' flowered for nearly 9 weeks.

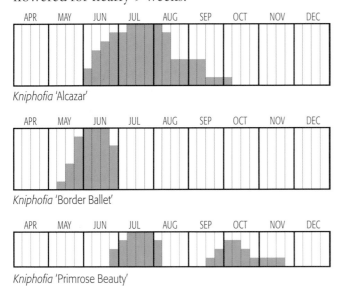

Kniphofia 'Alcazar'

Kniphofia 'Border Ballet'

Kniphofia 'Primrose Beauty'

Lamium

DEADNETTLE

The name *Lamium* was used by ancient Romans and is derived from the Greek *lamia*, a kind of flatfish, in reference to the flowers resembling the throat of that fish.

Lamium album

ARCHANGEL, SNOWFLAKE, WHITE DEADNETTLE

This perennial is native to Europe and Asia, from Spain, north to Norway, east across Russia, Kazakhstan, Mongolia, and China to Japan, and south to India. *Lamium album* grows usually in moist soils, in forest clearings and margins, thickets, along streams, and on grassy hillsides, at elevations to 2400 m. It has naturalized in parts of northeastern North America.

Lamium album forms clumps of decumbent, usually unbranched, leafy stems to 60 cm tall, growing from spreading rhizomes. The petiolate, ovate to ovate-lanceolate, softly hairy leaves have a cordate base, serrated or crenate margins, and reach 7 cm in length. The two-lipped, 2.5-cm-long, white or creamy flowers are held up to 16 in false whorls in the axils of upper leaves. Fruits are dark gray nutlets 3 mm long.

In the garden, *Lamium album* is valued as an easy-to-grow, low-maintenance ground cover. It is well suited for planting in any informal or naturalistic setting, where plants can spread freely without impeding other plants. In more confined and formal spaces, *L. album* can be allowed to weave through and in between other perennials in the front of a border. Preferably plant it in partial shade, although plants can tolerate full shade. Avoid planting in full sun, except in cooler climates and on moist sites. *Lamium album* thrives in a wide range of soils, but grows best in those that are moist and fertile. Trim back after the first flush of bloom to encourage new growth and possible repeat flowering. Plants are hardy to zones 3 or 4.

Despite its immense distribution range stretching across two continents, only a few regional variants of *Lamium album* have been described. Some of them, such as variety *barbatum* from eastern Asia, which has lower floral leaves that are petiolate, not subsessile like the typical form, are also treated as a separate species. In cultivation, a handful of variegated selections are grown, including 'Goldflake', 'Friday', and 'Pale Peril'.

In the wild, *Lamium album* blooms from April to September, depending on the region. Cultivated in Poznań, it flowered starting between 10 and 15 May and ending between 10 to 19 June. Similarly, at Longwood, the cultivar 'Pale Peril' began flowering in the second or third week of May and continued through the end of May or June. One year, it re-bloomed in July. During 3 years at Longwood, 'Pale Peril' averaged 7 weeks in bloom.

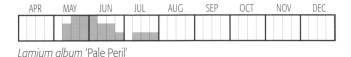

APR	MAY	JUN	JUL	AUG	SEP	OCT	NOV	DEC

Lamium album 'Pale Peril'

Lamium maculatum

SPOTTED DEADNETTLE, SPOTTED HENBIT

This plant is native to Europe, northern Africa, and Asia, from Portugal to north-central Russia and east to Gansu and Xinjiang Provinces in northwestern China. It grows in moist woodlands, in valleys, and on hills, at elevations up to 2700 m. *Lamium maculatum* has also naturalized in parts of North America.

Lamium maculatum forms spreading clumps of branched, sparsely white-pubescent stems to 50 cm tall, growing from stoloniferous rhizomes. The ovate, cordate, and petiolate leaves reach 9 cm in length, have crenate or dentate margins, and are often white-striped, blotched, or mottled. The two-lipped, 3-cm-long, deep purplish pink flowers are borne four to eight together in false whorls in the upper leaf axils. Fruits are brown nutlets.

In the garden, *Lamium maculatum* can be used as an effective ground cover (especially under trees and shrubs), for edging a border, in containers, and for filling tight corners. Although the wild type may be too vigorous and coarse for most situations, garden selections are more refined and less invasive. This species is valued for its exceptionally long flowering season. In warmer areas, its foliage may be retained through the winter. Preferably plant it in partial shade. Dense shade is tolerated, provided the site is not damp, but plants may be somewhat lanky and flower less. In colder climates, *L. maculatum* can be grown in full sun, as long as the soil is consistently moist. It thrives in any average garden soil that is moist and well drained. Plants

Lamium maculatum 'Beedham's White'

Lamium maculatum 'Check In'

Lamium maculatum 'Chequers'

Lamium maculatum 'White Nancy'

grown in dry locations tend to scorch in hot weather and develop bare patches. If foliage declines in summer heat, cut plants back to encourage new, fresh growth. *Lamium maculatum* can spread by self-seeding, underground stolons, or rooting aboveground stems, but it can be kept in check without much difficulty. Plants are hardy to zones 3 or 4.

In the wild, *Lamium maculatum* is a highly variable species, and several forms and varieties have been described in the past. In cultivation, more than 20 different variants have been selected and named. Most of them have foliage showing strong white, striped, or blotched patterns, and their flowers range from white in 'White Nancy' and pink in 'Check In' to deep rose-pink in 'Chequers' or purple in 'Immaculate'. Several cultivars, such as 'Beedham's White', 'Cannon's Gold', and 'Dellam', feature yellow variegated foliage.

Lamium maculatum often blooms in spring and summer, often into the fall. Plants grown in Germany and Poland flower from May to July. A similar bloom season has been observed in Chicago and St. Louis. At Longwood, bloom times for three cultivars were recorded. 'Chequers' was earliest to flower, usually starting in late April or the first week of May, but one year it was in bloom in the first week of April. 'Chequers' also had the longest bloom season, flowering continuously for 33 weeks, through the end of November or even into early December. The other cultivars, 'Beedham's White' and 'White Nancy', began blooming about a month after 'Chequers' and continued, on average, for only 7 and 10 weeks, respectively.

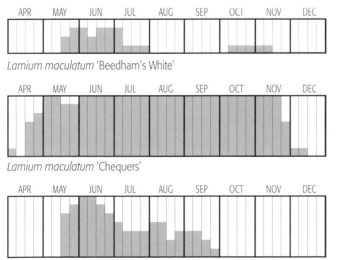

Lamium maculatum 'Beedham's White'

Lamium maculatum 'Chequers'

Lamium maculatum 'White Nancy'

Lathyrus

PEAVINE, VETCHLING, WILD PEA

The name *Lathyrus* was used by ancient Greeks and was derived from *la*, very, and *thoures*, stimulant, in reference to the irritating properties of the seeds.

Lathyrus latifolius

EVERLASTING SWEET PEA, HARDY SWEET PEA, LARGE-LEAVED LATHYRUS, PERENNIAL SWEET PEA

This plant is native to Europe, from Portugal, north to Poland, and east to southern Russia, and is naturalized further north. *Lathyrus latifolius* has been cultivated since at least the 16th century. Once

Lathyrus latifolius

Lathyrus latifolius

introduced into North America, it spread widely across the United States and Canada.

Lathyrus latifolius forms sprawling vines with broadly winged stems to 3 m long, prostrate or climbing by means of tendrils on the leaves, growing from a deep rootstock. The even-pinnate leaves have one pair of lanceolate or elliptic leaflets to 15 cm long, leaf-like stipules, and terminate in a branched tendril. The unscented, 3-cm-long, purple-pink flowers are held three to 12 in a raceme. Fruits are brown, glabrous legumes to 12 cm long.

In the garden, *Lathyrus latifolius* is used as a climber trained on walls, trellises, and fences, allowed to ramble over declining trees, hedges, or bare spots left by summer-dormant perennials. It can sprawl on the ground and cover difficult slopes. *Lathyrus latifolius* should be sited carefully, because its vigorous growth can smother other plants around it. The flowers, although not scented like those of the annual pea, are noted for being long-lasting. Plant *L. latifolius* in full sun, in any average garden soil that is well drained. This species is long-lived and does poorly after transplanting. *Lathyrus latifolius* may self-seed but rarely to the point of being a nuisance in the garden. Plants are hardy to zones 4 or 5.

Lathyrus latifolius varies markedly in the shape of leaflets, and flower colors can range from deep rose to pink and white. In cultivation, a number of color variants have been selected and named, including white 'Albus' and 'Weisse Perle', white flushed pink 'Blushing Bride', pink 'Rosa Perle', and purple-red 'Rote Perle'.

Lathyrus latifolius blooms in summer. Cultivated in Germany and the United Kingdom, it flowers from June to August. Similarly, plants grown in Poznań began flowering between 14 June and 2 July and ended between 13 August and 2 September. In Moscow, *L. latifolius* flowered even longer, from around 23 June until 25 September, on average. At Longwood, bloom start date varied by 4 weeks, between the second week of June and the second week of July. Flowering continued through mid or late September, averaging nearly 14 weeks in bloom in a season. Similar bloom duration was observed in Moscow.

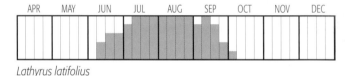

Lathyrus latifolius

Lavandula

LAVENDER

The name *Lavandula* is derived from the Latin *lavare*, to wash, in reference to the oil of lavender being used in a fragrant wash, known as lavender water.

Lavandula angustifolia

COMMON LAVENDER, ENGLISH LAVENDER, TRUE LAVENDER

This perennial is native to the Mediterranean region, but it has naturalized in other parts of Europe and northern Africa. *Lavandula angustifolia* grows usually in calcareous soils, on rocky slopes, montane scrub, and other open and dry areas with shallow soils and sparse vegetation, at elevations from 250 to 2000 m. It has been cultivated since antiquity.

Lavandula angustifolia forms a compact, rounded, evergreen shrub to 1 m tall and is grown as a perennial in northern climates. The gray-green, oblong to linear, entire leaves reach 6 cm in length. The young leaves are white-tomentose, strongly revolute, and often clustered in older leaf axils. The lavender or purple, 1-cm-long flowers are borne three to seven together in whorls forming interrupted, terminal spikes to 12 cm in length. Fruits are nutlets.

Lavandula angustifolia

In the garden, *Lavandula angustifolia* is valued as the most cold hardy and adaptable of the lavender species. Besides the traditional use in herb and kitchen gardens, *L. angustifolia* can be employed in a wide variety of situations, from edging beds and making low, informal hedges, to perennial borders. Its highly aromatic foliage remains evergreen in warmer climates, and both leaves and flowers can be dried for potpourri. Plant *L. angustifolia* in full sun. It grows best in light, alkaline, and rather dry soil of low fertility. Avoid damp sites with heavy soils that drain poorly. Deadhead after the first flush of flowers to encourage a rebloom, but do not prune past August because it will delay acclimation of the plants before winter. Trim in the spring, after the new leaves emerge, to just above the bases of the previous year's growth. *Lavandula angustifolia* is long lived and is best left undisturbed indefinitely. Under ideal conditions, it may self-seed. Plants are hardy to zones 5 or 6.

Lavandula angustifolia is highly variable, even within the same natural population. There are two subspecies recognized among plants in the wild. The typical subspecies *angustifolia*, from southern France and Italy, has calyces covered with wooly indumentum of long hairs, whereas subspecies *pyrenaica*, native to the Pyrenees and northeastern Spain, has calyces covered with felt-like indumentum of short hairs. In addition, variants with exceptionally long, interrupted spikes, found in the Dauphiné region of eastern France, are known as variety *delphinensis*. Furthermore, a natural hybrid between *L. angustifolia* and *L. latifolia*, named *L. ×intermedia*, occurs in France, Italy, and Spain and is also widely grown, supplying most of the world's lavender oil production. In cultivation, many forms have been selected. There are more than 150 named cultivars of *L. angustifolia*, with about half as many cultivars of *L. ×intermedia*. These selections vary in flower color from white 'Alba', pink 'Rosea', and lavender blue 'Munstead' and 'Provence', to deep violet blue 'Grosso', 'Hidcote', and 'Royal Velvet'. Some appear silvery gray due to particularly abundant indumentum on

Lavandula ×intermedia 'Provence'

Lavandula ×intermedia 'Provence'

calyces. Others have calyces showing purple color several weeks before the flowers open.

In the wild, *Lavandula angustifolia* blooms during June or July, depending on elevation, with subspecies *pyrenaica* flowering about 2 weeks earlier than subspecies *angustifolia*. Cultivated in St. Louis, it bloomed between the first week of June and the first week of July. Plants grown in Germany occasionally rebloom in late summer. At Longwood, bloom start date of the cultivar 'Munstead' varied by 5 weeks, between the third week of May and the last week of June. The first flush of bloom ended usually in late July. One year, though, plants flowered continuously from late May until the first week of November. In other years, plants rebloomed in August and September. On average, 'Munstead' was in flower for a little more than 14 weeks. The hybrid cultivar 'Grosso' began flowering in June, somewhat later than 'Munstead'. It usually bloomed through the end of July but occasionally into August or even September. Unlike 'Munstead', 'Grosso' never rebloomed and its bloom season averaged less than 10 weeks.

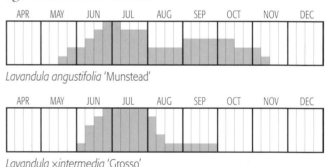

| APR | MAY | JUN | JUL | AUG | SEP | OCT | NOV | DEC |

Lavandula angustifolia 'Munstead'

| APR | MAY | JUN | JUL | AUG | SEP | OCT | NOV | DEC |

Lavandula ×intermedia 'Grosso'

Leucanthemum

SHASTA DAISY

The name *Leucanthemum* is derived from the Greek *leukos*, white, and *anthemon*, flower.

Leucanthemum ×superbum

SHASTA DAISY

This hybrid was developed at the turn of the 20th century by Luther Burbank, an American breeder, who crossed the Portuguese species *Leucanthemum lacustre* with *L. maximum* from the Pyrenees. The hybrid was named Shasta daisy after Mount Shasta, near Burbank's nursery in California.

Leucanthemum ×superbum forms upright to round clumps of stiff, glabrous stems to 1 m tall, growing from stoloniferous rhizomes. The oblanceolate to lanceolate, coarsely serrate leaves can reach 30 cm in length. The lower leaves are petiolate, whereas the upper ones are sessile. The 7-cm-wide flower heads, comprised of white ray florets and yellow disc florets, are borne singly atop long stems. Fruits are achenes.

In the garden, *Leucanthemum* ×*superbum* is well suited for planting as small groups in perennial borders or for naturalizing in meadows. It is valued for its prolific flowering, adaptability, and handsome deep green foliage that, in warmer climates, may hold well through the winter. Plant it in full sun or partial shade. A lightly shaded situation is preferred in areas with hot summers, particularly for double-flowered varieties. Stay clear of deep shade, where plants have lanky growth and flower less. *Leucanthemum* ×*superbum* thrives in fertile, moist, but well-drained soil. Avoid spots where soil stays waterlogged during winter, or where plants may be subject to prolonged droughts. Deadhead to maintain a neat appearance and to encourage rebloom. Cut back to basal foliage when all flowering is completed. Taller varieties may require staking to prevent flopping, but pinching stems in spring will keep them shorter and sturdier. *Leucanthemum* ×*superbum* is short-lived, especially in colder climates. Divide the plants regularly every 2 or 3 years to maintain their vigor or, especially when naturalized, allow them to regenerate through self-seeding. Plants are hardy to zones 4 or 5.

Leucanthemum ×*superbum* is represented in gardens by more than 50 cultivars. Among them are single-flowered forms, such as 'Becky' and 'Nordlicht'; anemone-centered, including 'Christine Hagemann' and 'Wirral Supreme'; double-flowered, 'Esther Read' and 'Fiona Coghill'; and double frilly types, such as 'Aglaia', which have unusually narrow and numerous ray florets. The tall varieties, such as 'Everest', can grow to 1.2 m tall, but the low-growing cultivars 'Little Miss Muffet' and 'Silberprinzesschen' reach only 30 to 45 cm in height. While the ray florets of most cultivars are white or creamy, those of 'Sonnenschein' are primrose yellow.

Leucanthemum ×*superbum* flowers during early summer and may rebloom in early fall. Bloom season and duration vary with the region, growing conditions, cultivar, and the age of the plant, with younger plants flowering longer. Diligent deadheading, especially of young plants, promotes repeat flowering and may extend bloom until the first frost. In St. Louis,

the cultivar 'Becky' flowered from the second or third week of June until the end of August or mid-September. At Longwood, 'Becky' started to bloom a little later, in late June or early July. Its flowering continued through the end of July and into mid-August, rarely until early September. Only once in 6 years, 'Becky' rebloomed weakly in September. On average, 'Becky' was in flower for 8 weeks.

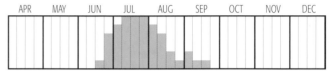

Leucanthemum ×*superbum* 'Becky'

Leucanthemum ×*superbum* 'Becky'

Liatris

BLAZING STAR, GAYFEATHER, SNAKEROOT
The name *Liatris* is of unknown derivation.

Liatris microcephala

SMALL-HEADED BLAZING STAR, SMALLHEAD GAYFEATHER
This perennial is native to the southern Appalachian Mountains in the United States, from Kentucky, west to North Carolina, and south to Alabama and Georgia. *Liatris microcephala* grows on rocky outcrops and slopes, along streams, and in open woodlands and oak barrens, at elevations from 200 to 600 m.

Liatris microcephala forms clumps of grass-like foliage and multiple stems to 80 cm tall, growing from globose corms with fibrous roots. The linear to lanceolate, entire leaves reach 20 cm in length, but become gradually reduced in size on the upper portion of the stems. The tiny, fluffy flower heads, comprised of four to six rose-purple disc florets, are arranged in loose to dense spike-like arrays atop leafy stems. Fruits are 3-mm-long achenes.

In the garden, *Liatris microcephala* should be reserved for open spots where it will not be crowded by more vigorous plants. Plant in a warm, sunny location, in rather dry and low-fertility soil that drains well. This species is well adapted to summer heat and drought. Avoid sites that stay damp in winter. Once plants begin flowering, the basal foliage starts to senesce. *Liatris microcephala* is hardy to zones 5 or 6, but in colder areas a light cover of mulch or compost is beneficial.

In the wild, *Liatris microcephala* blooms between July and October. Curiously, flowering begins first in the uppermost flower heads and then progresses down the stems. Cultivated at Longwood, *L. microcephala* started blooming in late July and early August. Rarely, plants flowered as early as the third week of July or were delayed until the third week of August. They usually bloomed through the end of September, but one year, flowering continued until the first week of November. On average, *L. microcephala* was in flower for 10 weeks.

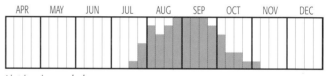

APR	MAY	JUN	JUL	AUG	SEP	OCT	NOV	DEC

Liatris microcephala

Liatris spicata

BUTTON SNAKEROOT, DENSE BLAZING STAR,
KANSAS GAYFEATHER, SPIKE GAYFEATHER
This plant is native to eastern North America, from Ontario, east to Maine, and south to Louisiana and Florida. It has also naturalized in other parts of North America. *Liatris spicata* grows in damp meadows, marshes, bogs, tamarack swamps, moist woods and other wet sites, at elevations to 1700 m. It has been cultivated since the 18th century.

Liatris spicata forms upright clumps of tufted foliage and stiffly erect, unbranched, leafy stems to 1 m (rarely 1.8 m) tall, growing from globose or elongate corms. The linear to oblanceolate leaves reach 35 cm in length, but become progressively smaller up the stem. The sessile flower heads, comprised of five to 14 rose-purple disc florets, are borne in dense spike-like arrays to 30 cm long. Fruits are 5-mm-long achenes.

In the garden, *Liatris spicata* can be planted in small clusters or large groupings in perennial borders, along edges of ponds and streams, or in wildflower meadows. It is valued for its lush tufts of grassy foliage and contrasting rigid, vertical flowering spikes, as

Liatris microcephala

well as for providing excellent cut flowers. Plant *L. spicata* in a sunny location. In warmer climates, it may benefit from light afternoon shade. It thrives in any average garden soil, but also tolerates wet conditions better than other blazing stars. The lower-growing varieties require no staking, but the taller ones, especially when grown in a shaded location, may need staking. Once flowering is completed, cut back stems to the basal leaves. Otherwise, allow the fluffy, brown seed heads to develop and extend the season of interest. Divide clumps every 4 or 5 years, if plant vigor declines. Plants are hardy to zones 3 or 4.

There are two botanical varieties of *Liatris spicata* recognized among the natural populations. The typical variety *spicata* is widespread in inland areas and in the mountains, whereas variety *resinosa* is found only in low-lying coastal areas. It differs in having narrower leaves that become abruptly reduced in size up the stem. Furthermore, intermediate forms are known from Alabama and Tennessee. In both varieties, marked dimorphism occurs, with some plants having larger flower heads than is typical. In cultivation, several color variants, from white 'Floristan Weiss' to deep purple 'Picador', were selected. While taller varieties are preferred for cut flowers, the dwarf

Liatris spicata 'Kobold'

Liatris spicata

ones, such as the popular 'Kobold', are better suited as garden plants.

In the wild, *Liatris spicata* blooms from July to November, depending on the region. Cultivated in Poznań, it flowered beginning between 6 and 19 July and ending between 10 and 25 August. Similarly, plants grown in Moscow bloomed from around 18 July until 28 August. At Longwood, *L. spicata* started to flower in mid-July and continued, on average, for 4 weeks, until early August. In comparison, plants in Moscow average about 6 weeks in bloom. The cultivar 'Kobold' is reputed to flower earlier than the species and occasionally rebloom in late summer. At Longwood, 'Kobold' began to flower about 3 weeks before the species. Its average bloom duration exceeded that of the species by more than 1 week, but no rebloom was observed.

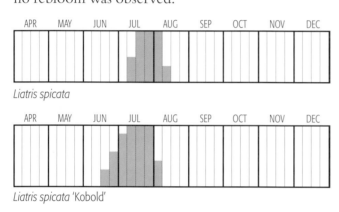

APR	MAY	JUN	JUL	AUG	SEP	OCT	NOV	DEC

Liatris spicata

APR	MAY	JUN	JUL	AUG	SEP	OCT	NOV	DEC

Liatris spicata 'Kobold'

Lilium

LILY

The name *Lilium* is derived from the Greek, *leiron*, ancient name of one of the lily species.

Lilium canadense

CANADA LILY, MEADOW LILY, WILD YELLOW LILY

This perennial is native to eastern North America, from Nova Scotia, west to Ontario, and south to Alabama and Georgia. *Lilium canadense* grows in woodland edges, moist meadows, bogs, swamps, along streams, and on roadsides, at elevations to 1400 m. It has been cultivated since the 16th century.

Lilium canadense forms erect, stout, leafy stems to 1.8 m tall, growing from a fleshy, rhizomatous rootstock with yellowish, few-scaled bulbs. The elliptic or lanceolate leaves reach 17 cm in length and are arranged in whorls, up to 12 leaves per whorl. The trumpet-shaped, nodding, butter yellow, dark-spotted

Lilium canadense

flowers are held on long, arched pedicles in umbellate inflorescences. Fruits are capsules to 5 cm long.

In the garden, *Lilium canadense* is valued for its simple, yet elegant, beauty. It is well suited for planting in perennial borders, near ponds and streams, and for naturalizing in moist meadows. Preferably, plant it in full sun. It grows best in well-aerated and well-drained soil that stays uniformly moist throughout the growing season. Plants are hardy to zone 3.

Lilium canadense is a quite variable species. In the past, variety *editorum* was designated to describe plants with wider leaves and narrower red tepals, found usually at higher elevations. This variety is no longer recognized because field observations showed these characteristics to be highly variable. This includes flower color, which can vary from yellow to red within the same population. Other designations that presently do not have a valid botanical standing include variety *flavorubrum*, distinguished by deep orange flowers with yellow throats, and variety *immaculatum*, with yellow, unspotted flowers. In cultivation, several of these color variants have been selected and given cultivar names, such as 'Redwing', which has scarlet flowers with yellow throats, and 'Golden Rule', with pure yellow flowers.

In the wild, *Lilium canadense* blooms from June to early August. Cultivated in Germany, it flowers at about the same time. At Longwood, *L. canadense* began flowering in the second or third week of July and continued through the end of July or into the first week of August. On average, *L. canadense* bloomed for a little longer than 3 weeks.

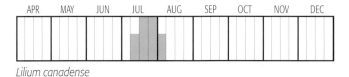

Lilium canadense

Lilium formosanum

FORMOSA LILY

This plant is native to Taiwan, where it grows on volcanic soils, in meadows, on grassy slopes, and along seashores, at elevations to 3500 m.

Lilium formosanum forms erect stems, purple-brown toward the base, reaching 1.5 m (rarely 1.8 m) in height, growing singly or two or three together from white or yellowish, scaly, stoloniferous bulbs. The linear or narrowly lanceolate leaves, to 20 cm long, are scattered along the stems. The fragrant, funnel-shaped, 10-cm-long flowers have white tepals, often tinged purple-red on the outside. They are borne singly or up to six held in terminal umbels. Fruits are 8-cm-long capsules.

In the garden, *Lilium formosanum* prefers warm and sunny locations. It rarely succeeds in areas where summers are cool and wet. Taller plants may require staking. Allow the large seed capsules to remain on the plants and provide interest through the fall. *Lilium formosanum* self-seeds easily under favorable conditions. Plants are hardy to zones 5 or 6, but in colder climates they tend to be short-lived or even biennial.

There are two varieties of *Lilium formosanum* recognized among natural populations. The typical variety *formosanum* has leaves and tepals to 15 cm long, whereas variety *microphyllum*, native to northern Taiwan, has leaves only 3 cm long and tepals to 8 cm long. A shorter and early-flowering variety *pricei*, found at higher elevations in Taiwan but also widely grown in the gardens, is currently considered to be

synonymous with variety *formosanum*. A number of superior but fairly similar seed strains have been selected in cultivation and given cultivar names, including 'Giant White', 'Kenya', and 'St. Louis'. In addition, *L. formosanum* has been hybridized with *L. longiflorum* in an effort to breed new types of Easter lilies.

In the wild, *Lilium formosanum* blooms from June to December, depending on elevation. In cultivation, it flowers in summer in warmer climates, but in colder areas flowering can be delayed until fall. At Longwood, bloom start date varied from the first to the last week of July, and plants flowered for nearly 3 weeks, on average.

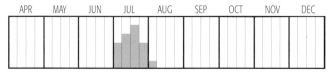

Lilium formosanum

Lilium speciosum

JAPANESE LILY, SHOWY LILY

This perennial is native to eastern Asia, from Guangxi east to Taiwan and north to Anhui in China and on Shikoku and Kyushu Islands in Japan. *Lilium speciosum* has been cultivated in Asia for centuries and since the 19th century in the West.

Lilium speciosum forms slender, wiry stems to 1.5 m (rarely 2 m) tall, growing from large yellowish to brownish bulbs. The lanceolate or oblong, petiolate leaves reach 18 cm in length and are scattered along the stems. The fragrant, nodding or outward facing, 15-cm-wide flowers have white tepals, flushed and spotted pink or crimson inside. They are held up to 30 in a leafy panicle. Fruits are subglobose capsules, about 3 cm wide.

Besides making a fine subject for a perennial border, *Lilium speciosum* does well planted in containers and is valued as an excellent cut flower. Plant it in a warm and sheltered spot in full sun or partial shade. Choose a location with fairly fertile, acidic, humus-rich, and well-drained soil. Plants are hardy to zones 4 or 5.

Several botanical variants of *Lilium speciosum* have been described among the natural populations. Variety *gloriosoides*, distinguished by narrower leaves and white flowers spotted scarlet red, is still recognized, but color variants designated as variety *album* and variety *rubrum* are presently considered as

Lilium speciosum 'Rubrum'

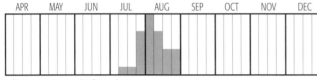

APR	MAY	JUN	JUL	AUG	SEP	OCT	NOV	DEC

Lilium speciosum 'Rubrum'

Lilium superbum

cultivars 'Album' and 'Rubrum', respectively. Furthermore, more than 100 other superior forms have been selected and named, including deep red 'Cardinal', lilac purple 'Grand Commander', and pink 'Attraction'.

In the wild, *Lilium speciosum* blooms in July and August. In cultivation, it is one of the later-flowering lilies. In colder climates, its flowering may even be delayed until early fall. At Longwood, the cultivar 'Rubrum' usually began to bloom in the last week of July or the first week of August, although one year, it was in flower in the second week of July. It bloomed for 4 or 5 weeks, into mid or late August.

Lilium superbum
AMERICAN TURK'S CAP LILY

This perennial is native to the eastern United States, from New Hampshire, west to Missouri, and south to Florida and Mississippi. It grows in acidic, humus-rich soils, in meadows, marshes, swamp edges, thickets, and moist woods. *Lilium superbum* has been cultivated since the early 18th century.

Lilium superbum forms leafy, purplish stems to 2 or 3 m tall, terminated in pyramidal inflorescences, growing from large, whitish bulbs with stout stolons. The lanceolate or narrowly elliptic leaves reach 26 cm in length and are arranged in whorls, evenly distributed along stems. The unscented, nodding flowers have orange-red, strongly spotted, and reflexed tepals to 10 cm long. The flowers are held on long pedicels, up to 40, in racemose inflorescences. Fruits are 5-cm-long capsules.

In the garden, *Lilium superbum* is best planted in larger groups and allowed to spread to form colonies. Use it in perennial borders, woodland edges, along pond margins, and wildflower meadows. Plant it in full sun, although in warmer climates light afternoon shade may be beneficial. *Lilium superbum* thrives in moist, deep, acidic, and humus-rich soils. Mulch around the plants to make sure that the soil stays cool and consistently moist. Plants are hardy to zones 4 or 5.

There are no botanical varieties of *Lilium superbum* recognized among natural populations, but plants show a wide range of flower color variations

Lilium superbum

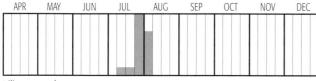

APR	MAY	JUN	JUL	AUG	SEP	OCT	NOV	DEC

Lilium superbum

from yellow to orange-red, less commonly red and purple-red. Furthermore, flowers can be variously suffused and spotted with red or purple. Mary Gibson Henry of Gladwyne, Pennsylvania, collected many such variants in the wild, including pure copper-colored 'Copper Head', blood red 'Howard Henry', or butter yellow and unspotted 'Norman Henry', which were introduced in the 1940s, but may no longer be in cultivation.

In the wild, *Lilium superbum* blooms from July to early August. Cultivated in St. Louis, it flowered in July. At Longwood, *L. superbum* began to bloom in late July, except for one year, when it was in flower unusually early, in the second week of July. It bloomed for 2 or 3 weeks, into the first week of August.

Lilium Asiatic Hybrids

This group includes hybrid lilies developed from several Asiatic species, including *Lilium amabile*, *L. dauricum*, *L. davidii*, *L. lancifolium*, *L. leichtlinii*, *L. maculatum*, *L. maximowiczii*, and others, as well as the European *L. bulbiferum*. Initially bred primarily for cut flowers, Asiatic Hybrids quickly gained popularity as easy-to-grow garden plants.

Asiatic Hybrids make up a very diverse group of cultivars, but in general are characterized by unscented, vividly colored flowers borne in racemes or umbels and narrowly ovate alternate leaves. They grow to about 1.2 m tall.

In the garden, Asiatic Hybrids, besides supplying some of the most highly prized cut flowers, can fit easily in a wide range of situations, from formal to naturalistic, from large scale to intimate. Plant Asiatic lilies in sheltered, sunny locations, although some varieties grow better in partial shade, especially in areas with hot summers. They can thrive in average, humus-rich garden soil that is well drained. Mulch

Lilium 'Granny'

Lilium 'Nepal'

Lilium 'Wowee'

well to keep soil cool during the summer. Transplant and divide every 3 to 5 years. Plants are hardy to zones 3 or 4.

Asiatic lilies are by far the largest group of hybrids. They are divided into three classes on the basis of the flower position: erect, horizontal, or nodding. Newer cultivars are often tetraploids. Furthermore, Asiatic Hybrids have been crossed with *Lilium longiflorum*, which has led to the development of cultivars known as LA Hybrids. Asiatic Hybrids vary widely in their colors, including white 'Bel Ami' and 'Nepal', yellow 'Connecticut King', orange 'Enchantment', coral 'Wowee', peachy 'Granny', deep red 'St. Tropez', and lavender pink 'Elf'.

Asiatic lilies bloom from June to August, depending on variety and the region. At Longwood, several cultivars were observed. They all flowered in June and early July. Some, like 'Nepal', began flowering in late June and continued often through the second week of July. Others, including 'Granny' and 'Wowee', in some years flowered as early as the first week of June but never bloomed past the first week of July. On average, Asiatic lilies were in flower for 2 or 3 weeks.

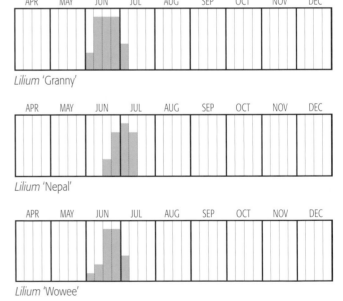

APR	MAY	JUN	JUL	AUG	SEP	OCT	NOV	DEC

Lilium 'Granny'

APR	MAY	JUN	JUL	AUG	SEP	OCT	NOV	DEC

Lilium 'Nepal'

APR	MAY	JUN	JUL	AUG	SEP	OCT	NOV	DEC

Lilium 'Wowee'

Lilium Oriental Hybrids

Oriental Hybrids include cultivars raised by intercrossing several species, native primarily to Japan, such as *Lilium alexandrae*, *L. auratum*, *L. japonicum*, *L. nobilissimum*, *L. rubellum*, and *L. speciosum*, and later also crossed with *L. henryi* from China. They gained

Lilium 'Black Beauty'

Lilium 'Muscadet'

Lilium 'Salmon Jewels'

a widespread popularity in the 1950s with the introduction of lime-tolerant cultivars, such as 'Black Beauty'. Like Asiatic Hybrids, many of the Oriental Hybrids, such as 'Star Gazer', were originally developed for cut flower production but later proved to be very useful garden plants.

Oriental Hybrids are characterized generally by large, wide-open, and heavily scented flowers, borne in racemes or panicles, and lanceolate, alternate leaves. They grow to 1.5 m tall.

Although not as hardy or easy to grow as Asiatic Hybrids, Oriental Hybrids can be successfully grown in perennial borders, among lower shrubs, or in containers. They are valued for their large, brightly colored, and fragrant flowers. Plant Oriental Hybrids in a protected, sunny location, preferably among other plants shading the soil, thus keeping it cool. They thrive in moist, humus-rich, acidic soils, but many cultivars can tolerate more alkaline soils as well. Oriental Hybrids perform best when planted in groups and left undisturbed for years, which allows them to produce more profuse bloom with each year. Plants are hardy to zone 4.

Not as numerous as Asiatic Hybrids, Oriental lilies nevertheless offer a great variety of flower colors and shapes. They are divided into four categories based on the form of the flower: trumpet-shaped, bowl-shaped, flat-faced, and strongly recurved. Flower colors range from the pure white 'Muscadet' and salmon pink 'Salmon Jewels' to crimson-maroon 'Black Beauty' and deep crimson 'Star Gazer'. Oriental lilies also have been crossed with varieties belonging to Trumpet Hybrids, which resulted in vigorous and large-flowered plants known as Orienpets, such as the 2- to 3-m-tall, crimson-colored 'Scheherazade' and 'Silk Road'.

Oriental Hybrids bloom mostly during July and August, but some varieties may flower as late as September. Several cultivars grown at Longwood bloomed from mid-July until early August. A relatively early flowering cultivar, 'Muscadet', began to bloom between the first and the third week of July and ended in the last week of July or the first week of August. In contrast, 'Black Beauty' rarely bloomed before the last week of July and often continued through the third week of August. Others, such as 'Salmon Jewels', were intermediate between these two cultivars. Their average bloom time ranged from 3 weeks for 'Salmon Jewels' to nearly 5 weeks for 'Black Beauty'.

Lilium Trumpet Hybrids

Trumpet hybrid lilies were developed from crosses between several trumpet-flowered *Lilium* species from Asia and from crosses between their progenies and *L. henryi*, a Chinese species with Turk's-cap type flowers. The first Trumpet Hybrids were raised in Germany in 1913 from crosses between *L. sulphureum* and *L. regale*, both species from western China. In 1916 in the United States, *Lilium sargentiae*, another species from western China, was crossed with *L. regale*, and more hybridization soon followed. Varieties developed in 1925 in Orleans, France, from crosses between *L. sargentiae* and *L. henryi* became known as Aurelian Hybrids.

Trumpet Hybrids are characterized by very vigorous growth, reaching in some cases to 2 m in height, and intensely scented flowers borne in large racemes or umbels. The flower form varies from distinctly trumpet-like to strongly recurved. Their elliptic or linear leaves are usually spirally arranged.

In the garden, Trumpet Hybrid lilies present themselves best in small groups placed in a prominent position in a perennial border. Their large flowers held on tall stems invariably attract attention, especially if set against a darker background. Site them where the scent of the flowers can be appreciated. Choose a sunny spot, sheltered from wind, although red and pink varieties may develop better color if given partial shade. Plant in good, fertile, humus-

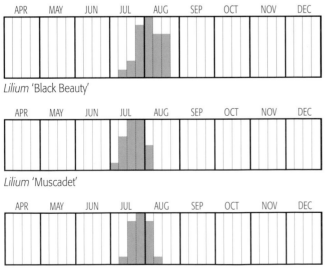

APR | MAY | JUN | JUL | AUG | SEP | OCT | NOV | DEC

Lilium 'Black Beauty'

Lilium 'Muscadet'

Lilium 'Salmon Jewels'

rich, and well-drained soil. Because most varieties grow tall and produce large inflorescences, they frequently require staking. Plants are hardy to zone 4, but protection of young shoots from late frosts may often be needed.

Among the large number of Trumpet Hybrid lilies, those derived only from the trumpet-flow-

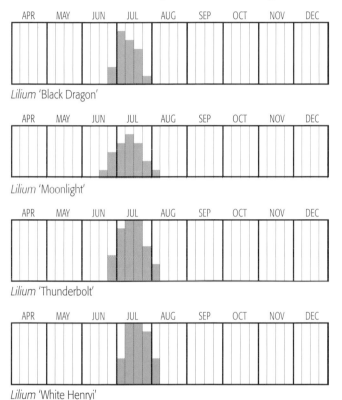

Lilium 'Black Dragon'

Lilium 'Moonlight'

Lilium 'Thunderbolt'

Lilium 'White Henryi'

ered species are regarded as purebred, as opposed to the hybrids developed from the crosses with *Lilium henryi*. Irrespective of the pedigree, they are divided into four classes based on the form of the flower: trumpet-shaped, bowl-shaped, flat, and distinctly recurved. Many cultivars are seed-grown strains, such as 'Black Dragon', with flowers white inside and purple-brown outside, and 'Moonlight', with chartreuse-yellow flowers. Others are clonally propagated, including cream-colored 'White Henryi' and yellow-orange 'Thunderbolt'.

Trumpet Hybrids bloom from the end of June until the end of August. Of several cultivars grown at Longwood, 'Moonlight' was the earliest, starting in some years as early as the third week of June, and

Lilium 'White Henryi'

Lilium 'White Henryi'

rarely flowering past mid-July. The latest to flower was 'White Henryi', beginning in early July and finishing in the last week of July or the first week of August. The average bloom duration varied from less than 3 weeks for 'Black Dragon' to a little more than 4 weeks for 'Thunderbolt'.

Limonium

MARSH-ROSEMARY, SEA-LAVENDER, STATICE

The name *Limonium* is derived from the Greek *leimon*, a meadow, in reference to the places where these plants are often found.

Limonium latifolium

BROAD-LEAVED SEA-LAVENDER, STATICE

This plant is native to southern Europe, from Bulgaria and Romania east to southern Russia. It grows in steppes and dry grasslands. *Limonium latifolium* has been cultivated since the 18th century. It is also known under the names *L. platyphyllum* and *L. gerberi*.

Limonium latifolium forms clumps of evergreen basal foliage and wiry, loosely branched, and wide-ly spreading flowering stems to 1 m tall, growing from a thickened taproot. The dark green, leathery, sparsely pubescent, oblong or elliptic leaves to 25 cm long are held on petioles of nearly equal length. The 6-mm-wide flowers have a blue-violet corolla and whitish calyx. They are borne in penciled, sub-spherical inflorescences to 60 cm wide. Fruits are capsules enclosed in calyces.

In the garden, *Limonium latifolium* is valued as an undemanding, long-lived, unassuming yet distinct perennial that easily fits with a wide range of plants, whether in perennial borders or in natural-istic meadows. Its bold foliar rosettes are offset by airy, haze-like mounds of myriads of tiny but long-lasting flowers. Cut stems are prized in dry flower arrangements. Plant *L. latifolium* in full sun, in any well-drained situation, although it performs best in deep, light, and moderately fertile soil. Avoid sites with heavy, rich, and wet soil, where plants grow weak and lanky stems. *Limonium latifolium* is excep-tionally drought and salt tolerant. Deadheading is not needed, as the plants bloom for a long time and

Limonium latifolium

retain a neat appearance even after flowering. *Limonium latifolium* is long-lived and is best left without transplanting or dividing indefinitely. Plants are hardy to zone 5, possibly zone 3.

There are no botanical varieties of *Limonium latifolium* recognized among the natural populations. In cultivation, only a handful of color variants have been selected and named, including light blue 'Blue Cloud', light pink 'Collier's Pink', and dark violet blue 'Violetta'.

In the wild, *Limonium latifolium* blooms from July to October. Plants in cultivation may begin flowering as early as May or June in certain areas. At Longwood, *L. latifolium* usually started to flower in the last week of June or in the first week of July. Rarely, flowering began as early as the second week of June or as late as the second week of July. On average, plants were in bloom for nearly 9 weeks, through July and into mid-August; but in some years they continued flowering for 12 weeks, into September. In comparison, the cultivar 'Violetta' grown at Longwood flowered a couple of weeks later, starting in the second week of July. 'Violetta' also averaged about 2 weeks less of bloom time.

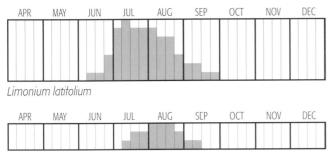

| APR | MAY | JUN | JUL | AUG | SEP | OCT | NOV | DEC |

Limonium latifolium

| APR | MAY | JUN | JUL | AUG | SEP | OCT | NOV | DEC |

Limonium latifolium 'Violetta'

Liriope

LILY-TURF

The name *Liriope* is for the nymph Liriope of Greek mythology.

Liriope muscari

BLUE LILY-TURF

This perennial is native to China, from Sichuan in the west, north to Shandong, and east to Taiwan. It grows in moist and shady places in forests, bamboo thickets, and scrub, at elevations up to 2000 m. *Liriope muscari* has also long been cultivated in Japan.

Liriope muscari forms dense clumps of tufted, grassy, evergreen foliage and erect flowering stems to 45 cm tall, growing from a fleshy, often tuberous rootstock with short rhizomes. The dark green, glossy, linear leaves reach about 45 cm in length. The lilac purple flowers are borne in clusters of three to eight, arranged in dense raceme-like inflorescences to 12 cm long, held on stiff scapes above the foliage. Fruits are capsules, splitting early and revealing fleshy, shiny black seeds to 8 mm in diameter.

In the garden, *Liriope muscari* makes an excellent plant for edging or as ground cover. It is well suited for little nooks in confined spaces of an urban garden, but it performs just as well filling large expanses in a woodland garden. Variegated forms can brighten up dark corners. Beyond the handsome foliage, *L. muscari* is valued for its late-season flowers and long-lasting, conspicuous, shiny black seeds. It thrives in partial shade, although in colder climates it can be grown successfully in full sun. Plants tolerate deep shade, but will spread more slowly and, in case of variegated forms, leaf coloration will be less pronounced. Plant *L. muscari* in any average garden

Limonium latifolium

Liriope muscari 'Variegata'

soil, provided it is well drained. Although it prefers moist and fertile conditions, *L. muscari* can adapt to drier situations. In warmer areas, the evergreen foliage remains attractive through the winter, but in the north the leaves usually look rather worn out and need to be trimmed in early spring. Clumps spread slowly and rarely need to be divided, unless flowering diminishes noticeably. Plants are hardy to zone 6, but in colder areas should be protected from desiccating winds with a light cover of mulch.

There are no botanical varieties of *Liriope muscari* recognized in the wild, but in cultivation more than 50 cultivars have been raised, primarily as chance seedlings. They vary in flower color from the deep purple of 'Royal Purple' to the pure white of 'Monroe White'. The low-growing 'Silvery Midget' grows only 20 cm tall, whereas vigorous 'Big Blue' reaches 45 cm in height. A number of cultivars, such as 'Gold Banded', 'Okina', and 'Variegata', feature variegated foliage.

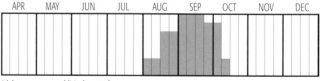

Liriope muscari 'Variegata'

In the wild, *Liriope muscari* blooms in July and August. Cultivated in Georgia, Illinois, and Missouri, it begins flowering in August. At Longwood, the cultivar 'Variegata' started to bloom between the first week of August and the first week of September. Flowering usually continued through the end of September and into early October. It averaged nearly 8 weeks in bloom.

Liriope spicata

CREEPING LILY-TURF, CREEPING LIRIOPE

This plant is native to eastern Asia, from Vietnam, north to Gansu and Hubei Provinces in China, and east to Korea and Japan. *Liriope spicata* grows in moist

Liriope muscari 'Variegata'

Liriope spicata 'Gin-ryu'

places in forests and on grassy hillsides, at elevations up to 1800 m. It has been cultivated in China as a medicinal plant for centuries.

Liriope spicata forms dense clumps of evergreen, mounded, grass-like foliage and erect flowering stems to 45 cm tall, growing from creeping stoloniferous rhizomes with fleshy, tuberous roots. The arching, linear leaves grow to 60 cm long and to 8 mm wide. The 6-mm-wide, pale lavender (rarely white) flowers are borne in clusters of three to five, arranged in terminal raceme-like inflorescences to 15 cm long, held at the foliage level. Fruits are capsules splitting to reveal subglobose, glossy black, fleshy seeds to 9 mm wide.

In the garden, *Liriope spicata* is used primarily as a rapidly spreading ground cover. It forms dense stands that can colonize even difficult areas on slopes, under shallow rooted trees, or on stream banks, but is considered too invasive for planting in a perennial border. Plant it in partial shade or, in cooler climates,

in full sun. Plants flower more profusely in sunny locations, but in hot summer weather may become scorched under such conditions. Preferably, choose a site with moist, fertile, and well-drained soil. Deadheading is not needed. Rather, allow the fruits to develop and display the attractive shiny black seeds. In warmer areas, leaves are evergreen, but elsewhere they may turn yellowish green or even brown during the winter and need to be cut back in early spring. Plants are hardy to zones 4 or 5.

Several botanical varieties and forms of *Liriope spicata* were described in the past, but currently they are considered synonymous with the species. In cultivation, only a few selections have been made, including white-flowered 'Alba', pale lavender 'Franklin Mint', and white-variegated 'Gin-ryu'.

In the wild, *Liriope spicata* blooms from May to July. Plants cultivated in Missouri and Ohio begin flowering in August. At Longwood, the cultivar 'Gin-ryu' started to bloom between the first and last

Liriope spicata 'Gin-ryu'

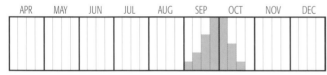

APR	MAY	JUN	JUL	AUG	SEP	OCT	NOV	DEC

Liriope spicata 'Gin-ryu'

week of September and continued through early October, rarely into the third week of October. It averaged nearly 5 weeks in bloom. In comparison, *L. spicata* grown in St. Louis flowered for 3 to 6 weeks.

Lobelia

LOBELIA

The name *Lobelia* commemorates Mathias de l'Obel (1538–1616), a French physician and botanist.

Lobelia cardinalis

CARDINAL FLOWER, INDIAN PINK, RED-BIRDS, RED LOBELIA, SCARLET LOBELIA

This plant is native to North America, from New Brunswick in Canada, south to Florida, and west to California and northern Mexico. *Lobelia cardina-*

Lobelia cardinalis

lis grows in wet soils in swamps, meadows, moist woods, and along streams and rivers. It has been cultivated since the 17th century.

Lobelia cardinalis forms erect clumps of basal foliage and rigid, unbranched, often reddish, leafy stems to 1.2 m tall, growing from a shallow rootstock. The oblong to lanceolate leaves are irregularly serrated, sessile or short-petiolate and reach 15 cm in length. The two-lipped, 3.5-cm-long, bright scarlet red flowers are borne in slender terminal racemes to 60 cm in length. Fruits are capsules opening at the top.

In the garden, *Lobelia cardinalis* is attractive to butterflies, hummingbirds, and people alike. Its stately and brilliantly colored flowers stand out in any situation. Use it in perennial borders or allow it to naturalize in wildflower and woodland gardens and near ponds and streams. Plant it in partial shade, although in cooler climates sunny locations are equally suitable. Choose a moist site with deep, humus-rich soil. Deadhead to maintain a neat appearance, but leave some fruits to produce and disperse seeds. Self-seeding occurs under favorable conditions and seedlings can be saved as replacements for the rather short-lived plants. Frequent dividing and transplanting are needed to maintain the plant's vigor and to extend its longevity. *Lobelia cardinalis* is hardy to zone 3, possibly 2, but in colder climates it benefits from a light winter protection.

Several botanical varieties of *Lobelia cardinalis* were described in the past, but they are no longer considered valid. In cultivation, flower color variants have been selected, including white 'Alba', pink 'Eulalia Berridge', and bright red 'Elmfeuer'. Cultivars such as 'Queen Victoria' feature purple foliage. Furthermore, *L. cardinalis* has been hybridized with *L. amoena* and *L. siphilitica*, two blue-flowered species, which resulted in a range of cultivars offering a wider color spectrum, including violet blue 'Butterfly Blue', bright purple 'Hadspen Purple', pink 'Rosenkavalier', and red 'Cherry Ripe'. Some of the hybrids are produced as seed strains with segregated colors, such as the Fan Series or the Kompliment Series.

In the wild, *Lobelia cardinalis* blooms from July to September. Similar bloom season was observed for cultivated plants in Germany and in Illinois, Missouri, and Ohio; but in the United Kingdom, flowering begins in late August and continues until frost. At Longwood, bloom usually started in late July, rarely as early as the second week of July or as late as the first week of August. Plants continued to flower through the end of August or into early September, averaging a little over 7 weeks in bloom.

APR	MAY	JUN	JUL	AUG	SEP	OCT	NOV	DEC

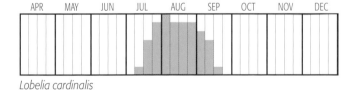
Lobelia cardinalis

Lobelia siphilitica

BIG BLUE LOBELIA, BLUE CARDINAL FLOWER, GIANT BLUE LOBELIA, GREAT LOBELIA

This perennial is native to eastern North America, from Manitoba, east to Maine, and south to Georgia and Texas. *Lobelia siphilitica* grows in wet areas, swamps, and moist woods. It has been cultivated since the 17th century.

Lobelia siphilitica

Lobelia siphilitica forms upright clumps of stiffly erect, unbranched, densely leafy stems to 1 m tall, growing from a shallow rootstock. The oval to lanceolate, sessile leaves are irregularly serrated and reach 15 cm in length. The 3-cm-long, two-lipped flowers have a smaller purplish upper lip and a larger blue lower lip, which frequently is marked with white stripes. Flowers are borne in slender, dense terminal racemes to 15 cm long. Fruits are capsules.

In the garden, *Lobelia siphilitica* is undemanding and easy to care for, provided its basic needs are met. It is well suited for traditional perennial beds but also for naturalizing beside streams and ponds, in wet meadows, or woodland gardens. Plant *L. siphilitica* in partial shade. In colder climates, it thrives in full sun as long as the soil is consistently moist. Choose a site with deep, fertile, constantly moist or even wet soil. *Lobelia siphilitica* tends to be short-lived, especially when grown in dry locations. Divide the plants every 2 or 3 years, or allow them to self-seed and

Lobelia siphilitica

save the young seedlings. Plants are hardy to zone 5, possibly zone 3.

Two botanical varieties of *Lobelia siphilitica* are recognized among the natural populations. The typical variety *siphilitica* is widespread in the eastern part of the range, whereas variety *ludoviciana*, a smaller plant with fewer flowers and narrower leaves, is found primarily west of the Mississippi River. In cultivation, a few flower color variants have been selected and introduced, including white 'Alba', light blue 'Blue Peter', and lilac 'Lilac Candles'. In addition, *L. siphilitica* has been hybridized with *L. cardinalis* as described above.

In the wild, *Lobelia siphilitica* blooms from August to September, somewhat later then *L. cardinalis*. Plants cultivated in St. Louis started flowering between mid-July and late August and finished between early September and late October. At Longwood, *L. siphilitica* flowered from mid or late August until mid or late September. Only once in 7 years, flowering started as early as the last week of July and continued as late as the first week of October. *Lobelia siphilitica* at Longwood averaged nearly 6 weeks in bloom.

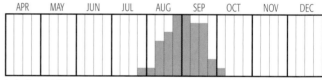

Lobelia siphilitica

Lychnis

CAMPION, CATCHFLY

The name *Lychnis* was used by ancient Greeks for these plants and was derived from the Greek *lychnos*, lamp, in reference to the use of the leaves as lampwicks.

Lychnis chalcedonica

JERUSALEM CROSS, LONDON PRIDE, MALTESE CROSS, SCARLET LIGHTNING

This perennial is native to central and eastern Russia, east to Mongolia and northern China. It has naturalized in parts of North America. *Lychnis chalcedonica* grows in open woodlands, meadows, and scrub. It has been cultivated at least since the 13th century.

Lychnis chalcedonica forms stout clumps of basal leaves and erect, unbranched, hispid stems to 1 m

Lychnis chalcedonica

Lychnis chalcedonica

tall, growing from a spreading rootstock. The ovate to lanceolate, 10-cm-long leaves are dark green, sparsely hispid, and clasping. The deep scarlet, 2.5-cm-wide flowers are borne in dense, terminal, rounded, cymose heads to 10 cm in width. Fruits are capsules enclosed by the calyx.

In the garden, *Lychnis chalcedonica* is valued as one of the truly scarlet red flowers, especially effective when planted in larger groups. Despite its radiant color, it combines easily with a wide range of plants in a perennial border. Plant it in full sun or, in warmer climates, partial shade. It thrives in light, fertile, consistently moist but well-drained soil. Avoid poor, dry soils, where foliage declines in hot weather and plants tend to be short-lived. *Lychnis chalcedonica* has rather brittle stems, so choose a location sheltered from wind, or plant it among other sturdy perennials that may provide support. Divide the clumps every 3 or 4 years, more often when grown in areas with hot and humid summers. Plants are hardy to zones 3 or 4.

There are no botanical varieties of *Lychnis chalcedonica* recognized currently, although in the past flower color variants, such as *rubra-plena* or *albiflora*,

were given such designations. In cultivation, several cultivars have been selected with unusual flower colors, such as white 'Hoarfrost' or pale pink 'Rosea'. There are also double-flowered forms, such as deep red 'Flore Pleno'.

In its native habitat, *Lychnis chalcedonica* blooms in early summer. Cultivated in Moscow, it began flowering, on average, around 20 June and finished around 17 August. Plants grown in Poznań bloomed a little earlier, starting between 3 and 26 June and ending between 14 July and 1 August. A similar June-to-August bloom season is observed in Germany and the United Kingdom, but in Chicago *L.*

Lychnis chalcedonica 'Rosea'

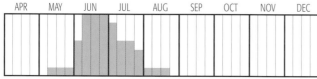

Lychnis chalcedonica

Lychnis coronaria

chalcedonica flowers in late May and June. At Long-wood, flowering usually began in early June, al-though one year plants were in bloom in the second week of May. Flowering continued, on average, for 7 weeks, through early or late July. Only once plants rebloomed in August. In comparison, *L. chalcedonica* in Moscow averaged 8 weeks in bloom.

Lychnis coronaria

DUSTY–MILLER, MULLEIN–PINK, ROSE CAMPION

This plant is native to southern Europe, northern Africa, and western Asia, from Italy east to Iran. *Lychnis coronaria* has naturalized in other parts of Europe as well as in North America. This species grows in open woodlands, thickets, scrub, and ex-posed rocky slopes. It has been cultivated since the 16th century.

Lychnis coronaria forms upright, silvery-wooly clumps of spreading, basal foliage and erect, stiffly branched stems to 1 m tall. The oblong or ovate leaves reach 12 cm in length. The basal leaves are petiolate, whereas the cauline ones are sessile. The magenta-pink, 2.5-cm-wide flowers are held on long pedicels, solitary or in few-flowered terminal inflorescences. Fruits are capsules.

In the garden, *Lychnis coronaria* stands out thanks to its silvery foliage and vividly colored flowers, both of which can brighten even the dullest corners. Use judiciously in a perennial border because plants die down after flowering. Plant *L. coronaria* in full sun, although light afternoon shade is tolerated. It thrives in any well-drained soil, including those that are dry and of low fertility. Cut back after flowering to pre-vent self-seeding and to extend longevity of other-wise short-lived plants. Alternatively, allow self-seed-ing and save young seedlings as replacements. *Lychnis*

Lychnis coronaria 'Alba'

coronaria at best lives for only a few years; often it is biennial, but the species perpetuates itself easily through self-seeding. Plants are hardy to zone 4.

There are no botanical varieties of *Lychnis coronaria* recognized among the natural populations. In cultivation, several color variants have been selected, including white 'Alba', pink-blushed 'Angel's Blush', or red-magenta 'Blood Red'. Some, like 'Blushing Bride' and 'Oculata', have white flowers with pink center. There is also double-flowered 'Flore Pleno' and variegated 'Hutchinson's Cream'. Furthermore, *L. coronaria* has been crossed with *L. flos-jovis* from the Alps to produce a hybrid *L. ×walkeri*, frequently represented in the gardens by the cultivar 'Abbotswood Rose'.

In the wild, *Lychnis coronaria* blooms from May to September, depending on the region. In cultivation, the flowering period can be extended through regular deadheading. Occasional rebloom may occur later in the season. Plants grown in Moscow flowered starting, on average, around 25 June and end-

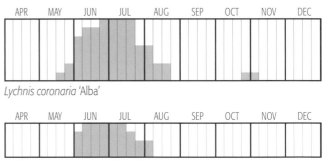

Lychnis coronaria 'Alba'

Lychnis coronaria 'Angel's Blush'

ing around 19 August. At Longwood, the cultivar 'Alba' usually began to bloom in late May and early June. Only once in 7 years, bloom was delayed until the last week of June. 'Alba' flowered, on average, for 9 weeks, into late July or early August, rarely until the third week of August. Rebloom occurred only one year, in late October. Another cultivar grown at Longwood, 'Angel's Blush', flowered during a similar period, but averaged less than 8 weeks in bloom. *Lychnis coronaria* cultivated in Moscow also flowered for 8 weeks, on average.

Lycoris

LYCORIS

The name *Lycoris* commemorates a Roman actress, the mistress of Mark Anthony.

Lycoris squamigera

AUTUMN-AMARYLLIS, AUTUMN LYCORIS, HARDY-AMARYLLIS, MAGIC-LILY, NAKED-LADY, NAKED-LILY, RESURRECTION-LILY

This perennial is native to eastern Asia, in China from Zhejiang north to Shandong, and east to Korea and Japan. *Lycoris squamigera* grows often in moist soils, in shady valleys, and along streams, at elevations to 1200 m.

    Lycoris squamigera forms clumps of strap-like, basal, foliage and stout, leafless flowering scapes to 70 cm tall, growing from large, ovoid, long-necked bulbs. The linear leaves are up to 40 cm long and 5

Lycoris squamigera

Lycoris squamigera

cm wide. They appear in the spring and die back in summer. The fragrant, rose-pink flowers, to 12 cm long, are borne in terminal umbels subtended by two lanceolate spathes. Fruits are rounded capsules.

In the garden, *Lycoris squamigera* is valued for large, showy, and fragrant flowers, which appear unexpectedly in late summer, long after the foliage dies back. Plant it among other perennials that hide the bare spots left when leaves disappear in summer. Use it in perennial borders, wildflower meadows, woodland gardens, and along streams or ponds. Choose a warm, protected, and sunny or partially shaded location. Plant in fertile, moist, and well-drained soil. *Lycoris squamigera* requires an ample supply of water in spring during the vegetative stage of growth. Watering can be withheld in summer when plants are dormant. Clumps of *L. squamigera* increase rapidly and can be divided every 4 or 5 years. Plants are hardy to zone 5, but in colder areas a light cover of mulch is recommended.

In the wild, *Lycoris squamigera* blooms in August. Plants cultivated in Germany flower during a similar season, whereas in St. Louis bloom may start as early as mid-July. At Longwood, the earliest flowering was observed in the second week of July. More often, however, bloom began in the second week of August. Flowering continued for 3 or 4 weeks, usually through the end of August, sometimes into the first week of September.

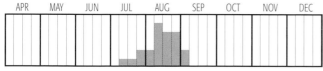

Lycoris squamigera

Lysimachia

LOOSESTRIFE

The name *Lysimachia* is derived from the Greek, *lysis*, releasing, and *mache*, strife, in reference to its soothing properties, or named after Lysimachos, king of Thrace.

Lysimachia ciliata

FRINGED LOOSESTRIFE, HAIRY LOOSESTRIFE

This perennial is native to North America, from Nova Scotia, west to British Columbia, and south to Florida and New Mexico. It has also naturalized

in parts of Europe. *Lysimachia ciliata* grows in moist woodlands, near ponds and lakes, and along streams and rivers, at elevations to 1800 m. It has been cultivated since the 18th century.

Lysimachia ciliata forms upright clumps of slender, erect stems to 1.2 m tall, growing from spreading rhizomes. The ovate-lanceolate, glossy leaves are fringed with hairs. Arranged in pairs or in whorls of four, the leaves reach 15 cm in length. The 2.5-cm-wide, light yellow, sometimes red-blotched flowers are borne singly or in pairs in axils of the uppermost leaves. Fruits are capsules.

Lysimachia ciliata is used primarily for naturalizing in the wild part of the garden, in meadows, on watersides, and similar informal settings, although the purple-leaved selections are suitable for traditional perennial borders as well. It is valued for willowy foliage that acquires attractive fall hues and for

Lysimachia ciliata 'Purpurea'

Lysimachia ciliata 'Purpurea'

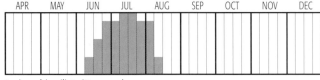

APR	MAY	JUN	JUL	AUG	SEP	OCT	NOV	DEC

Lysimachia ciliata 'Purpurea'

abundant softly colored flowers. Plant *L. ciliata* in full sun or partial shade. It thrives in any average garden soil that is consistently moist. It spreads vigorously, and needs to be divided regularly when grown in confined spaces. Plants are hardy to zone 5, possibly zone 3.

There are no botanical varieties of *Lysimachia ciliata* recognized among the natural populations, but in cultivation a couple of purple-leaved selections have been named, including 'Firecracker' and 'Purpurea'.

In the wild, *Lysimachia ciliata* blooms from June to August. Cultivated at Longwood, 'Purpurea' began flowering in mid to late June, although one year its bloom was delayed until the second week of July. It usually continued through the first week of August, rarely until the second week of that month. 'Purpurea' averaged a little more than 7 weeks in bloom.

Lysimachia ephemerum

LOOSESTRIFE

This plant is native to southwestern Europe, from Portugal west to southern France. *Lysimachia ephemerum* grows in moist meadows and near springs and streams. It has been cultivated since the 18th century.

Lysimachia ephemerum forms dense upright clumps of strong, erect, unbranched stems to 1.2 m tall, growing from spreading rhizomes. The gray-green leaves, up to 17 cm in length, are lanceolate to linear-spathulate and sessile. They are arranged in pairs. The starry, 1-cm-wide, white flowers are borne in dense, slender, erect, terminal racemes to 35 cm long, seldom with smaller axillary racemes at the base. Fruits are globose capsules.

In the garden, *Lysimachia ephemerum* is best suited for naturalizing in wildflower meadows, in open woodlands, and along streams or ponds. Its grayish foliage and airy white flowers create an overall informal and soothing effect. Plant *L. ephemerum* in full sun or partial shade. It thrives in any average garden soil as long as it is consistently moist. Avoid hot and dry sites with sandy soils. Deadheading is not necessary; rather, allow the mature seed heads to extend the season of interest. *Lysimachia ephemerum* increases slowly and does not require frequent dividing. Plants are hardy to zones 6 or 7, but in colder areas a light winter protection is beneficial.

In the wild, *Lysimachia ephemerum* blooms for several weeks from June to September. Cultivated at Longwood, it began flowering in mid-June to the first week of July, but in one year, its flowers did not open until the third week of July. *Lysimachia ephemerum* usually bloomed through late July, although once it was still in flower in the last week of August. It averaged a little over 5 weeks in bloom.

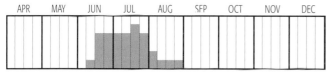

APR	MAY	JUN	JUL	AUG	SEP	OCT	NOV	DEC

Lysimachia ephemerum

Maianthemum

FALSE LILY–OF–THE–VALLEY, MAYFLOWER

The name *Maianthemum* is derived from the Latin *Maius*, May, and the Greek *anthemon*, flower, in reference to the time of bloom.

Maianthemum stellatum

LITTLE FALSE SOLOMON'S–SEAL, STARFLOWER,
STARRY FALSE LILY–OF–THE–VALLEY

This perennial is native to North America, from Newfoundland, east to Alaska, and south to northwestern Mexico, excluding the southeastern United States. It has also naturalized in parts of Scandinavia. *Maianthemum stellatum* often grows in moist soil in forest openings and woodland margins, at elevations to 3200 m.

Maianthemum stellatum forms upright clumps of erect, unbranched, straight or somewhat zigzag leafy stems to 80 cm tall, growing from stout fleshy rhizomes. The lanceolate to oblanceolate, sessile leaves, to 6 cm long, are light green above, dull glaucous below, and often folded lengthwise. The starry, creamy white flowers are held in erect terminal racemes to 5 cm in length. Fruits are globose berries, 5 mm in diameter, green with black stripes, maturing to red.

In the garden, *Maianthemum stellatum* is best suited for woodland gardens or along stream and pond

Maianthemum stellatum

Maianthemum stellatum

banks. In time it develops into large dense colonies and can provide an effective ground cover. Its starry flowers and red berries are rather understated but make a cheerful complement to the handsome foliage. Plant *M. stellatum* in a cool and shady location, in moist, humus-rich, and slightly acidic soil. It spreads widely, but unless the size of the colony needs to be restrained, no dividing is necessary. Plants are hardy to zones 3 or 4.

In the wild, *Maianthemum stellatum* blooms in May and June. In Alberta, Canada, the average bloom start date was 25 May. Plants cultivated at Longwood began flowering in the first or second week of May and usually continued until the end of that month, rarely until the first week of June. On average, *M. stellatum* was in bloom for a little more than 3 weeks.

Maianthemum stellatum

Manfreda

TUBEROSE

The name *Manfreda* commemorates Manfredo de Monte Imperiali, a 14th-century Italian herbalist.

Manfreda virginica

AMERICAN-ALOE, FALSE ALOE, RATTLESNAKE MASTER, VIRGINIAN-AGAVE

This perennial is native to North America, from Maryland, south to Florida, and west to Texas and northern Mexico. *Manfreda virginica* grows often in sandy, dry soils, in open woodlands, and on rocky glades, at elevations to 600 m.

Manfreda virginica forms rosettes of basal, spreading foliage and bracted, flowering scapes to 2 m tall, growing from a short cylindrical rhizome with numerous fibrous roots. The oblanceolate to linear-lanceolate leaves are stiff, somewhat succulent, glaucous green, often maroon speckled, and reach 40 cm in length. The slender, 4-cm-long, fragrant flowers have greenish yellow tepals and are held nearly erect in open spikes or racemes to 60 cm long. Fruits are globose capsules 1.5 cm in diameter.

In the garden, *Manfreda virginica* is best suited for naturalizing in a wildflower meadow or in a woodland edge. It also creates a most intriguing stand of

tall spires if planted closely as a group in a perennial border. Choose a warm spot in full sun or partial shade. *Manfreda virginica* thrives in any average garden soil, provided it is well drained. It adapts easily to dry conditions. Plants are hardy to zone 5, but in colder areas a light winter cover is recommended.

There are no botanical varieties of *Manfreda virginica* recognized among the natural populations, but variants with leaves speckled or spotted with purple are sometimes described as form *tigrina*. In cultivation, superior varieties are yet to be selected.

In the wild, *Manfreda virginica* blooms in summer. In cultivation, flowering sometimes extends into fall months. At Longwood, the bloom start date ranged from the last week of June to the last week of July. Flowering usually continued through the end of July

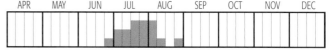

Manfreda virginica

Manfreda virginica

or into early August. One year, plants rebloomed in late August. On average, *M. virginica* was in flower for nearly 5 weeks.

Mazus

MAZUS

The name *Mazus* is derived from the Greek *mazos*, breast, in reference to protrusions in the flower throat.

Mazus reptans

MAZUS

This plant is native to the Himalayas, where it grows in moist places along the edges of woodlands and fields. It has been cultivated since the early 20th century. Some consider *Mazus reptans* to be synonymous with *M. miquelii* from Japan and southeastern China.

Mazus reptans forms spreading clumps of creeping or procumbent stems to 10 cm tall. The 1-cm-long leaves are lanceolate or elliptic and have coarsely serrated margins. The two-lipped lavender blue flowers are borne in two- to five-flowered terminal racemes. The lower lip of the flower is blotched white, yellow, and purple. Fruits are capsules.

In the garden, *Mazus reptans* is used primarily as a low ground cover to fill little nooks between rocks, paving stones, or along paths. Plant it in a sheltered location in full sun or partial shade. Choose a site with humus-rich, acidic, and consistently moist soil. Plants are hardy to zone 6.

There are no botanical varieties of *Mazus reptans* recognized, but in cultivation some color variants have been selected, including white-flowered 'Albus' and lavender-flowered 'Purperblau'.

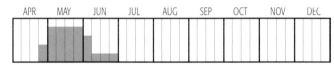

Mazus reptans 'Albus'

Mazus reptans

In the wild, *Mazus reptans* is a summer bloomer. At Longwood, the cultivar 'Albus' usually began flowering in the last week of April or the first week of May, although one year it did not bloom until the third week of June. On average, 'Albus' was in bloom for 5 weeks, through the end of May or June.

Mentha

MINT

The name *Mentha* is thought to be derived from Minthe or Menthe, a nymph of Greek mythology.

Mentha ×piperita

ORANGE MINT, PEPPERMINT

This perennial is a natural hybrid of two European species, *Mentha aquatica* and *M. spicata*. It is widespread in Europe as a garden escape, but has also naturalized in parts of Asia and North America. *Mentha ×piperita* often grows in wet places. It has been cultivated on a commercial scale as a source of peppermint oil since the 18th century.

Mentha ×piperita 'Chocolate'

Mentha ×piperita 'Chocolate'

Mentha ×*piperita* forms upright, spreading clumps of leafy, sometimes purple-tinged stems to 1 m tall, growing from rhizomatous or stoloniferous rootstock. The lanceolate to ovate, pungently aromatic leaves are long-petiolate, usually have serrate margins, and reach 9 cm in length. The lilac pink, 5-mm-long flowers are borne in dense verticillasters arranged in terminal spikes to 8 cm long. Fruits do not develop, as it is a sterile hybrid.

In the garden, *Mentha* ×*piperita* is grown primarily for its minty orange scent. It can be used for teas or garnish, as well as in potpourris. Beside herb or kitchen gardens, *M.* ×*piperita* makes an attractive ground cover for informal areas, woodland edges, or water margins. Before adding *M.* ×*piperita* to a perennial border, some consideration needs to be given to the fact that it spreads vigorously through the rhizomes. Plant it in full sun or partial shade. Preferably, choose a site with deep, fertile, loamy, and moist soil, although *M.* ×*piperita* can adapt to a wide range of conditions, except dry ones. Trim after bloom to improve the appearance and to encourage a new flush of vegetative growth. Plants are hardy to zone 3.

The most widely cultivated variant of *Mentha* ×*piperita* is the cultivar 'Citrata' known as lemon mint, bergamot mint, or eau de Cologne mint, recognized for its distinct fragrance. Sometimes it is treated as a hybrid form or as variety or subspecies *citrata*, with individual clones given names, such as 'Bergamot', 'Grapefruit', 'Lemon', 'Lime', and 'Orange', describing their fragrance. Ornamentally more distinct are several cultivars with variegated foliage, including 'Logee's' and 'Variegata', or with purple-tinged leaves, such as 'Chocolate'.

Mentha ×*piperita* blooms from mid to late summer. Cultivated in St. Louis, it flowered in July and August. At Longwood, the cultivar 'Chocolate' began to bloom between the first and the last week of August. Flowering continued through mid or late September. Once in 6 years, plants were still in bloom in the first week of October. On average, 'Chocolate' flowered for 6 weeks.

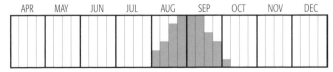

Mentha ×*piperita* 'Chocolate'

Mertensia

BLUEBELLS

The name *Mertensia* commemorates Franz Karl Mertens (1764–1831), a German botanist.

Mertensia virginica

ROANOKE BELLS, VIRGINIA BLUEBELLS, VIRGINIA-COWSLIP

This plant is native to eastern North America from Ontario, east to Maine, and south to Mississippi and Georgia. *Mertensia virginica* grows in moist meadows, rich woods, river floodplains, and along streams. It has been cultivated since the early 19th century.

Mertensia virginica forms erect clumps of basal foliage and upright or ascending, simple or branched, leafy stems to 70 cm tall, growing from fleshy, spindle-shaped rootstock. The glaucous green, elliptic to ovate leaves are summer deciduous. The basal leaves are long-petiolate and reach 20 cm in length; the cauline leaves are smaller and nearly sessile. The 3-

Mertensia virginica

Mertensia virginica

cm-long, tubular, nodding flowers are pink-purple in buds and open to rich blue. They are borne in loose, terminal racemes. Fruits are 3-mm-long wrinkled nutlets.

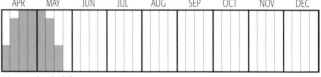

APR	MAY	JUN	JUL	AUG	SEP	OCT	NOV	DEC

Mertensia virginica

In the garden, a large patch of flowering *Mertensia virginica* is one of the most beautiful sights. It is often naturalized with spring bulbs and other early bloomers. Because *M. virginica* becomes dormant after flowering, interplant it with ferns or other perennials that can cover up the bare spot during the summer months. Choose a partially shaded location with a moist, acidic, humus-rich soil. *Mertensia virginica* spreads slowly through rhizomes and self-seeding and can be left undisturbed for many years. Plants are hardy to zone 5, possibly zone 3.

There are no botanical varieties of *Mertensia virginica* recognized in the natural populations. In cultivation, a few color variants have been selected, including white 'Alba' and pink 'Rubra'.

In the wild, *Mertensia virginica* blooms from March to May. Cultivated in Germany and Poland, it flowers in April and May. Plants grown in St. Louis started blooming between the end of March and mid-April and finished between the end of April and mid-June. At Longwood, flowering usually began between the first and the third week of April. Only once in 7 years, plants were in flower in the last week of March. *Mertensia virginica* bloomed until early or mid-May, averaging nearly 6 weeks of flowering time.

Monarda

BEEBALM, BERGAMOT, HORSEMINT

The name *Monarda* commemorates Nicolás Bautista Monardes (1493–1588), a Spanish botanist.

Monarda didyma

BEEBALM, BERGAMOT, HORSEMINT, INDIAN'S PLUME, MOUNTAIN-MINT, OSWEGO TEA, RED BALM

This plant is native to eastern North America, from

Monarda didyma

Monarda didyma

Quebec, west to Minnesota, and south to Georgia. It grows often in moist soils in rich woods, thickets, and along streams. It was used by Oswego Indians and the early American settlers as an herbal tea. *Monarda didyma* has been cultivated since the late 17th century.

Monarda didyma forms loose clumps of upright, sharply four-sided stems to 1.2 m tall, growing from creeping, stoloniferous rhizomes. The ovate to ovate-lanceolate, serrate leaves are softly pubescent, aromatic, and reach 15 cm in length. The bright scarlet red, 5- to 8-cm-long flowers, subtended by red-tinged bracts, are borne in dense, rounded terminal clusters. Fruits are oblong, smooth nutlets.

In the garden, *Monarda didyma* fits best where its spreading tendencies will not be a cause for concern, such as informal borders, wildflower meadows, or water and woodland edges. Choose a spot near a path, where the scent of foliage can be better enjoyed and where leaves can be conveniently picked for an occasional herbal tea. *Monarda didyma* is frequented by hummingbirds and brings scores of butterflies into the garden, giving enough reason to

Monarda didyma 'Gardenview Scarlet'

Monarda didyma 'Jacob Cline'

place it where these visitors can be easily observed. Plant it in a sunny or partially shaded location. This species thrives in any average garden soil as long as it is consistently moist throughout the entire growing season. Deadheading may prolong flowering, but cutting stems back will not result in rebloom or a new flush of growth; nevertheless, it may be necessary, if foliage becomes unsightly or diseased after flowering. *Monarda didyma* spreads rapidly and in confined spaces needs to be replanted and divided every 2 or 3 years to keep it in check. Alternatively, allow it to weave through other plants in a perennial border, to mimic the behavior of plants in the wild. *Monarda didyma* is hardy to zone 3.

There are no botanical varieties of *Monarda didyma* recognized among natural populations, but in cultivation a number of color variants have been selected. In addition, *M. didyma* has been hybridized with *M. fistulosa*, a purple-flowered species native to drier places, which not only widened the range of flower colors in resulting cultivars, but also improved their drought tolerance and disease resistance. More than 50 hybrid cultivars have been developed, but they are often listed as selections of *M. didyma*. Their flower colors range from white 'Schneewittchen' and pale pink 'Beauty of Cobham', to lilac 'Donnerwolke', purple 'Prärienacht', and red 'Jacob Cline'. They vary in height from 40-cm-tall 'Petite Delight' to 1.8-m-tall 'Comanche' and 'Mohawk'. Some, such as 'Gardenview Scarlet' and 'Colrain Red', have increased resistance to powdery mildew, which frequently afflicts *M. didyma*.

In the wild, *Monarda didyma* blooms from July to September. Cultivated in Moscow, it flowered starting, on average, around 10 July and ending around 1 September. Plants grown in Germany and Poland, however, are reported to start blooming in June. At Longwood, several cultivars were observed. While 'Jacob Cline' began flowering in June every year, sometimes as early as the first week of June, 'Beauty

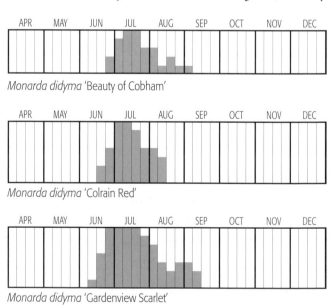

Monarda didyma 'Beauty of Cobham'

Monarda didyma 'Colrain Red'

Monarda didyma 'Gardenview Scarlet'

Monarda didyma 'Jacob Cline'

of Cobham' usually did not flower until the first week of July. Bloom duration averaged from about 6 weeks for 'Beauty of Cobham' and 'Colrain Red' to 9 weeks for 'Gardenview Scarlet' and more than 14 weeks for 'Jacob Cline'. In comparison, *M. didyma* in Moscow was in flower for 8 weeks, on average. The exceptionally long bloom season of 'Jacob Cline' resulted from this cultivar's ability to rebloom after being trimmed in late June or early July. Other varieties only rarely flowered into early September, whereas 'Jacob Cline' sometimes continued to bloom until early November.

Napaea

GLADEMALLOW

The name *Napaea* is derived from the Greek *nape*, a wooded valley, in reference to the habitat where this plant was believed to grow.

Napaea dioica

GLADEMALLOW

This perennial is native to eastern and central United States, from Vermont south to Virginia and west to Minnesota. *Napaea dioica* grows in mountain glades, shaded woodland clearings, moist prairies, alluvial meadows, on lake margins, and in other wet areas.

Napaea dioica forms coarse, robust clumps of erect stems to 2.5 m tall, growing from a large hollow taproot. The 25-cm-wide, orbicular leaves are palmately divided into five to 11 lobes, each lobe being further incised and serrated. The fragrant white flowers are dioecious, with male flowers having longer petals than female, up to 12 mm. They are borne in cymes arranged in panicles. Fruits are 6-mm-wide schizocarps breaking into several single-seeded mericarps.

Napaea dioica is well suited for all kinds of moist situations, in bog gardens, naturalized meadows, or along the margins of streams and ponds. It is valued for its large stature, lush foliage, and profuse flowers. Give preference to male plants, which have showier flowers. Plant it in full sun or partial shade. Choose a sheltered location, however, as the tall stems are vulnerable to wind damage. *Napaea dioica* thrives in humus-rich and consistently moist soil. Avoid sites subjected to periodic drought, if supplemental watering cannot be provided. Plants are hardy to zone 4.

There are no botanical varieties of *Napaea dioica* recognized currently among the natural populations,

Napaea dioica

Napaea dioica

but distinction between plants covered with stellate hairs, form *stellata*, and those with simple hairs, form *dioica*, was made in the past. In cultivation, no superior selections have been introduced.

In the wild, *Napaea dioica* blooms from June to August. Cultivated at Longwood, it began to flower in the first to the third week of June. Flowering continued through the end of July or into the first week of August, averaging a little more than 8 weeks in bloom.

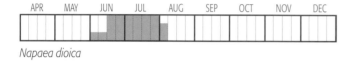

Napaea dioica

Nectaroscordum

HONEY–GARLIC

The name *Nectaroscordum* is derived from the Greek, *nectar*, the drink of the Olympian gods, and *skordon*, garlic, in reference to the nectaries on the ovary.

Nectaroscordum siculum

SICILIAN HONEY–GARLIC

This plant is native to southern Europe and western Asia Minor, from southern France and Sicily west to Crimea and Turkey. *Nectaroscordum siculum* has been cultivated since the 19th century.

Nectaroscordum siculum forms clumps of strap-shaped basal foliage and stout flowering scapes to 1.2 m tall growing from a white, ovoid, stoloniferous bulb. The linear, keeled, deeply channeled leaves grow to 40 cm long. The campanulate, pendulous flowers are green, with margins tinged white and purple. The flowers are held on long, arching pedicles and arranged up to 30 in loose umbels. Fruits are capsules.

In the garden, *Nectaroscordum siculum* is noted for its distinct, bold inflorescences, which stand out and draw attention in any perennial border, despite being only modestly colored. It is also well suited for both fresh and dry flower arrangements. Combine it with perennials that will produce lush foliage able to hide

Nectaroscordum siculum ssp. *bulgaricum*

Nectaroscordum siculum ssp. *bulgaricum*

the bare spot left by this plant's summer-deciduous leaves. Plant it in full sun, in an average garden soil that is well drained. A fair supply of moisture is beneficial in the spring, but no supplemental watering is needed after leaves senesce. *Nectaroscordum siculum* self-seeds easily under favorable conditions. If this becomes objectionable, deadhead spent flowers to prevent seed dispersal. Regular transplanting is not required, unless plants are spreading too far. Leaving the clumps undisturbed for several years improves their flowering with each passing year. Plants are hardy to zone 6.

There are two subspecies of *Nectaroscordum siculum* recognized in the natural populations. The typical subspecies *siculum* is found in the western part of the range, in France, Italy, and on the islands of Corsica, Sardinia, and Sicily. The more eastern subspecies *bulgaricum* is native to Bulgaria, Romania, Crimea, and Turkey. While subspecies *siculum* has whitish or cream flowers tinged with green and pale pink, subspecies *bulgaricum*, favored by gardeners, has greenish flowers, strongly tinged with purple and each tepal edged white.

In the wild, *Nectaroscordum siculum* blooms in spring and early summer. Plants of subspecies *bulgaricum* grown at Longwood usually started flowering in the second week of May. Only once in 6 years, they bloomed later, beginning from the last week of May. Flowering continued, on average, for 4 weeks, into early June, rarely until the third week of June.

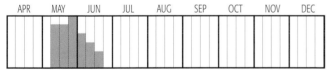

Nectaroscordum siculum ssp. bulgaricum

Nepeta

CATMINT

The name *Nepeta* was used for these plants by ancient Roman authors, probably after the town Nepete (today's Nepi), north of Rome.

Nepeta ×faassenii

BLUE CATMINT, FAASSEN'S NEPETA

This plant is a hybrid between *Nepeta racemosa* and *N. nepetella*. The latter species, native to southwestern Europe, southern Spain, France, Italy, and the Balearic Islands, has been cultivated since the 18th century. *Nepeta racemosa* was introduced from the Caucasus around 1803. The two species probably intercrossed before the end of the 19th century, but it was not until 1939 that the hybrid was given the name *N. ×faassenii*, after the Dutchman J. H. Faassen, in whose nursery it was allegedly found.

Nepeta ×faassenii forms bushy, spreading and billowy clumps of prostrate or upright stems to 60 cm tall. The oblong-ovate or lanceolate, gray-green, strongly aromatic leaves have coarsely crenate margins and reach 5 cm in length. The two-lipped, 1.2-cm-long, soft lavender to violet blue flowers are held in axillary verticillasters arranged in elongated and interrupted racemes.

In the garden, *Nepeta ×faassenii* is indispensable as an excellent edging plant that combines soft, silvery gray foliage with abundant and long-lasting flowers. It is well suited for a position in the front of a perennial border, as well as for underplanting roses and other low-growing flowering shrubs. *Nepeta ×faassenii* has smaller flowers than *N. racemosa*, but is more

Nepeta ×faassenii 'Dropmore'

floriferous and exhibits greater vigor. Plant it in full sun or, in warmer climates, partial shade. Choose a site with light, dry or moderately moist, and well-drained soil. Trim stems back after the first flush of flowers fades to encourage new growth and repeat bloom. *Nepeta ×faassenii* increases rapidly but not to the point of being invasive, so division is rarely needed. Plants are hardy to zone 5, possibly zone 3.

A number of superior selections of *Nepeta ×faassenii* have been named. Their flower colors range from white 'Alba' and 'Snowflake' to violet blue 'Kit Cat'. Many cultivars, including 'Blauknirps' and 'Blue Wonder', grow to about 35 cm tall, but others, such as 'Dropmore', can reach 60 cm or even more in height. Sources variably assign these cultivars to either *N. ×faassenii* or *N. racemosa*.

With a prompt removal of spent flowers, *Nepeta ×faassenii* can bloom from spring nearly continuously until fall. In Germany and Poland, it flowers from May until September. Similar bloom season was recorded in St. Louis. At Longwood, two selections of *N. ×faassenii*, 'Blue Wonder' and 'Dropmore', were observed. 'Blue Wonder' usually started to flower between the first and the last week of May, about a week earlier than 'Dropmore'. Their spring bloom continued until mid or late July, when flowering stems were cut back. Plants rebloomed within 3 to 6 weeks, but when trimming back was done after July, rebloom did not occur or was delayed until October. 'Blue Wonder' continued to flower for about a week longer than 'Dropmore', averaging more than 22 weeks in bloom, which gave it a 2-week advantage over 'Dropmore'.

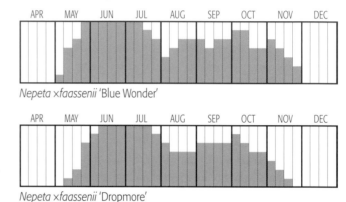

Nepeta ×faassenii 'Blue Wonder'

Nepeta ×faassenii 'Dropmore'

Nepeta ×faassenii 'Dropmore'

Nepeta grandiflora

CAUCASUS CATMINT, GIANT CATMINT

This perennial is native to the Caucasus, but locally naturalized elsewhere in eastern and central Europe. *Nepeta grandiflora* grows in montane meadows and scrub.

Nepeta grandiflora forms lax, upright clumps of erect, sparsely branched stems to 1 m tall. The oblong-cordate leaves are softly hairy, aromatic, have crenulate margins, and reach 10 cm in length. The 2-cm-long lavender blue flowers are borne in dense clusters arranged in interrupted, elongated spikes. Fruits are nutlets.

In the garden, *Nepeta grandiflora* is prized for having some of the richest blue flowers among cultivated catmints. It looks best combined with other perennials in a border, where its rather tall stems can lean on other plants. Plant in full sun or partial shade. *Nepeta grandiflora* thrives in any average garden soil that is well drained. Avoid sites with fertile, moist soil, especially if shady, because plants will produce lanky stems and will flop easily under such condi-

tions. Once established, *N. grandiflora* is quite tolerant of drought stress. Plants are hardy to zone 5, possibly zone 3.

There are no botanical varieties of *Nepeta grandiflora* recognized in the wild, but in cultivation several color variants have been selected, including indigo blue 'Bramdean', lavender blue 'Pool Bank', lavender purple 'Wild Cat', and pale pink 'Dawn to Dusk'.

Nepeta grandiflora blooms from early to late summer. Cultivated in Moscow, it flowered starting, on average, around 22 June and ending around 6 August. Plants grown in Poznań began to bloom at about the same time, around 24 June, but continued through the end of August. At Longwood, the cultivar 'Dawn to Dusk' opened flowers between the first and the third week of June. It bloomed through early (rarely late) July. In one year, after being cut back in the first week of June, plants rebloomed in the second week

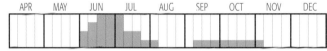

Nepeta grandiflora 'Dawn to Dusk'

Nepeta parnassica

of September. On average, 'Dawn to Dusk' was in flower for nearly 8 weeks. In comparison, *N. grandiflora* in Moscow averaged 7 weeks, whereas plants in Poznań averaged nearly 10 weeks in bloom.

Nepeta parnassica
CATMINT

This plant is native to southern Europe, from southern Albania west to Greece. *Nepeta parnassica* grows in dry meadows, on rocky slopes, and in other open places.

Nepeta parnassica forms upright, rather coarse clumps of erect or ascending, stout, glandular-sticky stems to 1.2 m tall. The oval, 3.5-cm-long leaves are aromatic, light gray-green, and have crenate margins. The 13-mm-long flowers are purple-blue or white, spotted with purple. They are borne in spike-like cymes to 8 cm long. Fruits are nutlets.

In the garden, *Nepeta parnassica* can be used like *N. grandiflora*. Its height predisposes *N. parnassica* to the center of the border, where surrounding plants may give it a little support. It is hardy to zone 5.

Nepeta parnassica is a summer bloomer, although in the United Kingdom it may flower through the early fall. Plants grown at Longwood usually began flowering in the third week of June, rarely a week earlier. They bloomed until late July or early August, although in one year flowering stopped in the first week of July, whereas in another it continued until the third week of August. *Nepeta parnassica* averaged 7 weeks in bloom at Longwood.

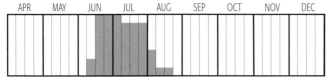

APR	MAY	JUN	JUL	AUG	SEP	OCT	NOV	DEC

Nepeta parnassica

Nepeta racemosa
PERSIAN CATMINT

This perennial is native to southwestern Asia, from Turkey east to Armenia, Azerbaijan, and northern Iran. *Nepeta racemosa* grows in open rocky places. It has been cultivated since the early 19th century.

Nepeta racemosa forms spreading clumps of decumbent, ascending or upright stems to 50 cm tall. The ovate, cordate, gray-green, strongly aromatic leaves have bluntly serrated margins and grow to 3.5

Nepeta racemosa 'Walker's Low'

cm long. The two-lipped, violet to lilac blue flowers reach 1.8 cm in length and are borne in dense verticillasters arranged in loose terminal racemes. Fruits are nutlets.

In the garden, *Nepeta racemosa* is used in a variety of situations, in the front of a perennial border, for edging beds or paths, naturalistic plantings, especially among rocks, and even as an informal ground cover. Plant it in full sun, although in warmer climates partial shade in the afternoon is beneficial. *Nepeta racemosa* thrives in any soil that is well drained and only moderately moist. It is very tolerant of drought. Trim back spent flowering stems to encourage prolonged or repeat bloom. Diligent and frequent trimming of spent flowers will also reduce self-seeding, which under favorable conditions can be quite prolific. Plants are hardy to zone 3.

Although *Nepeta racemosa* is a variable plant, only a few selections have been named, including white-flowered 'Snowflake', dense and bushy 'Walker's Low' with lavender-mauve flowers, and

Nepeta racemosa 'Walker's Low'

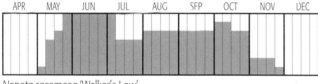

APR	MAY	JUN	JUL	AUG	SFP	OCT	NOV	DEC

Nepeta racemosa 'Walker's Low'

dwarf 'Little Titch' with pale lavender flowers. Additional cultivars were developed from crosses between *N. racemosa* and *N. nepetella*, named *N.* ×*faassenii*.

Nepeta racemosa blooms in the spring, but favorable conditions and regular trimming of spent flowering stems may extend the bloom season into early fall. Plants grown in Poznań began flowering on 26 June and ended on 20 July. Cultivated in St. Louis, *N. racemosa* bloomed from late April until late May and again from mid-June to early July. At Longwood, flowering of the cultivar 'Walker's Low' started between the first and the last week of May. Flowering usually diminished or ceased by early to mid-July. When cut back at that time, plants rebloomed with-

in 3 to 7 weeks and continued to flower through the end of October, rarely until the first frost in November. Plants that were cut back in late July did not rebloom until October. On average, 'Walker's Low' was in flower for over 21 weeks.

Nepeta sibirica
SIBERIAN CATMINT, SIBERIAN CATNIP

This perennial is native to Asia from the Altai Mountains in Siberia east to Russia's Far East and south to Ningxia and Qinghai Provinces in northern China. *Nepeta sibirica* grows on sunny slopes, at elevations between 1800 and 2700 m. It has been cultivated since the 18th century.

Nepeta sibirica forms upright clumps of erect, branched stems to 1 m tall, growing from creeping rhizomes. The lanceolate to oblong, shallowly cordate, aromatic leaves are bluntly serrated and grow to 15 cm long. The two-lipped, deep blue, 4-cm-long flowers are borne in lax verticillasters held in tiered racemes to 30 cm long.

Nepeta sibirica

Nepeta 'Joanna Reed'

In the garden, *Nepeta sibirica* is valued for its exceptional hardiness and vigor. It can be used in similar fashion as other catmints. Plant it in a sunny or partially shaded spot, in any average garden soil that is well drained. Avoid fertile and moist soil, where plants may produce rather lanky growth. Trim back stems after they finish flowering, which will encourage a new flush of growth and repeat bloom. *Nepeta sibirica* spreads rapidly and may require regular dividing to be kept in check, especially in confined spaces or in richer soils. Plants are hardy to zone 3.

A handful of superior variants of *Nepeta sibirica* are frequently grown in gardens, including lavender blue 'Six Hills Giant', reaching 1 m, and a shorter form, 'Souvenir d'André Chaudron', with medium blue flowers. Another selection, 'Joanna Reed', with iridescent blue-violet flowers, is thought to be a hybrid of *N. sibirica* with *N. ×faassenii*.

In the wild, *Nepeta sibirica* blooms in August and September. Cultivated in Poznań, it flowered

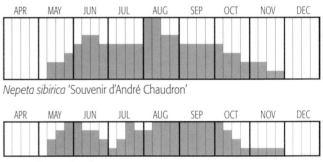

Nepeta sibirica 'Souvenir d'André Chaudron'

Nepeta 'Joanna Reed'

earlier, starting between 10 and 18 June and ending between 20 and 24 August. At Longwood, the bloom start date for 'Souvenir d'André Chaudron' varied greatly. In some years plants flowered as early as the second week of May, whereas in others the bloom was delayed until late July or the first week of August. When flowering occurred early and plants were cut back in mid-June, they rebloomed promptly and continued until the first frost. In contrast, in years when the spring bloom was delayed and subsequently plants were cut back

Nepeta stewartiana

in August or later, no rebloom took place. On average, 'Souvenir d'André Chaudron' was in flower for a little more than 15 weeks. The hybrid cultivar 'Joanna Reed', grown at Longwood, had a similar overall blooming season, but it consistently began flowering in May and consistently rebloomed after being cut back in June, averaging more than 21 weeks in bloom.

Nepeta stewartiana

CATMINT

This perennial is native to western China, from Yunnan north to Sichuan and west to Xizang. *Nepeta stewartiana* grows in montane forests and meadows, at elevations between 2700 and 3300 m.

Nepeta stewartiana forms upright clumps of erect stems to 1 m tall. The oblong to lanceolate leaves, to 10 cm long, have finely crenate margins and whitish pubescence underneath. The two-lipped, 2.5-cm-long, oblique flowers are violet blue and white-spotted on the lower lip. They are borne in loose verticillasters forming long terminal spikes. Fruits are oblong, brown nutlets.

In the garden, *Nepeta stewartiana* can be used in similar situations as other catmints. It resembles the better-known *N. sibirica* and has analogous requirements. Plants are hardy to zone 3.

In the wild, *Nepeta stewartiana* blooms from August to October. Cultivated at Longwood, it usually began flowering in May, but one year its bloom was delayed until the second week of July. When plants were cut back in late June or early July, they rebloomed within 7 to 10 weeks and then typically continued to flower until the first frost in November. Plants that were not cut back, however, bloomed just as long. *Nepeta stewartiana* averaged over 21 weeks in bloom.

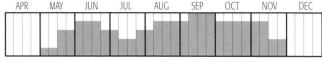

Nepeta stewartiana

Oenothera fruticosa 'Fyrverkeri'

Oenothera fruticosa ssp. *glauca*

Oenothera

EVENING–PRIMROSE

The name *Oenothera* was applied by the ancient Greeks to an unrelated plant used either for flavoring wine or giving off an aroma of wine.

Oenothera fruticosa

COMMON SUNDROPS, NARROWLEAF
EVENING–PRIMROSE

This plant is native to eastern North America, from Nova Scotia, south to Florida, and west to Oklahoma. *Oenothera fruticosa* grows in dry meadows, old fields, forest clearings, and along roadsides. It has been cultivated since the 18th century.

Oenothera fruticosa forms loose clumps of basal foliage and erect, slender, rarely branched, reddish stems to 60 cm tall. The ovate to lanceolate, sessile, and partially serrate leaves reach 10 cm in length. The bright yellow, 5-cm-wide, cup-shaped, four-petalled flowers, borne in terminal racemes, open during the day. Fruits are 1-cm-long, oblong, and prominently winged capsules.

In the garden, *Oenothera fruticosa* is used in perennial borders or naturalized meadows. It is valued primarily for its persistent flowering, but in addition its foliage takes on attractive reddish purple hues in the fall. Preferably plant it in full sun, although light afternoon shade is tolerated. *Oenothera fruticosa* thrives in moderately fertile and rather dry soils. Avoid sites with overly fertile and moist soil, where plants may flower less and instead spread aggressively. Deadheading is not needed, but if the foliage declines after flowering, plants can be cut back to the basal rosettes. *Oenothera fruticosa* is short-lived; occasionally it grows as biennial. Divide regularly every 4 years or so to maintain plant vigor and prevent uncontrolled spreading. Plants are hardy to zones 4 or 5.

Oenothera fruticosa is a variable species and there are two subspecies currently recognized among the natural populations. The typical subspecies *fruticosa* is distinguished by its pubescent leaves, whereas subspecies *glauca* differs in having broader, glaucous, and glabrous leaves and lighter color, lemon yellow flowers. Other previously described botanical variants, such as variety *linearis*, with narrower leaves and smaller flowers, or variety *fraseri*, with a dark purplish new growth, are no longer considered valid. In cultivation, several superior selections have been named.

Their flower color varies little, but some, such as 'Fyrverkeri', have particularly large flowers, to 7 cm wide. While the low-growing cultivars, including 'African Sun' and 'Cold Crick', reach only 30 cm in height, the taller 'Sonnenwende' and 'Hohes Licht' can exceed 60 cm. Some selections have brightly colored new growth: orange in 'Camel' or yellow in 'Erica Robin'.

In the wild, *Oenothera fruticosa* blooms from June to August. Cultivated in Germany, it flowers during a similar season. Plants grown in Poznań bloomed starting between 6 and 19 June and finishing between 1 and 23 July, whereas in Moscow *O. fruticosa* flowered from 22 June until 7 August. At Longwood, bloom began somewhat earlier, in late May and early June, and continued through the end of June or into early July. Only once in 7 years, sporadic rebloom was observed in mid to late July. At Longwood, *O. fruticosa* averaged 5 weeks in bloom; the cultivar 'Sonnenwende' also bloomed for 5 weeks, but about 1 week later than the species. In comparison, plants in Moscow were in flower for nearly 7 weeks. Another cultivar, 'Fyrverkeri', started to bloom after 'Sonnenwende', usually in the second week of June. Its bloom season was shorter, on average, only 3 weeks.

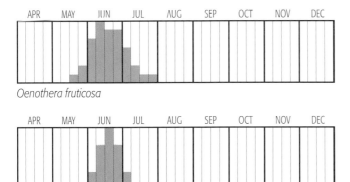

APR	MAY	JUN	JUL	AUG	SEP	OCT	NOV	DEC

Oenothera fruticosa

APR	MAY	JUN	JUL	AUG	SEP	OCT	NOV	DEC

Oenothera fruticosa 'Fyrverkeri'

APR	MAY	JUN	JUL	AUG	SEP	OCT	NOV	DEC

Oenothera fruticosa 'Sonnenwende'

Oenothera macrocarpa

MISSOURI EVENING–PRIMROSE, OZARK SUNDROPS

This perennial is native to the south-central United States, from Texas north to Illinois and Nebraska. It grows often in dry soils, in prairies, on rocky slopes, limestone glades, and along roadsides. *Oenothera macrocarpa* has been cultivated since the early 19th century.

Oenothera macrocarpa forms spreading, mounded clumps of decumbent to erect, reddish stems to 30 cm tall, growing from deep, stout taproots. The lanceolate to ovate, entire or serrate, silvery green leaves grow to 10 cm long. The funnel-shaped, light yellow flowers reach 12 cm in width and are borne singly in the leaf axils. They open in the afternoon and remain open the following morning. Fruits are orbicular capsules with very broad wings.

In the garden, *Oenothera macrocarpa* can be used in the front of a perennial border, for edging paths, on stone walls, as a ground cover, especially on rocky slopes, and for naturalizing in meadows and prairies.

Oenothera macrocarpa 'Lemon Silver'

The silvery foliage of *O. macrocarpa* emerges fairly late, so it combines effectively with many early-spring ephemerals. Plant it in full sun, in moderately fertile and rather dry soil that drains well. *Oenothera macrocarpa* tolerates drought very well, but declines rapidly when grown under excessively moist conditions. Deadheading is not needed. Following flowering, large, conspicuous fruits develop. *Oenothera macrocarpa* is short-lived and does poorly after transplanting, but it can self-seed readily. Plants are hardy to zones 4 or 5, but in colder climates they may benefit from a light cover in winter,

Oenothera macrocarpa is a highly variable species, and among the natural populations four subspecies are recognized. The typical subspecies *macrocarpa* is found throughout the species' range. The other three subspecies are restricted to Texas, Oklahoma, and Kansas. Subspecies *fremontii* is characterized by oblong fruits and smaller flowers. Subspecies *oklahomensis* is distinguished by its glabrous leaves, whereas the foliage of subspecies *incana* is strongly silvery canescent. In cultivation, a few superior selections featuring large pale yellow flowers and foliage in shades of gray- or silver-green have been named, including 'Greencourt Lemon', 'Lemon Silver', and 'Silver Blade'.

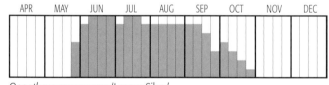

APR	MAY	JUN	JUL	AUG	SEP	OCT	NOV	DEC

Oenothera macrocarpa 'Lemon Silver'

Oenothera macrocarpa 'Lemon Silver'

In the wild, *Oenothera macrocarpa* blooms from May to July. Cultivated in Germany, it flowers from May to September. Plants grown in Poznań started to bloom between 13 and 28 June and finished between 25 August and 22 September, whereas those in Moscow flowered, on average, from 30 June to 5 September. At Longwood, the cultivar 'Lemon Silver' began flowering in the last week of May or early June. Its bloom continued through the end of September, sometimes even into October. Once in 7 years, 'Lemon Silver' was still in flower in the last week of October. It averaged more than 17 weeks in bloom.

Ophiopogon
MONDO GRASS

The name *Ophiopogon* is derived from the Greek *ophis*, snake, and *pogon*, beard, in reference to the tufted growth habit.

Ophiopogon planiscapus
MONDO GRASS

This plant is native to Japan, where it grows on open slopes and along forest margins.

Ophiopogon planiscapus forms dense, tufted clumps of grassy, arching foliage and flowering scapes to 20 cm tall, growing from a stoloniferous rootstock. The linear, 5-mm-wide, dark green leaves grow to 35 cm long. The 6-mm-long, white or lilac, campanulate flowers are borne in racemes rising slightly above the foliage. Fruits are capsules splitting early to expose fleshy, dull bluish black seeds.

In the garden, *Ophiopogon planiscapus* is valued as an excellent ground cover for smaller areas, as well as an outstanding edging plant along paths or in the front of a perennial border. Its main asset is the handsome, grassy leaves, but delicate flowers are a welcomed sight in early summer. In warmer climates, its foliage remains attractive through the winter, but in colder areas it may deteriorate in severe weather. Plant *O. planiscapus* in a warm, protected site in full sun or partial shade. It thrives in slightly acidic, humus-rich soils that are consistently moist but well drained. *Ophiopogon planiscapus* spreads slowly; therefore, plant it fairly closely if it is to be used as a ground cover. Plants are hardy to zone 7, possibly 5, but in northern areas they benefit from a light cover during the winter.

In cultivation, several variants of *Ophiopogon planiscapus* have been introduced. The most widely grown is 'Nigrescens', with exceptionally dark purple, nearly black foliage and pink flowers. A couple of white-variegated forms, such as 'Little Tabby' and 'Silver Ribbon', are also known.

Cultivated in St. Louis, *Ophiopogon planiscapus* bloomed from the first week of June until the end of June or mid-July. At Longwood, the cultivar 'Ni-

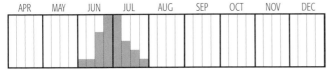

APR	MAY	JUN	JUL	AUG	SEP	OCT	NOV	DEC

Ophiopogon planiscapus 'Nigrescens'

Ophiopogon planiscapus 'Nigrescens'

grescens' usually began flowering in the third or fourth week of June, but once in 6 years it was in bloom in the first week of June. Its flowering continued, on average, for 4 weeks, into early July, rarely until the end of July.

Origanum

MARJORAM, OREGANO

The name *Origanum* is derived from the Greek *oros*, mountain, and *ganos*, joy, in reference to the habitat where many species grow.

Origanum laevigatum

SHOWY OREGANO

This perennial is native to southwestern Asia, from Lebanon, Syria, and Cyprus, north to Turkey. *Origanum laevigatum* grows often in dry meadows, open scrub, and on rocky slopes. It has been cultivated since the early 20th century.

Origanum laevigatum forms bushy, upright or sprawling subshrubs with slender, wiry, purplish stems to 60 cm tall. The ovate to elliptic, pubescent, scarcely aromatic leaves are gray-green, sometimes tinged purple, and reach 2 cm in length The pink to purple, 1.5-cm-long flowers are subtended by reddish purple bracts and borne in whorls arranged in loose spike-like inflorescences. Fruits are small nutlets.

In the garden, *Origanum laevigatum* is well suited for planting in the front of a perennial border, along paths and edging other hard surfaces, or for massing on rocky slopes. It produces small but profuse purplish pink flowers backed by purple-tinged calyces, bracts, and leaves. Plant it in a warm sunny location in light, moderately fertile, and well-drained soil. *Origanum laevigatum* tolerates drought and summer heat, but will quickly succumb to excessively humid or damp conditions. Cut plants back in early spring to remove stems that might have died over the winter and to keep their habit compact. *Origanum laevigatum* increases through underground rhizomes and rooting procumbent stems. It does not require regular dividing, except to control its spread. Plants are hardy to zones 5 or 6, but in colder climates may need a light winter protection.

In cultivation, a couple of color variants have been selected, including 'Herrenhausen', with lilac

Origanum laevigatum 'Herrenhausen'

Origanum 'Rotkugel'

flowers and purplish leaves, and 'Hopleys', with pinkish flowers and light green leaves. A variegated form, 'Silver Anniversary', features creamy yellow and white leaves and pink flowers. Furthermore, *Origanum laevigatum* has been hybridized with the European species *O. vulgare* to produce several cultivars, such as 'Rosenkuppel', with purple-flushed leaves, and 'Rotkugel', with deep purple bracts.

Origanum laevigatum blooms in late summer and fall. Cultivated in Germany, it flowers in August and September. The cultivar 'Herrenhausen' grown in St. Louis blooms from mid-July to late August or mid-September. The same cultivar at Longwood began flowering between the third week of July and second week of August. It usually continued blooming through the end of September or the first week of October, although in 1 of 4 years its flowering stopped in the last week of August. At Longwood 'Herrenhausen' averaged a little over 8 weeks in bloom. In comparison, two hybrid cultivars observed

at Longwood, 'Rosenkuppel' and 'Rotkugel', started to flower 1 or 2 weeks before 'Herrenhausen'. They also flowered later into the fall, averaging over 12 weeks in bloom for 'Rotkugel' and 13 weeks for 'Rosenkuppel'.

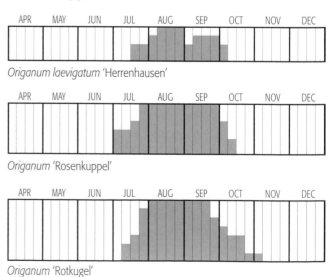

Origanum laevigatum 'Herrenhausen'

Origanum 'Rosenkuppel'

Origanum 'Rotkugel'

Paeonia

PEONY

The name *Paeonia* is derived from the Greek *paionia*, after Paeon or Paion, the physician to the gods.

Paeonia lactiflora

CHINESE PEONY, GARDEN PEONY

This plant is native to eastern Asia, from Gansu Province in northern China, north to Siberia, and east to Japan, Korea, and Russia's Far East. It grows in open woodlands, meadows, on dry rocky slopes, and along streams and rivers, at elevations from 400 to 2300 m. *Paeonia lactiflora* has been cultivated in the Orient for more than 1000 years and in the West since the late 18th century. The first Chinese selections of *P. lactiflora* arrived in Europe in the early 19th century. They were received enthusiastically because, in addition to having fragrant flowers, they introduced colors and forms unseen previously in the European species. Breeders, especially those in France, soon started to introduce their own varieties. Beginning in the early 20th century, hybrids were developed between *P. lactiflora* and other species, including European *P. officinalis* and *P. wittmanniana* from the Caucasus.

Paeonia lactiflora forms upright or mounded clumps of stout, glabrous, reddish brown stems branched above, reaching 1 m in height, and growing from a woody crown with thick, tuberous roots. The 30-cm-wide, long-petiolate, biternate leaves have lanceolate to ovate, entire or lobed leaflets to 16 cm long. The fragrant, bowl-shaped flowers, up to 10 cm wide, have eight to 13 white or pink petals surrounding a conspicuous boss of yellow stamens, and up to five large green or red carpels. Flowers are borne singly or several to the stem. Fruits are oblong follicles to 3 cm long.

In the garden, *Paeonia lactiflora* and its selections have enjoyed unwavering popularity since their introduction in the 19th century. Their sumptuous flowers are highly prized for bouquets. *Paeonia lactiflora* can be grown alone in large groups, combined with other perennials in borders, or mixed with spring-flowering shrubs. Although its flowering season is short, the foliage remains attractive through the rest of the season, and in some cases even colors well in the fall. Also, before flowering, emerging leaves are often colored deep mahogany and provide a striking

Paeonia lactiflora 'America'

companion for the early-spring bulbs. *Paeonia lactiflora* thrives in full sun, although in partial shade it may flower longer. Plant it in deep, fertile, humus-rich, moderately moist, and well-drained soil. Once established, *P. lactiflora* can tolerate summer drought, but still requires consistent moisture in spring before and during flowering. Varieties with large and double flowers usually require staking. Deadhead spent flowers to keep a neat appearance. Cut back the stems in the fall after frost. *Paeonia lactiflora* is long-lived, increases slowly, and needs several years to fully develop. Transplanting and dividing are not necessary, unless flowering or vigor declines. Plants are hardy to zone 5, possibly zone 3.

More than 1000 selections and hybrids of *Paeonia lactiflora* are in cultivation. Based on the form of their flowers, cultivars are classified as single-flowered, Japanese or Imperial, anemone-flowered, semi-double-flowered, or double-flowered. Single-flowered varieties, such as 'America', have five to 10

Paeonia lactiflora 'Cytherea'

Paeonia lactiflora 'Festiva Maxima'

Paeonia lactiflora 'Gold Rush'

Paeonia lactiflora 'Sarah Bernhardt'

petals surrounding numerous stamens in the center. In Japanese peonies, such as 'Gold Rush', petals surround numerous stamens transformed into showy staminoids, whereas in anemone-flowered cultivars, including 'Philoméle' and 'Primevère', anthers are transformed into petal-like petaloids. Forms with semi-double flowers, exemplified by 'Cytherea', have outer petals surrounding broad petals and stamens in the center, whereas the double-flowered ones, including 'Festiva Maxima' and 'Sarah Bernhardt', have all stamens transformed into petals. The flower colors range from white and pink to deep crimson and maroon.

In the wild, *Paeonia lactiflora* blooms in May or June. Flowering of plants cultivated in Germany, Poland, and the United Kingdom tends to concentrate in June, but the difference between the early- and the late-flowering cultivars may be 4 to 6 weeks. This allows for extending the bloom period by care-

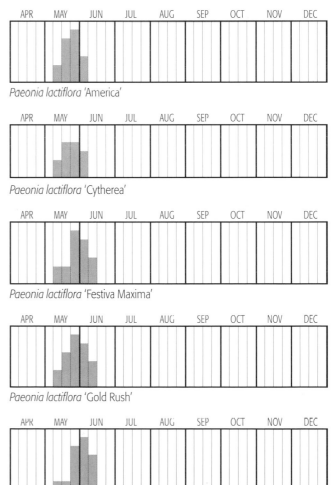

APR MAY JUN JUL AUG SEP OCT NOV DEC

Paeonia lactiflora 'America'

APR MAY JUN JUL AUG SEP OCT NOV DEC

Paeonia lactiflora 'Cytherea'

APR MAY JUN JUL AUG SEP OCT NOV DEC

Paeonia lactiflora 'Festiva Maxima'

APR MAY JUN JUL AUG SEP OCT NOV DEC

Paeonia lactiflora 'Gold Rush'

APR MAY JUN JUL AUG SEP OCT NOV DEC

Paeonia lactiflora 'Sarah Bernhardt'

fully selecting early-, mid-, and late-season cultivars, each of them expected to flower for about 2 weeks. At Longwood, several cultivars were observed, including early- to midseason 'America' and 'Cytherea', midseason 'Festiva Maxima' and 'Gold Rush', and mid to late-season 'Sarah Bernhardt'. While their overall bloom season spanned from the second week of May to the second week of June, the difference between the earliest in this group, 'Cytherea', and the latest, 'Sarah Bernhardt', was usually about 2 weeks. For all cultivars, the bloom start date varied by about 3 weeks between the earliest and the latest. 'America', for example, one year began flowering in the second week of May, whereas in another it was delayed until the first week of June. In comparison, 'America' in St. Louis started to bloom between the last week of April and the second week of May, which is 2 or 3 weeks before plants at Longwood. The average bloom duration of about 2.5 weeks was similar for all cultivars grown at Longwood.

Parthenium

WILD-QUININE

The name *Parthenium* is derived from the Greek *parthenos*, virgin, in reference to the fact that only the female ray florets produce fruits.

Parthenium integrifolium

AMERICAN FEVERFEW, PRAIRIE DOCK, WILD-QUININE
This perennial is native to the United States, from New York south to Georgia and west to Minnesota

Parthenium integrifolium

and Texas. *Parthenium integrifolium* grows often in dry soil, in open woodlands, glades, and prairies, at elevations to 500 m.

Parthenium integrifolium forms upright clumps of stout, striate stems, usually branched above, to 1.2 m tall, growing from a thickened, tuberous rootstock. The ovate to lanceolate, aromatic, hairy leaves grow to 35 cm long, have crenate to coarsely toothed margins, and are sometimes lobed near their bases. The 1-cm-wide flower heads are comprised of five (rarely six) white ray florets and 15 to 35 disc florets. They are arranged in corymb-like or panicle-like terminal arrays to 25 cm wide. Fruits are compressed, 4-mm-long achenes.

Parthenium integrifolium is best suited for cottage-style gardens or naturalistic meadow- or prairie-style plantings. Although its flowers are rather small, they are produced in sufficient numbers to make *P. integrifolium* a worthwhile subject for perennial borders. Plant it in full sun, in any average garden soil that is

Parthenium integrifolium

moderately moist and well drained. Deadhead spent flower heads to keep a neat appearance. Plants are hardy to zone 3.

In the wild, *Parthenium integrifolium* blooms from May to September, depending on the region. Cultivated in St. Louis, it flowered from May to August, whereas plants in Athens, Georgia, bloomed in June and July. At Longwood, flowering usually began in June, although in the first year after planting the bloom was delayed until the last week of August. One year, flowering stopped in July but returned in the second week of August. It usually continued through mid or late September. On average, *P. integrifolium* at Longwood was in flower for a little over 11 weeks. In comparison, plants in Athens bloomed for 3 to 4 weeks.

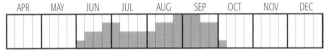

Parthenium integrifolium

Patrinia scabiosifolia 'Nagoya'

Patrinia

PATRINIA

The name *Patrinia* commemorates Eugène Louis Melchior Patrin (1742–1814), a French naturalist.

Patrinia scabiosifolia

SCABIOUS PATRINIA

This perennial is native to eastern Asia, from Taiwan, north to Japan and Sakhalin, and west to eastern Siberia. *Patrinia scabiosifolia* grows in open places, meadows, and grassy slopes from the seashore to 1400 m in elevation.

Patrinia scabiosifolia forms upright, loose clumps of basal foliage and erect, slender, leafy flowering stems to 1.8 m tall, growing from stout, short rhizomes. The basal leaves are oblong to ovate and deeply serrated or cleft, whereas the cauline leaves are pinnately parted with five to seven coarsely toothed leaflets. The 4-mm-wide yellow flowers are borne in cymes arranged in flat-topped open panicles. Fruits are 3-mm-long winged achenes.

In the garden, *Patrinia scabiosifolia* is used in perennial borders and naturalistic wildflower meadows. It is also highly regarded as a cut flower. Plant it in a warm and sunny or partially shaded location. *Patrinia scabiosifolia* thrives in deep, humus-rich, moderately moist, and well-drained soil. Deadhead

Patrinia scabiosifolia

spent flowers to prolong flowering, and cut back to basal foliage after all bloom is finished. *Patrinia scabiosifolia* is rather slow to establish, but it is long-lived and rarely needs division. It may self-seed under favorable conditions, but rarely in numbers high enough to be of concern. Plants are hardy to zones 5 or 6

Plants with especially thick and lustrous leaves, found among the wild population in central Honshu, Japan, are described as form *crassa*. In cultivation, a low-growing selection is known under the name 'Nagoya'. It reaches only 1 m in height, but otherwise resembles the species.

Patrinia scabiosifolia blooms in late summer and early fall. In the wild in Japan, it flowers from August to October. Plants cultivated in St. Louis started to flower between mid-June and the first week of July and ended in mid or late September. *Patrinia scabiosifolia* grown at Longwood flowered a couple of weeks later than in St. Louis. Their bloom start date varied between the second week of July and the second week of August. Flowering continued until the end of September, but in some years flowers were still present at the end of October. On average, *P. scabiosifolia* at Longwood flowered for 11 weeks. In comparison, bloom duration in St. Louis varied from 10 to 15 weeks.

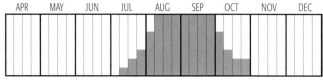

Patrinia scabiosifolia

Penstemon

BEARDTONGUE

The name *Penstemon* is derived from the Greek *pente*, five, and *stemon*, stamen, in reference to the flowers having the fifth stamen sterile.

Penstemon barbatus

BEARDLIP PENSTEMON, COMMON BEARDTONGUE

This plant is native to southwestern North America, from Colorado and Utah, east to Texas, and south to northern Mexico. *Penstemon barbatus* grows in scrub, in dry forests, and on rocky hills. It has been cultivated since the late 18th century.

Penstemon barbatus forms rounded to upright clumps of semi-evergreen, tufted basal foliage and erect or ascending, slender, branched flowering stems to 1.5 m tall, growing from a creeping rootstock. The lanceolate to linear leaves are glabrous, sometimes glaucous, have entire (rarely serrate) margins, and reach 15 cm in length. The two-lipped, tubular, 3- to 5-cm-long flowers are light pink to carmine. The lower lip is strongly reflexed and often bearded with yellow, bristly hairs. The flowers are held in open, pyramidal, terminal panicles. Fruits are capsules.

In the garden, *Penstemon barbatus* is best suited for informal borders, naturalistic plantings, and stony slopes. Plant it in full sun or partial shade, but avoid deep shade, where plants grow lanky and flower less. Choose a site with a light, moderately fertile, and moist soil that drains easily. Deadhead spent flowers to extend bloom, and cut the stems back to the basal foliage to maintain a neat appearance after flowering. Plants are hardy to zones 2 to 5, but in colder climates light cover in winter is recommended.

There are three subspecies of *Penstemon barbatus* recognized among the wild populations. From the typical subspecies *barbatus*, subspecies *torreyi* differs in having unbearded flowers and all leaves linear, whereas subspecies *trichander* stands out because of its hairy anthers. Several previously described botanical varieties, such as *coccineus* or *praecox*, are no longer considered valid and are best treated as cultivars or cultivar groups. In cultivation, several color variants, such as white 'Albus' or pink 'Carnea', are known. Furthermore, *P. barbatus* has been hybridized with blue-flowered *P. virgatus* and other species to produce a range of cultivars sometimes referred to as Barbatus Hybrids, including rose-purple 'Prairie Dusk' and scarlet 'Prairie Fire'. Some are produced as seed strains and offer a mix of colors, among them 'Navigator'.

Penstemon barbatus blooms in late spring to midsummer. Cultivated in Moscow, it flowered from around 20 June until 2 August. In Poznań, bloom began between 13 and 30 June and ended between 17 and 29 July, but plants that had suffered winter damage did not flower until early August or early September, depending on the degree of injury. In Georgia and Missouri, an earlier bloom season, from May to June, was observed. Similarly, at Longwood

Penstemon 'Prairie Dusk'

flowering of the cultivar 'Prairie Dusk' started in late May and continued through mid or late June, averaging 4 weeks in bloom. In comparison, plants in Moscow were in flower for 6 weeks, on average.

Penstemon digitalis

FOXGLOVE BEARDTONGUE, SMOOTH WHITE PENSTEMON

This plant is native to eastern North America, from Quebec, south to Georgia, and west to Texas and South Dakota. *Penstemon digitalis* grows in open forests and woodland margins, meadows, prairies, old fields, and along railroad tracks. It has been cultivated since the early 19th century.

Penstemon digitalis forms vigorous, dense clumps of erect or ascending, glabrous stems, often flushed with red, to 1.7 m tall. The elliptic to oblanceolate leaves often have serrate margins and reach 18 cm in length. The two-lipped, tubular, 3-cm-long, white flowers may be flushed pale pink or lavender and marked with purple nectar guides inside. They are borne in broad, open panicles to 30 cm long. Fruits are capsules.

In the garden, *Penstemon digitalis* is valued as an easy-to-grow, reliable summer bloomer that produces swarms of delicately colored flowers. Use it in large groupings in either formal perennial borders or naturalistic meadows or wild gardens. Plant it in full sun, in any average garden soil that is moderately

Penstemon digitalis 'Husker Red'   *Penstemon digitalis* 'Husker Red'

moist and well drained. Deadhead spent flowers to prolong flowering and to maintain a neat appearance. Plants are hardy to zone 5, possibly zone 3.

There are no botanical varieties of *Penstemon digitalis* recognized in the wild, but in cultivation, a number of superior selections have been named, including pure white 'Woodville White'; white, tinted bluish 'Ruby Tuesday'; and white, tinged pink 'Husker Red', which also features deep maroon leaves.

Penstemon digitalis blooms from the middle of spring to early summer. Cultivated in St. Louis, it flowered from late May until mid-June. Similarly, at Longwood the cultivar 'Husker Red' usually started to bloom in late May or early June, but once in 7 years it was in flower in the second week of May. Flowering continued through the end of June and often into the first week of July. On average, 'Husker Red' flowered for nearly 6 weeks at Longwood. In comparison, this cultivar in St. Louis bloomed for only 3 to 4 weeks.

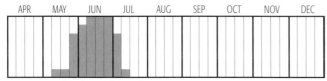

Penstemon digitalis 'Husker Red'

Perovskia

PEROVSKIA, RUSSIAN–SAGE

The name *Perovskia* commemorates Vasilii Alekseevich Perovski (1795–1857), a Russian general.

Perovskia ×hybrida

HYBRID PEROVSKIA

This hybrid was bred by crossing *Perovskia abrotanoides*, native to Turkmenistan and northeastern Iran, and *P. atriplicifolia*, from western Pakistan, Afghanistan, and Tibet. Both species are found growing on dry, rocky slopes and screes.

Perovskia ×hybrida forms an upright, fine-textured, open subshrub with stiff, erect, square, silvery pubescent stems that are woody at the base, to 1.5 m tall, growing from a deep rootstock. The aromatic, ovate leaves are deeply pinnately dissected, covered with gray-green pubescence, and reach 5 cm in length. The two-lipped, tubular, 1-cm-long, lavender blue flowers are borne in false whorls arranged in airy, terminal racemes or panicles to 40 cm long.

In the garden, *Perovskia ×hybrida* provides unique and striking foliage and texture effects. The silvery branches carry masses of light blue, airy flowers, creating a highly desirable element for compositions in perennial borders. Plant it in a warm, sunny location, as shading invariably causes plants to stretch and flop. *Perovskia ×hybrida* thrives in any average garden soil that is moderately moist and fertile and well drained. Avoid sites that stay damp, especially during the winter. *Perovskia ×hybrida* can tolerate extended periods of drought. It retains a neat, graceful appearance after flowering, even through the winter, when the silvery, withered stems take on ghostly qualities. Cut the stems back to about 15 cm off the ground in the spring, before new growth starts. *Perovskia ×hybrida* increases slowly and is best left undisturbed for many years. Plants are hardy to zone 5, but benefit from a light winter cover of boughs in colder climates.

Perovskia ×hybrida 'Longin'

Selections of *Perovskia* ×*hybrida* are preferred as garden plants because their inflorescences are often longer and showier than those of either parent. Because their origin is not always known, they are sometimes listed as selections of *P. atriplicifolia*. Flower colors vary little and include light blue 'Filigran' and violet blue 'Longin', whereas the leaves range from nearly entire in 'Blue Haze' to finely dissected in 'Blue Spire'.

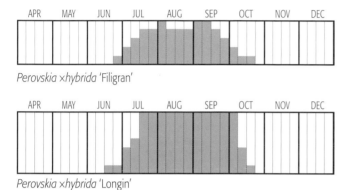

Perovskia ×*hybrida* 'Filigran'

Perovskia ×*hybrida* 'Longin'

Perovskia ×*hybrida* blooms for a long time during the summer. Cultivated in Illinois and Ohio, it flowers from July until September. Plants in St. Louis began flowering earlier, in mid-June. At Longwood, two cultivars were observed, 'Filigran' and 'Longin'. Both selections began flowering in early to mid-July, but 'Longin' continued to bloom at least through the first week of October, whereas 'Filigran' sometimes ended flowering in mid or late September. While 'Longin' averaged nearly 15 weeks in bloom, the flowering period of 'Filigran' was 3 weeks shorter.

Persicaria

KNOTWEED

The name *Persicaria* is derived from the Latin *persica*, peach, and *aria*, pertaining to, in reference to appearance of the leaves of some species resembling those of peach trees.

Perovskia ×*hybrida*

Persicaria affinis

HIMALAYAN FLEECE–FLOWER

This perennial is native to the Himalayas, from Pakistan, east to Sikkim, and north to Tibet. *Persicaria affinis* grows in alpine meadows, on grassy slopes, and on rocky slopes, at elevations of 4000 to 4900 m. It has been cultivated since the middle of the 19th century.

Persicaria affinis forms densely tufted mats of basal foliage and flowering stems to 30 cm tall, growing from creeping, somewhat woody rhizomes. The erect, mostly basal, lanceolate to spathulate leaves, to 10 cm long, have prominent white midveins and finely serrate margins. In the fall they turn bronze or red and persist through the winter. The tiny flowers are rose red and fade to white; they are borne in dense, erect, terminal spikes to 7 cm in length. Fruits are 3-mm-long shiny brown achenes enclosed in a persistent perianth.

In the garden, *Persicaria affinis* makes an excellent low and dense ground cover, attractive dark green in summer, bronzing in winter. It spreads rapidly but can be easily controlled. Use it in the front of a perennial border, among shrubs or rocks, along a path

or stream, or on the bank of a pond. *Persicaria affinis* grows best in full sun. Shaded plants do not develop into dense mats. Plant it in any average garden soil that stays consistently moist. *Persicaria affinis* is hardy to zone 3.

There are no botanical varieties of *Persicaria affinis* recognized among the natural populations, but in cultivation a few superior forms, including 'Superba', 'Darjeeling Red', and 'Donald Lowndes', have been selected. They feature flowers in shades of pink, rose, and red.

In the wild, *Persicaria affinis* blooms in July and August. Cultivated in Poland, it flowers from June to September, whereas in Germany from August to October. At Longwood, the cultivar 'Superba' usually began to bloom in late June or the first week of July, but in some years flowers opened as early as mid-May. Flowering continued through mid or late September, occasionally until the second week of October. On average, 'Superba' was in bloom for 16 weeks.

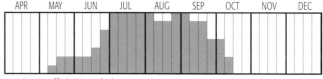

APR	MAY	JUN	JUL	AUG	SEP	OCT	NOV	DEC

Persicaria affinis 'Superba'

Persicaria virginiana

JUMPSEED

This plant is native to eastern North America, from Quebec, west to Ontario, and south to Florida and Texas, and in central Mexico. *Persicaria virginiana* grows in moist rich forests, thickets, and floodplains, at elevations to 500 m. It has been cultivated since the middle of the 17th century.

Persicaria virginiana forms rounded, bushy clumps of upright or arching, leafy stems, simple or branched above, to 1.2 m tall, growing from rhizomes. The elliptical to ovate leaves, to 25 cm in length, are marked with dark brown in the center. The tiny, 3-mm-long, greenish white to pink flowers are borne in slender terminal and axillary spikes to 30 cm long. Fruits are 3-mm-long, brown or cream-colored achenes.

In the garden, *Persicaria virginiana* is valued primarily for its attractive foliage. It performs well as a ground cover, providing a foil for taller perennials in a border, or in woodland margins. Preferably, plant it in partial shade, where markings on the leaves color

Persicaria affinis 'Superba'

Persicaria virginiana

Persicaria virginiana 'Painter's Palette'

Persicaria virginiana 'Painter's Palette'

Persicaria virginiana 'Painter's Palette'

best. *Persicaria virginiana* will also succeed in full sun provided that soils stay consistently moist. Choose a site sheltered from strong winds, which easily bruise the leaves. *Persicaria virginiana* thrives in fertile, moist, and well-drained soil, but it can adapt to a wide range of conditions. Because this species spreads rapidly through rhizomes and self-seeding, it should be monitored to prevent it from encroaching on neighboring plants. Plants are hardy to zones 4 or 5.

Persicaria virginiana is a variable species, but no botanical varieties are recognized among the natural populations. In cultivation, several forms with variegated or strongly blotched leaves have been selected, including 'Lance Corporal', with bold, dark brown markings on its leaves; 'Painter's Palette', with white-variegated and pink-blotched leaves; and 'Variegata', with irregular creamy white blotches and splashes on the leaves.

In the wild, *Persicaria virginiana* blooms from July to October. Cultivated in St. Louis, it flowered from July until September. At Longwood, the bloom start date varied by 6 weeks, from the second week of August to the last week of September. On average, plants flowered for nearly 5 weeks. The cultivar 'Painter's Palette' was as variable in its bloom start date, but it flowered a couple of weeks earlier than the species and averaged a little more than 6 weeks in bloom.

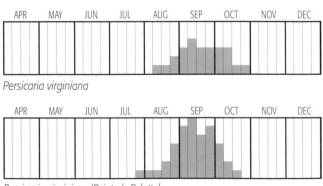

Persicaria virginiana

Persicaria virginiana 'Painter's Palette'

Petasites japonicus

Petasites

BUTTERBUR, SWEET COLTSFOOT

The name *Petasites* is derived from the Greek *petasos*, a broad-brimmed hat, in reference to the large, round leaves.

Petasites japonicus

FUKI, JAPANESE BUTTERBUR, SWEET COLTSFOOT

This perennial is native to eastern Asia, from Sakhalin in Russia, south to Japan's Ryukyu Islands, and west to Korea and eastern China, and it has naturalized in parts of Europe. *Petasites japonicus* often grows in wet soil in moist forests, thickets, grasslands, along streams, near ponds and lakes, and seaside scree, at elevations to 700 m. It has been cultivated in Asia as a vegetable for centuries.

Petasites japonicus forms vigorous, mounded clumps of bold basal foliage to 1 m tall and stout, bracteate stems to 20 cm tall in flower, extending to 1 m tall in fruit, growing from widely spreading

Petasites japonicus 'Purpureus'

rhizomes. The long-petiolate, reniform to orbicular leaves have dentate margins, and reach 80 cm in width. They appear after the flowers. The scented, milky white flower heads are held in dense corymbs atop short scapes covered closely with green, linear bracts. Male flower heads are comprised of tubular functionally staminate or bisexual inner florets and sterile peripheral florets, whereas female flower heads have nearly all florets pistillate. Fruits are cylindrical achenes with a 12-mm-long pappus.

In the garden, *Petasites japonicus* is grown for its very early flowers, followed by immense leaves. Thanks to its wide-spreading rhizomes, *P. japonicus* is capable of covering large areas in naturalistic woodland gardens, on moist banks of streams, ponds, or bogs. In small gardens, *P. japonicus* should be contained by planting in containers sunken in the ground or in spaces enclosed by hardscaping to limit its spread. Plant it in partial or full shade. When grown in full sun, plants often wilt during hot days even if well watered. *Petasites japonicus* thrives in a wide range of soils, provided they are consistently moist or wet during the entire growing season. It does not require regular dividing or transplanting, except to control its spread. Plants are hardy to zones 4 or 5.

Plants of *Petasites japonicus* ssp. *giganteus*, found in the wild on Hokkaido, on Honshu, and in Korea and northeastern China, have leaves to 1.5 m wide held on petioles to 2 m long and flowering scapes to 40 cm long. In cultivation, a couple of selections have been made, including 'Purpureus', with smaller

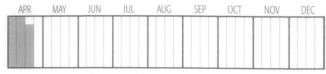

APR	MAY	JUN	JUL	AUG	SEP	OCT	NOV	DEC

Petasites japonicus 'Purpureus'

purple-tinged leaves, and 'Nishiki-buki', with leaves streaked and blotched with yellow.

In the wild in Japan, *Petasites japonicus* blooms from April to May. Similarly, plants cultivated in Moscow flowered, on average, from 19 April to 3 May. In St. Louis, flowering began between the second week of March and the first week of April and continued through the end of March or the third week of April. At Longwood, the cultivar 'Purpureus' was already in flower in the first week of April in all 6 years of observations, and it bloomed usually until the third week of April, averaging 3 weeks in bloom. In comparison, plants in Moscow flowered for 2 weeks, on average.

Phedimus

STONECROP

The name *Phedimus* is thought to be derived from the Greek *phaidimos*, shining, possibly in reference to the glossy leaves of some species.

Phedimus kamtschaticus

KAMCHATKA STONECROP, ORANGE STONECROP

This plant is native to northeastern Asia, from Kamchatka in Russia, south to Hokkaido in Japan, and

Phedimus kamtschaticus 'Weihenstephaner Gold'

west to Hebei in China. It grows in gravelly soil on rocky slopes, at elevations from 600 to 1800 m. It has been cultivated since the early 19th century. *Phedimus kamtschaticus* was classified previously as a species of *Sedum*.

Phedimus kamtschaticus forms open, spreading, semi-evergreen clumps of simple, erect or ascending leafy stems to 20 cm tall, growing from a thick, branched, and woody rootstock and slender rhizomes creeping on the surface. Young stems appear in late summer and flower the following spring. The 3.5-cm-long, glossy green and fleshy leaves are oblong to spatulate, sessile, and sharply serrate above the middle. The starry orange-yellow flowers, 1 to 2 cm wide, are arranged in open, flat, few-flowered terminal cymes. Fruits are follicles.

In the garden, *Phedimus kamtschaticus* is used as a loose ground cover for smaller areas, including green roofs, but may be even better suited to inhabit small nooks and crannies in stone walls, between rocks, pavers, or steps. Under favorable conditions, it remains attractive throughout the growing season, thanks to its glossy foliage and profuse bright flowers, followed by orangey follicles. Plant it in full sun, in any average garden soil that drains readily. Despite its succulent appearance, *P. kamtschaticus* does not tolerate prolonged droughts particularly well. Plants are hardy to zones 3 or 4.

Phedimus kamtschaticus is a highly variable species and several varieties have been described among wild populations, including *middendorffianus*, with narrow and deeply serrate leaves, *ellacombianus*, with wide and crenate leaves, and *selskianus*, with hairy leaves. These varieties are considered as separate species in some accounts. Plants widely grown in gardens are thought to represent variety *floriferum*, with more numerous but smaller flowers and densely branched habit. In cultivation, several superior forms have been selected, including 'Variegatus', with creamy-banded leaves, 'Weihenstephaner Gold', with golden yellow flowers, and 'Takahira Dake', with reddish stems.

In its native habitat in Japan and China, *Phedimus kamtschaticus* blooms from July to September. Cultivated in Germany and Poland, it flowers at about the same time. Plants grown in Moscow bloomed, on average, from 27 June to 25 July. At Longwood, the cultivar 'Variegatus' began flowering between the third week of May and the first week of June.

APR	MAY	JUN	JUL	AUG	SEP	OCT	NOV	DEC

Phedimus kamtschaticus 'Variegatus'

It usually continued to bloom through the end of June, but in one year flowers lasted until mid-July. On average, 'Variegatus' flowered for a little more than 4 weeks. Likewise, *P. kamtschaticus* in Moscow also averaged about 4 weeks in bloom.

Phlox

PHLOX

The name *Phlox* is derived from the Greek *phlox*, flame, and was applied by the ancient Greeks to a related plant, campion.

Phlox amoena

CHALICE PHLOX, HAIRY PHLOX

This perennial is native to the southeastern United States, from Kentucky and North Carolina south to Mississippi and Florida. *Phlox amoena* grows often in dry open forests, on rocky slopes, barrens, sandhills, and road banks.

Phlox amoena forms decumbent clumps of erect, simple or rarely branched pubescent stems to 30 cm tall. The elliptic or linear pubescent leaves have ciliate margins and reach 5 cm in length. The pink to lavender flowers, to 2 cm wide, are borne in compact, sessile, terminal cymes subtended by a leafy involucre. Fruits are papery capsules.

In the garden, *Phlox amoena* is best suited for informal plantings as an open, loose, and fast-spreading ground cover. Allow it to creep between other taller perennials and create a foil of soft stems, fine-textured foliage, and delicate flowers. Plant it in full sun or partial shade. Choose a site with moderately moist and fertile soil that is well drained. Cut *P. amoena* back after flowering to maintain a neat appearance. Plants increase vigorously, but regular dividing is not necessary except to restrict their spreading. *Phlox amoena* is hardy to zone 7.

There are two subspecies recognized among the natural populations. Subspecies *amoena* is distributed throughout the species' range, whereas subspecies *lighthipei* is found only on the coastal plains of South Carolina, Georgia, and Florida. In cultivation, although there are no selections named yet, plants may vary in their flower color from white to magenta-red.

In the wild, *Phlox amoena* blooms from April to June, depending on the region. Cultivated in Germany, it flowers in April and May. Plants grown in Moscow bloomed, on average, between 28 May and 19 June. At Longwood, the bloom start date varied by 4 weeks, between the second week of May and the second week of June. Flowering usually continued through late June, but often into the first week of July. Once in 6 years, *P. amoena* rebloomed weakly in the third week of July. On average, it flowered at Longwood for a little more than 5 weeks. In comparison, plants in Moscow were in bloom for 3 weeks.

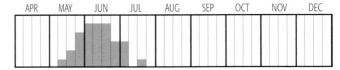

APR	MAY	JUN	JUL	AUG	SEP	OCT	NOV	DEC

Phlox amoena

Phlox bifida

CLEFT PHLOX, SAND PHLOX

This perennial is native to the United States, from Michigan, south to Tennessee, and west to Kansas. *Phlox bifida* grows in dry, stony soil in upland woods, on exposed cliffs, rocky slopes and ledges, sandhills, and dunes.

Phlox bifida forms tufted, spreading clumps of prostrate or ascending, leafy, rough-pubescent and much-branched stems to 30 cm tall, somewhat woody at the base. The stiff, narrowly linear leaves reach 6 cm in length. The purple to white flowers, to 2 cm wide, have deeply notched petals. They are borne on elongated filiform pedicels, in six- to 12-flowered loose cymes. Fruits are ovoid capsules.

In the garden, *Phlox bifida* is valued as a tough and floriferous perennial for a border, stone wall, stony bank, or naturalized wildflower meadow. Plant it in full sun, although light shade can be tolerated. *Phlox bifida* thrives in dry, sandy soils of low fertility, but it will succeed in any average garden soil provided it is well drained. Its leaves tend to senesce after flowering; cutting plants back will improve the appearance. *Phlox bifida* spreads gradually through trailing stems and self-seeding to eventually form large colonies. Plants are hardy to zone 4.

There are two subspecies of *Phlox bifida* found among wild populations. Subspecies *bifida*, found throughout the species' range, has glandular-pubescent inflorescences. Subspecies *stellaria*, with a distribution restricted to areas from Illinois south, is distinguished by glabrous or glandless inflorescences. In cultivation, a number of color variants have been selected, including white 'Minima Colvin', pink 'Petticoat', pale blue 'Thefi', powder blue 'Ralph Haywood', and violet blue 'Starbrite'.

In the wild, *Phlox bifida* blooms in April and May. Cultivated in Germany, it flowers during a similar season. Occasionally, it may rebloom later in the summer. Plants grown in St. Louis bloomed in May. At Longwood, the cultivar 'Minima Colvin' usually began flowering in early to mid-April, but one year its bloom was delayed until the first week of May. Flowering continued until mid or late May, rarely into the first week of June. On average, 'Minima Colvin' was in flower for nearly 6 weeks.

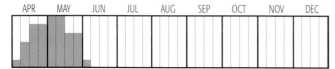

Phlox bifida 'Minima Colvin'

Phlox divaricata

BLUE PHLOX, WILD SWEET-WILLIAM,
WOODLAND PHLOX

This plant is native to North America, from Quebec, south to Florida, and west to New Mexico and South Dakota. *Phlox divaricata* grows in moist, rich deciduous forests, open woodlands and clearings, floodplains, and along roadsides and streams. It has been cultivated since the 18th century.

Phlox divaricata forms loose, spreading, semi-evergreen clumps of erect or decumbent, leafy, glandular-pubescent stems to 40 cm tall, growing from creeping rhizomes. The ovate-lanceolate or oblong leaves reach 5 cm in length. The slightly fragrant, blue-violet to lavender (rarely white), 3-cm-wide flowers are borne in loosely branched cymes. Fruits are ovoid capsules.

In the garden, *Phlox divaricata* is used as a loose ground cover that can intermingle with early-spring bulbs and other perennials in the front of a formal border or in naturalistic settings of an open woodland. Preferably, plant it in partial shade. Plants grown in full sun tend to senesce rapidly in summer, whereas those in deep shade produce rather lanky stems. *Phlox divaricata* performs best in fertile, consistently moist, humus-rich, and well-drained soil. Cut it back after flowering to remove senescing stems and encourage new growth. *Phlox divaricata* spreads through rhizomes and self-seeding to rapidly form large colonies. Plants are hardy to zones 3 or 4.

There are two subspecies of *Phlox divaricata* recognized among natural populations. The typical subspecies *divaricata*, found mostly in the eastern part of the range, has corolla lobes notched at the apex. Entire corolla lobes distinguish the subspecies *laphamii*, which is distributed throughout the species' range. In cultivation, a dozen or so superior forms have been selected and named. Their flower colors vary from creamy white 'Fuller's White' to pale blue 'Clouds of Perfume' and deep blue 'London Grove Blue'. The violet- or lavender-flowered cultivar 'Chattahoochee' is variably considered either a selection of *Phlox divaricata* or a hybrid between this species and *P. pilosa*.

In the wild, *Phlox divaricata* flowers from April to June, depending on the region. Cultivated in Germany, it blooms from April to June, whereas in Poland from May to July. Plants grown in St. Louis flowered from mid or late April until mid-May and rebloomed sporadically through mid-July. At Longwood, *P. divaricata* usually began flowering in the end of April and early May, rarely blooming as early as the third week of April or as late as the third week of May. It flowered through the end of May, rarely into early June. Once in 6 years, it rebloomed in late July and early August. On average, *Phlox divaricata* was in flower for nearly 6 weeks. Two cultivars of *P. divaricata*

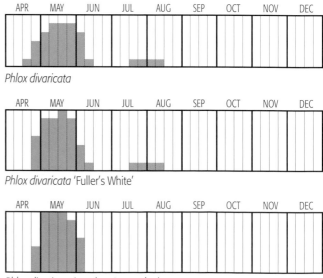

Phlox divaricata

Phlox divaricata 'Fuller's White'

Phlox divaricata 'London Grove Blue'

Phlox divaricata 'Fuller's White'

Phlox divaricata 'London Grove Blue'

observed at Longwood, 'Fuller's White' and 'London Grove Blue', flowered during the same season as the species. While 'Fuller's White' rebloomed once in 7 years, 'London Grove Blue' never did. The latter cultivar's bloom duration was a few days shorter than those of the species or 'Fuller's White'.

Phlox maculata
EARLY PHLOX, MEADOW PHLOX, SPOTTED PHLOX, SWEET-WILLIAM

This perennial is native to eastern North America, from Quebec south to Georgia, and west to Mississippi and Minnesota. *Phlox maculata* grows in moist meadows and woodlands, floodplains, and along streams and rivers. It has been cultivated since the 18th century.

Phlox maculata forms upright clumps of erect, hairy, usually red-mottled stems to 1 m tall, growing from slender, horizontal rhizomes. The linear-lanceolate to narrowly oblong leaves, to 12 cm long, are thick and dark glossy green. The fragrant, red-purple to pink flowers, to 2 cm wide, are borne in cylindrical or conical panicled cymes to 25 cm long.

In the garden, *Phlox maculata* is valued for its delightful fragrance, elegant flowers, and disease resistance. It is well suited for both formal perennial borders and informal cottage-style gardens, as well as for naturalizing in wildflower meadows. *Phlox maculata* attracts butterflies and hummingbirds and provides excellent cut flowers. Plant it in full sun or very light shade. It thrives in fertile, moist, humus-rich soils that drain easily, although it adapts well even to damp situations. *Phlox maculata* seldom requires staking. If flopping becomes an issue, trim plants back in the middle of spring to have smaller and bushier plants. This treatment will also delay the onset of flowering by a couple of weeks. Deadhead spent panicles to prolong the bloom, and cut stems back after flowering to encourage regrowth and possible sporadic rebloom. *Phlox maculata* spreads slowly through the rhizomes and self-seeding. Divide the clumps every 3 years or so to maintain plant vigor. Plants are hardy to zone 5, possibly zone 3.

Phlox maculata 'Natascha'

There are two subspecies of *Phlox maculata* recognized in the wild. The typical subspecies *maculata* is found throughout the species' range. The more southerly subspecies *pyramidalis* differs in smaller

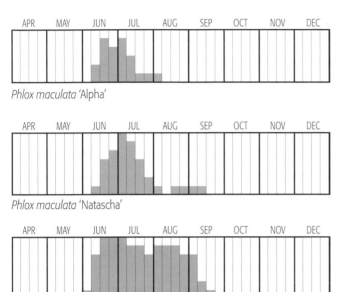

APR | MAY | JUN | JUL | AUG | SEP | OCT | NOV | DEC

Phlox maculata 'Alpha'

APR | MAY | JUN | JUL | AUG | SEP | OCT | NOV | DEC

Phlox maculata 'Natascha'

APR | MAY | JUN | JUL | AUG | SEP | OCT | NOV | DEC

Phlox maculata 'Rosalinde'

Phlox maculata 'Natascha'

flowers and leaves being more crowded on the stems; it also blooms 3 to 6 weeks later than subspecies *maculata*. In cultivation, several color variants have been selected, such as pure white 'Schneelawine', white-and-pink 'Natascha', rose-pink 'Alpha', or dark carmine-pink 'Rosalinde'. In the early 20th century, *P. maculata* was crossed with *P. carolina* by Georg Arends in Germany to produce early-flowering varieties, which became known as Maculata Hybrids.

In the wild, *Phlox maculata* blooms from June to August, depending on the region. Cultivated in Germany, it flowers from June to September. Plants grown in St. Louis bloomed sometimes in May, but more often their flowering fell in July, August, and September. At Longwood three cultivars of *P. maculata*, 'Alpha', 'Natascha', and 'Rosalinde', were observed. While all three selections began flowering in June, they differed markedly in their bloom duration. 'Alpha' averaged less than 4 weeks in bloom and never rebloomed after being cut back. 'Natascha' rebloomed twice in 7 years, and averaged 5 weeks in bloom. In contrast, 'Rosalinde' flowered nearly continually from June until early September, giving more than 11 weeks in bloom, on average.

Phlox paniculata

BORDER PHLOX, FALL PHLOX, GARDEN PHLOX, PERENNIAL PHLOX, SUMMER PHLOX

This plant is native to the eastern United States, from Maine south to Georgia, and west to Minnesota and Oklahoma. *Phlox paniculata* grows in open, rich, moist woodlands, thickets, and alluvial lowlands. Cultivated varieties are often found escaped in waste places and along roads. It has been cultivated since the mid-18th century.

Phlox paniculata forms upright clumps of stiff, erect, leafy stems to 2 m tall. The narrowly oblong to elliptic, glabrous or rarely pubescent and minutely ciliate leaves grow to 15 cm long. They are held on very short petioles or are sessile; the upper ones may be partially clasping. The sweetly fragrant, 2-cm-wide, tubular, red-purple to white flowers are held in dense, pyramidal, terminal panicled cymes to 20 cm in width. Fruits are ovoid capsules.

In the garden, *Phlox paniculata* is considered among the showiest of perennials. It offers a dazzling selection of fragrant flowers that can be incorporated in nearly every color scheme in a perennial

Phlox paniculata 'Eva Cullum'

Phlox paniculata 'Robert Poore'

border. Plant it in a sunny location with good air circulation, but one not exposed to strong winds. In areas with hot summers, light afternoon shade may be beneficial. *Phlox paniculata* thrives in deep, fertile, humus-rich, and moist soils. Stay away from sites with poor and dry soils or where plants will face competition from nearby trees. Provide supplemental watering during a drought, but avoid wetting the leaves, as this can favor foliar pathogens. Thin out the clumps in early spring, leaving only about the five strongest stems. Pinching stems before flower buds develop encourages branching and additional flowers. Deadhead regularly to prolong flowering and to prevent self-seeding. Cut back stems after all bloom is finished. *Phlox paniculata* usually does not require staking, except for cultivars with particularly large inflorescences grown in windy locations. Plants should be divided regularly, but the frequency depends on the fertility of the soil. When grown in rich soil, they can be left without dividing for 6 to 8 years or even longer, but in less fertile soils dividing may be required every 2 or 3 years. *Phlox paniculata* is hardy to zones 3 or 4, but in colder climates a light cover of mulch over the winter is recommended.

Although there are no botanical varieties of *Phlox paniculata* recognized in the wild, the species shows considerable variability of the flower color, which led to the selection of various color forms, first in France in the early 19th century. This sparked great interest among gardeners and breeders alike, and by the end of that century hundreds of cultivars had been named. Today, some 200 *P. paniculata* cultivars are grown by nurseries, whereas the species is rarely seen in cultivation. They include a wide range of colors from white 'David' and pink 'Eva Cullum', to purple 'Aïda' and cherry red 'Augustfackel'. Some may have a darker eye in the center of the flower, whereas others may have a lighter colored zone. There are also several selections with variegated foliage, such as 'Harlequin' and 'Norah Leigh'. Some cultivars, including pink 'Lizzy' and rosy 'Little Princess', grow to 50 cm tall, while others, such as purple 'Robert Poore', may reach 1.8 m in height. A number of cultivars have been developed by crossing *P. paniculata* with *P. maculata* and *P. divaricata*.

In the wild, *Phlox paniculata* blooms from July to October, depending on the region. Cultivated in Germany, it flowers from June to August. Plants

Phlox paniculata 'Norah Leigh'

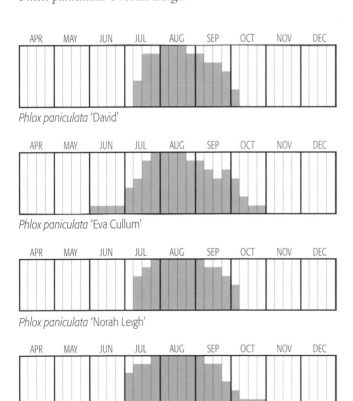

APR	MAY	JUN	JUL	AUG	SEP	OCT	NOV	DEC

Phlox paniculata 'David'

APR	MAY	JUN	JUL	AUG	SEP	OCT	NOV	DEC

Phlox paniculata 'Eva Cullum'

APR	MAY	JUN	JUL	AUG	SEP	OCT	NOV	DEC

Phlox paniculata 'Norah Leigh'

APR	MAY	JUN	JUL	AUG	SEP	OCT	NOV	DEC

Phlox paniculata 'Robert Poore'

grown in Chicago bloomed from July to September. Similarly, in Poznań it bloomed starting between 27 June and 10 July and finishing between 28 August and 8 September. At Longwood, four cultivars were compared, 'David', 'Eva Cullum', 'Norah Leigh', and 'Robert Poore'. All cultivars began flowering in July, but 'David' and 'Norah Leigh' were about a week later than 'Eva Cullum' and 'Robert Poore'. Once in 7 years, an unusually early bloom of 'Eva Cullum' was observed when flowers opened in the first week of June. Flowering of all four cultivars continued often through the end of September or into the first week of October. Occasionally, 'Eva Cullum', 'Norah Leigh', and 'Robert Poore' bloomed until mid-October. Their average bloom time varied from a little more than 10 weeks of 'David' to nearly 13 weeks in the case of 'Eva Cullum'.

Phlox stolonifera

CREEPING PHLOX

This perennial is native to eastern North America, from Ontario, east to Maine, and south to Georgia

Phlox stolonifera 'Bruce's White'

and Alabama. *Phlox stolonifera* grows chiefly in the mountains and piedmont areas, often on rocky slopes, in open moist woodlands, and along streams.

Phlox stolonifera forms mat–like spreading clumps of erect flowering stems to 40 cm tall and prostrate stolons. The lower evergreen leaves are often spatulate and reach 7 cm in length, whereas the upper ones on flowering stems are lanceolate or oblong and smaller. The fragrant, 2.5-cm-wide, purple to violet flowers are borne in open, loose, few–flowered, terminal cymes. Fruits are ovoid capsules.

In the garden, *Phlox stolonifera* is valued primarily as an adaptable and easy-to-grow ground cover for a woodland or shady informal border. It can also fill tight corners between rocks, near stone walls, or paths. *Phlox stolonifera* combines admirably with early-spring bulbs as well as ferns. Preferably plant it in partial shade. In colder climates, it can be grown successfully in full sun, but in southern areas shade is essential. It thrives in acidic, humus-rich, consistently moist, and well-drained soils. Cut plants back to the basal foliage after flowering to keep a neat appearance. *Phlox stolonifera* spreads rapidly through the stolons, but self-seeding may also take place under

Phlox stolonifera 'Pink Ridge'

favorable conditions. Regular dividing is not needed, except to control the spread. Plants are hardy to zone 4, possibly zone 2.

There are no botanical varieties of *Phlox stolonifera* recognized among the natural populations; nevertheless, plants may vary in their flower color. In cultivation, several such color variants have been selected, ranging from white 'Bruce's White', pink 'Home Fires', and dark mauve-pink 'Pink Ridge' to purple-blue 'Sherwood Purple' and mauve-blue 'Irridescens'.

In the wild, *Phlox stolonifera* blooms from April to June, depending on the region. Cultivated in St. Louis, it began flowering in the last week of April. At Longwood, two cultivars were observed, 'Home

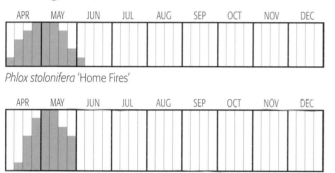

Phlox stolonifera 'Home Fires'

Phlox stolonifera 'Pink Ridge'

Fires' and 'Pink Ridge'. While 'Pink Ridge' usually started to flower in late April, 'Home Fires' often was in bloom a week earlier. Both cultivars continued to flower through mid or late May. One year, 'Home Fires' was still in flower in the first week of June. On average, 'Home Fires' bloomed for 6 weeks, and 'Pink Ridge' for 5 weeks.

Physostegia
FALSE DRAGONHEAD, LIONSHEART, OBEDIENT PLANT

The name *Physostegia* is derived from the Greek *physa*, a bladder, and *stege*, a covering, in reference to the inflated calyx.

Physostegia virginiana
FALSE DRAGONHEAD, OBEDIENT PLANT, STAY–IN–PLACE, VIRGINIA LIONSHEART

This plant is native to North America, from New Brunswick, west to Montana, and south to Florida and New Mexico. *Physostegia virginiana* grows in moist prairies and wet woodlands. It has been cultivated since the late 17th century.

Physostegia virginiana forms upright, dense clumps of glabrous, stiffly erect square stems to 1.8 m tall,

Physostegia virginiana 'Variegata'

Physostegia virginiana 'Miss Manners'

Physostegia virginiana 'Rosea'

growing from stoloniferous rhizomes. The lanceo-late to oblong, sharply serrate leaves reach 12 cm in length. The two-lipped, 3-cm-long, rose-purple to pink flowers are subtended by small leafy bracts. They are arranged in four vertical rows in spike-like terminal and axillary panicles to 45 cm long. Fruits are smooth, triangular nutlets.

In the garden, *Physostegia virginiana*, a vigorous grower, should be used where its rapid spread will be an asset and not a cause for concern. Naturalistic meadows and woodlands or large informal borders, where plants can be allowed some freedom to grow unrestrained, are perhaps the best situations. In small-er gardens, the spread of *P. virginiana* has to be care-fully monitored and often controlled. Plant it in full sun. Shady conditions promote lanky growth that

flops easily. *Physostegia virginiana* thrives in any aver-age garden soil that is consistently moist. To prevent flopping, stems can be trimmed in spring, which will result in shorter and sturdier plants. Deadhead regularly to prolong flowering and maintain a neat appearance. If foliage deteriorates after flowering, cut stems back to the ground. Where spreading be-comes excessive, divide the clumps every other year, discarding surplus rhizomes. Plants are hardy to zone 4, possibly zone 2.

There are two subspecies of *Physostegia virgin-iana* recognized currently. The typical subspecies *virginiana*, lacking floral bracts, tends to have a more northerly distribution, whereas subspecies *praemorsa*, with floral bracts present, is concentrated more in the southern areas. Other variants, such as *speciosa*, with larger, coarsely toothed leaves, or *candida*, with whitish flowers, are no longer considered botanically valid. In cultivation, a number of superior forms have been selected. They offer a choice of flower colors from white 'Summer Snow' and 'Miss Manners' to bright pink 'Rosea' and rosy crimson 'Rosy Spire'. In addition, variegated selections, such as white-edged 'Variegata' and gold-edged 'Olympic Gold', are available.

In the wild, *Physostegia virginiana* blooms from June to September, depending on the region. Cultivated in Germany, it flowers from July to September. Plants grown in Poznań began flowering between 24 June and 18 July and ended between 26 and 31 August. In Moscow, bloom started, on average, around 17 July and continued until 26 August. At Longwood, four cultivars were compared, 'Miss Manners', 'Rosea', 'Rosy Spire', and 'Summer Snow'. Of these cultivars, 'Miss Manners' was the earliest to flower, sometimes as early as late June. In contrast, 'Rosy Spire', which was the last to bloom, usually opened its flowers in mid or late September. While 'Miss Manners' often finished flowering by early September, 'Rosy Spire' continued usually through the end of October and sometimes even into late November. The early-flowering cultivars,

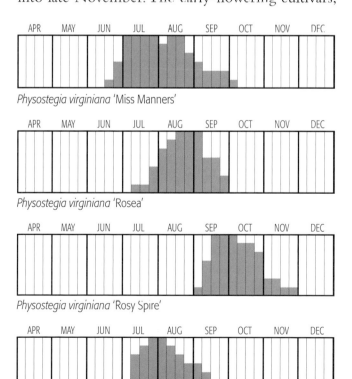

Physostegia virginiana 'Miss Manners'

Physostegia virginiana 'Rosea'

Physostegia virginiana 'Rosy Spire'

Physostegia virginiana 'Summer Snow'

such as 'Miss Manners' and 'Summer Snow', averaged about 10 weeks in bloom, whereas the later ones, 'Rosea' and 'Rosy Spire', averaged a little more than 7 weeks. In comparison, *P. virginiana* in Moscow was in flower for less than 6 weeks, on average.

Platycodon
BALLOON FLOWER

The name *Platycodon* is derived from the Greek *platys*, broad, and *kodon*, bell, in reference to the form of the flower.

Platycodon grandiflorus
BALLOON FLOWER, CHINESE BELL,
JAPANESE BELLFLOWER

This plant is native to eastern Asia, from southern Siberia and the Far East of Russia to northeastern China, Korea, and Japan. *Platycodon grandiflorus* grows in dry montane grasslands, scrub, and forest clearings. It has been cultivated in the West since the late 18th century, but it has been used as a medicinal plant in Asia for centuries.

Platycodon grandiflorus forms upright or rounded, compact clumps of erect, branched, leafy stems to 1 m tall, growing from deep, fleshy, stringy roots. The grayish green, lanceolate to ovate leaves are sharply serrate and reach 7 cm in length. The lower leaves are whorled, whereas the upper ones are alternate. The 7-cm-wide, broadly campanulate, bluish purple flowers open from round, inflated, balloon-like buds. They are held singly on long peduncles or in loose terminal cymes. Fruits are obovate, erect capsules.

In the garden, *Platycodon grandiflorus* is valued for its adaptability, longevity, and ease of care. Its flowers combine well with a wide array of perennials. Plant it in groups for stronger effect in the foreground of a border. *Platycodon grandiflorus* emerges late in the spring, so care needs to be taken not to damage it when cultivating soil. Choose a sunny location in northern climates, but plants require a partially shaded one in warmer areas. Also, pink-flowered varieties show color better when grown in light shade. This species thrives in slightly acidic, fertile, humus-rich soils that are well drained. Avoid damp sites with heavy, waterlogged soils. Deadhead spent flowers to prolong bloom season. Shorter varieties do not need staking, but the taller ones may flop. To avoid staking in such cases, trim stems in the middle

Platycodon grandiflorus

Platycodon grandiflorus 'Albus'

Platycodon grandiflorus 'Fuji'

of spring. This will delay flowering by a couple of weeks but will result in lower and sturdier plants. *Platycodon grandiflorus* is slow to establish and is best left undisturbed indefinitely. Rather than attempting to divide clumps, plants can be easily grown from seed. *Platycodon grandiflorus* is hardy to zones 3 or 4.

There are no botanical varieties of *Platycodon grandiflorus* currently recognized among the natural populations. Low-growing forms or varieties described in the past, such as 40-cm-tall *mariesii*, 25-cm-tall *pumilus*, or 15-cm-tall *apoyama*, no longer have a valid botanical status and are perhaps best treated as cultivars. In addition, there are many flower color variants in cultivation, including white 'Albus', pale pink 'Perlmutterschale', violet purple 'Misato Purple', and blue 'Sentimental Blue'. Furthermore, seed-grown strains, such as 'Astra' and 'Fuji', offer choices of white, pink, or blue flowers. A few cultivars, including 'Fairy Snow', 'Freckles', and 'Florovariegata', have white flowers veined, streaked, or spotted purple or blue. There are also double-flowered forms, such as 'Hakone Double Blue', which feature two rings of petals.

In the wild, *Platycodon grandiflorus* blooms in August and September. Cultivated in Moscow, it flowered, on average, between 15 July and 27 August. Likewise, plants grown in Poznań began flowering between 5 and 25 July and finished between 20 and 31 August. In contrast, in St. Louis flowering started several weeks earlier, between the last week of May and late June, and ended between mid-July and mid-October. At Longwood, two cultivars were observed, 'Albus' and 'Fuji'. While 'Albus' usually started to flower in mid or late July, 'Fuji' opened flowers between the last week of June and the second week of July. 'Albus' averaged 11 weeks in bloom, some-

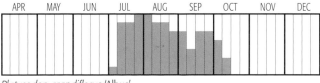

Platycodon grandiflorus 'Albus'

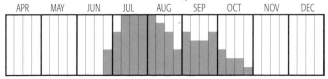

Platycodon grandiflorus 'Fuji'

times flowering as late as early October. 'Fuji', on average, bloomed 1 week longer, occasionally into late October. In comparison, *P. grandiflorus* in Moscow was in flower for about 7 weeks.

Polygonatum

SOLOMON'S-SEAL

The name *Polygonatum* is derived from the Greek *polys*, many, and *gony*, knee, in reference to the jointed appearance of the rhizome.

Polygonatum biflorum

SMALL SOLOMON'S-SEAL

This perennial is native to North America, from New Brunswick, west to Saskatchewan, and south to Florida, Texas, and northern Mexico. *Polygonatum biflorum* grows often in sandy soils, in rich deciduous forests, thickets, old fields, and along roadsides, at elevations to 3000 m.

Polygonatum biflorum forms upright clumps of erect or arching, unbranched stems to 2 m tall, growing from shallow, thick, slowly spreading rhizomes. The glabrous, elliptic-lanceolate to ovate leaves, to 20 cm long, are nearly sessile to clasping. The 2-cm-long, cylindrical, pendulous, white, often green-tipped flowers are held singly or up to 10 together in axillary clusters along and underneath the arching stems. Fruits are 1-cm-wide bluish black berries.

In the garden, *Polygonatum biflorum* performs splendidly in a naturalistic woodland or informal shaded border. Its gracefully arching, leafy stems remain attractive all season long, whereas the delicate flowers are followed by numerous berries set against a backdrop of elegant foliage, which turns buttery yellow in the fall. Plant it on a slope, where pendant flowers can be enjoyed better when viewed from below. Choose a cool, shady location with consistently moist, humus-rich, and well-drained soil. *Polygonatum biflorum* does not need to be regularly divided, and is best left undisturbed and allowed to spread slowly to form large colonies. Plants are hardy to zones 3 or 4.

Polygonatum biflorum is variable in its size, flower number, ecology, and ploidy level. The larger and coarser tetraploid plants have been described as variety *commutatum* and sometimes were treated as a separate species. The diploid plants of variety *biflorum*, besides being smaller in all their aspects, have only one to three flowers on each peduncle, compared to

Polygonatum biflorum

Polygonatum biflorum

Polygonatum biflorum var. *commutatum*

APR	MAY	JUN	JUL	AUG	SEP	OCT	NOV	DEC

Polygonatum biflorum

APR	MAY	JUN	JUL	AUG	SEP	OCT	NOV	DEC

Polygonatum biflorum var. *commutatum*

Polygonatum biflorum var. *commutatum*

two to 10 flowers in variety *commutatum*. Minor local variants of questionable validity include *melleum*, from Michigan and Ontario, with honey yellow flowers; *ramosum*, from Michigan and Indiana, which normally has long peduncles replaced by leafy branches bearing axillary flowers on very short peduncles; and several others. In cultivation, no superior selections have been named yet, but a dwarf form, growing to only 30 cm tall, is sometimes offered.

In the wild, *Polygonatum biflorum* blooms from April to June, depending on the region. It flowered in June when cultivated in Chicago and in May in St. Louis. At Longwood, the bloom start date varied by a month, from the second week of May to the second week of June. Flowering usually ended in the third week of June, but once in 7 years plants were still in bloom in the second week of July. *Polygonatum biflorum* averaged 5 weeks in bloom. In comparison, variety *commutatum* usually flowered at Longwood 3 weeks earlier, sometimes as early as the last week of April. It bloomed through late May or into the first week of June, averaging a little less than 5 weeks of flowering time.

Polygonatum odoratum

FRAGRANT SOLOMON'S-SEAL

This plant is native over an immense territory across Europe and Asia, from Portugal in the west to Japan in the east. *Polygonatum odoratum* often grows in open coniferous forests, in woodland edges, on shaded slopes, and along streams and rivers, at elevations from 500 to 3000 m.

Polygonatum odoratum forms upright clumps of erect and arching, distinctly angular, leafy stems to 1 m tall, growing from shallow, knobby, branched rhizomes. The glabrous, ovate to lanceolate leaves, to 12 cm long, are clasping or held on short petioles. The fragrant, 2.5-cm-long, cylindrical to campanulate, white, green-tipped flowers are borne one to four together, rarely more, in pendulous, axillary clusters along the stems. Fruits are blue-black berries to 10 mm wide.

In the garden, *Polygonatum odoratum* is valued as a long-lived, robust, and adaptable perennial. It can be naturalized in woodland settings, combined with other shade-tolerant perennials in a border, or even in larger containers. Following spring bloom, *P. odoratum* features elegant foliage that acquires yellow tints in the fall. Preferably, plant it in partial shade, although in moist situations full sun is tolerated. Avoid dry sites, whether in sun or shade. This species thrives in moist, humus-rich, well-drained soils. Once established, it can withstand competition from the roots of nearby trees. Plants spread slowly and are best left without dividing to develop into large colonies. *Polygonatum odoratum* is hardy to zones 3 or 4.

Several regional variants of *Polygonatum odoratum*, such as varieties *maximowiczii*, *pluriflorum*, or *thunbergii* from Japan, have been described, but their status is still uncertain. In cultivation, several distinct selections have been named, including variegated 'Byakko', 'Fireworks', and 'Variegatum'; double-flowered 'Flore Pleno'; and lemon-scented 'Lemon Seoul'.

In the wild, *Polygonatum odoratum* blooms in May and June. Cultivated in Germany, it flowers at about the same time. Plants grown in Poznań started to flower between 21 and 31 May and ended between 4 and 15 June. In a wet year, they bloomed for 25 days, but in a dry one for only 13 days. In Moscow, *P. odoratum* flowered, on average, from 25 May to 20 June. At Longwood, the cultivar 'Variegatum' usually began flowering in the last week of April or the first week of May. It continued to flower through the end of May, rarely until the first week of June, averaging a little more than 4 weeks in bloom. In comparison, 'Variegatum' grown in St. Louis flowered a couple of weeks earlier, from mid or late April until early or mid-May.

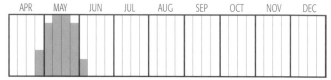

Polygonatum odoratum 'Variegatum'

Potentilla

CINQUEFOIL

The name *Potentilla* is derived from the Latin *potens*, powerful, in reference to the medicinal properties of some species.

Polygonatum odoratum 'Variegatum'

Potentilla recta

ROUGH-FRUITED CINQUEFOIL, SULFUR CINQUEFOIL

This perennial is native to Europe and Asia, from Spain east to Siberia. It has also widely naturalized in parts of North America. *Potentilla recta* often grows in river valleys, meadows, dry slopes, old fields, and waste places. It has been cultivated since the 17th century.

Potentilla recta forms robust, upright clumps of erect or ascending, stout, densely pubescent, branched stems to 75 cm tall. The palmate leaves have five to nine lanceolate, serrate, gray hairy leaflets to 10 cm long. The 2-cm-wide, pale yellow flowers are held in compact, terminal umbellate cymes. Fruits are one-seeded achenes.

In the garden, *Potentilla recta* can be used in formal perennial borders or in naturalized meadows. It is valued for its adaptability and profuse flowering. Plant it in full sun or partial shade, in any average garden soil. *Potentilla recta* self-seeds readily, sometimes to the point of being weedy, although cultivated varieties are somewhat less inclined to spread. Deadhead or cut back flowering stems to prevent seeds from developing. Plants are hardy to zones 3 or 4.

Potentilla recta is a quite variable species. Over the years, more than a dozen smaller species have been segregated from it, but currently they are thought to represent only regional or ecological variants. One of those segregates with very pale yellow flowers is widely cultivated as a variety *sulphurea*, but the validity of such a designation is questioned, and perhaps it is best to treat it as a cultivar. Other color selections grown in gardens include white 'Alba', butter yellow 'Macrantha', and bright canary yellow 'Warrenii'.

In the wild, *Potentilla recta* blooms from June to September. Cultivated in Germany and the United

Potentilla recta

Potentilla recta

Kingdom, it flowers from June until August. Plants cultivated in Poznań started to bloom between 14 and 25 June and ended between 22 July and 1 August. At Longwood, flowering began usually in the last week of May or in early June, but in one year plants opened flowers in the second week of May. The bloom continued through late June and into early July, rarely until early August. In most years, plants rebloomed between the last week of July and the first week of September. On average, *P. recta* was in flower for nearly 8 weeks.

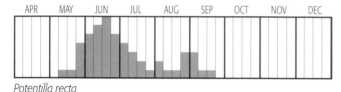

Potentilla recta

Potentilla thurberi

RED CINQUEFOIL, SCARLET CINQUEFOIL, THURBER'S CINQUEFOIL

This plant is native to southwestern North America, from New Mexico and Arizona south to northern Mexico, at elevations of 2000 to 3000 m. *Potentilla thurberi* grows in rich coniferous forests, moist meadows, and along streams.

Potentilla thurberi forms tight, mounded clumps of sprawling foliage and branched flowering stems to 75 cm tall. The palmately compound leaves have five or seven broadly oblanceolate, coarsely serrate leaflets to 5 cm long. The rose red to dark red, 2-cm-wide flowers darken toward the center to a blackish red eye. They are held in open, lax umbellate cymes. Fruits are achenes.

In the garden, *Potentilla thurberi* is well suited for planting in the front of a perennial border, informal cottage-style bed, on top of a stone wall, or among rocks on a slope. It is valued for its adaptability and the eye-catching, fiery flowers. Preferably, plant it in a light, moist, and well-drained soil, although it tolerates a wide range of situations. Established plants can withstand a periodic drought. Deadhead spent flowers to prolong bloom and to keep a neat appearance. *Potentilla thurberi* may self-seed under favorable conditions. Divide it every 3 years or so. Plants are hardy to zone 5.

There are three botanical varieties recognized throughout the distribution range of *Potentilla thurberi*. The typical variety *thurberi* has leaves sparsely

sericeous beneath, whereas leaves of variety *atrorubens* are densely silvery pubescent. Variety *sanguinea* differs in having basal leaves subpinnate rather than the usually palmate, like the other two varieties. The cultivar 'Monarch's Velvet', with raspberry red flowers, is widely grown.

In the wild, *Potentilla thurberi* flowers from July to October. Cultivated in St. Louis, it bloomed from June until August. At Longwood, flowering began in late June or early July. It continued until the first week of August, rarely mid-August. Once in 5 years, *P. thurberi* rebloomed in late September. On average, it was in flower for nearly 8 weeks.

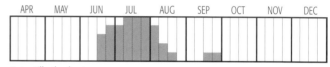

Potentilla thurberi

Primula

PRIMROSE

The name *Primula* is diminutive of the Latin, *primus*, first, in reference to the earliness of the flowers.

Primula kisoana

MOUNT KISO PRIMROSE

This perennial is native to central Honshu and Shikoku, Japan. It is extremely rare in the wild and is known from only a few locations. Reputedly *Primula kisoana* was originally collected on Mount Kiso, but it is not found there any more. Some of the population in Japan is believed to be the result of this plant escaping from gardens. *Primula kisoana* grows in moist meadows and on rocky slopes, at elevations of 800 to 1000 m. It has been cultivated in the West since the early 20th century and in Japan since at least the early 18th century.

Primula kisoana forms clumps of basal, deciduous foliage and stout, hairy flowering stems to 20 cm tall, growing from stoloniferous rhizomes. The orbicular, rather thick and wrinkled leaves, to 15 cm long, have a deeply cordate base and wavy to shallowly lobed margins. The 3-cm-long, flat-faced, rose-violet to pink flowers have deeply notched petals and are held in few-flowered, superimposed umbels. Fruits are capsules surrounded by a persistent calyx.

In the garden, *Primula kisoana* creates attractive, slowly spreading mats that can creep between other

Primula kisoana

Primula veris

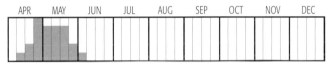

Primula kisoana 'Alba'

perennials and shrubs, exposed roots of trees, or rocks. Plant it in partial shade in any consistently moist and humus-rich soil. *Primula kisoana* increases slowly and does not need regular dividing, except for propagation purposes. Plants are hardy to zones 5 or 6.

A regional variant of *Primula kisoana*, densely covered with white hairs and found on the island of Shikoku, is sometimes designated as variety *shikokiana*. In cultivation, *P. kisoana* varies greatly in its flower color, and several color variants have been selected, including white 'Alba', magenta-pink 'Noshoku', and red 'Iyobeni'.

In the wild, *Primula kisoana* blooms in the middle of spring. Cultivated in Germany, it flowers in May. At Longwood, flowering of the cultivar 'Alba' began around mid to late April. It usually continued until the third week of May, rarely the first week of June. Bloom duration varied from 2 to 7 weeks, averaging 5 weeks.

Primula veris

COWSLIP PRIMROSE

This plant is distributed across Europe and Asia, from Spain north to Norway, south to Iran, and east to Siberia. *Primula veris* grows in moist meadows,

pastures, thickets, scrub, and on open slopes, at elevations to 3000 m.

Primula veris forms clumps of basal, lax, foliar rosettes and erect, green, shortly hairy flowering stems to 30 cm tall. The wrinkled, pubescent, ovate to oblong leaves, to 15 cm long, have irregularly crenate margins and white pubescent undersides. They are evergreen but summer dormant in dry climates. The sweetly scented, nodding, 2-cm-long, yellow flowers have orange spots at the base of the corolla lobes. They are borne in many-flowered, one sided, terminal umbels. Fruits are capsules.

In the garden, *Primula veris* makes an excellent subject for the front of a perennial border, but perhaps it is most effective when allowed to naturalize in meadows, parks, or open woodlands. Plant *Primula veris* in full sun or, in warmer climates, light shade. It thrives in moist, fertile, humus-rich, and well-drained soil but adapts to a wide range of situations. Plants are hardy to zone 5, possibly zone 3.

Over the immense distribution range of *Primula veris*, many regional variants have been described. In Europe, four subspecies are recognized. The typical subspecies *veris*, distributed throughout the species' range, has glabrescent or weakly hairy leaves and flowers to 1.2 cm wide. Subspecies *macrocalyx*, with flowers to 3 cm wide, is found in southern Russia and Crimea. Gray-tomentose leaves with winged petioles distinguish subspecies *canescens* from central and western Europe, whereas white-tomentose leaves with unwinged petioles are characteristic of subspecies *columnae* found in the mountains of southern Europe. In cultivation, a few forms, such as double-flowered 'Katy McSparron', have been selected and named. More significant, however, are numerous hybrids between *P. veris* and *P. vulgaris*, known as *P. ×polyantha*. These hybrids occur spontaneously where the two species grow together, and they have been cultivated at least since the early 16th century.

In the wild, *Primula veris* blooms from April to June. Cultivated in Germany and Poland, it flowers in April and May. Plants grown in Moscow bloomed, on average, from 3 May until 29 May. At Longwood, flowering began in late April or the first week of May. It continued until late May, rarely the first week of June. On average, *P. veris* bloomed for 5 weeks. In comparison, plants in Moscow were in flower for about 4 weeks.

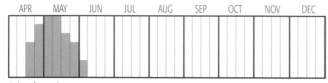

APR	MAY	JUN	JUL	AUG	SEP	OCT	NOV	DEC

Primula veris

Pulmonaria

LUNGWORT

The name *Pulmonaria* is derived from the Latin *pulmonarius*, suffering from lung disease, in reference to the spotted leaves resembling diseased lungs.

Pulmonaria Hybrids

HYBRID LUNGWORT

Several European species of *Pulmonaria*, including *P. angustifolia*, *P. longifolia*, *P. officinalis*, and *P. saccharata*, intercross easily when grown in close proximity. This led to the occurrence of spontaneous hybrid plants in gardens, from among which the first cultivars were selected around the middle of the 20th century. More recently, controlled crosses resulted in better-targeted and effective breeding of new cultivars.

Pulmonaria hybrids form rosettes of basal foliage and clumped flowering stems, growing from short creeping rhizomes with thick and fleshy roots. The lanceolate to oval, bristly hairy leaves are usually marked with silvery spots or blotches, sometimes covering the entire leaf blade. The basal leaves are held on long petioles, whereas the smaller and narrower cauline leaves are often sessile or partly clasping the stem. The 12-mm-long flowers are borne in nodding branched cymes. They open from pink, coral, or red buds; some forms retain this color, whereas others mature to white, purple, or blue. Fruits are 5-mm-long brownish nuts.

In the garden, *Pulmonaria* hybrids are among the earliest flowering perennials and so can complement early-spring bulbs. Use them in the front of an informal perennial border or as ground cover under deciduous trees and shrubs. Varieties with the strongly silver-patterned foliage can brighten the dark corners of a garden. The leaves remain attractive throughout the summer, provided the soil is consistently moist. Allow them to spread freely and form large colonies in time. Plant *Pulmonaria* hybrids in partial or full shade under deciduous trees.

Primula veris

Pulmonaria 'Blue Ensign'

Pulmonaria 'Cotton Cool'

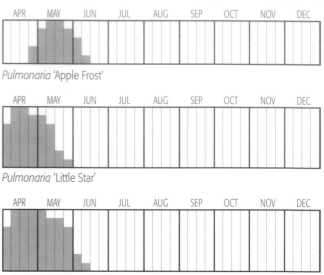

	APR	MAY	JUN	JUL	AUG	SEP	OCT	NOV	DEC

Pulmonaria 'Apple Frost'

	APR	MAY	JUN	JUL	AUG	SEP	OCT	NOV	DEC

Pulmonaria 'Little Star'

	APR	MAY	JUN	JUL	AUG	SEP	OCT	NOV	DEC

Pulmonaria 'Milchstrasse'

Pulmonaria 'Milchstrasse'

Avoid sites, however, that are shaded year-round by evergreen trees or shrubs. *Pulmonaria* hybrids thrive in cool, moist, humus-rich, and well-drained soils. Cut back stems after flowering and leaves, if they begin to decline in summer. *Pulmonaria* hybrids spread slowly and rarely require dividing. Plants are hardy to zones 3 or 4.

Pulmonaria hybrids in themselves make up a highly variable group of garden plants, but to complicate matters, they can further intercross and produce even more variable offspring. Named cultivars are variously attributed to one of the parent species or listed as hybrids of uncertain pedigree. They offer choices of plants with unspotted leaves, such as 'Blue Ensign', silver-spotted foliage, such as 'Apple Frost', or entirely silver, such as 'Cotton Cool'. Their flower colors vary from white 'Sissinghurst White', pale blue 'Blau Himmel', and pink 'Beth's Pink' to bright red 'Esther' and deep blue 'Little Star' and 'Milchstrasse'.

Pulmonaria hybrids bloom in early spring with flowers opening in succession over the course of several weeks. At Longwood, three cultivars were observed, 'Apple Frost', 'Little Star', and 'Milchstrasse'. While 'Little Star' began flowering in the first or the second week of April, 'Apple Frost' opened flowers 3 to 4 weeks later. Both of these cultivars averaged a little more than 5 weeks in bloom. In contrast, 'Milchstrasse', which started to flower with the early-blooming 'Little Star' but finished with the late-blooming 'Apple Frost', averaged nearly 8 weeks in bloom. In some years, 'Apple Frost' and 'Milchstrasse' were still in flower in early June.

Pulmonaria longifolia

JOSEPH-AND-MARY, LONG-LEAFED LUNGWORT, SPOTTED-DOG

This perennial is native to western Europe, from Portugal west to France and southern England. *Pulmonaria longifolia* grows often in clay soils, in woodlands, scrub, meadows, and among rocks, at elevations to 2000 m.

Pulmonaria longifolia forms tight clumps of basal, upright, semi-evergreen leaves and flowering stems to 30 cm tall, growing from a creeping rhizome. The

Pulmonaria longifolia 'Bertram Anderson'

Pulmonaria longifolia 'Roy Davidson'

narrowly lanceolate leaves have gray or white spots. The basal leaves, to 50 cm long and 6 cm wide, are held on long petioles in rosettes, whereas the few cauline leaves are smaller and narrower. The purple-blue flowers are borne in dense, drooping, terminal cymes. Fruits are 4-mm-long nutlets.

In the garden, *Pulmonaria longifolia* can be used in the front of a perennial border, for edging paths, or as a ground cover. Its prominently spotted leaves extend the season of interest beyond the bloom time. The foliage remains attractive through the entire growing season and, in warmer climates, even into winter. Plant in partial shade, although in colder climates full sun can be tolerated provided soil is adequately moist. *Pulmonaria longifolia* does not thrive in deep shade like some other lungworts. Choose a site with cool, moist, humus-rich, and well-drained soil. It increases slowly and rarely needs dividing unless growth and flowering decline noticeably. Plants are hardy to zone 5, possibly zone 3.

Pulmonaria longifolia is a variable species. Researchers have proposed segregating it into several subspecies, including *cevennensis*, *delphinensis*, and *glandulosa*, in addition to the typical subspecies *longifolia*. In cultivation, a number of variants have been selected, although some of them may be of hybrid origin. Most of them, including 'Ankum', 'Bertram Anderson', 'Dordogne', 'Majesté', and 'Roy Davidson', feature stronger silvery spotting or patterns on their leaves.

In the wild, *Pulmonaria longifolia* blooms from February to May, depending on the region. Cultivated in Moscow, it flowered, on average, from 27 April to 19 May. At Longwood, two cultivars were observed, 'Bertram Anderson' and 'Majesté'. Both varieties began flowering in mid or late April, but 'Bertram Anderson' usually bloomed through the

end of May, sometimes into the first week of June, whereas 'Majesté' rarely was in flower past the second week of May. On average, 'Majesté' bloomed for a little longer than 4 weeks, whereas 'Bertram Anderson' for more than 6 weeks. In St. Louis, these two cultivars started to flower about 2 weeks earlier than at Longwood, between the last week of March and mid-April; 'Majesté' continued to bloom for 3 to 4 weeks and 'Bertram Anderson' for 4 to 5 weeks. In comparison, *P. longifolia* grown in Moscow averaged about 3 weeks in bloom.

Pulmonaria rubra

BETHLEHEM-SAGE, CHRISTMAS-COWSLIP, RED LUNGWORT

This plant is native to the mountains of southeastern Europe, from Albania, across the Balkans, east to Ukraine. *Pulmonaria rubra* grows on slopes, often in moist deciduous, sometimes coniferous forests. It has been cultivated since at least the early 20th century.

Pulmonaria rubra forms tufted clumps of soft, distinctly light green, semi-evergreen basal foliage and bristly hairy flowering stems to 60 cm tall, growing from thin rhizomes. The oblong, nearly sessile leaves are not spotted, but covered with rough, long hairs. The basal leaves reach 35 cm in length, whereas the cauline ones are much shorter. The 1-cm-wide, coral red flowers are held in terminal paired cymes or small corymbs. Fruits are 4-mm-long nutlets.

In the garden, *Pulmonaria rubra* is valued for its abundant red flowers, unusual among lungworts. It creates an effective ground cover that remains evergreen in mild climates. The plants, however, may become summer dormant if subjected to drought. Allow it to spread among deciduous shrubs, taller perennials, and rocks, or use it to edge shaded paths. Plant it in partial or full shade, in cool, consistently moist, humus-rich soil. Avoid dry sites. Under favorable conditions, *P. rubra* spreads rapidly, but not to the point of becoming a nuisance. It self-seeds readily, which in case of clonal varieties necessitates the removal of feral seedlings. Regular dividing is not needed, unless the clumps become too crowded. Plants are hardy to zone 5, possibly zone 3.

There are no botanical varieties of *Pulmonaria rubra* currently recognized among the natural populations, although another species, *P. filarszkyana*, from the Carpathians, has been considered as its subspe-

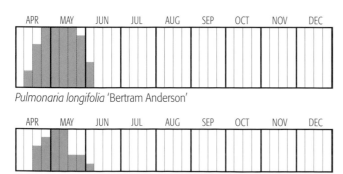

APR	MAY	JUN	JUL	AUG	SEP	OCT	NOV	DEC

Pulmonaria longifolia 'Bertram Anderson'

APR	MAY	JUN	JUL	AUG	SEP	OCT	NOV	DEC

Pulmonaria longifolia 'Majesté'

cies in the past. In cultivation, several flower color variants are known, ranging from white 'Albocorollata' and pale pink 'Prestbury Pink' to dark red 'Redstart' and 'Bowles' Red'. In addition, several cultivars have been selected for their decorative foliage, including 'David Ward', with creamy-edged leaves, and 'Rachel Vernie', with white-edged leaves.

In the wild, *Pulmonaria rubra* blooms from February to April, depending on the region. Cultivated in the United Kingdom, it is the earliest lungwort to flower, sometimes beginning in late January. Plants grown in Germany and Poland bloom in March and April. At Longwood, the cultivar 'David Ward' began to flower in the first or the second week of April. On average, it bloomed for a little more than 3 weeks, sometimes into the first week of May.

APR	MAY	JUN	JUL	AUG	SEP	OCT	NOV	DEC

Pulmonaria rubra 'David Ward'

Pulmonaria saccharata

BETHLEHEM LUNGWORT, BETHLEHEM-SAGE, JERUSALEM-SAGE

This plant is native to Europe, from the central Apennines north to the western Alps in France. It has naturalized in other parts of Europe and northeastern North America. *Pulmonaria saccharata* grows in moist forests and scrub. It has been cultivated since the 17th century.

Pulmonaria saccharata forms vigorous, dense to open clumps of soft hairy, semi-evergreen, basal foliage and flowering stems to 45 cm tall, growing from short creeping rhizomes. The elliptic leaves are heavily spotted with large white, overlapping blotches. The basal leaves reach 30 cm in length and 15 cm in width, whereas the cauline ones are much shorter and narrower. The funnel-shaped flowers open pinkish, turning to purple and blue as they mature. They are borne in terminal, branched cymes that elongate and become very lax in time. Fruits are 4-mm-long nutlets.

In the garden, *Pulmonaria saccharata* is most effective when planted in large groups and allowed to spread and create a ground cover under trees or shrubs. It is valued for the early and long-lasting prolific flowers, followed by attractive variously silvery-spotted or marbled foliage. The leaves may be

retained through the winter in mild climates, but require consistent moisture to stay attractive during the summer. Plant it in partial to full shade in cool, moist, humus-rich soil. Avoid dry and sunny situations. Cut back stems to basal foliage after flowering, unless self-seeding is to be encouraged. If leaves decline in dry summers, cut them off to keep a neat appearance. New foliage will emerge when cooler temperatures and rain return. *Pulmonaria saccharata* spreads slowly and rarely needs dividing, except when clumps become overcrowded and their vigor declines. Plants are hardy to zones 3 or 4.

There are no botanical varieties of *Pulmonaria saccharata* recognized among natural populations,

Pulmonaria saccharata 'Dora Bielefeld'

Pulmonaria saccharata 'Mrs. Moon'

but in cultivation numerous selections have been introduced. Those with particularly strongly silver-patterned leaves are collectively referred to as the Argentea Group. Some of the more notable forms include 'British Sterling', 'Excalibur', and 'Silverado'. Clonal selections vary in the color of fully open flowers from white 'Alba' and pink 'Dora Bielefeld' to light blue 'Mrs. Moon' and violet blue 'Sam Gamgee'. Many cultivars were developed through spontaneous hybridization of *P. saccharata* with other species of lungwort, and their assignment to one of the parent species is often tentative.

In the wild, *Pulmonaria saccharata* flowers from March to May. Cultivated in the United Kingdom, it begins to bloom often as early as February, but in Germany flowering usually starts in April. Similarly, in Chicago *P. saccharata* bloomed in April and May. At Longwood, the cultivar 'Dora Bielefeld' started to flower in the first or the second week of April and continued, on average, for nearly 6 weeks, until mid-May.

APR	MAY	JUN	JUL	AUG	SEP	OCT	NOV	DEC

Pulmonaria saccharata 'Dora Bielefeld'

Pulsatilla

PASQUE–FLOWER

The derivation of the name *Pulsatilla* is unclear, but it is thought to come from the Latin *pulsare*, to beat, in reference to the downy seed heads that are beaten about by the wind.

Pulsatilla vulgaris

COMMON PASQUE–FLOWER, COVENTRY–BELLS, FLAW–FLOWER, HILL–TULIP

This perennial is native to central and western Europe, from France, north to Sweden, and east to Ukraine. *Pulsatilla vulgaris* grows often in dry, calcareous soils in open forests, short grasslands, and montane meadows. It has been cultivated since before the 16th century.

Pulsatilla vulgaris

Pulsatilla vulgaris

Pulsatilla vulgaris forms tufted clumps of silky hairy basal foliage and upright flowering stems, to 15 cm tall at the time of flowering but expanding to 40 cm when in fruit. The 15-cm-long leaves are pinnately dissected into seven or nine lobes, these being further dissected two or three times into linear segments. The urn-shaped, nodding flowers are violet or purple (rarely pink or white), reach 9 cm in diameter, and are borne singly. Fruits are achenes topped by persistent long and feathery styles.

In the garden, *Pulsatilla vulgaris* is valued for its early large flowers, attractive silky foliage, and fluffy seed heads. Use it in the front of a perennial border, on open slopes, or in naturalistic meadows. Plant it in full sun or, in warmer climates, in partial shade. *Pulsatilla vulgaris* thrives in any average garden soil that is well drained, but it performs best in those that are light, rich in humus, calcareous, and moderately moist. Allow the spent flowers to develop feathery seed heads to extend the season of interest. *Pulsa-* *tilla vulgaris* does poorly after root disturbance, and it is best to leave it without dividing for many years. Plants are hardy to zone 5.

Pulsatilla vulgaris is highly variable in the wild. These regional variants are sometimes treated as varieties or subspecies of *P. vulgaris* or as separate species. The main divide appears to be between the western European forms, which are usually designated as subspecies *vulgaris*, producing leaves and flowers at the same time, and the eastern European subspecies *grandis*, producing leaves after flowering. The latter one, when recognized as a separate species, is known as *P. halleri*. In cultivation, several color variants have been selected, including white 'Alba' and 'Weisser Schwan', pink 'Barton's Pink', lilac blue 'Blaue Glocke', and red 'Eva Constance' and 'Röde Klokke'. Some of these cultivars are thought to have resulted from the hybridization of *P. vulgaris* with other species, such as *P. montana* or *P. rubra*.

Pulsatilla vulgaris 'Alba'

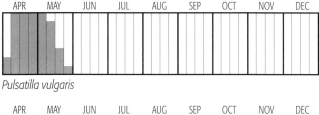

Pulsatilla vulgaris

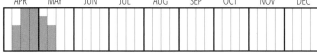

Pulsatilla vulgaris 'Alba'

In the wild, *Pulsatilla vulgaris* blooms from March to May, depending on the region. Plants grown in Chicago and St. Louis flowered in April and May. Cultivated in Poznań, subspecies *vulgaris* began to bloom between 1 and 5 May and ended between 28 and 30 May, but subspecies *grandis* bloomed about 2 weeks earlier. At Longwood, flowering started in the first or the second week of April and continued, on average, for nearly 6 weeks into mid-May, rarely late May. In comparison, the cultivar 'Alba' flowered at Longwood about 1 week later and averaged only 4 weeks in bloom.

Pycnanthemum
MOUNTAIN-MINT

The name *Pycnanthemum* is derived from the Greek *pyknos*, dense, and *anthemon*, flower, in reference to the densely arranged flowers.

Pycnanthemum incanum
COMMON MOUNTAIN-MINT, HOARY MOUNTAIN-MINT

This plant is native to eastern North America, from Ontario, east to New Hampshire, and south to Mississippi and Florida. *Pycnanthemum incanum* grows in upland dry woods, thickets, and old fields.

Pycnanthemum incanum forms upright clumps of pubescent, freely branched stems to 1 m tall, growing from spreading rhizomes. The aromatic, ovate to oblong, nearly sessile leaves to 10 cm long, have serrate margins and white-pubescent undersides. The two-lipped, purple spotted, whitish to pinkish flowers are subtended by conspicuous bracts and are borne in dense terminal or axillary cymose clusters to 3.5 cm wide. Fruits are nutlets.

In the garden, *Pycnanthemum incanum* is valued for late flowers complemented by the silvery bracts and upper leaves. The flowers are frequently visited by butterflies and moths. The leaves emit a spearmint-like aroma and have been used for flavoring teas. *Pycnanthemum incanum* spreads rapidly, so it is best suited for naturalized dry meadows or woodland edges, but with some monitoring it can also be used in large informal borders. Plant it in full sun or partial shade, in any average garden soil that is not excessively wet and drains readily. *Pycnanthemum incanum* adapts well to dry conditions. On moist sites, especially when shaded, plants become leggy and flop easily. To avoid staking, trim them back in the spring to encourage lower and bushier growth. Where *P. incanum* cannot be allowed to spread freely, it requires either regular replanting, or at least cutting off long rhizomes to keep the size of clumps or colonies in check. Plants are hardy to zones 3 or 4.

In the wild, *Pycnanthemum incanum* blooms from June to September. Similarly, plants cultivated in St. Louis flowered from July to September. At Longwood, the bloom start date varied by 5 weeks, from

Pycnanthemum tenuifolium

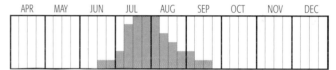

Pycnanthemum tenuifolium

Pycnanthemum tenuifolium forms compact clumps of erect, much-branched stems to 1 m tall, growing from spreading rhizomes. The aromatic, sessile, linear leaves, to 5 mm wide and 5 cm long, are firm and needle-like. The two-lipped, 5-mm-long white flowers are spotted with pink or violet. They are held in cymose clusters to 8 mm wide, arranged in compact corymbs. Fruits are nutlets.

In the garden, *Pycnanthemum tenuifolium* is best used in informal naturalistic settings, such as meadows, woodland edges, and along the banks of ponds or streams. There it can spread widely and create attractive late-flowering colonies. Plant it in full sun or partial shade in any average garden soil. *Pycnanthemum tenuifolium* adapts to a wide range of conditions, from dry to wet. Clumps spread readily, so unless allowed to naturalize, they need to be regularly divided. Plants are hardy to zone 5.

In the wild, *Pycnanthemum tenuifolium* blooms in summer, from June to September. Cultivated in St. Louis, it flowered from the second week of June until mid-October. At Longwood, flowering usually began in early July, although one year plants were in bloom in the third week of June. Bloom duration varied considerably, from 5 to 12 weeks, averaging a little less than 8 weeks. Flowers were rarely seen past August.

Pycnanthemum incanum

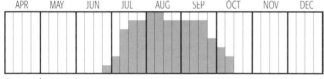

Pycnanthemum incanum

the last week of June to the first week of August. Flowering usually continued until mid or late September, but in 2 of 7 years plants were still in bloom in the second week of October. On average, *P. incanum* flowered for more then 11 weeks.

Pycnanthemum tenuifolium

NARROWLEAF MOUNTAIN-MINT, SLENDER MOUNTAIN-MINT

This perennial is native to eastern North America, from Ontario, east to Maine, and south to Texas and Florida. *Pycnanthemum tenuifolium* grows in dry to moist soils, in open woodlands, thickets, dry prairies, along streams, and in bogs.

Pycnanthemum virginianum

COMMON MOUNTAIN–MINT, VIRGINIA
MOUNTAIN–MINT, VIRGINIA–THYME, WILD–BASIL

This plant is native to eastern North America, from Quebec, west to North Dakota, and south to Georgia and Oklahoma. *Pycnanthemum virginianum* grows in upland woods, dry to wet thickets, and in moist prairies and meadows.

Pycnanthemum virginianum forms upright clumps of stiffly erect, much- branched, pubescent stems to 1 m tall, growing from spreading rhizomes. The aromatic, linear-lanceolate leaves, to 1 cm wide and 6 cm long, are glabrous and glossy. The two-lipped white flowers are borne in dense cymose clusters held in terminal corymbs. Fruits are nutlets.

In the garden, *Pycnanthemum virginianum* can be planted in an informal perennial border or wildflower meadow, along a woodland edge, or near ponds and streams. It grows and flowers best in full sun. This species thrives in any average garden soil that is moist and well drained. Shaded plants may be prone to flopping, but trimming them in late spring will result in shorter and stiffer stems. *Pycnanthemum virginianum* increases readily, calling for regular replanting unless grown in an area where it can spread unrestrained. Plants are hardy to zone 5, possibly zone 3.

In the wild, *Pycnanthemum virginianum* blooms from July to September. Cultivated in Germany, it flowers at about the same time. Likewise, plants grown in St. Louis bloomed from the third week of June until mid-September. At Longwood, *P. virginianum* usually flowered starting in early July and finished in late August. Rarely, bloom ended before August or continued into September. On average, it was in flower for nearly 7 weeks.

Ratibida

MEXICAN HAT, PRAIRIE CONEFLOWER
The derivation of the name *Ratibida* is unknown.

Ratibida pinnata

DROOPING CONEFLOWER, GRAY–HEAD CONEFLOWER,
GREEN CONEFLOWER, PINNATE PRAIRIE CONEFLOWER

This perennial is native to eastern North America, from Ontario, east to Massachusetts, and south to Louisiana and Florida. *Ratibida pinnata* grows on

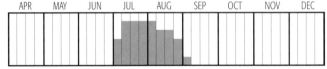

APR	MAY	JUN	JUL	AUG	SEP	OCT	NOV	DEC

Pycnanthemum virginianum

Pycnanthemum virginianum

Ratibida pinnata

prairies, in dry open woodlands, on limestone outcrops, and along roads, at elevations to 300 m.

Ratibida pinnata forms loose upright clumps of a few strongly erect branched stems to 1.5 m tall, growing from a stout rhizome or woody caudex with deep, wiry, fibrous roots. The pinnatifid leaves, divided into three to nine lanceolate, coarsely serrate to entire segments, reach 5 to 40 cm in length. The flower heads are comprised of five to 15 drooping yellow ray florets and many tiny brownish or purplish disc florets, which are borne on gray ellipsoid to ovoid cones to 2.5 cm high. They are held singly or up to 12 together on long peduncles well above the foliage. Fruits are 3 mm long achenes.

In the garden, *Ratibida pinnata* perform best when planted in large groupings in perennial borders or allowed to naturalize in wildflower meadows. The rather sparse and rough habit of *R. pinnata* makes it better suited for informal settings. It is valued for its unique, long blooming flower heads resembling little sombreros. Plant it in full sun, in any average garden soil that is well drained. *Ratibida pin-*

nata adapts well to dry and low-fertility situations. Cut plants back after flowering if their appearance becomes too ratty. Plants are hardy to zones 3 or 4.

In the wild, *Ratibida pinnata* flowers from May to October, depending on the region. Cultivated in St. Louis, it bloomed in June and July, sometimes August. Plants grown at Longwood began flowering in late June or early July, although one year unusually early blooms appeared in the first week of June. Plants usually flowered through late July or into early August. Cutting them back after flowering resulted in rebloom in 3 of 7 years. Those cut back in mid to late July rebloomed in 3 to 6 weeks, but plants cut back in mid-August flowered again 10 weeks later, in mid-October. On average, *R. pinnata* was in bloom for 7 weeks.

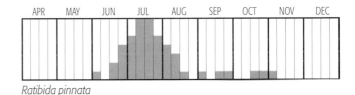

Ratibida pinnata

Ratibida pinnata

Rodgersia

RODGERSIA

The name *Rodgersia* commemorates John Rodgers (1812–1882), an American admiral.

Rodgersia aesculifolia

FINGERLEAF RODGERSIA

This plant is native to southeast Asia from Hebei in China, west to Xizang, and south to Myanmar. *Rodgersia aesculifolia* grows in moist forests, woodland edges, thickets, meadows, and on rocky cliffs, at elevations from 1000 to 3800 m. It has been cultivated since the early 20th century.

Rodgersia aesculifolia forms robust clumps of bold basal foliage and flowering stems to 1.8 m tall, growing from a thick rhizome. The palmately compound leaves, to 50 cm wide, have seven obovate to oblanceolate, coarsely serrate leaflets, each to 25 cm long. They are held on long, brown-pubescent petioles. The creamy white to creamy pink flowers are borne in cymose clusters arranged in pyramidal, loose panicles to 60 cm long, carried on stout stems well above the foliage. Fruits are ovoid reddish capsules.

In the garden, *Rodgersia aesculifolia* is valued for its grand foliage and large, plumy panicles. It is well suited for planting at watersides, boggy beds, and moist woodlands, as well as traditional perennial borders as long as they are protected from hot sun and given adequate moisture. Preferably, choose a partially shaded site sheltered from strong winds with fertile, humus-rich, and consistently moist soil. In dry situations leaves become easily scorched by sun. Deadhead after flowering to maintain a neat appearance. *Rodgersia aesculifolia* is long lived, spreads slowly, and rarely needs dividing. Plants are hardy to zones 4 or 5.

There are two varieties of *Rodgersia aesculifolia* recognized among natural populations. Variety *henrici* differs from the typical variety *aesculifolia* in having more leathery leaves and darker pink flowers. It is found in the western part of the distribu-

Rodgersia aesculifolia

tion range, in western Yunnan, Xizang, and Myanmar. In cultivation, *R. aesculifolia* easily hybridizes with other species of rodgersia. Several such hybrids have been named, including 'Irish Bronze', with pale pink flowers and bronze leaves, and 'Parasol', which features creamy flowers and leaves with narrow leaflets.

In the wild, *Rodgersia aesculifolia* starts flowering in May. Cultivated in Germany, it flowers in June and July. Plants grown in Poznań bloomed from 2 June until 12 July, whereas in Moscow they flowered a month later, between 2 July and 3 August. At Longwood flowering began in late May or early June and continued usually through mid-June, rarely into early July. On average, *R. aesculifolia* bloomed for nearly 4 weeks. In comparison, plants in Poznań were in flower for almost 6 weeks.

APR	MAY	JUN	JUL	AUG	SEP	OCT	NOV	DEC

Rodgersia aesculifolia

Rodgersia sambucifolia
ELDERBERRY RODGERSIA

This perennial is native to southwestern China, from Guizhou west to Sichuan and Yunnan. *Rodgersia sambucifolia* grows in montane forests, scrub, on grassy slopes, and rocky cliffs, at elevations from 1800 to 3700 m. It has been cultivated since the early 20th century.

Rodgersia sambucifolia forms bold clumps of basal leaves and glabrous flowering stems to 1.2 m tall, growing from blackish, creeping, thick rhizomes. The dull green, long-petiolate, pinnately compound leaves have three to 11 oblong-lanceolate, doubly serrate leaflets to 20 cm long. The creamy white to pink flowers are borne in cymose clusters arranged in panicles to 40 cm long. Fruits are capsules.

In the garden, *Rodgersia sambucifolia* performs admirably at waterside, along damp borders, or in shady woodlands, where given time and space it can create attractive colonies. Its large leaves and impressive panicles provide an all-season-long show. In

Rodgersia sambucifolia

Rodgersia sambucifolia

sunny locations, foliage takes on bronzy tones. *Rodgersia sambucifolia* grows best in partial shade, but it can tolerate full sun as long as the soil remains moist. Preferably, choose a site sheltered from wind, with fertile, humus-rich, consistently moist soil, but avoid locations with standing water. *Rodgersia sambucifolia* increases slowly and is best left without dividing for years. Plants are hardy to zone 6, possibly zone 4.

There are two varieties of *Rodgersia sambucifolia* described in its native range. The typical variety *sambucifolia* bears stiff and sharp hairs on the upper surfaces of the leaves. In contrast, leaves of variety *estrigosa*, found in the western part of the range, are glabrous above. In cultivation, a couple of superior selections have been made, including 'Rothaut', with bronzy foliage, and 'Kupferschein', with young leaves coppery green.

In the wild, *Rodgersia sambucifolia* starts blooming in May. Cultivated in Germany and Poland, it flowers in June and July. At Longwood, flowering began

in the last week of May or the first week of June. It continued until late June, rarely until the first week of July. On average, *R. sambucifolia* was in bloom for nearly 5 weeks.

Rudbeckia

CONEFLOWER

The name *Rudbeckia* commemorates Olaus Johannes Rudbeck (1630–1702) and Olaus Olai Rudbeck (1660–1740), father and son, Swedish botanists.

Rudbeckia fulgida

BLACK-EYED SUSAN, ORANGE CONEFLOWER,
PRAIRIE CONEFLOWER

This plant is native to the eastern United States, from Massachusetts south to Florida and west to Wisconsin and Texas. *Rudbeckia fulgida* grows in a wide variety of habitats from dry meadows and open rocky glades to moist and shady woods and bogs. It has been cultivated since the late 18th century.

Rudbeckia fulgida forms robust upright clumps of basal leafy rosettes and erect, branched flowering stems to 1.2 m tall, growing from creeping rhizomes. The lanceolate to ovate, slightly hairy leaves, to 15

APR	MAY	JUN	JUL	AUG	SEP	OCT	NOV	DEC

Rodgersia sambucifolia

Rudbeckia fulgida 'Viette's Little Suzy'

Rudbeckia fulgida 'Goldsturm'

cm long, have serrate or crenate margins. The lower leaves are long-petiolate, and the uppermost ones are sessile or clasping. The 7-cm-wide flower heads are comprised of 10 to 15 spreading yellow ray florets and numerous brownish purple disc florets forming a short cone. The flower heads are borne singly or several together in corymb-like arrays. Fruits are 3-mm-long achenes.

In the garden, *Rudbeckia fulgida* is valued as a floriferous, long-blooming, and adaptable summer performer. Because it spreads rapidly to form colonies, it is best suited to large spaces, such as wildflower meadows or woodland edges, but with some degree of monitoring it can be very effective in larger borders as well. Plant it in full sun or light shade. *Rudbeckia fulgida* thrives in fertile, humus-rich, moist and well-drained soil, but it can tolerate a wide range of conditions. Deadhead to prolong flowering. Alternatively, allow the seed heads to develop to extend the season of interest, self-seed, and provide some food for birds. *Rudbeckia fulgida* is long-lived and does not require regular dividing, except to control the spread. Plants are hardy to zones 3 or 4.

Rudbeckia fulgida is a highly variable species, and currently seven botanical varieties are recognized: *deamii, palustris, spathulata, speciosa, sullivantii,* and *umbrosa,* in addition to the typical variety *fulgida.* The wild variants are rarely cultivated and have been mostly replaced by superior garden selections with larger and more richly colored flowers, such as 'Goldschirm', 'Goldsturm', 'Pot of Gold', and the lower-growing 'Viette's Little Suzy'.

In the wild, *Rudbeckia fulgida* blooms from July to October. Cultivated in Poznań, it flowered from 18 July until 14 October. In Moscow flowering began almost a month earlier, around 19 June, on average, but continued only until 14 August. In the United States, blooms starts in July in Chicago and in late June in St. Louis. At Longwood, two cultivars were observed, 'Goldsturm' and 'Viette's Little Suzy'. They both began flowering in early or mid-July and continued until early September, rarely early October. While 'Viette's Little Suzy' averaged about 10 weeks in bloom, 'Goldsturm' flowered for about 1 week longer. In comparison, *R. fulgida* in Moscow was in bloom for a little more than 6 weeks on average.

Rudbeckia laciniata

CUTLEAF CONEFLOWER

This plant is native to North America, from Quebec, south to Florida, and west to Oregon and Arizona. *Rudbeckia laciniata* grows in moist meadows, old fields, and along streams and roadsides. It has been cultivated since the mid-17th century.

Rudbeckia laciniata forms robust, coarse, upright clumps of wiry, glabrous, often glaucous, branched stems to 3 m tall, growing from a woody crown with slender stolons. The pinnately lobed or compound leaves, to 50 cm long, have three to 11 widely serrat-

Rudbeckia laciniata 'Herbstsonne'

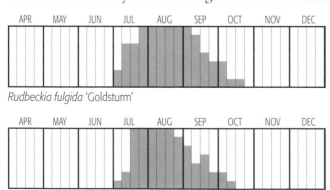

Rudbeckia fulgida 'Goldsturm'

Rudbeckia fulgida 'Viette's Little Suzy'

ed segments or leaflets, with cauline leaves becoming progressively less divided toward the tip of the stem. The basal leaves often wither before flowering. The 8-cm-wide flower heads are comprised of eight to 12 drooping yellow ray florets and numerous yellowish green disc florets forming a knob-like cone. Fruits are 4-mm-long achenes.

In the garden, *Rudbeckia laciniata* is among the most widely grown perennials. Its popularity is well deserved and can be credited to the plant's longevity, adaptability, and to the unmatched spectacle of summer bloom. It is well suited for the rear of a larger perennial border, at watersides, or near fences or sunny walls, which can provide support for plant's exceptionally tall stems. It thrives in full sun, in rich, moist, and well-drained soil. *Rudbeckia laciniata* often requires staking, especially the double-flowered forms. Alternatively, plants can be trimmed in late spring, which will result in shorter and bushier growth, with only a slight delay of flowering. Deadheading prolongs flowering, but may not be easily accomplished considering plant's remarkable height.

Space permitting, *R. laciniata* can be left undisturbed for long time; otherwise divide it every 4 years or so. Plants are hardy to zones 3 or 4.

Rudbeckia laciniata exhibits high variability among the natural populations, which has led to the designation of many botanical varieties, five of which are still recognized: *ampla*, *bipinnata*, *digitata*, *heterophylla*, and the typical *laciniata*. In cultivation, though, the wild forms are largely replaced by superior garden varieties, such as 'Herbstsonne', 'Juligold', and 'Soleil d'Or', including a few double-flowered selections, 'Golden Glow', 'Goldkugel', and 'Goldquelle', among them. Some of these cultivars are thought to be a result of hybridization of *R. laciniata* with *R. nitida*.

In the wild, *Rudbeckia laciniata* blooms from July to September. Cultivated in Moscow, it flowered

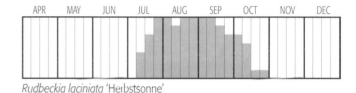

Rudbeckia laciniata 'Herbstsonne'

Rudbeckia laciniata 'Herbstsonne'

on average from 25 July until 15 September. Plants grown in Poznań started to bloom a little earlier, between 1 and 19 July, and ended between 3 and 11 September. At Longwood, the cultivar 'Herbstsonne' began flowering in mid or late July and continued until late September or early October. Once in 7 years, 'Herbstsonne' was still in flower in the last week of October. On average, 'Herbstsonne' bloomed for nearly 13 weeks.

Rudbeckia maxima
CABBAGE CONEFLOWER, GIANT CONEFLOWER, GREAT CONEFLOWER

This perennial is native to the south-central United States, from Louisiana and Arkansas west to Texas and Oklahoma. *Rudbeckia maxima* grows chiefly in moist open places, pine forests, prairies, pastures, and along roadsides, at elevations to 70 m. It has been cultivated since the early 19th century.

Rudbeckia maxima forms imposing, loose clumps of large, upstanding, basal leaves and a few stout flowering stems to 3 m tall, growing from rhizomes. The basal, ovate to elliptic, heavily glaucous green leaves are long-petiolate and reach 60 cm in length, whereas the cauline leaves become smaller, sessile, and clasping. The 8-cm-wide flower heads are comprised of 10 to 20 drooping yellow ray florets and several hundred maroon disc florets forming a blackish elongated cone to 7 cm long. The flower heads are held singly or several together in corymb-like arrays. Fruits are 7-mm-long achenes.

In the garden, *Rudbeckia maxima*, although coarse and wild in appearance, easily catches attention. It is admired for its impressive stature, bold bluish foliage, and contrasting flower heads held well above the crowd of other perennials. Choose a site where *R. maxima* can look its best without impeding surrounding plants, such as the rear of a large perennial

Rudbeckia maxima

Rudbeckia maxima

border, waterside, the edge of a moist woodland, or similar informal or naturalistic settings. Plant it in full sun, preferably in rich soil that is moist or even damp. Despite its exceptional height, *R. maxima* usually does not require support. Plants are hardy to zone 6, possibly zone 4.

In the wild, *Rudbeckia maxima* blooms from May to August. Cultivated in Germany, it flowers later, from August to September. At Longwood, flowering began between the second week of June and the first week of July. It continued until the end of July or early August. The latest bloom of *R. maxima* was observed in the third week of August. On average, it flowered for nearly 7 weeks.

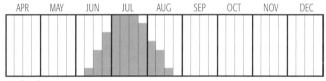

APR	MAY	JUN	JUL	AUG	SEP	OCT	NOV	DEC

Rudbeckia maxima

Rudbeckia subtomentosa

SWEET BLACK–EYED SUSAN, SWEET CONEFLOWER

This plant is native to the central and eastern United States, from Michigan, east to Massachusetts, and south to Texas and Alabama. *Rudbeckia subtomentosa* grows in prairies, lowlands, forest clearings, and along streams, at elevations to 300 m.

Rudbeckia subtomentosa forms clumps of stiff-branched, densely hirsute leafy stems to 2 m tall, growing from a stout, woody rhizome. The grayish green, lanceolate to ovate leaves are serrate, softly pubescent, and reach 30 cm in length. The lower, larger leaves usually have three or five lobes. The anise-scented, 10-cm-wide flower heads are comprised of 10 to 16 yellow disc florets and hundreds of purplish brown disc florets forming a hemispheric cone. The flower heads are held in loose, corymb-like or panicle-like arrays. Fruits are 3-mm-long achenes.

Rudbeckia subtomentosa

Rudbeckia subtomentosa 'Henry Eilers'

fahsa Wheaten Gold', with chocolate brown cones, and 'Henry Eilers', with unusual rolled petals.

In the wild, *Rudbeckia subtomentosa* blooms over a long period from July to September. Cultivated in St. Louis, it flowered from July to October. Plants grown at Longwood usually began blooming in late July or the first week of August. Once in 7 years, flowers opened in the second week of July. Flowering continued until mid-September, rarely into the first week of October. On average, *R. subtomentosa* was in bloom a little more than 9 weeks.

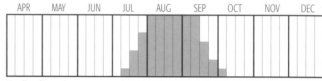

| APR | MAY | JUN | JUL | AUG | SEP | OCT | NOV | DEC |

Rudbeckia subtomentosa

Rudbeckia triloba

BROWN–EYED SUSAN, THREE–LOBED CONEFLOWER

This perennial is native to eastern North America, from Quebec, south to Florida, and west to Minnesota, Utah, and Texas. *Rudbeckia triloba* grows in open forests, alluvial thickets, rocky slopes, pastures, moist prairies, and on roadsides, at elevation to 1200 m.

Rudbeckia triloba forms dense rounded clumps of much-branched, moderately hairy stems to 1.5 m tall, growing from rhizomes. The basal, ovate to sub-cordate leaves are held on long petioles and reach 30 cm in length, whereas the cauline ones are short-petiolate or sessile and smaller. The larger leaves are often deeply trilobed or pinnatifid. The flower heads, 3 to 8 cm wide, are comprised of eight to 15 slightly reflexed yellow ray florets and numerous disc florets forming a purplish black cone. The flower heads are arranged in panicle-like arrays. Fruits are 2-mm-long achenes.

In the garden, *Rudbeckia triloba* is valued for exceptionally profuse flowering. It is well suited to informal perennial borders, cottage-style planting, wildflower meadows, or similar naturalistic settings. Plant *R. triloba* in full sun. It tolerates partial shade, but plants will grow taller and will be prone to flopping under such conditions. If this is the case, stake the plants or trim stems in late spring to encourage lower growth. This treatment will delay flowering slightly. Choose a site with moist, humus-rich, and well-drained soil, although *R. triloba* adapts to a wide

In the garden, *Rudbeckia subtomentosa* is valued for its reliability and a brilliant show of profuse long-lasting flowers. It can be used in either traditional perennial borders or naturalistic wildflower meadows and prairie style plantings. *Rudbeckia subtomentosa* thrives in full sun, but can also tolerate partial shade. Plant it in any average garden soil that is consistently moist and well drained. Stay away from extremely dry or damp places. Plants are hardy to zone 5, possibly zone 3.

There are no botanical varieties of *Rudbeckia subtomentosa* recognized among the natural populations, but in cultivation a couple of forms have been selected, including the tall and late-flowering 'Loo-

Rudbeckia triloba

range of situations. Deadhead to prolong flowering, and cut back later to prevent excessive self-seeding. *Rudbeckia triloba* is short-lived or even biennial in some situations. Therefore, allow some seed heads to mature, and save a few seedlings to use as replacements. Plants are hardy to zone 3.

There are three botanical varieties of *Rudbeckia triloba* recognized among the natural populations. The typical variety *triloba* is found throughout the species' range. Variety *pinnatiloba* is restricted to the southeastern United States and is distinguished by its larger pinnatifid leaves. Even more limited is the distribution of variety *rupestris*, found in Kentucky, Tennessee, and North Carolina and featuring larger flowers, with ray florets to 3 cm long and cones to 2

cm wide. In cultivation, only a couple selections have been made, including 'Prairie Glow', with reddish, yellow-tipped ray florets, and low-growing 'Takao'.

In the wild, *Rudbeckia triloba* blooms for a long time from July to October. Cultivated in St. Louis, it flowered at about the same time. For plants grown at Longwood, the bloom start date varied by 5 weeks between the first week of July and the second week of August. Flowering usually continued through the end of August, rarely until early October. One year, when plants were cut back in the last week of August, they rebloomed 2 months later. Cutting back in September did not result in repeat bloom. On average, *R. triloba* was in flower for a little more than 10 weeks.

Salvia

SAGE

The name *Salvia* is derived from the Latin *salvare*, to save or heal, in reference to the medicinal properties of certain species.

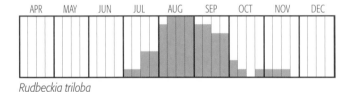

Rudbeckia triloba

Rudbeckia triloba

Salvia koyamae

Salvia koyamae

YELLOW SAGE

This perennial is native to Japan, where it has restricted distribution in central Honshu. It grows in the forests, at elevations of 800 to 1100 m. *Salvia koyamae* has been cultivated since the late 20th century.

Salvia koyamae forms lax, spreading clumps of decumbent, glandular hairy stems to 1 m tall, growing from creeping rhizomes. The light green, widely ovate, pubescent leaves have serrate margins and grow to 20 cm long. The pale yellow, 2.5-cm-long flowers are borne in distant few-flowered verticillasters arranged in leafy racemes to 30 cm long. Fruits are smooth brown nutlets to 2.5 mm long.

In the garden, *Salvia koyamae* creates a lush ground cover or a filler that weaves between other plants. Its handsome foliage provides a very pleasing backdrop for this plant's soft-colored flowers. The leaves remain attractive all season long, in mild climates even through the winter. Use it in a woodland garden to plant under trees and shrubs or in informal perennial borders. Choose a shady location, with deep, humus-rich, and moist soil. Under favorable conditions, *S. koyamae* increases readily. Regular dividing is usually not required, except to restrict the spreading. Plants are hardy to zone 6.

In the wild, in Japan, *Salvia koyamae* blooms from August to October. The bloom start date of the plants cultivated at Longwood varied greatly. In one year flowering began in the first week of July, whereas in another it was delayed until the first week of September. The early bloom in July and August, however, was rather weak compared to that in September. Flowering usually continued through the end of September, rarely until late October. On average, *S. koyamae* was in bloom for 9 weeks.

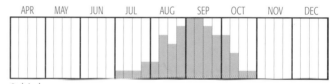

Salvia koyamae

Salvia koyamae

Salvia lavandulifolia

SPANISH SAGE

This plant is native to western Europe and northern Africa, from southern France, west to southern and eastern Spain, and south to Algeria. *Salvia lavandulifolia* grows in scrub on open dry hills.

Salvia lavandulifolia forms dense clumps of evergreen foliage and erect or ascending, sparsely leafed flowering stems to 50 cm tall, growing from a woody base. The whitish gray, lanceolate leaves, to 5 cm long, release a rosemary-like scent when crushed. The 2.5-cm-long flowers have lavender blue corollas and red-purple calyces. They are borne a few together in widely spaced whorls arranged in racemes. Fruits are nutlets.

In the garden, *Salvia lavandulifolia* fits admirably between rocks on an exposed slope, on top of a stone wall, or in containers. It is valued primarily for its silvery foliage, but the subtle flowers provide a fine complement. Plant *S. lavandulifolia* in an open, sunny site in any average garden soil that drains easily. It can tolerate drought well, but occasional deep watering is recommended. Plants are hardy to zone 5.

In the wild, *Salvia lavandulifolia* blooms in July. Similarly, plants cultivated in California flower in early summer. At Longwood, blooming began in mid or late May, but once in 6 years flowers opened in the first week of May. Flowering usually continued through late June, rarely early July. In some years, *S. lavandulifolia* rebloomed after 3 to 6 weeks. On average, it was in flower for more than 8 weeks.

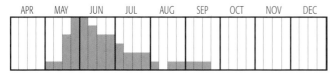

Salvia lavandulifolia

Salvia lyrata

CANCER WEED, LYRE–LEAF SAGE

This perennial is native to the eastern and central United States, from New York, south to Florida, and west to Illinois and Texas. *Salvia lyrata* often grows on sandy soils, in open upland woods, clearings, thickets, and along streams.

Salvia lyrata forms clumps of basal foliage and erect, maroon, flowering stems, to 60 cm tall, each with a pair of small leaves. The basal, pinnately lobed leaves, to 20 cm long, are often tinted purple in spring. Later this color is retained on leaf veins and margins. The lavender blue to purple, 2.5-cm-long flowers are borne in widely spaced whorls arranged in racemes, to 30 cm in length. Fruits are 2-mm-long obovoid nutlets.

In the garden, *Salvia lyrata* is primarily grown for its purple-tinted leaves, but light-colored flowers offer a welcome diversion from the rather somber looking foliage. Use it along the edge of a path or border, among rocks, in cottage-style plantings, or allow it to spread freely to establish colonies in a woodland, moist meadow, or along stream banks. Plant *S. lyrata* in full sun or partial shade, preferably in light and moist soil, although it can adapt to any average garden soil. Plants are short-lived but self-seed readily and usually renew themselves without special effort. *Salvia lyrata* is hardy to zone 6, possibly zone 4.

There are no botanical varieties of *Salvia lyrata* recognized in the wild, but in cultivation a couple of superior forms with stronger purple leaf color have been selected, including 'Burgundy Bliss' and 'Purple Knockout'.

Salvia lyrata 'Purple Knockout'

In the wild, *Salvia lyrata* blooms in May and June. Cultivated in the United Kingdom, it flowers in early to midsummer, although occasional flowers may appear until early fall. Plants grown in St. Louis began flowering in the second week of May. At Longwood, the cultivar 'Purple Knockout' started to bloom in mid to late May and usually continued until the first week of June. Once in 4 years, it rebloomed in late September. On average, 'Purple Knockout' flowered for a little more than 3 weeks.

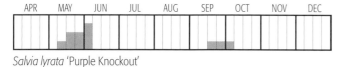

Salvia lyrata 'Purple Knockout'

Salvia nemorosa

PERENNIAL SALVIA, VIOLET SAGE, WOODLAND SAGE

This perennial is native to eastern Europe and western Asia, from Germany, south to Albania and Bulgaria, and east to western Siberia. *Salvia nemorosa* grows in woodlands, dry meadows, and along roadsides.

Salvia nemorosa forms broad bushy clumps of erect or ascending, lax, branched, leafy, often violet-red stems to 1.2 m tall, growing from a short woody rootstock with long stringy roots. The ovate to oblong leaves, to 10 cm long, have crenate margins and are held on short petioles. The 1.4-cm-long, lavender to violet flowers are borne in few-flowered whorls subtended by purple bracts and arranged in slender, branching racemes. Fruits are nutlets.

In the garden, *Salvia nemorosa* blooms freely and tirelessly. It combines easily with many of the taller perennials in a summer border. Choose a sunny location. It can tolerate light shade, but stems will become too lanky and floppy. This species thrives in cooler climates, where plants bloom longer and flower color is better. Preferably, plant *S. nemorosa* in fertile, moist, and well-drained soil. It can adapt to dry conditions, but avoid damp sites with heavy clay soil. The attractive purple bracts prolong interest after flowering. Cut stems back in midsummer to encourage a new flush of growth and possible rebloom. *Salvia nemorosa* is long-lived and does not require regular dividing. It is best to leave it undisturbed for years to develop into impressive clumps. Plants are hardy to zone 5, possibly 3, but in colder areas benefit from a cover of evergreen boughs.

Salvia nemorosa is a highly variable species in the wild, and two subspecies are currently recognized. The typical subspecies *nemorosa*, found throughout most of the range, has calyx covered with a closely appressed indumentum, whereas the subspecies *tesquicola*, distributed from Bulgaria to eastern Russia, has long and spreading hairs covering the calyx. In cultivation, the species has been largely replaced by superior garden selections, most, if not all, thought to be crosses with closely related *S. pratensis* and *S. amplexicaulis*, forming a complex hybrid swarm. These cultivars are variably listed with one of the parent species or under one of the hybrid designations *S. ×sylvestris* or *S. ×superba*. Cultivars show great variation in flower colors, from white 'Porzellan' and

Salvia ×sylvestris 'Blauhügel'

Salvia ×sylvestris 'Caradonna'

soft pink 'Rosenwein' to clear blue 'Blauhügel', indigo blue 'Mainacht', and deep purple-violet 'Ostfriesland'. Some cultivars, such as blue 'Haeumanarc' or violet blue 'Caradonna', may grow to only 30 cm tall, others, including blue 'Dear Anja' and rose 'Lapis Lazuli', may reach 70 or 90 cm in height.

In the wild, *Salvia nemorosa* blooms in June and July. Cultivated in Germany, it flowers at about the same time, but hybrids of *S. nemorosa* can flower as early as May or as late as August. Plants grown in Poznań started to bloom around 25 June and ended between 29 July and 20 August. At Longwood, four cultivars were compared, 'Blauhügel', 'Caradonna', 'Mainacht', and 'Ostfriesland'. They usually began flowering in May, with about a 2-week difference between the earliest, 'Mainacht', and the latest, 'Blauhügel'. The selection 'Mainacht' started to bloom between the last week of April and mid-May, whereas 'Blauhügel' began flowering between the second week of May and the first week of June. Plants were often cut back after the first flush of bloom in June and again in August. In nearly every case, they rebloomed within several weeks, although 'Caradonna' failed to repeat flowering in 2 of 6 years and both 'Blauhügel' and 'Mainacht' failed to rebloom in 1 of 7 years. Their average bloom time varied from about 20 weeks of 'Blauhügel' to more than 24 weeks of 'Ostfriesland'. The latter cultivar had a particularly strong fall showing, flowering reliably in October of every year and continuing sometimes until early December.

Salvia ×sylvestris 'Mainacht'

Salvia ×sylvestris 'Ostfriesland'

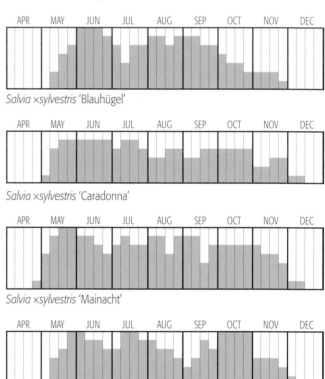

Salvia ×sylvestris 'Blauhügel'

Salvia ×sylvestris 'Caradonna'

Salvia ×sylvestris 'Mainacht'

Salvia ×sylvestris 'Ostfriesland'

Salvia uliginosa

BOG SAGE, MARSH SAGE

This plant is native to South America, from southern Brazil to Argentina and Uruguay. It often grows along damp watercourses, bogs, marshes, and other wet areas. *Salvia uliginosa* has been cultivated since the early 20th century.

Salvia uliginosa forms upright, lax clumps of erect, slender, branched stems to 2 m tall, growing from

Salvia uliginosa

shallow spreading fleshy stolons. The oblong-lanceolate leaves, to 10 cm long, have entire to serrate margins. They release a minty scent when crushed. The azure blue, 1.5-cm-long flowers have white throats. They are borne in seven- to 20-flowered whorls arranged in dense spike-like or panicle-like arrays to 12 cm in length. Fruits are nutlets.

In the garden, *Salvia uliginosa* is valued for its rare clear blue flower color. Although it is native to wet habitats, it adapts to a wide range of conditions. Its height and open habit allow it to be easily combined with a variety of plants in a perennial border, and the late flowering brings blue to a garden in late summer and fall. Plant it in a warm, sheltered, sunny or lightly shaded locations, where new growth will be protected from late frosts. *Salvia uliginosa* thrives in moist or even damp soil, but plants grown in average garden soil may be more manageable because of their lower height and slower spreading. Its slender growth usually needs support, either from the surrounding plants or staking. Plants are hardy to zone 8, possibly 6,

Salvia uliginosa

but in colder areas a protective cover of dry mulch may be required.

In the wild, *Salvia uliginosa* flowers in summer and into fall. In cultivation, its bloom start date varies considerably. In warmer climates, flowering may start in early June, whereas further north it may be delayed until August. Plants grown at Longwood began to bloom between the last week of July and the last week of August. They continued flowering until mid or late October, although in one year flowers were still open in the first week of November. On average, *S. uliginosa* was in bloom for about 12 weeks.

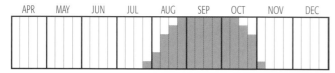

Salvia uliginosa

Salvia verticillata

LILAC SAGE, WHORLED CLARY

This perennial is native to central and southern Europe and western Asia, from France, south to Italy, and east to Russia. *Salvia verticillata* grows in meadows and woodland margins. It has naturalized in northern Europe and parts of northeastern North America.

Salvia verticillata forms spreading clumps of basal foliage and erect, leafy, flowering stems to 1 m tall. The oblong to ovate, or sometimes lyrate leaves, to 13 cm long, have irregularly and coarsely crenate margins and a rugose, pubescent surface. The lilac to dark purple flowers are borne in dense, widely spaced whorls arranged in branched, often arching, raceme-like arrays. The violet-tinged calyces persist long after flowering. Fruits are nutlets.

In the garden, *Salvia verticillata* can be used in the front of a perennial border, for underplanting roses and other shrubs, or naturalized in woodland margins. It is valued for its adaptability, grayish green foliage, and long-lasting flowers. *Salvia verticillata* grows best in full sun. Although it tolerates light shade, plants may produce lanky growth under such conditions. Plant it in any average garden soil, but avoid those that drain poorly. Deadhead to prolong flowering, and cut back to basal foliage when all bloom is finished to keep a neat appearance, prevent self-seeding, and encourage a repeat bloom. Plants are hardy to zones 5 or 6.

Salvia verticillata 'Purple Rain'

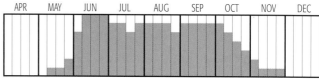

Salvia verticillata 'Purple Rain'

A naturally occurring, lower-growing variant of *Salvia verticillata* with unbranched inflorescences is sometimes segregated as subspecies *amasiaca*. In cultivation, a few superior forms have been selected, including 'Purple Rain', with reddish purple flowers, 'Smouldering Torches', with purple-tinted leaves, and white-flowered 'Alba'.

In the wild, *Salvia verticillata* blooms from June to September. Cultivated in Poznań, it began flowering between 22 and 27 June and ended between 29 and 31 July. Similarly, plants grown in Moscow bloomed, on average, from about 27 June until 30 July. In St. Louis, flowering started earlier, between mid-May and mid-June. At Longwood, the cultivar 'Purple

Rain' usually began to bloom in early June, rarely in mid-May. In some years, it flowered continuously from the first week of June until the first frost in November. In others, 'Purple Rain' rebloomed after being cut back at the end of June, in July, or in August. Plants that were cut back in early September or later did not rebloom. Flowering continued until early October, or sometimes early November, averaging nearly 20 weeks in bloom.

Sanguisorba

BURNET

The name *Sanguisorba* is derived from the Latin *sanguis*, blood, and *sorbeo*, to soak up, in reference to its medical use to prevent bleeding.

Sanguisorba obtusa

BOTTLEBRUSH-FLOWER, JAPANESE BURNET

This plant is native to Japan, where it grows in alpine meadows in northern Honshu. *Sanguisorba obtusa* has been cultivated since the late 19th century.

Sanguisorba obtusa forms upright clumps of erect or ascending, sparsely branched, leafy stems to 1.2 m tall, growing from stout creeping rhizomes. The gray-green, pinnately compound leaves, to 45 cm long, have 13 to 17 elliptic or oblong, serrate leaflets. The small reddish pink flowers are borne in nodding terminal spikes to 10 cm long. Fruits are achenes.

In the garden, *Sanguisorba obtusa* is valued for its attractive fluffy plumes of flowers, handsome gray-green foliage, and ease of care. It is well suited for planting in either a formal perennial border or in naturalistic woodland settings. Plant it in full sun or, in warmer climates, in partial shade. *Sanguisorba obtusa* thrives in moist or wet situations, but it can adapt to a wide range of soil conditions, except for dry ones. Deadhead spent flowers to maintain a neat appearance and to better show the attractive basal leaves. *Sanguisorba obtusa* is long-lived, but dividing it every 5 years or so will encourage vigorous growth. Plants are hardy to zones 4 or 5.

There are no botanical varieties of *Sanguisorba obtusa* recognized among the wild populations. In cultivation, one variegated selection named 'Lemon Splash' is known, although its affiliation with *S. obtusa* is uncertain.

In its native habitat in Japan, *Sanguisorba obtusa* blooms in August and September. Cultivated in Germany, it flowers at about the same time. In Chicago, flowering begins earlier, in July. At Longwood, the cultivar 'Lemon Splash' started to bloom between the first and the last week of August. Flowering usually continued until the first week of September, but once in 5 years plants were still in bloom at the end of September. On average, 'Lemon Splash' flowered for nearly 4 weeks.

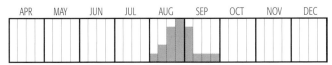

Sanguisorba obtusa 'Lemon Splash'

Sanguisorba officinalis

BURNET BLOODWORT, GREAT BURNET

This perennial is native to the temperate regions of Europe and Asia, from Spain east to Japan. *Sanguisorba officinalis* grows in moist meadows, open woods, forest edges, thickets, grassy slopes, damp ravines, and on stream banks, at elevations to 3000 m.

Sanguisorba officinalis forms upright clumps of erect, branched, reddish stems to 1.2 m tall, growing from stout creeping rhizomes. The pinnately compound leaves have seven to 25 oval to narrowly oblong, coarsely serrate leaflets, the largest to 7 cm long. The small, dark purple to dark red flowers are borne in erect, dense, ovoid to oblong spikes to 6 cm in length, opening first at the top. Fruits are achenes.

In the garden, *Sanguisorba officinalis* is most effective when planted in large groups in moist meadows or similar naturalistic settings, where plants can be allowed to roam freely. In more confined areas, its spread should be monitored and regularly controlled. Because the young leaves of *S. officinalis* are used in salad and soups, it may often be seen planted in herb or kitchen gardens. Grow it in full sun, in any average garden soil. Plants grown in sites with moist and rich soil may grow taller and require staking to prevent flopping. *Sanguisorba officinalis* self-seeds readily, so prompt deadheading is recommended to avoid problems with unwanted seedlings. Plants are hardy to zones 3 or 4.

With such an immense distribution range across two continents, it is not surprising that *Sanguisorba officinalis* shows great morphological variation. Regionally, different approaches were developed to account for this variability. In Japan, the previously described varieties *carnea*, *microcephala*, *montana*, and *pilosella* are now considered synonymous with the species. In China, on the other hand, several varieties are designated, including, *carnea*, *glandulosa*, *longifila*, and *longifolia*. In Europe, no botanical varieties are currently recognized. In cultivation, a few variants have been selected, including 'Tanna', with wine red flowers, 'Arnhem', with maroon flowers, and 'Shiro-fukurin', with cream-variegated leaves.

In the wild, *Sanguisorba officinalis* starts flowering from May to July, depending on the region. Cultivated in Moscow, it bloomed, on average, from 2 July to 25 August. In Poznań, flowering began about a month earlier, around 30 May, and ended between 22 and 25 June. Plants grown in St. Louis bloomed from the last week of June until late July or early August. At Longwood, the cultivar 'Tanna' started flowering around mid-July and continued until the end of that month, occasionally into early August. 'Tanna' averaged 3 weeks in bloom. In comparison, plants in Moscow were in flower for about 8 weeks, and those in St. Louis for 3 to 5 weeks.

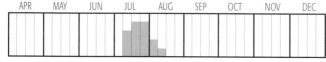

Sanguisorba officinalis 'Tanna'

Sanguisorba tenuifolia

ORIENTAL BURNET

This plant is native to eastern Asia, from eastern Siberia, east to Kamchatka, Japan, and Taiwan. *Sanguisorba tenuifolia* grows in forest margins, moist meadows, and on stream banks, at elevations of 200 to 1700 m. It has been cultivated since the late 19th century.

Sanguisorba tenuifolia forms upright clumps of mostly basal, feathery foliage and upright, branched flowering stems to 1.5 m tall, growing from slender rhizomes. The pinnately compound leaves have 11 to 19 serrate leaflets to 7 cm long. The reddish flowers are borne in erect or nodding, cylindrical spikes, opening from the top, to 7 cm in length. Fruits are achenes.

In the garden, *Sanguisorba tenuifolia* can be grown in situations similar to those described for the *S. officinalis*. Likewise, deadheading is recommended to

Sanguisorba tenuifolia 'Purpurea'

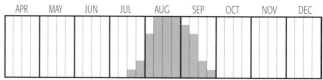

Sanguisorba tenuifolia 'Purpurea'

prevent excessive self-seeding. Plants are hardy to zone 4.

Several botanical varieties of *Sanguisorba tenuifolia* have been described in the past. Variety *grandiflora*, low-growing plants with greenish white flowers, occurs at higher elevations in Japan and the Far East of Russia. Also, white-flowered plants from China are known as variety *alba*. Other variants are considered to be synonymous with the typical variety *tenuifolia*. In cultivation, a few color variants have been selected, including pinkish 'Rosea', pinkish red 'Pink Elephant', and deep red-purple 'Purpurea'.

In the wild, *Sanguisorba tenuifolia* blooms from July to September. Cultivated in Germany, it flowers from August to September. The cultivar 'Pur-

Sanguisorba tenuifolia 'Purpurea'

purea' grown at Longwood usually began flowering in early August, rarely in late July. It continued to bloom until early September, occasionally late September. 'Purpurea' averaged a little more than 6 week of flowering time.

Santolina

LAVENDER–COTTON

The name *Santolina* is derived from the Latin, *sanctum linum*, holy flax, an old name given to *S. rosmarinifolia*.

Santolina rosmarinifolia

GREEN LAVENDER–COTTON, ROSEMARY
LAVENDER–COTTON

This perennial is native to southern Europe, from southern France west to Portugal. *Santolina rosmarinifolia* grows on dry gravelly or rocky slopes.

Santolina rosmarinifolia forms erect or ascending evergreen shrubs to 60 cm tall, growing from a procumbent rootstock. The bright green, very aromatic leaves are narrowly linear, to 5 cm long, and vary in form from entire to pectinate-pinnatifid. The 2-cm-wide, hemispherical flower heads are comprised of only yellow disc florets and no ray florets. They are held singly atop slender simple peduncles, leafless above, to 25 cm in length. Fruits are oblong achenes.

In the garden, *Santolina rosmarinifolia* is valued for its handsome, fine-textured foliage and the playful drumstick-shaped flower heads. Use it among rocks, on a south-facing stone wall, near terraces or patios, and in containers. If one is willing to give up flowers, *S. rosmarinifolia* can be easily sheared to make low hedging for perennial borders or seasonal beds. Plant it in full sun, in any average soil that is well drained. It tolerates dry and low fertility conditions. Plants are hardy to zone 7, and in colder areas good winter protection is essential. Alternatively, potted stock plants can be overwintered indoors.

There are two subspecies of *Santolina rosmarinifolia* recognized among the natural populations. The typical subspecies *rosmarinifolia*, found throughout

Santolina rosmarinifolia

most of the distribution range, is glabrous to sparsely tomentose, whereas subspecies *canescens*, restricted to the areas above 800 m in southern Spain, is densely white- to gray-tomentose. In cultivation, a few selections varying in flower and foliage color are grown, including 'Morning Mist', with silvery foliage, 'Lemon Fizz', with yellow-green foliage, and 'Primrose Gem', with pale yellow flowers.

Cultivated in Germany, *Santolina rosmarinifolia* blooms in July and August. Plants grown at Longwood began flowering between the first and the last week of June and continued until the third week of July, rarely into the first week of August. On average, *S. rosmarinifolia* bloomed at Longwood for a little more than 6 weeks.

APR	MAY	JUN	JUL	AUG	SEP	OCT	NOV	DEC

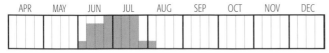

Santolina rosmarinifolia

Saponaria
SOAPWORT

The name *Saponaria* is derived from the Latin *sapo*, soap, and is a medieval name applied to *S. officinalis*.

Saponaria ×lempergii
LEMBERG'S SOAPWORT

This plant is a hybrid between *Saponaria cypria* from Cyprus and *S. sicula* var. *intermedia* (also known as *S. haussknechtii*), from the Balkans, developed in the mid-20th century by Fritz Lemberg in Austria.

Saponaria ×*lempergii* forms evergreen spreading clumps of procumbent or ascending, much-branched, fragile stems to 40 cm tall, growing from a woody rootstock. The lanceolate to oval, 1-cm-wide leaves are dark green and softly pubescent. The 2.5-cm-wide pink flowers are held in loose clusters.

In the garden, *Saponaria* ×*lempergii* is well suited for planting on open slopes, among rocks, on dry

Saponaria ×*lempergii* 'Max Frei'

Saponaria ×*lempergii* 'Max Frei'

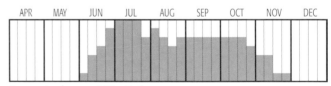

Saponaria ×*lempergii* 'Max Frei'

walls, or in the front of a perennial border. It is valued for its profuse, long-lasting, and brightly colored flowers accompanied by soft and grayish foliage. Plant it in full sun, in any average garden soil that drains well. It adapts easily to dry and poor soils, but it is intolerant of damp situations and high humidity. Cut back after the first flush of flowers to encourage a possible rebloom. Plants are hardy to zone 6, possibly zone 4.

The only selection of *Saponaria* ×*lempergii* is known as 'Max Frei'. It features pale pink flowers.

Cultivated in Germany, *Saponaria* ×*lempergii* blooms in August and September. The cultivar 'Max Frei' grown in St. Louis flowered from June until October. At Longwood, 'Max Frei' began to bloom between the first week of June and the first week of July. After being cut back in mid-June to the first week of August, plants rebloomed within 2 to 6 weeks. Plants that were cut back in mid-August or later did not rebloom. The repeat flowering usually continued through the end of October, sometimes until the first frost in November. 'Max Frei' averaged nearly 17 weeks in bloom.

Scabiosa

MOURNING-BRIDE, PINCUSHION-FLOWER, SCABIOUS
The name *Scabiosa* is derived from the Latin *scabies*, itch, in reference to the condition treated with these plants.

Scabiosa caucasica

CAUCASIAN SCABIOUS, PINCUSHION-FLOWER
This perennial is native to the Caucasus and southwestern Asia, from northeastern Turkey to north-

western Iran. *Scabiosa caucasica* grows in subalpine and alpine meadows and rocky places, at elevations to 2900 m. It has been cultivated since the early 19th century.

Scabiosa caucasica forms rounded clumps of gray-green foliage and simple or sparsely branched flowering stems to 80 cm tall. The basal leaves are lanceolate and entire, whereas the cauline leaves are pinnately lobed into linear segments. The flat flower heads, 7 to 10 cm wide, are held singly in long peduncles. They are comprised of lavender blue florets, with the marginal ones enlarged, and are subtended by a hairy involucre. Fruits are achenes enclosed by a persistent calyx.

In the garden, *Scabiosa caucasica* is used primarily in perennial borders. Its soft-textured grayish foliage and very showy flowers can be effectively combined with many other bolder perennials or grasses. Plant *S. caucasica* in a warm and sunny location. It grows best in light, fertile, calcareous, moderately moist, and well-drained soil, but it can adapt to a wide range of conditions, except for those excessively wet and poorly drained. Deadhead to prolong flowering and to maintain a neat appearance. *Scabiosa caucasica* is short-lived, especially when grown in hot and humid climates, and needs to be divided frequently, in some cases even every other year. Plants are hardy to zones 3 or 4, but in colder climates may benefit from a light winter cover of evergreen boughs.

The species *Scabiosa caucasica* is rarely cultivated in gardens, but numerous selections are available, offering a variety of colors: creamy white 'Loddon White', lavender blue 'Fama', dark blue 'Blauer Atlas', and violet 'Nachtfalter'.

In the wild, *Scabiosa caucasica* blooms in July and August. Cultivated in Germany, it flowers from June to September. Plants grown in Moscow bloomed, on average, from 30 June to 18 August. In Poznań, *S. caucasica* began flowering a little earlier, between 12 and 25 June, but ended at about the same time, on 20 or 21 August. An even earlier bloom, starting in mid-May, was recorded in St. Louis. At Longwood, the cultivar 'Fama' began flowering between the third week of May and the third week of June. Plants that were cut back in mid-June to mid-July resumed flowering within 2 to 4 weeks, but those cut back in the first week of August rebloomed only 13 weeks later, in November, whereas those cut back in the

last week of August did not rebloom at all. 'Fama' usually stayed in flower through the end of July, and only sporadically after the first week of August. It averaged nearly 10 weeks in bloom.

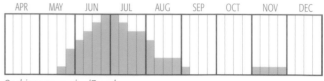

Scabiosa caucasica 'Fama'

Scabiosa columbaria
SMALL SCABIOUS

This perennial is native to Europe, western Asia, and northern Africa, from Portugal, north to Sweden, east to Russia and Turkmenistan, and south to Morocco, Algeria, Turkey, and Iran. *Scabiosa columbaria* often grows on calcareous soils on dry open hills. It has naturalized in parts of northeastern North America.

Scabiosa columbaria forms compact clumps of mostly basal foliage and branched, hairy stems to

Scabiosa caucasica 'Fama'

1 m tall. The basal leaves are oblanceolate to obovate, entire or occasionally lyrate-pinnatifid. The cauline leaves are progressively more pinnately dissected into linear segments. The 4-cm-wide domed flower heads are comprised of lilac blue (rarely pink or white) florets, the outer ones enlarged, and are held singly on long peduncles. Fruits are achenes.

In the garden, *Scabiosa columbaria* is valued for an exceptionally long bloom season that usually lasts until the first hard frost. It is well suited for planting in the front of a perennial border. Choose a warm and sunny site, although in climates with hot summers, partial shade may be preferred. Preferably, plant it in light, calcareous, fertile, and well-drained soil. Avoid situations with heavy clay or wet and poorly drained soil. Deadhead to prolong flowering. *Scabiosa columbaria* is short-lived and needs to be divided every 3 years or so. Plants are hardy in zone 3, but in severe climates require light winter protection.

There are three subspecies of *Scabiosa columbaria* recognized among wild populations in Europe.

The typical subspecies *columbaria*, found throughout the distribution range, has leaves covered with short hairs and flower heads subtended by involucral bracts shorter than the florets. In Italy and the northwestern part of the Balkans grows subspecies *portae*, distinguished by its long and dense hairs, whereas the Carpathians are home to subspecies *pseudobanatica*, differing in having involucral bracts at least as long as the florets. In cultivation, a number of flower color variants have been selected, including lavender pink 'Pink Mist', lavender blue 'Butterfly Blue', and intense blue 'Blue Buttons'.

In mild climates, *Scabiosa columbaria* blooms nearly all year-round in frost-free areas. Cultivated in the United Kingdom, it flowers from July to October, whereas in Ohio it blooms from May until October. At Longwood, two cultivars were observed, 'Butterfly Blue' and 'Pink Mist'. They both usually began flowering from mid-May to the first week of June, but occasionally as early as late April. They also both flowered nearly continuously through the entire

Scabiosa columbaria 'Butterfly Blue'

growing season, until the first hard frost in November or early December. On average, 'Butterfly Blue' and 'Pink Mist' were in bloom for 28 weeks.

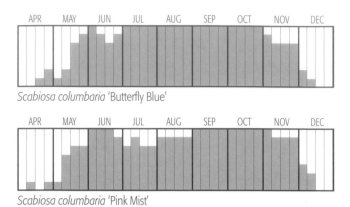

Scabiosa columbaria 'Butterfly Blue'

Scabiosa columbaria 'Pink Mist'

Scabiosa ochroleuca

CREAM SCABIOUS

This plant is native to Europe and western Asia, from Germany, south to Italy and Bulgaria, and east to Siberia. *Scabiosa ochroleuca* often grows in dry meadows and on stony slopes. It has been cultivated since the 16th century.

Scabiosa ochroleuca forms mounded clumps of fine grayish pubescent foliage and erect, wiry, much-branched, pubescent stems to 1 m tall, growing from a spindle-shaped rootstock. The basal leaves are obovate-lanceolate, entire to crenate. The lower cauline leaves are entire to lyrate, whereas the upper ones become pinnately dissected into linear lobes. The 4-cm-wide globular flower heads are comprised of primrose yellow florets, the marginal ones being enlarged. The flower heads are borne singly in long peduncles. Fruits are achenes.

In the garden, *Scabiosa ochroleuca* makes attractive mounds of soft-textured foliage and profuse and long-lasting flowers. It is well suited for traditional

Scabiosa columbaria 'Pink Mist'

Scabiosa ochroleuca

perennial borders, cottage-style plantings, or natu-ralized on open slopes or wildflower meadows. Plant in full sun, in any average garden soil that is well drained. This species is very adaptable and can toler-ate dry and low-fertility situations. It is short-lived but it self-seeds readily, and seedlings can be saved as replacement plants. *Scabiosa ochroleuca* is hardy to zone 7, possibly zone 5.

In the wild, *Scabiosa ochroleuca* blooms during the summer months. Cultivated in Germany, it flowers from June until October. Plants grown at Longwood began flowering between the second week of May and the last week of June. When cut back in mid to late July, they rebloomed within 2 to 3 weeks, but plants cut back in mid-August or later did not flower again. *Sca-*

biosa ochroleuca* often continued to flower until the first hard frost in November, averaging 19 weeks in bloom.

Senna

SENNA

The name *Senna* is derived from *sanã*, the Arabic name for one of the species.

Senna marilandica

MARYLAND SENNA, WILD SENNA

This perennial is native to the eastern United States, from Massachusetts, south to Florida, and west to Nebraska and Texas. *Senna marilandica* grows in moist open woodlands, thickets, swamps, on stream banks, and along roadsides.

Senna marilandica forms upright bushy clumps of erect, little-branched stems to 2 m tall, growing from a woody rootstock. The evenly pinnately compound leaves, to 27 cm long, have five to nine pairs of el-liptic or oblong leaflets, yellowish green above and somewhat glaucous below. The 1.5-cm-long yellow

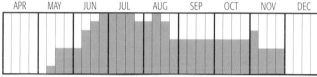

APR	MAY	JUN	JUL	AUG	SEP	OCT	NOV	DEC

Scabiosa ochroleuca

Scabiosa ochroleuca

Senna marilandica

flowers with conspicuous black anthers are borne in dense, erect, axillary racemes. Fruits are compressed legumes to 11 cm long.

In the garden, *Senna marilandica* is well suited for planting in the rear of a large perennial bed and for naturalizing in a wildflower meadow or along the edge of a woodland. Plant it in full sun or partial shade, in any average garden soil that is well drained. Established plants are quite tolerant of drought conditions. *Senna marilandica* is hardy to zone 5, although in cold climates young plants may benefit from a light winter protection.

In the wild, *Senna marilandica* blooms in July and August. Cultivated in Germany, it flowers at about the same time. Plants grown at Longwood began flowering between the first and last week of July and continued until early August, rarely until the end of August. On average, *S. marilandica* bloomed for a little more than 5 weeks.

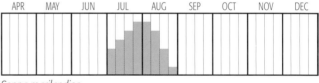

Senna marilandica

Silphium

ROSINWEED

The name *Silphium* is derived from *silphion*, a name used by ancient Greeks for another plant of uncertain identity that produced a resinous substance.

Silphium integrifolium

WHOLELEAF ROSINWEED

This plant is native to central North America, from Ontario, west to Wyoming, and south to Alabama and New Mexico. *Silphium integrifolium* grows in prairies, old fields, dry open woodlands, and along roadsides, at elevations to 600 m.

Senna marilandica

Silphium integrifolium

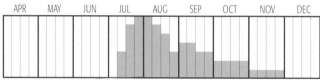

Silphium integrifolium

Silphium integrifolium forms imposing, coarse, upright clumps of erect, sturdy, sparsely branched, rough-hairy to glabrous stems to 2 m tall, growing from a woody, deep, sometimes creeping, rootstock. The lanceolate to ovate, sessile to nearly clasping leaves have entire or finely serrate margins and reach 23 cm in length. The starry 7-cm-wide flower heads are comprised of 12 to 36 yellow ray florets and numerous disc florets. The flower heads are arranged in broad, loose corymb-like arrays. Fruits are 1-cm-long achenes topped by short pappi.

In the garden, *Silphium integrifolium* may be too coarse for smaller perennial borders, but it is well suited for less formal situations, such as wildflower meadows and woodland margins, where plants can be allowed to naturalize. Plant it in full sun to partial shade, in any average garden soil that drains readily. Avoid excessively rich and moist sites, where plants tend to produce lanky growth prone to flopping.

Silphium integrifolium is slow to establish but long-lived, and it is best left without dividing for years. Plants are hardy to zone 5.

Silphium integrifolium is a variable species, and several botanical varieties have been described among the natural populations. Of those, currently only two are recognized. The typical variety *integrifolium* is characterized by flower heads with 12 to 22 ray florets, whereas variety *laeve* differs in having 20 to 36 ray florets. Both varieties can be found throughout most of the distribution range.

In the wild, *Silphium integrifolium* blooms from July to September. Cultivated in St. Louis, it flowered at about the same time. Plants grown in Germany begin flowering a little later, in August. At Longwood, *S. integrifolium* started to bloom in mid or late July and continued through the end of that month or until mid-August. Plants that were cut back at that time rebloomed in some years but not others. Occasionally, plants continued to flower through October and even until the first frost in November. On average, *S. integrifolium* was in bloom for 10 weeks.

Solidago
GOLDENROD

The name *Solidago* is derived from the Latin *solidus*, whole, and *ago*, resembling or becoming, in reference to the healing properties.

Solidago Hybrids
HYBRID GOLDENROD

In cultivation, *Solidago* species have been largely replaced by their hybrids. Breeding in this group of plants relied heavily on the North American *Solidago sphacelata* and European *S. virgaurea*, but other species, such as *S. caesia* and *S. juncea*, are thought to be involved as well. Low-growing varieties resulted from crosses with North American *S. missouriensis* and *S. ptarmicoides*.

Solidago hybrids are a varied group and can form tight or spreading clumps of typically erect stiff stems, branching only near the top, and ranging from 0.3 to 1.8 m in height. The linear, lanceolate, or ovate leaves can be glabrous or scabrous and reach 12 cm in length. The tiny yellow (rarely white) flower heads are held in arrays of various shapes, from corymb-like to those resembling panicles, racemes, or thyrses. Fruits are achenes.

In the garden, *Solidago* hybrids play a more important role than the species. Most of them do not show the same invasive tendencies as the wild species. They are valued as undemanding, robust, easy-to-grow plants well suited for late-summer or fall borders, wildflower meadows, and as cut flowers. Plant *Solidago* hybrids in full sun or partial shade, in any average garden soil. Avoid sites with excessively fertile or damp conditions, which may pro-

Solidago 'Goldstrahl'

mote rampant growth. Deadhead to prolong flowering and cut back stems to the ground once all bloom is finished. In more informal settings, leave the stems standing to provide interest during the winter months. Divide the spreading types every 2 or 3 years and the clump-forming types every 4 to 5 years. Plants are hardy to zone 5, possibly zone 3.

Solidago hybrids offer gardeners many subtle variations of yellow flowers, including pale primrose yellow 'Lemore', canary yellow 'Goldstrahl', and mimosa yellow 'Goldenmosa'. The arrangement of flowers varies as well, from flat and broad inflo-

rescences of 'Strahlenkrone' to plume-like arrays of 'Federbusch', whereas the height of the plants ranges from 30-cm-tall 'Golden Thumb' to 1.8-m-tall 'Golden Wings'.

Solidago hybrids bloom from the middle of summer to late fall. In Germany and Poland, they flower from July to September. In Moscow, the cultivar 'Strahlenkrone' bloomed, on average, from 17 August to 16 September, whereas 'Goldstrahl' bloomed from 29 August to 27 September. At Longwood, four cultivars were observed: 'Goldenmosa', 'Goldstrahl', 'Lemore', and 'Strahlenkrone'. The earliest to

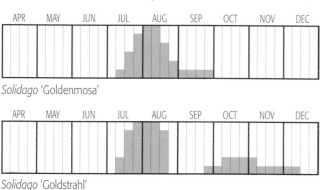

Solidago 'Goldenmosa'

Solidago 'Goldstrahl'

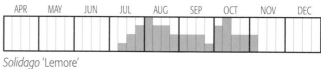

Solidago 'Lemore'

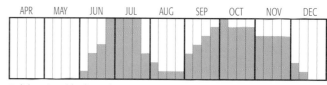

Solidago 'Strahlenkrone'

Solidago 'Lemore'

Solidago 'Strahlenkrone'

bloom was 'Strahlenkrone', which began flowering between the first and the last week of June, whereas the other three varieties were never in flower before the second week of July. 'Strahlenkrone' was usually cut back in mid to late July and flowered again from September until the first frost, averaging 17 weeks in bloom. 'Goldenmosa', 'Goldstrahl', and 'Lemore' flowered at about the same time in July and August, but differed in their ability to rebloom after being cut back. 'Goldenmosa' rebloomed only once in 6 years and averaged about 5 weeks in bloom; 'Goldstrahl' rebloomed twice and averaged more than 8 weeks of flowering; and 'Lemore' repeated flowering almost every year, with nearly 11 weeks of average bloom duration. In comparison, 'Strahlenkrone' and 'Goldstrahl' in Moscow were in flower for about 5 weeks.

Solidago caesia

BLUE–STEM GOLDENROD, WOODLAND GOLDENROD,
WREATH GOLDENROD

This perennial is native to eastern North America, from Quebec, south to Florida, and west to Wisconsin and Texas. _Solidago caesia_ grows in shaded woodlands, forest clearings, thickets, wet lowlands, and along streams, at elevations to 1000 m.

Solidago caesia forms loose clumps of erect or arching, slender, wiry, sparsely branched, purplish stems to 1 m tall, growing from woody caudex-like rhizomes. The sessile, lanceolate leaves, to 10 cm long, have entire to slightly serrate margins. The yellow flower heads, comprised of up to six rays florets and nine disc florets, are arranged in sessile clusters in leaf axils and in terminal raceme-like or panicle-like arrays. Fruits are 2-mm-long achenes topped by a 3-mm-long pappus.

In the garden, _Solidago caesia_ makes an attractive addition to traditional perennial borders, informal cottage-style plantings, or naturalized woodlands and meadows. Plant in full sun or partial shade, in any average garden soil. It even tolerates dry and poor soils if given a light shade. Deadhead spent flowers if self-seeding becomes a nuisances. Plants are hardy to zones 3 or 4.

There are two varieties of _Solidago caesia_ recognized throughout its range. The widely distributed typical variety _caesia_ has strongly arching stems and

narrower, longer leaves. Variety _zedia_, restricted to the southeastern United States, has only slightly arching stems and wider, shorter leaves.

In the wild, _Solidago caesia_ blooms from August to October. Cultivated in Germany, it flowers in September. Plants grown in St. Louis started to bloom between mid and late September and ended in mid-October. Similarly, at Longwood, flowering began in mid or late September and usually continued until the first week of October. On average, _S. caesia_ bloomed at Longwood for 4 weeks.

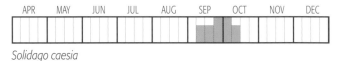

Solidago caesia

Solidago rugosa

ROUGH–STEMMED GOLDENROD,
WRINKLE–LEAF GOLDENROD

This plant is native to eastern North America, from Newfoundland, south to Florida, and west to Wisconsin and Texas. _Solidago rugosa_ grows often in wet soils, in open woodlands, thickets, old fields, bogs, and along roadsides, at elevations to 1800 m.

Solidago rugosa forms loose, spreading clumps of erect or arching, hairy stems to 2.5 m tall, growing from long-creeping rhizomes. The sessile, elliptical to lanceolate leaves, to 13 cm long, have deeply impressed veins and sharply serrate margins. The golden yellow flower heads, comprised of six to eight ray florets and four to six disc florets, are held in loose, conical panicle-like arrays to 40 cm long. Fruits are achenes to 1 mm in length, topped by a 2-mm-long pappus.

In the garden, _Solidago rugosa_ can be used in a similar fashion as _S. caesia_. It is valued for its adaptability and the fact that it does not spread as aggressively as many other goldenrods. Plant it in full sun, in any average garden soil. _Solidago rugosa_ can even be grown successfully in wet or damp situations. To reduce the ultimate height of the plants, cut the stems back in late spring. Divide clumps every 3 years or so to control their spread. Plants are hardy to zone 3.

Solidago rugosa is a highly variable species and is divided into two subspecies and five varieties, but distinctions between these variants are not always clear. The typical subspecies _rugosa_, more frequent

Solidago caesia

Solidago rugosa 'Fireworks'

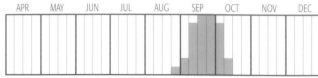

Solidago rugosa 'Fireworks'

in the northern part of the range, has thin, sharply toothed leaves; it is represented by variety *rugosa*, with hairy stems and leaves, and variety *sphagnophila*, which is glabrous. The more southern subspecies *aspera* has thick leaves that are bluntly serrate or nearly entire; it includes three varieties, *aspera*, with lanceolate leaves; *celtidifolia*, with ovate leaves; and *cronquistiana*, distinguished by its very narrow flower arrays. In cultivation, the most commonly grown is a low-growing selection named 'Fireworks', which reaches 1 m in height.

In the wild, *Solidago rugosa* blooms from July to November. Plants cultivated in Moscow started to flower, on average, around 15 August and ended on 20 September. At Longwood, the cultivar 'Fireworks' usually began flowering in mid-September, although once in 7 years flowers opened in the last week of August. Bloom continued until the first week of October, rarely until the second week. On average, 'Fireworks' flowered for a little more than 5 weeks. *Solidago rugosa* in Moscow also averaged about 5 weeks in bloom.

Solidago sphacelata 'Golden Fleece'

Solidago sphacelata

FALL GOLDENROD, FALSE GOLDENROD

This perennial is native to the eastern United States, from Virginia, west to Illinois, and south to Georgia and Mississippi. *Solidago sphacelata* grows often on calcareous soils, on rocky slopes, in open woodlands and old fields, at elevations to 1000 m.

Solidago sphacelata forms loose spreading clumps of basal foliage and ascending to erect and arching, leafy, flowering stems to 1.2 m tall, growing from a short caudex-like rhizome. The basal semi-evergreen leaves, to 12 cm long, are petiolate, cordate, and coarsely serrate. The cauline leaves become progressively smaller, shorter petioled, and less cordate. The yellow flower heads, comprised of three to six ray florets and a similar number of disc florets, are held in dense, narrow, panicle-like terminal arrays. Fruits are achenes 1 to 2 mm long with a short pappus.

In the garden, thanks to its dense and attractive basal foliage, *Solidago sphacelata* creates an effective ground cover when not in bloom. Plant in full sun, in any average garden soil that is well drained. This species can tolerate dry conditions and poor soils. Deadhead to extend flowering. Plants are hardy to zone 5.

There are no botanical varieties of *Solidago sphacelata* recognized among the natural populations. In cultivation, a low-growing and more freely flowering selection has been named 'Golden Fleece'.

In the wild, *Solidago sphacelata* blooms from August to September. In St. Louis, the cultivar 'Golden Fleece' started to flower between the last week of August and mid-September and continued until the end of September or mid-October. Similarly, at Longwood 'Golden Fleece' began flowering in the last week of August or the first week of September, but once in 7 years flowers were already open in the second week of August. Bloom usually continued until the first week of October, occasionally extending until the third week of October. On average, 'Golden Fleece' flowered at Longwood for a little more than 7 weeks. In comparison, plants in St. Louis averaged 5 to 6 weeks in bloom.

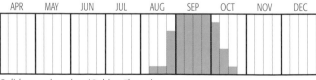

Solidago sphacelata 'Golden Fleece'

Spigelia

PINKROOT, WORM GRASS

The name *Spigelia* commemorates Adrian van der Spigel (1578–1625), a Dutch physician and botanist.

Spigelia marilandica

INDIAN PINK, STARBLOOM, WOODLAND PINKROOT

This plant is native to the southeastern and central United States, from Maryland, south to Florida, and west to Illinois and Texas. *Spigelia marilandica* grows in moist shaded woodlands, in thickets, and along stream banks. It has been cultivated since the early 18th century.

Spigelia marilandica forms upright loose clumps of erect, stiff, slender, unbranched stems to 60 cm tall. The sessile, ovate-lanceolate leaves have entire margins and reach 10 cm in length. The tubular, 5-cm-long flowers with five flaring acute lobes are carmine red outside and yellow inside. They are borne in one-sided terminal cymes. Fruits are 6-mm-long bilobed capsules.

In the garden, *Spigelia marilandica* is well suited for shaded borders or woodland settings. For best effect, plant it in large groups near paths or where it can be easily viewed. Choose a shaded location, although in northern climates *S. marilandica* can be successfully grown in full sun provided the soil is consistently moist. It thrives in humus-rich, slightly acidic, moist, and well-drained soils. Plants are hardy to zones 4 to 6.

In the wild, *Spigelia marilandica* blooms from May to July. Cultivated in Germany, it flowers later, from July to September. Plants grown in St. Louis bloomed from the last week of May until mid-June. At Longwood, flowering began between the third week of May and the third week of June. The bloom usually continued until the end of June, but in some years an occasional repeat flowering was observed between July and September. On average, *S. marilandica* was in bloom for a little more than 6 weeks.

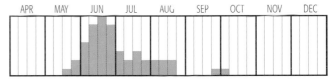

APR MAY JUN JUL AUG SEP OCT NOV DEC

Spigelia marilandica

Spigelia marilandica

Spigelia marilandica

Stachys

BETONY, HEDGE NETTLE, WOUNDWORT

The name *Stachys* is taken from the Greek, *stachys*, spike, in reference to the spikate inflorescence.

Stachys byzantina

DONKEY'S-EARS, JESUS-FLANNEL, LAMB'S-EARS, LAMB'S-TONGUE, WOOLLY BETONY, WOOLLY WOUNDWORT

This perennial is native to southeastern Europe and southwestern Asia, from northern Turkey and the Crimea east to the Caucasus and northern Iran. It grows on dry rocky slopes, in scrub, and margins of cultivated fields, at elevations to 2000 m. *Stachys byzantina* has been cultivated since the late 18th century.

Stachys byzantina

Stachys byzantina forms thick, mat-like clumps of white woolly foliage and stout, flowering stems to 80 cm tall. The oblong to elliptic leaves, to 10 cm long, are densely white-tomentose. In warmer climates leaves are retained through the winter. The 2-cm-long, pink to purple flowers are mostly obscured by the woolly calyces. They are borne in dense whorls widely spaced in spikes to 15 cm in length. Fruits are nutlets.

In the garden, *Stachys byzantina* is valued primarily for its soft-textured silvery foliage, and the flowering stems are sometimes removed entirely to maintain the uniform appearance of the foliar carpet. Use it for edging and softening hard corners, as a ground cover in open and dry situations, as a foil for other perennials in the front of a border, and for underplanting roses and other low shrubs. Plant it in full sun or, in areas with hot summers, in light afternoon shade. Choose a site with light, moderately fertile and moist soil that drains readily. Avoid situations where leaves may stay moist long after rain, which will quickly deteriorate their condition. Clean out declining foliage regularly throughout the season, or even cut back completely to encourage a new flush of growth. *Stachys byzantina* spreads steadily and needs dividing every 4 to 5 years, or more often if it becomes too rampant. Plants are hardy to zone 4.

In cultivation, several variants of *Stachys byzantina* have been selected and named. They differ chiefly in their leaf characteristics. The cultivar 'Sheila Macqueen' features larger and less woolly leaves, but 'Silver Carpet' grows shorter, narrower, and has strongly silvery white foliage. Leaves of 'Primrose Heron' emerge primrose yellow in spring and later mature

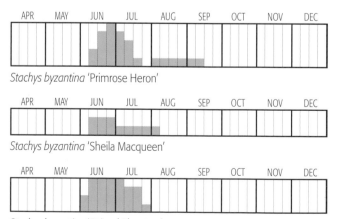

APR	MAY	JUN	JUL	AUG	SEP	OCT	NOV	DEC

Stachys byzantina 'Primrose Heron'

APR	MAY	JUN	JUL	AUG	SEP	OCT	NOV	DEC

Stachys byzantina 'Sheila Macqueen'

APR	MAY	JUN	JUL	AUG	SEP	OCT	NOV	DEC

Stachys byzantina 'Striped Phantom'

to gray-green, whereas those of 'Striped Phantom' are creamy variegated.

In the wild, *Stachys byzantina* blooms from June to September. Cultivated in Poznań, it started to flower between 14 and 25 June and ended between 29 July and 20 August. Plants grown in Moscow bloomed, on average, from 26 June to 27 July. *Stachys byzantina* flowers in Chicago in July and August, but in St. Louis blooming begins several weeks earlier, in May or early June. At Longwood, three cultivars were observed, 'Primrose Heron', 'Sheila Macqueen', and 'Striped Phantom'. All three started flowering in June, with 'Striped Phantom' usually being 1 week ahead of the two other varieties. They usually bloomed through mid July, rarely late July. Only one of the cultivars, 'Primrose Heron', rebloomed once after being cut back in July. Their average bloom duration varied from 3 weeks for 'Sheila Macqueen' to 5 weeks for 'Primrose Heron' and over 6 weeks for 'Striped Phantom'. In comparison, *S. byzantina* in Moscow was in flower for about 4 weeks.

Stachys macrantha

BIG BETONY, BIG-SAGE

This plant is native to southeastern Europe and southwestern Asia, from the Caucasus in Russia south to Turkey, Armenia, and northwestern Iran. *Stachys macrantha* grows in rocky slopes, scrub, or grasslands. It has been cultivated since the early 19th century.

Stachys macrantha forms dense, bushy clumps of basal wrinkled foliage and erect unbranched flowering stems to 60 cm tall. The broadly ovate, long-petiolate leaves, to 10 cm long, have cordate bases and crenate margins. The two-lipped, violet to purple, 4-cm-long flowers are borne in dense whorls widely spaced on erect spikes. Fruits are nutlets.

In the garden, *Stachys macrantha* is valued for its attractive and long-lasting floral display. Use it in smaller groups in the front of a perennial border, or allow it to spread and create an effective ground cover. Plant it in full sun or, in southern areas, in partial shade. It thrives in any average garden soil that is

Stachys byzantina

Stachys macrantha

Stachys macrantha

well drained. Deadhead to maintain a neat appearance and to prevent unwanted self-seeding. *Stachys macrantha* spreads rather quickly in fertile and moist soils and needs to be regularly divided. In dry and poor soils, the spread is slow and dividing is rarely required. Plants are hardy to zone 6, possibly zone 4.

There are a few color variants of *Stachys macrantha* cultivated in gardens. They include white 'Alba', rose-pink 'Rosea', and violet 'Violacea'. In addition, two vigorous superior forms have been named 'Robusta' and 'Superba'.

In the wild, *Stachys macrantha* blooms from June to August. Cultivated in Moscow, it flowered, on average, from 24 June to 27 July. Plants grown in Poznań started to bloom a little earlier, between 15 and 19 June and ended between 23 and 29 July. In Chicago and St. Louis, flowering begins in early June. At Longwood, *S. macrantha* started flowering between the second week of May and the second week of June. The first flush of bloom continued until mid-July. Plants that were cut back at that time usually rebloomed within 2 to 6 weeks, but those

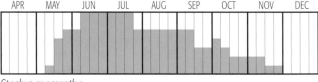

Stachys macrantha

that were not cut often continued to flower as well. In some years, *S. macrantha* kept on flowering until fall. Once in 7 years, it was still in flower at the end of November. On average, *S. macrantha* flowered for more than 17 weeks.

Stokesia

STOKES'–ASTER, STOKESIA

The name *Stokesia* commemorates Jonathan Stokes (1755–1831), an English physician and botanist.

Stokesia laevis

JASPER–BLUE STOKESIA, STOKES'–ASTER

This perennial is native to the southeastern United States, from North Carolina, south to Florida, and west to Louisiana. *Stokesia laevis* grows in pine

Stokesia laevis 'Silver Moon'

Stokesia laevis 'Blue Danube'

woods, forest clearings, savannas, and bogs, at elevations to 1000 m. It has been cultivated since the late 18th century.

Stokesia laevis forms upright loose clumps of leafy rosettes and erect or ascending, stiff, coarsely branched stems to 1 m tall, growing from a fleshy rootstock. The oblong-lanceolate, entire or serrate toward the base, evergreen leaves, to 20 cm long, often have pronounced white midrib. The 10-cm-wide flower heads are comprised of up to 35, rarely more, lilac blue florets. Marginal florets are larger and ray-like, whereas the inner ones are shorter and tubular. The flower heads are held singly or in few-flowered corymb-like terminal arrays. Fruits are glabrous achenes.

In the garden, *Stokesia laevis* is best suited for a position in the front of a perennial border. It is valued for its simple yet attractive foliage, which persists through winter in milder climates, and large fringed flower heads. Plant it in a warm, sunny location, although partial shade is also tolerated, with light, slightly acidic, and well-drained soil. Avoid sites where soil stays damp in winter. Staking is not needed, except for the tallest varieties. Deadhead individual flower heads to prolong flowering, and cut

back to the basal foliage after all bloom is finished. *Stokesia laevis* increases slowly and needs to be divided only when plant vigor decreases. It is hardy to zone 5, but in colder climates a light winter cover is recommended.

There are no botanical varieties of *Stokesia laevis* recognized among the natural populations, but in cultivation numerous color variants have been selected. They range from creamy white 'Silver Moon' and creamy yellow 'Mary Gregory' to lavender blue 'Blue Danube' and purple-blue 'Purple Parasols'. Whereas most of the cultivars grow between 35 and 60 cm high, some, such as 'Omega Skyrocket', may reach more than 1 m in height.

In the wild, *Stokesia laevis* blooms from June to September. The lower-growing forms tend to bloom early, from June to August, whereas the taller ones flower later, often starting in September. Cultivated in Germany and the United Kingdom, *S. laevis* flowers from June to September. Plants grown in Poznań began blooming between 28 June and 13 July and ended between 8 and 19 September. In St. Louis, flowering started earlier, between late May and early June and continued until mid or late July. At Longwood, four cultivars of *S. laevis* were observed, 'Blue Danube', 'Mary Gregory', 'Purple Parasols', and 'Silver Moon'. All four usually began to bloom in mid to late June, rarely as early as the second week of June. They differed, however, in their average bloom duration, which reflected to some degree their ability to rebloom after being cut back in July. 'Blue Danube', which

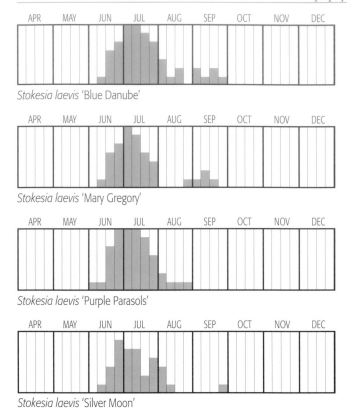

Stokesia laevis 'Blue Danube'

Stokesia laevis 'Mary Gregory'

Stokesia laevis 'Purple Parasols'

Stokesia laevis 'Silver Moon'

rebloomed in 4 of 7 years, averaged the longest in this group with a bloom time of 7 weeks, whereas 'Silver Moon' rebloomed only once and averaged less than 5 weeks in bloom. 'Mary Gregory' and 'Purple Parasols' were in flower for about 5 and 6 weeks, respectively.

Symphyotrichum

ASTER

The name *Symphyotrichum* is derived from the Greek *symphysis*, junction, and *trichos*, hair, in reference to the basal connation of bristles.

Symphyotrichum dumosum

BUSHY ASTER, CUSHION ASTER, LONG-STALKED ASTER, RICE-BUTTON ASTER

This perennial is native to eastern North America, from New Brunswick and Ontario, south to Georgia, and west to Texas. *Symphyotrichum dumosum* grows usually in wet meadows, bogs, marshes, swamps, moist woods, old fields, and on shores of lakes and ponds, up to 700 m in elevation. It has been cultivated since the early 18th century, and is naturalized in parts of Europe. This and other species of *Symphyotrichum* were previously classified as belonging to the genus *Aster*.

Symphyotrichum dumosum makes dense mounds of erect, slender stems to 40 cm tall, growing out of a creeping rhizome or sometimes a stout caudex. The basal, oblanceolate to spathulate, petiolate leaves reach 5 cm in length. The cauline, linear to oblanceolate leaves have very short petioles and reach 12 cm in length, but they become progressively shorter and sessile toward the end of the stems. The basal and the lower cauline leaves usually wither by the time of flowering. Flower heads, comprised of 15 to 33 pale lilac to white ray florets and 15 to 30 yellow to cream-colored disc florets, are arranged in open, diffuse, panicle-like arrays terminating ascending branches. Fruits are pink or gray, 2-mm-long achenes topped with a whitish pappus.

In the garden, *Symphyotrichum dumosum* can quickly fill in large areas under favorable conditions. Use it in perennial borders or allow it to spread freely in a wildflower garden. Plant it in full sun or, in areas with hot summers, in partial shade. It thrives in any average garden soil, but avoid planting in poor, gravelly, or dry soil. Provide additional water during dry spells. Divide and replant *S. dumosum*, while adding organic matter and fertilizer to enrich the soil, every 3 or 4 years. Plants are hardy to zone 4.

Symphyotrichum dumosum is a highly variable species, with five botanical varieties recognized currently in various parts of its geographic range: *dumosum*, *gracilipes*, *pergracile*, *strictior*, and *subulifolium*. In addition, it hybridizes in the wild with other *Symphyotrichum* species, including *S. lanceolatum* and *S. racemosum*. In cultivation, *S. dumosum* has been replaced mostly by its hybrids with *S. novi-belgii*, which have become known as Dumosum Hybrids, although they are often are listed under *S. novi-belgii*. These hybrids vary in height from 20-cm-tall 'Niobe' to 70-cm-tall 'Rosenfeld', and they offer a choice of single, semi-double, or double flowers. Their colors range from white 'Snowsprite' and rose pink 'Nesthäkchen' to blue 'Blaubux' and violet 'Audrey'.

In the wild, *Symphyotrichum dumosum* flowers between August and October. In cultivation in Germany, it blooms during the same months. In Moscow, flowering began, on average, around 13 September and ended around 12 October. At Longwood, the cultivar 'Nesthäkchen' began flowering in mid-September. Only once in 7 years, it flowered in the first week of September. It then bloomed, on average, for

Symphyotrichum dumosum 'Nesthäkchen'

Symphyotrichum laeve 'Bluebird'

a little over 4 weeks, until the end of September or early October. Similar bloom duration was reported from Moscow.

Symphyotrichum laeve

SMOOTH ASTER

This plant is native to North America, from Quebec to Manitoba, throughout the United States, and south to northern Mexico. *Symphyotrichum laeve* grows in dry, open deciduous forests and thickets, in tall grass prairies, montane meadows, rocky glades, clearings, and along roadsides, at elevations to 2400 m. *Symphyotrichum laeve* has been cultivated since the mid-18th century and has since naturalized in parts of Mexico, South America, and Europe.

Symphyotrichum laeve forms vigorous, strong clumps of erect, dark, glaucous stems to 1.2 m tall growing out of a short, thick woody caudex or a few long rhizomes. The basal, bluish green, thick, and smooth leaves, to 20 cm long, are broadly lanceolate to spatulate and petiolate. The ovate to linear, cauline leaves grow to 15 cm long, but are much reduced toward the ends of the stems, and are sessile or have short petioles. The basal and lower cauline leaves usually wither by the time of flowering. The 2.5-cm-wide flower heads are comprised of 13 to 23 blue or violet purple, seldom white, ray florets and 19 to 33 yellow, turning purplish red, disc florets. They are borne in broad, loose, freely branching, sometimes flat-topped panicle-like arrays. Fruits are deep purple to brown achenes, to 3.5 mm long, topped with a tawny or reddish pappus.

In the garden, *Symphyotrichum laeve* is valued as an easy-to-grow late bloomer that is not affected by maladies ravaging other garden asters. It is at home in a traditional perennial border, informal cottage-style garden, or in a naturalized wildflower area. Plant it in full sun, in any average, moderately moist, and well-drained soil. It is able to tolerate dry sites. *Symphyotrichum laeve* self-seeds easily, so if this is not desired, remove spent flower heads promptly. Plants are hardy to zones 3 or 4.

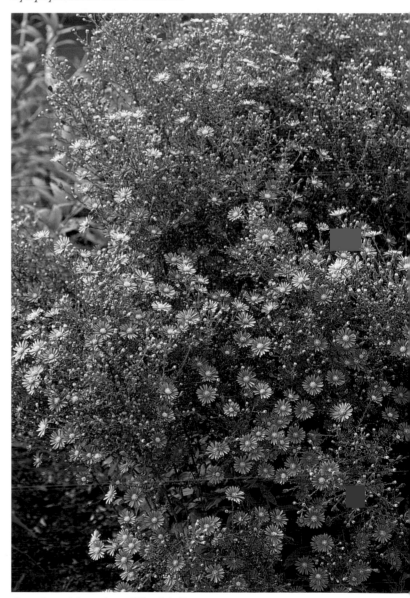

Symphyotrichum laeve 'Bluebird'

Symphyotrichum laeve is highly variable in the wild. Currently, four varieties are recognized in North America. Variety *laeve*, found in the eastern half of the range, has broader leaves conspicuously clasping the stems and strongly unequal involucral bracts. Similar to it is variety *geyeri*, native in the western half of the range; it differs in its involucral bracts being not as strongly unequal. Variety *concinnum*, found east of the Mississippi River, has narrower leaves only slightly clasping the stems. Native to the southeastern United States, variety *purpuratum* is unique in that its mostly linear leaves are persistent and do not wither by the time of flowering. The white-flowered form found occasionally in the wild was named *beckwithiae*, but it is no longer recognized. *Symphyotrichum laeve* hybridizes easily with several species of *Symphyotrichum*, including *S. novi-belgii* and *S. dumosum*. Garden selections offer several variations of the flower color, including rose-lilac 'Arcturus', lilac purple 'Calliope', and violet blue 'Bluebird'.

In the wild, *Symphyotrichum laeve* flowers from July to October, depending on the region. Cultivated in Germany, it blooms in September and October. In St. Louis, the cultivar 'Bluebird' flowered for 2 weeks in the first half of October. At Longwood, 'Bluebird' began flowering between the first and the last week of September and continued, on average, for 5 weeks into the middle or late October. Once in 7 years, it was still in bloom during the first week of November.

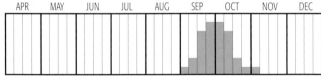

APR	MAY	JUN	JUL	AUG	SEP	OCT	NOV	DEC

Symphyotrichum laeve 'Bluebird'

Symphyotrichum lateriflorum

CALICO ASTER, ONE-SIDED ASTER, STARVED ASTER, WHITE WOODLAND ASTER

This plant is native to North America, from Quebec to Manitoba, south to Florida, and west to Texas. *Symphyotrichum lateriflorum* grows in deciduous and coniferous forests, along the edges of woodlands, in meadows, swamps, on stream banks and roadsides, usually in shaded locations, at elevations to 400 m. It has been cultivated since the early 19th century.

Symphyotrichum lateriflorum develops clumps or thickets of slender, ascending to erect, densely branched stems to 1.2 m tall, growing out of short rhizomes or a woody, branched caudex. The basal oblanceolate to spatulate and petiolate leaves reach 3.5 cm in length. The cauline, ovate to lanceolate leaves are sessile or on short petioles and reach 15 cm in length, but they become greatly reduced in size toward the tips of the stems. In the spring the leaves have a purplish tinge, which is retained on plants growing in full sun but fades to green in the shade. The basal and the lower cauline leaves wither by the time of flowering, whereas the upper cauline leaves turn a reddish color in the fall. The 1.5-cm-wide flower heads, comprised of eight to 15 white to pale purple ray florets and a similar number of yellow ray florets, are borne in clusters in leaf axils of the secondary, often horizontal, branches. Disc florets quickly change from yellow to pink or purple, creating the calico effect. Fruits are gray or tan, 2-mm-long achenes topped with a white to pink pappus.

In the garden, *Symphyotrichum lateriflorum* can be grown in extensive mass plantings in naturalized settings or as smaller groups in more traditional borders. Its attractive, dark, and fine-textured foliage allows it be used to create herbaceous, seasonal hedging. Plant it preferably in full sun, where the purple or bronze coloration of leaves and stems will be stronger and the flowering more profuse, but plants will tolerate dappled shade conditions. It thrives in any average garden soil as long as it is consistently moist and well drained. It requires only minimum care and rarely needs to be divided. Stems can be trimmed lightly in late summer, if lower-growing plants are favored. Plants are hardy to zone 5, possibly zone 3.

Much variation is encountered within the wild populations of *Symphyotrichum lateriflorum*, which led to a number of botanical varieties being recognized, including *lateriflorum* and *hirsuticaule* found throughout the distribution range, *angustifolium* and *tenuipes* in the northern end of the range, *horizontale* east of the Mississippi River, *flagellare* in Texas and Oklahoma, and *spatelliforme* in Florida. This wealth of natural diversity has resulted so far in only a small number of garden selections, with some cultivars, such as 'Coombe Fishacre', suspected of being hybrids with *S. novi-belgii*. Breeders have focused on

Symphyotrichum lateriflorum 'Lady in Black'

APR	MAY	JUN	JUL	AUG	SEP	OCT	NOV	DEC

Symphyotrichum lateriflorum 'Coombe Fishacre'

APR	MAY	JUN	JUL	AUG	SEP	OCT	NOV	DEC

Symphyotrichum lateriflorum 'Lady in Black'

APR	MAY	JUN	JUL	AUG	SEP	OCT	NOV	DEC

Symphyotrichum lateriflorum 'Prince'

Symphyotrichum lateriflorum 'Coombe Fishacre'

finding variants with better pink flower color, such as 'Coombe Fishacre'; stronger purple-colored foliage that does not fade to green, such as 'Lady in Black'; and those that grow lower, including 'Horizontalis' and 'Prince'.

In the wild, *Symphyotrichum lateriflorum* flowers between August and October. Similarly, when cultivated in Germany, it blooms from September until October. At Longwood, three selections of *S. lateriflorum* were observed: 'Coombe Fishacre', 'Lady in Black', and 'Prince'. Of these, 'Coombe Fishacre' was the earliest to flower, in some years as early as the third week of July, whereas the earliest bloom of 'Lady in Black' and 'Prince' was recorded in the last week of August and the second week of September, respectively. 'Coombe Fishacre' was also the longest flowering of this group, with over 9 weeks in bloom, compared to 5 weeks of the other two cultivars. When not cut back after the main flush of flowers, 'Coombe Fishacre' continued blooming, although weakly, until the first frost in late November, whereas the 'Lady in Black' and 'Prince', when left without cutting back, stopped blooming in late October or the first week of November, respectively.

Symphyotrichum novae-angliae

MICHAELMAS DAISY, NEW ENGLAND ASTER

This perennial is native to North America, from Quebec to Alberta, south to Alabama, and west to New Mexico. *Symphyotrichum novae-angliae* grows in sandy or loamy, rich, moist to wet soils, in meadows

Symphyotrichum novae-angliae 'Andenken an Alma Pötschke'

Symphyotrichum novae-angliae 'Purple Dome'

and prairies, shrubby swamps, thickets, edges of woods, and on roadsides, at elevations up to 1600 m. It has been cultivated since the early 18th century and has since naturalized in parts of Europe and North America.

Symphyotrichum novae-angliae forms robust clumps of few erect, stout, stiff stems that are densely leafed to the top and reach 1.8 m in height, growing out of a thick, woody, branched caudex or short and fleshy rhizomes. The entire, sessile, pubescent leaves reach 10 cm in length. The basal leaves are usually spatulate, whereas the cauline ones are oblong to lanceolate, clasping the stems, and become gradually reduced toward the ends of the stems. The lowermost leaves wither by the time of flowering. Flower heads, up to 6 cm wide, are comprised of 50 to 75 pink, carmine, violet, or blue ray florets and 50 to 110 yellow, changing to purple, disc florets. They are arranged in loose, leafy, corymb-like or panicle-like arrays. Fruits are dull purple or brown achenes to 3 mm long, topped by a tawny pappus.

In the garden, *Symphyotrichum novae-angliae* is valued as a long-lived, tough fall bloomer that has an imposing presence in either the perennial border or wildflower garden. Because its lower leaves often die off before flowering, in order to hide the bare lower portions of the stems plant *S. novae-angliae* in large groups or among other tall perennials. Choose for it a sunny location. Although it can tolerate partial shade, flower heads often close under low light conditions. *Symphyotrichum novae-angliae* grows best in humus-rich and moisture-retentive soil. When grown in consistently moist and fertile soil, it keeps its lower leaves longer. Divide the plants every 2 to 5 years to maintain their vigor. Taller varieties may require support in more formal settings, as their stems tend to flop under the weight of the flowers. Alternatively, pinching stems in early summer will result in a more compact habit. Flowers of *S. novae-angliae* are excellent for cutting. Remove spent flower heads if self-seeding becomes a nuisance. Plants are hardy to zones 3 or 4.

Within natural populations of *Symphyotrichum novae-angliae*, variants with different flower colors have been described as botanical forms, but these are no longer recognized as valid. Among cultivated plants, nearly 100 cultivars have been selected since its introduction 300 years ago, about half of which are still grown today. Garden selections offer sturdier plants, sometimes with semi-double flowers, in a range of brighter flower colors. Among them, violet purple or bluish purple, such as 'Purple Dome', dominate, but other cultivars offer colors ranging from white of 'Herbstschnee' and pink of 'Harrington's Pink' to rose of 'Andenken an Alma Pötschke' and ruby red of 'Septemberrubin'.

In the wild, *Symphyotrichum novae-angliae* flowers between August and October, rarely November, depending on the region. Cultivated in Germany and the United Kingdom, it blooms in September and October. Similarly, in Moscow the bloom started, on average, around 20 September and ended around 13 October. In contrast, in Poznań *S. novae-angliae* began flowering 2 months earlier, between 15 and 22 July and ended between 7 and 24 September. Even earlier bloom time was recorded in Georgia, in the United States, where cultivar 'Septemberrubin' started flowering in late May and continued through late June. In St. Louis, the cultivar 'Andenken an Alma Pötschke' flowered from early July to early or mid-October. Another cultivar, 'Purple Dome', began flowering in St. Louis several weeks after 'Andenken an Alma Pötschke', in late August. At Longwood, however, 'Andenken an Alma Pötschke', 'Purple Dome', and 'Septemberrubin' all flowered at about the same time. They usually bloomed between early to mid-September and mid-October. Only rarely did these cultivars flower in late July or early August. All three cultivars bloomed at Longwood for about 6 weeks.

Symphyotrichum novi-belgii
MICHAELMAS DAISY, NEW YORK ASTER

This plant is native to eastern North America, from Newfoundland to Quebec and south to Georgia. *Symphyotrichum novi-belgii* grows primarily in the coastal areas at elevations to 800 m, in open, moist sites, meadows, edges of thickets, along watercourses, in salt marshes, savannas, pine barrens, on sandy or stony seashores, and edges of sea cliffs. It has been cultivated since the end of the 17th century and has naturalized in parts of Australia, Europe, and Mexico.

Symphyotrichum novi-belgii forms loose to dense colonies or sometimes clumps of erect, stout to slender, often reddish stems to 1.5 m tall, growing out of creeping, long rhizomes. The nearly glabrous, entire, ovate to lanceolate leaves are sessile or petiolate and clasping the stems. The basal leaves reach 6 cm in length, whereas the lower cauline leaves can be up to 20 cm long, but they become progressively reduced toward the end of the stems. The lowermost leaves wither by the time of flowering. The 5-cm-

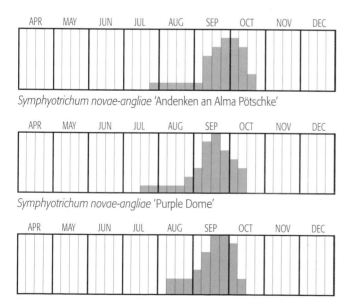

APR	MAY	JUN	JUL	AUG	SEP	OCT	NOV	DEC

Symphyotrichum novae-angliae 'Andenken an Alma Pötschke'

APR	MAY	JUN	JUL	AUG	SEP	OCT	NOV	DEC

Symphyotrichum novae-angliae 'Purple Dome'

APR	MAY	JUN	JUL	AUG	SEP	OCT	NOV	DEC

Symphyotrichum novae-angliae 'Septemberrubin'

Symphyotrichum novi-belgii 'White Climax'

Symphyotrichum novi-belgii 'Porzellan'

Symphyotrichum novi-belgii 'Porzellan'

wide flower heads are comprised of 15 to 35 purple or blue (rarely pink or white) ray florets and nearly twice as many yellow, turning brown to purple, disc florets. They are arranged in open to dense panicle-like arrays on ascending, leafy branches. Fruits are tan to brown achenes to 4 mm long, topped by a yellowish white pappus.

In the garden, *Symphyotrichum novi-belgii* is considered as perhaps the showiest of all fall-flowering perennials. Although most spectacular when used in masses or large groupings in wildflower meadows or similar naturalized areas, lower-growing selections make this species suitable even in more intimate settings of a small-scale perennial border. Plant it in an open position in full sun, in fertile, humus-rich, consistently moist soil. Water during dry spells, which impact flowering and lead to rapid decline. *Symphyotrichum novi-belgii* grows and spreads fast, and it can quickly exhaust the soil. Transplant and divide it every 3 to 5 years, or even more often if plants decline or die off in the center. In deep and rich soils such frequent transplanting may not be necessary. Taller varieties will usually require staking. As an alternative, stems can be trimmed once or pinched repeatedly before mid-July, resulting in more branched and shorter plants that will not need to be staked. Cut back or deadhead after flowering if self-seeding becomes a problem. Plants are hardy to zone 4.

Symphyotrichum novi-belgii is a variable species, and currently four botanical varieties in North America are recognized. The typical variety *novi-belgii* is found in the northern part of the range, south to West Virginia. Variety *villicaule* from Quebec, New Brunswick, and Maine differs in having densely pubescent stems. Variety *crenifolium* from Quebec and New Brunswick has broader and strongly clasping leaves. Reaching the furthest south, to the Carolinas, is variety *elodes*, which is unique in its especially narrow leaves. Several color variants, such as *albiflorus* or *roseus*, were found and described in the natural populations but are no longer recognized as valid. In the wild, *S. novi-belgii* hybridizes easily with a number of *Symphyotrichum* species, including *S. anticostense*, *S. ciliolatum*, *S. lanceolatum*, and *S. lateriflorum*. In cultivation, additional crosses have been made with species such as *S. dumosum*, *S. ericoides*, *S. laeve*, and others. The intense breeding has led to an astonishing number of about 1000 named cultivars, a third of which are still cultivated. Their height ranges from 60 cm, such as 'Professor Anton Kippenburg', to 1.2 m, such as 'Blaue Nachhut', whereas their flower heads vary in size from 2.5 to 5 cm and come with single or multiple rows of ray florets. The flowers come in a wide range of colors, including white 'White Climax', carmine red 'Patricia Ballard', chalky blue 'Porzellan', dark blue 'Sailor Boy', and purple violet 'Fuldatal'.

In the wild, *Symphyotrichum novi-belgii* flowers in August and September. Cultivated in Germany and the United Kingdom, plants bloom in September and October. In Poznań, flowering started between 24 and 29 August and ended between 8 and 17 October. Similarly, in Moscow *S. novi-belgii* flowered, on average, from around 26 August to 4 October. At Longwood, the cultivars 'Porzellan' and 'Professor Anton Kippenberg' bloomed from early September until late October or early November, whereas flowering of 'White Climax' began 2 or 3 weeks earlier, in mid to late August. 'White Climax' was also the longest blooming of the three cultivars observed at Longwood. On average, it flowered

for over 6 weeks, whereas 'Porzellan' and 'Professor Anton Kippenberg' were in flower for around 5 and 4 weeks, respectively. In comparison, plants grown in Moscow bloomed, on average, for just under 6 weeks. Cutting back or pinching for height control delays flowering. At Longwood, plants of 'White Climax' that were cut back in mid-August did not flower until mid-October, a nearly 2-month delay. They then continued flowering until the first hard frost at the end of November.

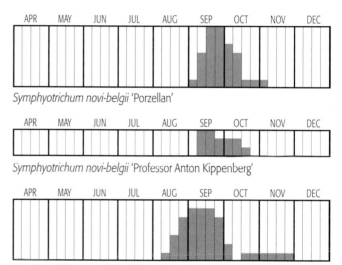

Symphyotrichum novi-belgii 'Porzellan'

Symphyotrichum novi-belgii 'Professor Anton Kippenberg'

Symphyotrichum novi-belgii 'White Climax'

Symphytum
COMFREY

The name *Symphytum* is derived from the Greek *syn*, together, and *phyton*, plant, in reference to the healing properties of these plants.

Symphytum officinale
BONESET, COMMON COMFREY, KNITBONE

This perennial is native to Europe and western Asia, from Portugal east to western Siberia. It has also naturalized in parts of North America. *Symphytum officinale* often grows on moist soils, along streams and rivers, and in damp meadows. It has been cultivated since antiquity.

Symphytum officinale forms coarse upright clumps of mostly basal foliage and erect, heavily branched, roughly hairy, winged stems to 1.2 m tall, growing from thick fleshy roots. The lower leaves are ovate-lanceolate, petiolate, and reach 25 cm in length. The upper leaves are smaller, oblong-lanceolate, and sessile. The 2-cm-long, tubular, nodding flowers range from violet to pink to white. They are borne in

Symphytum officinale

many-flowered scorpioid cymes. Fruits are 6-mm-long black nutlets.

Traditionally, *Symphytum officinale* was planted in herb gardens, but with newer selections featuring decorative foliage, it is now used in perennial borders, as a ground cover, or on banks of streams and ponds. Because it spreads rapidly, give it sufficient space to develop large colonies in a woodland or meadow. Do not combine it with less vigorous plants in a border, unless it can be carefully monitored and kept in check. Preferably, plant it in partial shade, although it tolerates full sun conditions provided that soil remains consistently moist. *Symphytum officinale* thrives in deep, fertile, humus-rich, and moist soil, but it can adapt to a wide variety of situations, including heavy clay soils and dry conditions. Cut back stems after flowering to encourage a possible rebloom. *Symphytum officinale* is long-lived and only infrequently needs dividing. It can grow back from sections of the roots. Plants are hardy to zones 4 or 5.

Symphytum officinale is a variable species, and several botanical varieties have been described in the past, including such color variants as *ochroleucum*, with creamy yellow flowers, or *purpureum*, with carmine flowers. These are not considered valid any more, and currently there are only two subspecies recognized in Europe. The typical subspecies *officinale*, found throughout the distribution range, is densely hairy, whereas subspecies *uliginosum*, restricted to east-central Europe, is only sparsely hairy. In cultivation, *S. officinale* has been hybridized with other comfreys, including *S. asperum* and *S. grandiflorum*, which led to the selection of several cultivars, such as 'Rubrum', with deep crimson red flowers, or 'Langthorns Pink', with pink flowers. Furthermore, variegated forms, including silver-edged 'Argenteum' or golden-leaved 'Belsay Gold', are available.

In the wild, *Symphytum officinale* blooms from May until July. Cultivated in Germany and the United Kingdom, it flowers at about the same time. Plants grown in Poznań began flowering between 28 May and 1 June and ended between 10 and 12 July. In St. Louis, *S. officinale* bloomed later, in mid-July. At Longwood, the hybrid cultivar 'Rubrum' usually started to flower in the second week of May, rarely in late May. The first flush of bloom lasted until early or late June, but plants continued to flower intermit-

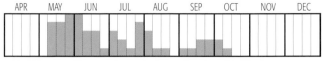

| APR | MAY | JUN | JUL | AUG | SEP | OCT | NOV | DEC |

Symphytum 'Rubrum'

tently until early August, and, in some years, even until early October. On average, 'Rubrum' was in bloom for a little more than 11 weeks.

Syneilesis

UMBRELLA–PLANT

The name *Syneilesis* is from the Greek *syneilesis*, rolling up.

Syneilesis aconitifolia

SHREDDED UMBRELLA–PLANT

This perennial is native to eastern Asia, from northern China east to Korea and Japan, where it grows in low-elevation woodlands.

Syneilesis aconitifolia forms open lax clumps of large finely cut leaves and erect, brownish, glabrous flowering stems to 1.2 m tall, growing from short creeping rhizomes. The lower leaves are peltate, pal-

Syneilesis aconitifolia

Syneilesis aconitifolia

mately parted into seven or nine bifid segments. They grow to 25 cm wide and are held on long petioles. The upper leaves are smaller, less divided, and not peltate. Young leaves are covered with silky or cobweb-like hairs. The 6-mm-wide flower heads, comprised of eight to 10 reddish florets, are arranged in dense, flat-topped, compound corymbs. Fruits are 5-mm-long achenes topped with a long pappus.

In the garden, *Syneilesis aconitifolia* is valued primarily for its unique leaves, which emerge in the spring, folded and cobwebby, resembling little umbrellas or mushrooms. Although this charm is brief, even fully expanded leaves can grace darker corners of a perennial border or woodland. Flowers are modest in their appearance but, nevertheless, enhance the overall fine-textured effect of the

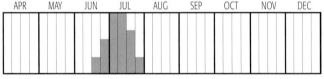

Syneilesis aconitifolia

plant. Site *S. aconitifolia* in a partially shaded spot, in moist yet well-drained soil. Once established, plants will tolerate periodic drought. *Syneilesis aconitifolia* spreads slowly and rarely requires dividing. Plants are hardy to zone 5.

In its native habitat in Japan, *Syneilesis aconitifolia* blooms in August. Plants cultivated at Longwood began flowering several weeks earlier, in late June or the first week of July. Bloom continued through mid-July, sometimes until late July. On average, *S. aconitifolia* was in flower for nearly 4 weeks.

Tanacetum parthenium

Tanacetum

TANSY

The name *Tanacetum* is thought to be derived from the Greek *athanasia*, immortality, in reference to the medicinal properties of some species.

Tanacetum parthenium

FEVERFEW, MATRICARIA

This plant is native to the Balkans, from Albania, north to Serbia, east to Bulgaria, and south to Greece, but has been naturalized widely beyond this area, in Europe, Asia, and the Americas. It grows in open rocky places, mountain scrub, hedges, and along roadsides. *Tanacetum parthenium* has been cultivated for medicinal use since antiquity and as an ornamental plant since the early 17th century, when a double-flowered form was discovered.

Tanacetum parthenium forms bushy rounded clumps of erect branched stems to 1 m tall, growing from a woody base. The strongly aromatic, oblong to ovate leaves, to 10 cm long, are pinnately divided into three to five pairs of ovate segments, which are further divided, crenate, or entire. The 2.5-cm-wide flower heads are comprised of 10 to 20 white ray florets and many yellow disc florets. The flower heads are arranged in dense corymb-like arrays. Fruits are 2-mm-long achenes.

In the garden, *Tanacetum parthenium* is valued for its ferny foliage and prolific blooms, which make for excellent cut flowers, fresh or dry. Use it for edging beds, in a perennial border, informal cottage-style plantings, or a naturalized wildflower meadow. Plant it in full sun, in any average garden soil that is moist yet well drained. When grown in rich fertile

Tanacetum parthenium

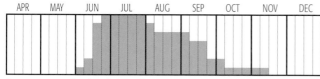

Tanacetum parthenium 'Aureum'

but in colder climates it benefits from a light winter cover.

There are no botanical varieties of *Tanacetum parthenium* recognized among the wild populations. In cultivation, a number of variants have been selected. The flower color varies little, from white of 'White Bonnet' to creamy yellow of 'Golden Ball'. Some, like 'Roya', have single flowers, but most, including 'Plenum', 'Rowallane', and 'Snowball', feature double flowers. In addition, a golden-leaved variety, 'Aureum', is grown widely.

Tanacetum parthenium blooms in mid to late summer. Cultivated in Moscow, it flowered from 22 June to 6 August. In Chicago and St. Louis, *T. parthenium* bloomed in July and August. At Longwood, the cultivar 'Aureum' began flowering in mid to late June, although once in 7 years flowers opened as early as the first week of June. Bloom usually continued until late August or early September, occasionally through October and into early November. On average, 'Aureum' flowered for a little more than 13 weeks. In comparison, *T. parthenium* in Moscow averaged less than 7 weeks in bloom.

Thalictrum

MEADOW–RUE

The name *Thalictrum* is derived from *thaliktron*, a name applied by ancient Greeks to a plant with compound leaves of uncertain identity.

Thalictrum aquilegiifolium

COLUMBINE MEADOW–RUE

This perennial is native to Europe and temperate Asia, from Spain, north to Sweden, and east to Kamchatka, Sakhalin, and Japan. *Thalictrum aquilegiifolium* often grows in acidic soils, in moist meadows, and woodland margins, at elevations to 3000 m. It has been cultivated since the early 18th century.

Thalictrum aquilegiifolium forms upright, tight clumps of glaucous, lacy basal foliage and erect, hollow stems to 1.5 m tall, growing from a short rootstock. The glaucous green, two- or three-pinnately compound leaves have 3-cm-long, suborbicular to oblong, three- to five-lobed leaflets. The apetalous flowers have greenish or white petaloid sepals and long, conspicuous, pink to purple stamens. They are borne in lax, feathery, corymbose panicles, to 20 cm

soil, plants may become somewhat lanky and require support to prevent flopping. Alternatively, trim them in late spring to encourage a lower and bushier growth habit. *Tanacetum parthenium* self-seeds freely. If this is not desired, deadhead flowers promptly. *Tanacetum parthenium* is short-lived, sometimes even biennial, so divide clumps frequently or save a few seedlings as replacement plants. It is hardy to zone 5, in length. The flowers are dioecious, with those on male plants being showier. Fruits are inflated winged achenes hanging on long pedicels.

In the garden, *Thalictrum aquilegiifolium* is considered among the most decorative meadow-rues. Its airy, fine-textured foliage and delicate profuse flowers, followed by attractive fruits, provide a long season of interest. Use it in a perennial border or allow it to naturalize in a wildflower meadow, open woodland, or near a pond or lake. Plant *T. aquilegiifolium* in partial shade or full sun, provided the soil is consistently moist. Avoid planting it in deep shade, where plants are short-lived. Choose a site with slightly acidic, fertile, humus-rich, moist, and well-drained soil. Allow the fruits to mature and extend interest, although under dry conditions flowering stems may deteriorate rapidly and are best cut back to the basal foliage promptly after bloom. Divide clumps every 5 years or so to maintain their vigor. Plants are hardy to zone 5.

Across the enormous distribution range of *Thalictrum aquilegiifolium*, several regional varieties have been described. The typical variety *aquilegiifolium* occurs in Europe and southwestern Asia and has flowers arranged in dense panicles. Variety *intermedium*, endemic to Japan, differs in having loose panicles. Variety *sibiricum*, found in northeastern Asia, is distinguished by having fewer achenes developing in each flower than either of the other varieties. In cultivation, several flower color variants have been selected, including white 'Album' and 'White Cloud', light pink 'Roseum', purple 'Purpureum', and deep dark purple 'Thundercloud'. 'Dwarf Purple' is a low-growing cultivar, reaching only 75 cm in height.

In the wild, the bloom season of *Thalictrum aquilegiifolium* varies greatly between May and September, depending on the region. Cultivated in Moscow, it flowered from 10 June to 6 July. Plants grown in Poznań flowered a couple of weeks earlier, starting between 25 May and 2 June and ending between 13 and 23 June. In the United States, bloom begins in early May in Missouri and late April in Georgia. At Longwood, the cultivar 'Purpureum' started to flower in mid to late May and continued until early to mid-June, although once in 7 years plants were still in bloom in the last week of June. On average, 'Purpureum' flowered for a little more than 4 weeks. *Thalictrum aquilegiifolium* in Moscow also averaged about 4 weeks in bloom.

Thalictrum aquilegiifolium

Thalictrum aquilegiifolium 'Album'

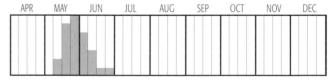

Thalictrum aquilegiifolium 'Purpureum'

Thalictrum dasycarpum

PURPLE MEADOW-RUE

This plant is native to North America from Quebec, west to Alaska, and south to Alabama and Arizona. *Thalictrum dasycarpum* grows in moist deciduous forests, damp thickets, wet meadows, and swamps, at elevations to 2500 m.

Thalictrum dasycarpum

Thalictrum dasycarpum forms upright, narrow clumps of fine-textured foliage and erect, stout, often purple stems to 2 m tall, growing from a thick short caudex. The leaves are three to five times ternately compound with ovate or obovate leaflets, to 6 cm long, and often lobed. The dioecious, apetalous flowers have four to six whitish sepals to 5 mm long and white to purplish stamens. They are arranged in many-flowered pyramidal corymbose panicles. Fruits are ovoid long-beaked achenes.

In the garden, *Thalictrum dasycarpum* is valued for its masses of delicate, creamy purplish flowers creating a subtle haze-like effect and for handsome lacy foliage. Together these provide an excellent background for more brightly colored perennials in a border or wildflower meadow. For planting in a border, choose male plants, which are showier and do not self-seed. *Thalictrum dasycarpum* thrives in partial shade or full sun, provided the site is adequately moist. Plant it in fertile, humus-rich, consistently moist but well-drained soil. Cut back stems after flowering if foliage turns yellow and declines. Plants are hardy to zone 3.

In the wild, *Thalictrum dasycarpum* blooms from April to July, depending on the region. Cultivated in St. Louis, it flowered for 2 weeks starting in the first week of April and again in late May. Plants grown at Longwood began flowering in late May or early June. Among the 7 years, the earliest bloom was observed in the third week of May. Flowering usually continued until late June, occasionally until the first week of July. On average, *T. dasycarpum* was in bloom for 4 weeks.

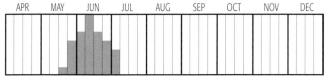

Thalictrum dasycarpum

Thalictrum rochebruneanum

LAVENDER MIST MEADOW-RUE

This perennial is native to Japan and South Korea. *Thalictrum rochebruneanum* grows in grassy highlands and in margins of deciduous forests, at elevations of 500 to 1500 m.

Thalictrum rochebruneanum forms upright slender clumps of stout, branched, glabrous, purplish stems to 4 m tall, growing from stoloniferous rhizomes. The glaucous leaves are three- to five-ternate with obovate to ovate, shallow-lobed leaflets to 3 cm long. The basal leaves usually wither at the time of flowering. The pendulous, apetalous, 12-mm-wide flowers have lavender sepals and long pale yellow stamens. They are held in open panicles to 15 cm in length. Fruits are 5-mm-long achenes.

In the garden, *Thalictrum rochebruneanum* is valued for its handsome foliage and graceful delicate flowers held at great heights, which makes it an excellent choice for the rear of a perennial border, a wildflower meadow, or the edge of a woodland. Plant it in large groups for best effect. Choose a

Thalictrum rochebruneanum

Thalictrum rochebruneanum

APR	MAY	JUN	JUL	AUG	SEP	OCT	NOV	DEC

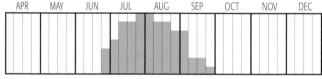

Thalictrum rochebruneanum

In its native habitat, *Thalictrum rochebruneanum* blooms in July and August. Cultivated in St. Louis, it started to flower in June and finished between the end of July and mid-September. Plants grown at Longwood began blooming a little later, usually in the last week of June or early July, but in one year flowering was delayed until the last week of July. *Thalictrum rochebruneanum* continued to bloom until late August or the first week of September, but occasionally flowers lasted until late September. On average, it was in bloom for a little more than 9 weeks.

Thalictrum speciosissimum
YELLOW MEADOW-RUE

This plant is native to Europe and northwestern Africa, from Portugal and Spain south to Algeria and Morocco. *Thalictrum speciosissimum* grows in meadows, grasslands, and on stream banks.

Thalictrum speciosissimum forms bold upright clumps of erect, robust, glaucous ridged and usually unbranched stems to 1.5 m tall, growing from creeping rhizomes. The strongly glaucous, two- or three-pinnately compound leaves have obovate to elliptic lobed leaflets to 7 cm long. The fragrant, apetalous flowers have four white or pale yellow, early-falling sepals and tufts of conspicuous bright yellow stamens. They are borne in upright compact pyramidal panicles to 25 cm long. Fruits are slightly compressed achenes.

In the garden, *Thalictrum speciosissimum* creates lush mounds of bluish lacy foliage topped by contrasting yellow fragrant flowers. It can be used in a variety of settings, from traditional perennial borders to informal cottage-style plantings, naturalistic meadows, and open woodlands. Plant it in partial shade, or full sun if soil is consistently moist. *Thalictrum speciosissimum* thrives in fertile, humus-rich, moist, and well-drained soils. It spreads slowly and only infrequently requires dividing. Plants are hardy to zone 5.

Thalictrum speciosissimum is sometimes considered to be a variant of a closely related European species, *T. flavum*, and is designated as its subspecies *glaucum* or, in cultivation, as the cultivar 'Glaucum'. One selection of *T. speciosissimum* that features chartreuse young foliage has been introduced under the name 'Illuminator'.

Thalictrum speciosissimum is a summer bloomer. Cultivated in Moscow, it flowered, on average, from 23 July to 26 August. Plants grown in Poznań started

partially shaded location, although *T. rochebruneanum* can adapt to full sun conditions provided it is grown in moisture-retentive soil. It thrives in cool, deep, humus-rich, and moist soils. Despite its impressive height, *T. rochebruneanum* usually does not require staking, except perhaps for shaded locations with fertile soil, which promote lanky growth. Plants are hardy to zone 6, possibly zone 4.

There are no botanical varieties of *Thalictrum rochebruneanum* recognized in the wild, but in cultivation one variant with violet sepals is known as 'Lavender Mist'.

Thalictrum speciosissimum

Thalictrum speciosissimum

to bloom several weeks earlier, between 22 June and 3 July and ended between 19 and 22 July. At Longwood, *T. speciosissimum* began flowering in the last week of May or the first week of June. Only once in 7 years, bloom was delayed until the second week of June. Flowering usually continued until late June, occasionally until the first week of July. On average, *T. speciosissimum* flowered for close to 4 weeks at Longwood. In comparison, plants in Moscow were in bloom for 5 weeks.

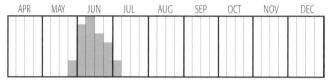

Thalictrum speciosissimum

Thermopsis

GOLDENBANNER

The name *Thermopsis* is derived from the Greek *thermos*, lupine, and *opsis*, appearance, in reference to the resemblance between these plants.

Thermopsis villosa

AARON'S-ROD, CAROLINA-LUPINE, SOUTHERN-LUPINE

This plant is native to the eastern United States, from West Virginia south to Georgia and Alabama. It is naturalized elsewhere in the region north to Maine. *Thermopsis villosa* grows in open places, dry woods, forest clearings, and ridges in low mountains.

Thermopsis villosa forms upright clumps of rigidly erect, sparsely branched, hollow, hairy stems to 1.6 m tall, growing from a taproot. The grayish green leaves are divided into three obovate or ovate leaflets to 10 cm long. The 12-mm-long yellow flowers are borne in dense, erect, terminal racemes to 30 cm in length. Fruits are densely villous, narrow pods to 5 cm long.

In the garden, *Thermopsis villosa* can be used in traditional perennial borders, where its narrow spike-like inflorescences provide a strong vertical element. It is also well suited for naturalizing in meadows, woodland edges, or parks. Its showy flowers are followed by attractive fruits, which extend the season of interest. Plant it in full sun or, in warmer climates, partial shade. Avoid deep shade, where plants flower less and develop weak, lanky growth prone to flopping. *Thermopsis villosa* thrives in light, deep,

Thermopsis villosa

fertile, and well-drained soils. It can adapt to a wide range of conditions, however, and once established it is fairly drought tolerant. Cut plants back in mid-summer when foliage begins to decline. *Thermopsis villosa* is slow to establish but long-lived and is best left undisturbed for years. Plants are hardy to zone 6, possibly zone 4.

In the wild, *Thermopsis villosa* blooms in May and June. Cultivated in Poznań, it began flowering between 25 and 27 June and ended between 15 and 19 July. Plants in St. Louis opened flowers several weeks earlier, in late May or the first week of June. At Longwood, *T. villosa* usually started to bloom in early June, although twice in 7 years it flowered in the last week of May. Bloom continued until late June, rarely to the first week of July. *Thermopsis villosa* averaged about 3 weeks in bloom at Longwood. Similar bloom duration was observed in Poznań and St. Louis.

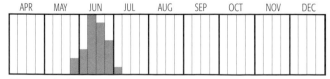

Thermopsis villosa

Tiarella

FOAMFLOWER

The name *Tiarella* is derived from the Latin *tiara*, turban, in reference to the shape of the fruit.

Tiarella cordifolia

ALLEGHENY FOAMFLOWER, FALSE MITREWORT

This perennial is native to eastern North America, from Nova Scotia, south to Georgia, and west to Minnesota and Mississippi. *Tiarella cordifolia* grows in moist, rich woods. It has been cultivated since the 18th century.

Tiarella cordifolia forms compact, dense clumps of basal foliage and slender, mostly leafless flowering stems to 30 cm tall, growing from stoloniferous rhizomes. The evergreen, broadly ovate, three- to seven-lobed leaves, to 10 cm wide, have cordate bases and serrate margins. The creamy white flowers, to 6 mm wide, have conspicuous, long, exerted stamens and are borne in dense racemes to 15 cm in length. Fruits are follicles to 1 cm long.

In the garden, *Tiarella cordifolia* is most effective when grown in large groups or as ground cover. Thanks to its stoloniferous nature, *T. cordifolia* spreads rapidly and forms large colonies. In areas with a mild

Tiarella cordifolia

Tiarella cordifolia

climate, foliage remains evergreen, taking on bronzy hues in winter. Plant it in a cool, shaded location, in a slightly acidic, humus-rich, moist, and well-drained soil. When properly sited, *T. cordifolia* does not need to be regularly divided, except to keep its spread in check. Plants are hardy to zone 3.

There are two principal variants of *Tiarella cordifolia* among the natural populations. The northern variety *cordifolia* is stoloniferous, whereas the southern variety *collina* does not produce stolons. The latter variety is sometimes considered as a separate species, *T. wherryi*. Both varieties and their selections are cultivated, as well as hybrids between them. Further-

more, *T. cordifolia* has been crossed with *T. trifoliata*, from the Pacific coast of North America, to develop an even wider range of cultivars. Nearly all breeding efforts have focused on selecting forms with decorative foliage, including 'Brandywine', 'Dark Eyes', 'Freckles', 'Marmorata', and 'Running Tapestry', which have leaves variously veined, blotched, spotted, or mottled with red, burgundy, or purple. In addition, some cultivars, such as 'Martha Oliver' and 'Oakleaf', feature deeply lobed leaves. Flower colors of garden selections vary from white in 'Moorgrün' and pink in 'Eco Red Heart' to pale lilac in 'Lilacina' and purple-red in 'Purpurea'.

In the wild, *Tiarella cordifolia* blooms from April to June. Cultivated in Germany, Poland, and the United Kingdom, it flowers at about the same time. Similarly, plants grown in Moscow bloomed, on average, from 14 May to 13 June. In St. Louis, flowering began between the last week of April and mid-May. At Longwood, *T. cordifolia* started to bloom in late April and continued until late May or the first week of June, although on one occasion plants were still in flower in the second week of June. On average, *T. cordifolia* bloomed for a little more than 6 weeks. In comparison, plants in Moscow were in flower for about 4 weeks.

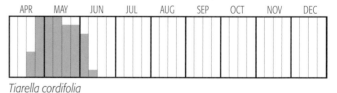

Tiarella cordifolia

Tradescantia

SPIDERWORT

The name *Tradescantia* commemorates John Tradescant (ca. 1570–1638) and his son John Tradescant (1608–1662), English gardeners and naturalists.

Tradescantia ×*andersoniana*

GARDEN SPIDERWORT, WIDOW'S-TEARS

The name *Tradescantia* ×*andersoniana* was coined in 1935 to describe a plethora of variable hybrids in cultivation and thought to be derived from several *Tradescantia* species found in eastern North America, including *T. ohiensis*, *T. subaspera*, and *T. virginiana*, and perhaps others. These hybrids are also known as the Andersoniana Group.

Tradescantia ×*andersoniana* forms dense tufted clumps of erect, fleshy, branched stems to 70 cm tall, growing from branched rhizomes. The linear to lanceolate leaves, clasping the stems, reach 45 cm in length. The 3- to 4-cm-wide, three-petalled flowers range from white and pink to purple and blue. They are borne in terminal umbels, subtended by linear-lanceolate leaf-like bracts.

In the garden, *Tradescantia* ×*andersoniana* makes an attractive and very distinct subject for a perennial border or woodland edge. It is valued for its handsome, spidery or grassy foliage and profuse and brightly colored flowers, which open over a long time. Plant it in full sun or, in warmer areas, in partial shade. Avoid heavily shaded sites, where plants are less floriferous. *Tradescantia* ×*andersoniana* thrives in slightly acidic, deep, humus-rich, and moist but well-drained soils, but it can also tolerate boggy conditions. Fertile soils may promote lanky growth with a tendency to flop. To avoid staking in such situations, trim plants in the middle of spring to encourage lower growth. Although individual flowers last only one day, they shed cleanly and do not require deadheading. After the first flush of bloom is finished, foliage often declines in midsummer. Cut plants back at that time to encourage growth of new foliage and a possible rebloom, but make sure plants are well watered. *Tradescantia* ×*andersoniana* is long-lived, and under favorable conditions it can spread to form large clumps. Divide it every 4 to 5 years, or more often if clumps become overcrowded. Plants are hardy to zone 5, possibly 3, but in colder climates they benefit from a light cover in winter.

There are dozens of cultivars of *Tradescantia* ×*andersoniana* from which to choose. Their spectrum of flower colors includes white 'Snowcap', pink 'Pauline', dark blue 'Zwanenburg Blue', carmine red 'Karminglut', and dark violet 'Leonora'. A number of cultivars feature decorative foliage, including golden yellow 'Blue and Gold', golden green 'Chedglow', and bluish green 'Concord Grape'. While tall selections, such as white-flowered 'Innocence', may exceed 60 cm in height, the low-growing ones, such as blue-flowered 'Little Doll', reach only 25 cm.

Tradescantia ×*andersoniana* blooms for several weeks in late spring and summer. Cultivated in Poland, it flowers from May to September. Plants grown in Moscow bloomed, on average, starting around

Tradescantia ×*andersoniana* 'Chedglow'

22 June and ending between 15 and 20 September. At Longwood, several cultivars were observed, including 'Chedglow', 'Concord Grape', 'Little Doll', and 'Snowcap'. The earliest to bloom was 'Concord Grape', which opened flowers between the third week of April and the third week of May. In comparison, the other three cultivars began blooming about 3 weeks later. There were significant differences between these varieties in their ability to rebloom, from 'Snowcap', which never rebloomed in 7 years, to 'Concord Grape', which rebloomed every year. As a result, 'Snowcap' averaged only 8 weeks in bloom, whereas 'Concord Grape' was in flower

Tradescantia ×*andersoniana* 'Chedglow'

Tradescantia ×*andersoniana* 'Snowcap'

Tradescantia ×*andersoniana* 'Concord Grape'

Tradescantia ×andersoniana 'Little Doll'

APR	MAY	JUN	JUL	AUG	SEP	OCT	NOV	DEC

Tradescantia ×andersoniana 'Chedglow'

APR	MAY	JUN	JUL	AUG	SEP	OCT	NOV	DEC

Tradescantia ×andersoniana 'Concord Grape'

APR	MAY	JUN	JUL	AUG	SEP	OCT	NOV	DEC

Tradescantia ×andersoniana 'Little Doll'

APR	MAY	JUN	JUL	AUG	SEP	OCT	NOV	DEC

Tradescantia ×andersoniana 'Snowcap'

for more than 20 weeks, on average. The remaining two cultivars, 'Chedglow' and 'Little Doll', averaged 11 and 15 weeks, respectively. In comparison, plants grown in Moscow bloomed for 13 weeks.

Tricyrtis

TOAD–LILY

The name *Tricyrtis* is derived from the Greek *treis*, three, and *kyrtos*, convex, in reference to the three outer tepals having sack-like nectaries at the base.

Tricyrtis hirta

HAIRY TOAD–LILY, JAPANESE TOAD–LILY

This perennial is native to Japan, where it grows on the islands of Honshu, Kyushu, and Shikoku on shaded rock cliffs and stream banks. *Tricyrtis hirta* has been cultivated in the West since the late 19th century.

Tricyrtis hirta forms compact clumps of arching or drooping, softly hairy, unbranched leafy stems to 1 m tall, growing from short rhizomes. The oblong to ovate, shortly pubescent leaves, to 15 cm long, clasp the stems. The 2.5-cm-wide campanulate flowers have six tepals, whitish to pale purple and spotted darker purple, the outer three with sack-like nectaries at the base. The tepals surround six large stamens and a pistil with branched stigma forming a conspicuous crown-like structure. The flowers are borne singly or two or three together in the upper leaf axils or in terminal cymes. The fruits are narrow capsules.

In the garden, *Tricyrtis hirta* is valued for its intriguing late-blooming flowers and elegant arching stems densely clad in leaves. It is well suited for shaded borders, along paths, on top of stone walls, and for naturalistic woodland gardens. Plant it where it can be observed in close proximity, revealing the unusual design of the floral structures. Choose a sheltered and partially shaded location. *Tricyrtis hirta* thrives in cool, slightly acidic, fertile, humus-rich, and consistently moist soil. Its stems arch naturally and may fall over after heavy rain. Because staking would be rather awkward in this situation, planting *T. hirta* in a raised position on a slope or atop of a wall will allow the stems to topple down gracefully. *Tricyrtis hirta* is long-lived, rarely needs dividing, and may self-seed under favorable conditions, but not to the point of becoming a nuisance. Plants are hardy to zones 4 or 5, but in colder areas they benefit from a light cover of dry mulch in winter.

A few botanical varieties of *Tricyrtis hirta* have been described in the wild, including variety *masamunei*, with glabrous leaves, and variety *albescens*, with white flowers. In cultivation, *T. hirta* frequently crosses with *T. formosana* from Taiwan, and many cultivars are suspected of being the result of this hybridization. Selections vary in the color of the tepals, as well as the color of the markings, which may take the form of spots or blotches or even coalesce into larger areas. Among popular varieties are 'White Towers', with pure white tepals, 'Lilac Towers', with white tepals and lilac spots, 'Sinonome', with creamy

Tricyrtis hirta 'Miyazaki'

Tricyrtis 'Sinonome'

Tricyrtis 'Sinonome'

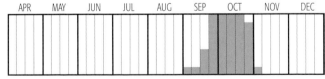

APR	MAY	JUN	JUL	AUG	SEP	OCT	NOV	DEC

Tricyrtis hirta 'Miyazaki'

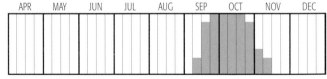

APR	MAY	JUN	JUL	AUG	SEP	OCT	NOV	DEC

Tricyrtis 'Sinonome'

white tepals and burgundy-purple spotting and blotching, and 'Miyazaki', with pink to white tepals and crimson spots. Furthermore, cultivars with decorative foliage have been selected and include 'Variegata', with white-edged leaves, 'Golden Gleam', which has yellow-green new leaves, and 'Miyazaki Gold', featuring yellow-edged leaves.

In its native habit in Japan, *Tricyrtis hirta* blooms from August to October. Cultivated in Germany and the United Kingdom, it flowers at about the same time. Plants grown in St. Louis bloomed from September until mid or late October. At Longwood two cultivars were observed, 'Miyazaki' and 'Sinonome'. They both flowered at about the same time, usually starting in late September and continuing through the end of October, occasionally into early November. Both 'Miyazaki' and 'Sinonome' averaged close to 7 weeks in bloom.

Uvularia grandiflora

Uvularia grandiflora

Uvularia

BELLWORT, MERRY-BELLS, WILD-OATS

The name *Uvularia* is derived from the Latin *uvula*, the pendant lobe in the posterior of the soft palate, in reference to the way flowers hang on the stem.

Uvularia grandiflora

BIG MERRYBELLS, LARGE-FLOWERED BELLWORT

This plant is native to eastern and central North America, from Quebec, south to Georgia, and west to Manitoba and Oklahoma. *Uvularia grandiflora* grows in rich, moist, deciduous forests, at elevations to 1100 m. It has been cultivated since the early 19th century.

Uvularia grandiflora forms clumps of several erect, arching stems, simple or sometimes sparsely branched, to 50 cm tall at flowering and to 1 m tall at maturity, growing from short, slender rhizomes with fleshy roots. The oblong to lanceolate leaves, to 13 cm long, are perfoliate and usually finely pubescent beneath. The campanulate, nodding, pale yellow flowers, to 5 cm long, have six slender, slightly

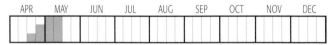

APR	MAY	JUN	JUL	AUG	SEP	OCT	NOV	DEC

Uvularia grandiflora

twisted tepals. They are borne singly or two to four together on a stem. Fruits are three-sided capsules.

In the garden, *Uvularia grandiflora* is best suited for naturalizing under a canopy of tall shade trees, but it can also be grown in a more formal setting of perennial borders. Plant it in partial to full shade, in light, humus-rich, moist, and well-drained soil. Plants are hardy to zones 3 or 4.

There are no botanical varieties of *Uvularia grandiflora* currently recognized among the natural populations. Previously described variety *pallida*, with pale yellow flowers, is best treated as a cultivar. Only a couple of clonal selections have been introduced so far, including pale yellow 'Sunbonnet' and medium yellow 'Susie Lewis'.

In the wild, *Uvularia grandiflora* blooms in April and May. Cultivated in Poland and the United

Kingdom, it flowers at about the same time. Similarly, plants grown in St. Louis bloomed in April and May. At Longwood, *U. grandiflora* began flowering between the third week of April and the first week of May and continued until the second week of May. On average, *U. grandiflora* was in bloom for 3 weeks.

Valeriana

VALERIAN

The name *Valeriana* is of medieval origin and is thought to be derived from Valeria, a classical name for one of the provinces of Pannonia.

Valeriana officinalis

CAT'S VALERIAN, COMMON VALERIAN,

GARDEN-HELIOTROPE, VERVAIN

This perennial is native to Europe and western Asia, from Portugal, north to Norway, and east to Russia, Turkey, and Iran. *Valeriana officinalis* often grows in calcareous soils in moist meadows, scrub, and woods. It has been cultivated since at least the Middle Ages.

    Valeriana officinalis forms robust clumps of basal foliage and erect, stout, fleshy, pubescent or glabrous, branching stems, to 2 m tall, growing from a thick, short rhizome, sometimes stoloniferous. The aro-

Valeriana officinalis

Valeriana officinalis

matic, pinnate or pinnatisect leaves, to 20 cm long, have up to 12 pairs of serrate, ovate to lanceolate leaflets or segments. The scented, tubular, pinkish or lavender flowers, 5 mm long, are borne in dense rounded terminal panicles, initially to 10 cm wide but expanding in time. Fruits are compressed achenes to 5 mm long.

In the garden, *Valeriana officinalis* has long been grown as a medicinal herb, but it is also a welcome addition to informal borders, cottage-style plantings, or wildflower meadows. It is valued for its aromatic foliage and delicately scented flowers, which create an airy effect. Plant it in full sun or partial shade, in any average garden soil that is well drained. *Valeriana officinalis* is fairly tolerant of both dry and wet conditions. Staking may be needed if plants are grown in rich and moist soils, especially if shaded. Foliage usually declines after flowering, so cut plants back to encourage a new flush of basal leaves. *Valeriana officinalis* may self-seed under favorable conditions. Plants are hardy to zones 4 or 5.

Valeriana officinalis is extremely variable in the wild, and diploid, tetraploid, and octoploid forms are known to occur. There are three subspecies recognized currently. The typical subspecies *officinalis* does not produce stolons, whereas subspecies *collina* and *sambucifolia* may develop stolons below or above the ground. The latter two subspecies differ in the leaves, with those of subspecies *collina* having many narrowly linear and entire leaflets, and those of *sambucifolia* having fewer, broader and serrate leaflets. In cultivation, variants with white and darker, rose-colored flowers are known.

In its native habitat, *Valeriana officinalis* blooms in late spring and early summer. Cultivated in Poznań, it began flowering between 31 May and 7 June and ended between 9 and 15 July. Plants grown at Longwood usually started to bloom in late May, sometimes as early as the second week of May or as late as the first week of June. Flowering continued until late June or early July. Once in 5 years, plants that were cut back in late June rebloomed in late July. On average, *V. officinalis* was in bloom for a little more than 6 weeks.

Valeriana phu

Valeriana phu

GARDEN-HELIOTROPE, VALERIAN

The native range of this perennial is uncertain. *Valeriana phu* is thought to have originated in northern Turkey, but it has long been naturalized in parts of Europe, Asia Minor, and the Caucasus. It has been used, along with *V. officinalis*, as a medicinal herb since antiquity.

Valeriana phu forms lush clumps of basal foliage and erect, sparingly leafy stems to 1.5 m tall, growing from short rhizomes. The basal leaves are simple, undivided or lobed, and reach 20 cm in length, whereas the cauline leaves are smaller and pinnately parted into seven or nine segments. The 4-mm-long, tubular, pinkish white flowers are held in flat-topped terminal panicles. Fruits are achenes.

Valeriana phu is chiefly grown in herb gardens, but a golden-leaved selection is often planted in perennial borders to add color in early spring, when few perennials are flowering. Plant it in full sun or partial shade, in any average garden soil that is moist and well drained. *Valeriana phu* may self-seed under favorable conditions. Plants are hardy to zones 5 or 6.

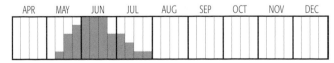

APR	MAY	JUN	JUL	AUG	SEP	OCT	NOV	DEC

Valeriana officinalis

Valeriana phu

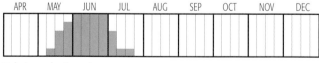

Valeriana phu 'Aurea'

There are no botanical varieties of *Valeriana phu* known in the wild. In cultivation, the species is rarely seen in ornamental gardens; it has been replaced by the cultivar 'Aurea', which has young foliage emerging yellow-green in spring and later maturing to light green.

Cultivated in Germany, *Valeriana phu* blooms from June to August. At Longwood, the cultivar 'Aurea' began flowering between the second week

of May and the first week of June. It continued to bloom through the end of June, sometimes into early July. 'Aurea' averaged a little more than 7 weeks in bloom.

Verbascum
MULLEIN

The name *Verbascum* was used by ancient Romans for mullein.

Verbascum chaixii
NETTLE-LEAVED MULLEIN

This perennial is native to Europe, from Spain, north to southern Poland, and east to central Russia. *Verbascum chaixii* grows in meadows and forest margins. It has been cultivated since the early 19th century.

Verbascum chaixii forms narrow upright clumps of woolly gray basal foliage and erect slender flowering stems, branched toward the apex, to 1 m tall. The ovate-oblong, crenate or slightly lobed basal leaves reach 30 cm in length and taper to long petioles, whereas the cauline leaves are smaller and short-petiolate to sessile. The 2.5-cm-wide pale yellow flowers have prominent clusters of purple-hairy stamens. The flowers are borne on short peduncles in erect terminal racemes or panicles. Fruits are globose capsules.

In the garden, *Verbascum chaixii*, with its narrow upright flowering spires, is well suited for traditional perennial borders, but it can also be naturalized on a larger scale on open slopes, wildflower meadows, or in similar informal settings. Plant it in full sun, in any average garden soil that is well drained. *Verbascum chaixii* is very adaptable and tolerates a wide range of conditions, except very moist ones. Cut back stems after flowering to encourage rebloom and to extend the longevity of the plant. This species is rather short-lived, sometimes even biennial. It self-seeds readily, and young seedlings can be saved as replacement plants. Plants are hardy to zone 5.

Three subspecies of *Verbascum chaixii* are recognized among the natural populations. The typical subspecies *chaixii* has flowers 15 to 22 mm wide and basal leaves slightly lobed toward the base. Subspecies *austriacum* differs in having basal leaves not lobed, whereas subspecies *orientale* has larger flowers, 20 to 25 mm wide. In cultivation, a few color variants have been selected, such as white-flowered 'Album', but many more cultivars have been raised

Verbascum chaixii 'Album'

Verbascum chaixii 'Album'

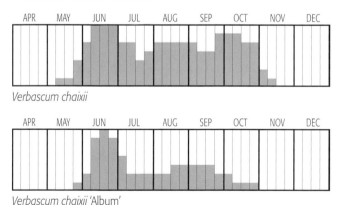

Verbascum chaixii

APR	MAY	JUN	JUL	AUG	SEP	OCT	NOV	DEC

Verbascum chaixii 'Album'

through hybridizing with several other mullein species, including *V. olympicum* and *V. phoeniceum*.

In the wild, *Verbascum chaixii* blooms in late spring and early summer. Cultivated in Germany, it flowers in July and August. Plants grown in St. Louis bloomed from mid-May until mid-June and again later in the summer or fall. At Longwood, the species *V. chaixii* was compared with its cultivar 'Album'. The species began flowering in the end of May and in early June. Once in 7 years, it opened flowers in

the second week of May. 'Album' bloomed a couple of weeks later, starting usually in the second week of June. The species responded well to cutting back, sometimes flowering continuously until November, and averaged more than 17 weeks in bloom. In contrast, 'Album' often failed to rebloom after being cut back in late June or early July, which reduced its average bloom duration to less than 9 weeks.

Vernonia

IRONWEED

The name *Vernonia* commemorates William Vernon (ca. 1666–1715), an English botanist.

Vernonia angustifolia

TALL IRONWEED

This plant is native to the southeastern United States, from North Carolina, south to Florida, and west to Mississippi. *Vernonia angustifolia* often grows in sandy soils, in savannahs, pine barrens, oak forests, and old fields, at elevations to 50 m.

Vernonia angustifolia

Vernonia angustifolia

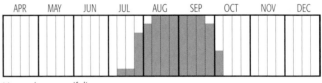

Vernonia angustifolia

Vernonia angustifolia forms upright clumps of erect, glabrescent to hirsute, leafy stems to 1.2 m tall. The lanceolate to linear leaves, to 12 cm long, are glabrous beneath. The flower heads, comprised of up to 20 (rarely more) purple disc florets, are held in compact corymb-like or panicle-like arrays. Fruits are 2.5-mm-long achenes with a whitish to purplish pappus.

In the garden, *Vernonia angustifolia* is best suited for wildflower meadows or informal plantings on the banks of ponds or lakes. In a perennial border it is valued chiefly for creating a lush backdrop for more refined perennials. Plant it in full sun, in any

Vernonia gigantea

average garden soil, although it performs best under moist conditions. Plants are hardy to zone 6.

In the wild, *Vernonia angustifolia* blooms from late June to August or early September. Plants grown at Longwood began flowering a month later, in late July or early August, although once in 7 years blooms opened in the second week of July. Flowering continued until the end of September, sometimes until the first week of October. *Vernonia angustifolia* averaged more than 10 weeks in bloom.

Vernonia gigantea

GIANT IRONWEED

This perennial is native to eastern North America, from Ontario, south to Florida, and west to Texas. *Vernonia gigantea* often grows in damp, rich soils on floodplains and in moist woods, at elevations to 300 m.

Vernonia gigantea forms upright clumps of erect, slightly pubescent or glabrous, leafy stems to 3 m tall.

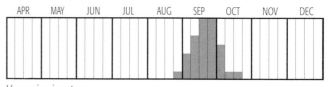

Vernonia gigantea

The sessile or short-petiolate, lanceolate leaves, to 30 cm long, have entire or finely serrate margins and sparsely hairy undersides. The 12-mm-wide flower heads are comprised of up to 24 (rarely more) purple disc florets. They are arranged in flattened, loose, corymb-like arrays. Fruits are 3-mm-long achenes tipped with a purplish, bristly pappus.

In the garden, *Vernonia gigantea* can be used in similar fashion as *V. angustifolia*. Plant it in full sun or shade. It thrives in any average garden soil, but consistent moisture is needed for plants to reach their height limits. On the other hand, if shorter plants are preferred, trim stems in late spring to encourage lower and bushier growth. Deadhead to minimize self-seeding. Plants are hardy to zone 5.

In the wild, *Vernonia gigantea* blooms from June to September, depending on the region. Cultivated in Germany, it starts flowering in August. Plants grown at Longwood usually began to bloom in early to mid–September, although once in 7 years flowers opened in the last week of August. They continued flowering through the end of September, sometimes into early October. On average, *V. gigantea* was in bloom for a little more than 4 weeks.

Vernonia noveboracensis

NEW YORK IRONWEED

This perennial is native to the eastern United States, from New Hampshire, south to Florida, and west to Ohio and Alabama. *Vernonia noveboracensis* grows in floodplains, moist meadows, marshes, old fields, thickets, on stream banks, and along roadsides, at elevations to 600 m.

Vernonia noveboracensis forms coarse, upright clumps of erect, glabrous or slightly hairy leafy stems to 2 m tall. The lanceolate to linear leaves, to 20 cm long, have entire or slightly serrate margins, a some-

Vernonia noveboracensis

Vernonia noveboracensis

what scabrous surface above, and glabrous or slightly pubescent beneath. The 12-mm-wide flower heads are comprised of up to 45 (rarely more) dull purple disc florets. They are held in loose corymb-like or panicle-like arrays to 20 cm wide. Fruits are 4-mm-long achenes tipped with a rusty purplish pappus.

In the garden, *Vernonia noveboracensis* can be used like *V. angustifolia*. Plant it in full sun or partial shade, in slightly acidic, fertile, and consistently moist soil. *Vernonia noveboracensis* can adapt to drier conditions, but plants do not grow as tall. If smaller plants are desired, trim the stems in late spring. This will delay flowering slightly but will result in plants only half the normal height. Deadhead to avoid prolific self-seeding, especially in moist situations. Plants are hardy to zone 5, possibly zone 3.

In the wild, *Vernonia noveboracensis* blooms from August to October. Cultivated in St. Louis, it flowered at about the same time. Plants grown in Poznań began to bloom around 20 August and ended between 7 and 17 October. At Longwood, bloom start date varied considerably, from the second week of July to the third week of August. Flowering usually continued until the end of August, sometimes into early September. *Vernonia noveboracensis* averaged a little more than 6 weeks in bloom.

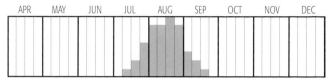

Vernonia noveboracensis

Veronica

SPEEDWELL

The name *Veronica* is of uncertain derivation but is thought to commemorate the Christian St. Veronica, in reference to markings on the flowers of some species resembling the image of Christ on her handkerchief.

Veronica incana

WOOLLY SPEEDWELL

This plant is native to eastern Europe and western Asia, south to the Crimea and east to Siberia. *Veronica incana* often grows in dry soils on the steppes and other open places. It has been cultivated since the late 18th century.

Veronica incana 'Saraband'

4

62

Veronica incana forms low clumps of silvery gray, semi-evergreen foliage and ascending flowering stems to 45 cm tall. The oblong to lanceolate, serrate or crenate, white-tomentose leaves reach 10 cm in length. The 6-mm-wide blue flowers are borne in dense terminal racemes to 20 cm long. Fruits are capsules.

In the garden, *Veronica incana* is valued as much for its silvery foliage as for the contrasting bright blue flowers. In milder climates the leaves are retained year-round, and plants can be used as a ground cover. Use in the front of a perennial border, on open slopes, in dry stone walls, and for edging paths. Plant it in full sun, in any well-drained soil, even poor soil. Avoid situations with cold, soggy soils and overhead irrigation, which both can cause the foliage to deteriorate rapidly and the plants to be short-lived. Plants are hardy to zone 5, possibly zone 3.

Veronica incana is often treated as a subspecies of *V. spicata*, from which it differs in being densely white-tomentose. In cultivation, many selections are thought to be the result of hybridization between these two species, but those with silvery or gray foliage are often listed under *V. incana*. While their foliage is more or less densely tomentose, flowers can vary from the pink of 'Minuet' and rosy pink of 'Barcarolle' to the purple of 'Silver Carpet' and violet blue of 'Saraband'.

In the wild, *Veronica incana* blooms in June and July. Cultivated in Moscow, it flowered, on average, from 17 June to 20 July. Plants grown in Poznań bloomed somewhat later, starting between 28 June and 10 July and ending between 22 and 30 July. At Longwood, the cultivar 'Saraband' began flowering in early or mid-June, but once in 7 years flowers opened in the last week of May. Bloom continued through mid or late July. Plants that were cut back in mid-July usually rebloomed within 2 weeks, but those cut back in early August did not. Occasionally, 'Saraband' kept on producing sporadic flowers through mid or late September. It averaged a little more than 10 weeks in bloom. In comparison, *V. incana* in Moscow was in flower for less than 5 weeks, on average.

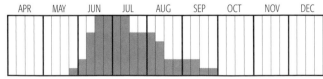

Veronica incana 'Saraband'

Veronica spicata
SPIKED SPEEDWELL

This perennial is native to Europe and Asia, from Spain, north to Norway, and east to Siberia, Kazakhstan, Kyrgyzstan, and Xinjiang in China. *Veronica spicata* grows in steppes, dry grasslands, and rocky slopes, at elevations to 2000 m.

Veronica spicata forms compact upright clumps of erect or ascending leafy stems to 1 m tall. The glossy green, lanceolate to oblong leaves, to 8 cm long, have serrate or crenate margins and taper to a short petiole. The 6-mm-wide blue flowers are held in dense terminal spike-like racemes to 30 cm long. Fruits are 3-mm-long capsules.

In the garden, *Veronica spicata* can be used in the front of a perennial border, among low-growing shrubs, for edging paths, on top of a wall, and as an attractive ground cover for a confined area. Plant it in full sun, although partial shade is tolerated as well.

Veronica spicata 'Blue Peter'

Choose a site with light, moderately fertile, well-drained soil. Avoid situations where soil is heavy and stays soggy in winter. If flopping of the taller forms becomes an issue, trim stems in the middle of spring to encourage shorter and more branched growth. Deadhead to encourage additional bloom. Cut back to basal foliage after all flowering is finished for a neater look. *Veronica spicata* is long-lived but needs regular dividing every 3 years or so. Plants are hardy in zone 5, possibly zone 3.

Veronica spicata is an extremely variable species, and a few of subspecies have been recognized. The typical subspecies *spicata* is found throughout the distribution range. Subspecies *orchidea*, from southeastern Europe, differs in having twisted lower corolla lobes, whereas subspecies *crassifolia*, native to the Balkans, is distinguished by longer leaf petioles. In cultivation, numerous color variants have been selected and additional cultivars were developed through hybridizing with *V. incana* and *V. longifolia*. Flower color choices include white 'Snow White', pink 'Erika', rose red 'Rotfuchs', and dark blue 'Blue Peter'. While most selections are about 50 cm tall, there are several low-growing cultivars available, such as 'Waterperry', reaching only 15 cm in height. A form with variegated leaves is named 'Noah Williams'.

Veronica spicata blooms from late spring to summer. Cultivated in Germany, it flowers in July and August. Plants grown in Moscow bloomed from 20 June to 9 August, on average. In Poznań, flowering started at about the same time, between 19 June and 4 July, and ended between 4 and 20 August. At Longwood, *V. spicata* was observed along with its two cultivars, 'Blue Peter' and 'Noah Williams'. The species and 'Blue Peter' began flowering in early or mid-June, but 'Noah Williams' did not bloom until late June. When *V. spicata* or its cultivars were cut back in July, they often rebloomed. However, when

Veronica spicata 'Blue Peter'

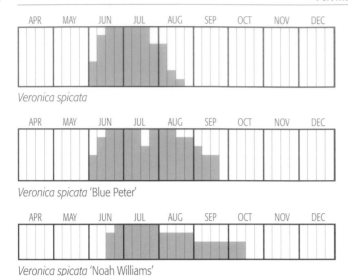

| | APR | MAY | JUN | JUL | AUG | SEP | OCT | NOV | DEC |

Veronica spicata

| | APR | MAY | JUN | JUL | AUG | SEP | OCT | NOV | DEC |

Veronica spicata 'Blue Peter'

| | APR | MAY | JUN | JUL | AUG | SEP | OCT | NOV | DEC |

Veronica spicata 'Noah Williams'

plants were cut back in August, no rebloom was observed. While the species usually ended flowering in late July or early August, 'Blue Peter' and 'Noah Williams' often continued to bloom until late September or early October. 'Blue Peter' and 'Noah Williams' averaged 15 and 13 weeks in bloom, respectively. In comparison, *V. spicata* was in flower for less than 9 weeks, on average.

Veronicastrum

CULVER'S ROOT

The name *Veronicastrum* is derived from *Veronica* and the Latin suffix *aster*, resembling, in reference to the similarities between these plants.

Veronicastrum virginicum

BLACKROOT, BOWMAN'S ROOT, CULVER'S PHYSIC, CULVER'S ROOT, OXADADDY, QUITCH

This plant is native to eastern North America, from Ontario, west to Manitoba, and south to Florida and Texas. *Veronicastrum virginicum* grows in low meadows, prairies, moist open forests, thickets, and along roadsides. It has been cultivated since the early 18th century.

Veronicastrum virginicum forms vertical clumps of erect, unbranched, usually glabrous stems to 2 m tall. The lanceolate, short-petiolate, sharply serrated leaves, to 15 cm long, are arranged in whorls of three to nine. The tubular, 8-mm-long, white to pinkish or purplish flowers are borne in erect, dense, terminal and upper axillary, spike-like racemes to 22 cm long. Fruits are ovoid capsules.

Veronicastrum virginicum

In the garden, *Veronicastrum virginicum* is well suited for larger perennial borders or naturalistic plantings along a woodland edge, in a meadow, or on the banks of a stream or pond. It is valued for its elegant, stately habit creating a strong vertical element and the distinct candelabra-like racemes held high above the surrounding perennials. Site *V. virginicum* among plants that will hide its rather bare base. Choose a sunny or, in warmer climates, partially shaded spot. Avoid deep shade, where plants will stretch excessively and flop easily. Plant it in fertile, humus-rich, consistently moist, and well-drained soil. Despite its considerable height, *V. virginicum* rarely needs staking. Deadhead to extend bloom and cut back after all flowering is finished to encourage a new flush of growth and a possible rebloom. *Veronicastrum virginicum* is long-lived and takes a few years to fully establish in a new location. Divide infrequently if the size of the clumps needs to be reduced. Plants are hardy to zones 3 or 4.

Veronicastrum virginicum 'Album'

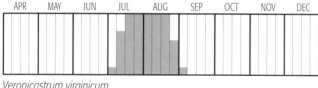

Veronicastrum virginicum

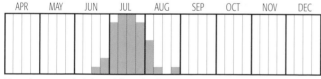

Veronicastrum virginicum 'Album'

There are no botanical varieties of *Veronicastrum virginicum* recognized among the natural populations. In cultivation, a number of color variants have been selected, including white 'Album' and 'Diane', pink 'Pink Glow' and 'Roseum', lavender 'Apollo' and 'Lavendelturm', and purple-blue 'Temptation'.

In the wild, *Veronicastrum virginicum* blooms from June to September. Cultivated in Germany, it flow-

ers at about the same time. Plants grown in Chicago and St. Louis bloomed in July and August. At Longwood, *V. virginicum* and its cultivar 'Album' were observed. While the species usually began to bloom in the second and third week of July, 'Album' opened flowers up to 2 weeks earlier. *Veronicastrum virginicum* continued to flower until late August, and in one year it was still in bloom in the first week of September. It averaged more than 7 weeks in bloom. In comparison, 'Album' bloomed only through the end of July, sometimes the first week of August, and its average bloom time was 2 weeks shorter than that of the species.

Viola

VIOLET

The name *Viola* is derived from the Greek *ion*, a flower that was borne under a foot of Io, an Argive princess, after she was changed by Zeus into a cow, and applied to violets, stocks, and wallflowers.

Viola cornuta

HORNED VIOLET, TUFTED VIOLET, VIOLA

This perennial is native to Europe, where it grows in the Pyrenees in France and Spain. *Viola cornuta* also naturalized in other parts of central and southern Europe. It has been cultivated since the 18th century.

Viola cornuta forms tufted or spreading clumps of prostrate and ascending stems to 30 cm tall, growing from a short creeping rootstock. The evergreen, ovate leaves, to 5 cm long, have shallowly crenate margins and large triangular stipules. The slightly fragrant, 3.5-cm-wide, slender-spurred, violet blue flowers are held on long peduncles in leaf axils. Fruits are three-chambered capsules.

In the garden, *Viola cornuta* makes an effective low ground cover or compact mounds when grown in the open, but it can also sprawl between and through taller plants. Plant it in full sun or partial shade, in any reasonably moist garden soil. *Viola cornuta* is relatively tolerant of hot and dry conditions. It self-seeds easily and spreads rapidly. Dividing is not needed except to control the spread. Plants are hardy to zones 5 or 6.

There are no botanical varieties of *Viola cornuta* recognized in the wild. In cultivation, many color variants have been selected. Furthermore, *V. cornuta* has been crossed with *V. gracilis* and *V. ×wittrockiana* to develop an even broader range of cultivars. Color choices include white 'White Perfection', creamy yellow 'Altona', lemon yellow 'Bullion', soft lavender 'Angerland', clear blue 'Blaue Schönheit', wine red 'Famös', mauve 'Irish Molly', and dark violet purple 'Germania'.

Viola cornuta blooms over a long time in summer. Cultivated in Poland and the United Kingdom, it flowers from May until August, and it may repeat flowering in the fall if cut back. Plants grown in Moscow bloomed, on average, from 6 May to 23 August. In St. Louis, *V. cornuta* flowered earlier, from April until June. At Longwood, the bloom start date of the hybrid cultivar 'Irish Molly' varied by 5 weeks, from the first week of May to the second week of June. Bloom continued until mid-July, sometimes mid-August. On average, 'Irish Molly' flowered at Longwood for 11 weeks. In comparison, *V. cornuta* in Moscow averaged more than 15 weeks in bloom.

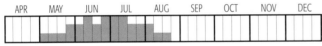

Viola cornuta 'Irish Molly'

Viola labradorica

ALPINE VIOLET, LABRADOR VIOLET

This plant is native to northern and eastern North America, from Newfoundland, west to Alaska, and south to Georgia and Alabama. *Viola labradorica*

Viola labradorica

grows primarily in subarctic moist forests and at higher elevations in the mountains further south.

Viola labradorica forms spreading clumps of erect or ascending, slender stems, to 10 cm tall, growing from a creeping, scaly rhizome. The broadly ovate, 2.5-cm-wide leaves have shallowly serrate margins and linear stipules. They are dark green, often tinged purple-violet, especially in cold weather. The 2-cm-wide flowers, held on long peduncles, are blue to lavender and suffused with darker purple. Fruits are subglobose capsules.

In the garden, *Viola labradorica* can establish a fine ground cover in a smaller area or fill tight spaces between stones or pavers. It also makes an innocuous companion plant for taller perennials. Space permitting, allow it to spread on its own and naturalize. Plant it in full sun in northern areas, but partial or full shade is recommended further south. *Viola labradorica* thrives in any average garden soil that is consistently moist. It spreads rapidly through the creeping rhizomes and self-seeding. Divide when needed to control the spread. Plants are hardy to zones 2 or 3.

In the wild, *Viola labradorica* blooms in July and August. Cultivated in Germany, it flowers a couple of months earlier, in April and May. Plants grown in Moscow bloomed, on average, from 23 May to 5 June. At Longwood, *V. labradorica* began flowering in mid-April. The first flush of flowers peaked in May, but often continued less profusely through June and into early July. Blooming ceased in the heat of summer, but it resumed with the return of cooler weather. This rebloom in some years lasted only a couple of weeks, but in others it continued for more than 2 months, occasionally into early November. On average, *V. labradorica* was in flower for 18 weeks.

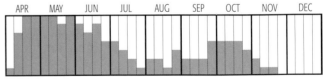

Viola labradorica

Viola striata

CREAM VIOLET, PALE VIOLET, STRIPED VIOLET

This perennial is native to eastern North America, from Ontario, south to Georgia and Alabama, and west to Wisconsin and Oklahoma. *Viola striata* grows in rich moist forests, meadows, and on stream banks, at elevations to 1000 m.

Viola striata forms spreading clumps of erect or decumbent, usually glabrous stems, to 30 cm tall, growing from short rhizomes. The orbicular to ovate leaves, to 3.5 cm wide, have cordate bases, finely crenate or serrate margins, and large fimbriate stipules. The creamy yellow flowers are marked with black or violet striation. They are held on slender peduncles in leaf axils. Fruits are ovoid capsules.

In the garden, *Viola striata* finds many applications, from making a dense vigorous ground cover, to filling nooks and crannies among rocks, in stone walls, or walkways, to naturalizing in a woodland. Plant it in partial shade, preferably in moist and humus-rich soil. It spreads rapidly through self-seeding. Dividing is needed only to restrain the spread. Plants are hardy to zone 3.

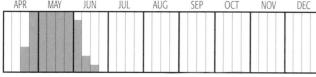
Viola striata

In the wild, *Viola striata* blooms in April and May. Cultivated in St. Louis, it flowered from the second week of April until late May. Plants grown at Longwood began to bloom in late April and continued until the first week of June, occasionally until mid-June. On average, *V. striata* flowered at Longwood for a little more than 7 weeks. Similar bloom duration was observed in St. Louis.

Yucca
YUCCA
The name *Yucca* is derived from the Carib *yuca*, cassava, an unrelated plant, and applied in error.

Yucca filamentosa
ADAM'S NEEDLE, BEARGRASS, NEEDLE-PALM, SILKGRASS, SPANISH BAYONET, SPOON LEAF YUCCA, THREAD-LEAVED YUCCA

This perennial is native to the eastern United States, from Maryland, south to Florida, and west to West Virginia and Louisiana, but has naturalized further north and west. *Yucca filamentosa* often grows in sandy

Viola striata

soils, in savannahs, on dry open slopes, beaches, sand dunes, and in old fields. It has been cultivated since the 17th century.

Yucca filamentosa forms tufted rosettes of evergreen spiky foliage to 1 m tall and flowering scapes to 4 m tall, growing from a short, woody, underground caudex. The lanceolate, sword-shaped, thick, rough, concave leaves, to 75 cm long, have curly thread-like filaments along the margins. The fragrant, nodding, 5-cm-long, creamy white flowers are often flushed red-brown in bud. They are borne in erect panicles, to 1.5 m long, terminating a stout scape. Fruits are oblong capsules to 5 cm in length.

In the garden, *Yucca filamentosa* can be used in perennial borders, mixed among shrubbery, combined with grasses, and naturalized margins of woodlands or on dry open slopes. It is valued for its distinct spiky foliage and imposing panicles of fragrant flowers. Preferably, plant *Y. filamentosa* in full sun, although it can tolerate partial shade as well. Choose a site with warm, light, and well-drained soil. Although plants can tolerate poor and dry soils, they flower better in reasonably fertile and moist ones. *Yucca filamentosa* is long-lived and does poorly after transplanting, so it is best left undisturbed for years. Plants are hardy to zone 5.

Several variants of *Yucca filamentosa* have been described among the natural populations, but they are no longer considered valid or their status has changed. Variety *smalliana*, from the southeastern United States, is currently regarded as a separate species, *Y. flaccida*. In cultivation, several selections have been made, although some of them are variably assigned to *Y. filamentosa* or *Y. flaccida* or as a hybrid between these two species. Cultivars such as 'Eisbär', 'Fontäne', and 'Schellenbaum' were selected for their particularly impressive inflorescences, while others feature variegated foliage, among them yellow-margined 'Bright Edge' and gold-striped 'Color Guard'.

In the wild, *Yucca filamentosa* blooms from May to July. Cultivated in St. Louis, it flowers in June and July. Plants grown in Poland bloom in July and August, and in the United Kingdom from August to October. At Longwood, the cultivar 'Color Guard' began flowering in early June and usually continued until the end of that month. One year, an additional late bloom occurred in late July. On average, 'Color Guard' was in flower for less than 4 weeks.

Yucca filamentosa

APR	MAY	JUN	JUL	AUG	SEP	OCT	NOV	DEC

Yucca filamentosa 'Color Guard'

Yucca filamentosa 'Color Guard'

Achieving Continuity of Bloom

As gardeners, we quickly learn from experience that each plant occupies a certain niche in the environment, characterized by a set of conditions, such as soil, moisture, light, or temperature, which we then attempt to approximate in cultivation. Much less appreciated is the fact that plants occupy a specific niche not only in space, but also in time. Each species has its developmental phases timed with the changes in the environment differently. The complex and intricate interactions between a plant and its surroundings allow it to have a temporal niche in which its flowering and other phenophases take place. As a result, different species blooming at different times can grow in the same location and share the same pollinators without competing for them. Thus, the temporal niches of various species are shifted with respect to each other but can also differ in their duration. Some species are known for their short bloom, whereas others produce flowers for most of the growing season.

In most natural plant communities, flowering of various species proceeds in a more or less orderly fashion from spring until fall, ensuring optimal conditions for cross-pollination. This does not mean that flowering is evenly distributed throughout the growing season. On the contrary, one should expect in any plant community that the number of flowering species will peak at a certain time and decline gradually after that. It is not uncommon for a temperate climate flora to have three-quarters of the species blooming in spring and the remaining quarter flowering in summer and fall.

Gardeners are faced with the same challenge, where cultivated plants making up an artificial community in a garden tend to concentrate their bloom around a particular season. In the case of perennials grown at Longwood Garden, nearly half of all taxa were in bloom in mid-July, compared to about only one in ten flowering in early May or late October. Yet, most gardeners desire to have an abundance of flowers all season long.

Several things can be done to get a little closer to that ideal. By creating conditions that permit each species in a garden to flower longer, we allow their bloom periods to overlap and, in effect, create an

Geranium sanguineum 'Max Frei'

impression of more flowers being present. Periods of dry and hot weather in summer may be accompanied by a decrease in flowering or even a complete cessation of bloom in many perennials. By choosing a moist site for species that are more sensitive to drought or growing a greater number of drought- and heat-tolerant species, we can ease this midsummer depression. A similar effect can be achieved by giving preference to long-blooming species over those that are in flower for only a brief period. At Longwood, nearly half of all perennials flowered, on average, for 5 weeks or fewer, but only one in ten was in bloom for more than 14 weeks.

Another solution is to hide or even replace perennials that are finished flowering with annuals or tender perennials that can provide extended bloom through summer and fall. This has to be done with a great deal of consideration, however. In addition to the extra labor and cost, it may lead to rather awkward plant combinations and may compromise the well-being of the perennials by rapidly growing annuals. A similar concept is planting early-spring and fall bulbs among perennials. This has to be executed just as thoughtfully to avoid situations where bulbs decline because of the competition of vigorous perennials, or where their

Adonis aestivalis

Muscari armeniacum 'Album'

Scaevola aemula 'Saphira'

Annuals, tender perennials, and bulbs that flower in early spring or fall can help to create a continuous bloom succession through the entire growing season.

foliage, senescing in the summer, becomes unsightly and detracts from the overall effect of the composition.

Yet another approach, widely popularized in recent years, is to rely to a greater extent on perennials with decorative foliage. Although this does not bring any more flowers into the garden, it assures a neat and pleasing appearance of perennial plantings even during the times when few plants are in bloom. Perennials that tend to die back or decline after flowering can be skillfully disguised by neighboring plants, as long as they are used sparingly and do not form large groups.

Similarly, the season of interest of many perennials can also be extended by allowing them to form fruits. In our desire to keep the garden appearance neat and tidy, we often rush to cutting back perennials soon after they finish flowering. But many of them, given the opportunity, develop attractive fruits of various sorts. Unlike shrubs and trees, many of which can dazzle us with sumptuous and colorful fruit display, perennials rarely develop fleshy and colorful fruits. Instead, dry types of fruits, such as achenes, capsules, or follicles that are subtly tinted or delicately textured, can provide interest when flowers are absent.

Ajuga reptans 'Burgundy Glow'

Brunnera macrophylla 'Jack Frost'

Amsonia hubrichtii

Perennials with decorative foliage are attractive even when not flowering.

Belamcanda chinensis   *Arisaema triphyllum*   *Pulsatilla vulgaris*

Fruits of some perennials provide interest beyond the bloom season.

The ultimate solution is to design perennial plantings from the very beginning with their bloom succession in mind. This approach requires detailed information about the flowering habits of the plants that are being considered. Although such information is specific to a particular region, regional differences should not be overemphasized. As observations made at Longwood Gardens indicate, parallels can be drawn between places, often as far away as southeastern Pennsylvania and Moscow, as long as they are within the same broadly defined temperate climate zone.

The scarcity of such information makes planning for bloom succession difficult, and only the most dedicated gardeners keep their own records to fine-tune plant compositions based on bloom times. This book attempts to fill this gap and provide gar-

deners with a tool that will permit staggering or layering flowering of various plants so that it can be distributed through the season according to individual needs. In most cases, making the flowering more evenly distributed from April to November, or at least broadening the midsummer bloom peak, would be a desirable outcome. Because in a typical perennial border, such as the one at Longwood, about five times as many perennials flower in mid-July as in early May or late October, a more uniform bloom distribution could be accomplished either by including more species and varieties that flower very early or very late in season or by repeating them in greater numbers throughout the garden.

In certain situations, the same information can be used to concentrate flowering in a particular season,

Designing perennial plantings with a bloom succession in mind allows gardeners to achieve continuous and harmonious floral display from spring through fall.

such as spring or fall, which may be preferred by those who spend summers away from home. On the other hand, gardens that receive many visitors during the summer vacation season would benefit from focusing on perennials that reliably flower during that time.

The charts that follow summarize the results presented individually in the encyclopedia and illustrate the time of year when plants flowered in all (dark gray), most (medium gray), or some (light gray) years. Plants are sorted first according the earliest date when their bloom was observed, then according to the latest date when they were in flower.

The charts provide a floral almanac gardeners can consult to create ever-blooming borders.

The bloom time data in the charts were gathered at Longwood Gardens, which is located in southeastern Pennsylvania (zone 6). To apply this information to perennials growing in other regions, choose a few indicator plants (one each for spring, summer, and fall) that you have experience with in your own garden, and compare its bloom time to the data shown in the chart. For instance, if an indicator plant blooms 2 weeks later in your garden than at Longwood Gardens, this 2-week offset can be applied to other plants that bloom in the same season as the indicator.

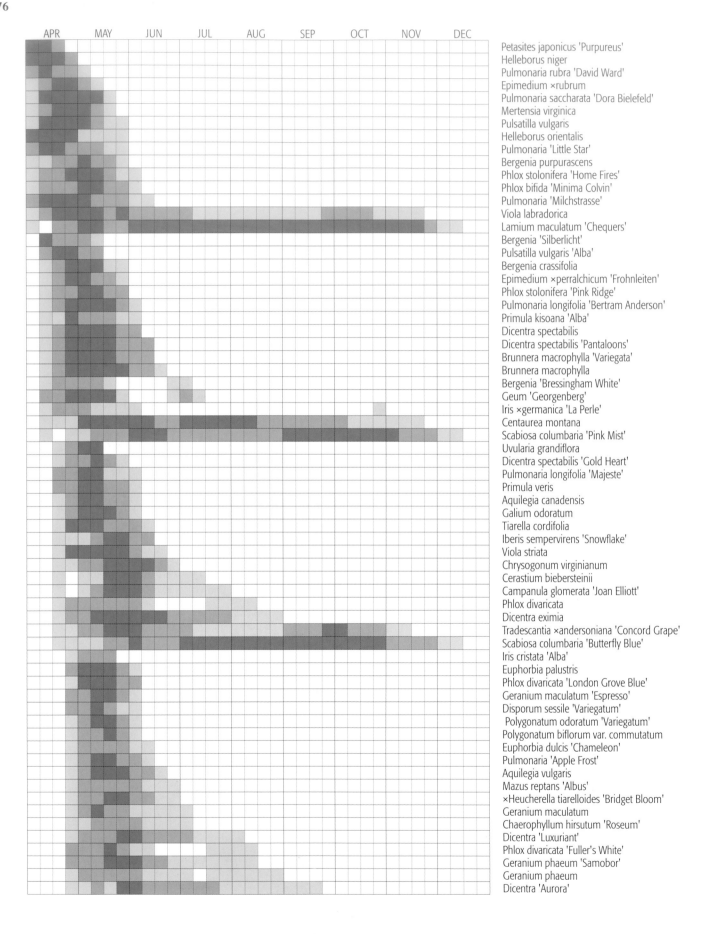

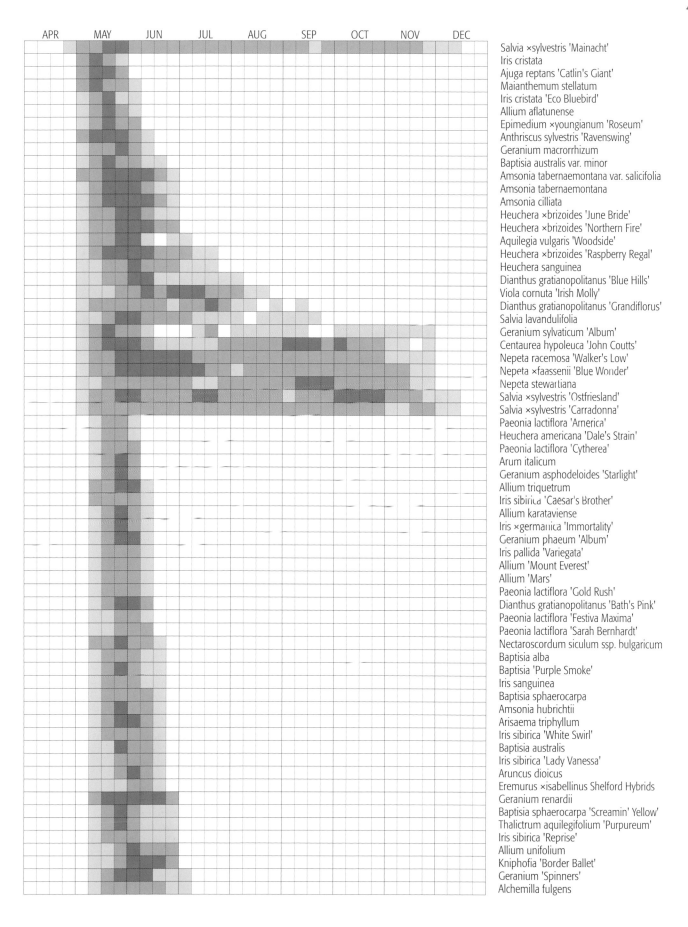

	APR	MAY	JUN	JUL	AUG	SEP	OCT	NOV	DEC	

Salvia ×sylvestris 'Mainacht'
Iris cristata
Ajuga reptans 'Catlin's Giant'
Maianthemum stellatum
Iris cristata 'Eco Bluebird'
Allium aflatunense
Epimedium ×youngianum 'Roseum'
Anthriscus sylvestris 'Ravenswing'
Geranium macrorrhizum
Baptisia australis var. minor
Amsonia tabernaemontana var. salicifolia
Amsonia tabernaemontana
Amsonia cilliata
Heuchera ×brizoides 'June Bride'
Heuchera ×brizoides 'Northern Fire'
Aquilegia vulgaris 'Woodside'
Heuchera ×brizoides 'Raspberry Regal'
Heuchera sanguinea
Dianthus gratianopolitanus 'Blue Hills'
Viola cornuta 'Irish Molly'
Dianthus gratianopolitanus 'Grandiflorus'
Salvia lavandulifolia
Geranium sylvaticum 'Album'
Centaurea hypoleuca 'John Coutts'
Nepeta racemosa 'Walker's Low'
Nepeta ×faassenii 'Blue Wonder'
Nepeta stewartiana
Salvia ×sylvestris 'Ostfriesland'
Salvia ×sylvestris 'Carradonna'
Paeonia lactiflora 'America'
Heuchera americana 'Dale's Strain'
Paeonia lactiflora 'Cytherea'
Arum italicum
Geranium asphodeloides 'Starlight'
Allium triquetrum
Iris sibirica 'Caesar's Brother'
Allium karataviense
Iris ×germanica 'Immortality'
Geranium phaeum 'Album'
Iris pallida 'Variegata'
Allium 'Mount Everest'
Allium 'Mars'
Paeonia lactiflora 'Gold Rush'
Dianthus gratianopolitanus 'Bath's Pink'
Paeonia lactiflora 'Festiva Maxima'
Paeonia lactiflora 'Sarah Bernhardt'
Nectaroscordum siculum ssp. bulgaricum
Baptisia alba
Baptisia 'Purple Smoke'
Iris sanguinea
Baptisia sphaerocarpa
Amsonia hubrichtii
Arisaema triphyllum
Iris sibirica 'White Swirl'
Baptisia australis
Iris sibirica 'Lady Vanessa'
Aruncus dioicus
Eremurus ×isabellinus Shelford Hybrids
Geranium renardii
Baptisia sphaerocarpa 'Screamin' Yellow'
Thalictrum aquilegifolium 'Purpureum'
Iris sibirica 'Reprise'
Allium unifolium
Kniphofia 'Border Ballet'
Geranium 'Spinners'
Alchemilla fulgens

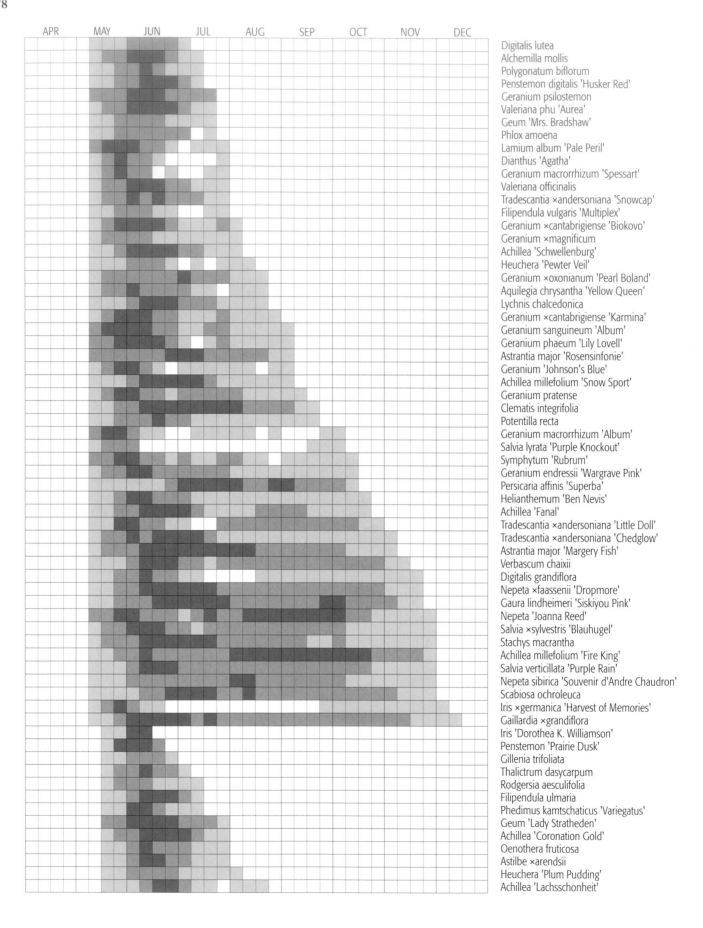

APR MAY JUN JUL AUG SEP OCT NOV DEC

Digitalis lutea
Alchemilla mollis
Polygonatum biflorum
Penstemon digitalis 'Husker Red'
Geranium psilostemon
Valeriana phu 'Aurea'
Geum 'Mrs. Bradshaw'
Phlox amoena
Lamium album 'Pale Peril'
Dianthus 'Agatha'
Geranium macrorrhizum 'Spessart'
Valeriana officinalis
Tradescantia ×andersoniana 'Snowcap'
Filipendula vulgaris 'Multiplex'
Geranium ×cantabrigiense 'Biokovo'
Geranium ×magnificum
Achillea 'Schwellenburg'
Heuchera 'Pewter Veil'
Geranium ×oxonianum 'Pearl Boland'
Aquilegia chrysantha 'Yellow Queen'
Lychnis chalcedonica
Geranium ×cantabrigiense 'Karmina'
Geranium sanguineum 'Album'
Geranium phaeum 'Lily Lovell'
Astrantia major 'Rosensinfonie'
Geranium 'Johnson's Blue'
Achillea millefolium 'Snow Sport'
Geranium pratense
Clematis integrifolia
Potentilla recta
Geranium macrorrhizum 'Album'
Salvia lyrata 'Purple Knockout'
Symphytum 'Rubrum'
Geranium endressii 'Wargrave Pink'
Persicaria affinis 'Superba'
Helianthemum 'Ben Nevis'
Achillea 'Fanal'
Tradescantia ×andersoniana 'Little Doll'
Tradescantia ×andersoniana 'Chedglow'
Astrantia major 'Margery Fish'
Verbascum chaixii
Digitalis grandiflora
Nepeta ×faassenii 'Dropmore'
Gaura lindheimeri 'Siskiyou Pink'
Nepeta 'Joanna Reed'
Salvia ×sylvestris 'Blauhugel'
Stachys macrantha
Achillea millefolium 'Fire King'
Salvia verticillata 'Purple Rain'
Nepeta sibirica 'Souvenir d'Andre Chaudron'
Scabiosa ochroleuca
Iris ×germanica 'Harvest of Memories'
Gaillardia ×grandiflora
Iris 'Dorothea K. Williamson'
Penstemon 'Prairie Dusk'
Gillenia trifoliata
Thalictrum dasycarpum
Rodgersia aesculifolia
Filipendula ulmaria
Phedimus kamtschaticus 'Variegatus'
Geum 'Lady Stratheden'
Achillea 'Coronation Gold'
Oenothera fruticosa
Astilbe ×arendsii
Heuchera 'Plum Pudding'
Achillea 'Lachsschonheit'

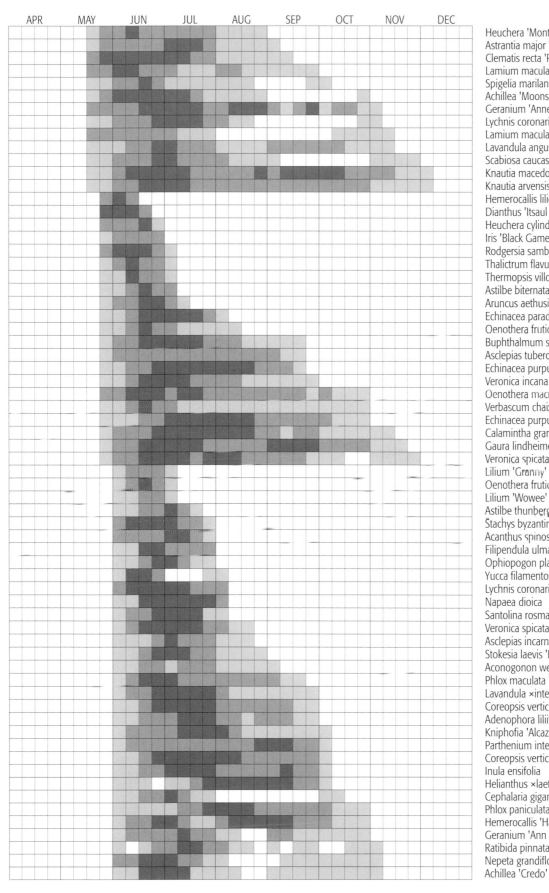

	APR	MAY	JUN	JUL	AUG	SEP	OCT	NOV	DEC

Heuchera 'Montrose Ruby'
Astrantia major 'Shaggy'
Clematis recta 'Purpurea'
Lamium maculatum 'White Nancy'
Spigelia marilandica
Achillea 'Moonshine'
Geranium 'Anne Thomson'
Lychnis coronaria 'Alba'
Lamium maculatum 'Beedham's White'
Lavandula angustifolia 'Munstead'
Scabiosa caucasica 'Fama'
Knautia macedonica
Knautia arvensis
Hemerocallis lilioasphodelus
Dianthus 'Itsaul White'
Heuchera cylindrica 'Greenfinch'
Iris 'Black Gamecock'
Rodgersia sambucifolia
Thalictrum flavum ssp. glaucum
Thermopsis villosa
Astilbe biternata
Aruncus aethusifolius
Echinacea paradoxa
Oenothera fruticosa 'Sonnenwende'
Buphthalmum salicifolium
Asclepias tuberosa 'Gay Butterflies'
Echinacea purpurea 'Leuchtstern'
Veronica incana 'Saraband'
Oenothera macrocarpa 'Lemon Silver'
Verbascum chaixii 'Album'
Echinacea purpurea 'White Swan'
Calamintha grandiflora 'Variegata'
Gaura lindheimeri 'Whirling Butterflies'
Veronica spicata 'Blue Peter'
Lilium 'Granny'
Oenothera fruticosa 'Fyrverkeri'
Lilium 'Wowee'
Astilbe thunbergii 'Professor van der Wielen'
Stachys byzantina 'Striped Phantom'
Acanthus spinosus 'Spinosissimus'
Filipendula ulmaria 'Variegata'
Ophiopogon planiscapus 'Nigrescens'
Yucca filamentosa 'Color Guard'
Lychnis coronaria 'Angel's Blush'
Napaea dioica
Santolina rosmarinifolia
Veronica spicata
Asclepias incarnata 'Ice Ballet'
Stokesia laevis 'Purple Parasols'
Aconogonon weyrichii
Phlox maculata 'Rosalinde'
Lavandula ×intermedia 'Grosso'
Coreopsis verticillata 'Golden Showers'
Adenophora liliifolia
Kniphofia 'Alcazar'
Parthenium integrifolium
Coreopsis verticillata 'Zagreb'
Inula ensifolia
Helianthus ×laetiflorus 'Lemon Queen'
Cephalaria gigantea
Phlox paniculata 'Eva Cullum'
Hemerocallis 'Happy Returns'
Geranium 'Ann Folkard'
Ratibida pinnata
Nepeta grandiflora 'Dawn to Dusk'
Achillea 'Credo'

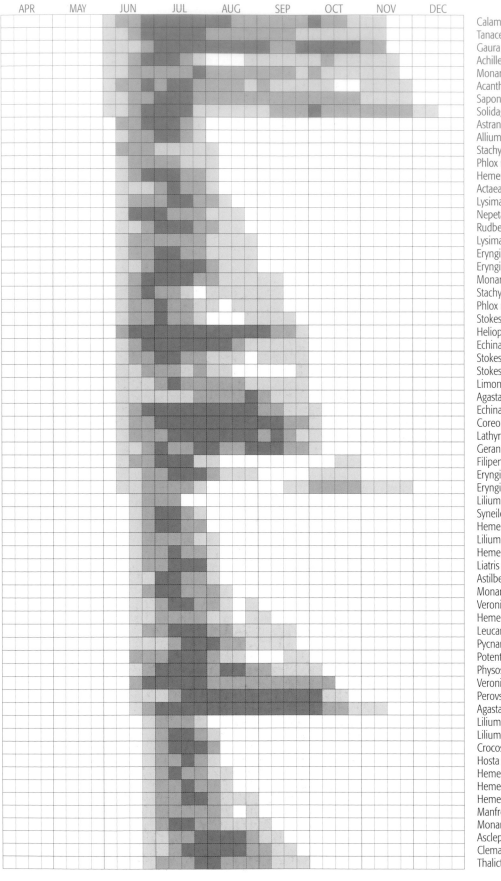

	APR	MAY	JUN	JUL	AUG	SEP	OCT	NOV	DEC	

Calamintha nepeta 'White Cloud'
Tanacetum parthenium 'Aureum'
Gaura lindheimeri 'Corrie's Gold'
Achillea millefolium 'Feurland'
Monarda didyma 'Jacob Cline'
Acanthus balcanicus
Saponaria ×lempergii 'Max Frei'
Solidago 'Strahlenkrone'
Astrantia major 'Rubra'
Allium sphaerocephalon
Stachys byzantina 'Sheila Macqueen'
Phlox maculata 'Alpha'
Hemerocallis 'Russian Rhapsody'
Actaea racemosa
Lysimachia ciliata 'Purpurea'
Nepeta parnassica
Rudbeckia maxima
Lysimachia ephemerum
Eryngium planum
Eryngium planum 'Blaukappe'
Monarda didyma 'Gardenview Scarlet'
Stachys byzantina 'Primrose Heron'
Phlox maculata 'Natascha'
Stokesia laevis 'Mary Gregory'
Heliopsis helianthoides 'Ballerina'
Echinacea tennesseensis
Stokesia laevis 'Blue Danube'
Stokesia laevis 'Silver Moon'
Limonium latifolium
Agastache nepetoides
Echinacea purpurea 'Magnus'
Coreopsis verticillata 'Moonbeam'
Lathyrus latifolius
Geranium wlassovianum
Filipendula rubra 'Venusta'
Eryngium yuccifolium
Eryngium agavifolium
Lilium 'Nepal'
Syneilesis aconitifolia
Hemerocallis 'Bertie Ferris'
Lilium 'Moonlight'
Hemerocallis 'Spindazzle'
Liatris spicata 'Kobold'
Astilbe chinensis 'Superba'
Monarda didyma 'Colrain Red'
Veronicastrum virginicum 'Album'
Hemerocallis thunbergii
Leucanthemum ×superbum 'Becky'
Pycnanthemum tenuifolium
Potentilla thurberi
Physostegia virginiana 'Miss Manners'
Veronica spicata 'Noah Williams'
Perovskia ×hybrida 'Longin'
Agastache 'Firebird'
Lilium 'Black Dragon'
Lilium 'Thunderbolt'
Crocosmia 'Lucifer'
Hosta ventricosa
Hemerocallis hakuunensis
Hemerocallis fulva
Hemerocallis citrina
Manfreda virginica
Monarda didyma 'Beauty of Cobham'
Asclepias incarnata
Clematis ×jouniana 'Mrs. Robert Brydon'
Thalictrum rochebruneanum

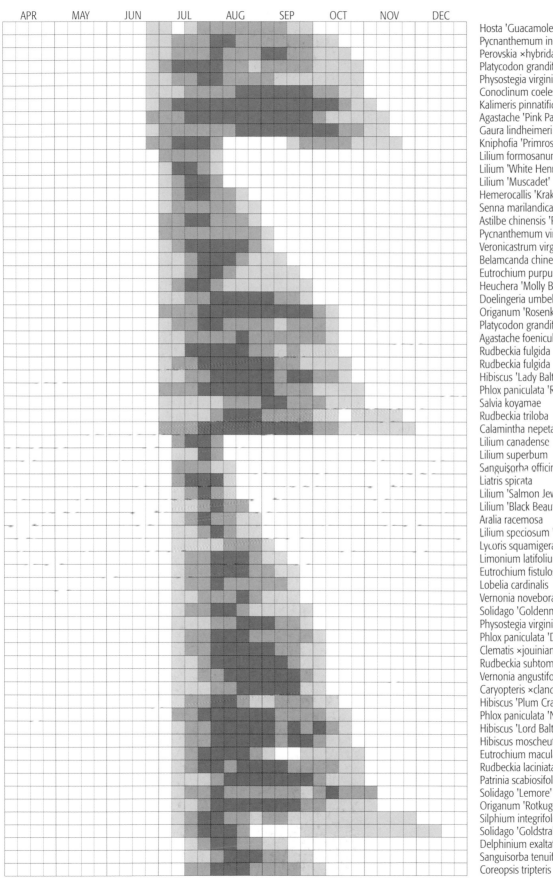

	APR	MAY	JUN	JUL	AUG	SEP	OCT	NOV	DEC	

Hosta 'Guacamole'
Pycnanthemum incanum
Perovskia ×hybrida 'Filigran'
Platycodon grandiflorus 'Fuji'
Physostegia virginiana 'Summer Snow'
Conoclinum coelestinum
Kalimeris pinnatifida 'Hortensis'
Agastache 'Pink Panther'
Gaura lindheimeri 'Dauphin'
Kniphofia 'Primrose Beauty'
Lilium formosanum
Lilium 'White Henryi'
Lilium 'Muscadet'
Hemerocallis 'Krakatoa Lava'
Senna marilandica
Astilbe chinensis 'Pumila'
Pycnanthemum virginianum
Veronicastrum virginicum
Belamcanda chinensis
Eutrochium purpureum 'Bartered Bride'
Heuchera 'Molly Bush'
Doelingeria umbellata
Origanum 'Rosenkuppel'
Platycodon grandiflorus 'Albus'
Agastache foeniculum
Rudbeckia fulgida 'Viette's Little Suzy'
Rudbeckia fulgida 'Goldsturm'
Hibiscus 'Lady Baltimore'
Phlox paniculata 'Robert Poore'
Salvia koyamae
Rudbeckia triloba
Calamintha nepeta
Lilium canadense
Lilium superbum
Sanguisorba officinalis 'Tanna'
Liatris spicata
Lilium 'Salmon Jewels'
Lilium 'Black Beauty'
Aralia racemosa
Lilium speciosum 'Rubrum'
Lycoris squamigera
Limonium latifolium 'Violetta'
Eutrochium fistulosum 'Gateway'
Lobelia cardinalis
Vernonia noveboracensis
Solidago 'Goldenmosa'
Physostegia virginiana 'Rosea'
Phlox paniculata 'David'
Clematis ×jouiniana 'Praecox'
Rudbeckia subtomentosa
Vernonia angustifolia
Caryopteris ×clandonensis 'Worcester Gold'
Hibiscus 'Plum Crazy'
Phlox paniculata 'Norah Leigh'
Hibiscus 'Lord Baltimore'
Hibiscus moscheutos 'Blue River II'
Eutrochium maculatum 'Purple Bush'
Rudbeckia laciniata 'Herbstsonne'
Patrinia scabiosifolia
Solidago 'Lemore'
Origanum 'Rotkugel'
Silphium integrifolium
Solidago 'Goldstrahl'
Delphinium exaltatum
Sanguisorba tenuifolia 'Purpurea'
Coreopsis tripteris

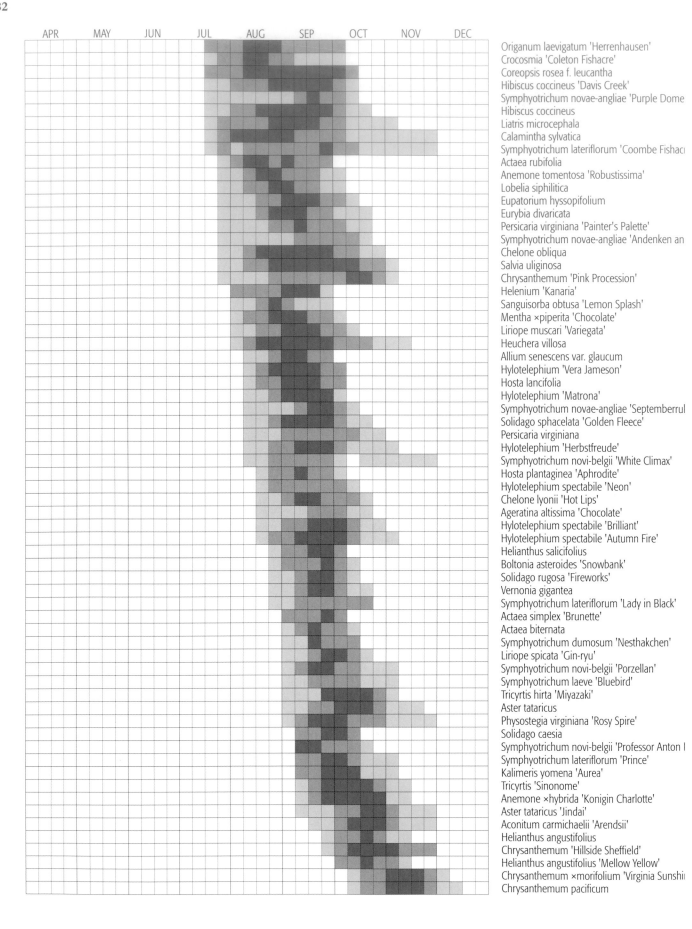

	APR	MAY	JUN	JUL	AUG	SEP	OCT	NOV	DEC	

Origanum laevigatum 'Herrenhausen'
Crocosmia 'Coleton Fishacre'
Coreopsis rosea f. leucantha
Hibiscus coccineus 'Davis Creek'
Symphyotrichum novae-angliae 'Purple Dome'
Hibiscus coccineus
Liatris microcephala
Calamintha sylvatica
Symphyotrichum lateriflorum 'Coombe Fishacre'
Actaea rubifolia
Anemone tomentosa 'Robustissima'
Lobelia siphilitica
Eupatorium hyssopifolium
Eurybia divaricata
Persicaria virginiana 'Painter's Palette'
Symphyotrichum novae-angliae 'Andenken an'
Chelone obliqua
Salvia uliginosa
Chrysanthemum 'Pink Procession'
Helenium 'Kanaria'
Sanguisorba obtusa 'Lemon Splash'
Mentha ×piperita 'Chocolate'
Liriope muscari 'Variegata'
Heuchera villosa
Allium senescens var. glaucum
Hylotelephium 'Vera Jameson'
Hosta lancifolia
Hylotelephium 'Matrona'
Symphyotrichum novae-angliae 'Septemberrubin'
Solidago sphacelata 'Golden Fleece'
Persicaria virginiana
Hylotelephium 'Herbstfreude'
Symphyotrichum novi-belgii 'White Climax'
Hosta plantaginea 'Aphrodite'
Hylotelephium spectabile 'Neon'
Chelone lyonii 'Hot Lips'
Ageratina altissima 'Chocolate'
Hylotelephium spectabile 'Brilliant'
Hylotelephium spectabile 'Autumn Fire'
Helianthus salicifolius
Boltonia asteroides 'Snowbank'
Solidago rugosa 'Fireworks'
Vernonia gigantea
Symphyotrichum lateriflorum 'Lady in Black'
Actaea simplex 'Brunette'
Actaea biternata
Symphyotrichum dumosum 'Nesthakchen'
Liriope spicata 'Gin-ryu'
Symphyotrichum novi-belgii 'Porzellan'
Symphyotrichum laeve 'Bluebird'
Tricyrtis hirta 'Miyazaki'
Aster tataricus
Physostegia virginiana 'Rosy Spire'
Solidago caesia
Symphyotrichum novi-belgii 'Professor Anton K'
Symphyotrichum lateriflorum 'Prince'
Kalimeris yomena 'Aurea'
Tricyrtis 'Sinonome'
Anemone ×hybrida 'Konigin Charlotte'
Aster tataricus 'Jindai'
Aconitum carmichaelii 'Arendsii'
Helianthus angustifolius
Chrysanthemum 'Hillside Sheffield'
Helianthus angustifolius 'Mellow Yellow'
Chrysanthemum ×morifolium 'Virginia Sunshine'
Chrysanthemum pacificum

Appendix: Metric Conversion Table and Hardiness Zones

Conversion Table for Length Measurements

To convert	Multiply by
Meters (m) to yards	1.09
Meters (m) to inches	39.4
Centimeters (cm) to inches	0.39
Millimeters (mm) to inches	0.04

Hardiness Zones Based on Average Annual Minimum Temperature

Temperature (°C)	Zone	Temperature (°F)
−45.6 and below	1	Below −50
−45.5 to −40.1	2	−50 to −40
−40.0 to −34.5	3	−40 to −30
−34.4 to −28.9	4	−30 to −20
−28.8 to −23.4	5	−20 to −10
−23.3 to −17.8	6	−10 to 0
−17.7 to −12.3	7	0 to 10
−12.2 to −6.7	8	10 to 20
−6.6 to −1.2	9	20 to 30
−1.1 to 4.4	10	30 to 40
4.5 and above	11	40 and above

Bibliography

Armitage, A. M. 1989. *Herbaceous Perennial Plants: A Treatise on Their Identification, Culture, and Garden Attributes*. Champaign, Ill.: Stipes.

Armitage, A. M. 2006. *Armitage's Native Plants for North American Gardens*. Portland, Ore.: Timber Press.

Bath, T., and J. Jones. 1994. *The Gardener's Guide to Growing Hardy Geraniums*. Portland, Ore.: Timber Press.

Bazzaz, F. A., and J. Grace. 1997. *Plant Resource Allocation*. London: Academic Press.

Beaubien, E. G., and D. L. Johnson. 1994. Flowering plant phenology and weather in Alberta, Canada. *International Journal of Biometeorology* 38: 23–27.

Benacchio, S. S. 1970. Phenological Development of Some Perennial Species as Related to Environmental Factors in Indiana. Ph.D. diss., Purdue University, West Lafayette, Ind.

Bennett, M. 2003. *Pulmonarias and the Borage Family*. Portland, Ore.: Timber Press.

Bird, R. 1994. *Border Pinks*. Portland, Ore.: Timber Press.

Clausen, R. R., and N. H. Ekstrom. 1989. *Perennials for American Gardens*. New York: Random House.

Clebsch, B. 1997. *A Book of Salvias: Sages for Every Garden*. Portland, Ore.: Timber Press.

Davies, D. 1992. *Alliums: The Ornamental Onions*. Portland, Ore.: Timber Press.

Davis, P. H., ed. 1965–1988. *Flora of Turkey and the East Aegean Islands*. Edinburgh: Edinburgh University Press.

Diels, L. 1917. Das Verhältnis von Rythmik und Verbreitung bei den Perennen des europäischen Sommerwaldes. *Berichte der Deutschen Botanischen Gesellschaft* 36: 6.

DiSabato-Aust, T. 1998. *The Well-Tended Perennial Garden: Planting and Pruning Techniques*. Portland, Ore.: Timber Press.

Evans, L. T., ed. 1969. *The Induction of Flowering: Some Case Histories*. Ithaca, N.Y.: Cornell University Press.

Fitter, A. H., R. S. R. Fitter, I. T. B. Harris, and M. H. Williamson. 1995. Relationship between first flowering date and temperature in the flora of a locality in central England. *Functional Ecology* 9: 55–60.

Flora of North America Editorial Committee, ed. 1993–. *Flora of North America North of Mexico*. New York: Oxford University Press.

Franklin Institute. 2007. Philadelphia Weather Data. http://www.fi.edu/weather/data/index.html

Galston, A. W., and P. J. Davies. 1970. *Control Mechanisms in Plant Development*. Englewood Cliffs, N.J.: Prentice-Hall.

Galston, A. W., P. J. Davies, and R. L. Satter. 1980. *The Life of the Green Plant*. Englewood Cliffs, N.J.: Prentice-Hall.

Goldblatt, P., J. Manning, and G. Dunlop. 2004. *Royal Horticultural Society Plant Collector Guide: Crocosmia and Chasmanthe*. Portland, Ore.: Timber Press.

Grainger, J. 1939. Studies upon the time of flowering of plants: anatomical, floristic and phenological aspects of the problem. *Annals of Applied Biology* 26: 684–704.

Grenfell, D. 1996. *The Gardener's Guide to Growing Hostas*. Portland, Ore.: Timber Press.

Grenfell, D. 1998. *The Gardener's Guide to Growing Daylilies*. Portland, Ore.: Timber Press.

Gusman, G., and L. Gusman. 2002. *The Genus Arisaema: A Monograph for Botanists and Nature Lovers*. Ruggell, Liechtenstein: A. R. G. Gantner Verlag KG.

Harding, A. 1993. *The Peony*. Portland, Ore.: Sagapress/Timber Press.

Harper, G., and L. Morris. 2006. Flowering and climate change. Part I. *Sibbaldia: The Journal of Botanic Garden Horticulture* 4: 71–86.

Heger, M., and J. Whitman. 1998. *Growing Perennials in Cold Climates*. Chicago: Contemporary Books.

Hellwig, Z. 1957. *Byliny w Parku i Ogrodzie*. Warsaw: Państwowe Wydawnictwo Rolnicze i Leśne.

Hewitt, J. 1994. *Pulmonarias*. Great Comberton near Pershore, U.K.: The Hardy Plant Society.

Hillman, W. S. 1962. *The Physiology of Flowering*. New York: Holt, Rinehart and Winston.

Iwatsuki, K., T. Yamazaki, D. E. Boufford, and H. Ohba, eds. 1993–. *Flora of Japan*. Tokyo: Kodansha.

Jelitto, L., and W. Schacht. 1990. *Hardy Herbaceous Perennials*. Portland, Ore.: Timber Press.

Kochmer, J. P., and S. N. Handel. 1986. Constraints and competition in the evolution of flowering phenology. *Ecological Monographs* 56(4): 303–325.

Köhlein, F. 1987. *Iris*. Portland, Ore.: Timber Press.

Köhlein, F., and P. Menzel. 1994. *Color Encyclopedia of Garden Plants and Habitats*. Portland, Ore.: Timber Press.

Komarov, V. L., ed. 1934–1960. *Flora SSSR*. Leningrad: Izdatelstvo Akademii Nauk SSSR.

Lambers, H., F. S. Chapin III, and T. L. Pons. 1998. *Plant Physiological Ecology*. New York: Springer-Verlag.

Leopold, A. C., and P. E. Kriedemann. 1975. *Plant Growth and Development*. New York: McGraw-Hill.

Leslie, A. C. 1982. *The International Lily Register*. London: The Royal Horticultural Society.

Longwood Gardens. 2001. *Perennials at Longwood Gardens*. Kennett Square, Pa.: Longwood Gardens.

Łukasiewicz, A. 1962. Morfologiczno-rozwojowe type bylin. Poznań *Towarzystwo Przyjaciół Nauk, Wydział Matematyczno-Przyrodniczy, Prace Komisji Biologicznej* 27(1).

Łukasiewicz, A. 1967. Rytmika rozwojowa bylin (ze szczególnym uwzględnieniem fenologii organów nadziemnych, *Poznańskie Towarzystwo Przyjaciół Nauk, Wydział Matematyczno-Przyrodniczy, Prace Komisji Biologicznej* 31(6).

Marcinkowski, J. 1991. *Byliny Ogrodowe: Produkcja i Zastosowanie*. Warsaw: Państwowe Wydawnictwo Rolnicze i Leśne.

McEwen, C. 1996. *The Siberian Iris*. Portland, Ore.: Timber Press.

Missouri Botanical Garden. 2007. Kemper Center for Home Gardening: Plants in Bloom. http://www.mobot.org/gardeninghelp/plantfinder/pib.asp.

Nau, J. 1996. *Ball Perennial Manual: Propagation and Production*. Batavia, Ill.: Ball Publishing.

Nold, R. 2003. *Columbines: Aquilegia, Paraquilegia, and Semiaquilegia*. Portland, Ore.: Timber Press.

North, F. 1969. *Perennials in a Cold Climate*. London: John Gifford.

Olsson, K., and J. Ågren. 2002. Latitudinal population differentiation in phenology, life history, and flower morphology in the perennial herb *Lythrum salicaria*. *Journal of Evolutionary Biology* 15: 983–996.

Ortloff, H. S., and H. B. Raymore. 1935. *Color and Succession of Bloom in the Flower Border*. Garden City, N.Y.: Doubleday, Doran and Co.

Page, M. 1997. *The Gardener's Guide to Growing Peonies*. Portland, Ore.: Timber Press.

Petit, T. L., and J. P. Peat. 2008. *The New Encyclopedia of Daylilies*. Portland, Ore.: Timber Press.

Primack, R. B. 1985. Patterns of flowering phenology in communities, populations, individuals, and single flowers. In: *The Population Structure of Vegetation*. Ed. J. White. Dordrecht, The Netherlands: Dr. W. Junk Publishers.

Quattrocchi, U. 2000. *CRC World Dictionary of Plant Names*. Boca Raton, Fla.: CRC Press.

Raunkiaer, C. 1934. *The Life Forms of Plants and Statistical Plant Geography*. Oxford: Claredon Press.

Rice, G., ed. 2006. *American Horticultural Society Encyclopedia of Perennials*. London: Dorling Kindersley.

Richards, J. 2003. *Primula*. Portland, Ore.: Timber Press.

Rogers, A. 1995. *Peonies*. Portland, Ore.: Timber Press.

Salisbury, F. B. 1963. *The Flowering Process*. New York: Pergamon Press.

Salisbury, F. B. 1971. *The Biology of Flowering*. Garden City, N.Y.: The Natural History Press.

Schmid, W. G. 1991. *The Genus Hosta*. Portland, Ore.: Timber Press.

Schmid, W. G. 2002. *An Encyclopedia of Shade Perennials*. Portland, Ore.: Timber Press.

Schöllkopf, W. 1995. *Astern*. Stuttgart: Verlag Eugen Ulmer.

Schulze, E. D., E. Beck, and K. Müller-Hohenstein. 2005. *Plant Ecology*. Berlin: Springer.

Schwartz, M. D., ed. 2003. *Phenology: An Integrative Environmental Science.* Dordrecht, The Netherlands: Kluwer Academic Publishers.

Serebriakov, I. G. 1959. Tipy razvitia pobegov u travianistykh mnogoletnikov i factory ikh formirovania. *Uchenie Zapiski Moskovskovo Gorodskovo Pedagogicheskovo Instituta imieni V. P. Potiomkina* C(5).

Sparks, T. H., E. P. Jeffree, and C. E. Jeffree. 2000. An examination of the relationship between flowering times and temperature at the national scale using long-term phenological records from the UK. *International Journal of Biometeorology* 44: 82–87.

Sparks, T. H., P. Croxton, and N. Collinson. 2006. The influence of a changing climate on the phenology of plants. *The Hardy Plant: Journal of the Hardy Plant Society* 27(1): 11–16.

Species Group of the British Iris Society, ed. 1997. *A Guide to Species Irises: Their Identification and Cultivation.* Cambridge: Cambridge University Press.

Stebbings, G. 1997. *The Gardener's Guide to Growing Irises.* Portland, Ore.: Timber Press.

Stephenson, R. 1994. *Sedum: Cultivated Stonecrops.* Portland, Ore.: Timber Press.

Still, S. M. 1994. *Manual of Herbaceous Ornamental Plants.* Champaign, Ill.: Stipes.

Sutton, J. 1999. *The Gardener's Guide to Growing Salvias.* Portland, Ore.: Timber Press.

Sutton, J. 2001. *The Plantfinder's Guide to Daisies.* Portland, Ore.: Timber Press.

Sweeney, B. M. 1969. *Rhythmic Phenomena in Plants.* London: Academic Press.

Szafer, W. 1970. Outline of the history of botany in Poland from the Middle Ages to the year 1918. In: *Essays in Biohistory.* Ed. P. Smit and R. J. C. V. ter Laage. *Regnum Vegetabile* 71: 381–388.

Thomas, G. S. 1990. *Perennial Garden Plants or the Modern Florilegium.* Portland, Ore.: Sagapress.

Tutin, T. G., V. H. Heywood, N. A. Burges, D. H. Valentine, S. M. Walters, and D. A. Webb, eds. 1964–1980. *Flora Europaea.* Cambridge: Cambridge University Press.

United States Department of Agriculture (USDA). 1990. USDA Plant Hardiness Zone Map. Miscellaneous Publication no. 1475. Washington, D.C.: Agricultural Research Service.

United States Department of Agriculture (USDA). 2007. Plants Database. http://plants.usda.gov.

Upson, T., and S. Andrews. 2004. *The Genus Lavandula.* Portland, Ore.: Timber Press.

Warburton, B., ed. 1978. *The World of Irises.* Wichita, Kans.: The American Iris Society.

Woodward, F. I. 1987. *Climate and Plant Distribution.* Cambridge: Cambridge University Press.

Wu, Z., and P. H. Raven, eds. 1994–. *Flora of China.* St. Louis: Missouri Botanical Garden Press.

Yeo, P. F. 2002. *Hardy Geraniums.* Portland, Ore.: Timber Press.

Zaitsev, G. N. 1978. *Fenologiia Travianistykh Mnogoletnikov.* Moscow: Nauka.

Index